LINGUISTIC DENSITY PLOTS
IN EZEKIEL

THE COMPUTER BIBLE
Volume XXVII-A

by

H. Van Dyke Parunak

BIBLICAL RESEARCH ASSOCIATES INC.

J. Arthur Baird
David Noel Freedman
Editors

To David Noel Freedman

        with gratitude for   encouragement provided,
                             opportunities offered,
                             counsel always available.

PREFACE

This work was supported by grant RO-32371-78-1495 from the National Endowment for the Humanities, a junior fellowship from the University of Michigan Society of Fellows, and computer services from the University of Michigan Computing Center. The methods and conclusions in this work are my own, and do not reflect the positions of the sponsoring agencies.

Financial sponsorship alone is not enough. The initial help and interest of Eric Andersen, Michael Coogan, Robin Cover, Paul Hanson, and Bruce Zuckerman, mentioned in <u>Linguistic</u> <u>Density</u> <u>Plots</u> <u>in</u> <u>Zechariah</u> (Parunak 1979), encouraged me in developing the methodology which these two volumes share. Francis Andersen and Yehuda Radday blazed many trails for my work in their own extensive labors. Anita Parunak continues to provide statistical guidance. John Hurd helped me sort out many of these ideas by providing a forum in the Computer-Assisted Research group of the Society for Biblical Literature. (The introductory chapters of this volume began as a report to that group in New York in 1979.) Peter Patton and Richard Whitaker showed personal as well as scholarly interest in my efforts. The editors of the Computer Bible series, David Noel Freedman and J. Arthur Baird, offered strong and continual encouragement.

I am indebted to the Württembergische Bibelanstalt, publishers of G. Lisowsky's <u>Konkordanz</u> <u>zum</u> <u>Hebräischen</u> <u>Alten</u> <u>Testament</u>, for permission to reproduce portions of that work.

Those who have worked with computers can appreciate the opportunities for error, both in coding the biblical text and in designing and writing the programs. The tremendous capacity of the machine multiplies our potential not only for research, but also for mistakes. I shall be grateful to readers who take the time to report to me mistakes that they find.

Two years ago, through the generosity of the Packard Foundation and in collaboration with R.E. Whitaker and the Claremont Graduate School, I had the privilege of supervising and releasing a comprehensive machine-readable edition of <u>Biblia</u> <u>Hebraica</u> <u>Stuttgartensia</u>. Readers who know of my role in that project might conclude that this book was prepared from that machine-readable text. In fact, the plots in this book were completed long before that project began, and my experience in coding Ezekiel by hand for this study persuaded me to pursue the more basic and comprehensive edition which that undertaking produced.

The largest part of this work is a collection of density plots of words and groups of words in Ezekiel. Readers already familiar with my methodology will find these helpful in studying the architectural and lexical structure of Ezekiel. The introductory chapters explain how the plots are computed and how they aid in exegesis.

* Chapter 1 shows how these plots are similar and dis-similar to conventional concordances.

* Chapters 2 and 3 discuss graphical and statistical methods for studying distributions of words in texts. These chapters tell how the plots in this work are computed, and suggest directions for further research.

* Chapter 4 describes coding conventions reflected in the plots, and explains the order of the plots in this volume.

* Chapter 5 suggests how to use the plots in studying Ezekiel.

To help readers locate plots of interest, the collection of plots itself begins with a complete ordered list of the words and groups of words plotted.

It is awe-inspiring to trace with Ezekiel God's justice as his glory abandons the sinful city (chapter 10), and his mercy and grace in returning to proclaim, "YHWH is there" (chapters 40-48). I send these plots forth with sober thankfulness for the vision of God and man that Ezekiel presents, and with the prayer that these plots might help make that ancient vision alive for modern readers.

Ann Arbor   H. Van Dyke Parunak
28 March 1984

TABLE OF CONTENTS

Page

PREFACE   5

PART I: THE METHOD

1. BEATING CONCORDANCES INTO PICTUREBOOKS 11

2. GRAPHICAL DISPLAY OF WORD DISTRIBUTIONS 19

3. STATISTICAL ANALYSIS OF WORD DISTRIBUTIONS 29

4. ORGANIZATION OF THE PLOTS 37

5. USING THE PLOTS 45

6. CONCLUSION 53

BIBLIOGRAPHY 55

PART II: THE PLOTS

LIST OF WORDS PLOTTED 59

PLOTS . . . . (unpaged)

PART I: THE METHOD

CHAPTER 1

BEATING CONCORDANCES INTO PICTUREBOOKS

The title of this chapter presumes two sorts of research tools. The first sort is the classical concordance. The second is a new sort of concordance, a "picturebook." We can tell the two apart by considering the fundamental task of a concordance. The task of a concordance is to show where a WORD occurs in a TEXT. This definition takes on two different nuances, depending on whether one emphasizes "word" or "text."

We can say, "The task of a concordance is to show where a WORD occurs in a text." This is the emphasis of the classical concordance. Classical concordances concentrate on the word. The text in which it happens to occur is secondary.

We can also give the definition this way: "The job of a concordance is to show where a word occurs in a TEXT. This is the emphasis of a new breed of concordance. The pictorial concordance tries to grasp the entire text as its structure is reflected in the distribution of a given word.

THE CLASSICAL (WORD-CENTERED) CONCORDANCE

Classical concordances, and also many computer-produced concordances, emphasize the individual word rather than the text. Exhibit 1-1 gives extracts from Lisowsky's concordance to the Hebrew Bible (1957) on the words ᵓāb "father," ᵓaḥôt "sister," and ᵓēm "mother." It duplicates only those portions of his listings which deal with Ezekiel. Each entry shows where a certain word, the TARGET WORD, occurs in the text. Exhibit 1-1 treats three target words-- "father," "sister," and "mother." Lisowsky sorts the references syntactically.

Computerized refinements of this classical style of concordance include the Key-Word-In-Context concordance, sometimes abbreviated KWIC. The classical concordance and its computerized offspring concentrate on the word or grammatical construction, rather than the text as a whole unit.

EXHIBIT 1-1.--Extracts from G. Lisowsky, Konkordanz zum Hebräischen Alten Testament (2te Auflage; Stuttgart: Württembergische Bibelanstalt, 1958, reprinted with permission).

אָב

Vater, Ahn / father, ancestor / pater, parens, progenitor

Ez 16,4	כְּנֵפֶשׁ הָאָב וּכְנֶפֶשׁ הַבֵּן
16,14	וַיֵּרָא אֶת־כָּל־חַטֹּאת אָבִיו
16,17	לֹא יָמוּת בַּעֲוֹן אָבִיו
16,18	אָבִיו כִּי־עָשַׁק עֹשֶׁק
16,19	לֹא־נָשָׂא הַבֵּן בַּעֲוֹן הָאָב
16,20	בֵּן לֹא יִשָּׂא בַּעֲוֹן הָאָב
20,4.18	אֶת־תּוֹעֲבֹת אֲבוֹתָם הוֹדִיעֵם
20,18	בְּחֻקֵּי אֲבוֹתֵיכֶם אַל־תֵּלֵכוּ
20,24	וְאַחֲרֵי גִלּוּלֵי אֲבוֹתָם
20,30	הַבְדֶרֶךְ אֲבוֹתֵיכֶם
20,36	נִשְׁפַּטְתִּי אֶת־אֲבוֹתֵיכֶם
20,42	לָתֵת אוֹתָהּ לַאֲבוֹתֵיכֶם
22,10	עֶרְוַת־אָב גִּלָּה־בָךְ
22,11	אֲחֹתוֹ בַת־אָבִיו
36,28	אֲשֶׁר נָתַתִּי לַאֲבוֹתֵיכֶם
44,25	לְאָב וּלְאֵם ס יִשַּׁמָּאוּ:
47,14	לָתֵתָּהּ לַאֲבֹתֵיכֶם

Als Subjekt:

Ez 22,3	הֵמָּה וַאֲבוֹתָם פָּשְׁעוּ בִי
5,10	אָבוֹת יֹאכְלוּ בָנִים בְּתוֹכֵךְ
16,3	אָבִיךְ הָאֱמֹרִי
16,45	וַאֲבִיכֶן אֱמֹרִי
18,2	אָבוֹת יֹאכְלוּ בֹסֶר
18,20	וְאָב לֹא יִשָּׂא בַּעֲוֹן הַבֵּן
20,27	גִּדְּפוּ אוֹתִי אֲבוֹתֵיכֶם
37,25	יָשְׁבוּ־בָהּ אֲבוֹתֵיכֶם

Als Objekt:

Ez 5,10	וּבָנִים יֹאכְלוּ אֲבוֹתָם
	וְעָשִׂיתִי בָךְ שְׁפָטִים
22,7	אָב וָאֵם הֵקֵלּוּ בָךְ

אָחוֹת cf. אֲחֻזָּה, אָח, אַחֲוָה

Schwester / sister / soror

Ez 1,9	חֹבֶרֶת אִשָּׁה אֶל־אֲחוֹתָהּ
1,23	אִשָּׁה אֶל־אֲחוֹתָהּ
3,13	מַשִּׁיקוֹת אִשָּׁה אֶל־אֲחוֹתָהּ
16,45	וַאֲחוֹת אֲחוֹתֵךְ אַתְּ
16,46	וַאֲחוֹתֵךְ הַגְּדוֹלָה
16,46	וַאֲחוֹתֵךְ הַקְּטַנָּה מִמֵּךְ
16,49	אִם־עֲשְׂתָה סְדֹם אֲחוֹתֵךְ
16,49	זֶה הָיָה עֲוֹן סְדֹם אֲחוֹתֵךְ
16,52	אֲשֶׁר פִּלַּלְתְּ לַאֲחוֹתֵךְ
16,56	סְדֹם אֲחוֹתֵךְ
23,4	וְאָהֳלִיבָה אֲחוֹתָהּ
23,11	וַתִּשְׁחֵת ס אֶת־תַּזְנוּתֶיהָ
	מִזְּנוּנֵי אֲחוֹתָהּ
23,18	נָקְעָה נַפְשִׁי מֵעַל אֲחוֹתָהּ
23,31	בְּדֶרֶךְ אֲחוֹתֵךְ הָלָכְתְּ
23,32	כּוֹס אֲחוֹתֵךְ תִּשְׁתִּי
23,33	כּוֹס אֲחוֹתֵךְ שֹׁמְרוֹן
44,25	לְאָח וּלְאָחוֹת ס יִשַּׁמָּאוּ:

Als Subjekt:

Ez 16,55	וַאֲחוֹתַיִךְ תָּשֹׁבְןָ לְקַדְמָתָן
23,11	וַתֵּרֶא אֲחוֹתָהּ אָהֳלִיבָה

Als Objekt:

Ez 16,51 ᵃ	וַתְּצַדְּקִי אֶת־אֲחוֹתַיִךְ
16,52	בְּצַדֶּקְתֵּךְ אֲחוֹתֵךְ
16,61	בְּקַחְתֵּךְ אֶת־אֲחוֹתַיִךְ
22,11	אִישׁ אֶת־אֲחֹתוֹ ס עִנָּה

אֵם

Mutter / mother / mater

Ez 16,44	כְּאִמָּה בִּתָּהּ
16,45	בַּת־אִמֵּךְ אַתְּ
21,26	עָמַד ס אֶל־אֵם הַדֶּרֶךְ
23,2	שְׁתַּיִם נָשִׁים בְּנוֹת אֵם־אַחַת
44,25	לְאָב וּלְאֵם ס יִשַּׁמָּאוּ:

Als Subjekt:

Ez 16,3	וְאִמֵּךְ חִתִּית
16,45	אִמְּכֶן חִתִּית
19,2	מָה אִמְּךָ לְבִיָּא
19,10	אִמְּךָ כַגֶּפֶן בְּדָמְךָ

Als Objekt:

Ez 22,7	אָב וָאֵם הֵקֵלּוּ בָךְ

THE PICTORIAL (TEXT-CENTERED) CONCORDANCE

Lately, biblical scholars have been turning their attention away from the analysis of individual words and constructions. They are focusing more on the text as a structural and literary unity. From this point of view, the data on "father" which Lisowsky has gathered might be more profitably displayed as Exhibit 1-2. The clusters of dots on this display show where and how strongly the word "father" is concentrated in the text.

The top of this display tells us that we are looking at a picture of Ezekiel 1-48. The target word is ᵓāb or "father," which occurs twenty-seven times in Ezekiel 1-48. Let us look at the rectangular area with the word "REFERENCE" at the top and bottom edges, and the word "DENSITY" at the right and left. The horizontal REFERENCE scale presents chapter numbers in Ezekiel. To conserve space, we print each chapter number of two digits with the tens digit over the units digit, rather than to its left. Thus the last chapter number, 48, appears at the right end of the scale as

4
8

The irregular horizontal spaces between these numbers reflect the varying lengths of the chapters. In this plot, each plus or dash on the reference scale represents thirteen verses of Ezekiel, possibly less if it is the last division in a chapter. For instance, chapter one has three horizontal spaces. The first covers 1:1-1:13; the second 1:14-26; and the third 1:27-28 (the end of the chapter). The number of verses per space, 13, is recorded at the left of the line just above the plot, in the form, "Each Column = 13 Verses."

The heavy black dots within the rectangle represent instances of the word "father." Each instance occurs in Ezekiel at the location indicated by the horizontal reference scale. For example, the word "father" first occurs in Ezekiel at 2:3. The chapter number "two" is at the left end of the lower reference scale. The heavy black dot just above this chapter number represents the occurrence of "father" at Ezekiel 2:3.

The vertical scale of the rectangle is labeled "DENSITY." This scale shows the concentration of the target word in the vicinity of each occurrence. For instance, consider the occurrence in chapter 36. The nearest other occurrence of the target word is in the next chapter. And these two occurrences are the only ones between chapters 22 and 44. The target word is very sparse in the vicinity of these occurrences. Thus they are assigned the lowest relative density, zero.

Linguistic Density Plot in Ezekiel 1 - 48

For 'āb 111 (27 times)

Each Column = 13 Verses. Separations are: Max = 4700.00, Mean = 998.93, Min = 14.50

CLUSTERS:

Start:	2: 3	5:10	16: 3	18: 2	18: 2	18: 2	18:14	18:17	18:17	18:19	18:20	20: 4	20: 4	20:18	20:30	22: 7	22:10
End:	22:11	5:10	22:11	20:42	18:20	18: 4	18:20	18:20	18:17	18:20	18:20	20:42	20:27	20:42	20:42	22:11	22:11
Count:	23	2	20	15	8	6	5	3	2	3	2	7	4	3	3	3	2
Width:	10974	9	4887	2945	1966	353	136	64	31	29	2	1008	596	230	323	78	31
Strength:	5.16	1.02	5.80	5.53	4.62	2.95	2.44	2.16	1.00	1.47	1.03	2.33	1.49	1.32	1.25	1.43	1.00

GAPS:

Start:	5:10	5:10	18: 2	18:20	22:11	37:25	37:25
End:	18: 2	16: 3	48:35	48:35	36:28	47:14	44:25
Count:	4	2	16	6	4	3	2
Width:	6601	4659	18934	16342	8570	6062	4500
Strength:	2.24	3.79	1.52	5.70	7.85	3.03	3.63

EXHIBIT 1-2 "father"

On the other hand, the highest dot in chapter 18 is very close to many other occurrences of the target word. We have assigned it a density of 24, the highest density in this particular plot.

Concentrations of the target word at other occurrences vary between the extremes measured in chapters 18 and 36. The height of the dot for each of these other occurrences shows how great the concentration is near that occurrence.

Such a plot gives us an intuitive "feel" for the structural significance of the word "father" in Ezekiel. It does not really contain more information than does Lisowsky. We could have gathered from Lisowsky, if we were so motivated, that the word "father" is concentrated in chapters 16 through 22 of Ezekiel, and that it is relatively rare elsewhere in the book. On the other hand, we might not have gathered this information from Lisowsky, if we were not looking for it. One advantage of the plot in Exhibit 1-2 is that the distribution of the points becomes inescapable. Furthermore, using certain conventions which we will shortly describe, we can measure this distribution quantitatively, and thus compare it with the distribution of other words in Ezekiel.

To see this, let us compare the plot for "father" with those for some other kinship terms. Exhibit 1-2 shows a peak of points on the plot for "father" midway between chapters 16 and 23. In Exhibit 1-3, we have a plot for the word, "sister." It shows clear peaks in chapters 16 and 23.

The first peak for "sister" contains the digit "3" at density 12. This digit indicates that three points are plotted on top of one another at this location. The digit "2" in the second peak indicates two points at the same location.

Exhibit 1-4 gives a plot for the word, "mother." Though the peaks are less pronounced than those for "father" and "sister," the word is clearly concentrated in chapters 16-23, with only one occurrence elsewhere in the book, in chapter 44.

These plots force us to see that all three kinship terms are concentrated in chapters 16 through 23 of Ezekiel. We might easily overlook this concentration from standard concordance articles. But once we are accustomed to the plots, it is impossible to view them and not notice the similarity of distribution among these three words.

Classical concordances, and their modern KWIC descendents, emphasize the individual word or construction. They are and will continue to be invaluable to lexicog-

Linguistic Density Plot in Ezekiel 1 - 48

For 'āhôt 114 (24 times)

Each Column = 13 Verses.   Separations are: Max = 12857.00, Mean = 1118.80, Min = 9.50 .

CLUSTERS:

Start:	1: 9	16:45	16:45	16:45	16:46	16:48	16:51	16:51	16:51	16:55	22:11	23: 4	23: 4	23:11	23:11	23:31	23:31
End:	23:33	23:33	16:61	16:49	16:46	16:49	16:56	16:52	16:61	16:56	23:33	23:33	23:18	23:11	23:18	23:33	23:32
Count:	23	20	12	6	4	2	5	2	3	2	8	7	4	3	3	2	
Width:	12528	5008	357	95	32	1	13	18	207	116	32	1060	602	279	143	40	16
Strength:	6.77	6.93	4.38	2.50	1.86	1.03	1.02	2.45	2.16	1.01	2.74	2.60	1.72	1.40	1.02	1.47	1.02

GAPS:

Start:	1: 1	1: 9	1:23	3:13	16:61	23:11	23:32	23:33	23:33
End:	16:45	16:45	16:45	23: 4	22:11	48:35	48:35	44:25	23:33
Count:	5	4	3	2	7	3	2		
Width:	7676	7520	7237	6592	4049	3591	15736	15309	15285	12857
Strength:	1.59	2.33	3.35	5.09	1.21	2.29	3.85	6.70	8.76	10.91

EXHIBIT 1-3 "sister"

Linguistic Density Plot in Ezekiel 1 - 48

For 'ēm 114 (10 times)

Each Column = 13 Verses.   Separations are: Max = 13476.00.   Mean = 2542.73.   Min = 12.50 .

REFERENCE

CLUSTERS:

Start:	16: 3	16: 3	16: 3	16:44	16:44	19: 2	21:26
End:	44:25	23: 2	19:10	16:45	16:45	19:10	23: 2
Count:	10	9	6	4	3	2	3
Width:	18786	5310	2721	943	25	137	876
Strength:	1.31	4.18	2.48	1.85	1.62	1.09	1.35

GAPS:

Start:	1: 1	19:10	22: 7	23: 2
End:	16: 3	48:35	48:35	44:25
Count:	2	6	4	3	2
Width:	6744	18504	16418	15915	13476
Strength:	1.80	1.44	2.44	3.47	4.71

EXHIBIT 1-4 "mother"

raphers and grammarians. The pictorial concordance displays
the overall structure of the entire text, as it is reflected
by the target word. Workers in structural analysis, content
analysis, rhetorical criticism, and redactional history will
find such displays a significant step forward (Parunak 1978:
549-571 and passim).

CHAPTER 2

GRAPHICAL DISPLAY OF WORD DISTRIBUTIONS

PREVIOUS WORK

The notion of a graphical display of the distribution of words is not new. John Smith computed such displays for some writings of James Joyce. Francis I. Andersen and A. Dean Forbes prepared similar plots for Biblical Hebrew literature. We can use the new plots more effectively if we understand how and why they differ from previous efforts.

DESCRIPTION OF PREVIOUS WORK

How shall we measure concentrations of a word in a text? Both previous approaches to the problem define a linguistic density as the number of occurrences of the target word in a section of text, divided by the length of that section of text.

$$\text{density} = \frac{\text{number of occurrences in section of text}}{\text{length of section of text}}$$

We want to see how this ratio changes as one looks at different parts of the text. Thus we cannot simply divide the total number of occurrences by the total length of the text. For the overall quotient does not vary with location in the text. Rather, we must look at a limited area of the text, and count the number of occurrences in this limited area.

We may illustrate by elaborating on a metaphor introduced by Andersen and Forbes. We can model a text as a series of asterisks (which represent occurrences of the target word) and periods (which represent other words).

. . . . * * . . . . * * * * . . . . . * . . . .

This picture shows the text as a whole. But we do not wish to compute the overall density. The text is like a parade, which is separated from us by a tall fence. We can only view the parade through a window in the fence. Thus, we can only see that portion of the parade which is visible through our window. As the parade passes by our window (or as we slide the fence past the text), we periodically count the occurrences of the target word that we can see through the window. For example, through a window of width 6, we might see this:

```
The overall
text:            . . . * * . . . * * * * . . . . . * . . . .

As seen
through the
window:                      * . . . * *
```

By dividing the observed number of occurrences by the width of the window, we can estimate the concentration of the target word at that location of the window. In the last display we have a concentration of three occurrences in a window of width six, or 0.5.

Previous approaches use a window of constant size, and differ only on how the window is moved about to cover the whole text. Thus we may call them variations of the "constant window width method."

In the late 1960's, John Smith divided the text of James Joyce's Portrait of the Artist as a Young Man into segments containing 500 words each (Sedelow 1970:96; Smith 1978:338-339). He plotted the number of times certain key words occurred in each segment. In terms of the fence illustration, Smith uses a window 500 words wide. He moves the window so that it neither overlaps itself nor leaves areas of text unviewed. The window is advanced over the text in steps equal to the window width. The following diagram suggests the sort of view one has of the text using Smith's approach. The window is six words wide, and advances in steps of six words. Note that the first position of the window happens to view two occurrences of the target word. The second position views four occurrences, and the third position, only one.

```
The overall
text:            . . . * * . . . * * * * . . . . . * . . . .

Successive
Views            . . * * . .
(Smith's                     . * * * * .
Method):                                 . . . * . .
```

F.I. Andersen (1976:25-31) and A.D. Forbes (1979) likewise use windows of constant width in their joint studies of Biblical Hebrew texts. But they allow more

flexibility in the length of the steps by which the window
is advanced over the text. If the size of these steps is the
same as the width of the window, successive views of the
text do not overlap, and their method becomes the same as
Smith's. But there are advantages to letting the successive
window positions overlap. The next display shows the view if
a six word window is advanced only four words at a time.
Note that the four word cluster in the text is viewed twice
in this method, once (partially) in the second window position, and once in the third.

```
The overall
text:             . . . * * . . . * * * . . . . * . . . . .

Successive
Views             . . * * . . .
(Andersen-            . . . * * *
Forbes):               * * * * . .
```

ANALYSIS OF PREVIOUS WORK

        The constant window width approaches of Smith,
Andersen, and Forbes have broken new ground. They reflect
the importance of thematic concentrations, and display these
concentrations in a helpful way. They are creative answers
to the needs posed by newer holistic approaches to exegesis.
Because of their importance, their behavior when applied to
a hypothetical cluster of words in a hypothetical text has
been analyzed in detail (Parunak 1981a). These approaches
have three undesirable side-effects.

  * First, they can give undue prominence to background
    occurrences which are not part of the main cluster of
    words. This is the problem of noise.

  * Second, the plotted peak representing the main cluster
    of words can appear flatter than it should.

  * Third, that peak can be wider than the cluster which it
    represents. Then we lose precision in locating the
    cluster in the text.

        All three problems (noise, peak flattening, and peak
broadening) result from using a constant window width to
compute density. If the window width selected is wider than
the actual width of a cluster of words, the plotted peak
will be broadened and flattened. If the window width is
narrower than a cluster, background points will appear as
noise. And it is impossible to select an optimum window
width which will avoid both of these problems. For clusters
even of a single target word in a single text will vary

greatly in width.

The density plots in this collection take two approaches to the problem of how to locate and measure concentrations of words without the distortions of noise, peak flattening, and peak broadening. The first approach, described in this chapter, is closely related to the constant window method of Smith, Andersen, and Forbes. The second, described in the next chapter, represents a completely new approach to the question. The two methods complement rather than challenge one another. Thus, the results of both are included on these plots.

CONSTANT OCCURRENCE METHOD

The first approach produces the patterns of dots in Exhibits 1-2, 1-3, and 1-4.

CONSTANT WIDTHS VS. CONSTANT OCCURRENCES

At the beginning of this chapter, we defined linguistic density as number of occurrences in a section of text, divided by length of the section of text. In the constant window method, we hold the length of the section of text constant, and count the occurrences which fall within it:

$$\text{density} = \frac{\text{observed number of occurrences}}{\text{length of constant section of text}}$$

The "constant section of text" is the constant width window. We have seen that this constant width window leads to distortion in the results.

We can fix the number of occurrences, instead of the window width:

$$\text{density} = \frac{\text{constant number of occurrences}}{\text{observed length of text}}$$

In the constant window method, we fix the length of text, and observe the number of occurrences in that length. In the constant occurrence method, we fix the number of occurrences, and observe the length of text in which they fall.

To measure linguistic density with constant occurrences, we note that each occurrence of the target word in the text (with the exception of the first and last) falls between two other occurrences of that word. We define its density as one occurrence divided by the average of its separations from each of the neighboring occurrences. For example, in the next diagram, the target word, represented by an asterisk, occurs at locations 2, 8, and 10 in the text.

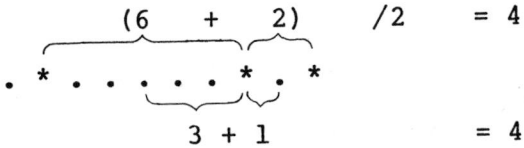

Consider first the numbers above the line of dots and asterisks. The second and eighth words are six words apart. 8 - 2 = 6. The eighth and tenth words are two words apart. 10 - 8 = 2. The average separation of the eighth word from its neighboring target words is thus (6 + 2)/2 = 4 words, and we define its density as one occurrence per four words.

The numbers below the dots and asterisks show how to view the average separation of a word from its nearest neighbors as a "window." We define a window which begins halfway between the second and eighth words, and ends halfway between the eighth and tenth words. For the eighth word in our example, this window is four words wide. As we move from one occurrence to the next, the width of this window changes, reflecting the characteristics of the data in the vicinity of the occurrence. Rather than forcing a window of our choosing on the data, we let them tell us what size window gives an optimal view.

Let us return to Exhibit 1-4, the plot for "mother." Just above the plot rectangle, a line of print begins, "Each Column = 13 Verses." The rest of the line gives three separations--a maximum, a mean, and a minimum. Two of these are actual window widths encountered in computing the plot. The maximum separation (or window width) corresponds to density zero. It is the variable window which surrounds the occurrence in chapter 44. The minimum separation or window surrounds the highest point in chapter 16, and corresponds to density 24. The third figure is the mean separation. This is the width the window would be if the occurrences of the target word were evenly distributed. Its density is indicated by the horizontal dotted line extending across the plot. In Exhibit 1-4, this line is at density one.

We have moved from a constant window width method to a constant occurrence method. The window width is no longer constant. It continually varies. But the number of occurrences within it is constant. In our example, we fix the number of occurrences at one, but we could as easily use another number. In each case, the window extends from halfway between the first occurrence in the window and the preceding occurrence, to halfway between the last occurrence in the window and the following occurrence. When we thus fix the number of occurrences and let the window width vary, the problems of noise, peak broadening, and peak flattening disappear (Parunak 1981a). (For probabilistic arguments leading to the same conclusion, see Pizer and Vetter 1966.)

Readers with a background in data analysis may wish to compare the constant occurrence method with the various techniques for smoothing sequences described in Tukey (1977:204-264).

The use of the constant occurrence method produces cleaner plots than does the constant window width method. Another advantage, more subtle but perhaps more important for the exegete, has been found in unexpected quarters. Medical radioisotope scans produce pictures made up of many discrete dots, in which clumps of dots relatively close together reveal medically significant information. These scans function in two dimensions much as our plots do in one, with dots in the scans filling the same role that occurrences of the target word do in the plots. In developing semi-automatic processing techniques for radioisotope scans, Pizer and Vetter (1968: 150-153; Vetter 1967) performed experiments on how humans perceive dot clusters. They found that the constant occurrence method (their "distance model") agrees much more closely with human perception of dots than does the constant window method (their "counting model"). In fact, the constant occurrence method did as well as the average human subject in their experimental task. Zahn (1971: 71) discusses the implications of their work in more detail.

In a text, even more than in a radioisotope scan, clusters of data points invite interpretation as meaningful constructs. Texts are written by perceiving people, for other people to perceive. We are interested in clusters of target words because of their perceptual effects on people. We want to plot a text in a way that will model and explain the effect of a text on a reader, and perhaps uncover how its author or authors perceived it. The work of Pizer, Vetter, and Zahn suggests that the constant occurrence method is much more likely to disclose perceptually relevant clusters than is the constant window method.

SOME TECHNICAL DETAILS

Endpoints.--The varying window width is computed from the separations of one occurrence of the target word from the nearest other occurrences of that word on either side. What should we do with the first and last occurrences in a text?

In these extreme cases, there is only one neighboring occurrence from which to compute a separation. Thus we cannot
compute a "window width" as the average of two separations.

    To simplify discussion, we imagine a text with ten
occurrences of the target word, and consider the tenth, the
last one before the end of the text. What shall we use as
the window width to compute the density at the tenth occurrence? Two solutions to this problem are possible. We might
use the single separation of the tenth from the ninth word.
Or we might take the average of the separation of the tenth
from the ninth word, and the distance from the tenth word to
the end of the text. The appropriate solution depends on how
close the tenth occurrence is to the end of the text.

* Suppose the tenth occurrence is closer to the end of
  the text than it is to the ninth occurrence. For example, the tenth occurrence might be four words from
  the end of the text, but eight words from the ninth
  occurrence. If we assign it to a window of width eight,
  its density is the same as it would be if there were
  another occurrence eight words after it. That is,
  taking the separation of eight as the window width
  yields the same size window as taking the average of
  two separations of eight. Lacking information to the
  contrary, we assume that the density is the same on
  both sides of the tenth occurrence. If the text were
  longer than it is, we would not be surprised to find
  another occurrence of the target word just as far after
  the tenth occurrence as the tenth occurrence now lies
  beyond the ninth occurrence.

* Now suppose the tenth occurrence is farther from the
  end of the text than it is from the ninth occurrence.
  For example, the tenth occurrence might be twelve words
  from the end of the text, but eight words from the
  ninth occurrence. In this case, we cannot assume that
  the density is the same on both sides of the tenth
  occurrence. We know that even if the text were longer
  than it is, the eleventh occurrence could not be closer
  than twelve words to the tenth, for we have those
  twelve words, and an eleventh occurrence of the target
  word is not among them. The window cannot be narrower
  than $(8 + 12)/2 = 10$, and we will clearly err if we use
  the single separation of 8 as the window width. In this
  situation, we use $(8 + 12)/2 = 10$ as the window width
  for the tenth occurrence.

Transforming and Scaling the Densities.--We may now compute,
for every occurrence of a target word in a text, a window
width w and a density 1/w. We might plot this density
linearly on the vertical scale of our diagrams. But the

resulting plots would not reflect the distribution of the target word as clearly as possible, for two reasons.

First, for any one target word, the densities computed for its various occurrences will not be evenly distributed between the minimum and maximum observed densities. More of the densities will be high than low. In terms of the plot, most of the points will appear at the upper part of the rectangle. This is because most target words occur in clumps, and are not uniformly distributed throughout the text. (The existence of these clumps is the motivation for the density plot technique in the first place.) The density of the clumped occurrences is, by definition, higher than average. Only a few occurrences, sprinkled in the open spaces between the clumps, will have low densities. If the occurrences in the open spaces should become more numerous than those in the clumps, the problem would not change. What previously were clumps would now be open spaces, while the former open spaces would become clumps. The majority of occurrences would still have above-average densities.

The second problem with plotting computed densities directly is that the range of densities computed for occurrences of one target word may vary greatly from the range for another target word. For instance, the densities computed for $m\u011bl\u014d^{\u0294}$ "fulness" in Ezekiel range from $1/6184 = 0.000162$ to $1/3614 = 0.000277$. Those for $^{\u0294}amm\u00e2$ "cubit" range from $1/1 = 1$ to $1/11228 = 0.000089$. If we give dimensions to the three inch vertical scale of the plot to accommodate the extreme densities of "cubit," the vertical distance between the extreme occurrences of "fulness" will be less than one thousandth of an inch. Since the vertical resolution of the printer used to produce the plots is only one eighth of an inch, the points for "fulness" would all be plotted at the same vertical location, revealing no information about the variation in density with location in the book. On the other hand, if the vertical scale were dimensioned to display the occurrences of "fulness" effectively, most of the occurrences of "cubit" would fall outside of the plot.

We solve these two problems by "re-expressing" the densities through two transformations. Such a systematic modification of values to make their visual display more orderly is a common and accepted technique of data analysis (Tukey 1978:57-96).

The first transformation must spread the densities evenly between their minimum and maximum observed values. We find by experiment that the square root of the density is distributed fairly evenly for most plots. So our vertical scale represents, not linear density, but the square root of the density.

The second transformation spreads the highest and lowest densities three inches apart on the vertical scale, and assigns the other densities to appropriate intermediate locations. (By "density" we now refer to the square root of the original 1/w.) Let us represent the maximum density as dmax, to be plotted three inches or twenty-five lines above the minimum density, dmin. A point with density d intermediate between dmin and dmax should fall between the points of extreme density. The number of lines between it and the point of density dmin is

$$25 * \frac{d - dmin}{dmax - dmin}$$

These two transformations greatly enhance the heuristic value of the plots. But they also obliterate some details of the untransformed data. To preserve this information, we record the maximum and minimum window widths (corresponding respectively to minimum and maximum densities) at the top of each plot. From these, we can readily estimate the actual density of each occurrence in the plot.

CHAPTER 3

STATISTICAL ANALYSIS OF WORD DISTRIBUTIONS

A good picture of the distribution of a word throughout a text can help us discover unusual concentrations and suspect that they mean something. Evaluating these suspicions requires other tools. The Bible scholar rightly invokes literary and linguistic criteria in deciding whether a constellation of occurrences is meaningful or not. We will demonstrate this process in Chapter 5. This chapter describes two other tools, of a more quantitative nature. One of these, cluster analysis, is used on the plots in this volume. The other, time series analysis, is not, and is a fruitful field for further research.

CLUSTER ANALYSIS AND STRENGTH COMPUTATION

There are straightforward ways to form a rough statistical estimate of how strong a cluster of words is in a text. Given a group of occurrences, we can compute how likely it is to have arisen by chance. In an interactive system, the user could specify a group of points which looks interesting, and receive an indication of its statistical significance. In a printed plot, though, we must try to anticipate which peaks are interesting, if we are to measure them statistically. For the plots in this volume, we use cluster analysis to isolate peaks and valleys automatically. Then we can list them with their strengths for the reader's reference.

CLUSTER ANALYSIS

Over the last twenty years, statisticians of a computational bent and biologists interested in taxonomy have developed techniques to discover clusters in collections of data. One of their products is single-linkage hierarchical clustering (Johnson 1967). Here is how it works:

Let us define a "thing" as either an occurrence of our target word, or else a cluster of such things which have already been grouped together. We assume that we have a way to measure the distance between any two things. We may reduce all of our target words to a series of nested clusters by following four steps.

1. Combine the closest two things into one new thing.

2. If all occurrences have been combined into one thing, stop.

3. Redefine the distances of all things to the new thing.

4. Go back to step 1.

The results of the cluster analysis appear at the bottom of each plot. Consider Exhibit 1-3, the plot for "sister." The section headed "clusters" lists the starting and ending verse for each important cluster in the plot. It also gives a "strength" figure that indicates the relative statistical importance of that cluster. Visually, we can see two dominant peaks in the density plot, one in chapter 16 and one in chapters 22 and 23. Two entries are circled in the table of clusters below the plot. Two of the highest strengths are 4.38 in a cluster of all the points in chapter 16, and 2.74 in a cluster in chapters 22 and 23.

With a few slight changes, the same procedure gives us the gaps in the data. These are areas that have no or very few occurrences of the target word. They appear on the plot as valleys rather than peaks. Refer again to Exhibit 1-3. The fourth entry is circled in the gap table at the bottom of the page. Here, we read that the gap between one occurrence at 3:13 and one at 16:45 has a strength of 5.09. This gap corresponds to the valley seen on the plot between these references.

STRENGTH COMPUTATION

Not all clusters or gaps discovered by the clustering process are equally significant. Each cluster or gap has with it a "strength" value. The larger this value is, the more significant is the cluster or gap to which it refers. We compute it with the help of some elementary statistical theory.

The motivation for our plots lies in the following assumption:

A group of words is more significant
when those words are bunched closely together
than when they are spread out.

We can readily explain a broad scattering of the target word throughout the text as an accident. When a small area of the text boasts an unusually high concentration of the target word, we seek a non-random explanation, such as emphasis by the author.

We might begin to measure the significance of a cluster by comparing its width with that of other clusters. Given two clusters of eight words each, the narrower one is surely the more significant. But most of our clusters contain different numbers of words. So we cannot directly compare their widths. Furthermore, to compare clusters of different target words, we must take into account the differences between the total numbers of each target word in the text. (We do not discard the absolute counts after correcting for them, though, but record them with each cluster we discover.)

Thus, we do not compare clusters directly with each other. Rather, for each cluster, we compute the expected width of a comparable randomly formed cluster. Then we can say how much narrower the observed cluster is than a comparable random one. By comparing observed clusters with theoretical random ones, we can correct for differences in the sizes of clusters and in the total numbers of target words. There is another advantage in measuring observed clusters in relation to random ones. The first question the peaks on the plots often raise is, "Are these just accidental congregations of words?" By adopting the average of random clusters as a reference point, we can address this question directly.

Let N be the total number of occurrences of the target word in a text W words long. If the N occurrences of the target word are linearly randomly distributed over the text, they will divide it into (N + 1) pieces, each of width W/(N + 1). The width of an average clump of two occurrences of the target word will be just W/(N + 1). A clump of three occurrences of the target word will be, on the average, 2W/(N + 1) words wide. In general, the EXPECTED WIDTH of a cluster of n such randomly distributed occurrences of the target word will be

$$\bar{w} = \frac{W * (n - 1)}{(N - 1)}$$

We compute this value for each observed cluster as a basis for comparison.

We need to standardize, not only our reference point, but also the ruler we use to measure how far our observed cluster width is from the corresponding average random cluster width. We do not measure this separation in words, but in terms of a statistical parameter called the standard deviation of the cluster width.

The formula for the standard deviation of cluster width is

$$S = W \sqrt{\frac{(n - 1)(N - n + 2)}{(N + 1)^2 \; (N + 2)}}$$

It is beyond our scope here to derive this form. Interested readers may study it further as W times the standard deviation of the probability to the left of the (n - 1)th order statistic (Mosteller and Rourke 1973:243).

Now we can define the strength of a cluster. The strength of a cluster is how much narrower a cluster is than the average corresponding random cluster, measured in standard deviations. If we observe a cluster of width w, its strength in terms of the expected width $\overline{w}$ and the standard deviation S is

$$\text{strength} = \frac{\overline{w} - w}{S}$$

The strength of a gap is how much wider a cluster is than the average corresponding random gap, measured in standard deviations, or

$$\text{strength} = \frac{w - \overline{w}}{S}$$

When a target word occurs ten or more times in a text, we can use the normal distribution to interpret the strength figures for clusters of five or more points. A peak with a strength of 1 has about a 16% chance of occurring randomly, from accidental causes. We arbitrarily select strength 1 as the cut-off point for the cluster and gap tables. Clusters and gaps which have strengths less than one do not appear in the tables. There is a 10% chance of randomness at strength 1.28. A cluster with strength 1.65 has a 5% chance of a random origin. Strength 2 indicates that only 2.3% of similar random peaks would be this narrow. A 1% chance of randomness exists at strength 2.33. For strength 3, the chance of randomness is on the order of one tenth of one percent.

It may help us to put these numbers into perspective if we look briefly at Exhibit 3-1, which presents "brother" in Ezekiel. This is an example of a word which is distributed almost randomly throughout Ezekiel.

Linguistic Density Plot in Ezekiel 1 - 48

For 'āḥ 111 (10 times)

Each Column = 13 Verses.   Separations are: Max = 4748.50.   Mean = 2542.73.   Min = 1388.50 .

REFERENCE

CLUSTERS:

Start:	11:15	18:10
End:	11:15	18:18
Count:	2	2
Width:	2	154
Strength:	1.09	1.02

GAPS:

Start:	18:18	18:18	18:18	24:23
End:	47:14	44:25	33:30	33:30
Count:	6	5	3	2
Width:	18096	16556	9497	4984
Strength:	1.33	1.64	1.41	1.05

EXHIBIT 3-1 "brother"

Our first clue that the plot lacks significant structure is the high level of the horizontal dotted line in the plot. This line indicates the average density expected in the case of linear random distribution. The expected density is computed from the expected mean window width $W/(N + 1)$. (This window width is given at the top of the plot as the mean separation.) For most target words, the expected density is less than the observed density of most or all occurrences. Here, it divides the ten points into two equal groups of five.

A second feature of this plot is that the points do not form clear "peaks," as they do in Exhibits 1-2, 1-3, and 1-4. The strength table confirms this subjective impression. There are no clusters that are significant at the 10% level (with strength 1.28 or greater). The only outstanding figure is the second gap strength, of 1.64. The most one can say is that the word "brother" may be unusually rare between chapters 18 and 44. Only five percent of all random distributions comparable to this one would have so few occurrences in a span this wide.

These results do not indicate that "brother" is an unimportant word in Ezekiel. They do suggest, though, that it does not function structurally the same way the other kinship terms do in Ezekiel 16-23. The contrast between the concentration of the other terms, and the relatively uniform distribution of "brother," is striking, and provides significant clues to the structure of Ezekiel. And though these comparisons are self-evident from the plots, they might well go long unnoticed on the pages of conventional, word-centered concordances.

TIME SERIES ANALYSIS

In this section, we point beyond the present volume to suggest an analogous discipline from which students of word distributions may borrow techniques and ideas.

Our study of distributions of words in a text has an analogy in the study of the distribution of galaxies in space. Our methods show us whether occurrences of a word are distributed evenly throughout a text or whether they are clustered together. When a word is not homogeneously distributed, its concentrations invite special study. Similarly, much effort in modern astrophysical research is devoted to asking whether galaxies are uniformly distributed throughout the universe, or whether they occur in statistically significant clumps. Basic questions of cosmology turn on whether or not the universe is homogeneous on a large scale.

Some studies of the distribution of galaxies in space use techniques similar to the window methods.

* For example, Abell (1958) places galaxies in clusters based on certain criteria. Among these criteria is the requirement that there be fifty or more galaxies in a circle of fixed radius about the center of the cluster. This criterion is analogous to the constant window method of computing linguistic densities.

* There are also astronomical analogs to the notion of a window which varies in size. Zwicky (1952) estimates the size of the predominant clusters of galaxies by computing the density of galaxies in regions of equal size and finding the size of region for which the variance of the density is a maximum. Zwicky (1961) and Turner and Gott (1976) identify the boundary of a cluster of galaxies, not as a region of fixed size, but as a region of whatever size is needed to contain a specified excess number of galaxies over the background density.

More recently, students of galactic clustering have used techniques of time series analysis to estimate the size and significance of groups of galaxies (Peebles 1980). In the strict sense, a time series is a series of measurements taken at different known times, and time series analysis seeks relationships between the values of the measurements and the times at which they were taken. Conceptually, the times at which measurements are taken are points along a line. The same techniques can be used to study the relationships among measurements along a geometric line instead of a chronological one. Once we learn to apply the techniques to a line, we can further extend them to two dimensions or even three.

Astronomers use an extension of time series techniques to the surface of a sphere to study the distribution of galaxies from the viewpoint of the earth. They prefer these techniques to window methods partly because the underlying mathematics allows conclusions drawn from a two-dimensional photograph of the night sky to be extended to the three-dimensional geometric space in which the stars are actually located. Such motives have little bearing on our problem. Furthermore, time series methods tend to yield information about the characteristic distances involved in irregularities of distribution, but they do not help locate the irregularities. We are interested in the locations as well as the sizes of clusters of words.

Because of the comparative simplicity of the window method and the clustering and strength analysis, we use these techniques in our charts. However, the more ways we can view data, the more we may learn from them. As computing power becomes less expensive and more widely available, time series analysis is a natural direction in which to extend the study of distributions of words in texts.

Bahcall (1977) and Peebles (1980: 138-142) are succinct surveys of the various methods used to study galactic distributions. Peebles (1980), Yu and Peebles (1969) and Peebles (1973) offer helpful explanations of the application of time series techniques to this problem. Bloomfield (1976) is a readable and accessible guide to time series in general.

CHAPTER 4

ORGANIZATION OF THE PLOTS

NOTATION

In Parunak (1979), the word or words presented in
each plot are printed in unpointed square script. Experience
with those plots shows that a vocalized transliteration is
preferable to unpointed script, and the plots in this volume
are labeled accordingly. The transliteration follows that
used in JBL and similar journals, with the exception (for
obscure historical reasons) that the letter between p and q
is written c rather than ṣ. Verbs are reduced to their (real
or hypothetical) triradical root, following BDB, and are
unvocalized. Matres lectionis have been used whenever they
are allowed in the heading of the appropriate BDB article,
whether or not they are historically correct. Our objective
is ready identification of forms, not an exposition of
morphology.

A morphological code follows each form. This code is
a restricted version of our full morphological code, which
in turn is derived from that used by Radday (1973:KEY).

In our full morphological code, each word in the
text is assigned a number of one or more digits. The first
digit (reading from the left) indicates the part of speech.
The significance of the next digit depends on what the part
of speech is. From Exhibit 4-1, we see that if the first
digit is a "1" (indicating a noun), the second digit indicates whether the noun is common or proper. But if the word
is a verb, with first digit "3," then the second digit
indicates the stem. Similarly, the meaning of the third
digit depends on the first two digits, and so on.

In Exhibit 4-1, certain digits are labeled
"N[umber]/Gen[der]," "State," "Affix," and "Person." The
following list explains these codes further.

EXHIBIT 4-1

Morphological Code for Hebrew

Digit: First	Second	Third	Fourth	Fifth	Sixth
1(Noun)	1(Generic)	Num/Gen	State	Affix	
	2(Proper)	1(Divine)			
		2(Personal)			
		3(Topogr.)			
		4(National)			
2(Modifier)	1(Adject)	Num/Gen	State	Affix	
	2(Prp.Adj.)				
	3(Adverb)	Affix			
3(Verb)	1(G)	1(Suffix)	Num/Gen	Person	Affix
	2(G-)	2(Prefix)			
	3(D)	3(Impertv)			
	4(D-)				
	5(Dt)	4(Act.Ptc.)	Num/Gen	State	Affix
	6(C)	5(Psv.Ptc.)			
	7(C-)				
	8(Irreg.)	6(Infintv)	1(Absolute)	State	Affix
			2(Construct)		
4(Prepn.)					
5	1(Interrog)				
	2(Interjct)				
	3(Conjnctn)	1(waw conj)			
		2(waw cons)			
6(Pronoun)	1(Personal)	Num/Gen	Person	Affix	
	2(Demonstr)				
7(Numbers)	1(Cardinal)	Num/Gen	State	Affix	
	2(Ordinal)				
8(Other)					

Num[ber]/Gen[der]:   Affix:
  1 masc. sing.   1 ה (article)
  2 masc. dual   2 ה enclitic
  3 masc. plural   3 י enclitic
  4 fem. sing.   4 ם enclitic
  5 fem. dual   5 ן enclitic
  6 fem. plural   6 ו enclitic

State: Person:
  1 absolute   1 first
  2 construct   2 second
  3 definite   3 third

    A few particles are coded with first digit "8," which is Radday's code for words which do not fit neatly into the other categories. Since each of these has its own distinct second digit, it is not necessary to list the codes here. The main significance of an "8" code in this work is that a word so marked is not classed in one of the first seven categories.

    We have listed participial formations as verbs rather than as nouns wherever possible, even when the verbal root is not otherwise attested in the required stem. Prepositions have been coded with "4" only when BDB describes them in the article heading as "prep." Words identified by BDB as "subst." or "n. m. used as prep." have been coded as masculine nouns.

    The words here displayed are not distinguished with respect to every detail of the morphological code. The number of cardinal numbers, and the number and gender of ordinal numbers and adjectives, are ignored. For example, the display for šĕlôšâ includes the occurrence of šĕlōšîm at 40:17. The singular and plural of nouns have been plotted together. Thus, on a display, the morphological code "111" means masculine generic noun, not just masculine singular generic noun. The code for a feminine noun of any number is "114." The line from top to bottom of Exhibit 4-1 divides those items of the morphological code which are reproduced on our plots (to the left of the line) from those (to the right) which are ignored.

ORDER OF THE ENTRIES

    The basic order of the entries is alphabetical, based on the consonantal skeleton (including matres lectionis) of the word. Consonantal homographs are then ordered on the numerical morphological code for the word. The multi-digit morphological code is to be "alphabetized" like a word, not read as a single numerical value. For instance, the code "6133" comes before the code "71," because the

first digit of one ("6") comes before the first digit of the
other ("7"). "71" is read "seven-one," not "seventy-one,"
and has no relationship to the quantity which is one less
than six dozen. If the first digits are the same, the words
are ordered on the basis of the second digits. Thus "31"
precedes "36."

We violate the ordering rules in the case of cardinal numbers and pronominal suffixes. The (syntactically)
masculine cardinal numbers precede the feminines, though (in
the range 3-10) they follow them lexically. Pronominal
suffixes follow the independent forms immediately . Thus -nî
follows ʾănî. The independent form ʾănaḥnû (ʾănû) does not
appear often enough in Ezekiel to warrant its own plot, so
-nû follows -nî after ʾănî.

This collection features combined plots of words
closely related to one another. In addition to plots of the
individual words, it offers combined plots of cardinal and
ordinal numbers; of each verbal root in its various stems
and within each stem in its various conjugations, and of
some other groups of related words. The first word listed in
the heading for a combined plot is that with the lowest
morphological code, and the entire combined plot occurs
where that word would occur in the order of the plots.
Combined plots precede the individual plots for the words
involved. When there are several combined plots, the more
inclusive ones precede the more limited ones. Thus, for
example, the plots for the verbal root yrd follow the order:
All occurrences; G stem; G suffix conjugation; G participle;
C stem.

Our statistical analysis suggests that plots based
on fewer than five points have questionable significance.
Thus words which occur fewer than five times in Ezekiel do
not have their own plots in this collection. They are included, though, in combined plots of words related to them,
and are listed in the headings of those plots.

An ordered list of all the plots in the volume
precedes the collection of plots themselves. By scanning
this list, users can determine the relative order of plots
of interest without remembering all the rules which we have
discussed.

HEADING

Within each plot, a heading presents the book and
chapter limits on which the plot has been computed. In the
present volume, these are Ezekiel 1-48, except in the case
of the conjunction waw. Then the word for which the plot is
computed is listed, together with its morphological code and

the number of times it occurs in the interval plotted.
Sometimes, we present several words on one plot. Then all
appear at this position.

    After listing the words plotted, the heading
presents four basic numbers which give some indication of
the scale of the plot.

* The first number ("13" throughout this collection,
  except for waw) tells how many verses are covered by
  each column of the plot. Ezekiel 1 contains 28 verses.
  Thus three columns are required to plot it. (The last
  column of each chapter will cover fewer than 13 verses,
  if the number of verses in the chapter is not evenly
  divisible by 13.)

* The three numbers labeled "Separations" describe the
  vertical scale of the plot. This arbitrary "density"
  scale is computed on the basis of the mean separation
  in words of an occurrence of the target word from each
  of the nearest occurrences on either side.

    - The maximum value of this mean separation is
      labeled "Max." The point or points corresponding
      to the maximum separation are plotted at density
      0.

    - The minimum value of the mean separation, "Min.",
      corresponds to points plotted at density 24 or 25
      (depending on how various quantities round off in
      the computations.)

    - The number labeled "Mean" is equal to the total
      number of verses in the book, divided by the
      number of occurrences of the target word plus one,
      and is the expected separation between words on
      the hypothesis of uniform random distribution.
      When this value falls between the maximum and
      minimum observed separations, a dotted line ex-
      tending completely across the plot shows its
      location on the density scale. The maximum and
      minimum are computed from the spaces between the
      words, while the mean is computed over the entire
      length of the book. When the first occurrence of
      the target word is far from the beginning of the
      book, or the last occurrence from the end of the
      book, the mean separation may be greater than the
      indicated maximum. This simply means that the
      points are clustered together in some limited area
      of the book.

DENSITY PLOT

The second component of an entry is the density plot itself. The horizontal "reference" scale shows where in the book a word occurs, while the vertical scale indicates the computed density. Within the plot, a bullet indicates a single occurrence of a word at a given plot location (column and row). Where two to nine words fall together at the same plotting point, a single digit gives the number of words that are thus superimposed. If ten or more words should pile up thus at one place, the plot shows an upper case "X."

STRENGTH TABLE

The third component of an entry is the table of strengths. These are computed both for clusters of points (corresponding roughly to peaks on the plot), and for "gaps," or stretches of text which have relatively few occurrences of the target word.

The strengths in our tables do not represent all the clusters or gaps which could be computed for the plotted data. It is reasonable to compute strengths only for clusters that are narrower than the average, and for gaps that are wider than the average. Furthermore, high strengths (indicating clusters and gaps formed by non-random influences) are more interesting than low strengths. Our plots will be less useful if we swamp the more interesting gaps and peaks in a sea of accidental ones.

We might draw the dividing line between "high" and "low" strength at 1.65, the 95% level on a normal approximation. But it is dangerous to leave too much of the decision concerning significance up to the computer. Our texts were written by people, not by machines. The final decision about whether a cluster or gap is random or intentional must be left to the human investigator. Thus we have recorded all clusters and gaps with strengths of 1.00 or greater. The possibility that a cluster or gap of such a low strength could have been formed randomly is greater than 15%. On solely statistical grounds this would lead one to reject such a peak as evidence of deliberate structuring. But competent analysis should not proceed on solely statistical grounds. Other evidence may lead a scholar to consider a (statistically) weak peak to be structurally significant.

Density (as indicated by the height of points in the plot) and strength are not the same. Density is computed entirely from the relative locations of three successive occurrences, irrespective of how many other occurrences there are in the book and how close these three points are to other occurrences. Strengths depend very much on the

total number of occurrences, and frequently take into account more points (in the case of clusters) or fewer points
(in the case of gaps) than does the density. Thus, a peak
whose highest point has a very high density may sometimes be
represented by a comparatively weak cluster. In such a case,
the analyst must weigh these data with other observations in
the text. Sometimes the overall dimensions of a peak may be
more important than how close together a few of its members
are. At other times, the repetition of a term several times
in quick succession may be more significant than the wider
relationships disclosed by the clusters. It is not a question of either density or cluster strength being "right" or
"wrong." Both are simply numerical parameters mechanically
derived from the text. Both are really meaningless unless
interpreted by a scholar in sympathy with the content of the
text.

CHAPTER 5

USING THE PLOTS

Linguistic density plots are a relatively new literary tool, and many scholars will be unsure at first how to use them. They have already been useful for two sorts of investigations, which we outline here by way of example. Other uses no doubt remain to be discovered.

STUDIES OF LITERARY STRUCTURE

The plots were devised in the first place to aid in studying the large scale literary structure of Ezekiel. They allow one to test hypotheses about concentration and distribution of words and other linguistic phenomena much more precisely and rapidly than by scanning the text by eye.

For instance, the plots of "sister," "mother," and "father" discussed in Chapter 1 show that these words are concentrated in chapters 16 and 23 of Ezekiel. A glance at these chapters shows that they have more in common than kinship terms. Both describe the apostasy of Israel under the metaphor of adultery, and the verbs nʾp and znh are common here, as are zimmâ and tôʿēbâ. A glance at the plots for these words shows that they are not only present, but concentrated, in these chapters, reinforcing the analyst's impression that these chapters correspond with one another. This correspondence, and the recurrence (though with lower density) of these terms in the intervening chapters, suggest that Ezekiel 16 and 23 form an internal inclusio (Parunak 1981b: 160-162). A close reading of the book confirms this analysis (Parunak 1978: 141-158).

Ezek 3:16-21 and 33:1-20 both use the metaphor of the watchman to describe Ezekiel's work. Exhibits 5-1 through 5-4 show some prominent words in these chapters: rāšāʿ "wicked," caddîq "righteous," mwt "to die," and hyh "to live." These plots offer graphic confirmation that the sections correspond with one another. We also learn something that we might not otherwise suspect: chapter 18 contains prominent concentrations of the same words, and should be compared with chapters 3 and 33 for structural connec-

For rāśā' 21 (28 times)

Linguistic Density Plot in Ezekiel 1 - 48

Each Column = 13 Verses.   Separations are: Max = 4908.00, Mean = 964.48, Min = 4.50 .

EXHIBIT 5-1 "wicked"

CLUSTERS:

Start:	3:18	3:18	3:19	3:18	3:18	3:18	3:19	18:20	18:20	18:20	18:20	18:23	21: 8	33: 8	33: 8	33: 8
End:	33:19	7:21	3:19	3:18	3:18	3:18	3:19	33:19	21:34	18:27	18:24	18:21	21: 8	33: 9	33:12	33: 8
Count:	28	7	6	4	3	2	2	9	11	5	4	2	2	9	8	2
Width:	17036	1853	48	21	9	4	2	9167	2326	147	78	30	524	275	139	8
Strength:	6.95	1.90	2.47	1.84	1.48	1.03	1.02	3.77	2.36	2.10	1.81	1.00	1.52	3.02	2.17	1.03

Start:	33: 8	33: 8	33:11	33:11	33:12	33:14
End:	33: 8	33: 9	33:11	33:12	33:19	33:15
Count:	2	2	6	3	5	2
Width:	5	43	48	77	43	15
Strength:	1.02	1.45	1.02	1.43	1.02	1.01

Linguistic Density Plot in Ezekiel 1 - 48

For caddiq 21 (16 times)

Each Column = 13 Verses.   Separations are: Max = 4931.00, Mean = 1645.29, Min = 19.00 .

REFERENCE

CLUSTERS:

Start:	3:20	3:20	3:21	13:22	18:5	18:20	18:24	21:8	33:12	33:12
End:	33:18	23:45	3:21	23:45	18:26	18:26	21:9	33:13	33:13	
Count:	16	12	3	2	9	6	5	2	3	2
Width:	16959	11688	46	4	7008	3253	446	133	61	132
Strength:	3.63	2.03	1.52	1.05	1.87	1.65	2.19	1.00	1.48	1.02

GAPS:

Start:	3:21	3:21	3:21	21:9	23:45	33:13	33:12
End:	48:35	18:5	13:22	48:35	33:12	48:35	
Count:	15	3	2	7	3	2	
Width:	26681	7441	4634	17112	7212	5139	9862
Strength:	1.45	1.95	1.92	2.29	1.84	3.09	5.23

EXHIBIT 5-2 "righteous"

Linguistic Density Plot in Ezekiel 1 - 48

For mwt 311 (6 times)   mwt 312 (29 times)   mwt 314 (3 times)   mwt 3161 (4 times)

Each Column = 13 Verses.   Separations are: Max = 7101.00, Mean = 650.47, Min = 4.00

REFERENCE

CLUSTERS:

Start:	3:18	3:18	3:18	3:18	3:18	3:19	3:18	3:20	3:20	5:12	6:12	6:12	17:16	18:17	18:17	18:24	18:24	18:26	18:31
End:	44:25	18:32	13:19	7:15	3:18	3:20	3:18	3:20	3:20	7:15	6:12	7:15	18:32	18:21	18:32	18:28	18:32	18:26	18:32
Count:	42	26	13	10	6	3	3	2	2	4	2	3	13	10	6	4	3	8	2
Width:	24338	8129	4657	1723	84	24	1	32	764	368	12	852	341	108	159	74	41	8
Strength:	2.62	3.90	1.66	2.40	2.34	1.43	1.02	1.42	1.01	1.10	1.05	1.00	3.67	3.21	1.71	2.28	1.74	1.41	1.01

Start:	24:17	33: 8	33: 8	33: 8	33: 8	33: 8	33:13	33:13	33:13	33:14
End:	33:27	33:27	33:11	33:18	33: 9	33:	33:18	33:15	33:14	33:14
Count:	15	11	10	5	4	3	5	4	8	2
Width:	5070	475	267	114	47	16	1	77	35	8
Strength:	2.04	3.38	3.25	2.03	1.77	1.44	1.02	2.06	1.78	1.45	1.02

EXHIBIT 5-3 "to die"

Linguistic Density Plot in Ezekiel 1 - 48

For hyh 311 (13 times)   hyh 312 (18 times)   hyh 314 (2 times)   hyh 3161 (9 times)
     hyh 3162 (1 times)   hyh 332 (2 times)   hyh 3362 (2 times)   hyh 3662 (1 times)

Each Column = 13 Verses.   Separations are: Max = 3968.00.   Mean = 570.82, Min =   6.00 .

REFERENCE

EXHIBIT 5-4 "to live"

CLUSTERS:

Start:	3:18	3:18	3:21	3:21	13:18	13:18	13:18	13:19	16: 6	16: 6	18: 9	18: 9	18:13	18:18	18:17	18:17	18:19
End:	47: 9	20:25	3:21	3:21	13:22	13:19	13:19	13:19	16: 6	20:25	18:32	18:24	18:13	18: 9	18:24	18:17	18:19
Count:	48	30	3	2	27	125	1013	4372	8	1375	503	315	17	2	156	50	1
Width:	25764	8992	97	27	4372	1013	125	27	4	315	17	21	13	9	4	2	1
Strength:	1.35	3.88	1.33	1.01	5.30	1.53	1.67	1.42	1.00	5.16	4.65	3.84	1.73	1.01	3.01	1.75	1.01

REFERENCE

Start:	18:21	18:21	3:21	18:21	18:27	18:28	20:11	33:10	33:13	33:13	33:12	33:15	33:15	33:13	37: 3	37: 3	18:17	18:19
End:	18:24	18:22	18:21	18:21	18:28	18:32	20:25	37:14	33:19	33:13	33:13	33:16	33:16	33:19	37:14	37:14	18:17	18:19
Count:	5	3	2	4	2	4	16	10	5	2	5	4	6	18	254	64	110
Width:	56	18	4	3	353	1	2688	205	87	13	63	18	1	63	6	254	64	110
Strength:	2.05	1.43	1.01	1.69	1.44	1.01	3.22	3.21	2.02	1.44	1.01	2.04	1.78	1.01	3.01	1.37	1.31

tions. The correspondence of 3:16-21 with chapter 18 and 33:1-20 is part of the general correspondence of the two judgment sections 3:16-7:27 and chapters 12-33 which inclose the second mar'at 'ĕlōhîm of chapters 8-11 (Parunak 1978: 118).

The analyst can use the plots in studying literary architecture in three ways.

* The analyst may note some similarity between two passages. This similarity can usually be articulated in terms of distinctive words or phrases. The plots for these words then show how strongly the passages correspond, and which other passages should also be taken into account in analyzing the structure.

* One may leaf through the plots with a given configuration of chapters in mind, looking for words that correspond among those chapters.

* Finally, perusal of the plots will often suggest correspondences which the analyst may check directly in the text. In each case, the plots provide a quick tool for generating and testing structural hypotheses.

STUDYING SEMANTIC STRUCTURES

Thus far, we compare concentrations of words to locate chapters that are similar to one another. We can reverse the process. It makes sense that words that are used in the same chapters deal with the same themes, and are thus in some sense similar to one another. This is certainly the case with the antonym pairs "wicked"/"righteous" and "to live"/"to die" that are characteristic of chapters 3, 18, and 33. Also, the two groups are clearly related to each other, at least within the context of judgment, since life and death are presented in these chapters as the consequences of wicked and righteous conduct. In chapters 16 and 23, as well, the words which indicate that the chapters are similar include a group of kinship terms which we can readily accept as related.

We must note that the similarity among words which occur in the same chapters is not the same as that which might be revealed through such techniques as componential analysis (Lyons 1977: 317-335). For instance, the kinship terms in chapters 16 and 23 do not occur together because they are kinship terms. If this were the case, "brother" would also be concentrated in these chapters, and we have seen that it is not. These words occur together, rather, because of their part in the larger semantic structure of

the discourse. In this case, the semantic structures under
consideration involve parents, daughters, and sisters, but
not brothers and sons. We can use the information gleaned
from such plots as these to construct semantic networks such
as those described in Parunak (1982). These networks reveal
the structure which is peculiar to the text under study.
They supplement other networks, such as those composed from
poetic parallelism, which may deal with more isolated
aspects of the lexicon.

CHAPTER 6

CONCLUSION

The promise of this technique is not fully realized by producing a fixed collection of plots and binding them in a book. These efforts are, at best, only illustrative. The method should be applied to grammatical phenomena, phrases, introductory formulae, and groups of synonyms, as well as to individual words. There are so many options that such plots should be produced on demand, to test hypotheses as they arise. It is gratifying to watch computers move into the study, and exciting to anticipate the day when scholars can call up a custom display as quickly as they can take down a bound volume from the shelf. Enterprises such as Paul Miller's Project GRAMCORD at Trinity Evangelical Divinity School and the Septuagint project directed by Robert Kraft at the University of Pennsylvania are developing textual and computational resources which will hasten that day.

We all have in our studies and on our desks, concordances of the classical variety. For questions of grammar and lexicon, we will continue to use them with profit. But the exegetical trends of rhetorical criticism, structural analysis, and thematic study demand that we forge new tools. We must bring the whole text, rather than just its component elements, into the foreground of our thought. The pictorial concordance, or linguistic density plot, offers us one answer to this challenge. It is time to beat our index cards into computer terminals and our concordances into picture books.

BIBLIOGRAPHY

Abell, George O., 1958. "The Distribution of Rich Clusters
of Galaxies." Astrophysical Journal Supplement
Series 31, 211-288.

Andersen, Francis I., 1976. "Style and Authorship." The
Tyndale Paper 21.

Bahcall, Neta A., 1977. "Clusters of Galaxies." Annual
Review of Astrophysics 15:505-540.

Bloomfield, Peter, 1976. Fourier Analysis of Time Series: An
Introduction. New York: John Wiley and Sons.

Forbes, A. Dean, 1979. Personal correspondence dated 30 May.

Johnson, S.C., 1967. "Hierarchical Clustering Schemes."
Psychometrika 32, 241-254.

Lisowsky, G., 1957. Konkordanz zum Hebräischen Alten Testament. 2te Auflage; Würtembergische Bibelanstalt,
Stuttgart.

Lyons, J., 1977. Semantics. 2 vols; Cambridge: Cambridge
University Press.

Mosteller, F., and R. E. Rourke, 1973. Sturdy Statistics.
Reading, MA: Addison-Wesley.

Parunak, H. Van Dyke, 1978. Structural Studies in Ezekiel.
Ann Arbor: University Microfilms.

_____, 1979. Linguistic Density Plots in Zechariah. The
Computer Bible 20; Wooster, OH: Biblical Research
Associates.

_____, 1981a. "Prolegomena to Pictorial Concordances."
Computers and the Humanities 15, 15-36.

_____, 1981b. "Oral Typesetting: Some Uses of Biblical
Structure." Biblica 62, 153-168.

_____, 1982. "Links, Chains, and Networks: Perspectives
for the Study of West Semitic Parallel Pairs,"
Afroasiatic Linguistics [in press].

Peebles, P.J.E., 1973. "Statistical Analysis of Catalogs of
          Extragalactic Objects. I. Theory." The Astrophysi-
          cal Journal 185, 413-440.

_____, 1980. The Large-Scale Structure of the Universe.
          Princeton: Princeton University Press.

Pizer, Stephen M., and H.G. Vetter, 1968. "Perception and
          Processing of Medical Radioisotope Scans." Pic-
          torial Pattern Recognition. Proceedings of Sym-
          posium on Automatic Photointerpretation. Ed. G.C.
          Cheng, R.S. Ledley, D.K. Pollock, and A. Rosen-
          feld. Washington: Thompson Book Co.

_____, and _____, 1966. "The Problem of Display in
          the Visualization of Radioisotope Distributions."
          Journal of Nuclear Medicine 7, 773-780.

Radday, Y.T., 1973. An Analytical Linguistic Key-Word-In-
          Context Concordance to the Books of Haggai,
          Zechariah and Malachi. The Computer Bible IV.
          [Wooster, OH:] Biblical Research Associates.

John B. Smith, 1978. "Computer Criticism." Style 12, 338-
          339.

Tukey, John W., 1977. Exploratory Data Analysis. Reading,
          MA: Addison-Wesley.

Turner, Edwin L., and J. Richard Gott III, 1976. "Groups of
          Galazies. I. A Catalog." Astrophysical Journal
          Supplement Series 32, 409-427.

Vetter, H.G., 1967. "Characterization of Geometric Imaging
          Properties of Gamma-Ray Detectors." International
          Journal of Applied Radiation and Isotopes 18, 231-
          235.

Yu, J.T., and P.J.E. Peebles, 1969. "Superclusters of
          Galaxies." The Astrophysical Journal 158, 103ff.

Zahn, C.T., 1971. "Graph-Theoretical Methods for Detecting
          and Describing Gestalt Clusters." IEEE Transac-
          tions on Computers C-20, 68-86.

Zwicky, Fritz, 1952. "Dispersion in the Large-Scale Dis-
          tribution of Galaxies." Publications of the
          Astronomical Society of the Pacific 64, 247-255.

_____, 1961. Catalogue of Galaxies and of Clusters of
          Galaxies, Volume 1. Pasadena: California Institute
          of Technology.

PART II: THE PLOTS

LIST OF WORDS PLOTTED

'āb 111

'bd 311,
'bd 312,
'bd 314,
'bd 331,
'bd 332,
'bd 3362,
'bd 361

'bd 311,
'bd 312,
'bd 314

'eben 114

'āgap 111

'ĕdôm 124

'ādôn 111

'ādām 111

'ădāmâ 114

'hb 311,
'hb 334

'ohŏlâ 12

'ohŏlîbâ 12

'ûlām 111

'ôpan 111

'ōzen 114

'āḥ 111

'eḥād 711,
'aḥat 714,
ri'šôn 721

'eḥād 711

'aḥat 714

'āḥôt 114

'ḥz 315

'aḥar 111

'aḥēr 21

'î 111

'ayil 111

'êlām 111

'ayin 111

'êpâ 114

'îš 111

'kl 311,
'kl 312,
'kl 313,
'kl 314,
'kl 3162,
'kl 322,
'kl 361,
'kl 362,
'kl 3662

'kl 311,
'kl 312,
'kl 313,
'kl 314,
'kl 3162

'kl 311

'kl 312

'oklâ 114

'al 23

'el 4

'ālâ 114

'ēlleh 6233

'ĕlōhîm 111

'almānâ 114

'elep 711

'ēm 114

'im 53

'ammâ 114

'mr 311,
'mr 312,
'mr 313,
'mr 314,
'mr 3161,
'mr 3162,
'mr 322

'mr 311

'mr 312

'mr 313

'mr 314

'mr 3162

'ănî 6111

-nî 6111

-nû 6131

'sp 311,
'sp 313,
'sp 315,
'sp 322,
'sp 323,
'sp 344

'ap 111

'âpîq 111

'ēcel 111

'arbā'â 711,
'arba' 714,
rĕbî'î 721,
rĕbî'ît 724

'arbā'â 711

'arba' 714

'erez 111

'ōrek 111

'erec 114

'ēš 114

'iššâ 114

'aššûr 12

'āšer 53

'ēt 4

'att 6142

-k 6142

'attâ 6112

-kā 6112

'attîq 111

'attem 6132

-kem 6132

-ken 6162

bĕ- 4

babel 12

beged 111

bad 111

bĕhēmâ 114

bw' 311,
bw' 312,
bw' 313,
bw' 314,
bw' 3162,
bw' 361,
bw' 362,
bw' 364,
bw' 3662,
bw' 371,
bw' 374

bw' 311,
bw' 312,
bw' 313,
bw' 314,
bw' 3162

bw' 311

bw' 312

bw' 313

bw' 314

bw' 3162

bw' 361,
bw' 362,
bw' 364,
bw' 3662,
bw' 371,
bw' 374

bw' 361

bw' 362

bw' 364

bw' 3662

bôr 111

baz 111

bzh 311

bzz 311,
bzz 314,
bzz 3162

bāḥûr 111

beṭaḥ 111

bayin 111

bayit 111

bēlet 111

bāmâ 114

bēn 111

bnh 311,
bnh 312,
bnh 314,
bnh 3162,
bnh 321,
bnh 322

bnh 311

binyān 111

b'r 314,
b'r 331,
b'r 332,
b'r 362

bq' 311,
bq' 3262,
bq' 331,
bq' 332,
bq' 344

biq'â 114

bōqer 111

bāqār 111

bqš 331,
bqš 332,
bqš 334,
bqš 342

bqš 332

br' 321,
br' 3262,
br' 3361

barzel 111

bĕrît 114

bāśār 111

bšl 311,
bšl 332,
bšl 334

bat 111

bat 114

gā'ôn 111

gab 111

gōbah 111

gābōah 21

gbh 311,
gbh 312,
gbh 361,
gbh 363

gĕbûl 111

gibbôr 21

gib'â 114

gādôl 21

gdl 312,
gdl 331,
gdl 351,
gdl 362

gôg 12

gôy 111

gôlâ 114

gzl 311,
gzl 312

gizrâ 114

gay' 111

galgal 111

glh 311,
glh 313,
glh 321,
glh 322,
glh 3262,
glh 331,
glh 332,
glh 3662

glh 311,
glh 313,
glh 321,
glh 322,
glh 3262

glh 331,
glh 332

gillûl 111

gam 23

gan 111

gepen 114

gēr 111

gešem 111

dābār 111

deber 111

dbr 324,
dbr 331,
dbr 332,
dbr 333,
dbr 334,
dbr 3361,
dbr 3362

dbr 331

dbr 332

dbr 333

dbr 334

dĕbaš 111

dāgâ 114

dālît 114

delet 114

dām 111

dmh 311,
dmh 321

dĕmût 114

dammeśeq 12

dārôm 111

derek 111

drš 311,
drš 312,
drš 314,
drš 3162,
drš 322,
drš 3261

drš 311,
drš 312,
drš 314,
drš 3162

drš 322,
drš 3261

drš 322

ha 51,
ha- 51

ha 51

ha- 51

hû' 6113

-hû 6113

hî' 6143

-hã 6143

hyh 311,
hyh 312,
hyh 313,
hyh 3161,
hyh 3162,
hyh 321

hyh 311

hyh 312

hyh 3162

hêkāl 111

hîn 111

hlk 311,
hlk 312,
hlk 313,
hlk 314,
hlk 315,
hlk 3161,
hlk 3162,
hlk 332,
hlk 351,
hlk 352,
hlk 354,
hlk 361,
hlk 362

hlk 311,
hlk 312,
hlk 313,
hlk 314,
hlk 315,
hlk 3161,
hlk 3162

hlk 311

hlk 312

hlk 313

hlk 314

hlk 3161

hlk 361,
hlk 362

hēm 6133

-hem 6133

hāmôn 111

hēn 6163

-hen 6163

hēn 84,	zimmâ 114	ḥzq 311,	ḥll 321,
hinnēh 84,		ḥzq 312,	ḥll 322,
hinnēh 84-	znh 311,	ḥzq 3162,	ḥll 3262,
	znh 312,	ḥzq 331,	ḥll 331,
hinnēh 84	znh 314,	ḥzq 332,	ḥll 332,
	znh 3162,	ḥzq 3362,	ḥll 334,
hinnēh 84-	znh 341	ḥzq 352,	ḥll 3362,
		ḥzq 361,	ḥll 344,
har 111	znh 312	ḥzq 364	ḥll 362
hrg 311,	znh 314	ḥṭ' 311,	ḥll 321,
hrg 312,		ḥṭ' 312,	ḥll 322,
hrg 314,	zāqēn 21	ḥṭ' 314,	ḥll 3262
hrg 315,		ḥṭ' 3162,	
hrg 322,	zār 111	ḥṭ' 331,	ḥll 331,
hrg 3262		ḥṭ' 3362	ḥll 332,
	zrh 312,		ḥll 334,
hrs 311,	zrh 322,	ḥṭ' 311,	ḥll 3362,
hrs 321,	zrh 3262,	ḥṭ' 312,	ḥll 344
hrs 324	zrh 331,	ḥṭ' 314,	
	zrh 332,	ḥṭ' 3162	ḥll 331
wē- 531-	zrh 3362		
		ḥṭ' 311	ḥll 332
wē- 532-	zrh 331,		
	zrh 332,	ḥṭ' 331,	ḥēmâ 114
zō't 6243	zrh 3362	ḥṭ' 3362	
			ḥml 312,
zebaḥ 111	zrh 331	ḥaṭṭā't 114	ḥml 3162
zbḥ 311,	zērôa' 114	ḥay 21	ḥml 312
zbḥ 312,			
zbḥ 314	zera' 111	ḥayyâ 114	ḥāmās 111
zeh 6213	ḥbl 311,	ḥyh 311,	ḥōmer 111
	ḥbl 314	ḥyh 312,	
zāhāb 111		ḥyh 314,	ḥāmissâ 711,
	ḥbš 311,	ḥyh 3161,	ḥāmēš 714,
zhr 321,	ḥbš 312,	ḥyh 3162,	ḥāmîšî 721,
zhr 361,	ḥbš 315,	ḥyh 332,	ḥāmîšît 724
zhr 3662	ḥbš 3161,	ḥyh 3362,	
	ḥbš 3162,	ḥyh 3662	ḥāmissâ 711
zhr 321	ḥbš 341		
		ḥyh 311,	ḥāmēš 714
zhr 361,	ḥag 111	ḥyh 312,	
zhr 3662		ḥyh 314,	ḥāmāt 12
	ḥōdeš 111	ḥyh 3161,	
zhr 361		ḥyh 3162	ḥācēr 114
	ḥādāš 21		
zkr 311,		ḥyh 311	ḥōq 111
zkr 312,	ḥômâ 114		
zkr 3162,		ḥyh 312	ḥuqqâ 114
zkr 322,	ḥws 311,		
zkr 3262,	ḥws 312	ḥyh 3161	ḥereb 114
zkr 361,			
zkr 364	ḥws 312	ḥayil 111	ḥrb 311,
			ḥrb 312,
zkr 311,	ḥûc 111	ḥîcôn 21	ḥrb 324,
zkr 312,			ḥrb 361,
zkr 3162	ḥzh 311,	ḥokmâ 114	ḥrb 371,
	ḥzh 312,		ḥrb 374
zkr 311	ḥzh 314,	ḥel'â 114	
	ḥzh 3162		ḥōrbâ 114
zkr 322,		ḥallôn 114	
zkr 3262	ḥāzôn 111		ḥrd 311,
		ḥālāl 111	ḥrd 312,
zkr 322	ḥāzāq 21		ḥrd 364,
			ḥrd 3662

ḥerpâ 114	yd' 311,	yc' 311,	viśrā'ēl 12
	yd' 312,	yc' 312,	
ḥittît 114	yd' 314,	yc' 313,	yšb 311,
	yd' 3162,	yc' 314,	yšb 312,
ḥtr 311,	yd' 321,	yc' 3162	yšb 314,
ḥtr 312,	yd' 322,		yšb 3162,
ḥtr 313	yd' 361,	yc' 311	yšb 321,
	yd' 362,		yšb 324,
ṭhr 311,	yd' 363	yc' 312	yšb 331,
ṭhr 312,			yšb 361
ṭhr 331,	yd' 311,	yc' 314	
ṭhr 332,	yd' 312,		
ṭhr 3362,	yd' 314,	yc' 3162	yšb 311,
ṭhr 344	yd' 3162		yšb 312,
		yc' 361,	yšb 314,
ṭhr 331,	yd' 311	yc' 362,	yšb 3162
ṭhr 332,		yc' 363,	
ṭhr 3362,	yd' 321,	yc' 364,	yšb 311
ṭhr 344	yd' 322	yc' 3662,	
		yc' 371,	yšb 312
ṭôb 21	yd' 361,	yc' 374	
	yd' 362,		yšb 314
ṭāmē' 21	yd' 363	yc' 361	
			yšb 321,
ṭm' 311,	yĕhûdâ 12	yc' 362	yšb 324
ṭm' 312,			
ṭm' 3162,	yhwh 121	yc' 3662	ytr 321,
ṭm' 321,			ytr 324,
ṭm' 324,	yôm 111	yr' 311,	ytr 361,
ṭm' 331,		yr' 312	ytr 362
ṭm' 332,	yld 311,		
ṭm' 333,	yld 312,	yrd 311,	ytr 321,
ṭm' 352	yld 361,	yrd 312,	ytr 324
	yld 3761	yrd 313,	
ṭm' 311,		yrd 314,	ytr 324
ṭm' 312,	yām 111	yrd 3162,	
ṭm' 3162,		yrd 361,	kĕ- 4
ṭm' 321,	yāmîn 114	yrd 362,	
ṭm' 324		yrd 363,	kābôd 111
	ynh 361,	yrd 3662,	
ṭm' 331,	ynh 362,	yrd 371	kĕbār 12
ṭm' 332,	ynh 3662		
ṭm' 333		yrd 311,	kebeś 111
	ya'an 111	yrd 312,	
ṭm' 331		yrd 313,	kōh 23
	ya'ar 111	yrd 314,	
ṭm' 352		yrd 3162	kōhēn 111
	yŏpî 111		
ṭum'â 114		yrd 311	kwn 321,
	yc' 311,		kwn 323,
ṭerep 111	yc' 312,	yrd 314	kwn 361,
	yc' 313,		kwn 362,
yĕ'ôr 111	yc' 314,	yrd 361,	kwn 363,
	yc' 3162,	yrd 362,	kwn 3662,
ybš 311,	yc' 361,	yrd 363,	kwn 374,
ybš 312,	yc' 362,	yrd 3662,	kwn 381
ybš 3161,	yc' 363,	yrd 371	
ybš 361	yc' 364,		kwn 361,
	yc' 3662,	yĕrûsālayim 12	kwn 362,
ybš 311,	yc' 371,		kwn 363,
ybš 312,	yc' 374	yarkâ 114	kwn 3662,
ybš 3161			kwn 374
		yrš 311,	
yād 114		yrš 312	kûš 12
			kāzāb 111

kî 53	krt 361	m's 311, m's 314	ml' 311
kōl 111	kaśdîm 12		ml' 314
klh 311,	ktb 312,	mābô' 111	
klh 312,	ktb 313,		ml' 322
klh 331,	ktb 315,	māgēn 111	
klh 332,	ktb 322		ml' 331,
klh 3362		midbār 111	ml' 332,
	kātēp 114		ml' 333,
klh 331,		mdd 311,	ml' 3361
klh 332,	lĕ- 4	mdd 312	
klh 3362			mĕlā'kâ 114
	lō' 23	mdd 311	
klh 331			mĕlô' 111
	lēb 111,	mdd 312	
klh 3362	lēbāb 111		milhāmâ 114
		middâ 114	
kĕlî 111	lēb 111		melek 111
		mâ 51	
klm 321,	lēbāb 111		min 4
klm 322,		mô'ēd 111	
klm 323,	lēbānôn 12		minhâ 114
klm 324		môrāšâ 114	
	lbš 311,		mispār 111
kĕlimmâ 114	lbš 312,	môšāb 111	
	lbš 315,		mē'aṭ 111
kēn 23	lbš 362	māwet 111	
			ma'al 111
kānāp 114	lbš 312	mwt 311,	
		mwt 312,	m'l 311,
kissē' 111	lbš 315	mwt 314,	m'l 3162
		mwt 3161,	
ksh 3262,	lēwî 12,	mwt 3662,	m'l 311
ksh 331,	lēwî 22	mwt 372	
ksh 332,			ma'ălâ 114
ksh 334,	lehem 111	mwt 311,	
ksh 3362,		mwt 312,	ma'an 111
ksh 344	lqh 311,	mwt 314,	
	lqh 312,	mwt 3161	ma'ărāb 111
ksh 331	lqh 313,		
	lqh 314,	mwt 311	ma'ăśeh 111
ksh 332	lqh 3161,		
	lqh 3162,	mwt 312	mappelet 114
kesep 111	lqh 321,		
	lqh 354,	mizbēah 111	miptān 111
kap 114	lqh 372		
		mĕzûzâ 114	mācôr 111
kĕpîr 111	lqh 311,		
	lqh 312,	maṭṭeh 111	mēcah 111
kpr 331,	lqh 313,		
kpr 332,	lqh 314,	mayim 111	micrayim 12
kpr 3362	lqh 3161,		
	lqh 3162	mikšôl 111	miqdāš 111
kōr 111			
	lqh 311	ml' 311,	māqôm 111
kĕrûb 111		ml' 314,	
	lqh 312	ml' 3162,	miqcōa' 111
krt 311,		ml' 322,	
krt 312,	lqh 313	ml' 331,	mar'eh 111
krt 341,		ml' 332,	
krt 361,	liškâ 114	ml' 333,	mrṭ 315,
krt 3662		ml' 3361	mrṭ 3162,
	mĕ'ōd 111		mrṭ 341
krt 361,		ml' 311,	
krt 3662	mē'â 714	ml' 314,	mērî 111
		ml' 3162	

mešek 12

māšāl 111

mšl 312,
mšl 313,
mšl 314,
mšl 3162,
mšl 334

mēšamâ 114

mišmeret 114

mišpāṭ 111

motnayim 111

mattānâ 114

nā' 23

nē'um 111

n'p 314,
n'p 331,
n'p 334

nb' 321,
nb' 323,
nb' 324,
nb' 3262,
nb' 351,
nb' 354

nb' 321,
nb' 323,
nb' 324,
nb' 3262

nb' 323

nābî' 111

negeb 111

neged 111

ngd 362,
ngd 363

nōgah 114

niddâ 114

nāhār 111

nwḥ 361,
nwḥ 362,
nwḥ 3662,
nwḥ 374

nwḥ 361,
nwḥ 362,
nwḥ 3662

nwḥ 361

nwḥ 362

naḥal 111

naḥălâ 114

nhm 321,
nhm 322,
nhm 331,
nhm 3362,
nhm 351

nĕḥōšet 111

nṭh 311,
nṭh 314,
nṭh 315

nṭh 311

nkh 361,
nkh 362,
nkh 363,
nkh 364,
nkh 3662,
nkh 371

nōkaḥ 111

nē'ûrîm 114

npl 311,
npl 361,
npl 314,
npl 3162,
npl 361,
npl 362,
npl 3662,
npl 381

npl 311,
npl 312,
npl 314,
npl 3162

npl 311

npl 312

npl 361,
npl 362,
npl 3662

nepeš 114

ncl 322,
ncl 332,
ncl 361,
ncl 362,
ncl 3662

ncl 361,
ncl 362,
ncl 3662

ncl 361

ncl 362

nēqāmâ 114

nś' 311,
nś' 312,
nś' 313,
nś' 3162,
nś' 322,
nś' 3261,
nś' 351,
nś' 352

nś' 311,
nś' 312,
nś' 313,
nś' 3162

nś' 311

nś' 312

nś' 313

nś' 3162

nś' 322,
nś' 3261

nāśî' 111

ntk 321,
ntk 361,
ntk 3662,
ntk 372

ntn 311,
ntn 312,
ntn 314,
ntn 3161,
ntn 3162,
ntn 321

ntn 311,
ntn 312,
ntn 314,
ntn 3161,
ntn 3162

ntn 311

ntn 312

ntn 314

ntn 3162

ntn 321

sbb 311,
sbb 321,
sbb 322,
sbb 361,
sbb 362,
sbb 374

sbb 311,
sbb 321,
sbb 322

sbb 322

sābîb 111

sgr 311,
sgr 315,
sgr 322,
sgr 323

sgr 311,
sgr 315

sĕdōm 12

sûs 111

swr 311,
swr 361,
swr 362,
swr 363

swr 361,
swr 362,
swr 363

shr 314

sîr 111

sap 111

'ebed 111

'bd 311,
'bd 312,
'bd 313,
'bd 314,
'bd 321,
'bd 322,
'bd 361

'bd 311,
'bd 312,
'bd 313,
'bd 314

'br 311,
'br 312,
'br 313,
'br 314,
'br 3162,
'br 322,
'br 361,
'br 362,
'br 3662

'br 311,
'br 312,
'br 313,
'br 314,
'br 3162,
'br 322

'br 312

'br 314

'br 361,
'br 362,
'br 3662

'br 362

'ebrâ 114

'ăbôt 111

'gb 311,
'gb 312

'ad 4

'ădî 111

'ēden 12

'ôd 23

'ôz 111

'āwel 111

'ôlām 111

'āwōn 111

'ôp 111

'zb 311,
'zb 324

'zb 311

'izzābôn 111

'ezrâ 114

'ayin 114

'îr 114

'êrōm 111

'al 4

'ōlâ 114

'lh 311,
'lh 312,
'lh 314,
'lh 321,
'lh 322,
'lh 361,
'lh 362,
'lh 3661,
'lh 3662

'lh 311,
'lh 312,
'lh 314,
'lh 321,
'lh 322

'lh 312

'lh 361,
'lh 362,
'lh 3661,
'lh 3662

'lh 361

'lh 3662

'ălîlâ 114

'am 111

'md 311,
'md 312,
'md 313,
'md 314,
'md 3161,
'md 3162,
'md 361,
'md 362,
'md 363

'md 311,
'md 312,
'md 313,
'md 314,
'md 3161,
'md 3162

'md 311

'md 312

'md 314

'ummâ 114

'ammôn 12

'ānān 111

'ēc 111

'ecem 114

'ereb 111

'erwâ 114

'ārēl 21

'śh 311,
'śh 312,
'śh 313,
'śh 314,
'śh 315,
'śh 3161,
'śh 3162,
'śh 321,
'śh 322,
'śh 324,
'śh 3262,
'śh 331

'śh 311,
'śh 312,
'śh 313,
'śh 314,
'śh 315,
'śh 3161,
'śh 3162

'śh 311

'śh 312

'śh 313

'śh 314

'śh 315

'śh 3162

'śh 321,
'śh 322,
'śh 324,
'śh 3262

'śh 322

'aśārâ 711,
'eśer 714,
'eśîrî 721,
'eśîrî 724

'aśārâ 711

'eśer 714

'ēt 114

'attâ 23

pē'â 114

pō'râ 114

peh 111

pōh 23

pwc 312,
pwc 321,
pwc 361,
pwc 362,
pwc 363,
pwc 3662

pwc 312,
pwc 321

pwc 321

pwc 361,
pwc 362,
pwc 363,
pwc 3662

pwc 361

pālîṭ 111

pāneh 111

pnh 311,
pnh 312,
pnh 314,
pnh 3162,
pnh 374

pnh 314

pēnîmî 21

par 111

pērî 111

par'ōh 111

prr 361,
prr 362,
prr 3662

prś 311,
prś 312,
prś 322

pārāṣ 111

peśa' 111

petaḥ 111

pth 311,
pth 312,
pth 314,
pth 315,
pth 3162,
pth 321,
pth 322

pth 311,
pth 312,
pth 314,
pth 315,
pth 3162

pth 321,
pth 322

pth 322

cō'n 114

cĕbî 111

cad 111

caddîq 21

cĕdāqâ 114

cwh 331,
cwh 3362,
cwh 341

côr 12

clḥ 312

cēlā' 114

cammeret 114

cph 314

cāpôn 114

qbc 312,
qbc 314,
qbc 322,
qbc 323,
qbc 331,
qbc 332,
qbc 334,
qbc 3362,
qbc 344

qbc 331,
qbc 332,
qbc 334,
qbc 3362,
qbc 344

qbc 331

qeber 111

qbr 311,
qbr 334

qādîm 111

qōdeš 111

qdš 321,
qdš 3262,
qdš 331,
qdš 332,
qdš 333,
qdš 334,
qdš 3362,
qdš 344,
qdš 351

qdš 321,
qdš 3262

qdš 331,
qdš 332,
qdš 333,
qdš 334,
qdš 3362,
qdš 344

qāhāl 111

qôl 111

qwm 311,
qwm 312,
qwm 313,
qwm 3362,
qwm 361

qwm 361

qômâ 114

qînâ 114

qîr 111

qin'â 114

qāneh 111

qsm 312,
qsm 314,
qsm 3162

qēc 111

qāceh 111

qr' 311,
qr' 312,
qr' 315,
qr' 322,
qr' 341

qr' 311,
qr' 312,
qr' 315

qrb 311,
qrb 312,
qrb 313,
qrb 331,
qrb 333,
qrb 361,
qrb 362,
qrb 3662

qrb 311,
qrb 312,
qrb 313

qrb 361,
qrb 362,
qrb 3662

qrb 362

qārôb 21

qeren 114

r'h 311,
r'h 312,
r'h 313,
r'h 314,
r'h 3162,
r'h 321,
r'h 322,
r'h 3262,
r'h 362,
r'h 364,
r'h 3662

r'h 311,
r'h 312,
r'h 313,
r'h 314,
r'h 3162,
r'h 321,
r'h 322,
r'h 3262

r'h 311,
r'h 312,
r'h 313,
r'h 314,
r'h 3162

r'h 311

r'h 312

r'h 314

rō'š 111

ri'šôn 721

rōb 111

rab 21

rbh 311,
rbh 312,
rbh 331,
rbh 361,
rbh 362,
rbh 363,
rbh 3661

rbh 361,
rbh 362,
rbh 363,
rbh 3661

rbh 361

rbh 362

reba' 111

regel 114

rûaḥ 114

rwm 311,
rwm 312,
rwm 314,
rwm 3162,
rwm 362,
rwm 363,
rwm 3662,
rwm 381

rwm 311,
rwm 312,
rwm 314,
rwm 3162

rwm 362,
rwm 363,
rwm 3662

rwm 362

rōḥab 111

rḥq 311,
rḥq 313,
rḥq 3162,
rḥq 332,
rḥq 361

ryq 361,
ryq 362

rkl 314

rēa' 111

ra' 21

rā'āb 111

r'h 311,
r'h 312,
r'h 314,
r'h 3162

r'h 312

r'h 314

ra'aš 111

r'š 311,
r'š 312,
r'š 361

ricpâ 114

rāqîa' 111

riqmâ 114	šbt 321, šbt 361	škb 311, škb 312,	šelem 111
rāśā' 21		škb 313, škb 314,	šēm 111
	šbt 361	škb 371, škb 373	
riš'â 114			šām 23
	šāw' 111		
śādeh 111		škb 311,	šemōnâ 711, šemōneh 714,
	šwb 311,	škb 312,	šemînî 721
śeh 111	šwb 312, šwb 313,	škb 313,	
	šwb 314,	škb 314	šāmayim 111
śwm 311, śwm 312,	šwb 3161, šwb 3162,		
śwm 313,	šwb 361,	škb 312	šmm 311, šmm 314,
śwm 3162,	šwb 362,		šmm 3162,
śwm 361, śwm 363	šwb 363, šwb 364,	škn 311, škn 312,	šmm 321, šmm 324
	šwb 3662,	škn 361	
śwm 311, śwm 312,	šwb 381, šwb 384,		šmm 311, šmm 314,
śwm 313,	šwb 3862	šālôm 111	šmm 3162
śwm 3162			
	šwb 311,	šelôšâ 711, šālôš 714,	šmm 311
śwm 311	šwb 312, šwb 313,	šelîšî 721, šelîšît 724	
	šwb 314,		šmm 321, šmm 324
śwm 312	šwb 3161, šwb 3162	šelôšâ 711	
			šmm 321
śwm 313	šwb 311	šālôš 714	
			šmm 324
ś'îr 12	šwb 312	šlḥ 311, šlḥ 312,	
		šlḥ 314,	šmm 361, šmm 362,
śāpâ 114	šwb 3162	šlḥ 315, šlḥ 3162,	šmm 364
		šlḥ 331,	
še'ôl 114	šwb 361, šwb 362,	šlḥ 332, šlḥ 3362,	šemāmâ 114
	šwb 363,	šlḥ 361	
še'ērît 114	šwb 364, šwb 3662		šemen 111
šēbeṭ 111		šlḥ 311, šlḥ 312,	šm' 311, šm' 312,
	šwb 361	šlḥ 314,	šm' 313,
šēbît 114		šlḥ 315, šlḥ 3162	šm' 314, šm' 3162,
šib'â 711,	šwb 362		šm' 321,
šeba' 714,		šlḥ 331, šlḥ 332,	šm' 322, šm' 361,
šēbî'î 721, šebî'ît 724	šḥt 312, šḥt 3162	šlḥ 3362	šm' 362, šm' 3662
šib'â 711		šlḥ 331	
	šḥt 324,		šm' 311, šm' 312,
šbr 311,	šḥt 331, šḥt 3362,	šulḥān 111	šm' 313,
šbr 314,	šḥt 362,		šm' 314, šm' 3162,
šbr 321, šbr 322,	šḥt 364	šelîšît 724	šm' 321,
šbr 324			šm' 322
	šḥt 331, šḥt 3362	šlk 361, šlk 362,	
šbr 311, šbr 314		šlk 363,	šm' 311, šm' 312,
	šḥt 3362	šlk 371, šlk 372	šm' 313,
šbr 311			šm' 314, šm' 3162
	šḥt 362, šḥt 364	šālāl 111	
šbr 321, šbr 322,			šm' 311
šbr 324	šḥt 364	šll 311, šll 314,	
šbr 321		šll 3162	
šabbāt 114			

šm' 312

šm' 313

šmr 311,
šmr 312,
šmr 313,
šmr 314,
šmr 3162

šmr 311

šmr 312

šōmrôn 12

šānâ 114

šĕnayim 711,
šĕttayim 714,
šēnî 721,
šēnît 724

šĕnayim 711

šĕttayim 714

ša'ar 111

šepeṭ 111

špṭ 311,
špṭ 312,
špṭ 314,
špṭ 3162,
špṭ 321,
špṭ 322

špṭ 311,
špṭ 312,
špṭ 314,
špṭ 3162

špṭ 311

špṭ 312

špṭ 321,
špṭ 322

špk 311,
špk 312,
špk 314,
špk 315,
špk 3162,
špk 3262

špk 311

špk 312

špk 314

špk 3162

šāpāl 21

šiqqûc 111

šeqel 111

šōreš 111

šrt 332,
šrt 334,
šrt 3362

šrt 334

šrt 3362

šiššâ 711,
šēš 714,
šiššî 721,
šiššît 724

šēš 714

šiššît 724

šth 311,
šth 312,
šth 314

šth 312

štl 311,
štl 312,
štl 315

tā' 111

tûbal 12

tāwek 111

tô'ēbâ 114

tôrâ 114

taznût 114

taḥat 111

taḥtôn 21

taḥtî 21

tkn 322

tāmîm 21

timōrâ 114

t'h 311,
t'h 312,
t'h 3162

ta'ar 111

tip'ārâ 114

tāpēl 111

tpś 314,
tpś 3162,
tpś 321,
tpś 322,
tpś 3262

tpś 314,
tpś 3162

tpś 321,
tpś 322,
tpś 3262

tĕrûmâ 114

taršîš 111,
taršîš 12

Linguistic Density Plot in Ezekiel 1 - 48

For 'āb 111 (27 times)

Each Column = 13 Verses.   Separations are: Max = 4700.00.   Mean = 998.93.   Min = 14.50 .

CLUSTERS:

Start:	2: 3	5:10	16: 3	18: 2	18: 2	18:14	18:17	18:17	18:19	18:20	20: 4	20:18	20:30	22: 7	22:10
End:	22:11	5:10	22:11	22:11	20:42	18:20	18:18	18:20	18:20	18:20	20:27	20:27	20:42	22:11	22:11
Count:	23	2	20	18	15	6	5	2	2	4	3	3	3	7	2
Width:	10974	9	4887	2945	1966	353	136	31	64	29	1008	596	230	323	78	31
Strength:	5.16	1.02	5.80	5.53	4.62	2.95	2.44	1.00	2.16	1.03	1.47	1.03	2.33	1.49	1.32	1.25	1.43	1.00

GAPS:

Start:	5:10	18:20	22:11	37:25	37:25
	18: 2	16: 3			
End:	48:35	48:35	36:28	48:35	47:14	44:25	37:25
Count:	4	2	16	6	4	3	2
Width:	6601	4659	18934	16342	8570	6942	6062	4500
Strength:	2.24	3.79	1.52	5.70	7.85	2.45	3.03	3.63

Linguistic Density Plot in Ezekiel 1 - 48

For 'bd 311 (4 times)   'bd 312 (1 times)   'bd 331 (1 times)
     'bd 332 (1 times)   'bd 3362 (1 times)
                              'bd 314 (2 times)
                              'bd 361 (4 times)

Each Column = 13 Verses.   Separations are: Max = 4527.50, Mean = 1864.67, Min = 295.00 .

CLUSTERS:

Start:	6: 3	25: 7	25: 7	25: 7	
End:	37:11	37:11	32:13	28:16	26:17
Count:	14	9	6	4	3
Width:	18292	6898	3588	1619	590
Strength:	2.50	2.29	1.73	1.42	1.32

GAPS:

Start:	7:26	7:26	12:22	12:22	34:16	37:11
End:	25: 7	22:27	22:27	19: 5	48:35	48:35
Count:	5	4	3	2	3	2
Width:	10634	8838	6631	4060	9055	7328
Strength:	1.02	1.15	1.22	1.25	2.24	3.13

Linguistic Density Plot in Ezekiel 1 - 48

For 'bd 311 (4 times)   'bd 312 (1 times)   'bd 314 (2 times)

Each Column = 13 Verses. Separations are: Max = 4632.00, Mean = 3496.25, Min = 1000.50 .

REFERENCE

DENSITY

CLUSTERS:

Start:	34: 4	34:16
End:	37:11	34:16
Count:	3	2
Width:	2001	274
Strength:	1.23	1.04

GAPS:

Start:	37:11
End:	48:35
Count:	2
Width:	7328
Strength:	1.24

Linguistic Density Plot in Ezekiel 1 - 48

For 'eben 114 (17 times)

Each Column = 13 Verses. Separations are: Max = 3392.00, Mean = 1553.89, Min = 42.50 .

```
CLUSTERS:

Start:      1:26   1:26  10: 1  10: 1  13:11  13:11  23:47  26:12  27:22  28:13  28:14
End:       40:42  28:16  13:13  11:19  13:13  28:16  28:16  28:16  28:16  28:16  28:16
Count:        17     14      5      3      4      6      5      4      3
Width:     22682  14856   1783    833   2396   1146    547     85     40
Strength:   1.08   1.85   1.66   1.12   1.86   1.02   1.72   1.49   1.02

GAPS:

Start:      1:26  13:13  16:40  28:16  38:22  40:42
           10: 1  23:47  23:47  48:35  36:26  48:35
End:       10: 1  23:47  23:47  48:35  36:26  48:35
Count:        2      4      3      5      2      3      2
Width:     3392   7285   5408  12601   4790   6331   4775
Strength:   1.25   1.09   1.14   2.39   2.20   1.59   2.19
```

Linguistic Density Plot in Ezekiel 1 - 48

For 'agap 111 (7 times)

Each Column = 13 Verses.   Separations are: Max = 8026.00. Mean = 3496.25. Min = 42.00

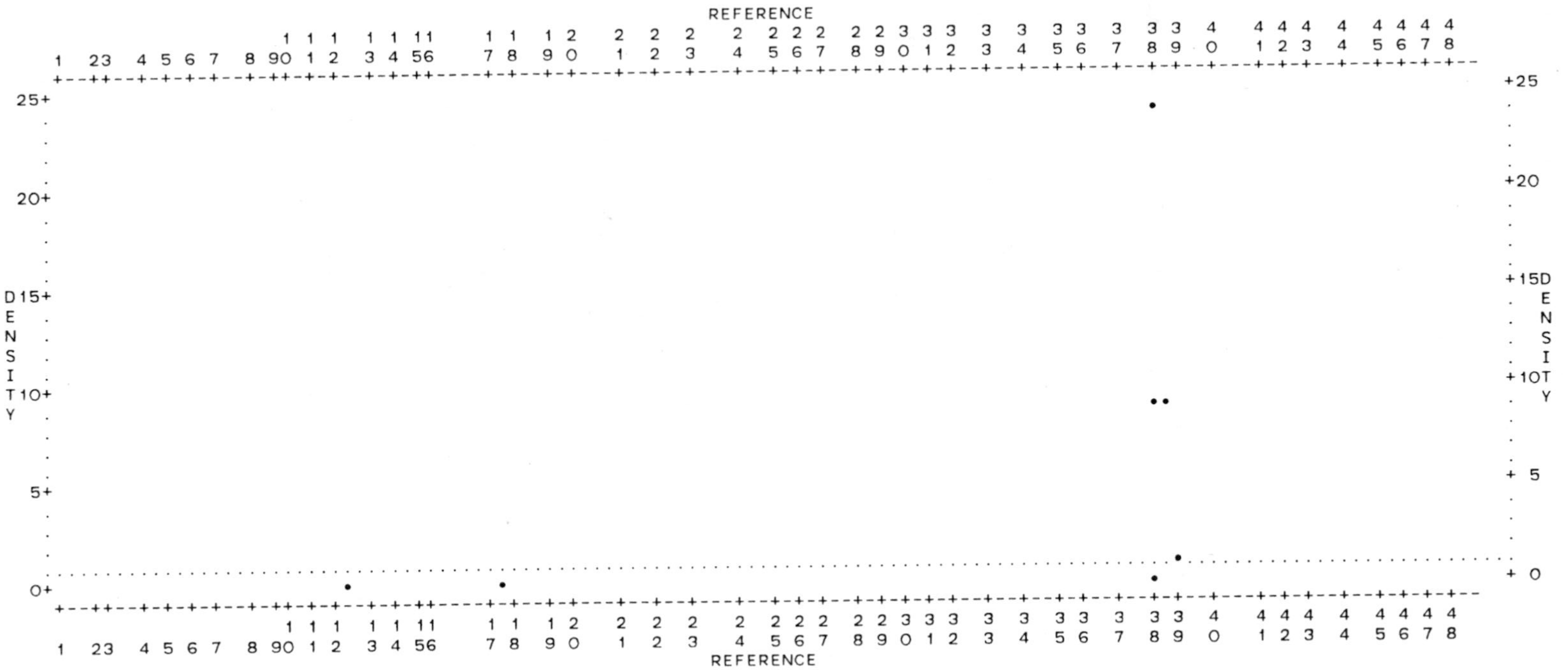

REFERENCE

CLUSTERS:

Start:	12:14	38: 6	38: 6	38: 6	38:22
End:	39: 4	38: 4	38: 9	38: 6	39: 4
Count:	7	5	3	2	2
Width:	16581	529	84	9	89
Strength:	1.08	2.88	1.71	1.13	1.10

GAPS:

Start:	1: 1	17:21
End:	38: 6	38: 6
Count:	4	2
Width:	21208	12648
Strength:	2.37	2.96

Linguistic Density Plot in Ezekiel 1 - 48

For `edôm 124 (7 times)

Each Column = 13 Verses.   Separations are: Max =   6928.50, Mean =   3496.25, Min =   17.50 .

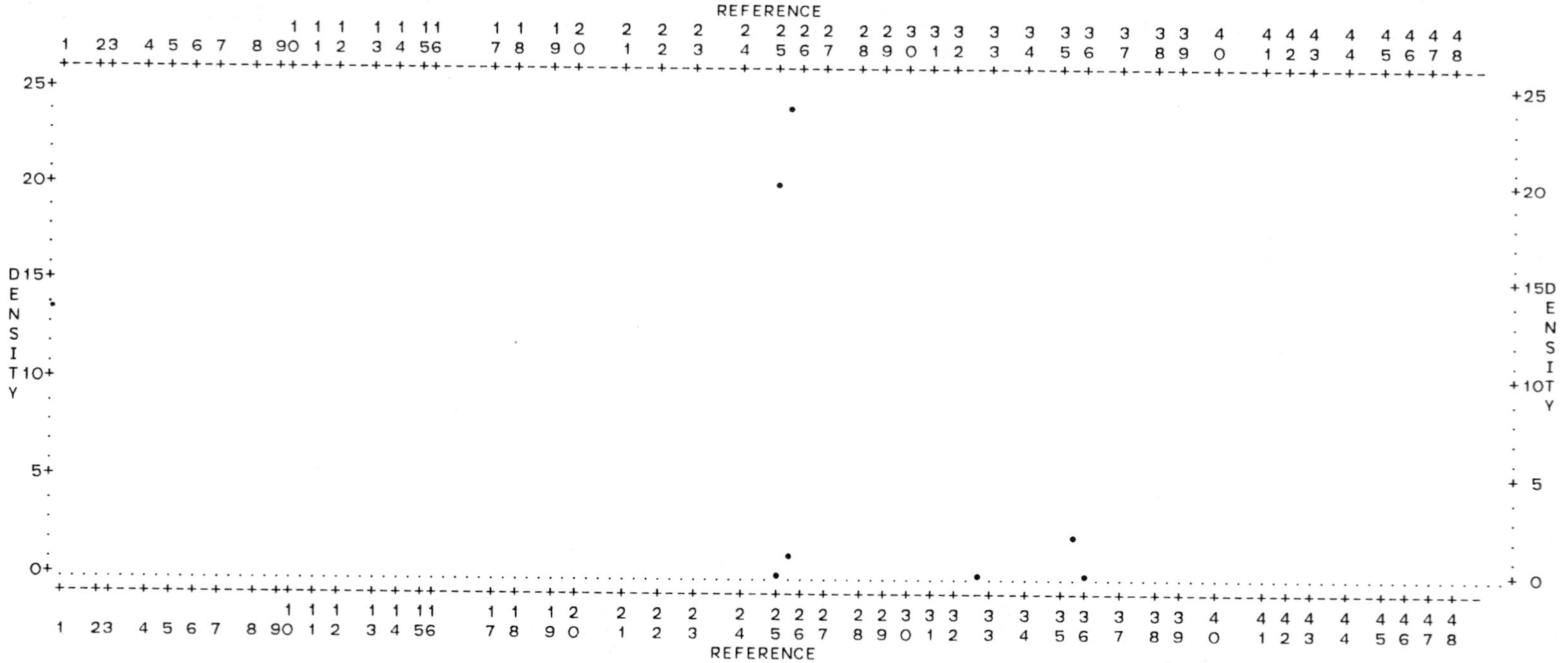

REFERENCE

REFERENCE

DENSITY

+25

+20

+15

+10

+5

0

CLUSTERS:

Start:	25:12	25:12	25:14	25:12	25:14	32:29	35:15
End:	36:5	25:14	25:14	25:13	25:14	36:5	36:5
Count:	7	4	2	2	3	2
Width:	5849	61	26	9	1999	141
Strength:	3.74	2.31	1.12	1.13	1.23	1.08

GAPS:

Start:	1:1	1:1	36:5
End:	25:13	25:12	48:35
Count:	3	2	2
Width:	13856	13830	8290
Strength:	1.69	3.35	1.55

Linguistic Density Plot in Ezekiel 1 - 48

For 'ādôn 111 (221 times)

Each Column = 13 Verses.   Separations are: Max = 1253.50, Mean = 125.99, Min = 14.00 .

CLUSTERS:

Start:	2: 4	5: 4	11: 7	12:10	12:10	12:19	12:28	13: 8	13: 8	14: 4	14: 4	14: 4	14: 4	14: 4	14: 8	14:11	14:18	14:18
End:	48:29	27: 3	13:20	11:21	13: 3	13: 3	13:13	13:20	13:13	27: 3	16:48	14:23	14:23	14:11	14:23	14:23	14:21
Count:	221	122	14	6	20	7	14	6	3	7	4	87	37	20	9	7	66	3
Width:	27181	13799	802	333	1397	417	226	305	45	117	54	8459	3629	1726	991	532	299	158	66
Strength:	3.03	1.54	1.89	1.06	1.90	1.11	1.45	1.48	1.16	1.20	1.11	2.60	1.31	1.27	1.46	1.50	1.01	1.04

Start:	18:23	18:23	18:32	20: 5	20: 3	20:27	20:27	20:27	20:36	23:46	25: 3	25:12	25:14	25:12	25:16	26: 7	28: 2	28: 2	29: 8	29: 8
End:	20: 5	18:32	20: 5	20: 5	22: 3	21: 5	22: 3	21: 5	27: 3	23:46	27: 3	25:16	26:14	25:16	25:16	27: 3	26: 7	33:27	39:29	30:22	30:22
Count:	8	5	5	3	5	3	6	3	6	3	4	5	3	5	8	4	12	10	33	18	8	6	7
Width:	552	213	213	40	1239	316	560	316	1528	868	479	144	108	266	217	82	3295	1425	719	426
Strength:	1.00	1.16	1.19	1.19	1.60	1.12	1.55	1.12	2.57	2.36	2.22	1.07	1.58	1.88	1.26	1.14	3.31	1.11	1.43	1.12	1.08

Clusters for 'ādōn 111, continued.

```
Start:    29:16  34: 2  34: 2  34: 2  34:30  34:30  34:30  34:30  36    36: 2  36: 4  36:13  36:13  36:13  36:32  37:19  39: 5  39: 5
End:      30: 6  39:29  37:12  34:20  36: 7  35:14  36     35: 3  36: 7  36: 5  36: 5  37:12  36:23  36:15  37:12  39:29  39:29  39:17
Count:    5      49     32     7      13     6      3      3      7      5      3      5      12     5      3      7      17     8      5
Width:    236    3713   2065   1154   411    508    270    45     182    101    43     788    222    52     373    1486   540    249
Strength: 1.07   3.02   2.83   2.36   1.13   2.36   1.29   1.25   1.16   1.88   1.61   1.17   1.46   1.12   1.12   1.25   1.09   1.04   1.02

GAPS:

Start:    1: 1   1: 1   1: 1   1: 1   1: 1   3:11   6: 3   6: 3   7: 5   8: 1   9: 8   11:21  11:21  11:21  18: 9  18:32  20: 5  20: 5  22:31
End:      6: 3   5: 7   5: 5   4:14   3:27   2: 4   3:27   12:28  11: 7  11: 7  11: 7  12:19  12:10  18:23  18:23  20: 3  20:31  20:30  20:27  23:32
Count:    10     7      6      5      4      2      17     4      2      3      7      3      2      2      2      4      3      2      4
Width:    2324   1997   1949   1750   1429   681    377    3098   2131   1755   1288   651    453    262    281    299    714    669    578    618
Strength: 3.22   4.08   4.74   4.99   4.85   4.42   1.99   2.23   4.52   6.36   5.85   4.18   1.13   1.08   1.23   1.37   1.55   2.35   3.59   1.10

Start:    22:31  22:31  27: 3  27: 3  27: 3  30:13  30:13  30:22  32:16  36: 4  36:33  37: 5  37: 5  37: 5  38:18  39: 8  39:17  39:20  39:25
End:      23:28  23:22  28:10  28: 2  28: 6  31:15  31:10  31:10  32:31  48:35  48:35  45: 9  43:18  38: 3  43:18  43:18  43:18  43:18  43:18
Count:    3      3      2      4      3      4      2      2      51     29     41     21     38     3      12     8      5      4      3
Width:    542    378    762    688    608    612    473    303    339    8343   7670   7484   5384   4215   3161   2884   2687   2601   2507
Strength: 1.63   2.00   1.77   2.46   3.83   1.07   1.24   1.40   1.69   2.61   3.65   4.04   2.98   3.16   4.36   6.11   8.76   10.27  12.73

Start:    39:29  43:18  44:15  44:27  45: 9  45:18  46: 1  46: 1  46:16  47:23
End:      43:18  45: 9  45: 9  48:35  48:35  48:29  48:29  47:13  47:13  48:29
Count:    2      3      2      9      7      5      9      5      2
Width:    2396   557    294    2075   1913   1806   1649   843    499    585
Strength: 18.09  1.72   1.33   3.05   3.80   4.22   4.59   3.33   2.96   3.65
```

Linguistic Density Plot in Ezekiel 1 - 48

For 'ādām 111 (132 times)

Each Column = 13 Verses.   Separations are: Max = 1367.00. Mean = 210.30. Min = 20.00 .

CLUSTERS:

Start:	1: 5	1: 5	1: 5	1: 5	1: 5	1: 5	1:26	2: 6	3: 6	3:10	4:12	4:15	8: 5	8: 5	8:12	10: 8	10: 8
End:	47: 6	34: 2	16: 2	8:17	16: 2	3: 4	1:10	3: 4	3: 4	5: 1	5: 1	5: 1	8:17	8: 8	8:17	16: 2	13: 2
Count:	132	103	49	27	19	11	77	185	64	832	123	57	281	76	118	2653	1391
Width:	26787	18478	6617	3444	1748	792	368	113	185	832	123	57	281	76	118	2653	1391
Strength:	2.59	2.90	2.99	2.11	2.46	2.05	2.04	1.04	1.58	1.18	1.41	1.23	1.67	1.17	1.02	2.00	1.63

Start:	10:21	11: 4	12:18	12: 2	13:17	14:13	14:13	19: 3	21: 2	21: 2	21:17	21: 2	28: 2	34:31	34:31	36:10	36:12	36:37
End:	11: 4	13: 2	12: 2	13: 2	16: 2	16: 2	14:19	20:27	23: 2	21:24	21:14	21:24	28:12	37:16	40: 4	36:14	36:17	37:16
Count:	7	3	4	9	7	4	8	12	4	3	6	9	6	22	15	5	3	6
Width:	578	230	950	578	450	162	868	418	240	118	554	173	118	1491	685	131	84	40
Strength:	1.36	1.11	1.27	1.08	1.61	1.30	1.11	1.68	1.08	1.02	1.08	1.27	1.02	1.95	1.73	1.83	1.29	1.52

Data for 'ādām 111, continued.

GAPS:

Block 1

Start	End	Count	Width	Strength
4:16	8: 5	5	1459	1.49
5: 1	8: 5	4	1415	2.18
5: 1	6: 2	2	460	1.19
7: 2	8: 5	2	627	1.99
8:17	10: 8	2	520	1.48
14:13	20: 3	10	3302	2.32
14:19	20: 3	8	3171	3.14
14:19	19: 3	6	2925	4.07
14:21	19: 3	5	2867	4.90
15: 1	19: 3	3	2788	6.01
16: 2	19: 3	3	2637	7.53
16: 2	17: 3	2	1393	5.66
20:27	21: 2	2	494	1.35
22:24	23:36	3	877	1.55
23: 2	23:36	2	690	2.29
26: 2	28: 2	4	1088	1.27
26: 2	27: 2	2	467	1.22
34: 2	34:31	2	670	2.20
36:14	48:35	23	8084	3.85
36:17	36:37	2	456	1.17

Block 2

Start	End	Count	Width	Strength
36:38	48:35	20	7565	4.22
39:17	48:35	10	5959	6.69
39:17	43: 7	4	2377	4.86
40: 4	43: 7	3	1987	5.32
40: 4	41:19	2	1360	5.50
43:18	48:35	6	3272	5.88
43:10	48:35	5	3479	5.28
44: 5	48:35	4	2975	6.53
44:25	48:35	3	2450	6.89
44:25	47: 6	2	1367	5.53

Linguistic Density Plot in Ezekiel 1 - 48

For 'adāmâ 114 (28 times)

Each Column = 13 Verses.   Separations are: Max = 2869.50, Mean = 964.48, Min = 13.50 .

```
CLUSTERS:

Start:     7: 2  11:17  12:19  20:38  21: 7  33:24  36: 6  36: 6  37:12  38:18  38:18  38:19  38:20
End:      39:28  13: 9  13: 9  21: 8  21: 8  39:28  37:21  36:24  37:21  38:20  38:20  38:20  38:20
Count:      28     4      3      4      2     15     12      6      3      4      3      2
Width:    19636   896    345    321     5    3964   1194    411    223    742     57     27      7
Strength:  4.94   1.28   1.22   1.65   1.02  3.73   3.24   1.88   1.17   2.11   1.82   1.46   1.02
```

```
GAPS:

Start:     1: 1   1: 1  12:22  13: 9  21: 8  25: 6  28:25  38:20  39:28
End:      12:19  11:17  20:38  18: 2  25: 3  33:24  33:24  48:35  48:35
Count:      4      3      2      4      3      4      3      4      2
Width:    5253   4702   4908   3080   2804   4596   5142   6376   5691
Strength:  1.51   2.14   2.30   2.26   1.97   2.06   1.44   1.90   2.23   5.07
```

Linguistic Density Plot in Ezekiel 1 - 48

For 'hb 311 (1 times)   'hb 334 (6 times)

Each Column = 13 Verses. Separations are: Max = 7894.50, Mean = 3496.25, Min = 17.00 .

REFERENCE

```
25+
     .
     .
20+
     .
     .
D 15+
E    .
N    .
S    .
I 10+
T    .
Y    .
     .
 5+
     .
     .
 0+
```

REFERENCE

CLUSTERS:

Start:	16:33	16:36	16:37	23: 5	23: 5
End:	23:22	16:37	16:37	23:22	23: 9
Count:	7	4	3	2	2
Width:	5043	102	34	10	314	71
Strength:	3.94	2.30	1.72	1.13	1.65	1.11

GAPS:

Start:	1: 1	16:37	23: 9	23:22
End:	16:33	48:35	48:35	48:35
Count:	2	5	3	2
Width:	7380	20487	15789	15546
Strength:	1.25	1.39	2.17	3.90

Linguistic Density Plot in Ezekiel 1 - 48

For 'ohŏlâ 12 (5 times)

Each Column = 13 Verses.   Separations are: Max = 7612.50, Mean = 4661.66, Min =   12.50 .

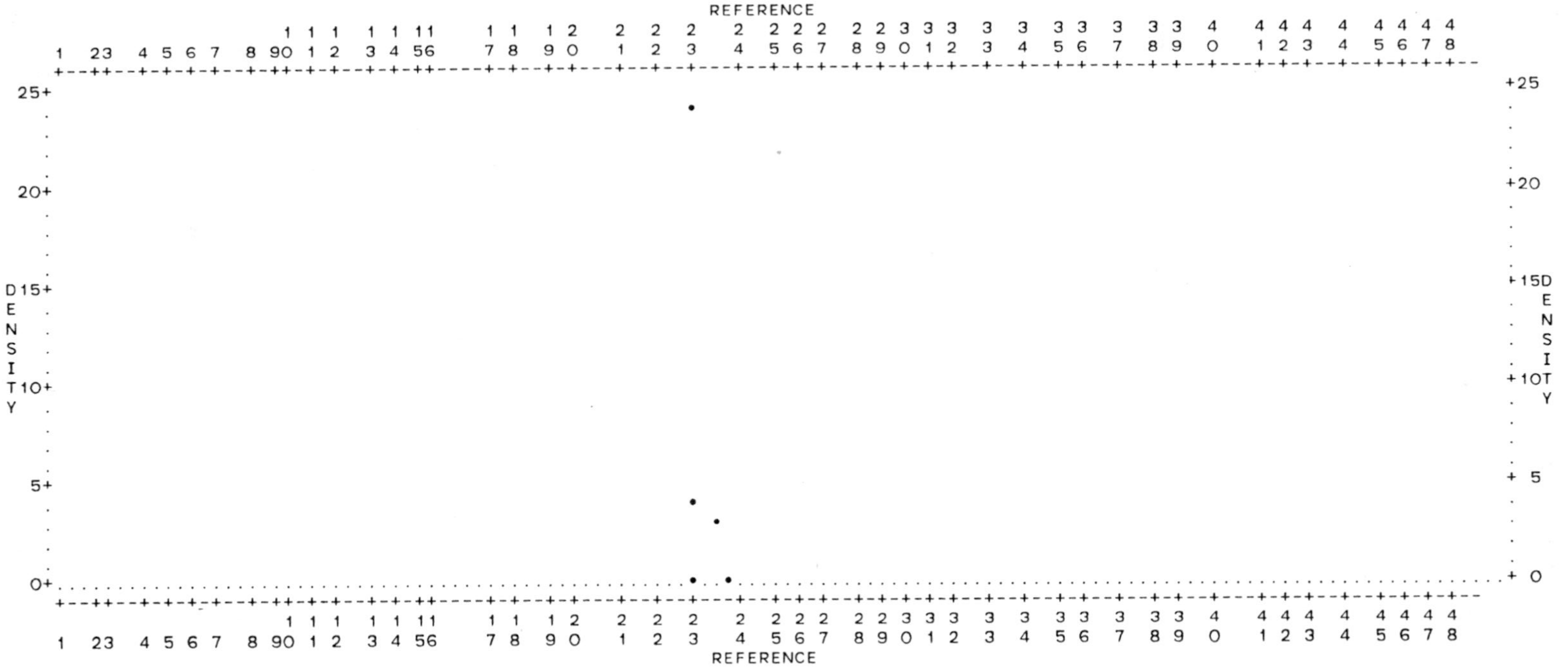

CLUSTERS:

Start:	23: 4	23: 4	23:36
End:	23:44	23: 5	23:44
Count:	5	3	2
Width:	844	25	6	178
Strength:	3.57	1.86	1.18	1.13

GAPS:

Start:	1: 1	23:44
End:	23: 4	48:35
Count:	2	2
Width:	12078	15047
Strength:	1.88	2.63

Linguistic Density Plot in Ezekiel 1 - 48

For 'oholiba 12 (6 times)

Each Column = 13 Verses.   Separations are: Max = 7611.00, Mean = 3995.71, Min = 69.50 .

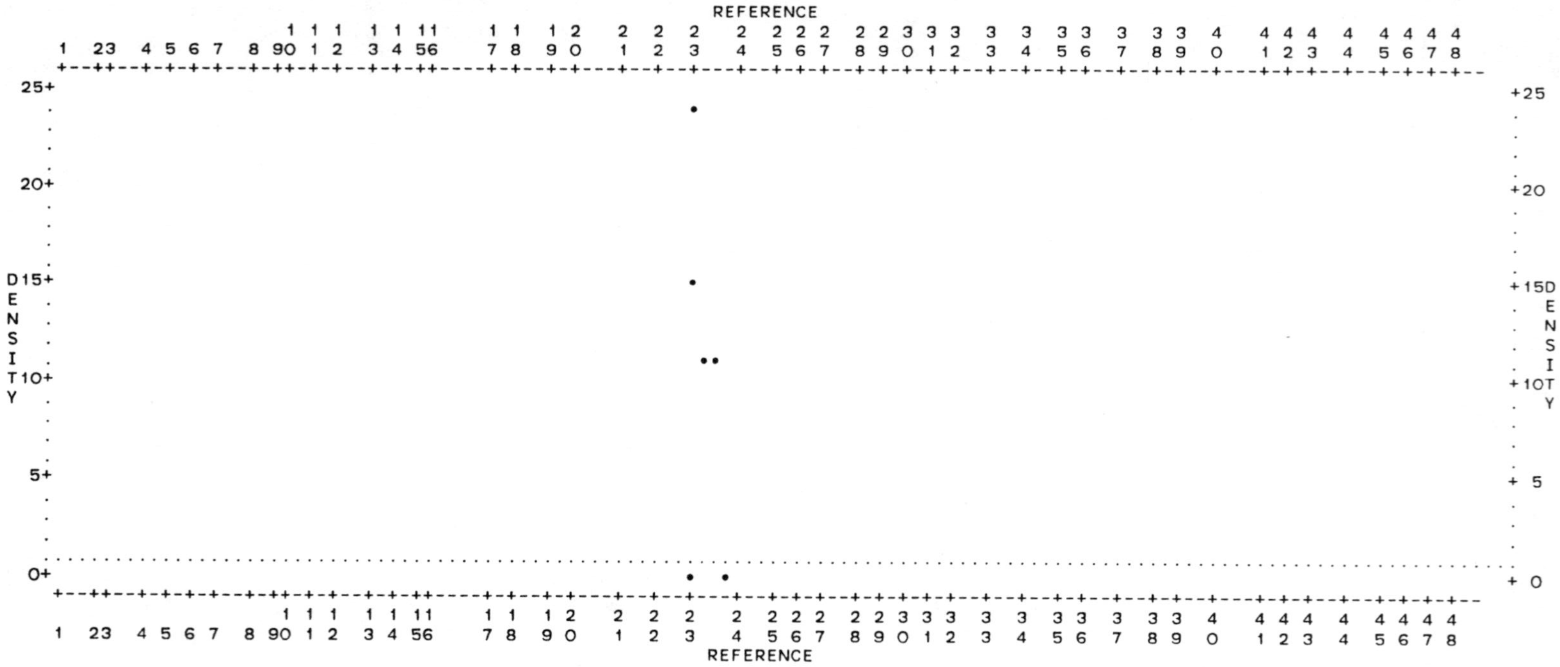

CLUSTERS:

Start:	23: 4	23: 4	23: 4	23: 4	23:36
End:	23:44	23:22	23:11	23: 4	23:44
Count:	6	4	3	2	2
Width:	844	332	139	19	178
Strength:	4.28	2.38	1.75	1.14	1.10

GAPS:

Start:	1: 1	23:44
End:	23: 4	48:35
Count:	2	2
Width:	12081	15044
Strength:	2.33	3.19

Linguistic Density Plot in Ezekiel 1 - 48

For 'Ôlām 111 (18 times)

Each Column = 13 Verses.   Separations are: Max = 19005.00. Mean = 1472.11, Min = 9.00 .

Density plot (vertical axis: DENSITY, scale +0, +5, +10, +15, +20, +25; horizontal axis: REFERENCE).

CLUSTERS:

```
Start:     8:16  40: 7  40: 7  40: 7  40: 7  40: 9  40: 9  40:29  40:39  40:48  40:48  41:15  41:15  41:25
End:      46: 8  46: 8  44: 3  40:15  40: 8  40: 8  40: 9  40:49  40:40  40:49  44: 3  40:48  41:26  41:26
Count:      18     17     15     11      5      4      2      6      3      2      4      3      2      2
Width:    22851   3846   2439    839    135     28      9     10    414    226     39   1262    198     15
Strength:  1.13   8.64   6.59   4.44   2.25   1.92   1.04   1.04   2.52   1.41   1.02   1.51   1.05   1.38   1.43   1.04
```

GAPS:

```
Start:     1: 1   1: 1   1: 1   8:16
End:      40:48  40: 8  40: 7  40: 7
Count:      11      4      3      2
Width:    23328  22526  22517  19005
Strength:  2.75   7.94  10.19  12.55
```

Linguistic Density Plot in Ezekiel 1 - 48

For 'Ōpan 111 (25 times)

Each Column = 13 Verses.   Separations are: Max = 11849.00, Mean = 1075.77, Min = 4.50 .

CLUSTERS:

Start:	1:15	1:15	1:15	1:16	1:15	1:19	1:19	1:19	1:20	1:21	1:21	10: 6	10: 6	10: 6	10: 9	10: 9	10:12
End:	11:22	3:13	1:21	1:16	1:21	1:19	1:20	1:21	1:20	1:21	11:22	10:10	10:10	10:10	10: 9	10: 9	10:19
Count:	25	11	10	4	11	6	4	2	2	14	13	7	6	4	2	2	6
Width:	4525	810	135	36	11	60	34	11	8	774	242	78	35	16	7	3	123
Strength:	14.84	3.79	3.72	1.85	1.02	2.50	1.85	1.03	1.03	4.90	4.72	2.81	2.51	1.86	1.03	1.03	2.47

Start:	10:12	10:16
End:	10:13	10:19
Count:	3	3
Width:	10	68
Strength:	1.49	1.03

Data for 'ôpan 111, continued.

GAPS:

Start:	1:21	3:13	10:13	10:16	10:19	11:22
End:	10: 6	10: 6	48:35	48:35	48:35	48:35
Count:	3	2	6	4	3	2
Width:	3616	2941	23811	23749	23698	23166
Strength:	1.02	1.80	8.68	11.93	15.02	21.33

Linguistic Density Plot in Ezekiel 1 - 48

For 'özen 114 (11 times)

Each Column = 13 Verses.   Separations are: Max = 5722.50, Mean = 2330.83, Min = 65.00

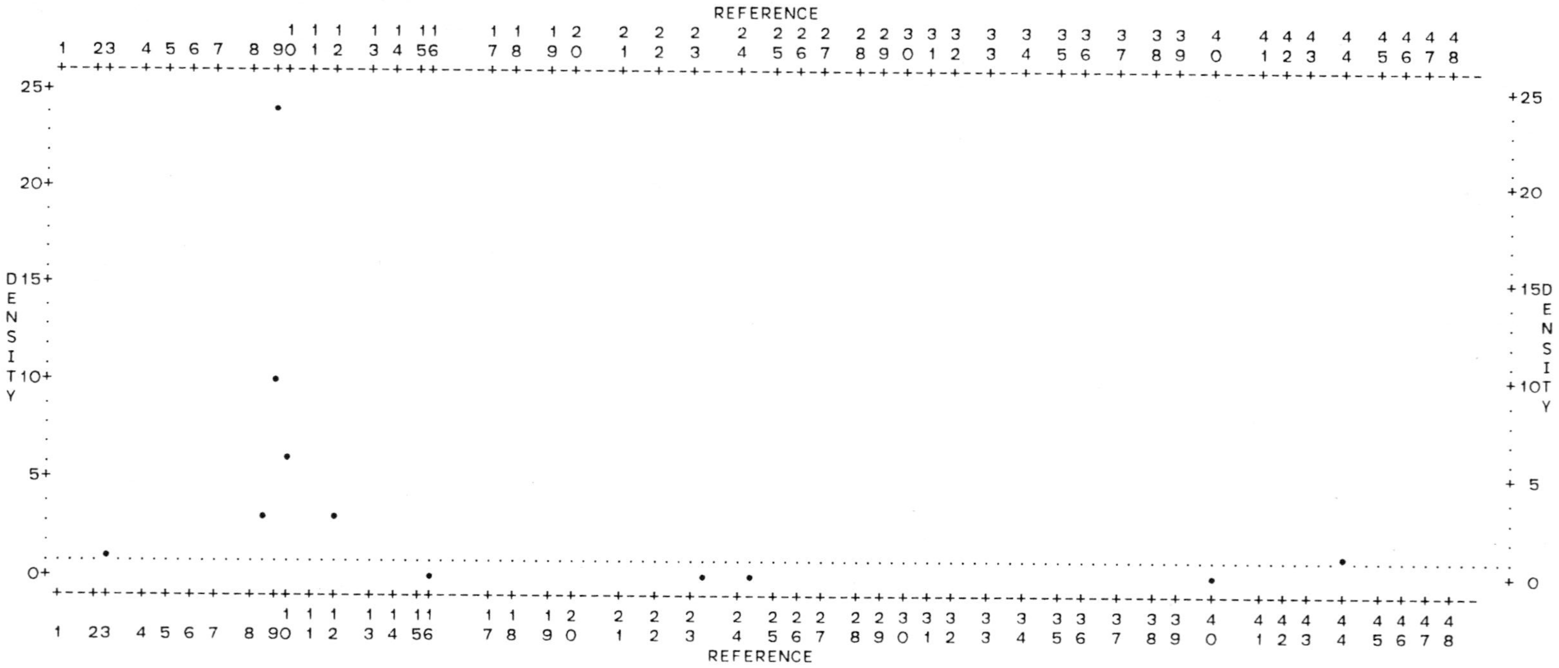

REFERENCE

(density plot, DENSITY axis scaled +25, +20, +15, +10, 5, 0)

REFERENCE

CLUSTERS:

Start:	3:10	8:18	8:18	8:18	8:18	
End:	16:12	16:12	12: 2	10:13	9: 5	9: 1
Count:	7	6	5	4	3	2
Width:	5925	3364	1301	573	130	12
Strength:	2.07	2.16	2.19	1.91	1.56	1.08

GAPS:

Start:	9: 1	9: 5	10:13	12: 2	12: 2	16:12	24:26	24:26
End:	48:35	48:35	48:35	48:35	23:25	23:25	48:35	40: 4
Count:	10	9	8	7	3	2	4	2
Width:	24366	24248	23805	23077	7626	5563	14409	8847
Strength:	1.00	1.53	1.95	2.34	1.02	1.50	2.20	3.03

Linguistic Density Plot in Ezekiel 1 - 48

For 'āḥ 111 (10 times)

Each Column = 13 Verses.   Separations are: Max = 4748.50, Mean = 2542.73, Min = 1388.50 .

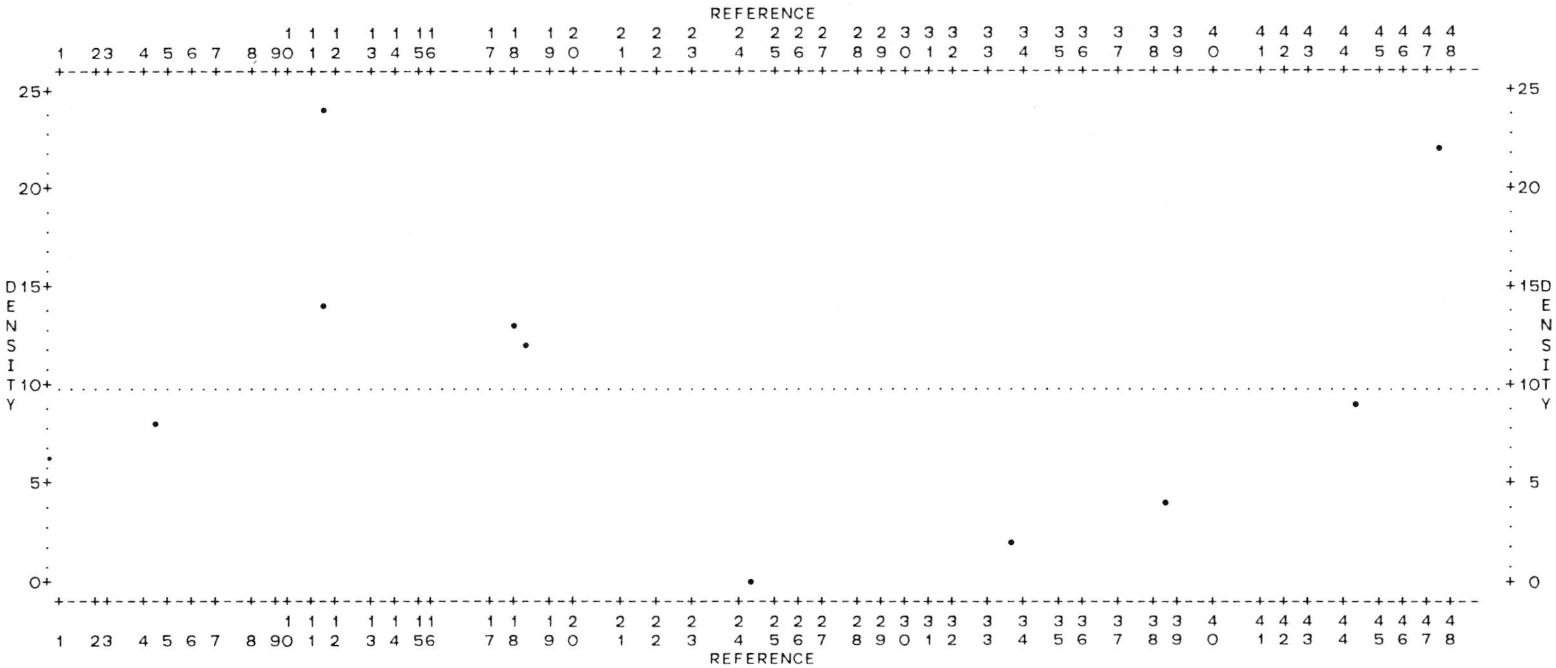

REFERENCE

CLUSTERS:

Start:	11:15	18:10
End:	11:15	18:18
Count:	2	2
Width:	2	154
Strength:	1.09	1.02

GAPS:

Start:	18:18	18:18	18:18	24:23
End:	47:14	44:25	33:30	33:30
Count:	6	5	3	2
Width:	18096	16556	9497	4984
Strength:	1.33	1.64	1.41	1.05

Linguistic Density Plot in Ezekiel 1 - 48

For 'ehād 711 (88 times)   'ahat 714 (19 times)   ri'šōn 721 (5 times)

Each Column = 13 Verses. Separations are: Max = 1869.00, Mean = 247.52, Min = 3.00

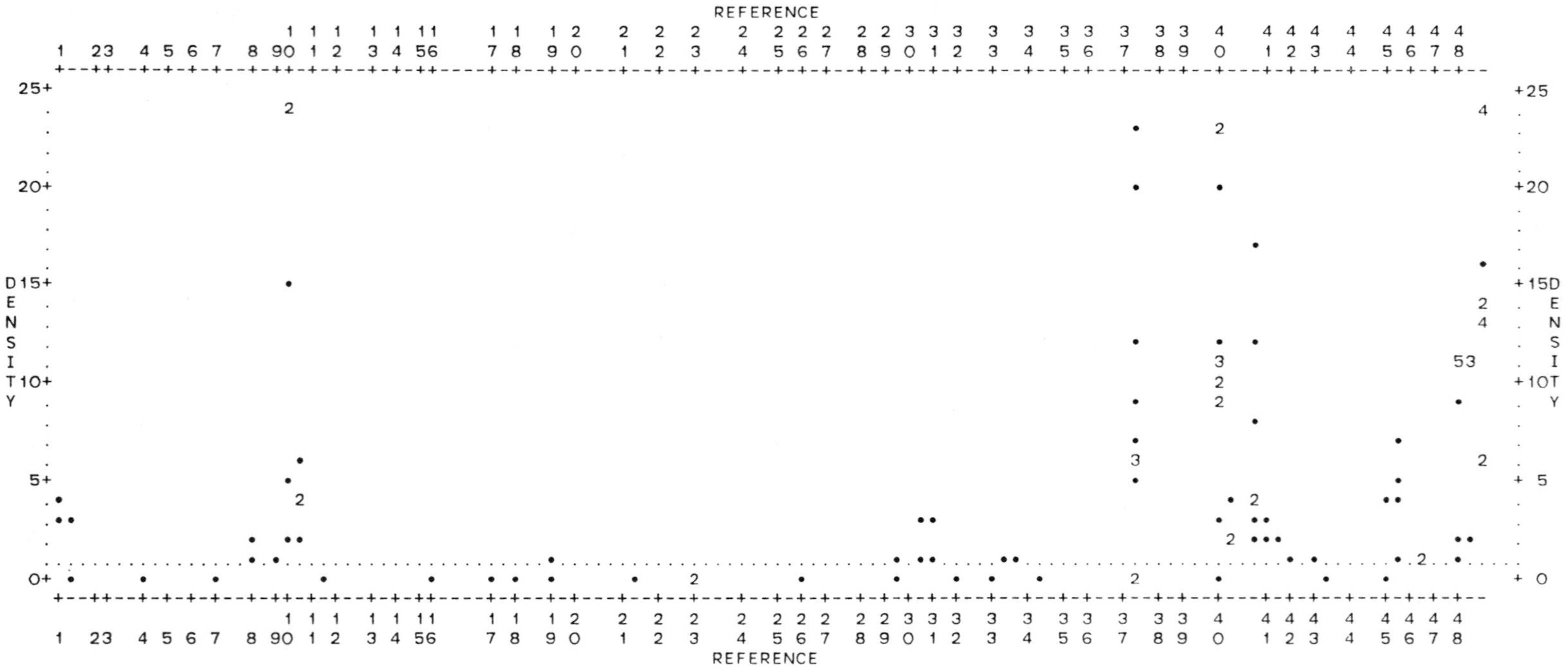

REFERENCE

(density scatter plot — vertical axis labelled DENSITY, scale +25, +20, +15, +10, +5, 0, 5; horizontal axis in verse columns)

REFERENCE

CLUSTERS:

```
Start:     1: 6   7: 5  10: 9  10: 9  10: 9  10:10  10:10     9  29:17  30:20  37:17  37:17  37:16  37:16  37:16  37:19  37:17  37:19  40: 5  40: 5
End:       1:16  11:19  10:21  10:14  10:10  10:10  43:14  48:34  31: 1  48:34  37:22  37:24  37:17  37:17  43:14  40:26  48:34  40:12  40:12  40: 8
Count:        4     14     10      9      7      5      4      9      4      4      5      4      6     11     40     16     73     16     13      9
Width:      192   2017    650    239     96     21    168  11963    168   2152    144     68     46    251   2152    431   7215    134    431     67
Strength:  1.30   1.43   2.22   2.59   2.36   2.00   1.74   7.41   1.36   3.88   1.74   1.60   2.21   2.98   4.63   3.69   8.42   3.51   3.69   2.84

Start:    40: 5  40: 6  40: 7  40: 6  40: 6  40:10  40:21  40:42  40:42  40:42  40:44  40:49  40:42  40:43  40:42  40:42  45:18  45: 7  45: 7  45: 7  48: 1  48: 5
End:      40: 7  40: 7  40: 7  40:12  40:26  40:26  40:42  40:43  40:44  40:49  43:14  48:34  40:42  40:42  40:42  48:34  45:21  45:15  45:21  46:22  48:34  48:34
Count:        7      5      5      3      4      6      3     13     11      7      5      3     33     25      8      3      7      6      8      3      3      5
Width:       41     16      7     36    123    765   1424    181     61     29     12   2126    898    284    147     56    649     97     49     24
Strength:  2.45   2.01   1.41   1.67   1.07   2.29   1.91   2.21   1.39   1.69   1.91   4.90   1.32   1.76   1.00   1.26   4.93   2.58   1.94   1.36
```

```
Clusters for 'ehãd 711, 'ahat 714, ri'sôn 721, continued.

Start:     48: 6  48:23  48:25  48:31  48:31  48:31  48:31  48:32  48:33  48:33  48:34
End:       48: 8  48:34  48:27  48:34  48:32  48:31  48:31  48:32  48:34  48:33  48:34
Count:         3     17      5      3     12      6      3      3      6      3      3
Width:        35    179     48     24     68     28      6      6     25      6      6
Strength:   1.33   4.13   1.94   1.36   3.41   2.24   1.41   1.41   2.25   1.41   1.41

GAPS:

Start:      1: 1   1: 1   1: 1   1: 1   1: 1   1: 1   1: 1   1: 6   1:16   1:16   1:16   1:16   1:16   1:16  10:14  10:21  11:19  11:19  11:19  11:19  11:19  11:19
End:       45:18  40: 6  37:17  29:17  10: 9  10: 9  10: 9  10: 9  10: 9  10: 9   8: 7   7: 5  29:17  29:17  29:17  29:17  19: 3  18:10  17: 7  16: 5  29:17
Count:        84     55     43     30     13     12     11      9      7      4      3      2     14     12      6      5      4      3      2      6      5
Width:     26060  22494  20778  15995   4082   4079   4076   3965   3778   3032   2411   1362  11823  11680   5027   4616   4104   3487   2057   6614
Strength:   4.76   6.97   8.20   7.70   1.37   1.74   2.15   2.95   3.90   5.43   5.54   4.54  10.29  11.53   7.03   7.48   7.98   8.66   7.37   9.97

Start:     19: 5  21:24  23:13  26: 1  29:17  29:17  30:20  31: 1  31: 1  31: 1  32: 1  32: 1  33:30  34:23  37:19  37:22  37:24  42: 4  43:14  43:14  45:21
End:       23: 2  29:17  29:17  29:17  37:17  37:17  37:17  37:16  37:17  33:24  33:24  33: 2  37:16  37:16  40: 5  40: 5  40: 5  43:13  45:11  45: 7  48: 1
Count:         3      2      3      2     13     11      9      7      4      3      2      9     11     14      5      5      3      3      7      4
Width:      2674   1765   3738   2013   4781   4309   4145   4110   1686   1233    725   2267   1681   1611   1546   1470   1290    642   1210   1193
Strength:   6.30   6.18   9.38   7.19   2.24   2.46   3.22   4.46   2.23   2.13   1.94   5.12   5.84   1.28   3.04   4.98   2.30   1.60   3.92   1.06
```

Linguistic Density Plot in Ezekiel 1 - 48

For 'eḥād 711 (88 times)

Each Column = 13 Verses.   Separations are: Max = 2052.00, Mean =   314.27, Min =   3.00 .

(DENSITY axis, vertical: +25, +20, +15 D, E, N, S, I +10 T, Y, +5, O; horizontal axis labeled REFERENCE, verse columns 1 through 48)

CLUSTERS:

Start:	8: 7	11:19	10: 9	10: 9	10: 9	10: 9	10: 9	10: 9	10: 9	9 10:14	37:16	37:16	37:17	37:17	37:17	37:19	37:19	37:19	40: 5
End:	11:19	11:19	10:21	10:14	10:10	10:10	10: 9	10: 9	10: 9	10:14	48:34	41:11	37:24	37:17	37:17	37:24	37:22	41:11	40:26
Count:	13	10	9	7	5	2	2	3	2	2	58	28	11	4	6	5	2	17	11
Width:	1396	650	239	96	21	9	3	3		7215	2863	251	46	11	68		144	1142	431
Strength:	2.35	2.45	2.69	2.42	2.02	1.75	1.00	1.00	1.00	7.56	7.56	3.10	2.24	1.75	1.00	1.82	3.43	2.91

Start:	40: 5	40: 7	40: 5	40: 6	40: 6	6 40:43	40:43	9 10:14	48: 1	48: 1	48: 3	5 48:	48: 5	48: 8	6 48:23	48:23	48:25	48:31	40: 5
End:	40: 7	40: 6	40: 7	40: 6	41:11	40:49	48:34	10:14	48: 1	48:34	48:	48: 5	48: 8	48:34	48:27	48:27	48:31	48:31	40:26
Count:	9	7	5	2	6	4	25	2	1	5	3	8	3	3	5	12	6	3	2
Width:	67	41	16	7	379	152	649	58	49	97	17	179	24	35	48	68	24	28	6
Strength:	2.90	2.49	2.03	1.42	1.75	1.48	5.26	2.64	1.97	1.38	4.28	1.97	1.35	1.38	1.97	3.49	2.27	1.42	1.00

```
Clusters for 'ehād 711, continued.

Start:    48:32 48:32 48:33 48:33 48:33 48:34 48:34
End:      48:32 48:32 48:33 48:33 48:34 48:34 48:34
Count:        3     2     6     2     6     3     2
Width:        6     3    25     6     6     3
Strength:  1.42  1.00  2.27  1.00  1.42  1.00

GAPS:

Start:     1: 1  1: 1  1: 1  1: 1  1:16  1:16  4: 9 10:14 10:21 10:21 11:19 11:19 11:19 19: 5 19: 5 19: 5 19: 5 19: 5
End:      37:17 10: 9 10: 7  9:10  8: 7  8: 7  8: 7 37:17 37:17 19: 3 19: 3 18:10 17: 7 37:16 33:24 31: 1 29:17 21:24
Count:       46    34    10     8     6     3     2    21    17     5     4     3     2    12     9     6     5     2
Width:    22494 20778  4082  4079  4076  3778  3032  1670 16606 16463 16428  5027  4616  4104  3487  8938  7252 11362  6616  1765
Strength:  5.66  7.30  1.40  1.85  2.36  3.24  5.49  4.36  8.38  9.12 10.06  6.17  6.90  7.95 10.20  7.61  8.36  8.14  8.77  4.66

Start:    23:13 29:17 26: 1 32: 1 32: 1 33:30 34:23 37:22 37:24 41:11 41:11 41:11 41:11 41:11 41:11 43:13 45:18 46:17
End:      29:17 37:17 33:24 33: 2 37:16 37:16 40: 5 40: 5 48: 4 48: 3 48: 1 45: 7 48: 1 48: 1 48: 1 45: 7 48: 7 48: 1
Count:        3     3    10     2     3     2     2     3     9    10     7     2     3     1     1     3     1     2
Width:     3740  2015  1233   725  2267  1681  1546  1470  3740  3728  3703  2226  1227  1247   720
Strength:  7.11  5.47  1.38  1.32  3.74  4.39  2.09  3.71  1.02  1.43  2.45  3.65  2.93  1.41  1.30
```

For 'aḥat 714 (19 times)

Linguistic Density Plot in Ezekiel 1 - 48

Each Column = 13 Verses.   Separations are: Max = 4841.00, Mean = 1398.50, Min = 6.00 .

CLUSTERS:

Start:	1: 6	1: 6	23: 2	40:10	40:10	40:10	40:12	40:42	41:24
End:	1: 6	46:22	46:22	43:14	40:42	40:12	40:42	43:14	
Count:	2	15	12	10	7	4	2	3	
Width:	5	14675	4168	2060	648	36	6	771	
Strength:	1.04	1.75	3.69	3.46	2.76	1.90	1.04	1.52	1.04	1.10

GAPS:

Start:	1: 1	1: 6	1: 6	1: 6	7: 5	16: 5	31: 1
End:	40:12	40:12	40:10	30:20	23: 2	40:10	
Count:	11	9	7	5	4	3	2
Width:	22595	22484	22451	16354	13756	9682	5272	5935
Strength:	2.82	3.77	5.02	4.40	4.38	3.75	2.91	3.40

Linguistic Density Plot in Ezekiel 1 - 48

For 'āḥôt 114 (24 times)

Each Column = 13 Verses.   Separations are: Max = 12857.00. Mean = 1118.80. Min =   9.50 .

CLUSTERS:

Start:	1: 9	16:45	1:23	16:45	16:45	16:45	16:46	16:46	16:48	16:51	16:51	16:51	16:55	22:11	23: 4	23:11	23:11	23:31
End:	23:33	23:33	23:61	16:49	16:61	16:46	16:46	16:49	16:49	16:56	16:61	16:52	16:56	23:33	23:18	23:11	23:33	23:32
Count:	23	20	12	6	4	2	13	6	18	5	40	16	32	8	7	4	3	2
Width:	12528	5008	357	95	32	1	13	1	207	116	40	279	16	1060	602	143	40	16
Strength:	6.77	6.93	4.38	2.50	1.86	1.03	1.02	1.02	2.45	2.16	1.47	1.72	1.01	2.74	2.60	1.40	1.47	1.02

GAPS:

Start:	1: 1	1: 9	1:23	3:13	16:61	16:61	23:11	23:32	23:33	23:33
End:	16:45	16:45	16:45	16:61	16:45	22:11	48:35	48:35	44:25	
Count:	5	4	3	2	2	4	7	4	3	2
Width:	7676	7520	7237	6592	4049	3591	15736	15309	15285	12857
Strength:	1.59	2.33	3.35	5.09	1.21	2.29	3.85	6.70	8.76	10.91

Linguistic Density Plot in Ezekiel 1 - 48

For 'ḥz 315 (17 times)

Each Column = 13 Verses.   Separations are: Max = 11757.00, Mean =   1553.89, Min =   9.00 .

```
                                                                              REFERENCE
        1  23  4  5  6  7   8  90 1 2   3 4 56   7 8   9 0   1 2   3 4   5 6 7 8   90 1 2   3 4   5 6   7 8   90 1 2   3 4   5 6 7 8
      +-+--+--+--+--+--+--+-+--+--+--+--+--+--+--+--+--+--+--+--+--+--+--+--+--+--+--+--+--+--+--+--+--+--+--+--+--+--+--+--+--+--+-+ +25
25+   .                                                                                                                              .
      .                                                                                              .                              .
      .                                                                                                                             .
20+   .                                                                                                                              +20
      .                                                                                                                             .
      .                                                                                                                             .
D15+  .                                                                                                   .        .               .  +15D
E     .                    .        .                                                                                                  E
N     .                                                                                                            .                   N
S     .              2     .                                                                 .               .                         S
I     .                                                                                      .                                      .  +10T
T10+  .                                                                                                                             .
Y     .                                                                                                                            .   Y
      .                                                                                                                             .
5+    .                                                                                             .   .                           .  +5
      .                                                                                                                             .
      .                                                                                                                             .
0+    +-+--+--+--+--+--+--+-+--+--+--+--+--+--+--+--+--+--+--+--+--+--+--+--+--+--+--+--+--+--+--+--+--+--+--+--+--+--+--+--+--+--+-+ + 0
        1  23  4  5  6  7   8  90 1 2   3 4 56   7 8   9 0   1 2   3 4   5 6 7 8   90 1 2   3 4   5 6   7 8   90 1 2   3 4   5 6 7 8
                                                                              REFERENCE
```

CLUSTERS:

```
Start:     41: 6  41: 6  44:28  44:28  44:28  45: 5  45: 7  45: 7  46:16  46:18  48:20  48:20  48:22
End:       48:22  41     48:22  41     46:18  45: 8  44:28  45: 8  45: 6  45: 8  46:18  46:18  48:22  48:21  48:22
Count:        17      2     15      7     11      2      3      2      4      3      2      2
Width:      4242       4   2163     11   1053    258     76     38     65     18      3     60     16      4
Strength: 10.22   1.05   7.34   4.54   2.99   2.30   1.05   1.52   1.05   1.92   1.53   1.92   1.05   1.04   1.05
```

GAPS:

```
Start:      1: 1   1: 1   1: 1
End:       46:18  45: 5  41: 6
Count:        12      6      2
Width:     26623  25770  23509
Strength:   3.04   6.26  14.93
```

Linguistic Density Plot in Ezekiel 1 - 48

For 'ahar 111 (25 times)

Each Column = 13 Verses.   Separations are: Max = 3174.00, Mean = 1075.77, Min = 178.00 .

CLUSTERS:

Start:	3:12	3:12	3:12	5: 2	12:14	12:14	20:16	20:16	20:16
End:	16:34	10:11	6: 9	6: 9	16:34	14:11	23:35	20:39	20:30
Count:	12	6	4	3	6	4	6	4	3
Width:	6340	3060	1403	565	2241	1065	2747	556	356
Strength:	2.06	1.09	1.06	1.10	1.47	1.25	1.24	1.55	1.25

GAPS:

Start:	16:34	23:35	23:35	23:35	23:35	33:31
End:	20:16	48:35	44:10	40: 1	29:16	40: 1
Count:	2	9	6	4	2	2
Width:	2568	15248	12436	9605	3257	3802
Strength:	1.44	2.67	3.32	3.70	2.10	2.63

Linguistic Density Plot in Ezekiel 1 - 48

For 'aḥēr 21 (5 times)

Each Column = 13 Verses.   Separations are: Max = 18239.00, Mean = 4661.66, Min = 509.00

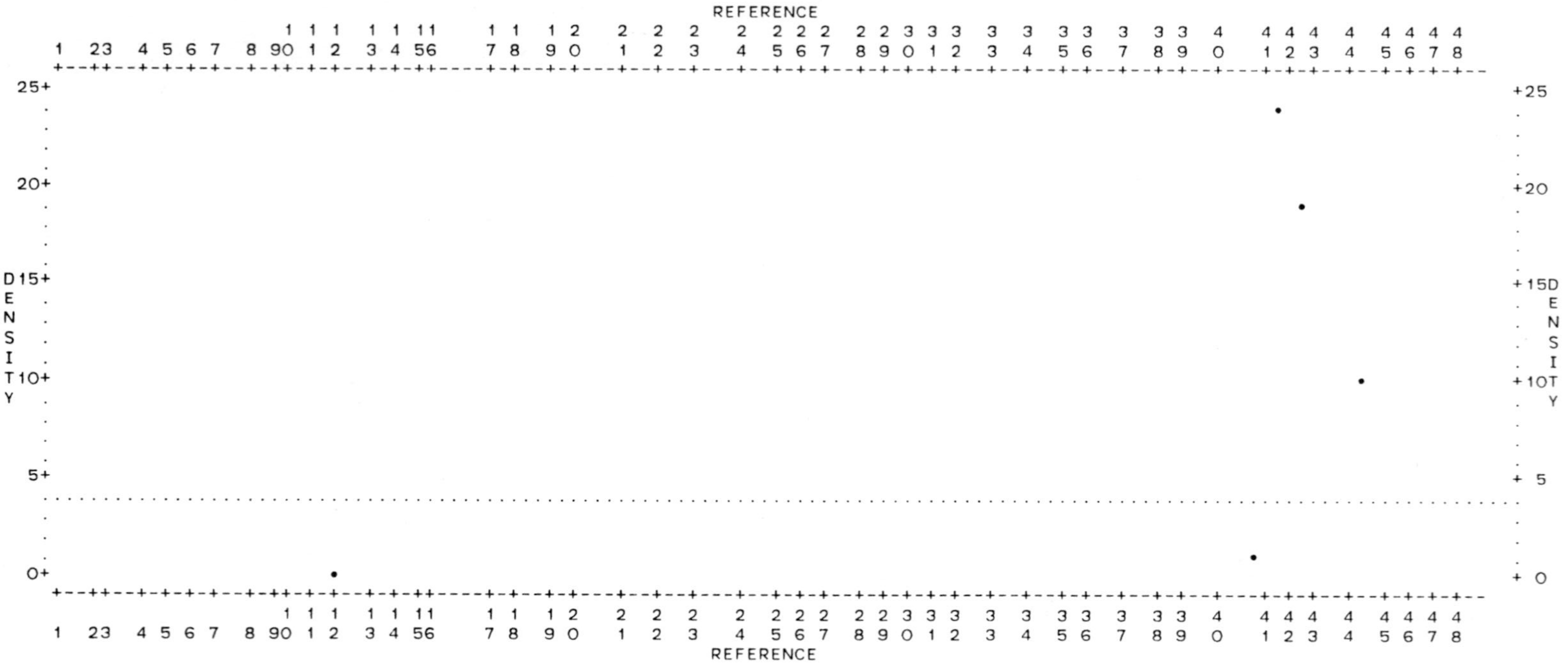

CLUSTERS:

Start:	40:40	40:40	41:24
End:	44:19	42:14	42:14
Count:	4	3	2
Width:	2245	1018	327
Strength:	2.22	1.66	1.10

GAPS:

Start:	1: 1	1: 1	12: 3
End:	41:24	40:40	40:40
Count:	4	3	2
Width:	23856	23165	18239
Strength:	1.86	2.77	3.44

Linguistic Density Plot in Ezekiel 1 - 48

For `ʃ 111 (9 times)

Each Column = 13 Verses.   Separations are: Max = 7179.50.   Mean = 2797.00.   Min = 37.00 .

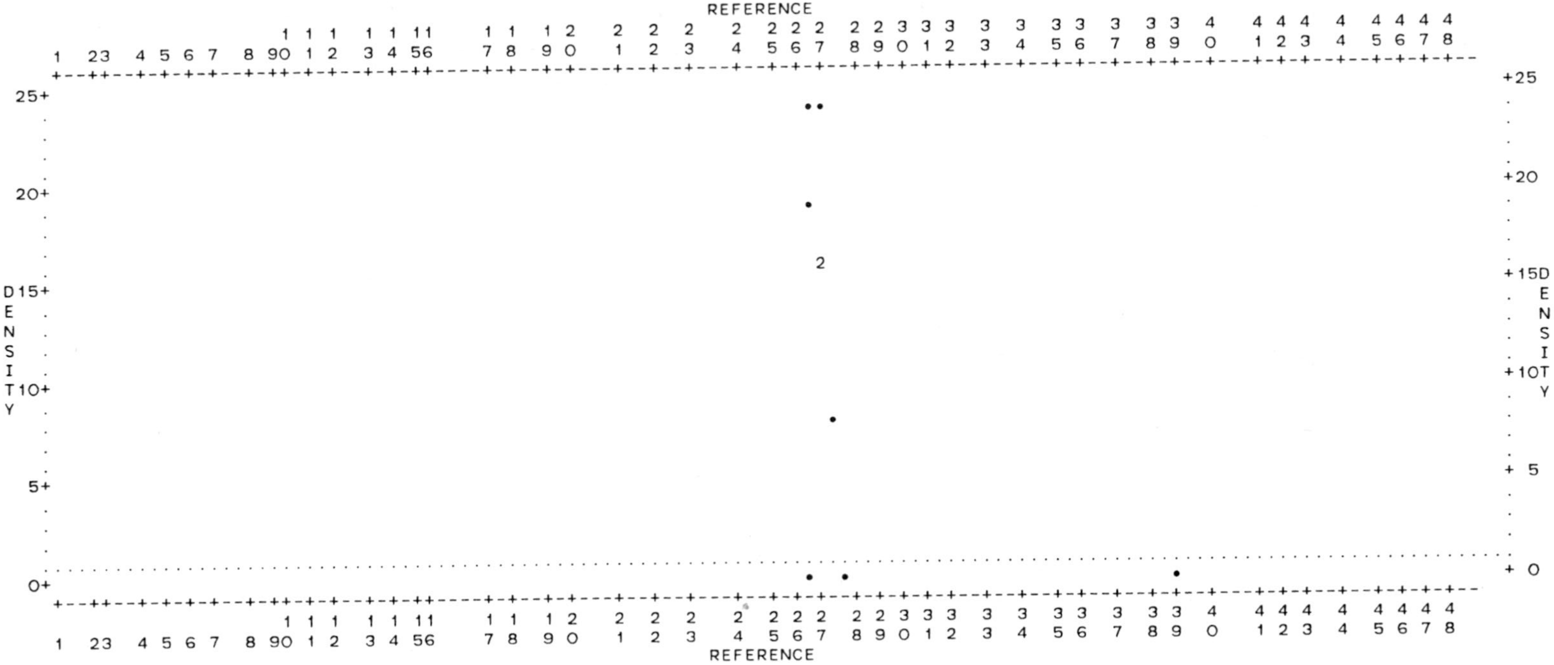

CLUSTERS:

Start: 26:15 26:15 26:15 26:18 27:15 27:15 27: 3 27: 3 27: 6
End: 39: 6 27:35 27:15 26:18 26:18 27:15 27: 7 27: 7 27: 7
Count: 9   8   7   3   2   4   3   3   2
Width: 7486   759   402   75   6   215   74   74   20
Strength: 4.41   4.86   3.96   1.63   1.10   2.11   1.63   1.63   1.09

GAPS:

Start: 1: 1   1: 1   27:15 27:35 27:35
End: 26:18 26:15 48:35 48:35 39: 6
Count: 3   2   4   3   2
Width: 14358 14289 13278 12921 6727
Strength: 2.59   4.54   1.26   2.17   1.55

Linguistic Density Plot in Ezekiel 1 - 48

For 'ayil 111 (37 times)

Each Column = 13 Verses.   Separations are: Max = 7400.50, Mean =   736.05, Min =   13.00 .

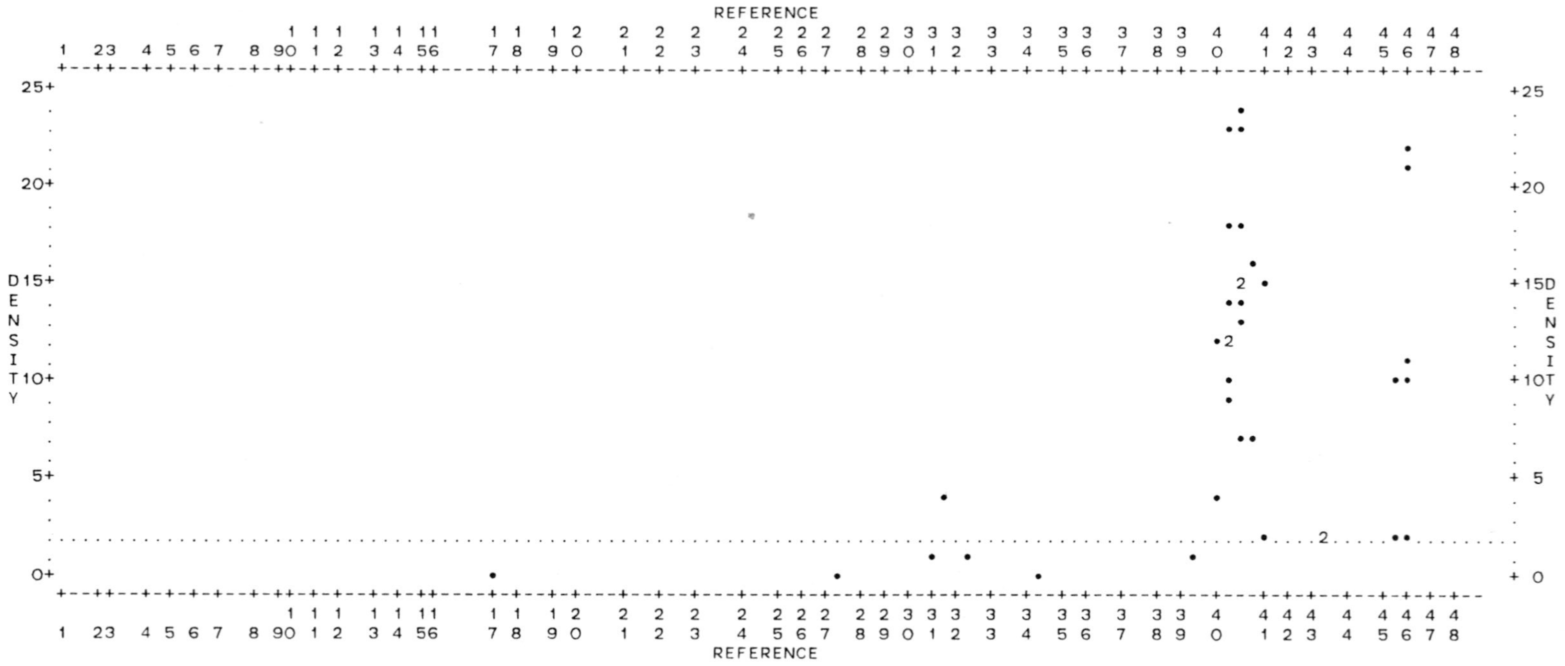

CLUSTERS:

Start:	17:13	39:18	39:18	40: 9	40: 9	40:14	40:14	40:26	40:26	40:34	40:37	40:37	40:48	40:48	40:49	43:23	45:23	46: 4
End:	46:11	46:11	41: 3	40:24	40:16	40:16	41: 3	40:38	40:33	40:38	40:37	40:38	41: 1	41: 3	41: 1	46:11	46:11	46:11
Count:	37	31	22	9	6	4	2	13	9	5	3	2	3	2	9	7	5	4
Width:	18058	4381	1378	787	306	144	50	538	222	114	72	26	8	105	58	16	1622	281	139
Strength:	8.43	9.69	6.32	2.79	2.33	1.78	1.01	3.98	3.10	2.08	1.44	1.01	1.01	1.74	1.41	1.00	2.33	2.53	2.04

Start:	46: 4	46: 4	46: 5	46: 6
End:	46: 7	46: 5	46: 6	46:10
Count:	4	7	2	2
Width:	41	6	10
Strength:	1.79	1.01	1.01

Data for 'ayil 111, continued.

GAPS:

Start:	1: 1	1: 1	1: 1	1: 1	1: 1	1: 1	31:14	31:14	32:21	34:17	46:11
End:	40:14	40: 9	31:11	27:21	17:13	40: 9	39:18	39:18	39:18	48:35
Count:	11	9	4	3	2	5	4	3	2	2
Width:	22634	22540	16843	14800	8382	5611	5130	4578	3103	1529
Strength:	7.74	9.11	12.11	13.32	10.66	1.93	2.41	3.10	3.30	1.10

Linguistic Density Plot in Ezekiel 1 - 48

For 'ēlām 111 (14 times)

Each Column = 13 Verses.   Separations are: Max = 11383.50. Mean = 1864.67. Min = 12.50 .

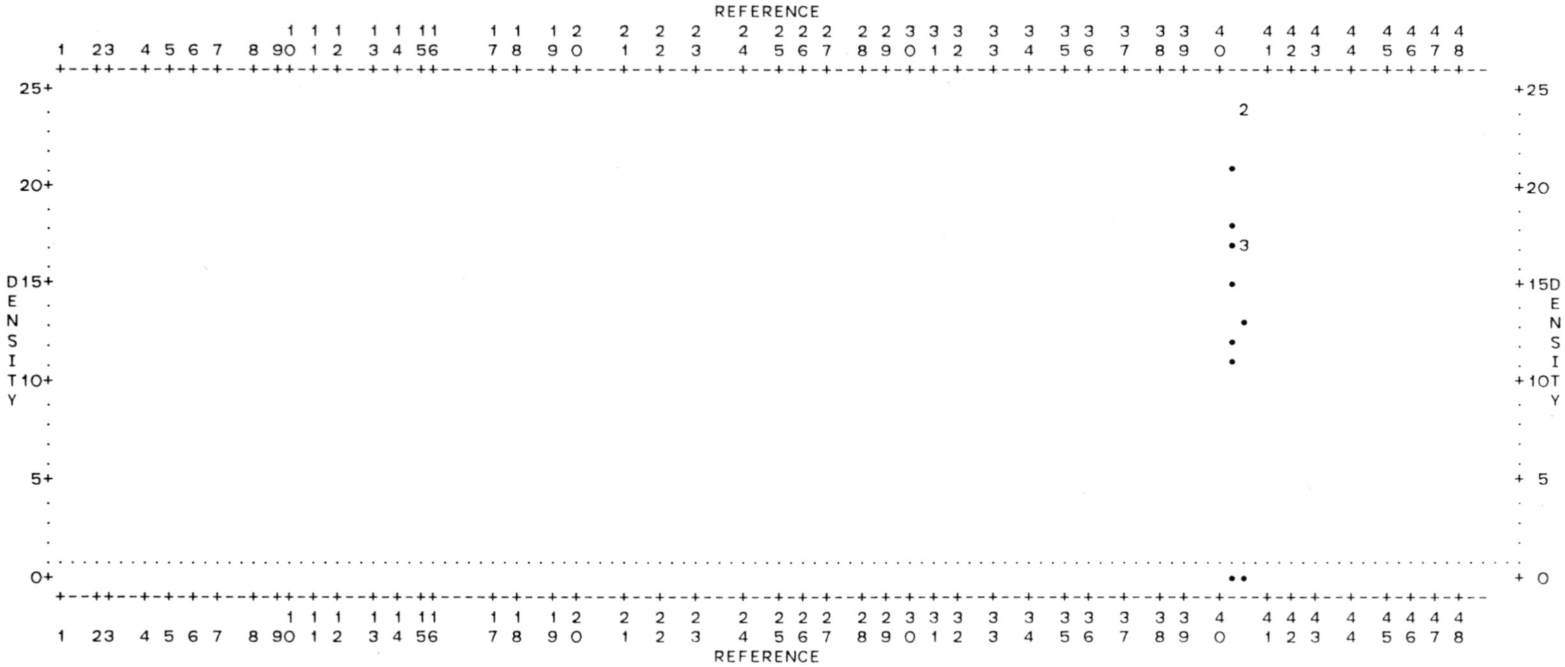

CLUSTERS:

Start:	40:16	40:21	40:21	40:22	40:22	40:24	40:24	40:29	40:29	40:30	40:31	40:33	40:33	40:33
End:	40:36	40:26	40:22	40:22	40:26	40:24	40:26	40:36	40:31	40:36	40:36	40:33	40:34	40:33
Count:	14	7	6	3	2	3	2	7	3	2	4	3	2	
Width:	402	207	116	43	21	33	11	124	27	13	61	25	11	
Strength:	10.02	3.20	2.79	1.55	1.05	1.55	1.06	3.22	1.55	1.06	1.97	1.55	1.06	

GAPS:

Start:	1: 1	1: 1	1: 1	1: 1	40:36
End:	40:24	40:22	40:21	40:16	48:35
Count:	6	4	3	2	
Width:	22849	22788	22766	22675	4892
Strength:	4.10	6.14	8.00	11.93	1.73

Linguistic Density Plot in Ezekiel 1 - 48

For 'ayin 111 (24 times)

Each Column = 13 Verses.   Separations are: Max = 4339.00, Mean = 1118.80, Min = 9.50 .

```
25+


20+


D 15+
E
N
S
I
T 10+
Y


  5+


  0+
```

REFERENCE

CLUSTERS:

Start:	3: 7	3: 7	7:14	7:14	13:10	13:15	13:15	13:16	26:21	33:28	34: 6	34: 6	38:11
End:	42: 6	13:16	13:16	9: 9	13:16	13:16	13:15	34:28	34:28	34: 8	34: 6	38:11	
Count:	24	9	8	4	3	9	6	3	2				
Width:	23036	4805	2879	977	136	19	4763	763	289	37	3	6	
Strength:	1.81	1.61	2.01	1.33	1.80	1.49	1.03	1.63	2.20	2.08	1.47	1.03	1.03

GAPS:

Start:	13:15	13:16	13:16	13:16	28:19	38:11	39:26	42: 6		
End:	34: 6	33:28	26:21	20:39	33:28	48:35	48:35			
Count:	9	8	6	4	3	2				
Width:	12946	12678	9311	8678	4775	2997	6630	5734	3981	
Strength:	1.56	2.06	3.22	3.34	4.32	3.40	1.74	1.83	2.34	2.66

Linguistic Density Plot in Ezekiel 1 - 48

For 'êpâ 114 (17 times)

Each Column = 13 Verses. Separations are: Max = 12954.50, Mean = 1553.89, Min = 6.00 .

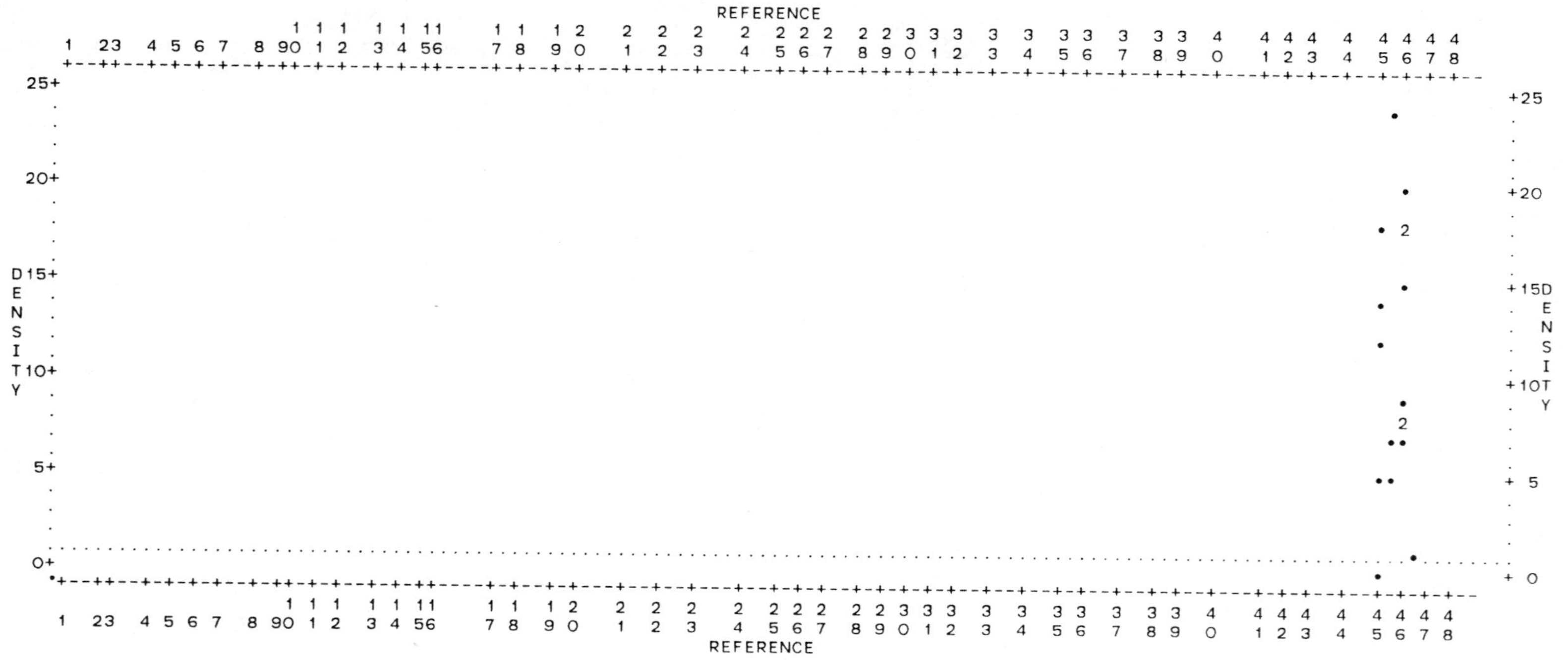

CLUSTERS:

Start:	45:10	45:10	45:10	45:10	45:13	45:24	45:24	45:24	45:24	46: 5	46: 5	46: 7	46: 7	46:11	46:11	46:11
End:	46:14	45:13	45:11	45:11	45:13	46:14	46: 7	45:24	45:24	46: 7	46: 5	46: 7	46: 7	46:14	46:11	46:11
Count:	17	5	3	2	2	12	8	3	2	5	2	3	2	4	3	2
Width:	624	57	22	8	6	351	184	12	4	52	14	21	4	90	17	4
Strength:	12.01	2.30	1.52	1.05	1.05	5.35	3.41	1.53	1.05	2.31	1.04	1.53	1.05	1.91	1.53	1.05

GAPS:

Start:	1: 1	1: 1	1: 1	1: 1	1: 1
End:	46:11	46: 7	45:24	45:13	45:10
Count:	15	12	7	5	2
Width:	26434	26336	26173	25951	25900
Strength:	1.75	2.95	5.57	7.39	16.56

Linguistic Density Plot in Ezekiel 1 - 48

For 'fs 111 (89 times)

Each Column = 13 Verses.   Separations are: Max = 1738.50, Mean = 310.78, Min = 5.50 .

CLUSTERS:

Start:	1: 9	1: 9	1: 9	1: 9	1:11	7:13	7:13	7:13	8:11	8:11	8:11	8:16	8:16	9: 1	9: 3	9:11	10:22	10:22	14: 1
End:	47:14	27:27	16:45	1:23	1:12	16:45	12:16	6:10	9: 6	8:12	6:10	9: 2	9: 9	9: 2	9: 6	10: 6	11:15	11: 2	16:45
Count:	89	70	44	6	3	36	23	18	16	12	6	4	9	2	6	4	3	13
Width:	26911	14746	7517	284	56	4819	2326	1146	620	377	44	246	121	28	87	133	277	52	1712
Strength:	1.01	5.40	3.99	1.89	1.66	4.23	3.57	3.60	3.69	3.16	1.33	2.68	1.85	1.71	1.60	1.51	1.24	2.02

Start:	14: 1	14: 1	14: 1	14: 7	14: 7	18: 5	18: 5	18: 5	18: 5	18: 8	18: 8	20: 1	21:36	22: 6	22:11	23:40
End:	14:18	14: 8	14: 4	14: 8	14: 7	18:16	23:14	27:27	18: 8	18: 8	20: 8	20: 8	21:36	22:11	22:11	24:23	23:45
Count:	10	7	4	3	2	5	26	18	4	9	8	3	6	5	3
Width:	417	191	55	54	1	84	6185	3542	204	74	1019	168	852	206	84	16	663	99
Strength:	2.70	2.28	1.66	1.31	1.00	1.24	1.20	1.51	1.75	1.62	1.71	1.00	1.04	1.68	2.00	1.91	1.39	1.32	1.20

```
Clusters for 'is 111, continued.

Start:     24:17  38:21  40: 3
End:       24:23  40: 5  40: 5
Count:         3      6      3
Width:       123    829     75
Strength:   1.15   1.07   1.26

GAPS:

Start:      1:23   1:23   4:17  11: 2  11:15  12:16  14: 7  14:18  16:45  16:45  18: 8  20: 8  20: 8  20:39  22:11  24:23  24:23
End:        8:11   7:13   7:13  14: 1  14: 1  14: 1  48:35  16:32  16:45  18: 7  18: 5  22: 6  21:36  21:36  48:35  40: 3  33:26
Count:         6      4      2      4      3      2     54      2      3     43      4      3      4      2     31     20     12     7
Width:      2940   2414   1028   1579   1354    781  21861    975   1080  19169   1793   1671    892  16347  10752   8881  4875
Strength:   2.06   2.81   2.33   1.22   1.69   1.52   3.73   2.15   1.05   4.18   1.63   2.42   1.88   5.08   4.05   5.68  4.11

Start:     24:23  27:27  27:27  33:30  33:30  40: 4  40: 5  40: 5  44: 2  44: 2  47: 3  47:14
End:       33:20  27:10  33: 2  33:30  39:14  48:35  46:16  48:35  44:25  45:20  48:35  48:35
Count:         6      4      3      2     11     10      6      5      3      2      3      2
Width:      4742   1112   3324   2899   3477   3143   5571   5520   4116   3657   1928   1180    620   1145   893
Strength:   4.74   2.60   4.54   5.26   6.73   6.60   9.21   2.67   3.09   3.81   3.99   5.26   1.29   1.00  1.20  1.89
```

Linguistic Density Plot in Ezekiel 1 - 48

For 'kl 311 (18 times)   'kl 312 (25 times)   'kl 313 (3 times)   'kl 314 (1 times)
     'kl 3162 (3 times)   'kl 322 (2 times)   'kl 361 (1 times)   'kl 362 (2 times)
     'kl 3662 (1 times)

Each Column = 13 Verses.   Separations are: Max = 2340.00. Mean = 490.70. Min = 8.50 .

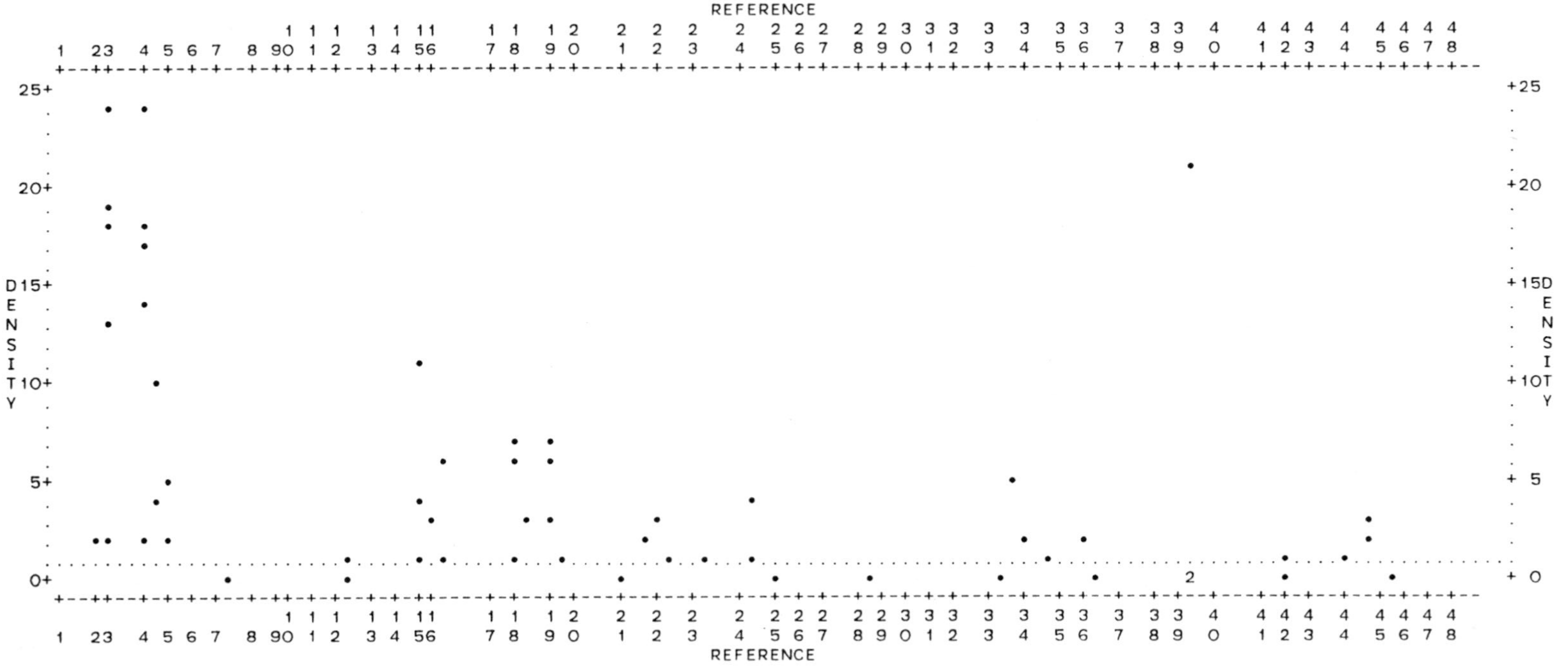

[Scatter / density plot: vertical axis labelled DENSITY with gridline markers 25+, 20+, D15+(15), 10+(T10+), 5+, 0+ and corresponding right-hand labels +25, +20, +15, +10, +5, +0; horizontal axis labelled REFERENCE with chapter reference numbers 1 through 48.]

CLUSTERS:

Start:	2: 8	2: 8	2: 8	2: 8	3: 8	3: 2	3: 1	3: 1	4: 9	4: 9	4: 9	4: 9	4: 9	4:13	5:10	12:18	15: 4	16:13	18: 2
End:	45:21	28:18	16:20	7:15	3: 3	3: 3	3: 1	3: 1	7:15	5:10	4:16	4:12	4:10	4:16	5:10	16:20	15: 7	16:20	22:25
Count:	56	41	24	16	6	5	2	1	10	9	7	4	2	3	9	8	6	3	12
Width:	25352	14634	6370	2132	96	44	27	1	1229	398	130	35	6	78	1920	538	69	168	3206
Strength:	2.42	2.97	2.72	3.23	2.26	2.04	1.41	1.01	2.37	2.76	2.49	1.75	1.00	1.33	1.00	1.25	1.34	1.20	1.51

Start:	18: 2	18: 2	19: 3	24:17	33:25	39:17	39:17
End:	19:14	18:15	19:14	25: 4	34: 3	39:19	39:18
Count:	8	4	4	3	3	3	2
Width:	865	230	194	295	262	23	7
Strength:	2.13	1.51	1.55	1.01	1.06	1.41	1.00

Data for 'kl 311, 'kl 312, 'kl 313, 'kl 314, 'kl 3162, 'kl 322, 'kl 361, 'kl 362, 'kl 3662, continued.

GAPS:

```
Start:      4:10   5:10   5:10   5:10   7:15  12:19  16:20  19:14  19:14  19:14  24:22  25: 4  28:18  36:14  39:18  39:19  39:19  39:19
End:       48:35  39:17  36:13  12:18  15: 4  18: 2  36:13  33:25  21:33  33:25  33:25  39:17  48:35  48:35  44:29  42: 5
Count:        50     34     32      5      3      2     15     11      3      2      4      3      2      2      9      8      5      2
Width:     26281  19966  17795   4531   3149   2318   1352   1534  10327   8799   1805   1203   4879   4680   2934   2159   5916   5900   3535   1905
Strength:   1.75   2.08   1.41   2.73   3.20   3.78   1.78   2.16   2.18   2.78   1.21   1.47   4.15   5.47   5.06   3.45   1.55   2.04   1.67   2.93
```

```
Start:     44:31  45:21
End:       48:35  48:35
Count:         3      2
Width:      2316   1838
Strength:   1.97   2.79
```

Linguistic Density Plot in Ezekiel 1 - 48

For 'kl 311 (18 times)   'kl 312 (25 times)   'kl 313 (3 times)   'kl 314 (1 times)
    'kl 3162 (3 times)

Each Column = 13 Verses.   Separations are: Max = 2340.00, Mean = 548.43, Min = 9.00 .

CLUSTERS:

```
Start:      2: 8   2: 8   2: 8   3: 1   3: 1   4: 9   4: 9   4: 9   4:13   4: 9   5:10  12:18  15: 4  15: 4  18: 2  18: 2
End:       44:31  22:25  16:20   3: 3   3: 3   7:15   5:10   4:16   4:16   4:10   5:10  16:20  15: 7  22:25  19:14  18:15
Count:        50     32     21     10      9     44    130      9      3      6      5      3     11      8
Width:     24874  11110   6370   2132    398   1229   2132     44     78    130     35     78   1920    538   3206    865    230
Strength:   2.65   3.11   2.42   2.95   2.82   2.50   2.52   1.39   1.35   1.76   1.00   1.69   1.00   1.58   1.47   2.22   1.55

Start:     19: 3  24:17  33:25  33:25  39:17  39:17
End:       19:14  25: 4  36:14  34: 3  39:19  39:18
Count:         4      3      6      3      2      7
Width:       194    295   1540    262     23      7
Strength:   1.58   1.06   1.04   1.10   1.42   1.00
```

Data for 'kl 311, 'kl 312, 'kl 313, 'kl 314, 'kl 3162, continued.

GAPS:

Start:	4:10	5:10	5:10	5:10	5:10	7:15	12:19	16:20	19:14	19:14	19:14	19:14	19:14	22:25	24:22	25: 4	28:18	36:14	39:18	39:19
End:	48:35	39:17	36:13	15: 4	12:18	12:18	15: 4	18: 2	36:13	33:25	24:17	22: 9	21: 3	24:17	33:25	33:25	33:25	39:17	48:35	48:35
Count:	46	31	29	5	3	2	2	2	13	9	5	3	2	2	4	3	2	2	8	7
Width:	26281	19966	17795	4531	3149	2318	1352	1534	10327	8799	3824	2039	1203	1483	4879	4680	2934	2159	5916	5900
Strength:	1.28	1.84	1.26	2.24	2.72	3.28	1.49	1.83	2.27	3.12	1.56	1.25	1.21	1.73	3.54	4.75	4.43	2.99	1.55	2.08

Start:	39:19	39:19	44:31
End:	44:29	42: 5	48:35
Count:	5	2	2
Width:	3535	1905	2316
Strength:	1.28	2.52	3.28

Linguistic Density Plot in Ezekiel 1 - 48

For 'kl 311 (18 times)

Each Column = 13 Verses. Separations are: Max = 5078.50, Mean = 1472.11, Min = 73.50 .

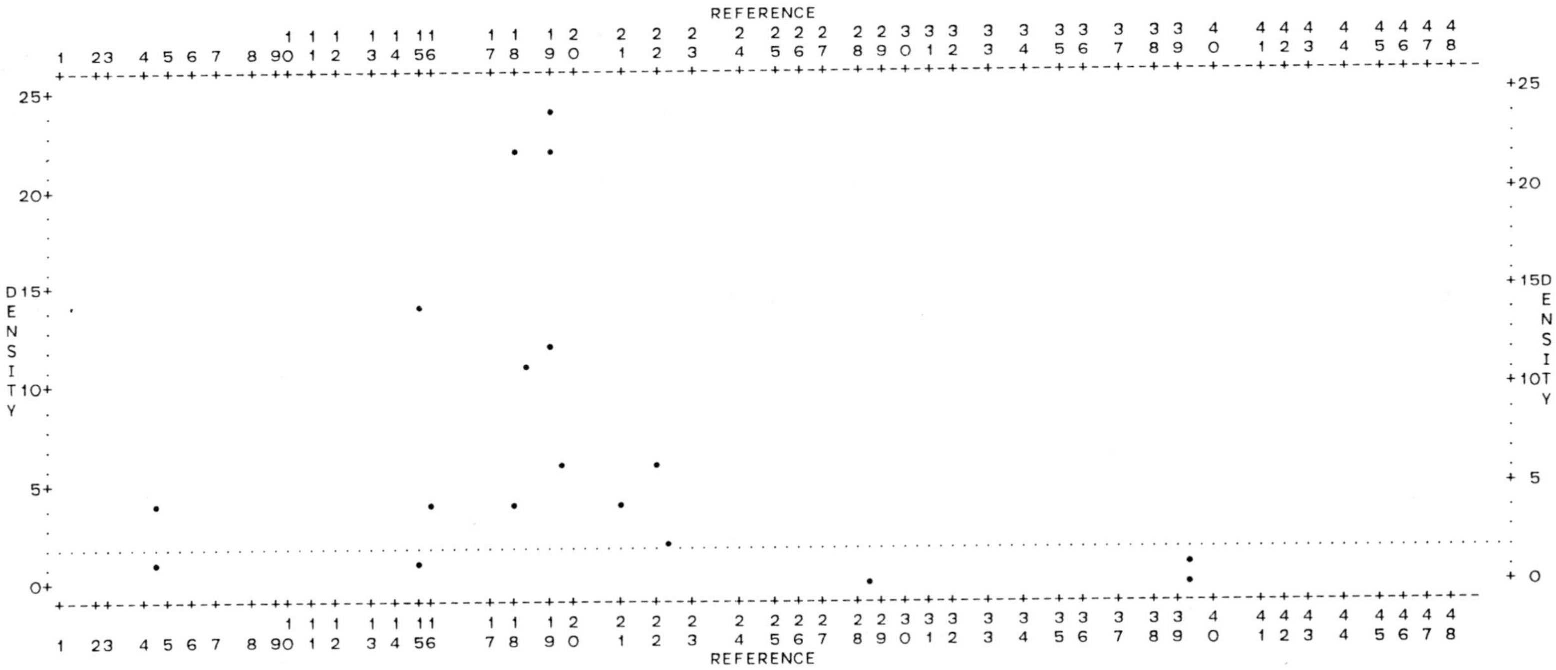

CLUSTERS:

Start:	4:14	4:14	4:14	15: 4	15: 4	15: 4	18: 6	18: 6	18:11	19: 3	19: 3	19:12	39:17
End:	39:19	19:14	4:16	19:14	16:13	15: 5	19:14	18:15	18:15	19:14	19: 6	19:14	39:19
Count:	18	12	2	10	3	2	7	3	2	4	2	2	2
Width:	20307	7786	50	2937	370	22	810	175	69	194	47	21	23
Strength:	2.45	2.72	1.01	3.30	1.34	1.03	2.75	1.44	1.00	1.85	1.02	1.03	1.03

GAPS:

Start:	4:16	19:14	19:14	22:25	28:18	39:19
End:	15: 4	48:35	39:17	39:17	39:17	48:35
Count:	2	8	6	3	2	2
Width:	4799	18421	12498	10157	6633	5900
Strength:	2.38	2.69	1.86	3.75	3.69	3.17

For 'kl 312 (25 times)

Linguistic Density Plot in Ezekiel 1 - 48

Each Column = 13 Verses.   Separations are: Max = 3346.00, Mean = 1075.77, Min = 9.00 .

CLUSTERS:

Start:	3: 3	3: 3	4: 9	4:10	4:10	5:10	12:18	24:17		
End:	18: 2	7:15	5:10	4:13	4:12	5:10	12:19	25: 4		
Count:	13	9	8	7	5	2	2	3		
Width:	7808	2036	1205	398	52	6	34	30	295	
Strength:	1.90	2.64	2.67	2.18	1.47	1.03	1.02	1.00	1.29	

GAPS:

Start:	5:10	7:15	12:19	12:19	15: 7	18: 2	24:22	25: 4	36:14	44:31
End:	48:35	12:18	48:35	44:29	24:17	24:17	42: 5	33:25	39:18	48:35
Count:	19	2	16	14	4	3	8	7	2	2
Width:	25889	2318	22710	20345	8113	6692	10506	4689	10307	4680
Strength:	2.62	1.19	2.47	2.36	2.84	3.16	1.24	3.49	1.69	3.48

Width:	4087	2166	2316
Strength:	1.34	1.05	1.19

Linguistic Density Plot in Ezekiel 1 - 48

For 'okîā 114 (10 times)

Each Column = 13 Verses.   Separations are: Max =   4240.00, Mean =   2542.73, Min =   67.00 .

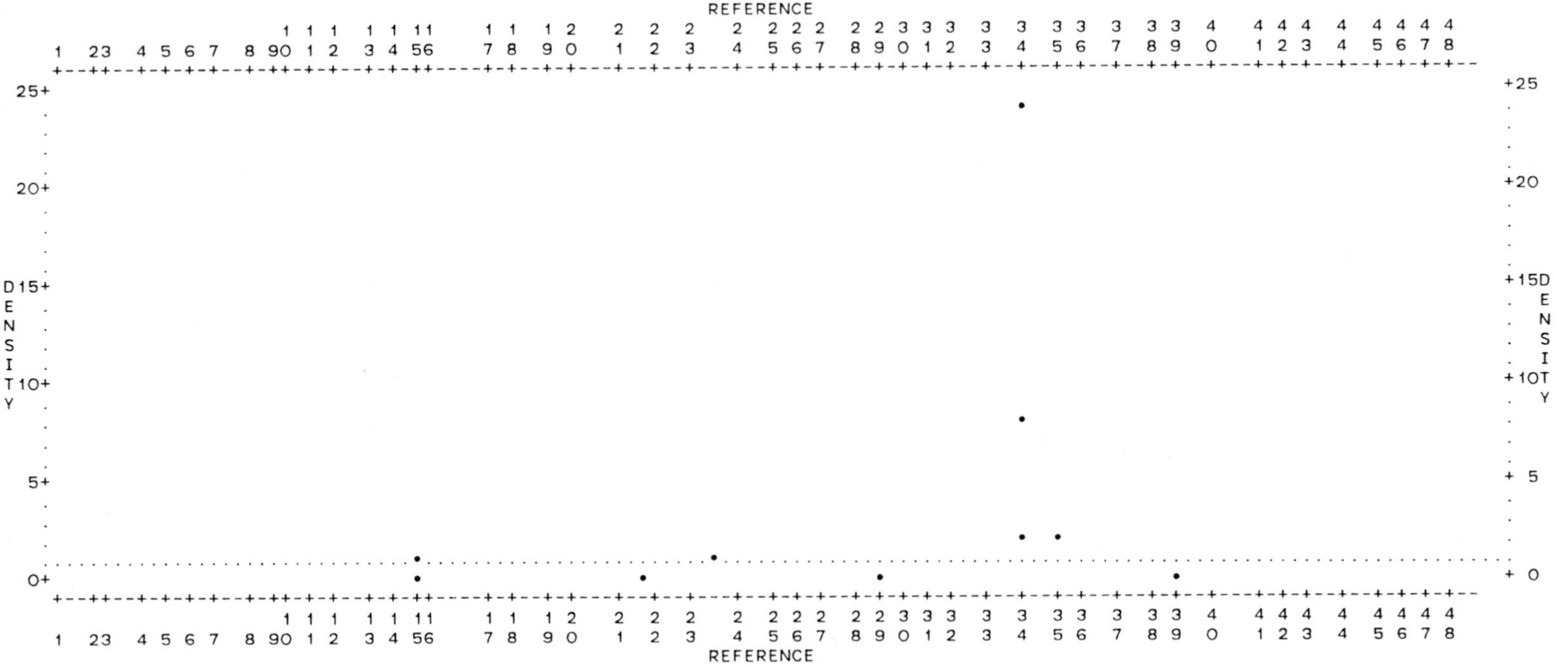

CLUSTERS:

Start:	15: 4	15: 4	34: 5	34: 5	34: 5
End:	39: 4	15: 6	39: 4	35:12	34:10	34: 8
Count:	10	2	5	4	3	2
Width:	15149	56	3095	829	134	58
Strength:	2.48	1.07	1.82	1.89	1.58	1.07

GAPS:

Start:	1: 1	35:12	39: 4
End:	15: 4	48:35	48:35
Count:	2	3	2
Width:	6606	8480	6214
Strength:	1.75	1.08	1.58

For 'al 23 (14 times)

Linguistic Density Plot in Ezekiel 1 - 48

Each Column = 13 Verses. Separations are: Max = 8977.50, Mean = 1864.67, Min =   6.00

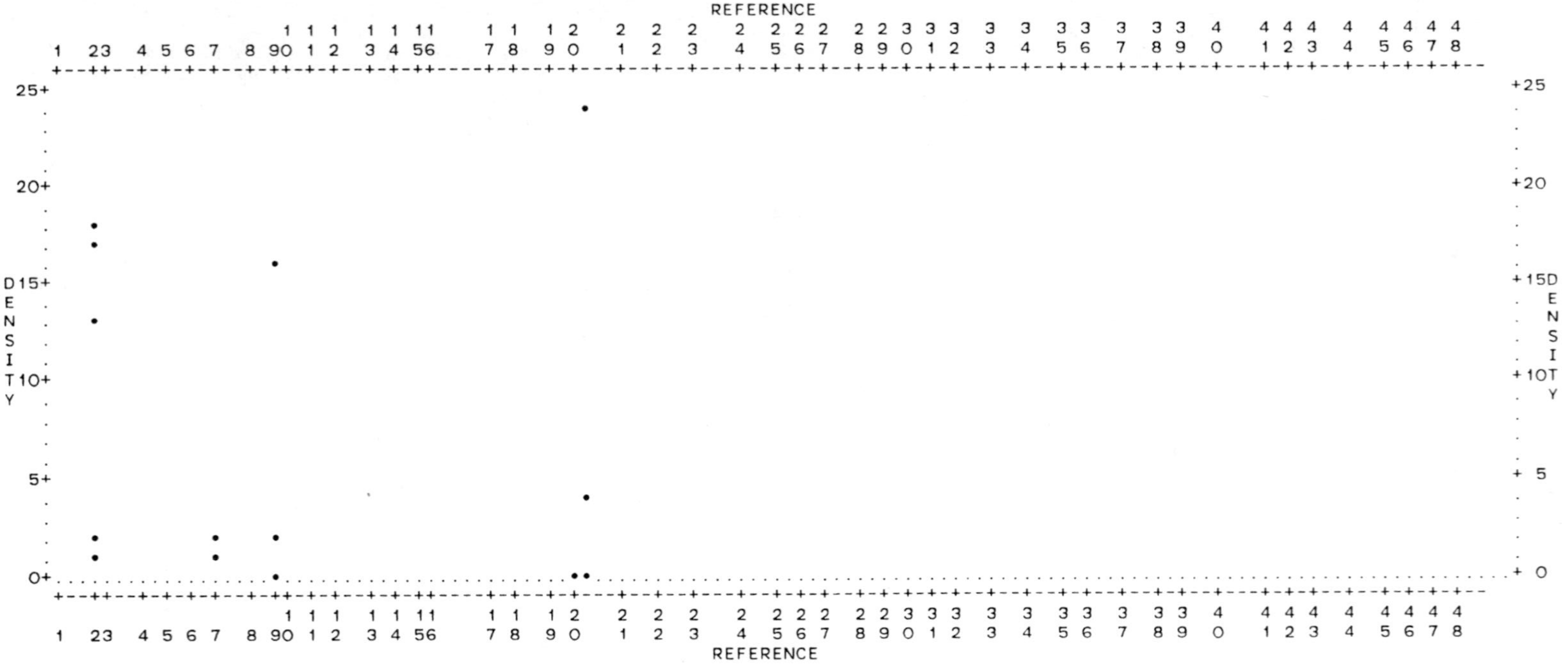

REFERENCE
(vertical density axis: +25, +20, +15, +10, +5, 0 — labelled D E N S I T Y)

CLUSTERS:

Start:	2: 6	2: 6	2: 6	2: 6	7:12	9: 5	9: 5	20: 7	20:18
End:	20:18	9: 6	2: 8	2: 2	7:12	9: 6	9: 5	20:18	20:18
Count:	14	10	5	4	2	3	3	4	2
Width:	9313	3049	62	30	926	26	292	12	6
Strength:	6.27	4.00	2.39	1.98	2.11	1.55	1.06	1.89	1.56	1.06

GAPS:

Start:	7:12	9: 5	9: 6	20:18
End:	48:35	48:35	20: 7	48:35
Count:	9	7	3	2
Width:	25135	24234	6252	5972	17949
Strength:	2.92	3.80	1.06	2.35	9.22

Linguistic Density Plot in Ezekiel 1 - 48

For 'el 4 (503 times)

Each Column = 13 Verses.   Separations are: Max =   319.00, Mean =   55.50, Min =   3.00 .

CLUSTERS:

Start:	1: 3	1: 3	1: 9	1: 9	1:23	2: 1	2: 2	2: 6	2: 8	2: 6	2: 8	3: 3	3: 3	3: 4	3: 3	3:10
End:	16:43	7:18	1:10	1:12	2: 4	2: 3	2: 3	3: 7	3: 3	3: 3	3: 1	3: 7	3: 4	3: 6	3: 3	3:16
Count:	158	73	25	45	9	6	4	20	6	9	11	7	4	23	4	10
Width:	7609	2908	72	1110	239	47	15	233	40	71	85	47	17	138
Strength:	1.91	2.49	1.35	3.78	1.31	1.86	1.57	3.46	1.31	1.66	2.70	2.11	1.55	1.49	2.18

Start:	3:10	3:11	3:13	3:15	3:22	6: 1	7:12	7:12	7:26	7:26	8: 3	8: 7	8:12	8:13	8:13
End:	3:11	3:11	3:16	3:16	3:24	6: 2	7:18	7:14	8:17	10:11	8: 9	8: 9	8:16	8:16	8:14
Count:	6	12	4	3	4	3	110	14	28	18	6	9	6	5	3
Width:	36	67	32	113	52	63	152	473	1012	2763	120	81	49	20
Strength:	1.95	1.60	1.00	1.32	1.19	1.23	1.35	1.24	1.18	1.65	1.73	1.69	1.27	1.01	1.87	1.58	1.56	1.15

Clusters for 'el 4, continued.

```
Start:     9: 3   9: 3   9: 7  10: 1  10: 2  12:17  12:17  12:17  12:17  12:26  13: 8  13: 8  13:13  14: 1  14: 1  14: 4  16:61
End:      10: 2   9: 4  10: 2  10: 2  13:10  12: 2  13:20  13:20  12:23  13:    13:20  12:10  13:13  14: 7  14:    14:    17:12
Count:        9      3      6      4      3      8      1      3      3      3      6      5      9      8      7      3     10
Width:      253     18    152     29     11     21    643    237    125     59    296     31     93    173     79     30    322
Strength:  1.22   1.18   1.01   1.43   1.27   1.14   1.73   1.58   1.23   1.11   1.23   1.01   1.16   1.47   1.29   1.02   1.07

Start:    17: 4  17: 4  18: 6  18: 6  19: 1  20: 1  20:10  20:27  20:30  20:35  20:42  21: 1  21: 1  21: 6  21: 6  21: 7  21:33
End:      17:    17:    18:    18:    20:10  20:10  20:28  20:30  20:28  20:35  20: 2  21:    21:    21: 9  21: 7  21:17  21:35
Count:        4      3      6      3     14      8      5      5     24      9      5      3      3      9      5      3      5
Width:       49     21    492     14    220     97     30     94    731    281    373    146     64     17     30    104     47
Strength:  1.22   1.14   1.16   1.87   1.15   1.12   1.02   1.12   2.09   1.04   1.97   1.91   1.72   1.73   1.55   1.30   1.06   1.24

Start:    23:36  23:42  23:44  23:44  24:    24: 1  24: 2  24: 2  24:15  24:18  24:23  24:26  25: 3  25: 3  30:20  30:25  31:    31: 1
End:      23:44  23:44  23:44  23:44  24:    24:    24:    24:20  24:24  24:20  24:26  25:    25:    31:    30:25  31:    31: 2  31: 2
Count:        9      6      6      4      6      5      4      4      5      8      3      3      3      8      5      5      2      4
Width:      187     46     12    687     18     61     14     99     80    223    142     80     17    220     93     50     15     57
Strength:  1.64   1.87   1.60   1.13   1.45   1.38   1.23   1.10   1.31   1.41   1.13   1.59   1.25   1.95   1.49   1.55   1.57

Start:    31: 6  31: 7  31: 7  31:12  31:13  31:14  31:17  31:18  32:    33:    33: 1  33:21  33:21  33:23  37: 3  37: 3  37: 9  39:28  43: 7
End:      32: 6  31:14  31:12  31: 8  31:14  32:    31:18  32:    33:    33: 2  34:    33:23  33:27  33:21  37:12  37:    37:    48:32
Count:       15      7      5      8      7      5      7      3      3      3     10     16      7      4      9      9      3      5
Width:      439    190    103     30     51     33     81     13    325    119    450    227    131     44     25     38     10     31
Strength:  1.64   1.62   1.07   1.02   1.20   1.27   1.02   1.24   1.05   1.13   1.58   1.64   1.49   1.27   1.09   1.33   1.01   1.28  3.29  4.22

Start:    39:28  40:14  40:16  40:16  40:18  40:23  40:23  40:26  40:28  40:31  40:31  40:37  40:39  40:39  40:39  40:40  40:42  40:43  40:45  40:46  40:49  41:    41:15  41: 7  42: 4
End:      41:12  40:16  40:18  40:16  41: 1  41:12  40:37  40:28  40:32  40:37  40:32  40:42  40:40  40:45  41:12  41: 1  41:    41: 6  43: 7  42: 4
Count:     1348     41      7      3      5      9     10      3      3      9     14     15     21     69    478    243    127    120     83     16     31    286
Width:     1348     41      7      3      5      9     25    272     29    120    127    243    478    711  2.58
Strength:  2.58   1.94   1.09   1.47   1.25   1.37   2.67   1.11   1.22   1.36   2.42   2.25   1.14   1.38   2.03   1.25   1.36   1.20   1.25   1.20   1.04   3.23

Start:    41:15  41:17  41:19  41:19  41:22  41:22  41:25  41:26  42:    42: 1  42: 1  42: 7  42: 7  42:13  42:19  43:    43:    43:13  43:13  43:19  44:    44: 2  44:13
End:      41:19  41:19  41:19  41:19  41: 4  41:26  41:26  41:26  42:    42:    42: 2  42:14  42:14  42:14  43:    43: 7  43: 7  43:13  44:13  43:20  44:13  44: 2
Count:        5      4      3     11      4      5      6      5     15     59     20    170     65    139    644    163     40     31
Width:      100     42     12    135     66     58     31    368    170    644    139    289   1486    163
Strength:  1.09   1.29   1.25   2.41   1.40   1.52   1.77   1.40   1.99   1.52   1.20   1.20   1.05   1.83   1.89   1.53   1.54   1.31   1.23   1.31   1.10   1.30

Start:    44: 2  44: 6  44: 6  44:    44:15  44:15  44:16  44:17  44:19  44:19  45:    45:    46:19  46:19  46:19  46:19  46:20  46:20  46:21  47: 2  47: 8
End:      44: 6  44:    44:    45:19  45:    44:15  44:17  44:17  44:21  44:19  45:    45: 7  46:21  47: 2  46:20  46:20  46:21  47: 8  47:    47:    47:
Count:        6      5      7     20     13      8      3      4      4      3      9      7      6     16     24     19      8      6     16     60     37
Width:      124     70     20    792    148    396     59     45     22     19    289    646    157   1486    644    289    139     52     16     60     52
Strength:  1.24   1.37   1.15   1.10   1.64   1.42   1.26   1.13   1.11   1.33   1.06   1.52   1.84   1.89   1.10   1.53   1.82   1.20   1.75   1.34   1.18

GAPS:

Start:     1: 1   1: 1   1: 3   1:12   1:12   1:12   1:12   3:11   3:11   3:11   3:11   3:11   3:11   3:16   3:22   3:22   3:23   4: 8   4:15  4:16   5: 4
End:      42: 1  41:25  41:25  41: 1  42: 2  41:23  37: 3  40:16  41:25  29:10  31: 9  20:42  29:10  3:22   6: 2   6: 1   6: 1   4:15   5: 4   5: 4   6: 1
Count:      423    417    115    402    390    370    378    337    255    163    245    312    163     14      2     13     12      3      4    129    359
Width:    23919  23859  21622  21622  14798  19534  22821  22822  15613  14798   9595    337    378   9595    995    986    975    390    402  1.31   5.47
Strength:  1.08   1.63   1.06   1.62   2.32   3.30   2.79   5.07   2.43   1.03   1.38   2.02   1.91   1.91   1.68   2.00   1.69   1.31   2.05

Start:     6: 2   6: 2   6: 9   7: 1   7: 6   7: 6  7:18   7:18   7:26  10:11  10: 7  10: 7  10: 2  10: 2  10: 7  11:11  11:21  11:11  11:14  12:12  12:12
End:       6: 9   6:13   7: 4   7:12   7: 6   7:12  7:26   8: 3   8: 3  10:22  10:22  11:25  11: 8  10: 7  12:    11:24  11:24  11:21  11:14  12:17  12:17
Count:      161    268    210    120    285    151    114    992    809    291    981    455    487    229    348    413    170    125
Width:      161    268    210    120    285    151    114    992    809    291    981    455    487    229    413    348    170    125
Strength:  1.89   1.05   1.25   1.15   2.21   1.71   1.04   1.04   1.46   2.29   1.31   1.72   1.13   3.12   1.43   1.89   1.02   1.24
```

Gaps for 'el 4, continued.

```
Start:    13: 2  13: 9  13: 9  14: 7  14: 7  14:12  14:12  14:22  15: 1  16: 1  16: 5  16:29  16:29  16:33  16:37  16:43  17: 8  17: 8
End:      17: 8  17: 1  17: 1  14:21  14:28  14:19  14:19  16:25  16:25  16:61  16:25  16:61  16:61  16:61  16:61  16:61  20:42  20:27
Count:    40     38     33     4      11     7      7      5      4      6      2      6      6      2      5      3      36     27
Width:    2787   2667   2528   1963   1149   338    271    151    719    661    429    796    731    651    540    390    2387   1971
Strength: 1.87   1.88   2.47   4.92   3.41   1.78   2.03   1.71   4.49   5.15   6.73   4.19   4.60   5.05   5.47   6.03   1.40   1.91

Start:    17: 8  18: 6  17:12  18: 1  18:12  18:12  18:15  20: 7  20:10  20:10  20:18  20:30  21:23  21:26  21:33  21:35  22: 1
End:      18: 6  18: 1  18: 1  20:27  20: 2  19: 4  19: 1  20:27  20:27  20:15  20:27  20:35  21:33  21:33  23:44  22:17  22:17
Count:    5      3      3      22     12     4      2      7      4      2      2      2      3      2      23     5      4
Width:    489    374    304    1473   850    613    601    500    403    128    218    132    211    160    1571   346    289
Strength: 2.41   3.35   4.47   1.23   1.31   2.07   2.61   1.23   2.46   1.30   2.92   1.37   1.27   1.87   1.37   1.11   1.27

Start:    22: 1  22: 9  22:13  22:20  22:20  22:23  22:23  23:12  23:17  23:17  23:17  23:36  23:44  24: 4  24:15  24:18  24:20  25: 3  25:25
End:      22:13  23:16  22:20  23:12  23: 1  23: 1  22:20  23:44  23:42  23:39  23:27  23:10  23:17  24:18  24:15  24:18  29:10  27:31  26:
Count:    3      2      7      5      3      3      6      8      4      4      2      3      2      3      3      4      20     3      10
Width:    222    144    518    444    254    187    124    598    564    494    423    256    2912   303    284    225    2421   2200   1341
Strength: 1.41   1.58   1.36   2.00   1.82   2.36   1.22   1.43   2.31   3.41   3.98   3.61   2.85   1.42   2.20   3.05   3.55   4.83   5.10

Start:    25: 6  26: 1  26: 2  27:31  27: 3  27:29  27:31  27:32  28:11  28: 1  28:20  28:21  28:21  29: 1  29:10  29:10  29:10  29:10
End:      26: 1  27:31  26:20  36: 9  27:31  29:10  28:20  32:17  28:20  33:    28:26  29:10  28:20  31: 2  31: 2  31:    29:17  29:18
Count:    2      2      3      9      3      10     5      17     3      2      3      5      9      3      9      8      2      6
Width:    271    972    448    3133   502    851    478    747    370    197    381    129    206    812    800    164    621
Strength: 3.88   4.73   2.93   1.78   4.99   2.12   7.61   1.94   3.30   2.54   1.43   1.31   1.20   1.89   2.82   1.95   2.78

Start:    29:18  30:20  30: 1  31: 1  31:18  31:14  32: 2  32: 2  32:17  32:18  32:24  33: 2  33: 2  33:10  33:11  33:12  33:27  33:31  34: 2
End:      30:25  30:30  37: 9  36: 9  33: 1  33:    32:17  32: 6  33:    34:13  33:    33:10  33:21  33:21  33:21  33:21  33:31  34:    34:13
Count:    5      2      2      2      3      11     6      16     17     2      3      16     5      3      2      3      3      13     2
Width:    586    459    351    3918   679    835    325    1061   231    462    202    236    196    193    116    274
Strength: 3.29   4.44   5.32   2.07   3.25   1.61   2.72   1.07   3.15   2.16   2.63   1.59   2.52   1.04   1.08   2.07

Start:    34: 2  34:10  34:13  35: 1  36: 9  36: 9  36: 9  36:16  36:20  36:20  36:20  36:29  37:    37: 9  37:19  37:21  38: 2  38: 2  38: 3
End:      34:13  36: 9  35: 1  36: 9  37:    37: 8  37: 7  36:24  36:24  36:37  37: 3  38: 4  40: 2  40:16  38:    38: 1  40:    40:
Count:    2      8      5      3      9      7      11     3      2      3      4      4      19     2      4      2      7      8      3
Width:    173    922    395    500    677    781    264    524    453    120    229    2085   1774   307    220    1219   1197
Strength: 2.11   3.65   1.56   4.96   1.97   1.29   3.75   2.73   2.98   1.15   3.12   2.83   3.03   1.46   2.96   5.69   6.39

Start:    38: 3  39:28  38:12  38:12  39:15  40: 2  40:14  40: 6  40:18  40:18  40:26  43:    43: 7  43:13  43:16  44: 4  44: 2  45: 7  45:19
End:      39:28  39:28  39:15  39: 1  39:    40:14  40:14  40:14  40:18  40:23  43:13  43:13  44:    46:19  48:35  45: 7  46:19  48:35
Count:    6      5      4      3      2      11     2      4      4      2      3      2      35     7      2      11     12
Width:    1120   1022   915    638    331    283    242    167    190    122    273    216    2405   153    307    566    1051   1041
Strength: 6.82   7.23   7.81   6.72   4.96   1.21   1.66   2.00   1.00   1.19   2.06   2.88   1.65   1.75   1.46   1.15   2.02   2.36

Start:    47: 8  47: 9  48: 1  48: 1  48: 1  48:12  48:20  48:28
End:      48: 1  47:16  48:35  48:12  48:28  48:21
Count:    5      4      2      7      2      3
Width:    359    346    671    392    204    123
Strength: 1.23   1.86   2.36   2.50   3.58   2.67   1.20
```

For 'alã 114 (5 times)

Each Column = 13 Verses. Separations are: Max = 9741.50, Mean = 4661.66, Min = 34.00 .

Linguistic Density Plot in Ezekiel 1 - 48

CLUSTERS:

Start:	16:59	17:13	17:18
End:	17:19	17:16	17:19
Count:	5	4	2	2
Width:	512	133	65	26
Strength:	3.63	2.62	1.16	1.17

GAPS:

Start:	17:19
End:	48:35
Count:	2
Width:	19457
Strength:	3.75

Linguistic Density Plot in Ezekiel 1 - 48

For `elleh 6233 (46 times)

Each Column = 13 Verses.   Separations are: Max = 3306.50, Mean = 595.11, Min = 16.00

REFERENCE

D
E
N
S
I
T
Y

+25
+20
+15
+10
+5
0

REFERENCE

CLUSTERS:

Start:	4: 6	14: 3	14: 3	14:14	16:30	17:12	17:12	18:10	18:10	33:24	36:20	37: 3	37: 3	40:24	40:24	40:24	40:24	40:28
End:	18:13	18:13	16: 5	14:18	14:18	18:13	17:18	18:13	18:11	37:18	37:18	37: 5	48:30	43:18	40:35	40:29	40:29	
Count:	17	13	5	4	3	8	3	6	3	19	10	7	5	3	3	4	2	12
Width:	7304	2891	795	398	1551	540	156	2498	795	5013	1850	352	795	172	218	93		
Strength:	1.15	2.41	1.40	1.40	1.81	1.95	1.26	1.15	2.05	2.90	2.20	2.10	1.42	1.95	2.48	1.71	1.00	

Start:	40:32	40:35	45:25	46:24	48: 1	48: 1
End:	40:35	40:33	47: 9	47: 9	48:30	48:16	48:30
Count:	3	2	9	4	3	5	3	2	8
Width:	63	12	1668	759	202	585	295
Strength:	1.38	1.00	2.03	1.00	1.21	1.59	1.09	1.00

Data for 'ēlleh 6233, continued.

GAPS:

```
Start:     1: 1   1: 1   4: 6   9: 5  11: 2  18:11  18:11  18:11  18:11  18:13  18:13  18:13  24:19  37:11  37:18  43:18  43:18
End:      14:14   8:15   8:15  14: 3  14: 3  40:32  40:28  40:24  37: 3  37: 3  36:20  23:30  36:20  33:24  40:24  40:24  46:24  45:25
Count:        7      3      2      3      2     17     15     13      6      5      3      2      3      2      3      2
Width:     6304   3496   1919   2272   1600  14171  14097  14016  11621  11577  11134   3747   6613   4910   2223   2043   2052   1495
Strength:  2.02   2.82   2.27   1.32   1.72   2.43   3.12   3.90   5.97   6.90   7.77   5.40   6.65   7.40   1.26   2.48   1.05   1.54
```

Linguistic Density Plot in Ezekiel 1 - 48

For 'elōhîm 111 (36 times)

Each Column = 13 Verses. Separations are: Max = 3208.00, Mean = 755.95, Min = 21.00 .

REFERENCE

(density plot, vertical axis labeled from 0 to +25, with DENSITY marked along the axis)

CLUSTERS:

Start:	1: 1	8: 3	8: 3	8: 3	10:19	10:19	11:20	20: 5	20: 5	20: 5	28: 2	28: 2	28: 2	28: 2	31: 8	31: 8	34:24	
End:	44: 2	14:11	11:24	9: 3	11:24	10:20	11:24	20:20	31: 9	28: 9	28:26	28:16	28: 9	28:13	31: 9	34:24	37:27	
Count:	36	9	8	3	5	2	3	26	15	11	8	7	4	3	3	2	6	
Width:	24909	3020	1615	431	563	12	73	15249	7127	1711	515	374	260	116	80	42	18	2002
Strength:	1.50	1.62	2.06	1.05	1.74	1.01	1.40	1.71	1.57	1.52	2.90	2.68	2.55	1.73	1.00	1.39	1.43	1.00	1.14

Start:	34:24	34:31
End:	39:22	40: 2
Count:	3	3
Width:	161	213
Strength:	1.31	1.26

Data for 'ĕlōhîm 111, continued.

GAPS:

Start:	1: 1	1: 1	10:20	11:24	11:24	14:11	20:20	31: 9	40: 2	40: 2	44: 2
End:	8: 3	8: 3	28: 2	20:19	20: 5	20: 5	28: 2	34:24	48:35	43: 2	48:35
Count:	3	2	10	5	3	2	2	2	4	2	2
Width:	3232	3208	10804	5177	4837	3432	5042	2278	5623	1945	3036
Strength:	1.67	3.33	2.05	1.52	3.24	3.63	5.82	2.06	2.70	1.61	3.09

Linguistic Density Plot in Ezekiel 1 - 48

For 'almānâ 114 (6 times)

Each Column = 13 Verses.   Separations are: Max = 6940.50. Mean = 3995.71. Min = 10.00 .

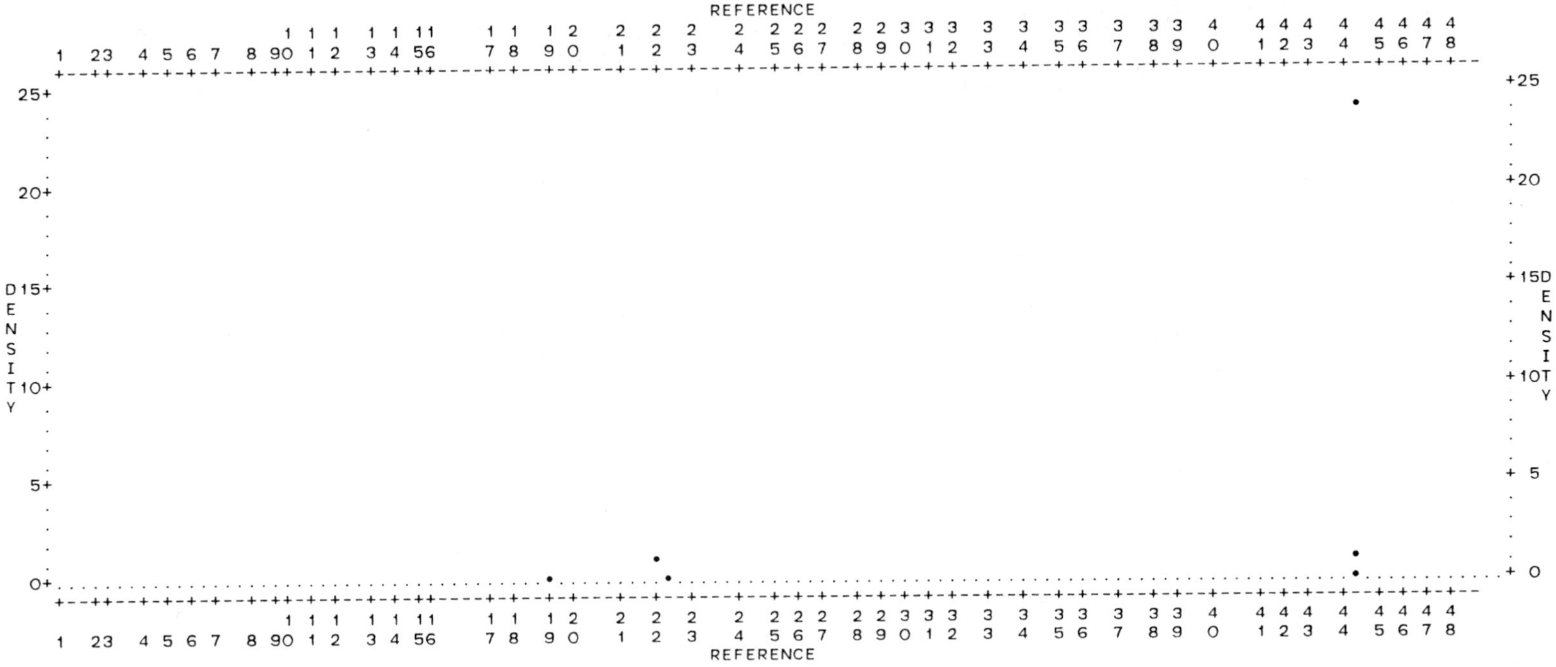

CLUSTERS:

Start:	19: 7	22: 7	44:22	44:22
End:	22:25	22:25	44:22	44:22
Count:	3	2	3	2
Width:	2490	329	20	3
Strength:	1.23	1.05	1.78	1.15

GAPS:

Start:	1: 1	1: 1	1: 1	22:25
End:	44:22	44:22	19: 7	44:22
Count:	6	5	2	2
Width:	25463	25446	9404	13552
Strength:	1.22	1.93	1.56	2.76

Linguistic Density Plot in Ezekiel 1 - 48

For 'elep 711 (40 times)

Each Column = 13 Verses.   Separations are: Max = 12840.00, Mean = 682.20, Min =   5.00 .

REFERENCE

CLUSTERS:

Start:	45: 1	45: 1	45: 1	45: 3	45: 3	45: 5	45: 5	45: 6	47: 3	47: 3	47: 4	48: 8	48: 8	48: 8	48: 8	48: 9	48:10	48:10	48:10
End:	48:35	45:45	45:45	45:45	45:45	45:45	45:45	48:35	47:47	47:47	48:35	48:16	48:10	48:16	48:35	48: 9	48: 9	48:10	48:10
Count:	40	8	4	2	4	2	4	2	32	4	5	28	7	17	28	7	3	2	2
Width:	2288	111	45	5	29	4	7	1129	30	12	8	561	209	62	32	17	5	4	7
Strength:	26.15	2.87	1.78	1.01	1.79	1.01	1.01	10.80	1.79	1.00	1.01	8.72	5.08	2.64	1.43	1.01	1.01	1.80	1.01

Start:	48:13	48:16	48:13	48:13	48:13	48:13	48:16	48:16	48:18	48:18	48:20	48:18	48:18	48:18	48:20	48:21	48:30
End:	48:16	48:15	48:13	48:13	48:13	48:13	48:16	48:16	48:18	48:35	48:20	48:20	48:18	48:21	48:21	48:35	48:33
Count:	10	6	4	2	2	2	4	2	11	6	4	2	4	2	2	5	3
Width:	96	45	15	5	2	9	25	8	82	40	8	11	2	5	12	86	50
Strength:	3.38	2.38	1.80	1.01	1.01	1.79	1.79	1.01	2.35	1.78	1.01	1.00	1.01	1.01	1.00	2.06	1.41

Data for 'elep 711, continued.

GAPS:

Start:	1: 1	1: 1	1: 1	1: 1	1: 1	1: 1	1: 1
End:	48:18	48:13	48: 9	45: 5	45: 3	45: 1	
Count:	31	23	15	6	4	2	
Width:	27644	27525	27429	25756	25715	25674	
Strength:	3.75	5.81	8.73	15.82	21.05	37.53	

Linguistic Density Plot in Ezekiel 1 - 48

For 'ēm 114 (10 times)

Each Column = 13 Verses.   Separations are: Max = 13476.00, Mean = 2542.73, Min = 12.50 .

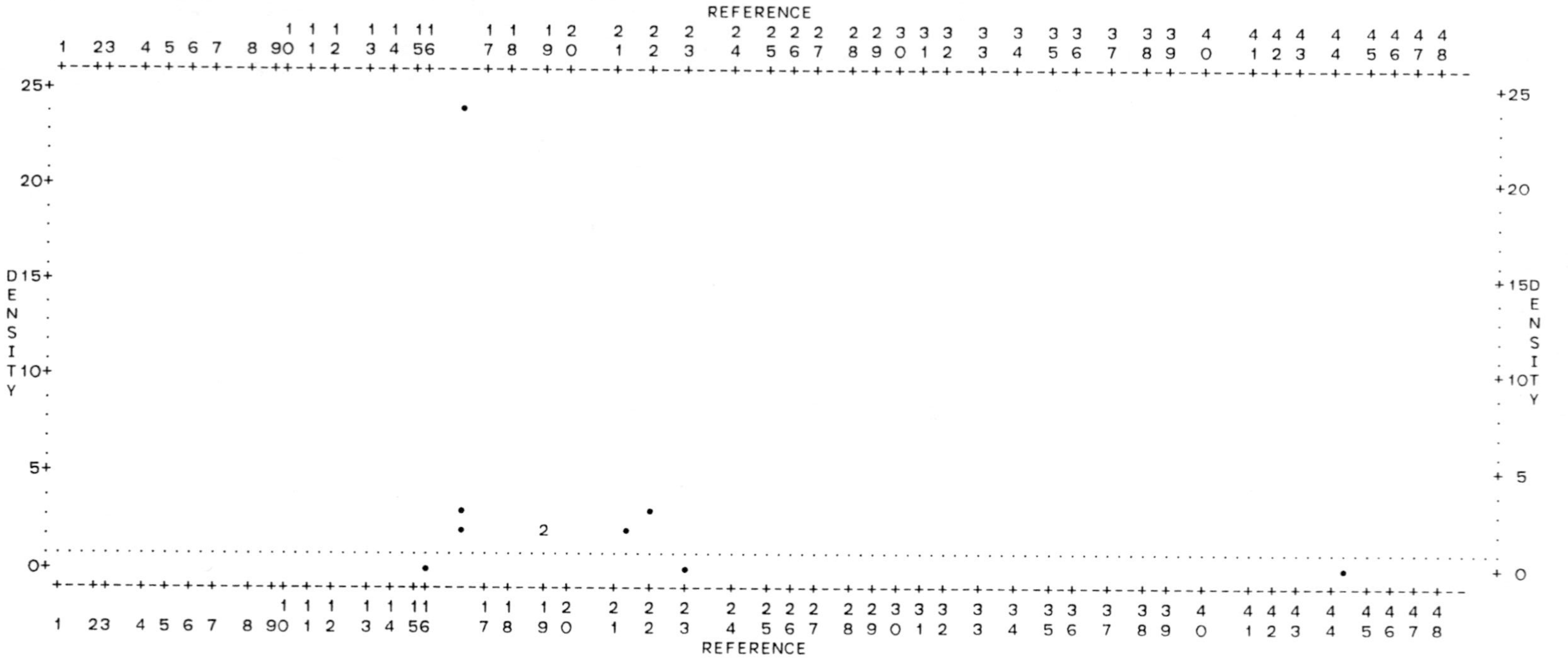

REFERENCE

DENSITY

REFERENCE

CLUSTERS:

Start:	16: 3	16: 3	16: 3	16:44	19: 2	21:26
End:	44:25	23: 2	19:10	16:45	19:10	23: 2
Count:	10	9	6	3	2	3
Width:	18786	5310	2721	943	137	876
Strength:	1.31	4.18	2.48	1.85	1.03	1.35

GAPS:

Start:	1: 1	19:10	22: 7	23: 2	23: 2
End:	16: 3	48:35	48:35	44:25	
Count:	16	2	6	4	2
Width:	6744	18504	16418	15915	13476
Strength:	1.80	1.44	2.44	3.47	4.71

Linguistic Density Plot in Ezekiel 1 - 48

For 'im 53 (37 times)

Each Column = 13 Verses. Separations are: Max = 3494.50, Mean = 736.05, Min = 32.00 .

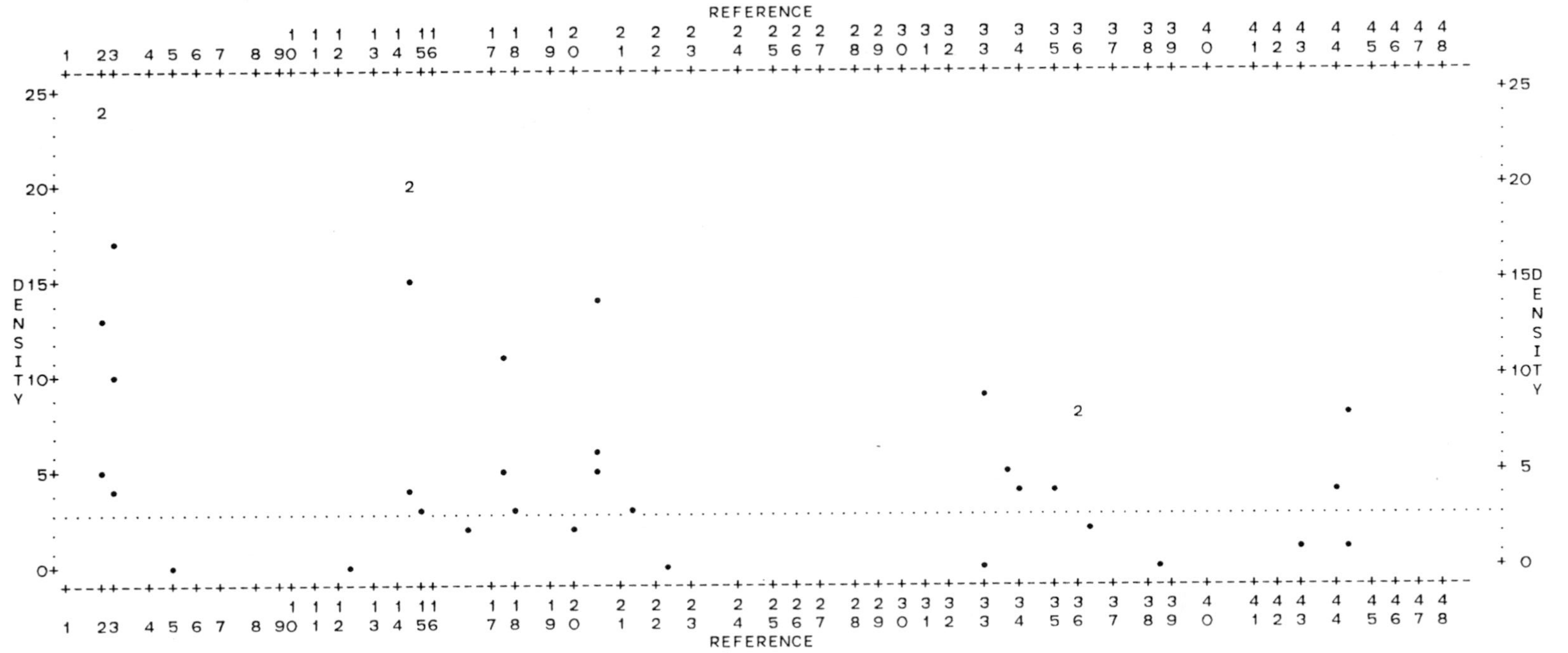

CLUSTERS:

Start:	2: 5	2: 5	2: 5	2: 5	2: 5	2: 5	2: 7	3: 6	3:11	12:23	12:23	12:23	14:16	14:16	14:16	14:20	16:48	17:16	20: 3	20: 3
End:	44:25	22:14	5:11	3:11	2: 7	2: 5	2: 7	3:11	3:11	22:14	18: 3	15: 3	15: 3	14:20	14:16	14:20	18: 3	18: 3	22:14	20:39
Count:	37	24	8	7	4	2	2	3	2	16	10	6	5	4	2	2	4	3	6	4
Width:	24839	10994	1419	372	67	3	3	126	3	6338	3353	1247	239	98	3	3	945	262	2058	909
Strength:	1.65	2.71	2.14	2.47	1.77	1.02	1.02	1.34	1.02	2.14	1.71	1.60	1.96	1.74	1.02	1.02	1.04	1.20	1.07	1.07

Start:	20:31	33:11	33:11	33:11	33:11	35: 6	36: 5	44:10
End:	20:39	38:19	36:22	34: 8	33:11	36:22	36:22	44:25
Count:	3	9	8	4	2	4	3	3
Width:	164	3525	2025	673	6	702	390	383
Strength:	1.30	1.29	1.80	1.27	1.01	1.24	1.08	1.08

Data for 'im 53, continued.

GAPS:

```
Start:     3:11   3:11   5:11  14:20  20:33  20:39  21:18  22:14  36: 7  36:22  36:22  38:19  44:25
End:      14:16  12:23  12:23  48:35  33:11  33:11  33:11  33:11  44:22  44:10  43:11  43:11  48:35
Count:        4      3      2     26     13      5      4      3      2      6      5      4      3      2      2
Width:     5292   4284   3237  21521  11584   7633   7501   6989   6352   5703   5399   5085   4450   2950   2444
Strength:  2.55   2.81   3.48   1.46   1.32   3.41   4.38   5.51   7.83   1.33   1.78   2.38   2.97   3.08   2.38
```

For 'ammā 114 (88 times)

Linguistic Density Plot in Ezekiel 1 - 48

Each Column = 13 Verses.   Separations are: Max = 11228.00.   Mean = 314.27.   Min = 1.00 .

Density plot (vertical axis labelled D E N S I T Y, scale +25, +20, +15, +10, +5, 0; horizontal axis REFERENCE, columns 1–4 series of verse groupings).

CLUSTERS:

```
Start:    40: 5  40: 5  40: 5  40: 5  40: 7  40:11  40:11  40:12  40:13  40:15  40:19  40:19  40:23  40:27  40:29  40:33
End:      47: 3  42: 8  40:36  40:15  40: 9  40:15  40:12  40:12  40:36  40:36  40:25  40:36  40:25  40:36  40:30  40:36
Count:       88     74     29     14      9      9      2      3     15      6      3      6      3      9      5      4
Width:     4382   1585    640    203     90     73     27     29    361    143     51     42     51    176     61     60
Strength: 52.54  18.86   5.95   3.72   1.90   2.89   2.27   1.37   3.76   2.10   1.32   1.34   1.00   2.77   1.73   1.65

Start:    40:42  40:42  40:42  40:47  40:48  41: 1  41: 7  40:11  40:15  40:36  40:25  40:36  40:36  41: 8  41:11  41:12
End:      42: 8  41: 5  40:49  40:48  40:49  41:    41: 5  40:12  40:    40:    40:    40:    40:    41:12  41:12  41:12
Count:       45     25     11      3      8     20      7      5      3      7      5      3     20      9     11     15
Width:      841    284    166     12     50    473     89     38     16     10     41     20    124     68     24     48
Strength:  8.80   5.54   3.19   1.40   2.70   4.55   3.83   2.49   1.41   2.02   2.49   1.41   3.24   2.21   1.38   1.97
```

Clusters for 'ammā 114, continued.

Start:	41:12	41:22	42: 2	42: 2	42: 7	43:13	43:13	43:13	43:13	43:13	43:13	43:13	43:14	43:14	43:14	43:14	43:14
End:	41:14	42: 8	42: 4	42: 4	42: 8	47: 3	45: 2	43:17	43:15	43:13	43:13	43:15	43:14	43:14	43:15	43:15	43:14
Count:	4	9	7	4	3	14	13	12	10	5	3	2	1	2	5	2	3	2
Width:	27	235	114	38	16	2249	1115	99	52	9	2	1	20	3	7	3
Strength:	1.72	2.70	2.39	1.69	1.40	1.76	2.63	3.46	3.12	2.04	1.43	1.00	1.00	2.02	1.00	1.42	1.00

GAPS:

Start:	1: 1	43:14	43:15	43:17	45: 2	45: 2
End:	40: 5	48:35	48:35	48:35	48:35	47: 3
Count:	2	7	6	4	3	2
Width:	22453	3335	3331	3284	2268	1134
Strength:	71.23	1.95	2.59	4.39	3.75	2.63

Linguistic Density Plot in Ezekiel 1 - 48

For 'mr 311 (189 times)   'mr 312 (65 times)   'mr 313 (24 times)   'mr 314 (12 times)
    'mr 3161 (1 times)   'mr 3162 (71 times)   'mr 322 (1 times)

Each Column = 13 Verses.   Separations are: Max = 964.00, Mean = 76.84, Min = 2.50 .

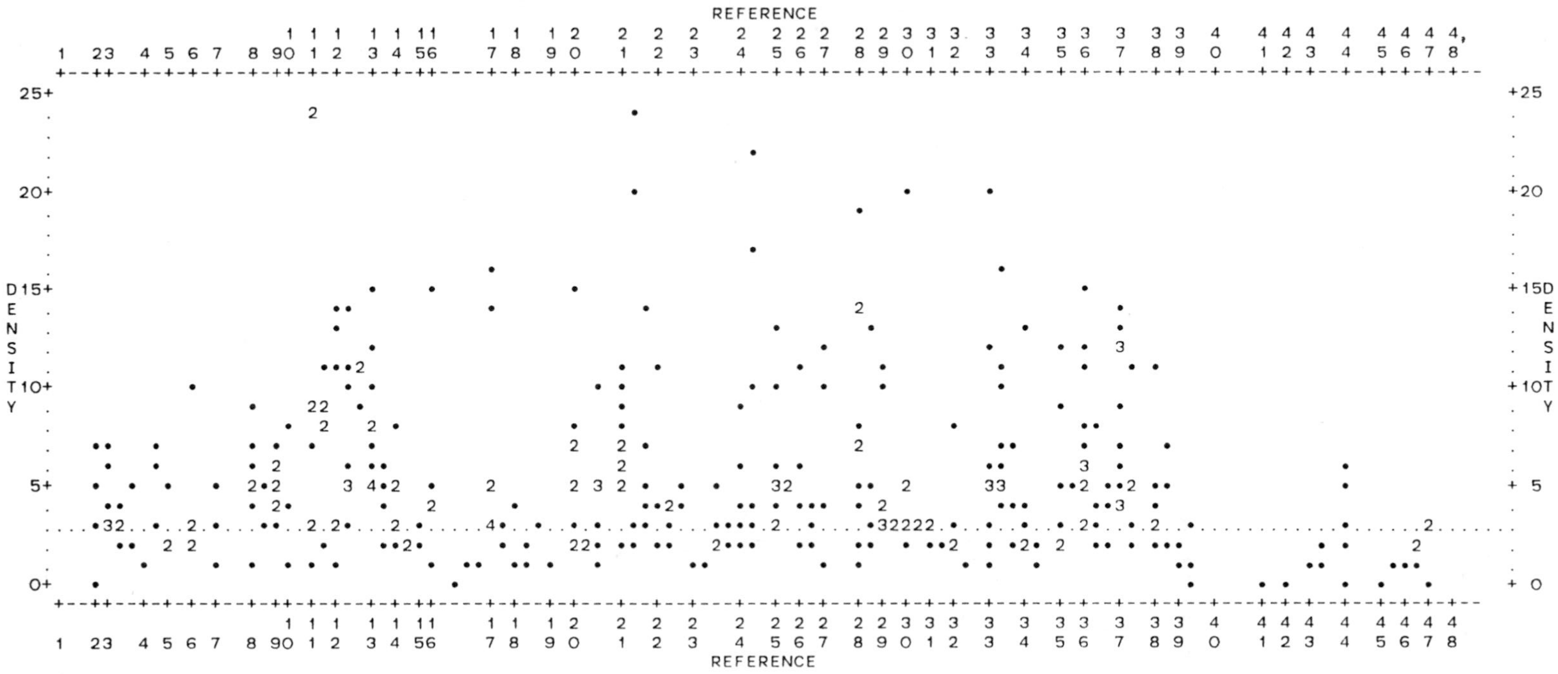

REFERENCE

(vertical axis label: DENSITY; scale markers +25, +20, +15, +10, +5, 0)

CLUSTERS:

Start:	2: 1	2: 1	2: 1	2: 1	8: 1	8: 5	8: 5	8: 5	8:12	8:12	9: 1	9: 7	9: 7	9: 8	9:11
End:	47:13	27: 3	16: 6	3:27	16: 6	11:17	10: 6	8:17	8: 9	8:13	10: 6	9: 9	9: 9	9: 9	10: 2
Count:	363	219	112	16	81	34	20	9	4	5	3	11	3	3	3
Width:	26459	13889	6228	832	3566	1419	755	279	94	118	32	405	240	76	42
Strength:	12.53	3.98	3.41	1.10	4.25	2.65	2.16	1.56	1.02	1.23	1.11	1.51	1.47	1.16	1.02

Start:	11: 2	11:17	11: 2	11: 5	2: 1	3:10	4:13	6: 1	8: 1	11:16	12: 1	12: 8	12:17	12:21	12:26
End:	11:17	11:11	11: 7	11: 7	3:27	3:11	4:16	6: 3	16: 3	11:17	12: 6	13: 3	12:19	12:23	12:26
Count:	14	7	5	4	16	3	4	3	23	4	47	20	7	3	4
Width:	292	74	32	8	832	86	68	23	405	35	1950	597	249	103	71
Strength:	2.60	2.07	1.80	1.67	1.36	2.00	1.09	1.22	1.20	1.48	3.25	2.64	2.75	1.91	1.54

REFERENCE

Clusters for 'mr 311, 'mr 312, 'mr 313, 'mr 314, 'mr 3161, 'mr 3162, 'mr 322, continued.

```
Start:    13: 1  13: 6  13:10  13: 7  13: 6  13: 6  16: 1  16: 1  16:36  16:59  17: 1  17: 9  17:11  20: 2  20: 2  20: 2  20: 2
End:      13: 3  13:20  13:13  13: 8  13:13  13: 3  16: 6  16: 3  27: 3  17:12  17:12  17:11  17:12  20: 2  20:21  20: 8  20: 5
Count:      3      3     12      3      4      5      4      3    107     12     14      3      3      3      8      5      3
Width:     19    338    150     33     12     50    100     81   7053    355     79     11    497    162     52   2070
Strength: 1.23  2.02  1.92  1.48  1.30  1.36  1.35  1.12  1.64  1.20  1.49  1.31  1.13  1.86  1.66  1.30  1.11

Start:    20:27  20:27  20:27  20:27  20:29  20:29  21: 1  21: 1  21:12  21:13  21:23  21:29  21:33  22: 1  23:22  24: 1
End:      27: 3  23: 1  21:14  20:32  20:30  20:30  21:14  21:14  21:14  21:14  21: 2  21:33  21:33  22: 3  23:27  24: 3
Count:    4262    740    158     87     24    250    117     14     55     10    337     96     14     22   2070     40
Width:    1825     21      4     77     37     21      8      6      5      9      3      5      3     22    ...    32
Strength: 2.65   2.15   2.38   1.32   1.08   1.19   2.75   2.09   1.16   1.72   1.92   1.66   1.36   1.38   1.28   2.04  1.11

Start:    24:15  24:15  24:20  24:20  24:21  25: 1  25: 1  25:12  26: 1  28: 1  28: 1  28: 1  28: 1  28: 1  28: 1
End:      27: 3  25: 8  24:21  24:21  24:21  25: 8  25: 8  25:12  26: 3  32:17  28:12  29:13  28:12  28: 2  28: 2
Count:    1166    441    105     31     15      6    168     29    661    218      7      4    125     10    186
Width:      28     13      6      5      4      8      7      3    266     21     40     68   2355    831    17
Strength: 2.36   1.83   1.63   1.80   1.62   1.35   1.56   1.51   1.47   1.34   1.22   1.41   2.11   2.22   1.60  1.34

Start:    28: 6  28:11  28:20  28:20  29: 1  29:17  29:17  30: 1  30: 1  32: 1  33: 1  33: 8  33:10  33:10  33:20
End:      28:12  28:12  29: 3  28:22  29: 3  29: 3  30:13  30: 6  30: 6  32: 3  34:20  33:12  33:11  33:10  33:20
Count:      98    461    226     15     42    336    194     71      6     38   1213    126     64     24      7
Width:       6     13      8      3      4      9      6      3      7      7     28      9      4      7    177
Strength: 1.67   1.29   1.54   1.27   1.42   1.00   1.11   1.35   1.20   1.06   2.24   1.71   1.55   1.59   1.35  1.52

Start:    33:20  34: 2  33:23  33:23  33:25  34: 1  35: 1  35:10  35:10  35: 3  35: 3  36: 1  36: 1  36: 3  36: 6
End:      33:27  33:24  33:24  33:25  34: 2  39:25  36:22  35:14  35:14  35: 4  35: 7  36: 7  36: 5  36: 3  36: 7
Count:     361    153     34     11     15     57   2929    781    481    243     90     28    189    108    247
Width:      13      9      5      3      5      3     43     23     17     18     10      7     31     12     33
Strength: 2.14   2.06   1.78   1.31   1.27   2.60   3.45   2.49   1.16   1.24   1.05   1.15   1.89   1.80   1.11  1.21

Start:    36:20  36:22  36:33  36:33  37: 1  37: 9  37: 9  37:15  37:18  38: 1
End:      36:22  37:21  37: 5  37: 5  37: 4  37:21  37:12  37:21  37:19  38: 3
Count:      34    577    186     34     17    304     84     31    140     79
Width:       3     20      8      5      3     12      7      4      9     22     40
Strength: 1.10   2.71   1.74   1.78   1.25   2.15   2.02   1.50   1.09   1.22  1.04

GAPS:

Start:     1: 1   1: 1   1: 1   2: 10  2: 10  2: 10  5: 10  5: 11  6: 3   6: 11  11:17  11:17  14: 6  14: 6  14:17
End:       3:11   2: 4   2: 2   11: 1  12: 1  12: 8  11: 5  11: 1  6:11   12: 8  12: 1  12: 1  14: 1  15: 1  14:17
Count:     1047    676    596    802    697    621    554    507    465    372    358    197    559    477    286
Width:       10      4      2      8      5      5      8      2      5      3      3      3      6      1      3
Strength:  1.56   3.36   6.76   1.31   2.54   4.31   6.22   1.30   1.24   3.84   1.88   1.56   1.02   1.10   1.21

Start:    14: 6  14:12  16: 6  16: 1  16: 6  16: 6  16:44  16:59  17:12  17:12  17:12  18:29  18:19  18:25  20: 8  20:30  20:32
End:      14:12  21:29  17: 1  17: 1  16:59  16:36  16:59  16:36  17:12  20: 1  20: 2  20: 3  20:27  20:21  21: 1  21: 1
Count:      178   1393   1283   1163   1313    608    327    162    916   1255   1265   1273    471    318    371    464    395
Width:        2      8      5      2     14     11     10      6      2      2      6      5      4      2      3      4    332
Strength:  1.31   4.25   6.38   7.04   1.15   6.92   3.25   2.47   1.10   3.11   2.92   3.14   2.00   2.52   1.02   1.23  1.64

Start:    20:39  21: 1  22: 3  22:17  22:28  22:28  22:28  23: 1  23:28  24:21  26: 1  26:15  27: 1  28: 9  28:12  28:20  30: 7  31: 2
End:      21: 1  21:29  22:23  22:17  24: 3  23:35  23:32  23:28  23:22  25: 1  28: 1  28: 1  26:15  48:35  28:20  28:20  33:43  33:10
Count:      193    286    395    267   1102    740    686    610    531    367    165    168    177    594  12754    184   1868   1359
Width:        2      3      4     11      5      6      5      3      4     13      2     11      2    139      2     20     13     10
Strength:  1.50   1.21   1.23   2.47   1.39   2.08   2.47   2.86   3.48   3.77   1.14   1.18   1.30   6.74   3.02   1.39   1.25   1.66
```

Gaps for 'mr 311, 'mr 312, 'mr 313, 'mr 314, 'mr 3161, 'mr 3162, 'mr 322, continued.

```
Start:    31: 2  31: 2  31: 2  32: 2  32: 3  32: 3  34: 2  34: 2  34: 2  34:11  36:22  37:19  37:21  38: 3  38:17  39: 1  39: 1
End:      33:10  31: 1  31:10  31: 1  33: 1  33: 1  34:10  35: 1  35: 1  35: 1  36:33  38: 1  38: 1  38:10  39: 1  48:35  39:17
Count:      12      9      4      2      5      4      2      7      6      4      3      3      2      2      2     24      2
Width:    1354   1143    450    170    683    655    168    354    687    673    162    466    262    307    249    183   6287   330
Strength: 2.02   2.45   1.65   1.20   2.45   3.20   1.18   3.61   1.20   1.69   1.10   1.77   2.40   2.30   2.24   1.00   1.37  12.68  3.29

Start:    39:17  39:25  39:25  43: 7  43:18  43:18  44: 6  44: 9  44: 9  44: 9  44: 9  44: 9  44: 9  46: 1  47: 1  47: 8  47:13
End:      48:35  43:18  41: 4  43:18  44: 5  48:35  48:35  47: 6  46:20  45:18  45:    46:16  45:    46:16  48:35  47:13  48:35
Count:      22      6      5      2      3     16     12      9      8      6      5      3      2      2      3      2
Width:    5953   2677   2501   1928   1273   3270    290   1836   1765   1552   1441    940    753    344   1057    914
Strength: 12.71  13.45  14.36  16.39  15.60  7.27   1.25   5.68   6.10   6.85   7.42   7.26   8.81   3.47   8.34  10.91
```

For 'mr 311 (189 times)

Linguistic Density Plot in Ezekiel 1 - 48

Each Column = 13 Verses.   Separations are: Max = 1422.50, Mean =   147.21, Min =   6.00

REFERENCE

CLUSTERS:

Start:	2: 4	5: 5	9: 5	11: 5	11:15	12: 9	12:19	12:28	13:18	13:13	15:	6 20:	20:27	21: 3	21: 3
End:	47:13	14: 6	11:17	11: 7	11:17	13: 8	12:23	13:	13:20	13:13	16:	3 20:	22:28	21:14	21:14
Count:	189	3	24	6	3	16	10	5	8	3	4	3	20	7	4
Width:	26379	83	2367	245	27	51	1046	511	285	125	85	73	81	188	44	1746	737	228
Strength:	6.27	1.02	1.54	1.51	1.29	1.17	2.12	1.89	1.04	1.59	1.01	1.20	1.06	1.03	1.00	1.57	1.73	1.62	1.85	1.36

Start:	21:12	21:29	21:29	21:33	23:22	23:22	23:22	23:46	23:22	24:21	25:12	25:12	26:15	27: 3	28: 2
End:	21:14	22:28	22: 3	21:33	21:33	47:13	39:25	30:22	27: 3	24: 9	25:16	25: 3	27: 3	27: 3	30:22
Count:	3	9	7	5	14	111	102	47	27	5	4	7	4	13	6	3	20
Width:	44	720	217	96	14640	9777	4097	2070	248	128	149	661	266	108	218	19	1425
Strength:	1.21	1.12	1.88	1.69	1.35	1.55	5.04	3.08	2.52	1.24	1.16	1.15	2.24	1.74	1.32	1.59	1.33	2.25

Clusters for 'mr 311, continued.

```
Start:    28: 2  28:22  28:22  29: 3  29: 3  29: 3  29: 8  29:19  30: 2  31:10  31:10  34: 2  35:12  35:12  35:12  36: 3  36: 3  36: 1  36: 3  36: 1  36: 4  36: 6  36:33
End:      29: 3  28:12  28:25  29: 3  29:30  30:22  30:    30: 6  30:    39:25  36:22  36:22  36:22  36: 7  36: 3  36: 3  36: 2  36: 3  36: 7  36: 6  36:33  39:25
Count:    10     4      6      3      3      10     7      4      6      55     33     22     14     12     108    31     12     119    33     22
Width:    588    178    213    85     21     719    407    152    66     5377   3229   1460   566    266    108    31     12     119    33     1894
Strength: 1.71   1.04   1.61   1.01   1.32   1.40   1.34   1.14   1.10   2.81   1.95   2.57   2.63   2.86   2.18   1.91   1.36   1.61   1.26   1.88
```

```
Start:    36:33  36:33  37: 3  37: 6  37: 4  37: 9  38: 3  38:14  38:14  44: 6  44: 9
End:      38:11  37:12  37:12  37:12  37:12  38:11  38:17  38:17  44: 9
Count:    15     9      3      6      4      5      9      3      3
Width:    1021   357    71     180    74     175    266    81     78
Strength: 1.96   2.01   1.07   1.71   1.45   1.05   1.10   1.03   1.04
```

GAPS:

```
Start:    1: 1   1: 1   1: 1   1: 1   1: 1   2: 1   2: 4   3:11   3:27   3:27   3:27   3:27   3: 7   5: 9   7: 5   9: 9   11:17  16: 3  16: 3  16: 3
End:      17: 3  13:18  11: 5  3:27   3:11   2: 4   3:11   3:27   11: 5  5: 7   5: 5   11: 5  11: 5  9: 5   11: 5  9: 5   12: 9  17: 3  16:59  16:36
Count:    47     35     18     6      4      2      12
Width:    8119   5783   4432   1424   1047   676    367    373    3004   891    568    520    2104   1728   1015   583    363    1393   1261   706
Strength: 1.55   1.00   3.33   2.12   2.39   3.60   1.49   1.53   2.92   1.03   1.32   2.54   3.44   5.09   5.92   2.97   1.47   3.76   4.67   3.81
```

```
Start:    17:22  18:25  20: 5  22: 3  22: 3  22: 3  22: 3  22: 3  22:28  27: 3  30:22  32: 3  32:28  32:11  32:11  39: 1  39: 1  39: 2  39: 1  39:25
End:      18:19  20:27  24:    23:32  23:28  23:22  22:19  23:22  23:22  28:12  31:10  33:17  33:10  33:10  48:35  44: 6  39:17  44: 3
Count:    3      2      2      6      5      4      2      9      13
Width:    574    421    1605   1189   1113   949    295    446    776    602    303    1051   883    703    496    6287   3355   330    2845
Strength: 1.35   1.86   2.91   1.05   1.39   1.80   2.00   1.00   2.03   1.32   1.06   1.58   1.74   1.97   2.37   9.18   9.51   1.24   12.34
```

```
Start:    39:25  43:18  44: 6  44: 9  44: 9  46: 1  46:16  47:13
End:      43:18  48:35  48:35  45:18  45: 9  48:35  48:35  48:35
Count:    2      8      7      3      2      4      3      2
Width:    2507   2925   2854   940    753    1757   1413   914
Strength: 16.11  4.96   5.56   3.12   4.13   5.21   5.41   5.23
```

For 'mr 312 (65 times)

Linguistic Density Plot in Ezekiel 1 - 48

Each Column = 13 Verses.   Separations are: Max = 2617.50, Mean =   423.79, Min =   8.50 .

REFERENCE

REFERENCE

CLUSTERS:

Start:	2: 1	2: 1	2: 1	2: 1	3: 1	3: 1	3:22	4:13	8: 5	8: 5	8:12	9: 4	9: 7	11: 2	20: 7
End:	47: 8	28: 9	16: 6	4:16	3:10	3: 4	4:16	4:16	11:13	8: 9	8:17	9: 9	9: 9	11:13	21:12
Count:	65	47	33	12	6	3	6	4	21	14	4	6	4	3	8
Width:	26316	14619	6228	1203	415	188	64	488	68	3566	1333	279	94	118	231	55	206	1192
Strength:	1.37	3.10	4.29	2.71	1.88	1.52	1.33	1.80	1.68	3.12	3.56	2.55	1.65	1.61	2.08	1.59	1.35	1.09	1.68

Start:	20: 7	20: 7	37: 3	37: 3	37: 3	42:13	46:20
End:	20:29	20:13	38:13	37:18	37:11	37: 4	44: 5	47: 8
Count:	6	3	7	6	5	3	5	4
Width:	578	181	930	346	174	17	869	245
Strength:	1.70	1.13	1.64	1.96	1.86	1.41	1.01	1.44

Data for 'mr 312, continued.

GAPS:

Start:	4:16	10: 2	10: 2	11:13	11:13	16: 6	16: 6	16: 6	16: 6	21:12	21:12	24:20	24:20	28: 9	28: 9	37:11	37:11	37:18	37:18	37:18
End:	8: 5	48:35	37: 3	16: 6	13:15	37: 3	37: 3	24:19	20: 7	24:19	23:36	37: 3	28: 2	37: 3	33:27	47: 6	44: 2	44: 2	43:18	42:13
Count:	2	41	25	4	2	18	17	12	2	4	2	5	2	3	2	12	8	7	6	4
Width:	1459	24049	16540	2225	1144	13636	13626	6569	2892	2485	1827	7041	1687	5235	3163	6256	4291	4119	3897	3324
Strength:	2.47	4.25	3.87	1.33	1.72	4.30	4.67	1.49	5.91	1.70	3.36	6.55	3.02	7.48	6.56	1.25	1.25	1.60	1.96	2.88

Start:	38:13	38:13	44: 5	47: 8
End:	42:13	41: 4	46:20	48:35
Count:	3	2	2	2
Width:	2740	2085	1678	1057
Strength:	3.22	3.97	3.00	1.51

For 'mr 313 (24 times)

Linguistic Density Plot in Ezekiel 1 - 48

Each Column = 13 Verses.   Separations are: Max =   3965.00, Mean =   1118.80, Min =   32.00 .

Linguistic density scatter plot. Vertical axis labelled DENSITY with scale markers +25, +20, +15, +10, +5, 0; horizontal axis numbered by verse column 1 through 48. "REFERENCE" marked along the baseline.

CLUSTERS:

Start	End	Count	Width	Strength
6:11	39:17	24	19501	4.18
6:11	24:21	16	10904	2.18
11:16	14: 6	9	3566	2.10
11:16	14:14	8	1437	2.59
12:10	12:11	4	428	1.64
12:23	11:17	2	31	1.01
12:23	12:11	3	22	1.01
12:23	13:11	4	760	1.45
17: 9	17:12	3	313	1.29
17:12	17:12	3	79	1.45
17:12	17:12	2	10	1.03
28: 2	33:25	6	3255	1.06
33:10	33:11	4	338	1.69
33:10	33:12	3	64	1.46
33:10	33:11	2	24	1.01

GAPS:

Start	End	Count	Width	Strength
1: 1	11:16	3	4644	1.61
6:11	11:16	2	2515	1.29
17:12	48:35	14	19627	1.85
33:11	48:35	6	9946	1.29
33:12	48:35	5	9632	3.52
33:25	48:35	4	9906	2.70
36:22	48:35	3	7930	3.82
39:17	48:35	2	5953	4.49

Linguistic Density Plot in Ezekiel 1 - 48

For 'mr 314 (12 times)

Each Column = 13 Verses.   Separations are: Max = 4048.50, Mean = 2151.54, Min = 67.50

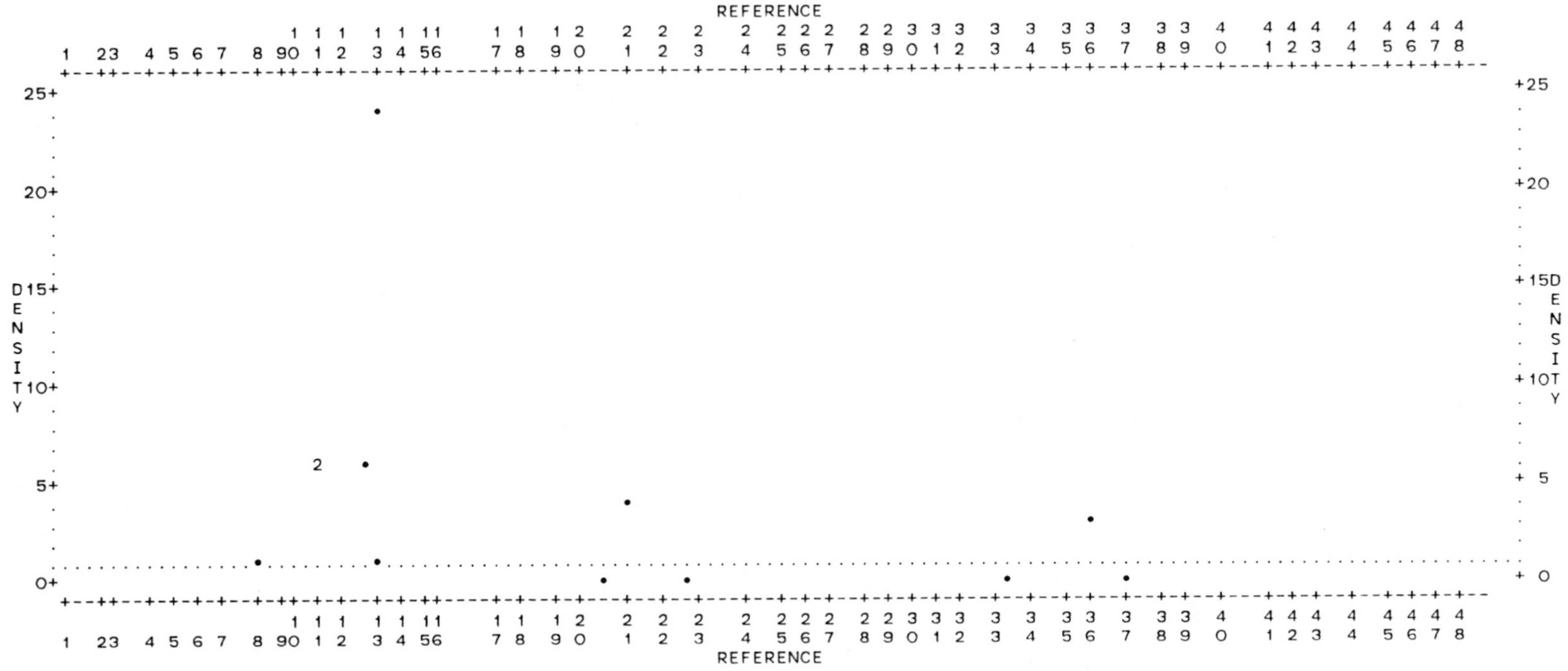

CLUSTERS:

Start:	8:12	8:12	8:12	8:12	11: 3	12:27	13: 6	20:32
End:	37:11	22:28	13: 7	11: 5	11: 5	13: 7	13: 7	22:28
Count:	12	9	6	3	2	3	2	3
Width:	17197	8528	2102	991	135	29	23	1586
Strength:	2.39	2.38	2.37	1.22	1.54	1.06	1.06	1.00

GAPS:

Start:	13: 7	13: 7	21: 5	22:28	37:11	
End:	48:35	20:32	48:35	33:24	48:35	
Count:	8	2	6	3	2	
Width:	22428	4840	17177	7905	6349	7333
Strength:	1.97	1.34	1.76	1.33	2.10	2.60

Linguistic Density Plot in Ezekiel 1 - 48

For 'mr 3162 (71 times)

Each Column = 13 Verses.   Separations are: Max =   3583.00, Mean =   388.47, Min =   26.00 .

REFERENCE

(density plot grid with vertical scale marks: 25+, 20+, D15+ / E N S I T10+ Y, 5+, 0+ and horizontal reference axis labelled in columns)

REFERENCE

CLUSTERS:

Start:	3:16	3:16	3:16	9: 1	11:14	12:17	12:26	16:44	21: 1	21: 1	24: 1	25: 1	28: 1	33: 1
End:	38: 1	27: 1	16: 1	13:10	13:10	13:22	13:10	27: 1	21:23	23: 8	27: 8	26: 1	38: 1	33: 1
Count:	71	43	20	12	9	16	3	23	16	8	4	8	4	28
Width:	19971	13303	5561	3106	2010	1009	396	6796	3743	1335	416	1413	399	6045
Strength:	13.42	1.86	1.26	2.04	1.92	2.03	1.85	1.16	1.56	1.42	1.14	1.34	1.17	2.80

Start:	28: 1	32:17	33: 1
End:	32:17	34: 1	
Count:	10	18	10
Width:	2355	3336	787
Strength:	1.05	2.35	2.50

Start:	33: 1	33: 8	33:21	33:21	35: 1
End:	33:14	33:14	33:24	36:20	35:12
Count:	5	4	5	3	
Width:	347	198	309	52	747	220
Strength:	1.60	1.47	1.65	1.34	1.07	1.03

Data for 'mr 3162, continued.

GAPS:

Start:	1: 1	3:18	3:18	3:18	7: 1	16: 1	16: 1	18: 2	20: 5	23: 1	33:24	35:12	37:18	38: 1
End:	3:16	9:11	9: 1	6: 1	9: 1	17: 1	16:44	20: 2	21: 1	24: 1	48:35	48:35	48:35	48:35
Count:	2	5	4	2	2	3	2	2	2	2	12	7	3	2
Width:	1153	2711	2432	1129	977	1393	946	916	1032	995	9651	8486	7166	6845
Strength:	1.99	1.54	1.93	1.93	1.53	1.14	1.45	1.37	1.67	1.58	4.56	6.80	11.87	16.85

For 'anî 6111 (169 times)

Linguistic Density Plot in Ezekiel 1 - 48

Each Column = 13 Verses.   Separations are: Max = 1583.50, Mean = 164.53, Min = 12.50 .

The vertical axis is labelled DENSITY (reading 0+, 5+, T10+, 15+, 20+, 25+) and the horizontal axis is labelled REFERENCE. The right-hand scale reads +0, +5, +10, +15, +20, +25. The plot area is a scatter of dots with occasional "2" and "3" markers indicating overplotted points.

CLUSTERS:

Start:	1: 1	1: 1	2: 3	4: 5	5: 8	5: 8	5:11	5:13	6: 7	12:11	13: 7	13: 7	13: 7	13: 7	13:21	13:21	14: 7		
End:	44:28	30:26	3: 3	7: 9	6: 3	7: 9	5:11	6: 3	7: 9	12:25	18: 3	22:22	30:26	15: 7	14: 4	15: 7			
Count:	169	120	5	15	14	6	4	3	7	6	53	28	85	15	4	7			
Width:	25583	16610	232	1236	749	303	92	32	163	364	197	294	6302	3145	11077	1140	504	132	536
Strength:	8.92	3.02	1.31	1.81	2.44	1.99	1.42	1.28	1.17	1.26	1.05	1.12	2.56	2.28	1.97	1.65	1.22	1.28	1.22	1.44

Start:	14: 7	14: 7	14:11	14:16	14:20	16:43	16:60	17:16	17:21	17:24	17:21	18: 3	20: 3	20:19	20:19	20:23	20:31	20:31	22:14
End:	14:20	14:11	14:20	14: 7	14: 9	16: 3	16:62	18: 3	17:22	18: 3	22:22	22:21	20:15	20:26	20:38	20:26	20:33	20:38	22:22
Count:	7	4	3	7	9	8	3	8	6	3	25	18	5	9	5	3	4	3	
Width:	291	98	41	95	1057	262	116	62	25	49	2226	308	857	491	190	79	158	39	160
Strength:	1.76	1.40	1.24	1.01	1.67	2.09	1.15	1.95	1.31	1.21	2.31	1.07	1.82	1.44	1.08	1.18	1.18	1.25	1.18

Clusters for 'anf 6111, continued.

```
Start:     22:14  23:34  24:24  24:24  28: 2  28:22  28:22  28:22  28:22  29: 6  32:15  32:15  34: 8  34:24  34:24  34:24  34:24  34:30  35: 9  35:12
End:       22:16  30:26  27: 3  25:11  30:26  29: 9  29: 3  29: 9  29: 6  29: 9  40: 4  35:15  34:20  35: 6  34:27  35: 6  35: 4  35:15  35:15
Count:         3     32     10      5     18      3      5      8     11      3     46     21     17      5     12      3      7      5      5      3
Width:        37   3919    971    306   1524    732    349    199     61     78   5026   2153    844    309    461    844     80    258    117    131     74
Strength:   1.26   1.42   1.06   1.08   1.98   1.81   1.88   1.41   1.16   1.08   2.51   1.65   2.86   1.07   2.56   1.84   1.07   1.33   1.62   1.10

Start:     36: 7  36: 7  36: 7  36:32  36:32  36:36  36:36  37:12  37:12  37:12  38:23
End:       40: 4  37:28  37: 6  37: 6  36:38  36:38  37:28  37:21  37:14  39: 7  39: 7
Count:        25     17     10      6      4      3      5      7      5      3      4
Width:      2669   1355    776    244    128     51    443    220     61    136     45
Strength:   1.71   2.04   1.47   1.59   1.29   1.20   1.37   1.34   1.16   1.26   1.22

GAPS:

Start:      1: 1   1: 1   2: 8   2: 8   2: 8   3: 3   3: 3   7: 9   8: 1   8: 1   8:18   9:10   9:10  14:20  14:20  14:20  15: 7  16:62  18: 3  18: 3
End:        5:11   2: 3   5:11   5:11   5: 8   4: 5   4: 5   7:27  11:10   9: 8   8:18  11:10  11: 5  16:62  16:60  16:43  16:43  17:16  20: 5  18: 3
Count:        10      2      8      8      4      3      2      9      8      3      2      3      3      6      5      3      7      3      5      3
Width:      2111    626   1341   1318   1258   1170    683    352   1370    644    423    664    582   1619   1566   1193    948    360    992    931
Strength:   1.31   2.81   1.43   2.03   2.71   3.64   3.16   1.14   1.51   1.36   1.57   1.45   2.54   2.20   2.79   3.74   4.78   1.19   2.87   4.68

Start:     21:22  22:14  22:16  22:16  22:16  22:22  22:22  26: 6  26: 6  26: 6  26:14  27: 3  29: 9  30:26  30:26  30:26  30:26  34:15  36:36  36:36
End:       22:14  48:35  25: 5  24:24  24: 9  23:49  23:34  28: 2  28: 9  28: 2  28: 2  28: 2  34:15  33:27  33:11  32:15  32:15  48:35  48:35  44:28
Count:         3     85      9      7      4      4      3     15      4      3      2      3      9      8      5      4      2     43     23     21
Width:       568  16278   1968   1791   1483   1175   1360   1131   1012    839    612   3071   2279   1765   1405    769   3071   9063   7606   5221
Strength:   1.03   2.29   1.43   2.03   2.54   4.22   3.66   3.07   1.45   1.83   2.20   2.73   1.30   2.65   4.51   4.66   3.69   2.33   5.55   2.80

Start:     37:21  37:23  37:28  39: 6  39: 7  39:22  39:28  40: 4  44:28
End:       38:23  38:23  44:28  44:28  44:28  44:28  44:28  44: 5  48:35
Count:         4      3      8      7      5      4      3      2
Width:       790    691   3803   3778   3453   3321   3167   2594   2374
Strength:   1.05   1.56   2.45   6.23   7.06   8.61  10.03  12.30  14.85  13.50
```

Linguistic Density Plot in Ezekiel 1 - 48

For -nf 6111 (846 times)

Each Column = 13 Verses.   Separations are: Max =   383.00, Mean =   33.02, Min =   2.50 .

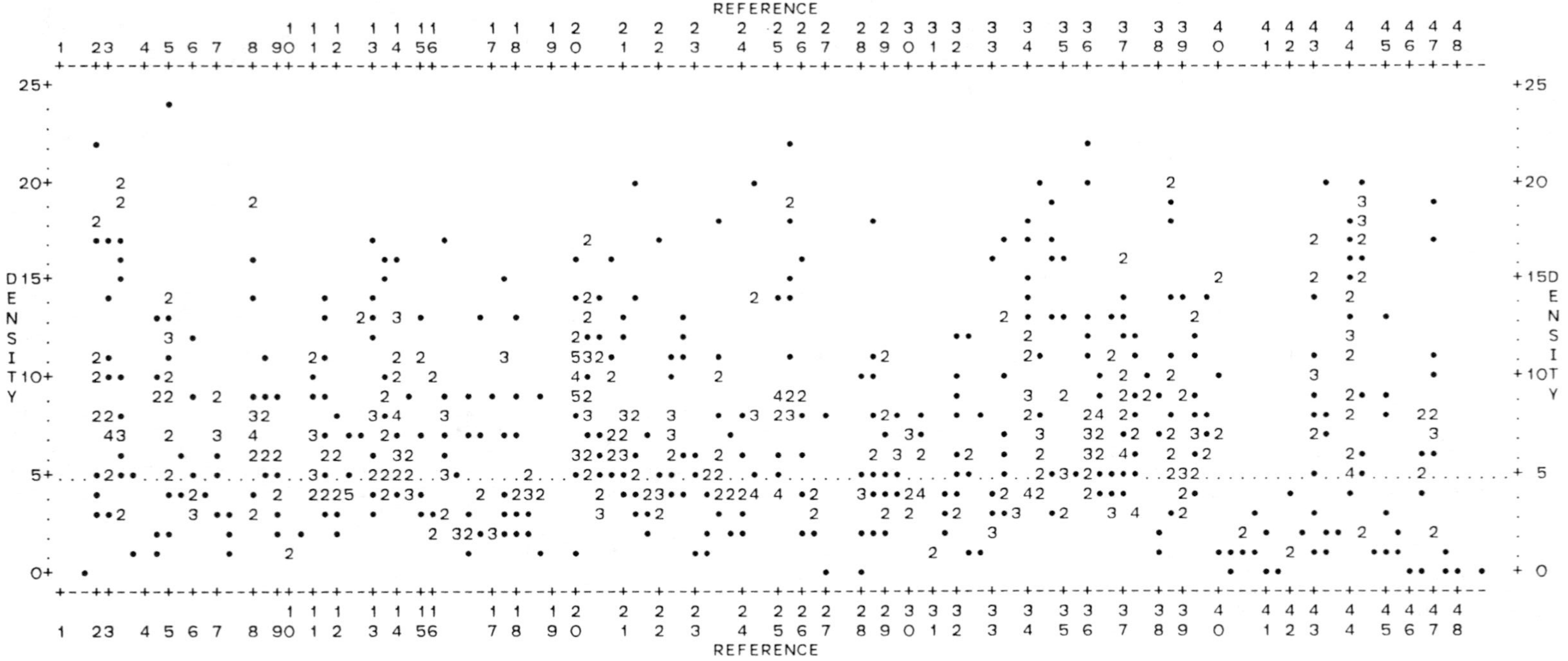

Density plot grid (vertical axis labels: 25+, 20+, D15+, E, N, S, I, T10+, Y, 5+, O+; right-hand axis spells DENSITY vertically: +25, +20, +15D, E, N, S, I, +10T, Y, 5, O). The horizontal axis is labelled REFERENCE.

CLUSTERS:

Start:	1:28	1:28	1:28	1:28	1:28	1:28	1:28	2:2	2:2	2:2	2:2	2:2	2:2	2:7	3:1	3:1	3:2	3:7	3:7	3:10	3:11	3:14
End:	48:29	27:3	16:3	7:14	3:27	3:18	2:4	2:3	2:3	2:3	2:2	3:4	2:3	3:4	3:3	4:3	3:3	3:27	3:18	3:12	3:12	3:18	3:14
Count:	846	481	225	89	45	21	11	8	6	4	4	4	3	6	10	7	4	3	24	14	54	8	14
Width:	27273	13891	6138	2294	840	311	92	44	22	12	22	6	10	154	76	31	24	10	472	219	54	78	239
Strength:	13.52	4.11	2.97	2.08	2.87	2.39	2.29	2.14	1.93	1.51	1.27	1.44	1.50	1.18	1.19	1.77	1.83	1.17	1.10	1.75	1.17	1.75	1.60

Start:	3:14	3:16	3:17	3:16	3:18	3:22	3:22	3:23	4:14	4:14	4:14	4:14	5:7	5:5	5:5	5:6	5:11	5:11	5:13	5:13
End:	3:14	3:18	3:18	3:17	3:18	3:27	3:24	3:24	7:14	6:3	5:1	4:14	5:8	5:7	5:8	5:7	6:3	5:16	5:16	5:13
Count:	4	11	3	3	10	8	6	4	44	30	16	6	4	10	6	3	14	10	7	5
Width:	15	26	11	124	59	19	44	86	1133	591	285	29	26	48	54	140	239	75	22
Strength:	1.46	1.27	1.17	1.75	1.53	1.97	1.97	2.09	1.35	2.09	1.65	1.21	1.27	1.58	1.50	2.13	1.10	1.59	1.52	1.66

Clusters for -nf 6111. continued.

BLOCK 1

Start:	5:13	6: 1	6: 3	7:22	7:22	7:22	7:22	8: 1	8: 1	8: 1	8: 1	8: 3	8: 3	8: 5	8:12	8:17	11:12	11:12	11:13	11:20
End:	5:13	6: 3	6: 3	16: 3	10: 2	8: 9	8: 3	8: 3	8: 4	8: 1	8: 3	8: 3	8: 3	8: 9	9: 1	9: 5	12: 1	11:17	11:14	12: 1
Count:	3	4	4	136	35	17	10	8	15	3	8	8	3	7	10	65	17	52	32	9
Width:	5	39	17	3686	906	312	186	70	186	18	8	18	94	183	65	317	124	52	32	121
Strength:	1.29	1.04	1.04	2.19	1.14	1.65	1.12	1.84	1.46	1.23	1.41	1.23	1.28	1.01	1.15	1.61	1.22	1.53	1.16	1.53

BLOCK 2

Start:	11:20	11:24	11:24	12: 1	12: 7	12: 7	12:25	12:28	12:28	13: 1	13: 7	13: 9	13: 9	13:13	13:13	13:18	13:18	13:19	13:23
End:	11:20	11:24	12: 1	13:21	13: 3	16: 3	13: 3	13: 1	13: 3	13:16	13:10	13: 9	13:13	13:13	13:21	13:19	13:21	13:20	16: 3
Count:	3	5	5	17	39	7	3	4	3	12	7	5	4	14	9	3	12	11	36
Width:	14	36	16	1727	900	75	82	22	45	208	63	33	21	114	37	12	114	11	771
Strength:	1.10	1.45	1.06	2.64	1.78	1.43	1.31	1.34	1.31	1.42	1.67	1.49	1.35	1.61	1.43	1.14	1.61	1.17	2.01

BLOCK 3

Start:	13:23	13:23	14:14	14:16	14:16	14:16	14:16	15: 6	16: 6	16: 8	16:15	16:16	16:17	16:17	16:18	16:19	16:62	16:63	17:19
End:	14:16	14:14	14: 8	14:16	14:13	14:13	14: 8	16: 3	27: 3	16: 3	16:16	16:21	16:21	16:19	16:19	17: 3	16:62	16:63	17:19
Count:	22	5	5	10	4	8	3	3	3	256	4	8	21	8	3	3	34	74	6
Width:	391	65	4	78	23	148	104	33	256	7609	4	96	40	61	10	34	16	74	46
Strength:	2.02	1.01	1.25	1.75	1.32	1.50	1.16	1.49	1.84	1.84	1.44	1.54	1.39	1.07	1.19	1.13	1.06	1.53	1.61

BLOCK 4

Start:	17:19	17:19	18: 9	18: 9	20: 1	20: 1	20: 1	20: 1	20: 3	20: 5	20: 5	20: 6	20: 8	20: 8	20: 9	20:11	20:11	20:11	20:13
End:	17:19	17:19	18: 9	27: 3	20:24	20: 3	20: 3	20: 6	20: 4	20: 5	20: 3	20: 9	20: 5	20: 3	20: 9	20:24	20:17	20:15	20:13
Count:	3	12	3	3	45	17	3	3	17	3	11	5	44	18	3	30	15	11	35
Width:	12	196	15	119	578	102	39	17	192	40	11	18	161	110	30	66	35	45
Strength:	1.14	1.31	1.08	3.82	4.10	1.97	1.40	1.04	2.20	1.39	1.17	1.01	1.33	2.11	1.20	1.63	3.50	2.45	1.46

BLOCK 5

Start:	20:13	20:13	20:16	20:17	20:19	20:19	20:20	20:21	20:21	20:22	20:24	20:24	20:27	20:28	20:36	20:36	20:39	20:40	20:41	20:44	20:44
End:	20:13	20:17	20:24	20:21	20:20	20:21	20:20	20:21	20:24	20:24	20:24	21: 3	20:28	21: 1	20:40	21: 1	20:40	20:40	21: 3	21: 1	21: 3
Count:	13	25	15	4	5	40	55	10	3	6	24	4	17	6	8	3	45	11	9	6	4
Width:	13	139	75	21	232	40	55	10	24	516	24	272	144	62	28	338
Strength:	1.12	1.28	2.63	1.35	1.20	1.39	1.48	1.19	1.42	1.55	1.19	1.30	1.95	1.57	1.62	1.28	1.39	1.23	1.34	1.65

BLOCK 6

Start:	21: 5	21:10	21:12	21:14	21:17	21:22	21:22	21:22	21:22	22: 8	22: 8	22: 8	22:12	22:13	22:17	22:20	22:26	22:30	22:30	23:18	23:35	23:35
End:	21:10	21: 6	21:14	21:23	21:23	21:23	21:23	21:23	23: 4	22: 5	22:23	22:23	22:13	22: 9	22:17	22:23	23: 1	23: 1	23:41	23:27	23:41	23:35
Count:	7	5	11	18	106	16	7	25	14	25	5	11	3	9	128	54	201	11	5	37	156	27
Width:	94	50	183	18	106	7	535	289	25	10	128	54	201	11	5	37	2131	77	156	27
Strength:	1.28	1.23	1.41	1.01	1.13	1.44	1.25	1.61	1.18	1.19	1.46	1.17	1.24	1.26	1.43	1.37	1.67	1.25	1.21

BLOCK 7

Start:	23:37	23:37	23:39	24: 9	24: 9	24:13	24:14	24:16	24:18	24:20	24:21	24:21	24:21	25: 1	25: 3	25: 3	25: 6	25: 6	25: 6	25:12	25:14	25:14
End:	23:41	23:39	27: 3	24:21	25: 4	24:16	24:16	24:21	24:21	24:21	24:21	25: 4	25: 4	25: 4	25: 4	25:16	25:16	26: 7	25:16	25:16	25:15
Count:	7	5	5	53	19	5	13	6	7	17	7	5	34	33	13	34	27	114	242	60	31
Width:	92	49	1280	445	232	44	51	17	56	138	33	397	783	242	114	60	31	17
Strength:	1.31	1.25	1.89	1.07	1.20	1.33	1.12	1.54	1.42	1.25	1.14	1.14	1.64	2.78	2.36	2.48	2.40	2.06	1.74

BLOCK 8

Start:	25:14	25:15	26: 1	26: 3	28: 1	28: 1	28:20	28:22	28:24	28:24	28:25	29: 1	29: 3	29: 3	29: 3	32: 8	32:14	33: 7	33:20
End:	25:15	25:16	26: 3	26: 3	28:20	39: 1	29: 3	28:22	28:24	28:26	28:25	29: 3	29:10	29: 4	29: 3	32:17	32:15	33: 8	34:12
Count:	3	3	9	9	225	14	38	14	56	10	5	10	4	24	3	5	17	3	29
Width:	8	6	48	126	6610	235	138	10	56	18	51	40	24	186	57	17	596
Strength:	1.23	1.27	1.48	1.58	1.85	1.64	1.06	1.61	1.14	1.61	1.21	1.02	1.30	1.35	1.01	1.12	1.13	1.04	1.17	1.91

BLOCK 9

Start:	33:20	33:22	33:23	33:22	33:22	34: 6	34: 6	34: 8	34: 8	34: 8	34: 8	34:10	34:10	34:10	34:10	34:11	34:11	34:15	34:15	34:15	34:15	34:15
End:	33:27	33:23	33:23	33:22	33:22	34:10	34: 8	34: 8	34: 8	34:10	34: 8	34:12	34:11	34:10	34:11	34:11	36:23	34:27	34:20	34:15	34:17
Count:	9	7	4	16	10	16	95	47	13	34	12	6	5	5	3	4	9	57	23	13	8	5
Width:	150	71	20	161	95	47	13	34	12	6	46	24	120	2783	1191	440	263	104	45
Strength:	1.22	1.57	1.37	1.19	2.63	2.26	1.28	1.12	1.77	1.14	1.19	1.29	1.30	3.43	2.75	1.87	1.16	1.45	1.31

Clusters for -nf 6111, continued.

```
Start:     34:17  34:17  34:30  34:30  34:30  35:    35:10  35:10  35:13  36:    36:    36:    36:12  36:14  36:20  36:22  36:27  36:27
End:       34:17  35:    34:31  34:31  35:    35:1   35:9   36:    36:9   36:    36:7   36:23  36:18  36:18  36:23  39:    39:1   37:15
Count:     3      10     9      6      4      11     20     34     3      8      6      5      3      7      5      49     63     28
Width:     7      111    61     28     13     121    360    669    34     61     27     10     14     114    87     65     1516   562
Strength:  1.25   1.88   2.18   1.85   1.49   1.17   2.01   1.87   2.26   1.95   1.87   1.55   1.53   1.03   1.37   1.25   2.12   1.95

Start:     36:27  37:5   36:27  36:27  36:37  36:37  37:    37:13  37:13  37:13  37:19  37:23  37:24  37:26  37:28
End:       37:5   36:28  36:27  37:    37:    37:5   37:    37:13  37:15  37:14  38:    38:    37:25  37:25  38:
Count:     16     31     3      15     9      4      3      5      4      18     16     16     6      4      4
Width:     315    .      31     115    62     21     .      45     18     868    332    176    77     40     19
Strength:  1.41   1.18   1.08   1.60   1.05   1.35   .      1.31   1.34   1.34   1.28   1.93   1.49   1.02   1.50

Start:     38:14  38:17  38:16  38:16  38:16  38:16  39:    39:    39:17  39:17  39:19  39:20  39:23  39:28
End:       38:17  38:17  38:16  38:16  39:    38:20  39:    39:    39:21  39:21  39:21  39:21  39:27  39:29
Count:     8      6      6      4      3      5      7      4      8      6      6      4      10     4
Width:     90     48     25     9      10     15     30     24     383    225    41     21     128    36
Strength:  1.61   1.58   1.28   1.21   1.52   1.80   1.20   2.40   2.16   1.72   1.67   1.35   1.71   1.09

Start:     39:29  40:    42:13  43:    43:    43:    43:    43:    43:18  43:19  43:19  43:19  43:27  44:
End:       39:29  40:    43:    43:    43:    43:7   43:    44:27  44:11  43:19  43:19  43:19  44:    44:
Count:     3      6      18     16     9      8      5      4      24     19     19     3      6      6
Width:     13     61     358    200    75     24     32     47     473    269    19     13     122    45
Strength:  1.12   1.40   1.50   2.32   1.79   1.63   1.16   1.92   1.83   2.34   1.01   2.41   1.31

Start:     44:7   44:7   44:    44:    44:12  44:12  44:12  44:13  44:15  44:15  44:16  44:16  44:23  44:24  44:24  45:    45:    45:8
End:       44:7   44:11  44:    44:    44:16  44:27  44:16  44:    44:15  44:15  44:16  44:16  44:27  44:24  44:24  45:    45:    45:9
Count:     4      8      4      9      16     23     11     13     5      4      6      5      8      5      9      5      3
Width:     20     67     8      359    116    26     49     20     23     103    19     10     41     16
Strength:  1.37   1.88   1.54   1.44   1.21   2.40   2.99   1.60   1.17   2.70   1.51   1.92   1.69   1.23   1.17   1.70   1.19   1.37   1.06

Start:     46:18  46:21  47:    47:
End:       46:21  47:    47:    47:
Count:     5      12     8      7
Width:     65     160    76     32
Strength:  1.01   1.86   1.77   1.46

GAPS:

Start:     1:1    1:1    1:1    1:1    1:1    3:18   3:18   3:24   3:24   3:24   3:24   3:24   3:27   3:24   3:24   4:16   5:8    5:13   6:3
End:       3:14   3:2    2:    1:2    1:28   3:23   3:22   5:6    4:16   4:16   4:14   4:14   4:14   4:16   4:14   5:    5:11   8:1    6:
Count:     29     17     6      2      2      169    129    627    444    436    400    386    321    409    590    145    67     25     20
Width:     1099   846    621    618    612    179    169    627    444    436    400    386    321    409    590    162    975    835
Strength:  1.01   2.42   6.18   7.37   8.98   1.39   2.89   1.34   1.48   2.34   4.06   5.01   8.71   3.30   16.87  3.37   1.14   1.45

Start:     6:3    6:    7:    7:8    7:8    7:14   7:22   8:9    8:18   9:    9:1   9:1   9:11   9:    9:    10:2   10:19  10:13  11:17  12:
End:       7:    6:9    8:1   7:22   8:1    7:22   8:1    8:12   8:8    9:8   11:   11:1  11:    11:1  11:7  10:19  10:    10:13  11:20  12:25
Count:     287   105    417   410    294    158    273    109    211    199   118   67    456    538   518   318    217    72     519
Width:     287   105    417   410    294    158    273    109    211    199   118   67    456    538   518   318    217    72     519
Strength:  1.09   2.16   2.71   3.32   3.40   3.77   4.42   2.28   1.19   1.74  2.56  1.01  4.91   3.52  3.96  5.39   5.56   1.16   1.07

Start:     12:1   12:    12:    12:10  13:    14:21  15:    15:    16:    16:    16:    16:8   16:17  16:14  16:29  16:18  16:27  16:30
End:       12:13  12:    12:7   12:13  13:    14:23  15:    16:    16:    16:    16:8   16:    16:    18:17  18:    17:19  16:42  16:36
Count:     6      129    68     80     86     86     163    144    167    110   42    49    31     39    1864  1707   1436   1417   1246  333  167  111
Width:     252    129    68     80     86     86     163    144    167    110   42    49    31     39    1864  1707   1436   1417   1246  333  167  111
Strength:  1.17   2.89   1.04   1.40   1.59   2.06   3.34   1.18   2.31   2.48  2.56  2.47  2.50   2.27  3.96  3.69   3.04   2.86   2.34  3.04  2.15 2.34
```

Gaps for -nl 6111, continued.

```
Start:    16:37  16:42  16:42  16:42  16:42  16:43  16:43  16:43  16:50  16:43  16:43  17:22  17:20  17:11  17:11  18: 3  18: 4  18: 9  18: 9  18:25
End:      16:42  17:19  17:19  16:63  16:63  16:59  16:48  16:59  16:59  16:48  16:43  18: 1  18: 1  17:17  17:19  18: 9  18: 9  18:17  18:17  18:29
Count:    2      17     16     10     9      7      4      3      2      6      5      2      3      2      3      2      3      9      9      2
Width:    132    907    900    492    483    447    347    106    189    401    383    144    177    102    86     84     153    142    69
Strength: 2.98   2.89   3.19   1.97   2.34   3.08   4.33   2.19   4.71   3.19   3.80   3.34   2.36   2.07   1.59   1.53   1.85   3.28   1.07

Start:    18:29  18:29  18:30  18:32  20:28  20:28  20:28  20:33  21:22  21:22  21:23  21:23  21:23  21:33  21:36  22: 3  22: 8  22:13  22:31
End:      20: 5  20: 3  20: 1  20: 1  20:36  20:36  20:30  20:36  22:12  21:12  21:29  21:29  21:36  21:36  22: 8  22: 8  22:12  22:17  23:22
Count:    9      6      4      3      5      2      2      6      13     4      6      7      6      7      8      8      389    69     8
Width:    415    375    353    329    277    220    67     76     538    285    124    276    68     289    245    163    102    77
Strength: 1.61   2.84   4.44   5.62   7.38   1.32   1.01   1.28   1.24   1.62   2.74   2.17   1.04   1.12   1.11   1.07   1.31   1.80

Start:    23:    23:    23:18  23:22  23:28  23:28  23:41  23:41  24: 1  24: 6  24: 9  24:21  24:24  26: 7  26: 7  26:15  26:19
End:      23: 5  23:18  23:28  23:25  23:35  23:32  23:49  24:13  24:13  24:13  24:13  24:24  28:22  26:14  26:19  26:19  28:22
Count:    6      4      3      3      8      2      3      5      3      8      2      2      17     7      6      2      13
Width:    371    304    245    86     127    73     157    248    202    215    78     84     1371   169    280    106    1087
Strength: 2.79   3.58   6.41   2.02   1.59   1.29   1.19   1.94   1.75   1.79   1.25   1.34   1.53   6.44   4.10   3.16   2.19   6.08

Start:    26:19  28:10  28: 2  28: 3  28:11  28:12  29:    29: 3  29: 8  30:    30: 6  30:25  30:25  31: 1  31: 1  31:10
End:      26:21  28:10  28: 2  28: 6  28:24  28:20  29: 9  29:13  29:13  30:    32:    31:18  31:18  31:15  31:15  31:10
Count:    9      7      2      2      6      5      2      8      3      2      8      6      6      3      3      2
Width:    864    68     596    623    216    199    180    215    150    77     83     540    478    361    316    177
Strength: 6.45   1.04   17.05  11.93  2.04   2.84   4.44   1.25   1.79   1.31   1.50   3.54   4.24   4.58   5.35   4.34

Start:    31:16  32:    32: 3  32:10  32:10  32:15  32:15  32:17  32:17  33: 1  33: 8  33: 8  33:23  33:23  33: 8  33:23
End:      31:18  32:    34:10  34: 8  33: 7  32:32  33: 7  32:31  32:32  33: 7  33:22  33:20  33:13  33:11  34: 8  34: 6
Count:    2      2      36     9      12     6      9      3      2      3      6      6      92     10     8      8
Width:    76     93     1447   652    566    410    397    347    322    141    336    296    398    92     167    364
Strength: 1.28   1.80   1.08   1.52   2.65   3.24   3.32   4.01   6.01   8.74   3.25   1.19   1.77   1.52   1.77   2.15   1.01

Start:    33:23  34: 1  33:25  33:27  33:29  33:31  34: 2  35:    35: 3  35:    36:23  37:15  37:15  37:21  38: 3  38: 3  38: 3
End:      34: 1  34: 1  34: 1  34: 1  34: 1  34: 1  34: 6  35:10  35:13  35:13  36:32  37:19  37:19  37:23  38:16  38:14  38:10
Count:    5      5      5      7      3      2      6      3      3      2      2      6      6      6      3      3      3
Width:    268    230    189    129    67     77     74     132    82     199    82     98     86     98     335    329    271    151
Strength: 1.39   1.47   1.56   1.33   1.01   1.31   1.22   1.40   1.46   1.40   1.00   1.28   1.46   1.21   1.59   1.95   1.69   2.22   4.38   3.56

Start:    38:21  39: 1  39: 8  39: 8  39:13  39:13  39:13  39:23  40: 2  40: 2  40: 2  40: 3  40: 4  40: 4  40: 4  40: 4  40:35  40:48
End:      39: 1  39: 5  39:13  39:10  43:19  43: 8  43: 6  43: 6  43: 6  43:    42: 1  40:45  40:28  40:32  40:17  40:24  40:45  42: 1
Count:    2      2      2      2      58     51     35     23     22     14     12     5      873    599    523    439    291    207    574
Width:    67     78     131    68     2782   2492   2430   2223   2027   2019   1546   1530   873    599    523    439    291    207
Strength: 1.01   1.34   1.38   1.04   3.73   3.71   4.58   5.83   8.50   8.87   9.45   9.98   8.37   7.08   7.42   7.98   7.80   5.25   6.70

Start:    41:    41: 1  41:22  42:    42:    42:    42: 1  42: 1  43:    43:    43: 8  43: 8  43: 8  43:19  43:19  44:16  44:16  44:24  44:45
End:      42:    41:22  43:    43:    43: 1  43:    43: 5  43: 3  43: 1  43: 1  43:18  43:18  43:18  44:    43:27  44:24  44:24  44:23  45: 8
Count:    4      3      8      7      5      8      2      2      213    82     286    248    239    215    247    159    168    162    140    345
Width:    516    441    358    464    450    413    371    286    213    82     286    248    239    215    247    159    168    162    140
Strength: 7.29   8.03   9.83   2.67   3.12   4.25   4.75   1.08   5.44   1.46   1.75   2.44   5.50   3.80   1.10   3.80   1.19   2.04   3.22   4.30

Start:    44:24  45:    44:27  45:    45: 9  45: 9  46:18  45:15  45:18  46:    46:16  47:    47: 6  47: 7  47:14  47:14  47:23  48:11
End:      44: 1  45: 8  47: 6  47:    45:21  45: 9  46:18  45:15  46:18  46:16  46:16  47: 1  48:35  48:35  48:29  48:35  48:29  48:29
Count:    3      2      8      19     13     6      4      6      2      2      2      5      8      7      6      5      3
Width:    340    278    994    905    802    743    581    501    344    106    143    1055   1077   1072   1055   885    779    585    383
Strength: 5.86   7.41   2.88   4.47   5.78   7.84   8.43   9.31   9.41   2.19   3.31   10.63  8.74   9.66   11.42  11.90  11.12  10.59
```

For -nO 6131 (15 times)

Linguistic Density Plot in Ezekiel 1 - 48

Each Column = 13 Verses.   Separations are: Max = 6686.50, Mean = 1748.13, Min =   2.50

REFERENCE

CLUSTERS:

Start:	8:12	24:19	33:10	33:10	33:10	33:21	35:12	37:11	37:11		
End:	40:1	40:1	37:18	33:24	33:10	33:24	37:18	36:2	37:11	37:11	
Count:	15	13	12	11	5	3	6	2	4	3	2
Width:	18870	8910	4305	2799	321	11	72	1322	169	93	
Strength:	2.49	4.10	4.74	4.47	1.55	1.06	1.02	2.35	1.91	1.55	1.00	1.06

GAPS:

Start:	1:1	1:1	1:1	11:15	11:15	37:18	40:1
End:	33:10	33:10	8:12	33:10	24:19	48:35	48:35
Count:	6	5	2	3	2		
Width:	18012	18009	3444	13373	8768	7161	5655
Strength:	2.94	3.75	1.03	4.40	1.63	2.37	

Linguistic Density Plot in Ezekiel 1 - 48

For 'sp 311 (1 times)   'sp 313 (1 times)   'sp 315 (1 times)   'sp 322 (1 times)
    'sp 323 (1 times)   'sp 344 (1 times)

Each Column = 13 Verses.   Separations are: Max = 8400.00. Mean = 3995.71, Min = 1409.00 .

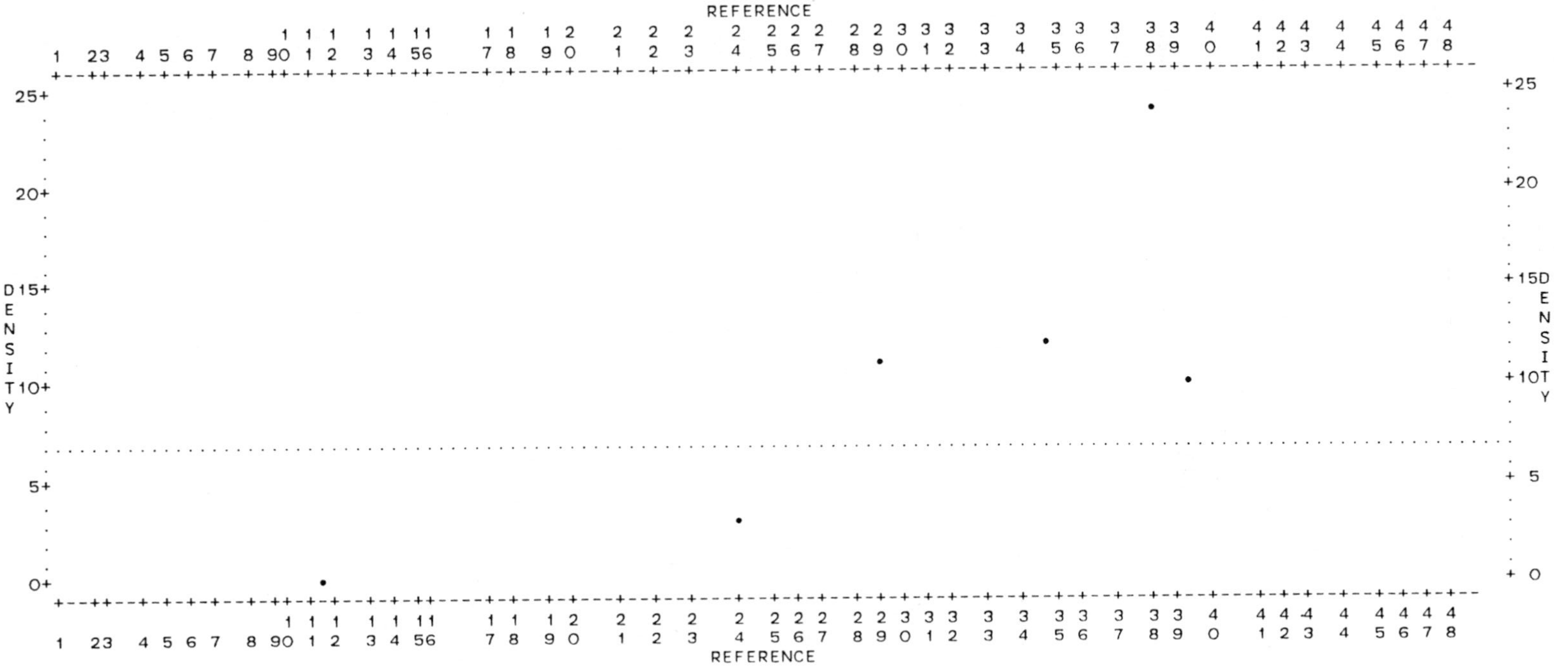

CLUSTERS:

Start:	24: 4	34:29
End:	39:17	39:17
Count:	5	3
Width:	8941	2818
Strength:	1.43	1.15

GAPS:

Start:	1: 1	11:17
End:	24: 4	24: 4
Count:	3	2
Width:	13088	8400
Strength:	1.14	1.27

Linguistic Density Plot in Ezekiel 1 - 48

For 'ap 111 (15 times)

Each Column = 13 Verses. Separations are: Max = 3826.50, Mean = 1748.13, Min = 245.00 .

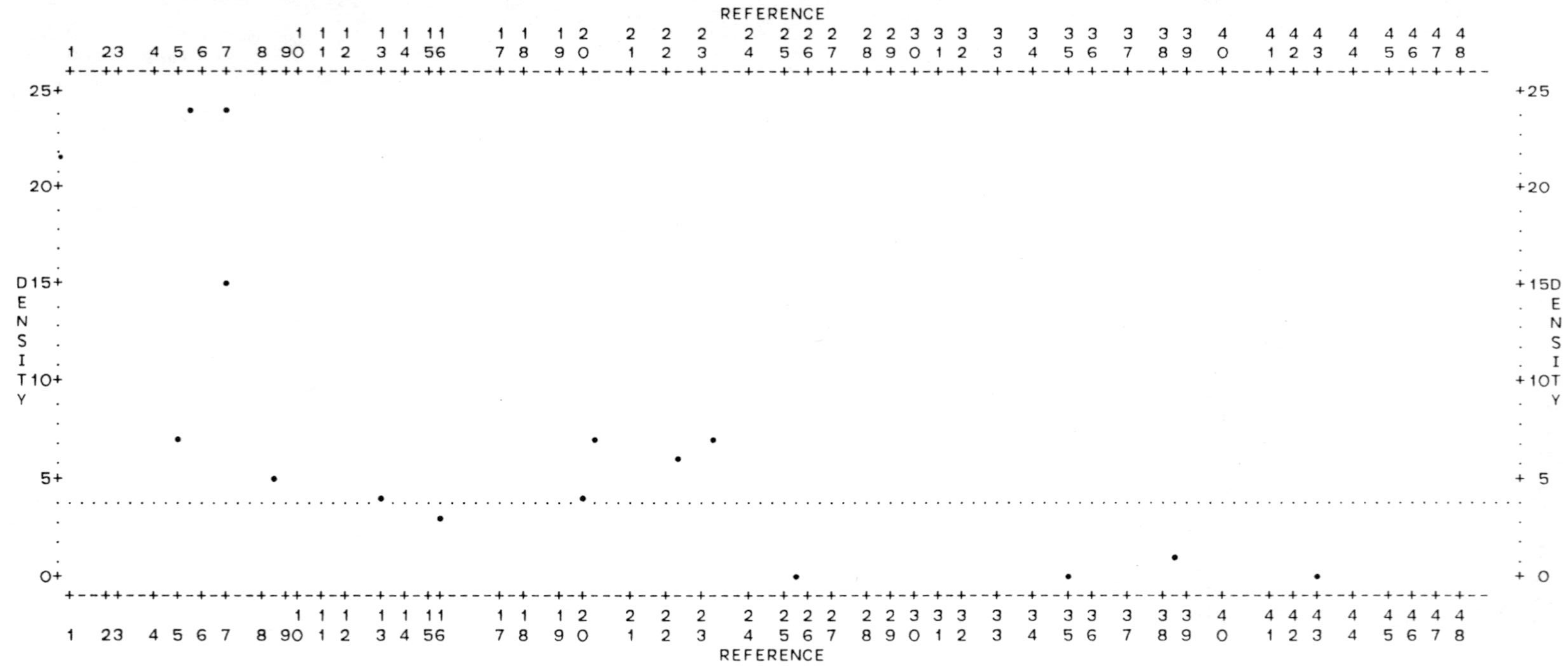

CLUSTERS:

Start:	5:13	5:13	5:13	5:13	7: 3	
End:	25:14	16:12	8:17	7: 8	5:15	7: 8
Count:	12	7	5	4	2	2
Width:	11726	4783	1406	580	63	90
Strength:	2.38	1.73	1.90	1.76	1.02	1.00

GAPS:

Start:	7: 8	20:21	23:25	25:14	38:18	43: 8
End:	48:35	48:35	48:35	35:11	48:35	48:35
Count:	13	8	6	5	2	3
Width:	25222	17867	15454	14076	5553	3502
Strength:	1.44	1.67	2.13	2.41	1.30	1.06

Linguistic Density Plot in Ezekiel 1 - 48

For 'āpîq 111 (7 times)

Each Column = 13 Verses.   Separations are: Max = 14541.00, Mean = 3496.25, Min = 162.00 .

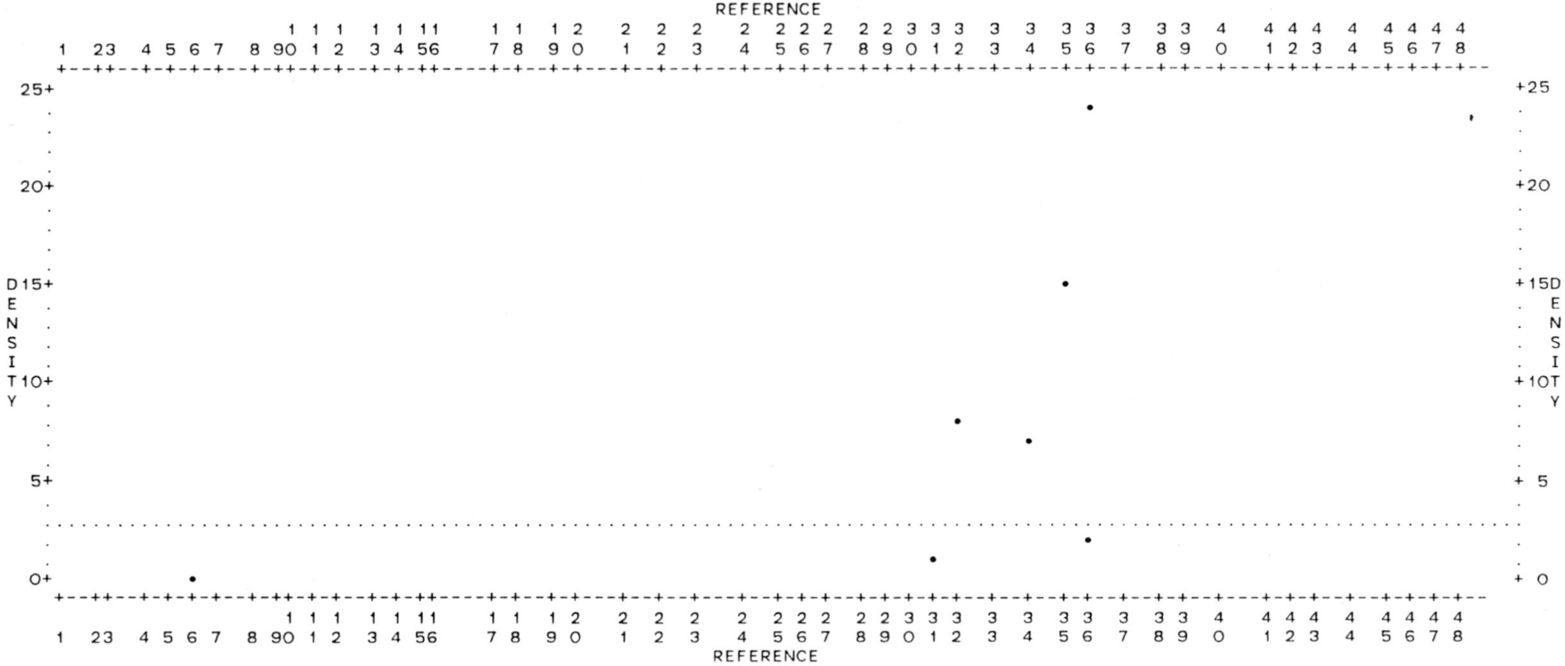

CLUSTERS:

Start:	31:12	31:12	34:13	35: 8	36: 4
End:	36: 6	32: 6	36: 6	36: 6	36: 2
Count:	6	2	4	3	2
Width:	2840	324	849	324	83
Strength:	3.24	1.02	2.13	1.65	1.10

GAPS:

Start:	1: 1	6: 3	36: 6
End:	31:12	31:12	48:35
Count:	3	2	2
Width:	16878	14541	8251
Strength:	2.44	3.58	1.54

Linguistic Density Plot in Ezekiel 1 - 48

For 'ēcel 111 (14 times)

Each Column = 13 Verses.   Separations are: Max =   8881.50. Mean =   1864.67. Min =   5.00 .

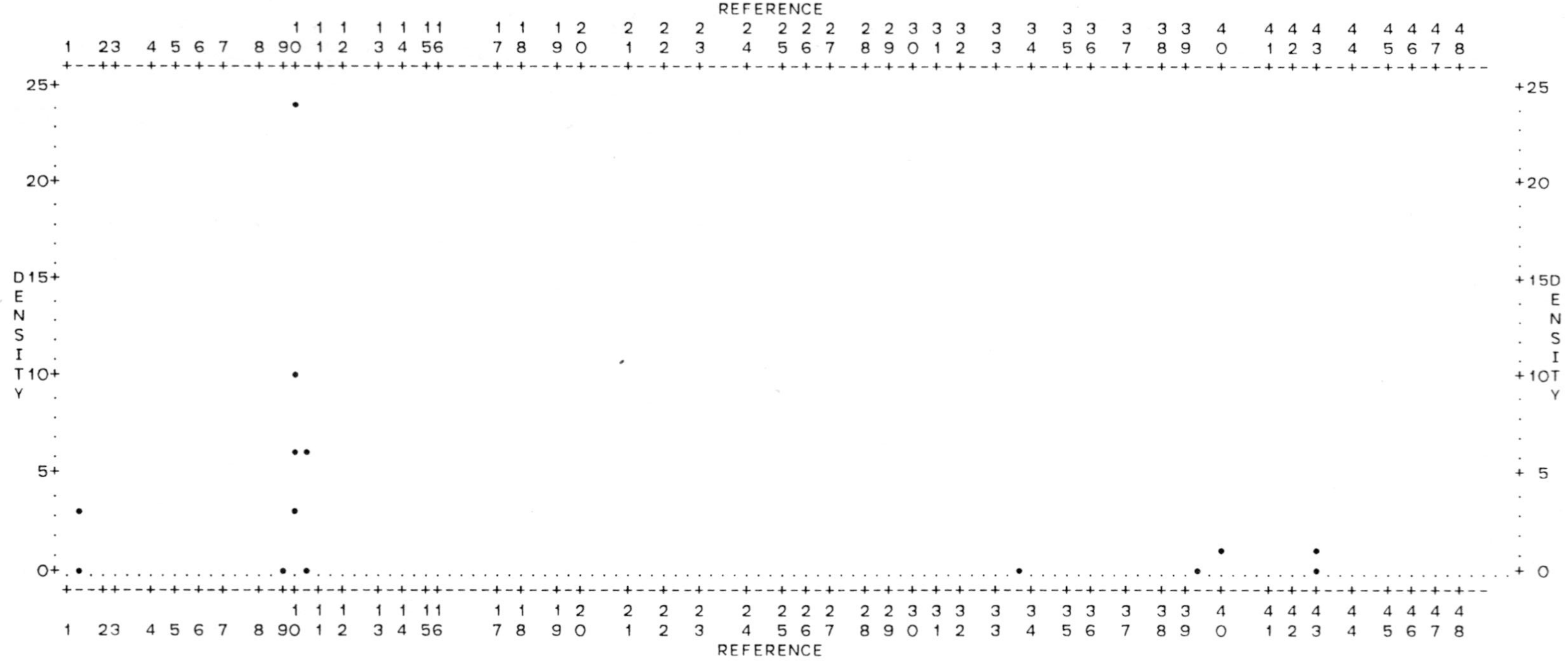

CLUSTERS:

Start:	1:15	1:19	9: 2	10: 6	10: 6	9	10: 9	10:16	9	10:16	39:15	43: 6
End:	10:16	10:16	10:16	10: 6	10: 9	10:	9	10: 9	10:16	43: 8	43: 8	
Count:	9	2	7	6	4	3	2	4	2			
Width:	3942	72	566	196	55	10	4	20	2454	61		
Strength:	3.14	1.02	3.10	2.76	1.98	1.56	1.06	1.05	1.12	1.03		

GAPS:

Start:	10: 9	10: 9	10:16	10:16	10:16	
End:	48:35	48:35	39:15	33:30		
Count:	10	9	7	5	3	2
Width:	23892	23886	23745	20156	17763	14242
Strength:	2.07	2.57	3.66	4.10	5.90	7.09

Linguistic Density Plot in Ezekiel 1 - 48

For 'arbā'â 711 (40 times)   'arba' 714 (18 times)   rēbî'ît 721 (2 times)   rēbî'ît 724 (1 times)

Each Column = 13 Verses.   Separations are: Max = 5781.00, Mean = 451.13, Min = 3.00 .

Density/Reference scatter plot with horizontal density axis labelled (bottom to top): `O+`, `5+2`, `.3`, `Y`, `T10+`, `I`, `S`, `N`, `E`, `D15+`, `20+`, `25+`; and right-hand scale `O`, `+5`, `Y`, `+10 T`, `I`, `S`, `N`, `E`, `+15 D`, `+20`, `+25`. Bottom axis labelled REFERENCE (verse columns 1 through 48).

CLUSTERS:

Start:	1: 1	1: 1	1: 1	1: 1	1: 5	1: 6	1: 8	1:10	1:15	10: 9	10: 9	10:12	10:21	29:11
End:	14:21	7: 2	1:18	1:10	1: 6	1: 6	1:10	1:10	10:21	10:14	10:21	10:14	10:21	29:13
Count:	25	15	13	9	3	3	5	2	4	10	9	6	3	3
Width:	6460	2642	340	191	102	16	56	14	61	2395	241	114	32	42
Strength:	2.54	2.49	3.64	2.89	1.65	1.42	2.01	1.42	1.70	1.34	2.85	2.23	1.38	1.38

Start:	37: 9	40: 1	40:41	40:41	41: 5	42:20	43:14	43:15	43:17	43:17	43:20	45:19	46:21	46:22	48:16
End:	48:34	43:20	40:41	40:42	43:20	43:20	43:17	43:17	43:17	43:17	43:20	45:19	46:22	46:22	48:34
Count:	33	16	6	5	3	9	7	2	16	5	2	5	2	9	
Width:	7355	2436	1157	308	18	503	41	25	1858	655	37	19	361		
Strength:	4.02	2.86	1.14	1.72	1.41	2.94	2.55	2.05	3.25	1.96	2.04	1.41	2.74		

Clusters for 'arbā'å 711, 'arba' 714, rēbî'ît 721, rēbî'ît 724, continued.

Start:	48:16	48:16	48:30
End:	48:20	48:16	48:34
Count:	5	4	4
Width:	101	25	70
Strength:	1.96	1.75	1.69

GAPS:

Start:	1:16	1:17	1:17	1:18	1:18	7: 2	10:21	10:21	10:21	10:21	10:21	10:21	10:21	10:21	14:21	29:13	29:13	29:13	43:20
End:	10:10	10:10	10: 9	10: 9	4: 6	10: 9	48:35	43:17	43:17	43:16	40:41	40:41	29:12	29:11	29:11	40: 1	37: 9	45:19	45:19
Count:	7	6	5	4	2	2	40	20	19	18	9	8	4	3	4	2	3	2	2
Width:	3799	3783	3755	3725	1245	1423	23662	20360	20356	20351	18865	18860	11583	11562	9408	7256	6407	4674	1328
Strength:	1.04	1.59	2.25	3.13	1.78	2.18	3.56	7.25	7.64	8.06	12.91	14.07	13.52	17.12	20.17	7.80	8.84	9.51	1.97

Linguistic Density Plot in Ezekiel 1 - 48

For 'arbā'ā 711 (40 times)

Each Column = 13 Verses.   Separations are: Max = 5783.50, Mean = 682.20, Min = 6.50

CLUSTERS:

Start:	1: 6	1: 6	1: 6	1: 6	1: 8	1:10	1:10	1:15	10: 9	10: 9	10:10	10:12	29:11	40:41
End:	14:21	4: 6	1:18	1:10	1: 8	1:10	1:10	1:16	14:21	10:21	10:11	10:14	29:13	48:34
Count:	19	11	10	6	2	3	2	4	8	7	5	2	3	18
Width:	6363	1488	243	94	48	14	6	61	2395	236	96	1	42	4773
Strength:	2.76	2.87	3.30	2.34	1.41	1.45	1.01	1.76	1.46	2.52	2.05	1.42	1.02	3.20

Start:	40:41	40:41	40:42	43:16	45:21	46:21	46:21	46:22	48:16
End:	41: 2	40:41	40:41	43:17	48:34	46:23	46:22	46:22	48:34
Count:	4	3	2	2	12	6	3	2	6
Width:	253	18	5	13	1827	624	37	19	70
Strength:	1.59	1.44	1.01	1.00	2.96	1.97	2.10	1.44	1.75

Data for 'arbā'ā 711, continued.

GAPS:

Start:	1:17	1:18	4: 6	10:21	10:21	10:21	10:21	14:21	29:13	43:17
End:	10: 9	10: 9	10: 9	48:35	46:22	40:41	29:12	29:11	40:41	45:21
Count:	4	3	2	24	14	6	4	3	2	2
Width:	3755	3725	2480	23662	22412	18865	11588	11567	9408	7256	1447
Strength:	1.51	2.53	2.69	3.72	6.74	10.94	8.48	10.97	13.10	9.87	1.14

Linguistic Density Plot in Ezekiel 1 - 48

For 'arba' 714 (18 times)

Each Column = 13 Verses. Separations are: Max = 9005.50, Mean = 1472.11, Min = 8.00 .

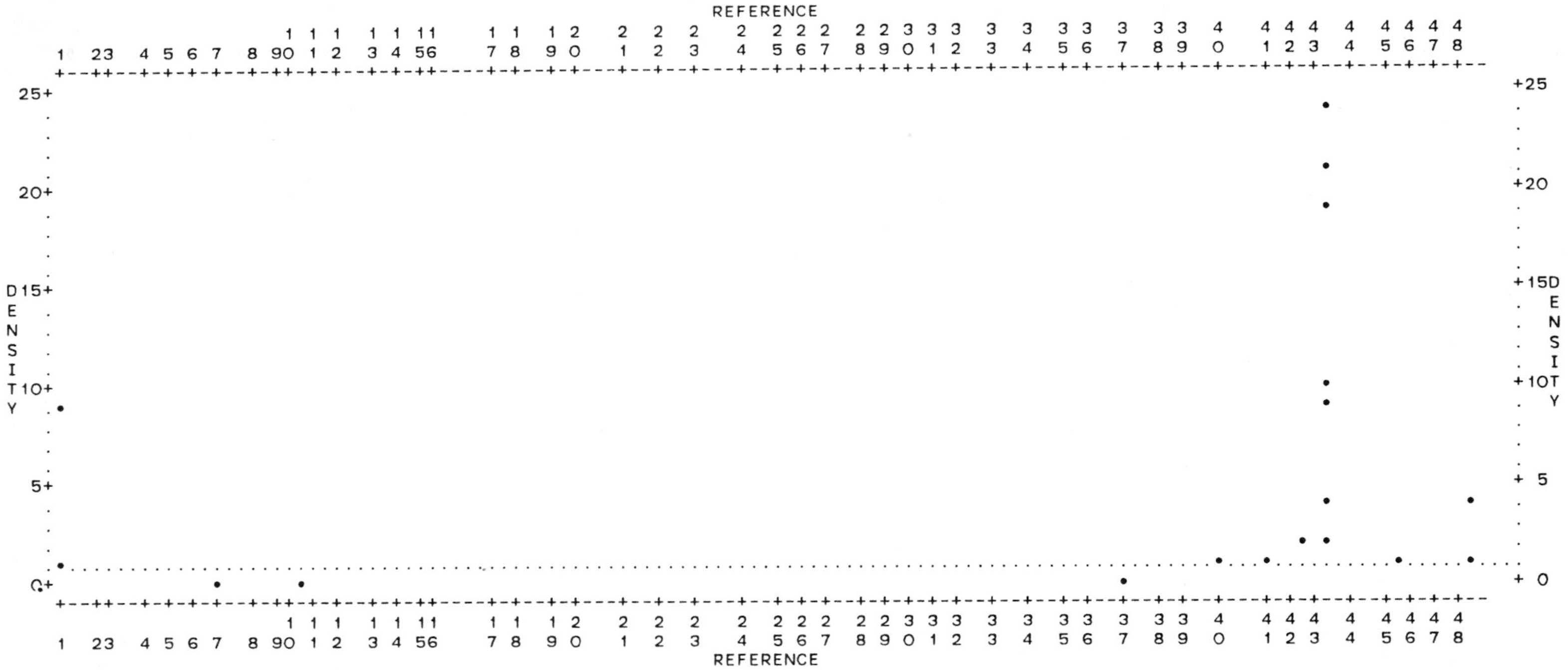

CLUSTERS:

Start:	1: 5	37: 9	37: 9	40: 1	42:20	43:14	43:14	43:14	43:14	43:17	43:20	48:16
End:	1: 6	48:16	43:20	43:20	43:20	43:20	43:17	43:15	43:15	43:17	43:20	48:16
Count:	2	14	11	10	8	7	5	3	2	2	2	2
Width:	16	7011	4169	2436	503	129	37	16	7	4	5	17
Strength:	1.04	4.17	3.37	3.46	3.24	2.99	2.29	1.52	1.04	1.05	1.05	1.04

GAPS:

Start:	1: 1	1: 1	1: 6	1: 6	1: 6	1: 6	10:21	10:21
End:	43:17	43:14	43:14	42:20	41: 5	40: 1	40: 1	37: 9
Count:	13	10	8	7	6	5	3	2
Width:	24663	24630	24522	24148	23372	22215	18011	16278
Strength:	2.31	3.64	4.71	5.26	5.81	6.40	7.84	10.60

Linguistic Density Plot in Ezekiel 1 - 48

For 'erez 111 (6 times)

Each Column = 13 Verses. Separations are: Max = 5653.50, Mean = 3995.71, Min = 238.00 .

REFERENCE

```
25+                                                                                   +25

20+                                                                                   +20

D15+                                                                                  +15 D
E                                                                                         E
N                                                                                         N
S                                                                                         S
I                                                                                         I
T10+                                                                                  +10 T
Y                                                                                         Y

 5+                                                                                    +5

 0+                                                                                    +0
```

REFERENCE

CLUSTERS:

Start:	17: 3	17: 3	17:22	27: 5	31: 3
End:	31: 8	17:23	17:23	31: 8	31: 8
Count:	6	3	2		
Width:	8619	476	33	2255	101
Strength:	2.54	1.68	1.14	1.28	1.12

GAPS:

Start:	1: 1	31: 8
End:	17: 3	48:35
Count:	2	2
Width:	8144	11206
Strength:	1.19	2.08

Linguistic Density Plot in Ezekiel 1 - 48

For 'örek 111 (42 times)

Each Column = 13 Verses. Separations are: Max = 11251.50, Mean = 650.47, Min = 9.00 .

CLUSTERS:

Start:	31: 7	40: 7	40: 7	40: 7	40:18	40:18	40:25	40:29	40:33	40:33	41:12	41:12	41:12	41:12	41:12	41:12	42:20	42:20
End:	48:18	43:17	41: 4	40:30	40:30	40:21	40:30	41: 4	40:42	41: 4	43:17	42:20	41:15	41:13	42: 2	41:22	41:22	42:20
Count:	42	41	28	15	6	3	3	7	4	13	11	7	4	13	2	3	2	7
Width:	10885	5136	2163	951	468	257	101	11	422	165	142	627	1027	285	33	117	10	246
Strength:	17.77	19.43	7.55	4.12	2.62	2.21	1.35	1.00	2.38	1.27	1.68	3.29	3.58	2.47	1.78	1.01	1.00	1.58

Start:	42: 7	42: 7	43:16	45: 1	45: 1	45: 1	45: 1	45: 5	46:22	48: 8	48: 8	48: 8
End:	42:11	43:17	48:18	45: 7	45: 7	45: 3	45: 1	48:18	48:13	48:13	48:10	48:13
Count:	3	2	2	13	6	3	2	7	5	3	55	6
Width:	62	14	1968	159	41	72	913	234	117	2	117	6
Strength:	1.39	1.01	1.00	3.08	2.28	1.41	1.01	1.38	2.04	2.23	2.02	1.40	1.01

Data for 'örek 111, continued.

GAPS:

```
Start:     1: 1   1: 1   1: 1   1: 1   1: 1   1: 1   1: 1   1: 1
End:      45: 1  42: 7  41:12  40:29  40:20  40:18  40: 7  31: 7
Count:       31     25     18      9      6      5      3      2
Width:    25670  24019  23638  22959  22747  22713  22502  16753
Strength:  3.17   4.01   6.10  10.82  14.42  16.41  23.87  25.33
```

Linguistic Density Plot in Ezekiel 1 - 48

For 'erec 114 (197 times)

Each Column = 13 Verses. Separations are: Max = 800.00. Mean = 141.26, Min =   7.00 .

```
                                        REFERENCE

 25+                                                                                    +25

 20+                                                                                    +20

D15+                                                                                    +15 D
E                                                                                           E
N                                                                                           N
S                                                                                           S
I                                                                                           I
T10+                                                                                    +10 T
Y                                                                                           Y

 5+                                                                                     + 5

 0+                                                                                     + 0

     1 23 4 5 6 7 8 90 1 2 3 4 56 7 8 90 1 2 3 4 5 6 7 89 0 1 2 3 4 5 6 7 89 0 1 2 3 4 5 6 7 8
                                        REFERENCE
```

CLUSTERS:

```
Start:    11:15  11:15  12: 6  12:12  12:12  12:19  12:19  14:13  14:13  14:13  14:15  14:15  14:16  19: 4  19: 4  20: 5  20: 5
End:      11:17  11:16  12:20  12:15  12:15  12:20  12:20  14:19  14:19  14:17  14:17  14:17  14:19  19:13  19:13  20:10  20:15
Count:        4      3      7      3      3     42      3      8      6      5      4      3     22     13      9      4     42
Width:       53     30    299    166     65  11562    101    471    146     88     51   3804   1267    584    165    282    137
Strength:  1.52   1.27   1.61   1.73   1.09   2.58   1.41   1.79   1.70   1.53   1.35   2.78   2.34   2.17   1.57   1.34

Start:    20: 8  20:23  20:32  20:32  20:38  20:40  20:42  25: 7  28:17  28:17  29:12  29:12  29:14  29:19  30: 5  30:11  30:11  30:23  30:23
End:      20:10  20:42  20:42  20:38  20:42  20:42  20:42  29: 5  30:13  29:14  29:12  29:14  30:13  30:13  30:12  30:12  31:18  30:26  31:12
Count:        3      9      4      7      5      3     63     45     19     10      8     59      9      5     26      8      5      6      6
Width:       35    483    250    111     51    165   4083   2446    974    555    201   2446   1280    507    177
Strength:  1.24   1.65   1.75   1.28   1.10   1.81   3.87   4.57   2.75   1.73   2.15   2.13   3.41   1.31   1.38
```

Clusters for 'erec 114, continued.

```
Start:    31:12  32: 4  32: 4  32: 4  32:15  32:23  32:23  32:23  32:25  32:32  33:    33: 2  33:24  33:24  33:24  33:24  34:25  36:18  36:18  37:22
End:      31:14  33: 3  32:18  32: 9  32:18  32:18  32:24  32:27  32:27  33: 3  33: 3  33:24  36:35  34:29  33:29  33:26  34:29  36:35  36:20  40: 2
Count:       3     18      8      5      3     10      3      6      3      4      3      3     13      6      4      7      3             48     19
Width:      65    671    293    103     80    295    132     28     70     67     29   2008    889    121    102    363            1438
Strength: 1.09   3.11   1.89   1.65   1.01   2.36   1.84   1.28   1.06   1.47   1.27   1.76   1.70   1.87   1.32   1.42           1.93

Start:    37:22  38:20  38: 8  39:12  39:12  39:14  39:14  39:16  39:16  45: 1  45: 4  45: 8  47:13
End:      38:20  38:11  40:    39:12  39:18  39:16  39:16  39:18  46: 9  45: 8  45: 4  47:21  47:15
Count:      10      3      9      7      6      4      3      9      5      3
Width:     692     71    418    125     74     47     21    715    199     69    152     38
Strength: 1.40   1.06   1.82   2.12   2.03   1.55   1.31   1.06   1.31   1.07   1.47   1.23
```

GAPS:

```
Start:     1: 1   1: 1   1: 1   1: 1   1: 1   1: 1   1: 1   1:21   5: 6   5: 6   5: 6   6:     7: 7   8:17   9: 9   9: 9  10:19  11:17  12:20  12:20  12:20  12:20
End:      29:14  20: 6  14:17  14:16  11:16   9: 5   5: 5   5: 5   7:21   6:14   6: 8   7:21   9: 9  10:16  11:15  12:    14:16  14:15  14:13
Count:      98     51     37     36     23     18      6      6      2      6      2      2      4      2      5      4      3
Width:   15935   9698   6369   6362   4660   3842   1962   1559   1056    631    464    306    283    364    376    294   1077   1040    982
Strength: 2.25   3.05   1.67   1.87   2.49   2.59   4.03  10.08   1.12   1.75   2.29   1.16   1.00   1.58   1.66   1.08   1.83   2.54   3.52

Start:    13:14  14:17  14:17  14:19  14:19  16:    16:29  17:    17:    17:13  19:    20:42  20:42  20:42  22:30  22:30  23:19  23:19  23:19  23:27
End:      14:13  20: 6  17: 4  15: 8  17: 4  17: 4  20:    17:    19: 4  19: 4  26:20  21:35  21:24  25: 7  25: 7  23:15  23:48  23:48  23:48
Count:       2     14      6      5      3      3      3      8      2      5      3      3      7      2      5      3      3      2
Width:     563   3322   1778   1741    285   1416    845   1533   1347   1205    987    755    508   1735    284   1369    620    434
Strength: 2.99   3.02   3.44   4.21   1.01   5.71   5.00   2.80   4.65   6.01   2.27   2.38   2.60   2.60   1.01   2.88   1.69   2.07

Start:    24: 7  25: 9  25: 9  26:20  26:20  26:20  26:20  27:33  28:18  33: 3  33: 3  36:    36:35  38:20  39:13  39:14  39:14  39:15
End:      25: 7  26:16  26:11  28:17  27:29  27:17  28:17  29:    29: 5  33:24  36:18  36:18  37:22  39:12  48:35  47:14  45: 1  45: 1
Count:       2      3      8      5      3      3      2      2      5      2      3              8      5      2     31     12     11
Width:     572    526    415    954    525    298    355    316    496    285    918    579    328   6030   6002   5126   3693   3680
Strength: 3.06   1.22   1.94   1.39   1.22   1.11   1.51   1.23   2.52   1.01   1.26   3.11   1.32   2.52   2.96   3.53   4.70   5.22

Start:    39:16  39:18  39:18  40: 2  41:20  42:    43:14  43:    45: 8  45: 8  46: 9  47:21  48:14
End:      45: 1  41:16  41:16  41:16  45: 1  45: 1  45: 1  45:    47:14  47:13  47:13  48:12  48:29
Count:      10      9      4      2      5      6      2      7      6      2
Width:    3654   3603   1656   1363   1881   1656   1355   1234   1047   1205    689    283    306
Strength: 5.76   6.33   5.08   8.68   4.71   5.08   5.40   1.13   6.44   1.60   3.89   1.00   1.16
```

Linguistic Density Plot in Ezekiel 1 - 48

For 'ēš 114 (47 times)

Each Column = 13 Verses.   Separations are: Max = 3057.50, Mean = 582.71, Min = 5.50

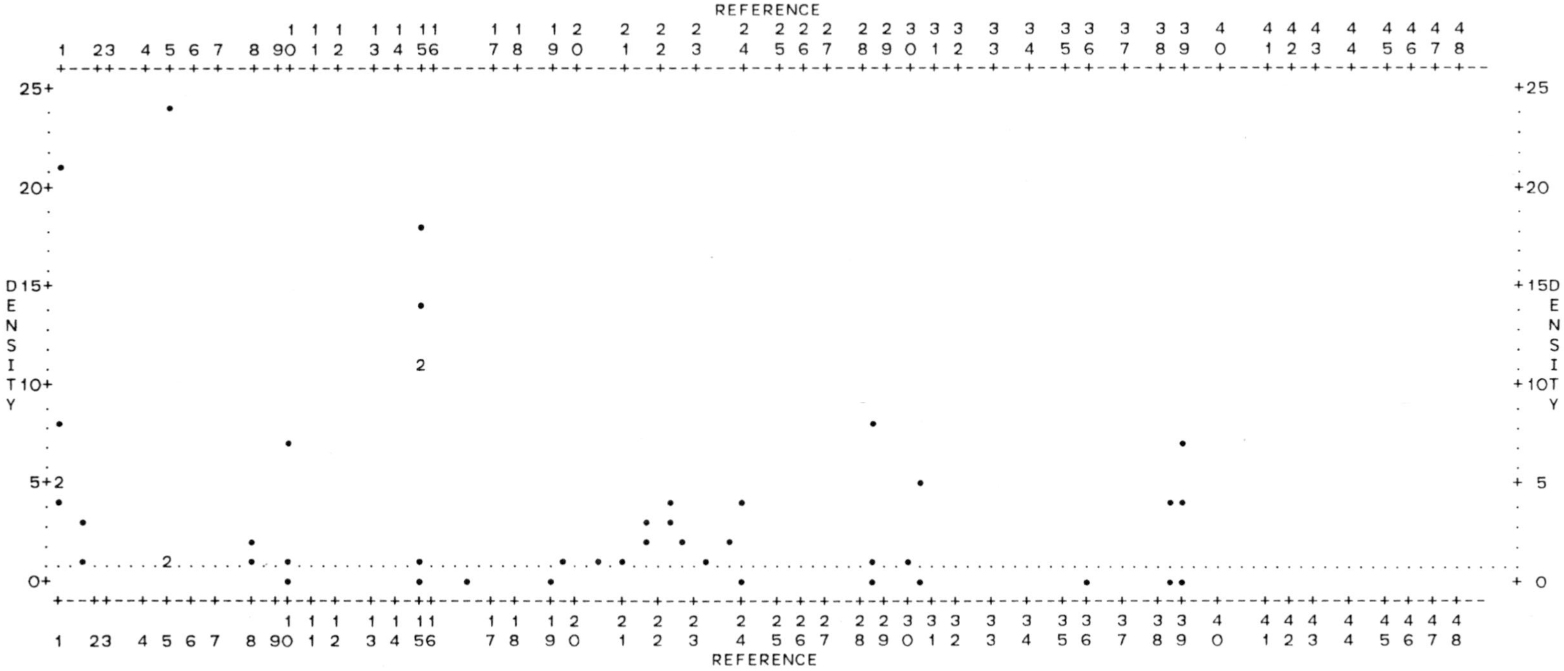

Linguistic density plot (rotated). Vertical axis labelled DENSITY (+25, +20, +15, +10, +5, 0); horizontal axis labelled REFERENCE with verse-column numbers.

CLUSTERS:

Start:	1: 4	1: 4	1: 4	1: 4	1: 4	1: 4	1:13	1:13	1:13	1:13	2: 8	2:10	2:15	4:15	4:15	4:15	4:15	6 15: 7
End:	39:10	24:12	10: 7	5: 4	1:27	1:13	1:13	1:13	1:13	24:12	8: 8	2:10	24:12	15: 7	16:41	15: 5	15: 7	7 15: 7
Count:	47	35	15	10	7	5	3	3	2	7	5	3	20	7	6	3	2	2
Width:	21802	13188	3971	1872	489	192	15	11	859	106	6655	973	76	29	19	3
Strength:	6.26	3.64	2.30	2.16	2.27	1.93	1.44	1.44	1.01	1.33	1.00	1.32	2.25	1.90	2.32	1.42	1.00	1.43	1.01

Start:	19:12	21:36	22:20	23:25	28:14	30: 8	38:19	39: 6
End:	24:12	22:31	24:12	24:12	28:18	30:16	39:10	39:10
Count:	13	9	5	4	3	3	5	3
Width:	3732	1853	621	228	719	1067	79	151	319	103
Strength:	1.88	1.88	1.54	1.17	1.06	1.51	1.36	1.26	1.82	1.32

Data for 'ēs 114, continued.

GAPS:

Start:	1:27	5: 4	10: 7	15: 7	16:41	19:14	21:37	24:12	30:16	30:16	30:16	30:16	30:16	39:10
End:	5: 4	8: 2	15: 4	48:35	19:12	48:35	28:14	48:35		39: 6	39: 9	38:19	36: 5	48:35
Count:	2	2	2	28	3	2	25	21	2	6	5	3	2	2
Width:	1372	1240	2562	21290	2847	1950	18428	16548	2071	5458	5373	5157	3274	6097
Strength:	1.38	1.15	3.46	2.80	2.10	2.39	2.22	2.48	2.60	2.08	2.75	4.99	4.71	9.66

Linguistic Density Plot in Ezekiel 1 - 48

For 'issâ 114 (22 times)

Each Column = 13 Verses.   Separations are: Max = 7084.00, Mean = 1216.09, Min = 34.50 .

CLUSTERS:

Start:	1: 9	16:30	16:30	16:30	16:30	18: 6	18: 6	22:11	23:44	23:44		
End:	24:18	18:15	16:41	16:34	16:32	18:15	24:18	23:10	24:18	23:48		
Count:	20	15	8	4	2	4	2	7	3	2		
Width:	13227	6049	1592	252	69	27	174	1773	602	464	84	9
Strength:	4.56	3.93	2.63	1.76	1.46	1.02	1.80	2.20	1.13	1.65	1.45	1.03

GAPS:

Start:	3:13	9: 6	18:15	23:44	24:18	33:26			
End:	8:14	16:30	48:35	48:35	44:22	44:22			
Count:	2	2	13	4	5	2			
Width:	2395	3588	19212	2684	15043	14968	14588	12073	7084
Strength:	1.01	2.03	1.61	1.26	3.80	4.66	5.68	5.99	5.03

Linguistic Density Plot in Ezekiel 1 - 48

For 'assor 12 (9 times)

Each Column = 13 Verses.   Separations are: Max = 6056.50, Mean = 2797.00, Min = 36.50 .

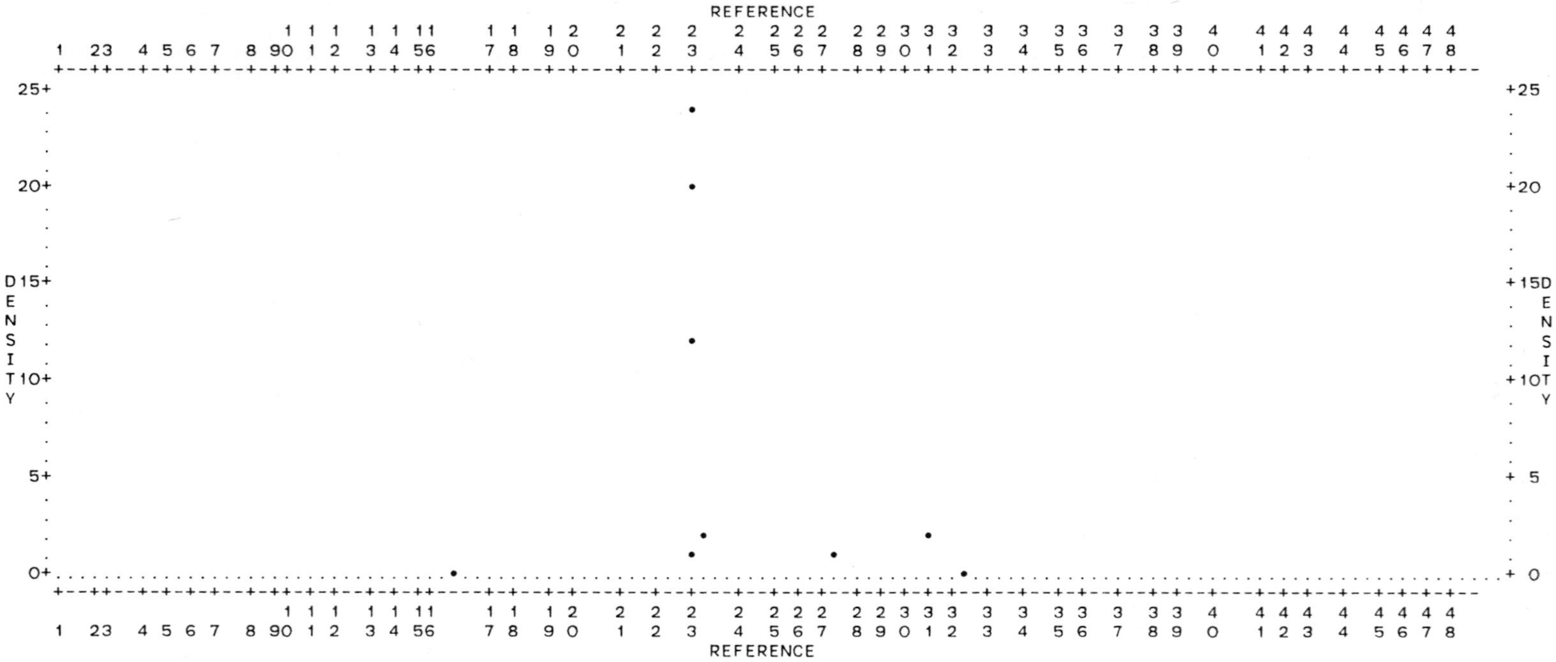

CLUSTERS:

Start:	16:28	16:28	23: 5	23: 5	23: 9	
End:	32:22	23:23	23:12	23: 7	23:12	
Count:	9	6	5	4	2	2
Width:	10203	5161	341	125	22	52
Strength:	3.60	2.09	2.62	2.13	1.09	1.08

GAPS:

Start:	1: 1	1: 1	23:23	32:22
End:	23: 5	16:28	48:35	48:35
Count:	3	2	5	2
Width:	12112	7292	15516	10474
Strength:	1.93	1.77	1.04	3.03

Linguistic Density Plot in Ezekiel 1 - 48

For 'aser 53 (342 times)

Each Column = 13 Verses.   Separations are: Max = 373.50, Mean = 81.55, Min = 4.50 .

REFERENCE

DENSITY axis (vertical): +25 +20 +15 +10 +5 0

REFERENCE

CLUSTERS:

Start:	1:12	1:12	1:25	5: 6	5: 6	5:14	6: 9	6: 9	8: 3	8: 3	8: 3	8:12	9: 2	9:11	11:23
End:	48:29	14: 7	2: 3	7:15	5:16	5:16	6:13	6: 9	14: 7	11:17	8:17	8:14	9: 6	11:17	14: 7
Count:	342	90	5	17	9	4	6	3	52	28	13	3	5	15	24
Width:	27622	5887	156	927	276	51	139	9	2876	1454	529	45	139	814	1287
Strength:	1.60	2.07	1.04	1.18	1.65	1.37	1.48	1.33	2.38	1.83	1.62	1.02	1.15	1.09	1.55

Start:	11:23	13: 3	11:23	11:24	12: 7	12: 7	12:10	13:12	13:19	14:22	14:22	16:36	16:36	16:37	16:48	16:50
End:	13: 3	12:16	12:16	12: 2	12: 2	12:12	12:12	13:20	13:20	18:31	15: 2	16:45	16:37	17: 3	16:52	16:52
Count:	15	11	11	4	5	5	6	6	44	26	16	4	3	10	87	41
Width:	651	379	379	29	114	209	45	222	2768	1616	672	219	373	57	373	41
Strength:	1.64	1.71	1.34	1.16	1.30	1.41	1.41	1.02	1.38	1.07	1.47	1.04	1.78	1.33	1.49	1.44

Clusters for 'aser 53, continued.

```
Start:    16:51 17:16 17:16 17:19 18:14 18:21 18:21 18:24 18:24 18:26 18:26 20: 6 20: 9 20:21 20:21 20:26 20:26 20:41 21:30
End:      16:52 18:31 17:20 17:20 18:31 18:31 18:24 18:24 18:28 18:31 20:36 20:11 20:36 20:29 20:28 20:43 20:43 20:43 22:14
Count:        3    18     5     3    13    11     7     4     4     3     3    16     7     9     4     3     4     4     9
Width:       15   844   108    35   384   225    86    22    29    16    30   756   242   378    90    40    62    62   405
Strength:  1.28  1.65  1.34  1.11  2.14  2.32  2.03  1.58  1.16  1.05  1.15  1.51  1.24  1.04  1.09  1.06  1.29  1.29  1.08

Start:    22:13 22:14 23:18 23:20 26:17 26:19 32:23 32:24 33:18 33:29 33:27 33:27 35:11 35:11 35:11 35:11 36:   36:18 36:18 36:21 36:22
End:      22:14 23:18 23:20 23:22 26:19 26:19 32:30 32:24 48:29 40:22 33:29 33:27 35:11 35:15 35:12 37:10 36:   36:36 37:10 36:23 36:23
Count:        3    20     4     3     4     3     4     4   126    49    23    19    64     5     4     5     4    15    13     7     5     3
Width:       20   818   805    73    29    47   201   351   412   448  8398  3344  1152   304    74    25    35   637   385   304   111    51    16
Strength:  1.24  1.66  2.19  1.21  1.16  1.40  1.44  2.16  3.30  2.95  2.77  1.40  1.25  1.08  2.47  1.73  1.21  1.19  1.24  1.68  2.14  1.91  1.69  1.27

Start:    36:27 36:36 37:18 37:25 39:17 39:21 39:23 40:40 40:40 40:40 40:40 40:42 41:   41:   41:   41: 9 41:12 41:15 41:22 42:   42:   42:
End:      36:36 36:31 37:18 37:21 39:17 39:23 40:   40:40 40:46 43:22 44:25 40:46 41:15 41:12 41:   43:22 42:16 42:   42:21
Count:        6     4     7     4    11     5     5     4     7     8    12     5     5     5     9     9     5     6     6     3     4     1
Width:      173    82   228    93   438   116    35   532   143    69   119   510  4684  2376  1637  1152   107    50    12    26   113   373    16   975    98   373   124    47
Strength:  1.29  1.15  1.31  1.07  1.48  1.29  1.11  1.61  1.74  1.24  1.27  1.45  2.94  2.93  2.41  1.25  1.35  1.38  1.31  1.62  1.40  2.75  1.40  2.71

Start:    42: 7 42:15 42:11 42:13 42:13 42:13 43: 1 43:11 43:   43:   44: 5 44:   44:   44: 9 44:10 44:12 44:15 46:18 46:18 46:20 46:24 47:   47: 5 47: 9 47:
End:      42:15 42:15 42:13 42:13 42:13 43: 1 43:11 43:   43:   44: 5 44:25 44:15 44:12 44:10 44:15 46:18 46:18 46:20 46:24 47:   47: 5 47: 9 47:
Count:       10     8     5     3     3     8     4     4     3     5     4     8     7     4     3     9     9     9     5     9     9     3
Width:      194   124    61    11    27   227    35   532    17    65   269   143    61   329   124    47   975   373   113    98    24
Strength:  2.23  2.09  1.63  1.32  1.18  1.61  1.48  1.61  1.26  1.61  1.41  1.74  1.30  1.67  1.24  1.40  2.71  2.75  1.62  1.40  1.20

Start:    47:13 48:11 48:
End:      47:23 48:11 48:11
Count:       11     6     4     5     3
Width:      428   206    66    93    12
Strength:  1.52  1.11  1.26  1.43  1.31

GAPS:

Start:    1: 1  1: 1  3: 3  3: 6  3: 6  3:23  3:23  4:10  4:13  5:16  6:11  6:13  7:15 12:16 13: 3 13:20 14: 5 14: 7 15: 6
End:      1: 1  1:12  4: 1  4: 9  4: 7  4: 9  4: 9  5: 3  5: 6  6: 2  7:15  7:15  8: 3 12:25 13:12 14:22 14:22 14:22 16:37
Count:        5     2     8     7     3     9     2     3     5     6     4     9     3     2     5     3     8     6
Width:      491   309   228   802   744   334   207   291   235   196   375   309   334   184   632   448   402   825
Strength:  1.01  1.26  1.79  1.08  1.28  1.48  1.53  1.10  1.88  1.40  1.84  2.79  3.09  1.25  1.88  2.47  3.93  1.18

Start:    15: 6 15: 6 16:14 16:17 16:19 16:20 16:36 16:59 17: 3 17:16 17:19 17:20 17:20 18:14 18:27 18:28 18:31 20:26 20:26
End:      16:37 16:36 16:19 16:17 16:19 16:36 17:16 17: 4 18:14 18:18 18:20 18:21 18:14 20: 9 20: 6 20: 3 20: 6 48:11 48:35
Count:        7     5     3     4     3     4     5     5     6     5     9     4     6     6     3     6     9   194   183   151
Width:      818   805   448   412   351   322   443   308   541   511   435   352   589   569   503   417 17758 17266 16728 14103
Strength:  1.66  2.19  1.44  2.16  3.30  2.95  1.40  2.77  1.32  1.89  2.36  3.32  2.30  1.62  2.95  4.11  2.16  2.04  2.50  2.50

Start:    20:26 20:26 20:43 20:43 20:43 21:30 21:34 21:30 22: 4 22:13 22:13 22:14 22:14 23: 9 23: 7 23:18 23:28 23:28 23:28 23:40
End:      42:13 42: 1 36:22 22: 4 21:34 21:30 22: 2 23:28 22:13 23:19 23:19 23:18 23: 7 23:18 36:22 36:24 24:21 24:21 24:21
Count:      145   136   130    85    32    17    58     6     4     5     2     9     6     8    17     4
Width:    13923 13701 13366  9851   817   701   607   429   168   918   703   688   669   454  7469  4958  2321   857   607   731
Strength:  2.92  3.65  3.89  4.62  1.65  2.31  3.86  4.26  1.05  1.16  1.63  2.23  3.01  4.57  1.06  5.02  5.61  3.19  1.33  2.57

Start:    23:40 24:18 24:22 24:22 24:24 24:24 26:   26: 6 26:17 26:18 26:19 27:27 27:27 28:25 28:25 29: 3 29: 3 29:20 31:10
End:      24:18 24:   27:27 26:17 26:17 26:   26: 2 26:17 27:27 27:27 32:24 28:25 29:20 29:18 29:13 32:24 31: 9 32:24
Count:        3     2     9     5     4     2     4     2    15     7     5     4     2     6     2
Width:      547   289  1456   881   833   489   262   566   549   528  2629  1160   637   507   466   249  1459   716   731
Strength:  3.33  2.54  3.52  3.42  4.18  5.00  2.21  2.28  3.35  5.48  4.98  3.39  6.82  1.11  1.57  2.05  4.16  7.79  1.78
```

Gaps for 'aser 53, continued.

```
Start:    31:10 31:14 31:14 32:24 32:24 32:30 32:30 33:16 33:27 33:27 33:27 33:27 33:27 33:29 34: 2 34: 2 34:21 36: 5 36: 7 36:36
End:      32:23 32:23 32: 9 36:22 36:21 33:27 33:13 33:27 36: 4 36:21 35:11 35:11 35:11 35:11 35:11 34:12 34:11 36:18 36:18 37:18
Count:        4     3     2    26    24     4     2     2    11    17     7     6     5     4     2     2     3     2     4
Width:      690   602   354  2505  2470   833   679   417   219  1250  1630  1055  1043   998   855   418   241   285   211   443
Strength:  3.16  3.81  3.34  1.18  1.57  1.73  3.08  4.11  1.68  1.71  1.02  2.85  3.51  4.14  4.34  1.95  4.13  1.05  1.58  1.40

Start:    36:36 37:10 37: 7 37:18 37:25 37:25 37:25 38: 8 39: 8 40: 4 40: 4 40: 4 40: 6 40: 6 40: 6 40:22 43: 4 43: 7 43:11 43:11
End:      37: 7 37:18 39:21 39:19 39:17 38:20 38:17 38:17 39:17 40:44 40:42 40:45 40:42 40:40 40:20 40:40 44: 9 44: 9 44: 9 43:19
Count:        2     2    10     9     4     8     2     8     7     7     6     5     4     2     8     2     9     7     5     2
Width:      177   191  1093  1058   567   481   242   214   818   785   743   693   265   370   787   738   625   215
Strength:  1.16  1.34  1.48  1.77  2.29  2.76  1.96  1.62  1.26  1.66  2.08  2.57  3.18  2.25  3.54  1.01  1.25  1.84  1.63

Start:    43:22 44:15 44:15 44:15 44:15 44:22 44:25 44:25 48:11 48:11
End:      44: 9 46:20 46:18 46: 7 46: 4 46: 4 46: 4 45:13 48:35 48:22
Count:        3     5     2    10     7     6     4     3     2     4     2
Width:      333   207  1393  1355  1070  1010   825   747   406   480   266
Strength:  1.47  1.53  1.86  2.57  2.93  3.32  4.12  5.08  3.98  1.67  2.26
```

For 'ēt 4 (701 times)

Linguistic Density Plot in Ezekiel 1 - 48

Each Column = 13 Verses. Separations are: Max = 417.00, Mean = 39.84, Min = 3.00

CLUSTERS:

Start:	1:11	1:23	2: 6	3: 1	3: 8	3:21	3:27	4: 3	4: 4	5: 2	5: 2	5: 2	5: 3	6: 9	8:12	8:17
End:	48:20	20:44	3: 3	3: 3	3:10	4: 6	4: 1	4: 6	4: 5	5:11	5: 6	5: 4	5: 4	6: 9	8:18	8:18
Count:	701	298	16	10	4	14	4	6	5	11	6	4	3	3	9	4
Width:	27470	10467	145	38	45	288	44	89	51	84	45	19	155	56	47
Strength:	7.46	2.62	1.79	1.52	1.07	1.61	1.09	1.54	1.35	1.29	1.29	1.07	1.45	1.29	1.04

Start:	8:17	9: 7	9: 9	10: 3	10: 7	10:16	10:22	11: 7	11: 7	11:17	11:17	11:17	12:12	12:12	13:14	13:15	13:19	13:19	13:20
End:	8:17	9: 9	9: 5	10: 4	10: 4	11: 1	10:22	11: 1	11:25	11:10	11:18	11:25	12:16	12:13	13:15	13:15	13:21	13:21	13:20
Count:	3	5	5	3	8	5	15	199	15	4	5	9	4	3	3	20	11	7	6
Width:	19	75	70	21	168	41	384	6208	199	43	177	31	83	22	48	243	79	30
Strength:	1.07	1.05	1.11	1.03	1.48	1.05	1.14	3.54	1.17	1.10	1.26	1.61	1.60	1.41	1.03	1.05	1.23	1.64	1.90

Clusters for 'ët 4, continued.

```
Start:    13:20  14:22  14:22  14:22  14:22  14:22  15: 7  16:15  16:20  16:20  16:21  16:25  16:25  16:29
End:      13:21  16:43  16: 8  16: 2  16: 2  16: 2  16:16  16:26  16:22  16:22  16:22  16:25  16:25  16:43
Count:    4      43     17     14     8      7      4      6      10     12     6      3      3      14
Width:    16     1141   381    214    101    40     30     55     125    230    47     22     27     342
Strength: 1.49   2.12   1.62   2.13   1.69   2.04   1.29   1.62   1.96   1.58   1.41   1.33   1.17   1.23

Start:    16:29  16:33  16:37  16:37  16:40  16:37  16:37  16:50  16:50  16:50  16:51  16:53  16:53  16:57  16:57  16:59  16:60  16:61  16:62  17:17
End:      16:33  16:43  16:43  16:40  16:43  16:37  16:37  17:21  20: 4  16:54  16:51  16:54  16:53  16:58  16:58  16:61  16:61  16:62  17:21  17:21
Count:    5      3      5      9      7      4      4      18     56     4      37     4      3      11     8      3      8      5      3      20
Width:    79     19     37     177    91     33     111    38     260    104    22     37     10     93     62     17     39     3      17     412
Strength: 1.00   1.07   1.65   1.26   1.51   1.25   3.91   3.06   2.57   1.38   1.01   1.19   1.23   2.43   2.06   1.26   1.50   1.10   1.10   2.01

Start:    17:12  17:14  17:14  17:13  17:17  17:17  17:16  17:16  20:    20: 4  20:44  20:13  20:13  20:11  20:11  20:12  20:13  20:13  20:15  20:17  20:19
End:      17:21  17:17  17:14  17:13  17:17  17:17  17:16  17:16  20:    20:44  20:44  20:13  20:13  20:11  20:11  20:13  20:13  20:20  20:20  20:20  20:19
Count:    14     7      3      4      3      5      7      4      20:    4      55     34     18     3      5      8      100    48     5      20
Width:    204    44     10     23     44     10     29     55     938    544    294    145    71     12     14     100    48     5      3      9
Strength: 2.20   2.00   1.24   1.39   1.46   1.23   1.63   1.54   1.30   4.31   3.45   2.36   1.97   1.79   1.55   1.15   1.17   1.70   1.39   1.24

Start:    20:21  20:28  20:26  20:23  20:21  20:21  20:21  20:26  20:24  20:23  20:28  20:27  20:27  20:34  20:35  20:34  20:37  20:36  20:40  20:44  20:41  20:41  20:42  20:42  20:42  20:43  20:42
End:      20:28  20:23  20:21  20:21  20:24  20:20  20:26  20:24  20:28  20:28  20:39  20:37  20:35  20:44  20:41  20:41  20:42  20:44  20:43  20:42
Count:    16     11     123    64     4      3      11     4      56     22     10     3      4      8      5      23     11     27     103    5      3      11     6      53     26     14
Width:    219    123    64     18     4      11     50     21     56     267    362    8      34     66     23     103    27     11     36     6      53     26     14
Strength: 2.47   2.19   1.79   1.46   1.21   1.01   1.00   1.03   1.29   1.01   1.74   2.68   1.23   2.02   1.39   2.35   1.66   1.14   1.67   1.24   1.21   1.20   1.21   1.64   1.67   1.15

Start:    22: 8  22:15  22:12  22:11  22:11  22:12  22:11  22: 8  23:17  23:23  23:24  23:17  23:21  23:34  23:35  23:34  23:39  23:35  23:35  23:36  23:37  23:36  23:39  24:27  24:25  24:25  24:25  26:19  26:20
End:      22:12  22:12  22:11  22:11  22:11  22:12  23:17  23:29  23:29  23:23  24: 2  23:21  23:35  23:35  23:35  23:39  23:39  23:37  23:36  24:27  24:25  24:25  26:20  26:19  26:20
Count:    5      78     44     16     29     4      12     278    131    73     362    5      17     42     16     111    13     8      9      5      3      4      36     11     38     26     3
Width:    125    78     44     16     16     29     728    278    131    73     362    17     42     16     57     26     9      11     36     4      53     11     38     22
Strength: 1.16   1.01   1.79   1.12   1.21   1.09   1.87   1.21   1.40   1.08   1.74   2.68   1.47   2.11   1.12   2.68   1.67   1.24   1.20   1.17   1.21   1.01

Start:    28:24  31: 4  29:    29:10  29:13  30:    30:    30:12  31: 4  30:22  30:22  30:22  30:25  30:23  30:22  30:22  30:26  30:25  30:24  30:25  31:16  31:18  32:25  33: 7  32:16  32:16  32:15  32:18  32:21  32:27
End:      31: 4  29:    29:14  29:14  30:12  31: 4  30:12  31: 4  30:25  30:22  30:23  30:25  30:26  30:24  30:25  31:18  33: 7  32:21  33:
Count:    39     3      5      6      24     5      14     169    91     54     9      17     10     42     4      5      89     41     42     5      19     296
Width:    1156   16     89     14     499    58     91     169    54     17     10     26     13     64     682    89     41     42     296
Strength: 1.49   1.12   1.23   1.15   2.21   1.27   2.45   2.64   2.35   1.78   1.58   1.17   1.35   1.51   1.05   2.51   1.19   1.23   1.13   1.47   2.52

Start:    32:27  32:32  32:30  32:28  32:29  32:29  32:30  32:32  32:31  33:    33:    33:20  34: 2  33:32  33:30  34:12  35:12  36:37  33:12  33:30  33:30  33:30
End:      32:32  32:30  32:30  32:29  32:29  32:30  32:32  32:32  33:    33:    34:    34:12  36:37  34:23  33:31  33:30  33:33  34:34
Count:    12     5      5      4      21     44     10     44     114    64     24     151    5404   593    358    172    24     77     51     30     38     2
Width:    134    78     37     21     114    44     8      10     64     358    172    77     1233   2144   5404   593    358    15     47     4      8
Strength: 2.31   1.65   1.53   1.42   1.26   1.44   1.23   1.28   1.38   1.51   1.32   2.67   2.79   2.48   2.61   2.97   2.67   1.66   1.52   1.13   1.12   2.20

Start:    34: 2  34: 4  34: 4  34: 4  34: 7  34: 8  34: 8  34:10  34:14  34:14  34:14  34:16  34:16  34:16  34:16  34:21  34:23  34:23  36:23  36:24  36:24  36:25  36:29
End:      34: 4  34: 4  34: 4  34:12  34: 8  34: 8  34:12  35:12  34:16  34:16  34:16  34:16  34:23  34:23  36:24  36:27  36:29
Count:    5      3      3      9      44     21     5      5      6      6      19     53     194    594    64     114    8      7      45     13     39     17
Width:    24     11     13     137    44     21     9      71     19     11     53     194    594    151    64     37     77     7      107    107    313    40
Strength: 1.69   1.21   1.17   1.61   1.09   1.42   1.24   1.10   1.76   1.64   1.63   1.15   1.51   1.32   1.28   1.19   1.26   1.63   1.65   1.07   1.17   1.16   1.14

Start:    36:29  36:30  37:12  37:12  37:12  37:14  37:12  37:19  37:19  37:21  37:24  37:21  37:26  37:28  39:10  39:15  39:10  39:10  39:11  39:11  39:11
End:      36:30  38:    37:12  37:19  37:14  37:12  37:12  37:19  38:    37:21  37:24  37:22  37:26  37:28  39:40  40:14  39:12  39:12  39:12  39:11  39:11
Count:    3      27     180    635    51     14     10     18     415    128    224    11     45     50     494    758    117    56     24     8
Width:    22     635    180    51     14     10     137    18     415    194    224    11     45     11     494    758    313    117    56     24     8
Strength: 1.01   2.00   1.50   1.66   1.15   1.08   1.17   1.08   1.41   1.13   1.39   1.21   1.07   1.37   1.90   2.19   1.63   1.79   1.16   1.60   1.38   1.26
```

```
Start:    39:21 39:21 39:21 39:24 39:26   40: 4 40: 4 40: 4 40: 4   42:15 42:15   43: 8 43: 8 43: 8 43: 8   43:11 43:11 43:11 43:11   43:20 43:20 43:20 43:20
End:      40: 3 39:27 39:27 39:27 39:27   40: 6 40:14 40:14 44:24   43:17 43:17   43:10 43:10 43:11 43:11   43:17 43:17 43:17 43:24   44: 7 44: 3 43:27 43:27
Count:      13     9     3     6     5       10    51    18    13      12     7        4     3     5     3       11    18    12     7       33    12    18     5
Width:     265   142    15    64    32      214  1320   485   242     127    69       36    12    33    11      744   321   173   105      296    80    45    10
Strength: 1.55  1.57  1.14  1.51  1.26     1.21  2.47  1.18  1.72    2.37  1.74     1.20  1.19  1.58  1.21     2.41  2.19  2.02  1.37     1.77  2.12  1.43  1.23

Start:    43:24 43:27   43:26 43:27   43:27 44     44: 7 44     44:11 44:11   44:11 44:12   44:19 44:23   44:24 44:24   45:17 45:17   45:17 45:18   46:12 46:12   46:12 46:13   46:12 46:12
End:      43:27 44: 1   43:27 44: 1   44:    44     44:    44   44:11 44:12   44:24 44:24   44:20 44:24   44:24 44:24   45:17 45:18   45:17 45:18   46:24 46:24   46:15 46:15   46:13 46:12
Count:       4     3       3     5       4     3     7     6       3    15      336    23        4    38        8   120       6    75       34     9      296    80       15     9       45    10
Width:      37    12      55    17      109   130   379   412     135   308    610   286      216    87       93   142     219   207      885  1372     296  1180      179   111      555   304
Strength: 1.19  1.19    1.30  1.48    1.01  2.25  2.02  1.77    2.37  6.72   3.15  3.66    1.39  1.17    1.32  1.09    1.43  2.25    1.57  1.92    1.77  2.18    3.48  1.77    3.24  2.67

Start:    46:14 46:15   46:15 46:20   46:20 46:20   46:20 46:20   47:13 47:23
End:      46:15 46:15   46:18 46:20   46:20 46:20   46:20 46:20   47:14 47:23
Count:       4     3       5     4       4     5       3     7       3     7
Width:      16     6      64    17      17    98      84   404     207   123
Strength: 1.49  1.30    1.19  1.48    1.48  1.44    1.09  1.69    1.07  1.19

GAPS:

Start:     1: 1   1: 1   1: 1   1: 1   1:11   1:11   1:24   1:24     3: 3   3: 3   3: 8   3:27    3:10  3:10  3:10  3:10    3:10  3:10  3:17  3:19    3:27  3:21  3:27    4:15   5: 2     5: 9   5: 9   5: 9   5: 9    5: 9   5: 5     9     9     9   10: 4   10:22  10:14  13:10  13:21
End:      16: 2   3: 1   3:27   3: 1   1:17   1:23   2: 2   2: 2     3: 8   3:27   3:27  3:27    3:21  3:19  3:17  3:10    3:10  3:17  3:19  3:17    3:27  3:27  3:27   14:22   5: 9     5: 9   5: 9   6:14   8:12    6: 5   5: 9    10: 2  10: 3  10: 3  10:22   10: 4  14: 9  13:10  13:21
Count:     158    28     14      1      7      3      3      3         2      9      7   118     283   154     4     2       4     7    283   219       7    11    23    5086     541     96   387   311   136      6    11       10     3     3     353     111     9    244   294
Width:    6718  1417    828   227   202   454   148   168     94    437   105   5086   1555   154   283   219     401   142   437   219   401   311     96   541    387  1384   311   136  1180     85     111   207    179   141    353   244   294
Strength: 1.05  1.67   2.17  1.55  1.44  6.64  2.70  1.56   1.34   1.05  1.62  1.07   1.68  2.85  2.36  2.46    1.66  1.09  1.05  2.46  1.66  1.25   1.39  1.13  1.02   2.75  1.25  2.40  2.18    1.12  1.77    2.25  1.08   1.16   5.11  1.06

Start:     5:16   6: 2     6: 9   6: 9     6:14   6:14   7: 3   7: 8     7:18   7:24   7:27   7: 8     8: 3   8: 3     8: 7   8:12   8:12   8:17    8:17   8:18   9: 7   9:10    10: 2  10: 3  10: 3  10:22   17:21  18:11
End:       6: 5   6: 2     6:14   6:14     8: 3   7:22   7:22   7:18     7: 8   7: 3   8: 3   8: 2     8: 7   8: 2     8: 7   8:12   8: 9   8:17    9: 7   9: 7   9:10  10: 3    10: 3  10:22  10: 4   10:22   17:21  18:11
Count:     114    2       130   145       412   379   331   225     140   183   264   216     93    87    207     216   156    85      3     4    281    141     93   141   219   353
Width:     114    135     308   145       412   379   331   225     140   183    87   216     93    85    207     93   156    85    281   141    207   179     93   141   111   459
Strength: 1.85  2.25     6.72  1.15     1.77  2.02  2.15  2.57   2.50  3.58  1.31  1.39    1.32  1.17  2.25    1.39  2.90  1.12   2.33  1.08  1.24  1.77    1.77  1.24

Start:    10: 4  10: 6     10: 6  10: 7    10: 7  11: 7    11:11  11:11   11:13  11:18   11:20  11:22   11:25  12: 6   12:13  12:15   12:16  12:23   12:23  12:23   12:25  13:21
End:      10:17  10:17     10:16  10:16    11: 7  11:11    11:17  11:13   11:17  12:12   12:12  12:12   12:12  12:14   13:22  12:15   12:23  13:15   13:22  13:10   13:10  13:21
Count:      251    4        227   202       98   138      138    376     404   358     319    258     29     133    1384   149    129   533    387    278   244
Width:      251  202       227    98      138   440     138    376    404   358    319   258    149   133   1384   149    129   533   387   278   244   294
Strength: 1.14  1.55     2.16  1.44     1.44  1.02    1.02  3.52    1.69  2.49    3.16  2.89    1.22  2.32    1.29  1.22    2.22  1.46    2.11  3.51    5.11  1.06

Start:    14: 4  14: 5     14: 9  14: 9    16: 2  16: 4    16: 4  16: 5    16: 5  16: 8    16:15  16:33   16:39  16:40   16:43  17: 4    17: 7  17:16   17:16  17:16   17:16  17:21   17:21  18:11
End:      14:22  14: 9     14:22  14:22    16:20  16:18    16:18  16:18    16:15  16:15    16:37  16:37   16:50  16:50   16:50  17: 7    17: 7  20:11   20: 4  20:11   18:19  18:19   18:11  18:11
Count:      162    130       308   379      412   331      331   282     140   86      86    264    156    242    156    92       25     27    1376   1368   459   281
Width:      162  130       308   412      412   331     331   282    140   86     86   264    156   242    156    92      25     27   1376  1368  1180   459
Strength: 1.45  2.25     6.72  2.02     1.77  2.15    2.15  2.35    2.50  1.14    1.31  1.77    2.90  1.77    2.14  1.29    1.70  2.14    2.14  2.18    1.24

Start:    17:21  18: 2     18:15  18:19    18:19  18:19    18:19  18:21    18:21  18:21   18:31  20: 1   20: 4  20: 8    20:28  20:28   20:28  20:43   20:43  20:44   21:16  21:17   21:25  21:25
End:      18: 2  18:11     18:19  20: 4    20: 4  20: 1    18:30  18:30    18:27  18:30   20: 1  20: 8   20: 8  20:34    20:20  20:34   21:25  21:25   21:16  21:16   21:25  21:25   22: 2  22: 2
Count:      120    86        90   308      581   563      234   190     143   302     108    145    127   302     20     6      335    506    145    308    156   132
Width:      120   86        90   612      581   563     330   190    234   302    108   145    127   302   1157   506    335   506   308   308   156   132
Strength: 2.00  1.14     1.24  6.72     3.51  4.09    4.44  1.65    2.58  1.95    1.70  1.15    2.17  2.33    2.20  3.45    4.53  6.72    1.34  1.34    2.30  2.30    2.25  1.24

Start:    21:25  21:34     22: 2  22: 2    22: 2  22: 2    22:21  22:21    23:11  23:29   23:29  23:34   23:36  24:25   23:36  23:37    23:38  23:39   23:39  23:39    23:47  24:25
End:      21:34  22:11     22: 8  23:22    23:19  23:23    23:19  22:29    23:17  23:34   29:16  26:16   24:25  25:16   23:45  24:25    24:25  23:45   23:45  23:39    24:13  24:13
Count:      201    148       114   604      547   330     330   172     94    88      1555  1199    762   785     739   762     739   161    133    555   304
Width:      201  148       114   604      547   330     330   172    94   88     2972  1199   762   785    739   762    739   161   133   555   304
Strength: 4.03  1.20     1.85  1.26     2.03  4.44    4.44  3.30    1.34  1.19    1.68  1.03    2.07  1.22    2.72  3.13    1.22  1.43    1.43  2.32    3.24  2.67
```

Gaps for 'ēt 4. continued.

```
Start:     24: 2  24: 2  24:16  24:16  24:27  25: 5  25: 7  25: 9  25:16  25:17  26: 4  26: 4  26:16  26:20  26:20  26:20  27: 5  27: 5  27: 5
End:       24:13  24: 8  24:25  24:21  25: 2  25:14  25:14  25:14  26:16  26:16  26:11  26:16  29: 5  29: 4  29: 4  28:24  28:24  28: 6  27:26
Count:     3      2      3      2      4      4      3      2      4      5      2      3      15     12     11     10     7      5      6      2
Width:     229    136    203    103    110    195    153    103    331    352    138    251    1413   1316   1303   1287   1119   1032   669    376
Strength:  2.64   2.40   2.18   1.57   1.75   1.08   1.57   3.06   2.41   2.45   3.03   2.45   5.79   6.69   7.23   7.81   9.05   10.98  10.47  8.43

Start:     28:14  28:25  28:26  29: 4  29: 5  29:14  29:20  29:20  29:20  30:26  31: 4  31:18  32: 7  32:21  33: 4  33: 5  33: 6
End:       28:24  28:25  28:26  29: 4  29:12  29:14  30:10  30: 9  30: 5  31:16  31:15  32:12  32:24  32:12  33:30  33:30  33:30
Count:     2      3      3      2      3      7      6      3      5      6      3      5      2      11     10     9      7
Width:     223    151    100    157    123    354    333    177    105    383    274    260    82     107    634    616    594    539
Strength:  4.59   1.25   1.49   1.36   2.07   1.17   1.50   1.72   1.62   2.06   3.44   1.26   1.04   1.67   1.88   2.16   2.45   3.08

Start:     33: 6  33: 7  33:20  33:22  34:27  34:27  34:30  35: 5  35:10  35:10  35:12  35:12  36:33  36:37  37:12  38: 4  38: 6  38: 6
End:       33:22  35: 7  33:20  35: 5  34:27  35: 5  36:24  36:11  36:11  37:37  36: 3  37:12  37:12  39:10  39:10  38:22  38:15
Count:     4      4      2      4      3      5      13     6      5      3      3      2      2      14     11     9      6      5
Width:     402    359    309    197    156    96     1240   681    404    353    211    123    348    563    701    654    406    228    152
Strength:  4.09   4.95   6.75   1.11   1.34   1.39   1.02   1.48   2.30   2.43   2.32   2.07   4.76   2.04   1.28   2.17   2.32   2.62   2.80

Start:     38:16  38:17  38:22  38:22  39:14  39:14  39:14  39:14  39:14  39:14  39:14  39:15  39:26  39:27  40: 6  40: 9  40:14  40:14
End:       39:14  38:22  39: 4  39:  46:15  46:15  45:17  45:17  44:11  43:10  39:21  39:21  40:42  40:42  40:42  40:42  40:42  40:28
Count:     3      2      2      3      2      2      3      2      7      2      3      21     19     10     8      5      2
Width:     142    105    87     6006   4713   4581   4578   4081   4078   4075   3217   2529   141    112    968    722    680    581    296
Strength:  1.09   1.62   1.17   2.86   1.29   1.27   1.38   1.40   1.51   1.62   1.21   3.22   1.08   1.80   1.50   3.05   3.82   5.30   6.42

Start:     40:32  40:38  40:42  40:42  40:42  40:42  40:42  40:47  41: 4  41:13  42:18  42:18  43:11  43:11  44: 7  44:24  44:24  45: 4
End:       40:42  43:10  43: 7  42:15  41: 1  40:47  41: 1  43: 7  42:15  43: 3  43:20  43: 7  44:11  45:17  45:17  45:17  45: 1  45:17
Count:     3      2      15     9      3      3      2      3      3      2      3      17     6      5      2      3      5      8
Width:     210    121    1170   974    171    91     740    548    154    91     206    115    87     855    535    526    147    299    183
Strength:  2.02   4.85   7.59   8.72   1.61   1.27   11.73  12.75  1.31   1.27   2.23   1.87   1.17   1.37   3.77   4.61   2.68   3.89   3.58

Start:     45:17  45:18  46:12  46: 2  46: 2  46: 2  46:15  46:18  46:20  46:20  46:20  46:24  47:14  47:22  47:23
End:       46:12  45:20  46: 2  46:12  46:12  46:18  47:14  48:35  48:35  47:14  47:13  47:13  48:35  47:23  48:20
Count:     7      4      2      3      2      2      16     15     5      4      3      2      6      5      3      2
Width:     426    205    180    139    217    211    82     1286   1290   391    381    370    300    887    743    699    417
Strength:  1.91   1.23   1.77   2.47   2.43   4.28   1.04   4.93   4.53   2.91   3.79   5.15   6.52   4.44   7.34   11.00  9.46
```

Linguistic Density Plot in Ezekiel 1 - 48

For 'att 6142 (11 times)

Each Column = 13 Verses. Separations are: Max = 8051.00, Mean = 2330.83, Min = 47.00 .

CLUSTERS:

Start:	16: 7	16:58	16:45	16:45	16:52	16:52	16:55
End:	23:35	16:58	16:48	16:58	16:58	16:52	16:58
Count:	11	9	7	3	2	4	2	51
Width:	5873	1128	313	94	11	146	22	51
Strength:	6.03	4.79	3.52	1.57	1.08	2.03	1.07	1.06

GAPS:.

Start:	1: 1	16:52	16:58	23:35
End:	16: 7	48:35	48:35
Count:	2	6	4	2
Width:	6853	20112	19988	15243
Strength:	2.10	2.21	3.86	6.02

Linguistic Density Plot in Ezekiel 1 - 48

For -k 6142 (443 times)

Each Column = 13 Verses.   Separations are: Max = 4033.00, Mean = 63.00, Min = 2.00

REFERENCE

```
                                                                              +25
                                                                              +20
                                                                              D15+
                                                                              E
                                                                              N
                                                                              S
                                                                              I
                                                                              T10+
                                                                              Y
                                                                              +5
                                                                              0+
```

REFERENCE

CLUSTERS:

Start:	5: 8	5: 8	5: 8	5: 8	5: 8	5: 9	5:11	5:12	5:14	5:14	5:17	5:12	5:11	5:12	5:17	5:14
End:	36:15	7: 9	5:12	5:17	5:12	5:10	5:12	5:12	5:17	5:15	5:17	5:12	5:12	5:17	5:17	5:17
Count:	443	41	19	12	7	4	5	3	32	5	3	12	7	10	7	4
Width:	17877	746	256	115	55	24	38	17	99	32	12	130	56	90	38	65
Strength:	112.25	4.67	3.35	2.80	2.10	1.51	1.70	1.22	1.81	1.44	1.27	4.23	2.73	3.71	2.82	3.04

Start:	7: 8	7: 8	7: 8	7: 3	7: 3	7: 3	7: 3	7: 4
End:	7: 9	7: 8	7: 8	7: 9	7: 6	7: 9	7: 7	7: 7
Count:	10	6	9	4	5	12	22	4
Width:	40	20	256	22	12	130	27	15
Strength:	2.81	2.10	1.32	3.22	3.04	4.23	2.28	1.59

Start:	16:3	16:3	16:3	16:4	16:3	16:5	16:5	16:6
End:	16:31	16:63	16:18	16:8	16:7	16:8	16:6	16:6
Count:	86	175	54	7	10	17	23	14
Width:	613	1358	354	25	56	90	38	23
Strength:	9.08	14.83	6.94	2.30	2.73	3.71	2.82	1.89

```
Clusters for -k 6142, continued.

Start:     16: 7  16: 8  16: 9  16:10  16:10  16:12  16:14  16:14  16:14  16:15  16:15  16:17  16:17  16:19
End:       16: 8  16: 8  16:13  16:13  16:13  16:13  16:14  16:16  16:16  16:15  16:15  16:17  16:17  16:31
Count:         7      3     15     27      8     19     12     50      8     25      3      4     15     32
Width:        38     16     71    188     16     93     50     41     16     10     10     27     15    239
Strength:   2.21   1.23   3.49   4.65   1.58   2.90   2.36   2.41   1.30   1.80   1.30   1.48   1.24   5.07

Start:     16:19  16:20  16:22  16:22  16:22  16:22  16:23  16:24  16:25  16:25  16:27  16:27  16:30  16:33
End:       16:26  16:20  16:24  16:26  16:26  16:24  16:24  16:26  16:25  16:26  16:27  16:29  16:31  16:39
Count:        20      5     15     86     43     10      5      6      3      3     12     38     26     89
Width:       152     47     80     43     19     17     10     32      5      7     77      7     51    714
Strength:   3.89   1.63   3.30   2.61   1.85   1.57   1.30   1.85   1.30   1.57   2.98   1.33   1.79   9.13

Start:     16:33  16:33  16:34  16:36  16:36  16:36  16:36  16:37  16:39  16:39  16:39  16:40  16:40  16:41
End:       16:34  16:34  16:34  16:39  16:36  16:37  16:38  16:39  16:39  16:41  16:43  16:41  16:40  16:41
Count:         9      5      4     13      7      4      6     16     29      6     18      6      3      3
Width:        43     21     16     86     34     10     17    240     16     56    104     31     10     14
Strength:   2.61   1.83   1.58   3.11   2.24   1.34   1.25   4.72   1.21   3.08   3.50   2.02   1.30   1.25

Start:     16:43  16:43  16:46  16:46  16:47  16:49  16:51  16:51  16:51  16:52  16:52  16:52  16:53  16:55
End:       16:49  16:45  16:46  16:46  16:49  16:46  16:55  16:51  16:52  16:52  16:52  16:52  16:55  16:57
Count:        13     26      5     11      4      4     15      4     11     29      8      5      4     61
Width:       120     65     23     21     38     29     98    278     54     18     29     13     22    158
Strength:   2.95   2.48   1.82   1.83   1.46   1.63   3.38   5.60   2.92   2.27   1.56   1.35   1.53   4.26

Start:     16:57  16:57  16:60  16:60  16:61  16:61  16:61  16:63  16:63  16:63  21: 8  21: 8  22: 7  21:34
End:       16:59  16:58  16:63  16:61  16:61  16:62  16:63  16:63  16:63  36:15  22:16  21: 8  22:16  21:34
Count:         4      3     14      8      4     15      6      4     12      3    227     39     20      9
Width:        23      9     80     32     12     42      4     29    223   9080    882     37    208     66
Strength:   1.52   1.31   3.30   2.47   1.59   1.94   1.24   1.46   1.27   7.77   4.07   5.27   3.68   2.48

Start:     22: 4  22: 7  22: 4  22: 4  22: 9  22: 9  22:11  22:12  22:13  22:13  22:15  22:15  23:21  21:35
End:       22: 7  22: 5  22: 7  22: 7  22:10  22:16  22:14  22:14  22:14  22:16  22:16  22: 7  23:21  21:36
Count:        11      7      5      3      4     17      7      3      5      5      3     57   1275     32
Width:        78     40     23      9     58    128     52     10     14     25      7    448   1275      7
Strength:   2.80   2.20   1.82   1.31   2.08   3.55   1.59   2.75   1.80   1.33   1.86   5.76   5.11   2.01

Start:     23:22  23:22  23:23  23:25  23:25  23:25  23:26  23:26  23:27  23:28  23:28  23:28  23:29  23:29
End:       23:27  23:24  23:27  23:27  23:25  23:25  23:27  23:27  23:40  23:29  23:29  23:30  23:29  23:29
Count:         3     18      9     15      8      5      3      7      3     25     13     10      7      5
Width:         7     96     80     61     28     15     27      3     19    170     75     47     13      9
Strength:   1.33   3.82   3.54   1.31   2.49   1.88   2.28   1.33   1.88   4.47   3.16   2.78   1.90   1.34

Start:     23:33  23:35  24:13  24:13  24:13  25:25  26: 3  26: 3  26: 3  26: 3  26: 3  26: 8  26: 8  26: 8
End:       23:35  25: 5  24:14  24:14  24:13  25:25  26:21  26:14  27:36  26:14  26:14  26:14  26:14  26:10
Count:         5      3     13      7      6     26      6     21     36    119    229     21      9      8
Width:        48     10     44     21     10     52    417    128   1050   1788    417    128     76     31
Strength:   1.62   1.30   2.17   1.54   1.30   1.87   1.79   1.34   1.24  10.89  10.28   5.00   4.11   1.30

Start:     26:11  26:14  26:12  26:12  26:13  26:14  26:15  26:15  26:16  26:17  26:18  26:18  26:19  27: 4
End:       26:11  26:14  26:12  26:12  26:14  26:21  26:17  26:21  26:17  26:19  26:20  26:21  26:20  27: 4
Count:         9     10      7     12      3     13      5      8      9      5     20     18     83     38
Width:        41     22      6     10    158     10     53    158     75     44    576    231     18    102
Strength:   1.31   2.81   1.34   1.62   2.77   1.30   1.58   1.32   2.21   1.65   8.91   5.72   1.21   3.80
```

```
Clusters for -k 6142, continued.

Start:    27: 7  27: 7  27: 7  27: 8  27: 9  27: 9  27:10  27:10  27:10  27:11  27:12  27:12  27:14  27:15  27:15  27:15  27:17  27:17  27:17
End:      27: 9  27: 8  27: 7  27: 7  27: 9  27: 9  27:16  27:12  27:11  27:12  27:13  27:16  27:15  27:16  27:16  27:16  27:28  27:22  27:20
Count:       11      7      3      4      4     10      6     10      4     15     16      9      3      4      3      9     45      9      6
Width:       56     32     15      9     16    120     42     21     12     36     65     16      9     22      7    194    325     69     38
Strength:  2.91   2.25   1.24   1.65   1.58   4.01   2.80   2.09   1.62   1.99   2.68   1.23   1.31   1.53   1.33   5.09   6.17   2.46   1.97

Start:    27:17  27:18  27:19  27:20  27:21  27:22  27:22  27:24  27:26  27:26  27:27  27:27  27:27  27:30  27:30  27:31  27:33  27:33  27:34
End:      27:18  27:20  27:20  27:22  27:24  27:25  27:24  27:25  27:27  27:28  27:27  27:27  27:28  27:32  27:36  27:32  27:33  27:33  27:36
Count:        3      3     13     17      6     39     22      3      6     59      8      4     12      4     14      5    110     56     12
Width:        7     13     17    111     39     14     23      4     22      4      8     12      7     34     42    110     23     56     32
Strength:  1.33   1.26   1.22   4.30   1.96   1.25   1.96   1.34   3.69   2.53   1.67   1.62   1.57   2.46   3.16   1.52   2.53   1.27   2.01

Start:    27:34  27:34  28:13  28:13  28:16  36:13
End:      27:35  27:34  28:22  28:17  28:17  36:15
Count:        4      3      6      4      3      4
Width:       14      7    169     64     24     34
Strength:  1.60   1.33   1.03   1.14   1.14   1.42

GAPS:

Start:     1: 1   1: 1   1: 1   1: 1   1: 1   1: 1   1: 1   1: 1   5:17   5:17   5:17   5:15   5:11   5:10   7: 9   7: 9   7: 9   7: 9   7: 9   7: 9   7: 9   7: 9   7: 9   7: 9   9: 7   9: 7   9:16:52
End:       7: 9   7: 4   7: 3   7: 3   5:17   5:15   5:11   5:10   5: 8   7: 3   7: 3   7: 2   16    16:22  16: 9  16: 6  16:16  16: 3  16: 4   7: 9   7: 9   9: 7   9:16  16: 3  16: 3  22: 5   45
Count:       39     28     23     22     19     16      9      7      2      8      7      2             63     33     21     19     16      4
Width:     2775   2687   2663   2660   2289   2222   2115   2086   2038    360    366    360   4396   4131   4049   4041   4030   3956   3949   3660
Strength:  1.02   3.11   4.43   4.74   4.41   5.32   9.13  11.15  31.41   2.69   4.71  11.15   1.06   6.16  10.14  11.11  12.87  34.67  61.81   2.24

Start:    16:52  16:61  16:61  16:61  16:63  16:63  16:63  16:52  22:16  22:16  22:15  22:16  22:16  23:40  24:14  24:14  24:14  25: 4  25: 4  25: 4
End:      21:35  21:35  21:34  21:34  21:34  21:21  21:21  21:36  23:21  23:21  23:22  23:21  23:22  24:13  24:13  24:25  24:25  25: 4  25: 3  26: 3
Count:       34     15     14     12     11      4      3      2      5      6      4      2      2      3      4      3      2      4      3
Width:     3527   3360   3356   3327   3322   3269   3013   2744    682    688    707    711    707    530    416    352    341    315    356    345
Strength:  4.16  10.69  11.34  12.77  13.68  28.35  32.51  42.64   9.84   6.32   3.62   2.82   2.41   4.54   5.60   1.49   2.41   4.00   1.53   4.47

Start:    27:27  27:34  27:36  27:36  28:22  29: 8  29: 8  36:14  36:15
End:      48:35  48:35  48:35  28:13  28:13  48:35  36:13  48:35  48:35
Count:       37     17     14      8      6      2      4      2
Width:     13071  12925  12900    732    279    239    324  12162   4074   8078   8054
Strength: 29.84  48.22  54.04   1.75   1.71   2.79   4.14  84.67  63.80  72.62 127.12
```

Linguistic Density Plot in Ezekiel 1 - 48

For 'attâ 6112 (62 times)

Each Column = 13 Verses.   Separations are: Max = 2768.50, Mean = 443.97, Min = 14.50 .

Linguistic density plot with vertical DENSITY axis (0+, 5+, 10+, D15+, 20+, 25+) and horizontal REFERENCE axis (verse/chapter references). The right-hand scale reads +25, +20, +15, +10, +5, +0 with the word DENSITY spelled vertically.

CLUSTERS:

```
Start:      2: 6   2: 6   2: 6   2: 6   2: 6   2: 6   2: 6   3:19   3:19   3:19   3:25   4: 9  11:13  11:13  12: 2  12: 2  21:11  21:11  21:30  24:19
End:       43:10  28:15  13:17   9: 8   5: 1   3: 5   5: 2   5: 1   4: 3   4: 4   4: 4   5: 1  13:17  12: 9  12: 4  21:24  22: 2  28:15
Count:        62     40     24     18     15     11      8      8     11      8      4      9      5      6      5      4      3      3      8
Width:     23784  14628   5060   3110   1141    632    315    209     85    155    206   1167    451    167    555    240    170   1926
Strength:   5.37   1.58   3.05   2.85   3.49   2.97   2.54   1.35   1.50   1.67   1.58   1.11   1.55   1.56   1.33   2.05   1.46   1.17   1.07
```

```
Start:     27: 2  28: 2  28: 9  32: 2  32: 2  32: 2  32: 2  32:28  33: 9  33: 9  33:10  33:10  37: 3  37: 3  38: 7  38:13
End:       28:15  28:15  28:15  32: 9  43:10  36: 1  33:30  33:12  33:30  33:12  33:10  40: 4  38:17  38:17  38:17  38:17
Count:         6      5      5      3     22     10      8      6      7      5      3      2     11      7      5      3
Width:       874    226    109   1968   7376   2435   1345    788    391    146     82     29   1038    274    115
Strength:   1.42   1.81   1.26   1.93   1.18   1.27   1.60   1.82   1.93   1.91   1.67   1.40   1.00   1.58   1.76   1.26
```

Data for 'attä 6112, continued.

GAPS:

Start:	3:21	5: 1	12: 3	12: 4	12: 9	13:17	13:17	21:33	21:33	22: 2	24:25	24:25	28:12	28:15	28:15	33:10	36: 1	38:17	39: 4
End:	21:11	11:13	21:11	21:11	21:11	21:11	19: 1	24:19	28: 2	24:19	28: 2	27: 2	33: 7	33: 7	32:28	48:35	37: 3	48:35	48:35
Count:	19	5	6	5	4	3	2	6	3	2	3	2	5	4	3	18	2	7	5
Width:	9593.	2752	5986	5943	5843	5127	3555	3780	2080	1960	1586	938	2645	2582	2337	1780	9973	917	6467	6235
Strength:	1.01	1.14	3.98	4.88	6.05	6.91	7.11	1.65	1.94	3.46	1.13	1.12	1.01	1.67	2.36	3.05	1.56	1.08	3.70	5.22

Start:	39:17	40: 4	43:10
End:	48:35	48:35	
Count:	4	3	2
Width:	5961	5537	3481
Strength:	6.21	7.58	6.94

Linguistic Density Plot in Ezekiel 1 - 48

For -kā   6112 (291 times)

Each Column = 13 Verses.   Separations are: Max = 1846.50.   Mean =   95.79.   Min =   2.50 .

REFERENCE

REFERENCE

REFERENCE

CLUSTERS:

Start:	2:1	2:1	2:1	2:1	2:1	2:1	2:1	2:6	2:6	2:8	3:3	3:6	3:6	3:6	3:10	3:10	3:17	3:20			
End:	44:30	13:17	10:2	5:3	3:22	3:3	2:4	2:1	8:8	8:8	3:3	3:11	3:7	3:9	3:11	3:10	3:22	3:22			
Count:	291	83	68	60	27	11	4	7	151	63	17	13	385	104	58	13	10	3	18	45	6	3
Width:	25038	5169	3329	1315	718	269	68	151	63	13	385	104	16	58	104	13	22	8	164	45		
Strength:	20.33	3.65	4.49	6.60	3.80	2.31	1.32	1.82	1.29	1.32	2.91	1.98	2.68	1.32	1.25	1.63	1.48	1.08			

Start:	3:24	5:3	3:24	4:10	3:24	4:5	3:24	4:1	3:27	4:1	3:24	3:25	3:24	4:1	3:26	4:3	4:3	4:6	4:7
End:	5:3	4:1	4:10	4:5	4:1	4:3	4:1	3:26	4:1	3:25	3:24	3:24	4:9	4:4	4:8	4:10	4:9	4:10	3:10
Count:	33	26	14	9	5	5	3	4	5	3	12	5	3	3	3	12	3	5	5
Width:	548	315	185	84	27	14	5	37	27	60	104	18	27	10	20	104	20	69	135
Strength:	4.93	4.54	3.14	2.55	1.87	1.32	1.32	1.51	1.68	2.64	3.05	1.34	1.21	1.35	1.26	1.89	1.65	1.61	1.32

+25 +20 +15 D E N S I +10 T Y 5 0

```
Clusters for -kā   6112, continued.

Start:    11:15 11:15 12: 3 12: 3 12: 4 19: 2 19: 2 21: 2 21: 2 21: 7 21: 7 24: 2 24: 2 24:16 24:16 24:17 24:17 24:26
End:      12: 9 11:15 12: 9 12: 6 12: 6 44:30 33:32 21:24 21:12 21:12 21: 9 24:17 25: 7 24:17 24:16 24:17 24:17 25: 7
Count:    10    5     3     7     6     132   208   8     7     3     3     8     85    19    7     35    10    11
Width:    429   132   80    51    9218  16313 418   192   35    98    44    314   700   208   35    17    10    191
Strength: 1.53  1.38  1.90  1.43  4.73  4.09  1.00  1.64  1.15  1.14  1.09  1.42  2.60  6.73  2.32  1.29  1.68  2.57

Start:    24:26 25: 2 28:13 28:13 28:15 28:16 28:17 28:17 28:18 28:18 28:18 28:18 28:18 28:21 29: 2 29: 2 29: 2 28:13
End:      25: 3 25: 7 28:14 28:14 28:16 28:17 28:17 28:21 28:18 28:18 28:18 28:21 28:19 29:21 29:10 29:21 29: 9 28:17
Count:    3     8     5     4     17    22    10    64    27    15    6     13    4     13    18    105   58    14
Width:    40    46    34    17    50    656   360   47    69    137   48    28    10    13    472   203   58    99
Strength: 1.12  2.49  1.83  1.63  2.68  3.36  7.66  4.17  3.16  2.92  2.69  1.86  1.66  1.86  3.18  3.72  2.44  3.39

Start:    29: 5 29: 5 29: 7 29: 7 32: 4 32: 7 32: 4 32: 4 32: 8 32: 5 32: 6 32: 5 32: 8 32: 9 32: 3 32:12 33: 2 33:30
End:      29: 5 29: 5 29:10 29: 7 32:12 33:32 32:12 32: 7 32:10 32: 6 32: 7 32: 6 32:12 32: 9 32: 3 32:10 33:32 33:32
Count:    4     3     5     3     36    14    16    48    28    4     9     15    40    3     5     13    752   85
Width:    27    9     75    16    1888  90    35    78    78    5     12    20    17    752   85    13    7     85
Strength: 1.57  1.35  1.61  1.29  2.75  3.42  1.83  2.69  2.36  1.64  1.32  1.26  1.80  1.22  1.29  2.11  1.22  2.11

Start:    33:30 33:31 35: 1 35: 9 35: 4 35: 4 35: 5 35: 5 35: 8 35: 8 35: 6 35: 6 35: 8 35:11 35:12 35:11 35:11 35:14
End:      33:31 33:31 35: 4 36:12 35:15 35:10 35:15 35:15 35:10 35:15 35: 3 35: 3 35:10 35:11 35:13 35:12 35:11 35:15
Count:    5     3     24    263   16    51    31    6     16    84    13    8     7     29    9     84    752   85
Width:    49    15    76    584   149   51    31    16    29    84    13    8     29    9     84    43    82    85
Strength: 1.75  1.30  4.85  4.27  3.41  2.01  1.85  1.64  1.29  2.34  1.32  1.36  1.32  1.86  2.11  1.09  1.58  1.31

Start:    37:16 40: 4 37:16 37:18 37:17 37:17 38:17 38: 9 38: 2 38: 4 38: 2 38: 3 38: 6 38: 8 38:12 38:13 38:15 38:16
End:      37:20 37:20 37:18 37:17 37:18 37:17 39: 4 39: 8 38:10 38: 4 38:17 38:10 38: 7 38:10 38:13 38:17 38:17 38:17
Count:    6     40    71    125   149   263   624   394   184   48    33    21    91    20    171   43    82    46
Width:    75    125   71    1012  149   584   624   394   184   48    33    21    91    20    171   43    82    46
Strength: 1.92  1.93  1.37  4.89  4.32  3.67  4.78  3.68  2.97  2.03  1.35  1.36  1.66  1.26  1.99  1.09  1.58  1.07

Start:    39: 1 39: 4 39: 3 39: 1 39: 2 39: 2 39: 3 39: 4 44:23 44: 4 44: 4 44: 5 44: 5
End:      39: 4 39: 4 39: 4 39: 9 39: 3 39: 3 39: 9 40: 4 44: 6 40: 4 40: 4 44: 6 44: 5
Count:    39    39    15    18    5     15    13    7     6     5     9     5     5
Width:    64    15    219   21    18    15    13    5     24    219   31    9
Strength: 2.72  1.64  1.35  1.30  1.91  1.36  1.35  1.90  1.88  1.22  1.85  1.35

GAPS:

Start:    1: 1 2: 1 4: 8 5: 1 5: 1 6: 2 7: 7 8: 5 9: 8 8: 9 9:11 11:15 11:15 11:15 11:15 11:15 11:15 11:15
End:      2: 1 9: 8 9: 8 6:11 6:11 9: 8 9: 8 9: 9 11:15 11:15 48:35 32: 6 29: 5 29: 4 29: 7 29: 4 28:18 11:15
Count:    2     18    5     4     2     3     3     2     3     3     223   105   101   99    96    95    87    85
Width:    604   2184  645   638   589   391   1096  555   789   680   23354 12580 11101 11094 11081 11078 10811 10799
Strength: 5.31  1.45  1.37  2.12  2.94  3.08  6.70  4.80  4.42  6.11  2.99  1.22  1.96  2.21  2.58  2.71  3.45  3.72

Start:    11:15 28:18 28:17 28:17 28:13 28: 5 28: 5 28: 3 25: 7 28: 5 28: 3 24:17 24:17 13:17 13:17 12:18 13: 4 13:17
End:      28:18 28:17 28:17 28:16 28:13 28: 5 28: 5 28: 3 24:17 28: 3 24:17 24:17 24:16 13:17 13:17 13:17 13:17 24:16
Count:    84    82    76    75    66    57    55    53    52    49    47    40    31    30    29    26    27    14
Width:    10796 10787 10763 10760 10688 10558 10545 10538 10535 10519 10512 9114  8740  8737  8734  8709  537   7554
Strength: 3.86  4.13  5.01  5.16  6.56  8.07  8.46  8.88  9.10  9.77  10.25 9.67  11.82 12.19 12.57 13.80 2.55  18.71
```

Gaps for -kā   6112, continued.

```
Start:     13:17 13:17 19:10 19:10 21: 3 21: 9 21:12 21:24 21:24 24:17 25: 7 25: 7 25: 7 29: 7 29:10 29:10 29:10 29:21
End:       21: 3 19:10 19: 2 19: 2 21: 2 24:16 24:16 24: 2 24:16 24:26 28: 3 28: 2 28: 2 32: 4 32: 2 32: 2 32: 2 32: 2
Count:        6     3     2     3     8     5     4     3     2           7     3     2    12     9     4           3
Width:     4975  3693  3556  1277  2574  2471  2417  2191  1912   195  1395  1379  1366  1346  1394  1322  1309  1280  1011
Strength: 21.20 25.97 36.24  8.05  7.61 10.98 12.92 14.83 19.02  1.03  3.53  6.62  8.71 13.09  1.09  2.08  3.16  6.02  6.07

Start:     29:21 31: 2 32:12 32:12 33: 9 33:12 33:17 33:31 33:32 33:32 35:15 35:15 35:15 35:15 35:15 36:12 37:20 39: 3
End:       33: 2 33:30 33: 7 33: 2 33:30 33:30 33:30 35: 3 35: 2 35: 3 37:18 37:17 37:17 37:17 37:16 37:16 38: 2 48:35
Count:        2     8     4     3     2     4     3     2     6     5     7     6     4     3     2           2    18
Width:      549  1147   649   604   480   469   395   275   785   777   741   721  1278  1272  1262  1251  1210   889   263  6245
Strength:  4.74  1.90  2.19  3.05  4.01  1.09  1.50  1.87  1.44  2.07  4.07  6.54  3.03  3.73  4.62  5.84  7.55  8.30  1.74 12.06

Start:     39: 3 44: 5 39: 3 39: 4 40: 4 40: 4 40: 4 40: 4 44: 5 44: 5 44: 5 44:30 48:35
End:       40: 5 40: 4 40: 4 40: 4 44: 5 43:23 48:35 48:35 48:35 48:35 48:35
Count:       13     5     3     2     7     6     4     3     2
Width:     3278   676   661   651  2594  2589  2572  2384  2963  2955  2941  2327
Strength:  6.56  1.53  3.47  5.81  8.70  9.95 17.65 23.96 13.58 16.18 20.39 23.36
```

Linguistic Density Plot in Ezekiel 1 - 48

For 'attiq 111 (5 times)

Each Column = 13 Verses.   Separations are: Max = 11851.00, Mean = 4661.66, Min = 15.00 .

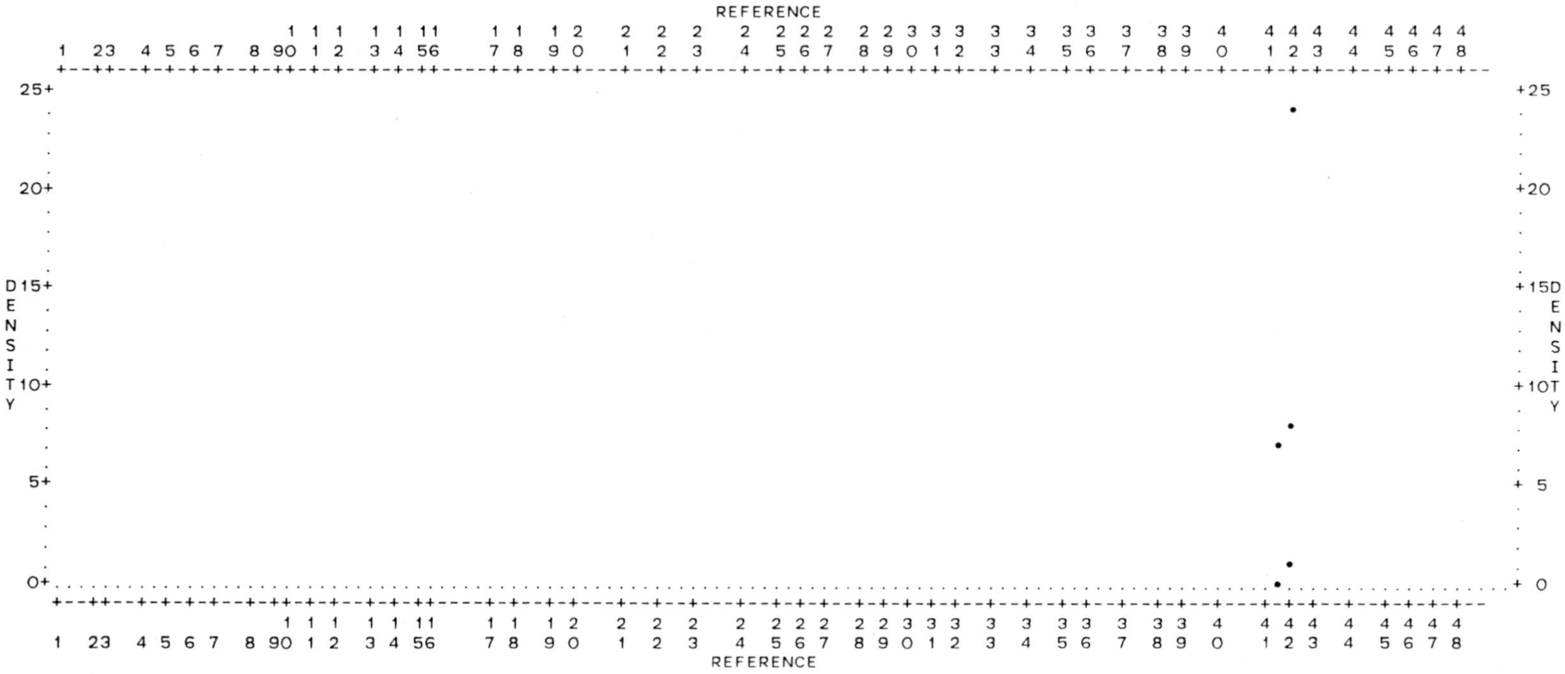

CLUSTERS:

Start:	41:15	41:15	42: 3	42: 3
End:	42: 5	41:16	42: 5	42: 3
Count:	5	2	3	2
Width:	294	20	30	3
Strength:	3.68	1.17	1.86	1.18

GAPS:

Start:	1: 1	1: 1
End:	42: 3	41:15
Count:	4	2
Width:	23945	23681
Strength:	1.88	4.82

Linguistic Density Plot in Ezekiel 1 - 48

For 'attem 6132 (12 times)

Each Column = 13 Verses. Separations are: Max = 4625.00, Mean = 2151.54, Min = 9.50 .

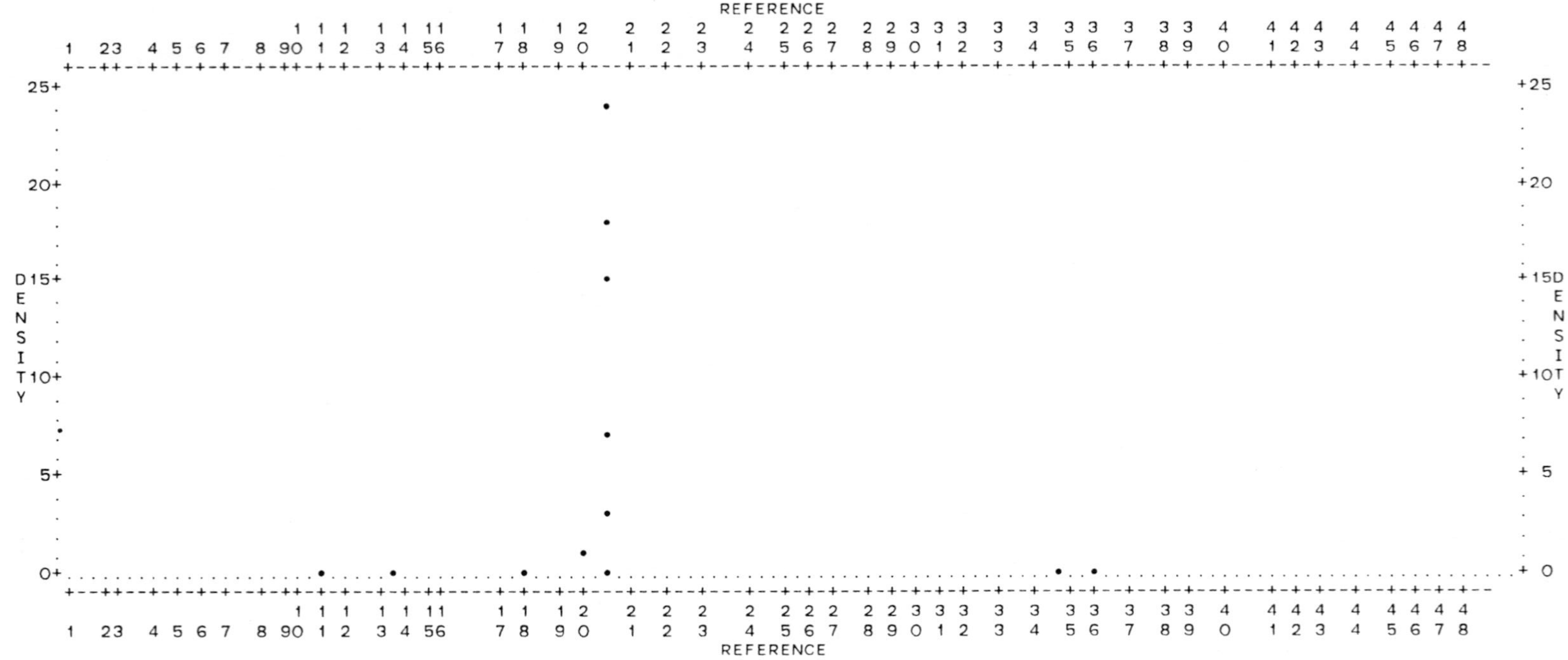

CLUSTERS:

Start:	11:11	11:11	18: 2	20: 3	20:29	20:29	20:29	20:30	20:30
End:	36: 8	20:39	20:39	20:39	20:39	20:32	20:31	20:31	20:30
Count:	12	10	8	7	6	5	4	3	2
Width:	15232	5982	1844	898	216	80	46	19	6
Strength:	3.12	3.87	3.54	3.22	2.89	2.47	2.03	1.58	1.07

GAPS:

Start:	1: 1	20:30	20:31	20:32	20:39	20:39	36: 8
End:	11:11	48:35	48:35	48:35	48:35	34:31	48:35
Count:	2	7	6	5	4	2	2
Width:	4534	17636	17623	17589	17453	8732	8203
Strength:	1.19	1.26	1.88	2.60	3.49	3.30	3.03

Linguistic Density Plot in Ezekiel 1 - 48

For -kem 6132 (236 times)

Each Column = 13 Verses. Separations are: Max = 2370.00, Mean = 118.02, Min = 3.00

CLUSTERS:

Start:	5: 7	5: 7	5: 7	5: 7	5: 7	5:16	5:16	5:16	5:16	6: 3	6: 3	6: 4	6: 4	6: 6	6: 6	6: 6	6: 6	6: 8	9: 5
End:	47:22	24:24	14:23	6: 9	6: 9	5:17	5: 7	6: 9	6: 9	6: 4	6: 4	6: 4	6: 6	6: 6	6: 6	6: 7	6: 7	9:14:23	12:25
Count:	236	132	56	24	21	4	3	21	17	6	3	8	10	3	10	5	13	32	20
Width:	25253	11499	4528	443	185	3	9	99	21	9	17	8	63	39	76	20	621	2797	1648
Strength:	14.95	4.39	2.56	4.23	4.31	1.36	1.67	3.93	2.18	1.36	1.37	1.37	3.06	2.56	1.37	1.93	1.34	1.40	1.20

Start:	11: 5	11: 5	11: 5	11: 5	11: 7	11: 7	11: 9	11:17	11:17	11:17	11:17	13:19	13:19	18: 2	18: 2	18:25	18:29	18:30
End:	12:25	11:19	11:12	11:10	11: 7	11:10	11: 7	11:10	11:12	11:19	11:17	13:21	13:19	14: 6	20:44	18:31	18:31	18:31
Count:	19	16	12	9	3	6	4	10	4	49	16	3	54	6	10	8	7	5
Width:	940	292	128	79	23	43	24	39	49	258	548	49	2027	621	4830	122	48	24
Strength:	2.46	3.34	3.06	2.64	1.28	2.09	1.18	1.50	1.32	1.27	1.48	1.12	5.59	1.27	4.76	2.29	2.31	1.91

```
Clusters for -kem 6132, continued.

Start:     18:31  20: 3  20:18  20:27  20:27  20:30  20:30  20:31  20:33  20:33  20:35  20:35  20:37  20:39  20:39  20:39  20:40  20:40  20:40  20:40
End:       18:31  20:44  20:44  20:44  20:32  20:32  20:31  20:32  20:34  20:34  20:36  20:38  20:38  20:44  20:44  20:42  20:42  20:41  20:41  20:40
Count:         3     44      4     37      8     17      3     24     10      4     25      7     13     19     11      3      8      5     20      3
Width:        12   1073     52    461    138    254     24     49     77     10     46     25     13    165     99     18     49     20      9
Strength:   1.34   5.72   1.48   5.81   2.24   2.31   1.31   1.62   2.84   1.35   2.32   1.62   1.34   4.07   2.96   1.31   2.53   1.93   1.36

Start:     20:41  20:42  20:42  20:42  20:44  20:44  21:29  21:29  21:29  22:19  22:20  22:20  22:21  33:11  33:19  33:11  33:20  33:26  33:25
End:       20:42  20:44  20:43  20:44  20:44  20:44  21:29  22:22  21:29  22:22  22:21  22:21  22:24  33:11  39:19  47:22  33:26  33:26  33:25
Count:         3      8      5     24     11      3      5     11      3      6      4      3      6     85     79    104      4    123     14
Width:        23     49     24     11    597     13     11      7     15     38      8      6     30   9204   4033    104   4033    123     14
Strength:   1.28   2.53   1.91   1.34   1.59   1.35   1.37   1.95   1.37   1.55   1.37   1.38   1.69   1.93   6.07   3.28   6.07   1.13   1.33

Start:     34:18  34:18  34:18  34:18  35:13  35:13  35:13  36: 3  36: 3  36: 7  36: 7  36: 8  36: 9  36: 9  36:11  36:11  36:11  36:22
End:       34:31  34:21  34:19  34:18  35:13  37:25  39:17  36:36  36: 3  36:11  36:13  36:10  36:11  36:10  36:13  36:12  36:11  36:36
Count:         8      7      6      3     12      3     48     12      5      7      7      3      9      4     47     17      8     31
Width:       288     66     33     11    859   1532     64    106    378    116     58     28     12     55     23     11      8    304
Strength:   1.75   2.25   2.13   1.35   6.48   7.36   6.28   1.56   3.31   3.09   2.28   1.60   1.34   1.81   1.69   1.66   1.37   5.36

Start:     36:22  36:22  36:23  36:23  36:24  36:25  36:25  36:25  36:26  36:26  36:26  36:28  36:28  36:31  36:31  36:31  36:32  36:32  36:33
End:       36:29  36:25  36:23  36:24  36:25  36:29  36:27  36:26  36:26  36:27  36:26  36:28  36:29  36:31  36:33  36:32  36:32  36:33  36:33
Count:        20      7      7      3     13      8      4      3      3     22     12     34     21     10     55     10      6      4     23
Width:       181     73     27     13    100     43     12      7      4     22     12     34     21     99     55     23      6      4    533
Strength:   4.18   2.22   2.15   1.34   3.30   2.54   1.68   1.37   1.34   1.63   1.34   1.87   1.64   2.90   2.96   2.17   1.69   1.63   2.80

Start:     37: 5  37: 5  37:12  37:12  37:12  37:13  37:13  37:14  37:14  43:27  43:27  43:27  44: 6  44: 6  44: 7  44: 7  44: 8  45: 1  45: 9  45: 9  45:10  47:14
End:       37:14  37: 6  37:12  37:12  37:12  37:14  37:13  37:14  37:14  43:27  45:21  44: 8  44: 8  44: 7  44: 4  44: 3  45:21  45:12  45:12  45:10  47:22
Count:        15      5     10     53      3     17      9     26      3      9    225      8      6      7      3      3     32      3      9      3     33    165
Width:       222     22     12     53      7     17     26    100      3    499   1237     63      9      9      4     71    499     33     71     33    165
Strength:   3.34   1.92   1.34   2.91   1.37   2.16   1.36   3.30   1.37   1.06   1.43   2.02   1.36   2.19   1.34   1.39   1.22   1.69   1.22   1.63   2.15

Start:     47:21  47:22
End:       47:22  47:22
Count:         6      3
Width:        36     19     11
Strength:   2.12   1.30   1.35

GAPS:

Start:       1: 1   1: 1   1: 1   1: 1   1: 1   1: 1   1: 1   1: 1   1: 1   6: 6   6: 9   9: 9  11:17  11:19  11:19  11:19  14: 6  14: 6  14: 6  14: 6
End:        36:11   6: 5   6: 4   6: 4   6: 4   5:16   5:16   5: 7  11: 5  11: 5   9: 5  13: 8  13: 8  12:11  12:22  20:33  20:31  18:31  18:30
Count:       159     15     13     12     10      6      5      2      3      3      2     13      8      8      9     29     23     11      9
Width:     19827   2382   2363   2359   2355   2260   2265   2002   2026   1996   1288    857    824    342    574   4309   4234   3175   3163
Strength:   1.38   1.70   2.38   2.77   3.22   6.42   7.65  16.02  10.60   9.95   1.02   1.50   2.03   1.90   1.71   3.11   5.47   6.77

Start:      14: 6  14: 6  14:23  18: 3  18: 3  18: 3  18: 3  20: 7  20: 7  20:44  21:29  21:29  24:23  24:23  24:23  24:23  24:23  24:23  24:23  24:23  24:23
End:        18: 2  14:22  18: 2  18:25  18:29  18:25  18:31  20:18  20:18  21:29  24:21  22:22  24:21  36: 9  36:11  36: 8  34:18  33:25  33:25
Count:          4      2      2      2      5      3      2      3      3      8      3      8      3     25      9     23     10      6      5
Width:        398   2566   2141    546    472    715    333    274    558   2165    497   1583   6308   6347   6290   5490   5490   4870   4860
Strength:    2.37  10.91  17.20   1.86   3.00   1.82   1.03   1.32   3.73   4.36   3.22   6.35   5.19   7.01  12.46  12.77  16.42  18.78

Start:      24:24  24:24  33:25  33:25  33:26  34:21  34:31  37:14  37:14  37:14  37:14  39:17  44: 7  44: 8  44:30
End:        24:24  33:20  33:15  34:18  34:18  34:31  34:18  35:13  48:35  43:27  43:27  39:17  44:30  44:30  47:14
Count:          4      3      2      4      2     30     27      6      5      8      6      2     13      2      8
Width:       4740   4550    616    609    599    467    245   6527   7252   4333   4175   4171   2804   2031   1011    531    513   1457
Strength:   27.15  37.70   1.28   2.24   4.08   1.38   1.07   6.10   6.44  11.42  13.75  15.83  22.85   1.54   1.77   3.35   2.05
```

Gaps for -kem 6132, continued.

Start:	45: 9	45:10	45:12	45:21	47:22	47:22
End:	47:14	47:14	47:14	47:14	48:35	48:35
Count:	5	4	3	2	3	2
Width:	1202	1183	1145	965	721	714
Strength:	3.12	4.08	5.47	7.20	2.92	5.06

Linguistic Density Plot in Ezekiel 1 - 48

For -ken 6162 (15 times)

Each Column = 13 Verses. Separations are: Max = 4266.50, Mean = 1748.13, Min = 3.00 .

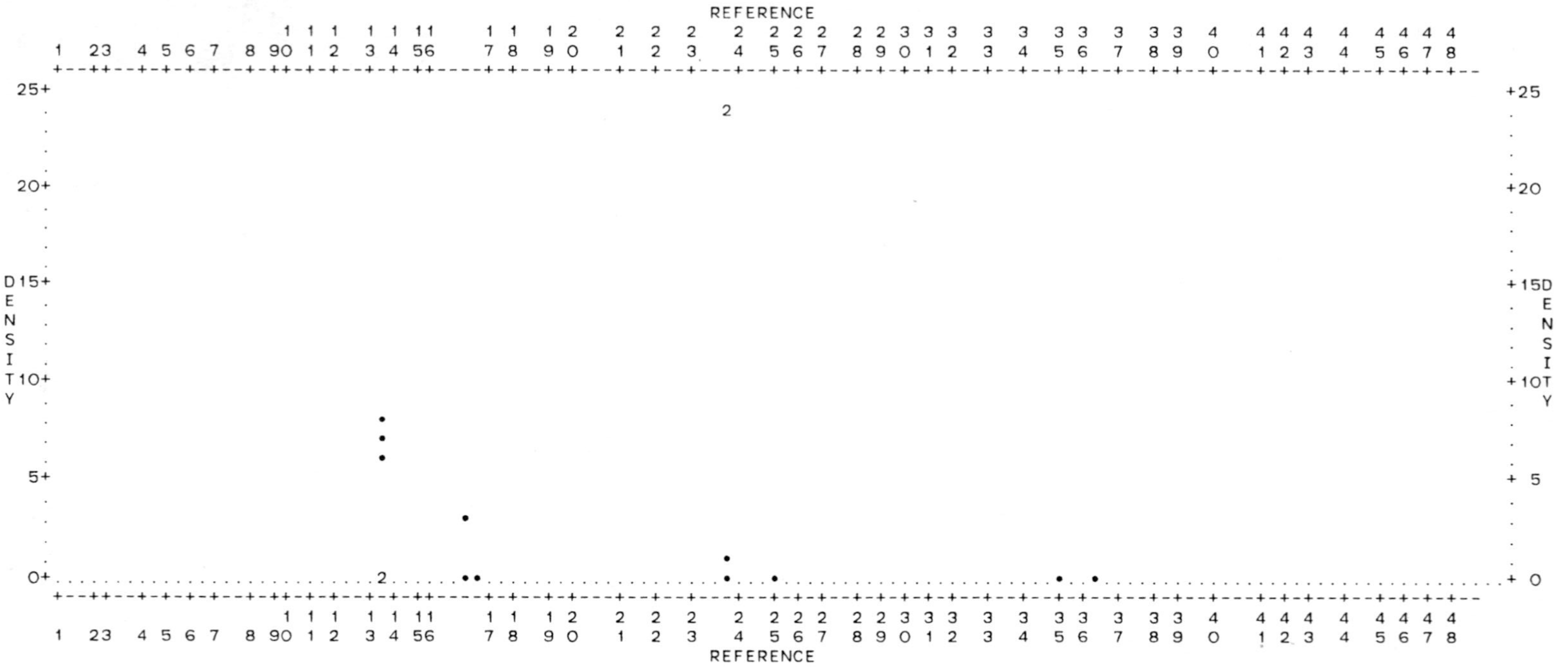

CLUSTERS:

Start:	13:18	13:18	13:18	13:18	13:20	13:21	16:45	16:45	23:48	23:48	23:48	23:48	23:49
End:	36:14	16:55	13:23	13:21	13:21	13:21	16:55	16:45	36:14	25: 4	23:49	23:49	23:49
Count:	15	8	5	4	3	2	3	2	7	5	4	3	2
Width:	14068	2121	144	95	47	7	249	4	6877	637	10	6	2
Strength:	4.63	3.00	2.33	1.94	1.53	1.06	1.44	1.06	1.09	2.16	1.97	1.55	1.06

GAPS:

Start:	1: 1	1: 1	16:55	23:49	23:49	23:49	25: 4	36:14
End:	13:20	13:18	23:48	48:35	48:35	35:11	35:11	48:35
Count:	3	2	2	6	5	3	2	2
Width:	5864	5816	5070	14956	14952	6419	5792	8085
Strength:	1.05	2.47	2.02	1.97	2.70	1.30	2.46	3.85

Linguistic Density Plot in Ezekiel 1 - 48

For bě- 4 (1182 times)

Each Column = 13 Verses.   Separations are: Max =   166.50,   Mean =   23.64,   Min =   2.00 .

REFERENCE

Vertical axis legend (top to bottom): +25 · +20 · +15 D E N S I T +10 Y · +5 · · O

D E N S I T Y (left axis label)

CLUSTERS:

Start:	1: 1	1: 1	1: 1	1: 1	1:16	1:16	1:16	1:16	1:20	1:20	4: 9	4: 9	4: 9	4: 9	4:16	4:16	4:16	4:16	5: 2
End:	48:22	34:29	1: 3	1: 1	1:25	1:21	1:19	1:17	1:21	1:21	8:11	7: 4	5:17	8: 9	5:17	4:17	4:16	4:16	5: 3
Count:	1182	917	6	43	13	100	45	13	4	5	68	1036	630	101	45	6	32	11	5
Width:	27751	19211	43		183		13		12	26	1036			1776	630	259	108		40
Strength:	5.12	7.19	1.41		1.23	1.58	1.03	1.01	1.42	1.44	2.91	2.91	2.66	2.59	2.66	1.26	1.71	1.67	1.14

REFERENCE

Start:	5: 4	5:11	5:11	5:11	5:12	5:12	5:13	5:13	5:13	5:15	5:15	5:15	5:16	1:20	1:21	4: 9	6: 6	6: 7	6: 8	6: 8	6: 9
End:	5:17	5:17	5:14	5:12	5:12	5:11	5:13	5:13	5:14	5:15	5:15	5:17	5:17	1:21	1:21	5:17	6:13	7: 4	6: 9	6: 3	6:13
Count:	19	19	11	6	4	6	3	3	5	3	3	12	8	4	8	23	20	4	6	4	100
Width:	176	176	37	28	7	28	18	8	28	12	12	65	25	65	62	308	188	62	29	13	100
Strength:	2.35	2.50	1.97	1.42	1.19	1.40	1.28	1.16	1.40	1.22	1.73	1.60	1.53	2.01	1.37	1.92	2.55	1.37	1.68	1.25	2.24

Clusters for be- 4. continued.

```
Start:     6:11  6:11  6:11  6:12  6:12  6:12  7:15  7:15  7:15  7:15  7:15   8: 1   8: 1   8: 1   8:18   8:18   8:18   9: 3   9: 3   9: 3   9: 4  10:10  10:10
End:       6:13  6:12  6:12  6:13  6:13  6:13  7:19  7:15  7:15  7:16  7:27   8: 1   8: 1   8: 1   8:25   8:18   8:18   9: 9   9: 9   9: 9   9: 5  10:20  10:16
Count:       10     6     4     4    11           89    38    16     7    23      5     3      5   1800   210    87     12    39     11     11    193    102
Width:       50    21     9    22    11          175    93    48                          72    39
Strength:  2.29  1.83  1.50  1.18  1.07         1.21  1.18  1.33  1.19  1.50   1.25  1.45  1.25   1.10   1.37   1.20   1.04   1.49   1.04   1.07   1.10   1.01

Start:    10:10 10:10 10:10 11:10 11:16 12:   12:12 12:15 12:11 12:10 12:    12:10 12:10 12:11 12:11 12:12 12:12 12:15 12:15 12:16 12:16 12:18
End:      10:11 10:11 10:11 11:10 12:25 12:   12:12 12:12 12:12 12:25 12:12  12:15 12:12 12:12 12:12 12:12 12:12 12:15 12:15 12:19 12:19 12:18
Count:        4     3     3     4     8    41                 7     8    12      8     6     3     7     3     9     3     3    11    73     9
Width:       26    13    12    20     8   726    82    41   318   122    45     23
Strength:  1.08  1.01  1.04  1.23  1.16  1.49  1.60  1.60  1.28  1.65  1.76   1.92  1.79  1.16  1.13  1.13  1.13  1.07  1.07  1.18  1.18  1.13

Start:    13: 4 13: 5 13:13 13:13 14:   14:   16:   16:   16:10 16:   16:   16:12 16:15 16:13 16:14 16:14 16:31 16:31 16:33 16:40 16:56 16:57 17: 9 17: 9 21:30
End:      13:13 13:15 13:13 13:13 14:   14:   16:   16:10 16:   16:   16:   16:15 16:15 16:14 16:14 16:14 16:31 16:31 16:34 16:41 16:57      17:30 23:31 21:30
Count:        9    42    23    10     3    12    36    11    54    93    57     6     6     4     8    19     5    34     4     4    35          583   222   148
Width:       99    42    99    13   222   136   610   231    38   175    93    48    57    20    34    19   285    13    57                  10923  4361  2995
Strength:  1.34  1.72  1.79  1.10  1.22  1.22  1.57  1.35  1.78  1.15  1.32  1.15  1.15  1.23  1.16  1.25  1.60  1.01  1.25  1.33  1.19   1.19   6.98  2.72  1.79

Start:    17:13 17:16 17:16 17:17 17:17 17:17 18:17 18:17 18:   18:22 18:24 18:22 18:24 18:24 18:31 19:   19:   19:   19:   19:   19:11 19:11 19:12
End:      17:17 17:17 17:17 17:17 17:17 17:21 18:17 18:27 18:19 18:27 18:27 18:27 18:24 18:24 20: 1 20: 1 19: 9 19:10 19:   19:   19:   19:12 19:12
Count:        9     3     3     5    11     5    36    16     5    76   107     7     6     3    20    14     9     5     3     9    72     9     9
Width:       99    88   189    38     6    42   610   231    56   107   107    42    34                285    35   138   138
Strength:  1.72  1.58  1.39  1.18  1.22  1.07  1.57  1.35  1.10  1.22  1.22  1.10  1.17  1.07  1.60  1.99  1.13  1.25  1.19  1.13  1.75  1.11  1.12

Start:    19:13 20:   20:   20: 5 20:   20:19 20:11 20:15 20:17 20:19 20:21 20:21 20:23 20:25 20:25 20:30 20:31 20:31 20:33 20:33 20:38
End:      20: 1 21:30 21:30 20:31 20:19 20:19 20:19 20:19 20:17 20:31 20:23 20:31 20:23 20:26 20:25 20:31 20:31 21: 2 21: 3 21:30 20:38
Count:        6     3     5    40    23    14    91    91   282    17     8     3     5     9     3    44     8    28    366    94
Width:       40    88  1632   691   373   189   610   282    91                44    21                884    28    10
Strength:  1.47  1.25  2.00  1.58  1.33  1.39  1.18  1.18  1.02  1.13  1.18  1.16  1.13  1.06  1.13  1.20  1.16  1.42  2.23  1.67

Start:    20:33 20:34 20:34 20:39 20:39 20:39 20:39 20:40 20:41 20:41 20:43 20:43 20:43 20:44 21:24 21:16 21:24 21:26 21:26 21:29 21:34
End:      20:34 20:33 21: 3 20:44 20:41 20:40 20:39 20:40 20:41 20:44 20:43 20:44 20:43 21:17 21:17 21:30 21:28 21:27 21:27 21:21 23:31
Count:        7     3     4    15     8    26    54     4     7    67     4    18     7    25   132    80    10    25     6     4    74
Width:       38     8    10   136   222    54          12                67    18         132    80    45
Strength:  1.79  1.16  1.47  1.85  2.21  1.08  1.78  1.08  1.10  1.28  1.19  1.28  1.19  2.06  1.11  1.87  1.66  1.75  1.52  1.03  2.20

Start:    21:34 22:   21:34 21:34 22:   22:   22:   22:   22:   22:   22:   22:20 22:20 22: 9 22: 9 22: 9 22:18 22:21 22:22 23:   23:14 23:14 23:24 23:31
End:      22:27 22:   21:37 21:35 22:   22:   22:   22:   22:13 22:12 22:10 22:27 22:22 22:12 22:13 22:18 22:22 22:22 23:10 23:15 23:31
Count:       41    17     8     5     9     6    38    94    38    24     7    11     7    85   164   348    46   133    17    76     9    13
Width:      579   210    71    34    12    94   164   348             85   133
Strength:  2.49  1.78  1.50  1.27  1.04  1.42  1.51  1.42  1.51  1.74  1.55  1.38  1.30  1.46  1.55  1.74  1.65  1.38  1.30  1.13  1.13  1.36

Start:    23:24 23:28 23:30 23:30 23:37 23:37 24:   24:   24:17 24:18 24:21 24:21 25:   25:13 25:13 25:14 25:17 25:17 25:17
End:      23:25 23:31 23:31 23:31 34:29 29: 7 24:   24:18 24:18 24:18 26: 1 26:20 25:   25:15 25:14 25:14 26: 1 25:17 25:17
Count:       59    13     4    11   361 6454   170     4    27    53    29   976  108    50    17     9    26    73     3
Width:       59    64    11  6454  361 6454                27    53   529   976  108    50    17     9    26    73
Strength:  1.11  1.33  1.23  1.07  5.50  3.43  1.22  1.06  1.06  1.51  1.07  1.51  1.94  1.28  1.30  1.13  1.04  1.73  1.13

Start:    25:17 26:   26: 5 26: 7 26: 7 26: 7 26: 7 26:10 26:10 26:11 26:10 26:15 27:   27:   27: 4 27: 8 27:10 27:16 27:18 27:18 27:21 27:24
End:      26:   26:20 26:11 26:11 26:11 26: 9 26: 7 26:11 26:11 26:11 26:15 26:15 27:   28:10 27:22 27:13 27:22 27:20 27:18 27:22 27:22 28:10
Count:        3    24    14    88    47    17     5     4     6    21    10     3     9    91    55   100   330   108    45    35    71   393
Width:        8   370   136    88    47    17              21    10          91    55    91  1289   746   330
Strength:  1.16  1.54  2.01  1.98  1.63  1.63  1.22  1.20  1.20  1.20  1.10  1.22  1.76  3.89  3.12  1.72  1.04  1.94  1.03  1.25  1.18  2.61
```

Clusters for bd- 4, continued.

Band 1 (clusters 27:24 – 28:17)

Start:	27:24	27:24	27:24	27:24	27:27	27:27	27:27	27:32	27:32	28: 2	28: 2	28: 4	28: 4	28:13	28:13	28:13	28:14	28:14	28:17
End:	27:36	27:31	27:26	27:24	27:27	27:31	27:33	27:36	27:33	28:10	28: 5	28: 5	28: 5	29: 7	28:23	28:16	28:16	28:15	28:23
Count:	22	16	8	5	8	15	6	12	6	10	59	4	7	36	20	8	5	3	12
Width:	218	145	45	16	72	72	53	53	59	133	133	7	17	501	232	68	24	12	136
Strength:	2.59	2.29	1.92	1.65	1.49	1.67	1.19	1.22	1.04	1.12	1.42	1.30	1.19	2.36	2.12	1.55	1.48	1.04	1.58

Band 2 (clusters 28:22 – 29:20)

Start:	28:22	28:22	28:22	28:22	28:26	28:26	29: 1	29: 1	29: 7	29: 7	29:11	29:11	29:11	29:11	29:12	29:12	29:15	29:17	29:20
End:	28:23	28:22	28:23	28:23	29: 1	29: 1	29: 1	29: 1	34:29	32:32	31: 3	30:10	30:10	29:12	29:12	29:17	29:17	29:17	30:10
Count:	34	3	5	8	16	8	3	1	3353	1906	803	430	136	30	46	5	4	7	206
Width:	227	18	9	71	24	16	4	5	191	127	59	30	11	4	24	34	5	34	30
Strength:	2.10	1.07	1.61	1.13	1.39	1.50	1.48	1.25	4.27	3.81	3.23	2.02	1.34	1.33	1.35	1.13	1.27	1.19	2.20

Band 3 (clusters 30:4 – 31:1)

Start:	30: 4	30: 4	30: 6	30: 6	30: 7	30: 8	30:12	30:12	30:16	30:17	30:18	30:18	30:18	30:20	30:20	30:20	30:21	30:25	30:25	30:26	31: 1
End:	30: 5	30: 4	30: 9	30:10	30: 7	30: 9	30:20	30:12	30:20	30:18	30:20	30:18	30:18	30:20	30:20	30:21	30:21	30:31	30:25	30:26	31: 1
Count:	36	5	8	11	4	4	337	16	144	33	31	8	6	13	3	156	72	41	21	3	1
Width:	36	5	8	11	4	4	337	16	144	33	31	8	6	13	3	156	72	41	21	3	1
Strength:	1.23	1.47	2.14	1.87	1.28	1.23	2.62	2.31	2.18	1.60	1.33	1.16	1.22	1.40	1.56	1.75	1.54	1.22	1.73	1.54	1.22

Band 4 (clusters 31:5 – 32:4)

Start:	31: 5	31: 5	31: 6	31: 6	31: 8	31: 8	31: 8	31:16	31:16	31:17	31:17	31:18	31:18	32: 1	32: 2	32: 2
End:	31:12	31:12	31: 8	31: 8	31:11	31:11	31:18	32: 4	31: 9	31:17	31:18	31:18	31:18	32: 1	32: 4	32: 4
Count:	1045	436	237	155	46	27	12	56	7	91	162	53	26	90	42	10
Width:	68	36	15	9	6	4	3	11	3	9	17	9	6	8	5	8
Strength:	2.86	1.89	1.99	1.35	1.04	1.06	1.04	1.47	1.01	1.46	2.29	1.73	2.03	1.96	1.43	1.10

Band 5 (clusters 32:7 – 33:27)

Start:	32: 7	32: 7	32:12	32:12	32:22	32:22	32:22	32:24	33: 3	33:12	33:12	33:13	33:21	33:21	33:21	33:27	33:27
End:	32:32	32:12	32:32	32:12	32:27	32:25	32:23	33: 3	33:22	33:13	33:13	33:14	33:21	33:22	33:30	33:27	33:27
Count:	557	101	258	18	135	70	25	29	458	217	30	91	44	78	24	5	3
Width:	32	8	18	8	12	8	8	4	29	10	6	9	6	8	5	3	3
Strength:	1.35	1.02	1.48	1.08	1.59	1.52	1.11	1.01	1.64	1.90	1.83	1.66	1.22	1.06	1.18	1.39	1.48	1.25

Band 6 (clusters 34:12 – 38:22)

Start:	34:12	34:13	34:13	34:14	34:21	34:21	34:21	36:17	36:18	36:19	36:22	36:23	37:22	37:23	37:23	38:14	38:17	38:18
End:	34:21	34:14	34:14	34:14	34:21	34:21	34:14	36:23	36:19	36:23	36:23	37:23	37:23	37:23	37:23	38:22	38:18	38:19
Count:	210	74	23	8	153	7	12	153	13	42	8	55	206	126	91	206	53	25
Width:	14	8	7	4	3	7	3	13	5	4	6	4	8	9	10	17	5	10
Strength:	1.14	1.45	1.50	1.19	1.36	1.19	1.10	1.01	1.31	1.10	1.18	1.18	1.16	1.71	1.18	1.82	2.03	1.46	1.38

Band 7 (clusters 39:6 – 42:19)

Start:	39: 6	39: 6	39:11	39:15	39:23	39:23	39:23	39:21	39:21	39:26	39:26	39:27	40: 1	40: 1	40: 1	40: 1	42:12	42:16
End:	39:15	39:11	39:11	39:15	39:23	39:40	40: 6	39:21	40: 2	39:28	39:27	40: 1	40: 2	40: 1	40: 1	40: 1	42:12	42:19
Count:	710	209	128	66	20	373	24	237	17	126	91	8	37	23	7	3	10	38
Width:	39	15	13	9	6	26	8	63	11	5	9	4	7	8	10	4	5	18
Strength:	1.31	1.38	1.90	1.84	1.85	1.49	1.16	1.03	1.08	1.55	1.18	1.13	1.53	1.35	1.19	1.16	1.10	1.18

Band 8 (clusters 43:7 – 47:22)

Start:	43: 7	43: 7	43: 8	43:21	43:23	44:18	44:18	45:16	45:16	45:16	45:17	45:20	45:20	45:25	45:25	46: 8	46: 8	46:11
End:	43: 8	43: 8	43:23	43:21	43:23	44:18	44:19	45:16	45:17	45:18	45:17	45:21	45:22	45:25	45:25	46:16	46:11	46:16
Count:	82	7	29	62	26	883	5	309	21	49	19	34	5	3	8	536	30	220
Width:	7	4	10	5	8	51	39	309	7	4	8	5	4	5	8	30	18	71
Strength:	1.02	1.01	1.10	1.05	1.08	1.82	1.16	1.55	1.75	1.59	1.52	1.27	1.33	1.01	1.16	1.18	1.87	2.00	1.23

Band 9 (clusters 46:8 – 47:22)

Start:	46: 8	46: 9	46: 9	46:10	46:11	46:12	46:12	46:13	46:14	46:21	46:21	47:22	47:22
End:	46:11	46:40	46:11	46:10	46:14	46:14	46:12	46:14	46:23	46:23	47: 1	47:22	47:22
Count:	12	16	6	8	3	38	96	14	27	37	4	8	14
Width:	24	16	6	8	3	38	96	14	27	37	3	8	14
Strength:	1.04	1.77	1.33	1.16	1.10	1.18	1.10	1.38	1.06	1.19	1.42	1.80	1.38	1.16

Data for be- 4, continued.

GAPS:

```
Start:     1: 1   1: 1   1: 1   1: 1   1: 2   1: 2   1: 3   1: 3   1: 3   1: 3   1: 3   1:21   1:21   1:24   1:25   1:28   1:28   1:28   1:28   1:28   1:28   1:28
End:      19: 9   1:20   1:17   1:17   1:16   1:16   1:15   1:12   1: 9   1: 1   1: 9   1:28   1:24   1:28   1:28   5:15   5:15   5:13   5:12   5:13   5:12   5: 2
Count:     383     13      8      7      6      6      5      3      2      2      6      6      3      3      2     63     62     57     53     57     53     36
Width:    9441    379    312    306    299    287    267    235    192    117    117     58     92    172     75   1657   1654   1651   1611   1569   1569   1305
Strength:  1.07   1.16   1.83   2.24   2.71   3.19   3.64   4.00   4.31   3.93   3.93   1.01   1.43   1.32   2.15   1.05   1.17   1.30   1.65   2.03   2.03   3.46

Start:     1:28   1:28   1:28   2: 3   2: 5   2: 9   3: 3   3: 3   3: 4   3:10   3:10   3:10   3:10   3:10   3:10   3:10   3:10   3:18   3:19   3:25   3:25   3:25
End:       4:16   4:16   3:10   3:10   3: 3   3: 2   3: 9   3: 3   3:10   4:16   4:16   4:16   3:25   3:24   3:24   3:24   3:14   3:19   3:25   3:24   4:16   4:10
Count:      33     31      6      6      3      3      9      2     21     22     11      6      4      3      3      3     10      5      4      3     11      5
Width:     1249   1242   453    369    223    179     96    126     22    780    785    355    200    144    128    109     88    420    301    128    420    301
Strength:  3.73   4.16   3.95   4.74   3.70   3.92   3.04   3.04   3.10   2.92   2.68   2.92   1.54   1.82   1.38   1.03   1.83   1.38   2.70   1.38   2.92   4.36

Start:     3:27   3:27   4: 9   4: 9   4:10   4: 9   5:16   5:16   5:16   5:16   5:17   5:16   6: 6   6: 7   6:13   6:13   7: 8   7: 8   7:13   7:27   8: 1   8: 7
End:       4:10   4: 9   4: 9   4: 1   4: 9   4: 2   6: 6   6: 8   6: 7   6: 6   6: 6   6: 3   6: 3   6: 2   7: 8   7: 5   7: 8   7:13   7:19   7:27   8: 3   8: 1
Count:      4      3      3      2      3      2      9      6      4      3     10      3      3      2      7      5      8      3      4      3      2      1
Width:     276    244    142    203    145     54    301    290    249    276    138    171    181    188    175    175    173    108     81    175    175    105
Strength:  5.00   5.87   4.98   5.11   1.59   1.26   1.24   1.50   1.84   1.76   1.50   2.13   2.43   1.82   1.69   1.30   1.02   1.80   2.40   1.06   1.06   1.71

Start:     8: 8   8:12   8:11   8: 2   8:18   8:12   9: 4   9: 5   9: 5   9: 5   9:11  10:17  10:19  10:20  11:10  11:12  11:16  11:20  11:24  11:24  11:24  11:24
End:       8:12   8:18   9: 2   9: 6   9: 2   9: 1  10:10  10: 9  10:10  10: 5   9:11  11: 1  11: 1  11: 1  11:16  11:16  11:24  11:24  11:24  11:24  12: 5  12: 4
Count:      2      2      6      8      2     11     14     11     10      9      2      3      3      2      6      4      2      2      2      5     12      3
Width:      54    203    145    227    381    331    408    276    381    212     84    325    325     96    100    225    175     94    527    513    119    105
Strength:  1.26   1.59   5.11   2.05   1.18   1.26   1.93   1.29   1.08   1.47   3.21   1.44   1.72   3.04   3.21   3.75   3.21   1.38   1.28   1.42   1.16   1.71

Start:    12: 2  12: 2  12:19  12:19  12:19  12:19  12:23  13: 9  13: 5  13: 9  13:13  13:15  13:13  13:19  13:21  13:21  14: 8  14: 8  14: 8  14:15  14: 7  14:17
End:      12:19  13: 1  13: 7  13: 5  13: 6  12:23  13: 3  13: 3  13: 9  13:13  13:13  13:15  14: 1  13:19  14: 4  14: 4  14: 7  14:15  14:14  15: 7  14:17  14:17
Count:      2      4      5      6      8      3      2      5      5      9      5     96     57     96    145    209    527    527     18     17      7      7
Width:     245    227     76    119    284    212     61    221    111    166    544     73     86    209    145     73    124     83    124    513    215    215
Strength:  1.26   2.05   2.19   2.43   1.00   2.47   1.56   1.67   3.67   2.13   2.15   2.41   1.50   1.14   2.06   1.14   1.28   2.49   1.44   1.42   1.25   1.47

Start:    16:34  16:34  16:36  16:36  16:41  16:43  16:43  16:43  16:43  16:43  16:47  16:47  16:56  16:56  16:56  16:57  16:57  16:57  16:61  16:22  16:24  16:24
End:      16:40  16:40  16:39  16:39  16:56  16:56  16:53  16:51  16:47  16:31  16:51  16:47  17:17  17:17  16:31  17: 4  16:60  16:21  17: 4  16:29  16:29  16:27
Count:      5      4      3      2      9     11      9      7      4     11      2      2     17     15      5      5      2      3      4      3      3      2
Width:     161    152    119     82    367    309    253    191     87    341    88    522    511    337    203    166    146    124    83    124     96     59
Strength:  1.39   1.97   2.13   2.44   1.36   1.79   1.91   2.92   2.66   2.80   2.70   1.52   2.04   3.37   2.28   2.31   2.94   1.28   2.49   1.44   1.44   1.47

Start:    17:10  17:13  17:21  17:21  17:21  17:21  17:21  17:21  17:23  18: 8  18:27  20: 1  20: 5  20:27  20:27  20:30  20:31  18:13  18:17  18:24  18:20  19: 9
End:      17:13  17:21  19: 9  18:24  18:20  18:17  18:13  18:18  18:18  18:18  18:31  20: 5  20: 7  20:30  20:27  20:33  20:33  18:17  18:13  18:24  18:22  18:13
Count:      2      2     32     20     14     11      9      8      3      7      3      5      2      3      5      2      4      7     75     78     48     67
Width:      65     50    879    581    469    426    400    306    151     78     95     81     87    121    122     57    122     75     94     67    167     78
Strength:  1.72   1.09   1.12   1.28   1.90   2.54   3.15   2.83   3.09   2.27   2.44   2.40   1.39   4.10   1.23   1.39   1.23   2.15   2.95   1.81   1.52   1.00

Start:    20:38  20:39  20:43  20:43  20:44  21: 3  21: 3  21:11  21:11  21:11  21:16  21:17  21:17  21:17  21:17  21:24  21:26  21:29  21:30  22:16  22:18  23: 3
End:      20:39  21:26  21:17  20:43  21: 3  21:11  21:11  21:11  21:17  21:16  21:21  21:26  21:25  21:24  21:17  21:34  21:34  21:34  22:18  22:20  22:20  23:14
Count:      2      2     15     10      6      3      2      4      2      5      2      5      3      5      2      3      3     85     72     87    130     77
Width:      50    518    349    225    143    128     99    165    120    157    147    165    85    130     99    165     72     85     72     87    130     61
Strength:  1.09   2.12   1.92   2.01   1.77   2.85   4.39   1.18   2.62   1.48   2.09   2.97   1.11   4.48   3.16   2.02   1.17   1.11   2.02   1.13   1.17   2.23
```

Gaps for be- 4. continued.

STRIP 1

Start:	23:17	23:17	23:21	23:25	23:31	23:31	23:31	23:39	23:39	23:39	23:42	24: 6	24: 7	24:13	24:18	24:18
End:	23:25	23:24	23:24	23:28	24: 1	23:38	23:37	23:47	23:45	23:45	23:45	24:12	24:11	24:16	24:23	24:21
Count:	6	5	4	2	12	6	8	6	4	3	3	4	2	3	2	2
Width:	177	170	149	79	390	146	137	211	157	125	71	122	77	49	91	65
Strength:	1.10	1.58	1.89	2.32	1.65	1.82	2.67	1.74	2.09	2.31	1.98	1.23	2.23	1.05	1.29	1.72

STRIP 2

Start:	24:27	24:27	25: 4	25: 6	25:10	26: 1	26: 1	26: 5	26: 6	26: 6	29:17	29:17	29:20	29:17	29:17
End:	24:27	25: 4	25: 3	26: 1	26: 5	26:12	26:15	26:17	26:15	26: 3	29: 2	29:11	29:15	29:21	29:20
Count:	3	2	3	5	2	6	5	2	3	2	7	4	5	3
Width:	97	80	96	99	57	49	85	82	56	164	104	88
Strength:	1.47	2.36	3.04	1.53	1.39	1.05	1.11	2.44	1.34	1.46	1.68	2.70	1.43

STRIP 3

Start:	32: 4	32:12	32:17	32:32	32:32	33:21	33:22	33:27	33:27	33:30	33:30	33:33	34: 6	34: 4	34:21
End:	32: 7	32:15	32:22	33: 4	33: 3	33:27	33:27	36:23	37:22	34:12	33:31	34: 4	34:12	34:34	34:21
Count:	2	2	3	3	4	22	54	8	5	86	50	79	167	147	1070
Width:	52	57	85	66	89	101	78	1678	2496	605	453	402	348	175	123
Strength:	1.17	1.39	1.11	1.77	1.23	3.25	2.52	3.36	1.20	1.00	2.21	2.91	1.69	1.71	2.25

STRIP 4

Start:	34:21	34:21	34:21	34:21	34:21	34:21	34:25	34:27	34:29	35: 5	35: 5	35:11	35:11	35:13	35:13	36: 6	36: 6
End:	36:23	36:17	36: 5	35:11	35: 5	35: 5	34:24	34:35	35: 5	35:11	36: 5	35:35	36: 4	35:36	36: 3	36:17	36:17
Count:	30	22	18	13	10	9	3	2	2	6	2	5	4	5	3	3
Width:	1053	920	706	668	434	307	303	88	68	209	152	230	208	175	97	210
Strength:	2.91	3.40	3.94	2.74	1.83	1.32	1.70	1.20	1.85	1.71	3.12	3.93	2.85	3.34	3.80	3.08	7.86

STRIP 5

Start:	36:23	36:23	36:23	36:27	36:28	36:28	36:31	36:31	36:33	37:10	37:13	37:13	37:14	37:14	37:14
End:	37: 1	36:26	36:19	37: 1	37: 1	36:30	37: 1	36:38	36:38	37:13	37:22	37: 5	37:19	37:19	37:17
Count:	24	10	25	7	6	4	4	3	7	5	2	5	3	2
Width:	815	322	55	238	226	58	152	129	93	172	218	77	161	147	121	83
Strength:	2.41	1.53	1.30	1.65	2.03	1.43	1.97	2.43	2.91	2.07	1.63	1.94	2.11	1.30	1.39	1.84	2.19	2.49

STRIP 6

Start:	37:22	37:22	37:25	37:25	37:28	37:28	38: 4	38:11	38:19	38:21	38:22	39: 9	39: 9	39:11	39:11	39:15
End:	38:17	38:16	37:28	37:26	38:14	38:10	38:	38:21	39:	38:21	39: 6	39:23	39:21	39:21	39:21	39:21
Count:	20	15	83	50	314	194	140	80	94	62	138	292	246	209	60	128
Width:	593	574	513	314	50	4	2	372	312	230	292	246	209	60	128
Strength:	1.40	1.77	2.06	1.05	1.09	3.70	2.99	2.76	2.36	2.95	1.60	4.81	1.07	1.00	1.53	2.41	3.36	1.51	4.39	1.26

STRIP 7

Start:	39:26	40: 1	40: 1	40: 4	40: 5	40: 5	40: 6	40:22	40:28	40:39	40:43	40:43	40:44	40:49	41:17	41:17
End:	43:22	41:17	40:22	40:22	40:22	40:21	40:21	41:17	40:38	40:42	41: 6	41:	41: 6	41: 6	43:22	41:17
Count:	59	30	24	396	348	328	302	930	314	608	92	507	269	252	133	222	1066	29
Width:	2579	1510	1418	484	348	328	302	930	314	608	92	507	269	252	133	222	1066	681
Strength:	6.87	6.55	7.78	2.45	5.25	6.76	8.39	11.76	9.31	7.97	7.08	2.87	7.36	6.11	4.83	2.41	4.60	3.36	8.37	3.26	3.21

STRIP 8

Start:	41:17	41:17	42:	42:10	42:17	42:19	42:19	43:	43: 8	43: 8	43: 9	43:16	43:17	43:18	43:23	43:23	43:23
End:	42:12	42: 3	42: 3	42:12	43: 7	43: 7	43: 7	43:22	43:22	43:16	43:13	43:16	43:21	43:21	45:17	45:17	45:17
Count:	367	308	210	51	190	168	149	81	375	351	115	169	102	75	1222	1219	1216
Width:	367	308	210	51	190	168	149	81	375	351	115	169	102	75	1222	1219	1216
Strength:	5.76	7.79	7.86	1.13	1.35	2.36	3.03	2.40	1.54	2.42	2.98	2.80	3.62	3.29	2.01	2.15	1.69	1.85	2.02

STRIP 9

Start:	43:23	43:23	44:	44:	44: 3	44: 7	44:10	44:10	44:15	44:17	44:19	44:21	44:24	45: 1	45: 2	45: 3	45: 8	45:22	45:22	46:11
End:	43:23	44:	44: 2	44:27	44:	44:17	44:17	44:14	44:17	44:14	44:17	44:24	44:27	45:17	45:16	45:16	45:16	45:25	45:25	46:12
Count:	19	6	2	2	5	9	3	6	2	3	6	2	4	16	14	3	8	2
Width:	545	193	122	70	274	203	123	106	51	643	362	351	318	291	165	51	53
Strength:	1.19	1.40	2.22	1.94	1.26	1.26	1.59	2.25	3.46	1.13	2.18	2.80	3.80	1.17	1.26	4.40	6.03	7.28	5.96	1.13	1.22

Gaps for be- 4, continued.

Start	End	Count	Width	Strength
46:15	47:22	20	706	2.50
46:15	46:21	5	160	1.37
46:16	46:19	3	95	1.41
46:19	46:21	2	67	1.81
46:22	47:22	14	48	1.00
46:22	47:22	2	539	2.72
46:23	47: 3	3	104	1.68
47: 3	47:22	2	84	2.53
47: 3	47:22	9	418	3.42
47: 3	47:22	8	412	3.94
47: 3	47:22	5	397	5.27
47: 3	47:22	6	389	6.22
47: 4	47:22	4	379	7.52
47: 4	47:22	3	333	8.54
47: 7	47:14	2	202	7.52
47: 7	48:35	12	710	5.76
47:22	48:35	11	704	6.27
47:23	48:21	9	477	4.31
47:23	48:10	3	203	4.64
47:23	48: 8	2	152	5.41

Start	End	Count	Width	Strength
48:11	48:21	6	258	2.64
48:15	48:15	2	68	1.85
48:15	48:18	4	170	2.41
48:18	48:21	2	65	1.72
48:20	48:21	2	62	1.60
48:22	48:35	2	216	8.12

Linguistic Density Plot in Ezekiel 1 - 48

For babel 12 (20 times)

Each Column = 13 Verses.   Separations are: Max = 5685.00, Mean = 1331.90, Min = 22.00 .

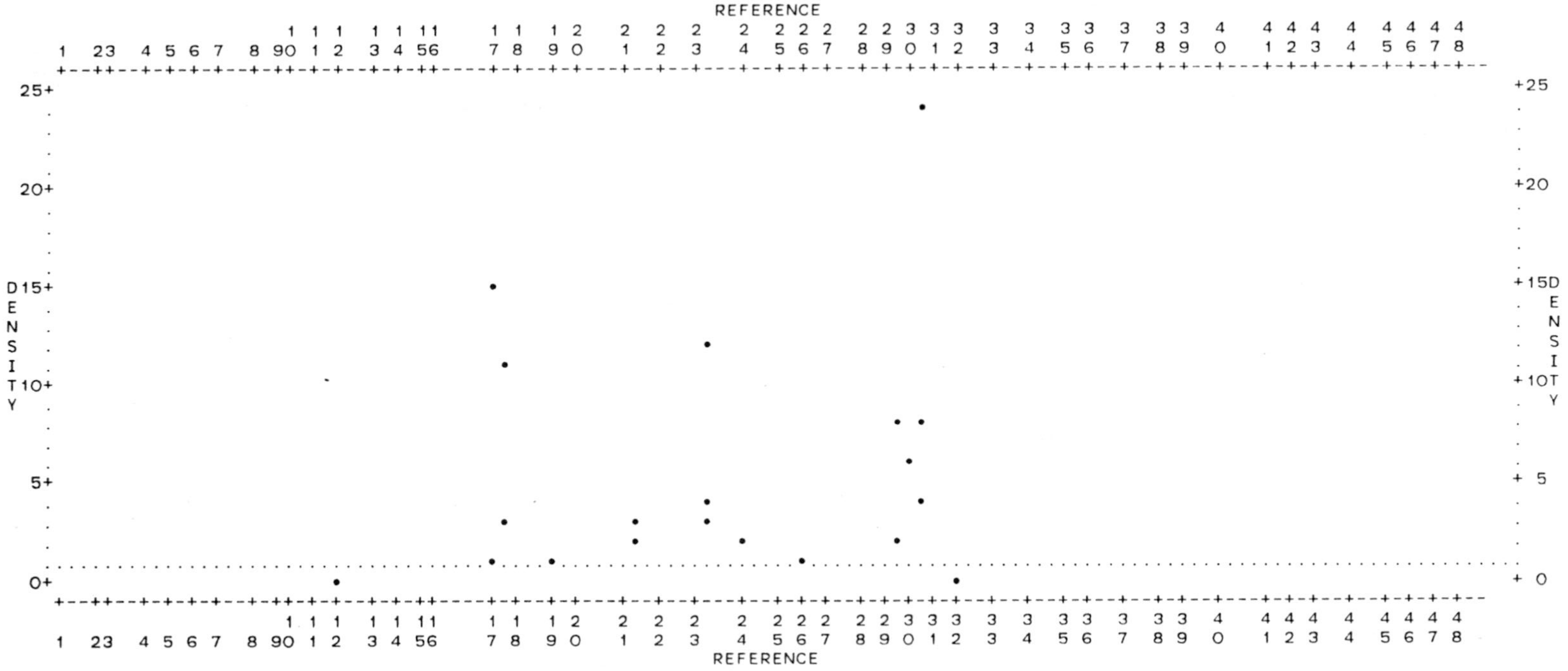

REFERENCE

(scatter density plot with horizontal axis columns labelled 1 through 48 and vertical axis 0+ to 25+, with reference markers +25, +20, +15, +10, +5, 0 and letters D E N S I T Y on the right margin)

REFERENCE

CLUSTERS:

Start:	12:13	12:13	17:12	17:12	17:12	21:24	23:15	23:15	23:15	23:15	29:18	29:18	29:18	30:24	30:25
End:	32:11	21:26	21:26	19: 9	17:20	21:26	26: 7	24: 2	23:23	23:17	32:11	30:10	30:25	29:19	30:25
Count:	20	8	7	5	4	2	12	5	4	3	7	6	3	44	18
Width:	12171	6040	2830	1104	195	17	5014	764	1808	149	1296	588	283	1.49	1.03
Strength:	7.50	1.16	1.91	1.80	1.82	1.03	3.23	1.54	1.50	1.43	2.48	2.39	1.35	1.01	

GAPS:

Start:	1: 1	1: 1	30:25	32:11
End:	17:12	12:13	48:35	48:35
Count:	3	2	3	2
Width:	8346	5136	11370	10662
Strength:	3.24	2.99	4.97	7.34

Linguistic Density Plot in Ezekiel 1 - 48

For beged 111 (14 times)

Each Column = 13 Verses. Separations are: Max = 4933.00, Mean = 1864.67, Min = 12.00 .

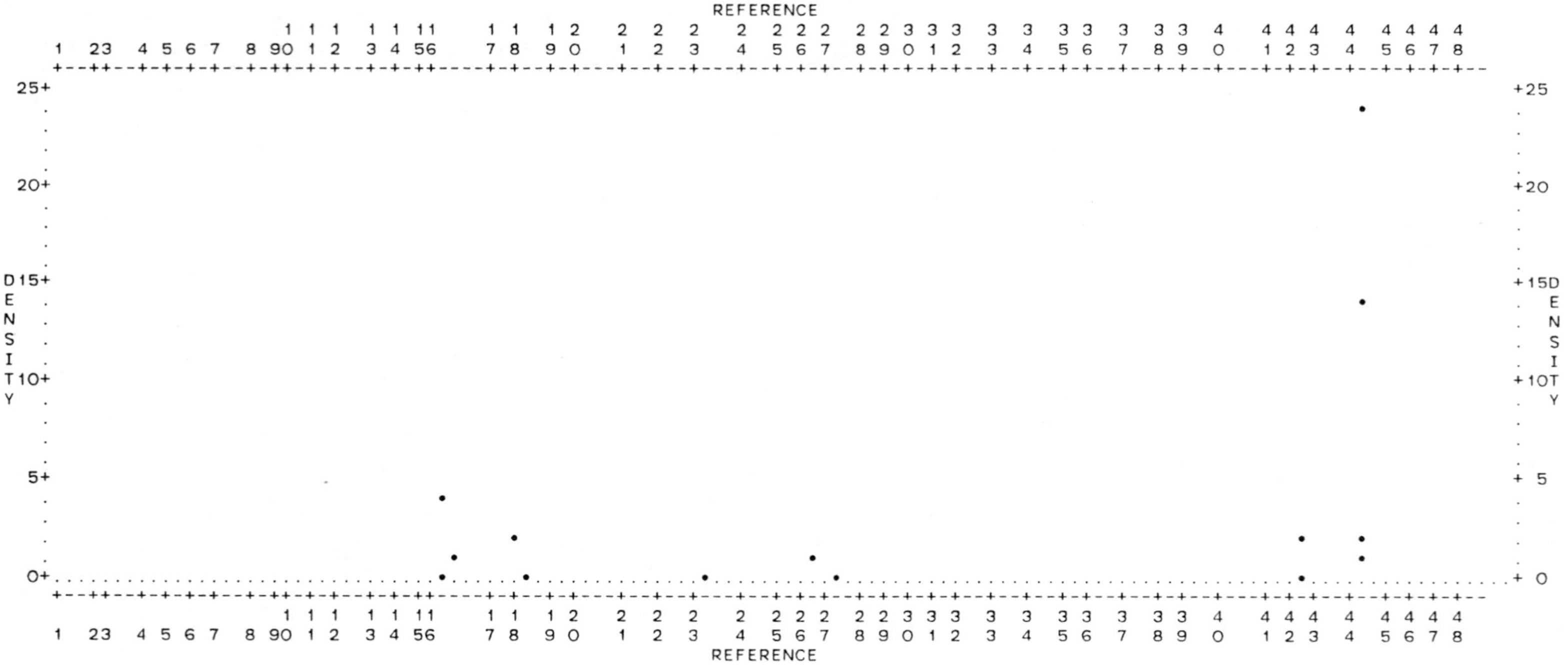

CLUSTERS:

Start:	16:16	16:16	16:16	16:16	16:16	42:14	42:14	44:17	44:19	44:19
End:	44:19	27:20	18:16	16:39	16:18	44:19	42:14	44:19	44:19	44:19
Count:	14	8	5	3	2	6	2	4	3	2
Width:	18378	7745	1909	502	46	1245	10	74	24	8
Strength:	2.46	1.52	1.79	1.35	1.04	2.45	1.06	1.97	1.55	1.06

GAPS:

Start:	1: 1	1: 1	16:18	18:16	27:20
End:	42:14	16:16	42:14	42:14	42:14
Count:	10	2	8	5	2
Width:	24172	7039	17087	15224	9388
Strength:	2.15	2.96	1.15	2.51	4.31

Linguistic Density Plot in Ezekiel 1 - 48

For bad 111 (10 times)

Each Column = 13 Verses.   Separations are: Max = 9881.50, Mean = 2542.73, Min =   66.50 .

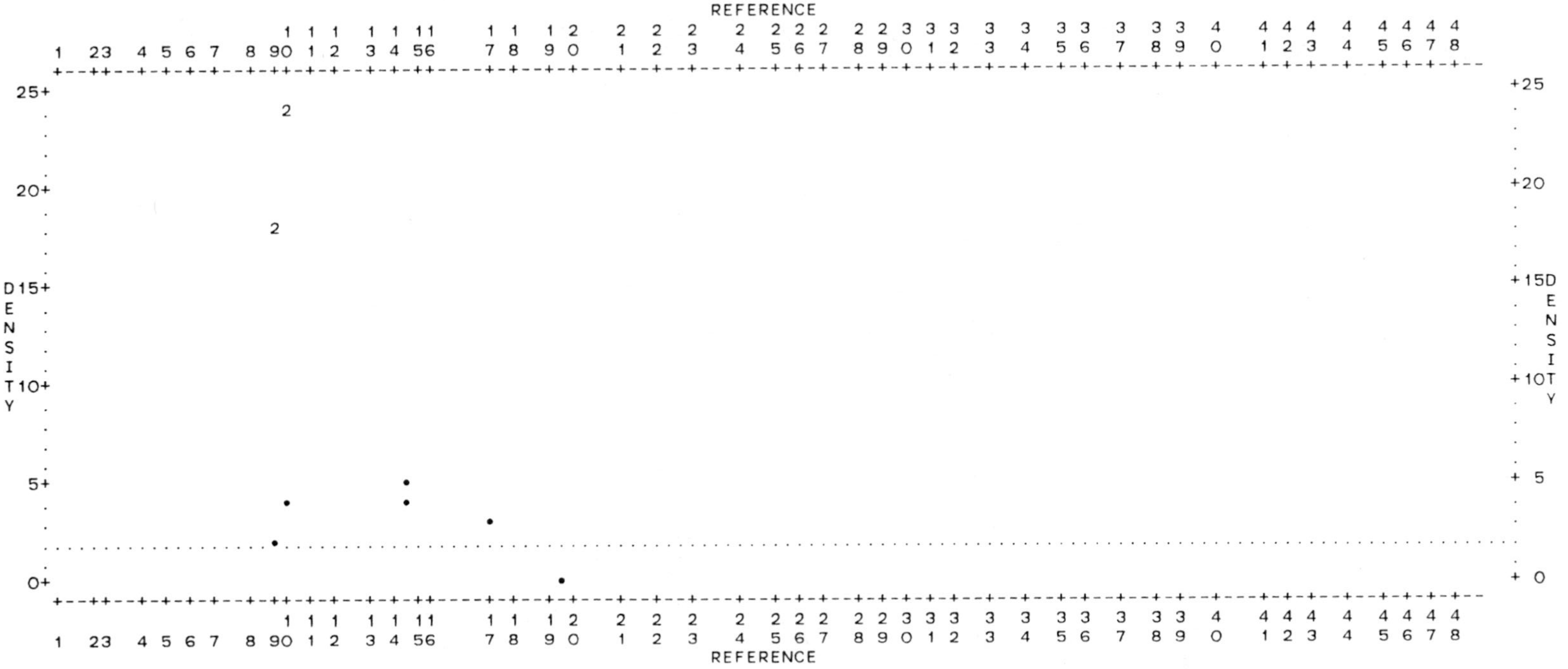

REFERENCE

REFERENCE

CLUSTERS:

Start:	9: 2	9: 2	9: 2	9: 2	9:11	9:11	10: 6	14:16
End:	19:14	14:18	10: 7	9: 3	10: 7	10: 2	10: 7	14:18
Count:	10	8	6	2	4	2	2	48
Width:	5897	2759	405	34	174	40	41	48
Strength:	5.45	3.87	3.06	1.08	2.07	1.08	1.07	1.07

GAPS:

Start:	10: 2	10: 7	14:18	19:14
End:	48:35	48:35	48:35	19:14
Count:	8	6	4	2
Width:	24051	23917	21563	18425
Strength:	1.60	2.78	3.87	6.84

Linguistic Density Plot in Ezekiel 1 - 48

For bēhēmā 114 (12 times)

Each Column = 13 Verses.   Separations are: Max = 5832.00, Mean = 2151.54, Min = 52.00 .

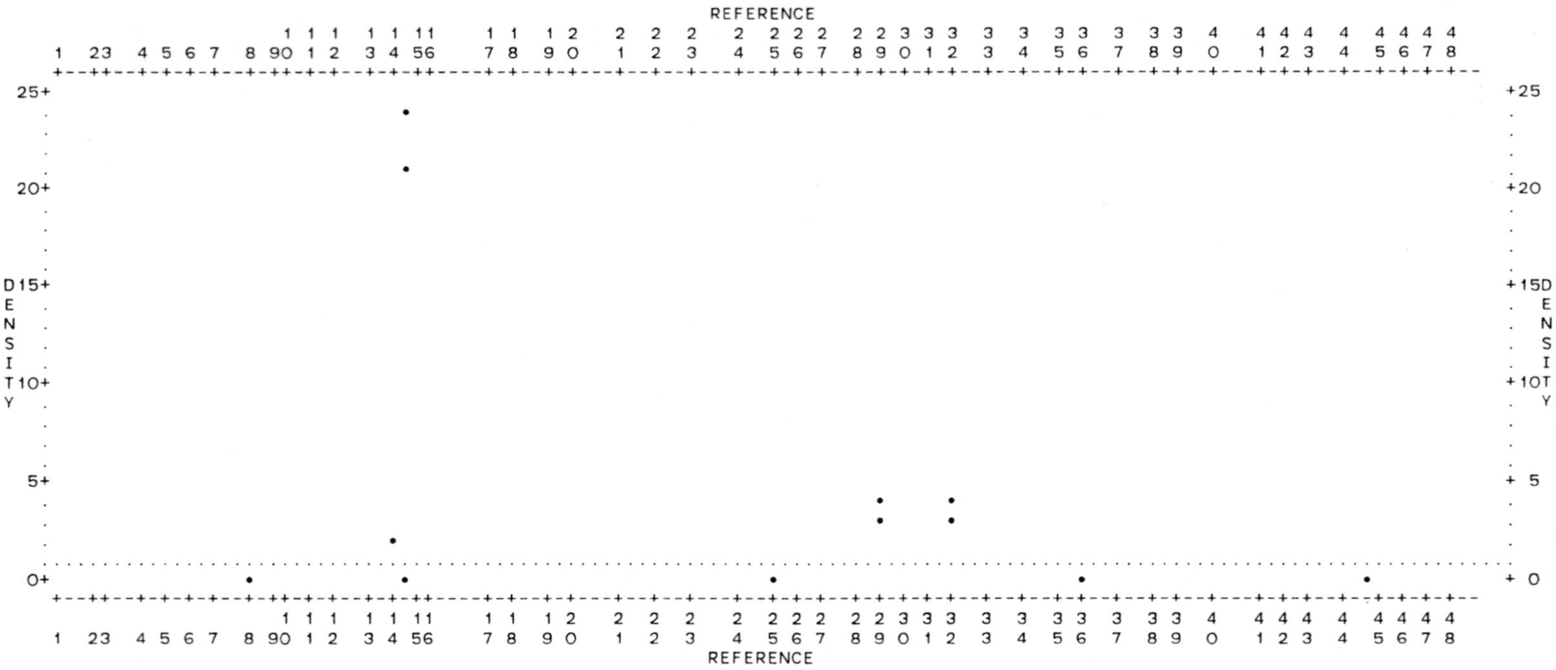

CLUSTERS:

Start:	8:10	14:13	14:17	14:17	25:13	29: 8	29: 8	32:13
End:	14:21	14:21	14:21	14:19	32:13	32:13	29:11	32:13
Count:	5	4	3	2	5	4	2	2
Width:	3113	189	104	46	3485	1539	56	15
Strength:	1.59	1.98	1.55	1.05	1.48	1.56	1.05	1.07

GAPS:

Start:	14:21	14:21	32:13	32:13	36:11
End:	29: 8	25:13	48:35	44:31	44:31
Count:	3	2	4	3	2
Width:	9322	7376	10620	8302	5832
Strength:	1.86	2.62	1.32	1.48	1.84

Linguistic Density Plot in Ezekiel 1 - 48

```
For  bw' 311 (47 times)     bw' 312 (37 times)    bw' 313 (8 times)    bw' 314 (11 times)
     bw' 3162 (25 times)    bw' 361 (16 times)    bw' 362 (30 times)   bw' 364 (5 times)
     bw' 3662 (5 times)     bw' 371 (1 times)     bw' 374 (2 times)

Each Column = 13 Verses.  Separations are:  Max =  612.00, Mean =  148.78, Min =    1.50 .
```

Linguistic Density Plot (REFERENCE axis, density values along vertical scale: 0+, 5+, T10+, D15+, 20+, 25+)

CLUSTERS:

```
Start:       1: 4   5:17   7: 2   7: 5   7: 6   7:22   7:22   7:22   8: 3   8: 7   8:14  10: 2  17: 3  17:12  19: 4  19: 4
End:        47:15   7:12   7:12   7: 7   7: 7  10: 9   8:10   7:26   8:10  10: 6  10: 6  10: 6  17:20  17:13  20: 3  19: 9
Count:        187     11      9      6      3     24     16      8      4      8      8      4      6      3      5      3
Width:      27048    533    180     16   2550    974    315    140     47    562    104     36    402     31    254     86
Strength:    2.98   2.09   2.45   2.22   1.38   2.28   1.88   1.19   1.19   1.24   1.34   1.25   1.04   1.27   1.16   1.01

Start:      20:28  20:28  20:35  20:42  21:12  21:30  23:17  23:39  23:39  23:42  23:44  33:21  33:21  33:30  36: 8  36: 8
End:        22: 4  20:42  20:38  22: 4  22: 4  21:12  23:44  23:40  23:44  23:44  34:13  33: 4  33:22  33:33  41: 6  39:17
Count:         15      6      4      3      9      5     10      7      3      4      6      5      3      4      8      8
Width:       1261    384    186     66    586    224    607    113     34     37     46     92    598    300   7329   3714
Strength:    1.53   1.09   1.01   1.10   1.47   1.26   1.68   1.26   1.38   1.60   1.26   1.71   1.14   1.65   2.85   1.71

Start:      36:36  39:17
End:        41:15  39:17
Count:         35     22
Width:       2245
Strength:    1.37
```

```
Start:    36: 8  36:20  37: 5  37: 9  38: 8  38: 8  38:15  40: 1  40: 1  40: 1  40:48  42: 1  42: 1  42: 1  43: 2  44: 2
End:      36:24  36:22  37:12  37:12  39:17  38:13  38:18  41: 6  40:40  41: 6  47:15  44:27  43: 5  44:27  44: 5  44: 9
Count:    6      5      4      4      8      11     8      4      5      3      34     19     8      4      11     6
Width:    332    118    182    83     779    139    284    347    130    172    3204   1652   450    65     632    200
Strength: 1.25   1.62   1.03   1.02   1.55   1.20   1.96   1.21   1.58   1.07   2.20   1.71   1.53   1.49   1.87   1.65

Start:    44: 2  44:16  46: 2  46: 2  46: 8  46: 8  46: 9  47: 8  47: 8
End:      44: 4  44:27  47:15  46:10  46:10  46: 4  46:10  47:15  47: 9
Count:    4      5      15     10     9      4      4      5      3
Width:    37     244    875    407    183    60     21     38     20
Strength: 1.60   1.19   2.26   2.14   2.45   2.54   1.66   1.59   1.32
```

GAPS:

```
Start:    1: 1  1: 1  1: 1  1: 4  1: 4  4: 1  3:24  3:24  6: 3  6: 3  10: 6  11:18  12:16  12:16  14: 1  14:22  14:22  14:22
End:      7: 6  7: 5  3:24  3:24  3:11  3: 4  5:17  7: 5  7: 2  7: 7  11: 1  14:22  14: 1  13: 2  19: 9  17:12  17: 3  16: 7
Count:    14    13    7     6     3     3     2     6     2     7     3      10     3      13     8      6      2      2
Width:    2714  2712  1348  971   829   546   521   1346  301   326   1813   1310   759    393    2922   1820   1613   318
Strength: 1.50  1.86  1.27  2.05  2.54  2.68  2.51  1.83  1.02  1.19  1.09   1.16   2.20   1.64   2.28   2.01   2.65   1.14

Start:    16: 8  16:16  16:33  17:12  17:13  17:13  17:20  20:15  22: 4  22: 4  23:24  23:24  23:44  23:44  23:44  23:44  24:26
End:      17: 3  17: 3  17: 3  19: 2  19: 1  19: 3  19: 3  20:28  23:39  23:17  23:39  23:17  33:33  33: 3  33: 6  30: 9  24:14  24:26
Count:    4      3      2      5      3      3      2      2      5      3      2      19     26     17     12     9      2      8
Width:    1253   1085   750    1088   1071   990    826    306    1301   929    807    336    5641   5359   4963   5636   4907   3359
Strength: 3.16   3.77   4.05   1.67   2.44   3.31   4.57   1.05   2.40   3.02   4.44   1.26   2.52   3.48   3.81   2.77   4.44   3.60

Start:    24:26  26: 7  26:10  26:10  28: 7  28: 7  30:11  30:11  32:11  33: 6  33:33  33:33  34:13  36:24  37:12  37:21  39: 8  41: 6
End:      26: 7  30: 9  30: 4  27:26  29: 4  29: 8  30: 4  32: 9  33: 2  33:21  36:20  36: 8  36: 8  37: 5  38: 8  39:17  40: 1  42: 9
Count:    2      6      9      4      3      2      5      9      2      2      2      9      8      5      8      5      1      3
Width:    542    2105   1984   704    974    615    1524   951    494    365    1438   926    378    574    351    528    312    551
Strength: 2.65   4.15   4.72   3.74   3.23   3.14   3.16   5.41   2.32   1.45   4.12   5.24   1.54   1.32   1.36   1.10   1.09   1.21

Start:    41: 6  42: 1  44:27  44:27  46:10  46: 2  47: 9
End:      43: 5  44: 2  46: 2  46: 2  48:35  48:35  47:15
Count:    2      2      3      8      2      3      2
Width:    411    570    800    677    1005   1549   857
Strength: 1.76   2.84   2.40   3.56   1.31   3.38   4.78
```

Linguistic Density Plot in Ezekiel 1 - 48

For bw' 311 (47 times)   bw' 312 (37 times)   bw' 313 (8 times)   bw' 314 (11 times)
     bw' 3162 (25 times)

Each Column = 13 Verses.   Separations are: Max = 1302.00, Mean = 216.82, Min = 1.50 .

REFERENCE

REFERENCE

CLUSTERS:

Start:	1: 4	1: 4	7: 2	7: 2	7: 2	7: 2	7: 5	7: 2	7: 6	7: 6	7: 7	7: 6	8: 9	9 10:	10:	2 10:	2 10:	2 21:12	21:12	21:30
End:	47:15	13: 9	13: 9	10: 6	7:26	7:12	7: 7	7:12	7: 7	7: 7	7: 7	7:26	10: 6	10: 6	10: 6	22: 4	21:25	22: 4	21:30	21:34
Count:	128	32	24	20	12	9	7	6	3	1	3	4	8	9	4	5	3	4	5	3
Width:	27048	5537	2956	1380	451	180	83	16	45	670	104	36	586	241	224	94				
Strength:	1.60	1.12	2.16	3.15	2.82	2.62	2.35	2.25	1.28	1.00	1.40	1.00	1.52	1.47	1.31	1.94	1.10	1.11		

Start:	23:17	23:17	23:39	23:39	24:14	30: 4	32:11	33: 3	33:21	36:20	36:22	38:18	41: 3	41: 3	41: 3	42: 3
End:	26:10	23:44	23:44	23:44	24:26	47:15	33:33	33:33	33:22	36:22	38:11	43:11	44:27	43: 4	43: 4	43: 4
Count:	13	8	6	3	4	61	12	7	6	5	3	17	31	8	6	6
Width:	1861	607	113	34	266	10954	1251	300	28	76	70	284	3680	2128	912	296
Strength:	1.03	1.63	2.04	1.31	1.03	1.67	1.65	1.93	1.33	1.55	1.56	1.68	2.72	1.65	1.08	1.66

```
Clusters for bw' 311, bw' 312, bw' 313, bw' 314, bw' 3162, continued.

Start:    42: 9  43: 2  44: 2  44: 2  44:16  44:21  46: 2  46: 2  46: 8  46: 9  47: 8  47: 8  47: 9
End:      42:14  43: 4  44:27  44: 9  44:27  44:27  46:10  46:10  46:10  46: 9  47:15  47: 9  47: 9
Count:        3      3      9      4      5      3     14      8      4      4      5      3
Width:      110     51    632    200    244    120    875    183     21     28    186     38     20
Strength:  1.06   1.26   1.86   1.21   1.46   1.03   2.63   2.62   1.70   1.68   1.60   1.65   1.36

GAPS:

Start:     1: 4   3:24   4:14   7: 7   7:26   8:10  10: 3  10: 3  11:16  11:18  11:18  11:18  11:18  11:18  14: 7  16: 8
End:       3: 4   7: 2   7: 2  33:33  23:44  23:40  23:40  21:12  11:16  21:12  16: 7  14: 1  16: 7  12:16  21:12
Count:        3      4      3     67     41     39     32     20     17      2      7      4      3      2     10
Width:      829    546   1346    874  15834   9815   9735   9465   8874   6963    646   6215   2137   1262    896    503    796    702   4036
Strength:  1.30   1.52   1.87   2.78   3.05   1.24   1.00   1.33   1.50   2.05   3.27   1.99   3.39   1.61   1.65   1.52   1.32   1.19   2.25   3.33

Start:    16: 8  16:16  16:16  16:33  17:12  20: 3  20: 3  22: 4  23:44  23:44  23:44  23:44  24:26  24:26  26:10  30: 9  30: 9  33:33
End:      20: 1  20: 1  17: 3  17: 3  20: 1  21:12  20:29  23:39  23:17  33:33  33:22  33: 6  33: 3  30: 4  30: 3  32:11  36:20
Count:        6      5      3      2      2      4      2     19     15     12     10      6      3      2      3      2      3
Width:     2692   2524   1085    750   1232   1301    682    807   5641   5636   5359   4963   4907   4273   2604   1984   1548   1029   1438
Strength:  3.39   3.89   2.14   2.47   4.71   1.75   2.15   2.74   1.74   2.03   3.04   3.76   4.72   6.73   7.15   8.21   3.67   3.77   3.31

Start:    33:33  36:22  37:10  38:15  38:18  39:17  40: 6  41: 6  43: 4  44:27  46:10  47: 9  47:15
End:      36: 8  37: 9  38: 8  42:12  41: 3  41: 3  41: 3  42: 9  44: 2  46: 2  47: 8  48:35  48:35
Count:        2      2      9      6      5      3      2      2      3      2      2      3
Width:     1224    525    641   2679   1994   1404    962    551    584    800    677    506    857
Strength:  4.67   1.43   1.96   1.59   1.92   2.42   3.20   3.46   1.55   1.70   1.20   2.13   1.34   1.88   2.97
```

Linguistic Density Plot in Ezekiel 1 - 48

For bw' 311 (47 times)

Each Column = 13 Verses.   Separations are: Max = 1707.00, Mean =   582.71, Min =   1.50 .

Density density plot grid. Left (vertical) axis marked: 25+, 20+, D15+ / E / N / S / I / T10+ / Y, 5+, 0+ (spelling DENSITY). Column headers across top and bottom run as verse-column indices 1–48. Two REFERENCE baselines are shown.

CLUSTERS:

Start:	1: 4	1: 4	4:14	7: 2	7: 2	7: 2	7:25	7: 5	7: 2	7: 6	6: 7	7: 6	7: 6	21:30	36:20	46: 2
End:	24:14	7:25	7:25	7:12	7:12	7: 7	11:18	14: 7	11:16	21:12	7: 7	7: 7	24:14	22: 4	36:22	47: 9
Count:	30	13	12	11	9	7	6	3	6	5	7	7	9	5	3	4
Width:	13224	3023	1316	442	180	83	16	1584	2576	4780	1997	586	2368	224	66	717
Strength:	1.88	2.29	3.03	3.31	3.00	2.58	2.37	1.75	1.76	2.21	2.47	1.57	1.53	1.17	1.37	1.06

GAPS:

Start:	1: 4	7: 2	1: 4	7: 7	7: 7	7:12	7:25	11:18	14: 7	17:12	20: 1	21:12	21:12	23:44	24:14	30: 9	33:33
End:	7: 2	4:14	7: 7	48:35	21:12	11:16	21:12	21:12	21:12	21:12	48:35	36:20	30: 4	36:20	30: 4	36:20	36:20
Count:	3	2	3	41	40	12	8	5	24	13	26	7	2	3	2	4	2
Width:	2581	1707	25247	25241	8095	6215	4780	15987	9062	17030	7081	3238	2870	3722	1980	1442	
Strength:	1.77	1.96	1.30	1.61	1.00	1.51	2.21	1.29	1.19	1.23	2.71	2.59	2.04	4.00	2.44	2.04	1.50

```
Gaps for bw' 311, continued.

Start:      36:22  36:22  36:22  39:  8  39:  8  44:  2
End:        47:  8  43:  2  38:15  43:  2  41:  3  46:  2
Count:          10      5      2      3      2      2
Width:        6859   4226   1371   2481   1620   1302
Strength:     1.03   1.71   1.38   1.64   1.81   1.25
```

For bw' 312 (37 times)

Linguistic Density Plot in Ezekiel 1 - 48

Each Column = 13 Verses. Separations are: Max = 2714.50, Mean = 736.05, Min = 37.50

Linguistic Density Plot for bw' 312 (37 times) in Ezekiel 1 – 48. DENSITY (vertical axis) against REFERENCE (horizontal axis).

CLUSTERS:

Start:	2: 2	7:26	9: 2	23:17	32:11	38: 8	44: 2	44: 2	46: 8
End:	10: 6	10: 6	24:26	47: 9	38:11	47: 9	44:16	44:25	47: 9
Count:	8	5	3	19	9	9	4	4	5
Width:	3415	929	370	1241	9656	75	2036	593	388	599
Strength:	1.00	1.46	1.10	1.23	1.60	1.39	2.10	1.71	1.50	1.33

GAPS:

Start:	1: 1	1:: 1	3:24	10: 1	16: 8	16: 8	16: 8	23:44	24:26	33:31	38: 9	38:11	40: 6
End:	44: 2	38: 8	7:26	13: 9	38: 8	33: 4	23:39	20:38	33: 4	32:11	36:20	44: 2	44: 2
Count:	30	26	2	14	9	3	4	5	3	2	4	3	2
Width:	24928	21249	1748	1576	10964	14365	5923	5429	3625	4937	3754	1503	3646	2458
Strength:	1.88	1.33	1.41	1.17	2.77	2.25	3.07	3.95	4.02	2.82	1.44	1.06	1.19	2.13	2.40

Linguistic Density Plot in Ezekiel 1 - 48

For bw' 313 (8 times)

Each Column = 13 Verses.   Separations are: Max = 8335.50, Mean = 3107.78, Min = 236.50 .

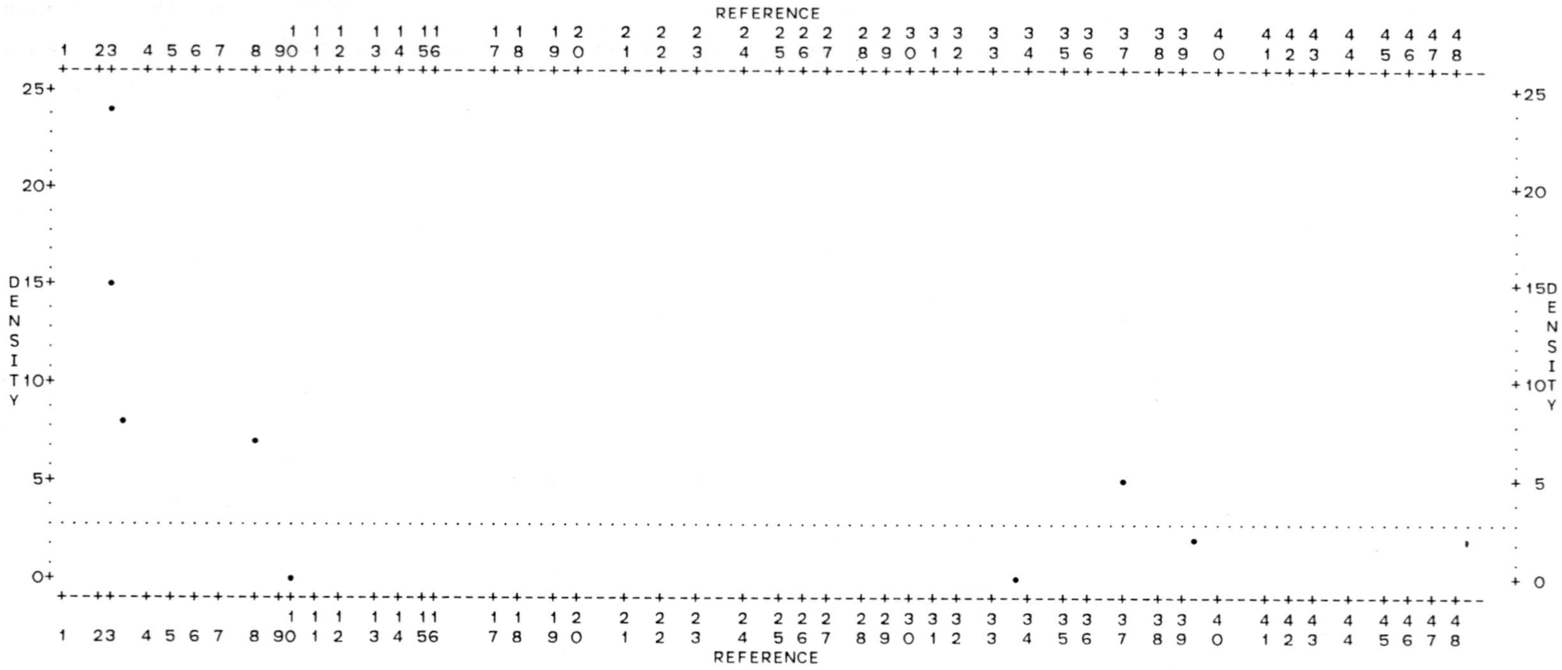

CLUSTERS:

Start:	3: 4	3: 4	3: 4
End:	10: 2	3:24	3:11
Count:	5	3	2
Width:	3028	473	142
Strength:	2.13	1.56	1.06

GAPS:

Start:	3:11	3:24	10: 2	10: 2	39:17
End:	48:35	48:35	48:35	33:30	48:35
Count:	8	7	5	3	2
Width:	26934	26603	24048	16671	14562	5941
Strength:	1.40	1.90	2.64	2.84	4.12	1.01

Linguistic Density Plot in Ezekiel 1 - 48

For bw' 314 (11 times)

Each Column = 13 Verses.   Separations are: Max = 3763.00, Mean = 2330.83, Min = 794.00 .

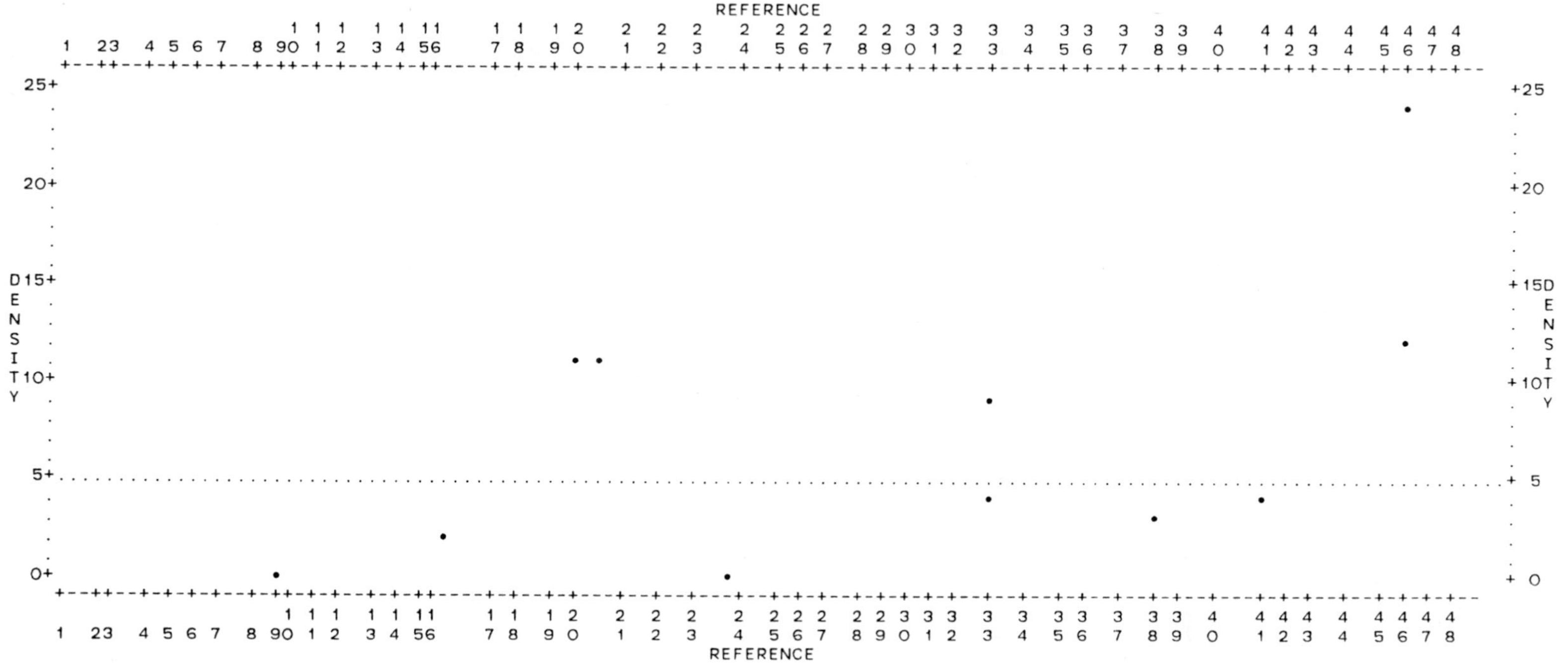

CLUSTERS:

```
Start:     33: 3  46: 9
End:       33: 6  46: 9
Count:         2      2
Width:        56     11
Strength:   1.06   1.08
```

GAPS:

```
Start:      1: 1  23:40
End:       46: 9  33: 3
Count:        11      3
Width:     26381   4996
Strength:   1.06   1.24
```

Linguistic Density Plot in Ezekiel 1 - 48

For bw' 3162 (25 times)

Each Column = 13 Verses.   Separations are: Max = 3694.00, Mean = 1075.77, Min = 29.00

REFERENCE (axis)

DENSITY (axis)

CLUSTERS:

Start:	10: 3	21:24	21:24	33:22	33:22	33:22	42: 9	42: 9	44:17	46: 8	46: 8
End:	47:15	26:10	22: 3	21:25	47:15	36: 8	33:33	47:15	44:27	43: 3	42:14	44:27	47:15	46:10	46: 9
Count:	25	7	4	2	16	4	3	11	7	4	3	2
Width:	23155	3034	337	8833	1504	277	3064	1512	273	110	223	752	58	13
Strength:	1.85	1.50	1.68	2.74	1.00	1.30	2.93	2.17	1.34	1.42	1.71	1.43	1.45	1.02

GAPS:

Start:	1: 1	1: 1	1: 1	16:33	22: 3	24:24	26:10	33:33	36: 8	38:18
End:	33:22	21:24	10: 3	21:24	33:22	33:22	42: 9	42: 9	42: 9
Count:	11	4	2	5	3	2	4	3	2
Width:	18279	11140	3957	3753	6802	4769	4105	5492	4265	2515
Strength:	2.87	4.60	2.78	2.58	1.28	1.82	2.92	1.31	1.47	1.38

Linguistic Density Plot in Ezekiel 1 - 48

For bw' 361 (16 times)   bw' 362 (30 times)   bw' 3662 (5 times)
     bw' 371 (1 times)   bw' 364 (5 times)
                                 bw' 374 (2 times)

Each Column = 13 Verses.   Separations are: Max = 1586.00, Mean = 466.17, Min = 14.00

CLUSTERS:

Start:	5:17	5:17	5:17	7:24	14:17	14:22	17: 4	17:12	19: 4	19: 4	19: 9	20:28	20:35	32: 9	36:24	38:16	40: 1
End:	46:19	17:20	12:13	8:16	14:22	14:22	17:20	17:20	19:15	19: 9	19: 9	20:42	20:42	46:19	39: 2	39: 3	46:19
Count:	59	18	11	7	3	3	9	5	3	2	4	9	25	7	3	2	15
Width:	24352	6247	2841	1206	428	249	157	181	388	574	86	384	1264	9390	186	233	4304
Strength:	4.17	1.03	1.36	1.48	1.60	1.06	1.20	1.16	1.29	1.44	1.31	1.00	1.29	2.02	1.16	1.11	1.08	1.46

Start:	40: 1	40: 1	40: 1	40: 1	40:28	40:28
End:	44: 7	41: 1	40:17	40: 4	40: 3	41: 1	40:35
Count:	14	10	5	4	3	5	3
Width:	2718	1043	347	86	28	464	143
Strength:	2.26	2.46	1.69	1.68	1.40	1.56	1.22

Data for bw' 361, bw' 362, bw' 364, bw' 3662, bw' 371, bw' 374, continued.

GAPS:

Start:	1: 1	12:13	14:22	14:22	20:37	20:37	20:42	20:42	20:42	20:42	23:42	23:42	28: 7	28: 7	30:11	30:11	33: 2	34:13	41: 1	44: 7
End:	5:17	14:17	17:12	17: 4	40: 1	38:16	38:16	37: 5	27:26	23:22	27:26	26: 7	37: 5	36:24	36:24	32: 9	36:24	36:24	48:35	48:35
Count:	2	2	3	2	20	17	16	13	5	2	3	2	8	7	5	2	3	2	7	3
Width:	2292	1234	1834	1627	11858	10994	10847	9864	4249	1806	1995	1213	5309	4931	3812	951	2313	1258	4586	2911
Strength:	3.98	1.67	1.40	2.53	1.80	2.23	2.48	2.98	2.66	2.92	1.65	1.62	1.77	1.98	2.17	1.05	2.14	1.72	1.66	3.07

Linguistic Density Plot in Ezekiel 1 - 48

For bw' 361 (16 times)

Each Column = 13 Verses.   Separations are: Max = 3211.00, Mean = 1645.29, Min =   391.50 .

```
                                    REFERENCE

25+
 .
 .
20+
 .
 .
D15+
E .
N .
S .
I .
T10+
Y .
 .
5+
 .
 .
0+

                                    REFERENCE
```

CLUSTERS:

Start:	7:24	14:22	20:35	34:13	36:24	38:16
End:	40: 2	14:22	20:37	40: 2	37:21	40: 2
Count:	16	2	7	4	3	2
Width:	19277	6	39	3490	2041	783	871
Strength:	2.54	1.05	1.03	2.02	1.15	1.18	1.13

GAPS:

Start:	20:37	20:37	23:22	27:26	39: 2	40: 2
End:	36:24	34:13	34:13	34:13	48:35	48:35
Count:	5	4	3	2	3	2
Width:	9633	8375	6422	3979	6260	5622
Strength:	1.09	1.36	1.47	1.50	1.39	2.56

For bw' 362 (30 times)

Linguistic Density Plot in Ezekiel 1 - 48

Each Column = 13 Verses. Separations are: Max = 6047.50, Mean = 902.26, Min = 43.00 .

```
CLUSTERS:

Start:     5:17   5:17   5:17   8: 3  11: 1  14:17  17:12  19: 4  19: 4  40: 1  40: 1  40: 1  40:28
End:      46:19  20:28  11:24   8:16  11:24  20:28  17:13  17:13  20:28  19:19  46:19  44: 3  41: 1  40:35
Count:       30     17      8      4      9      3      5      3      2     12     11      8      5      3
Width:    24352   7953   2546   1206    272   3878    487    224    880     86   4304   2625   1043    347    464    143
Strength:  1.49   2.62   1.82   1.44   1.66   1.54   1.08   1.30   1.01   1.64   1.41   1.02   2.37   2.76   2.55   1.19   1.89   1.36

GAPS:

Start:     1: 1   1: 1  11:24  14:17  19: 9  19: 9  20:10  20:28  20:28
End:       8: 3   5:17  17: 4  17:17  40: 1  40: 1  40: 1  33: 2  20:28
Count:        3      2      3      2      5     17      4      3      2
Width:     3226   2292   3313   1784  18518  12889  12528  12095   7557
Strength:  1.16   1.59   1.24   1.00   1.65   5.59   6.71   8.47   7.61
```

Linguistic Density Plot in Ezekiel 1 - 48

For bw' 364 (5 times)

Each Column = 13 Verses. Separations are: Max = 11752.00, Mean = 4661.66, Min = 851.50 .

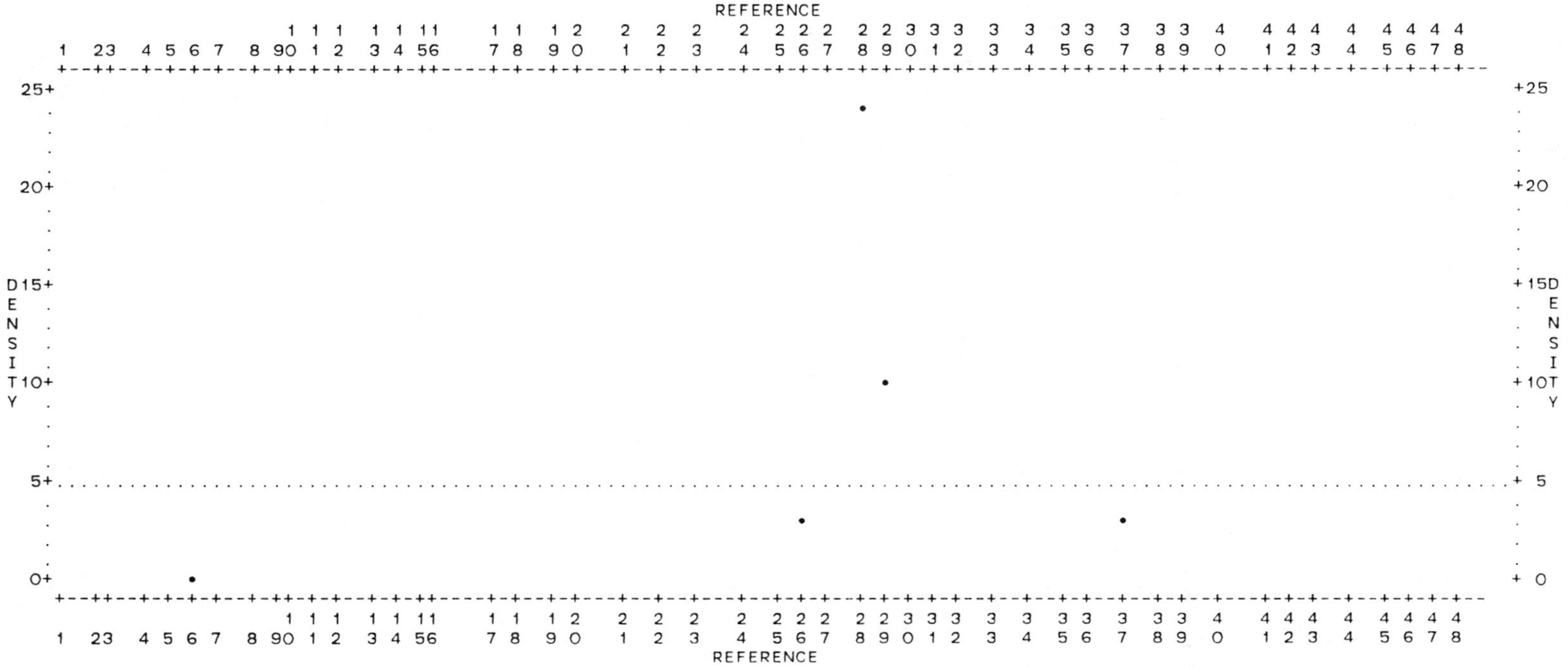

CLUSTERS:

Start:	26: 7	26: 7	28: 7
End:	37: 5	29: 8	29: 8
Count:	4	3	2
Width:	6397	1703	615
Strength:	1.43	1.52	1.02

GAPS:

Start:	6: 3
End:	26: 7
Count:	2
Width:	11752
Strength:	1.79

Linguistic Density Plot in Ezekiel 1 - 48

For bw' 3662 (5 times)

Each Column = 13 Verses.   Separations are: Max = 5446.00, Mean = 4661.66, Min = 3537.00 .

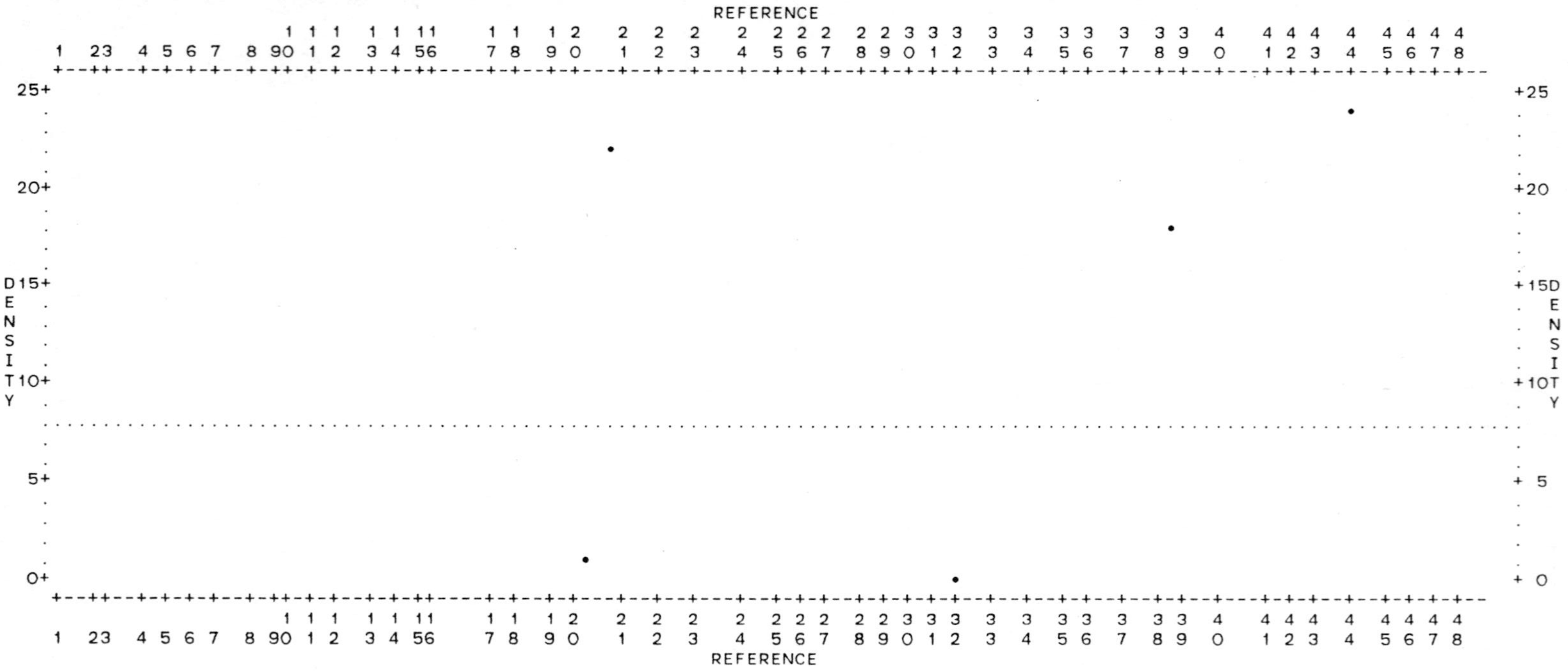

CLUSTERS:

Start: 20:15
End: 20:42
Count: 2
Width: 690
Strength: 1.00

GAPS:

Start: 1: 1
End: 20:15
Count: 2
Width: 9939
Strength: 1.33

Linguistic Density Plot in Ezekiel 1 - 48

For bôr 111 (10 times)

Each Column = 13 Verses. Separations are: Max = 7210.50, Mean = 2542.73, Min = 44.00 .

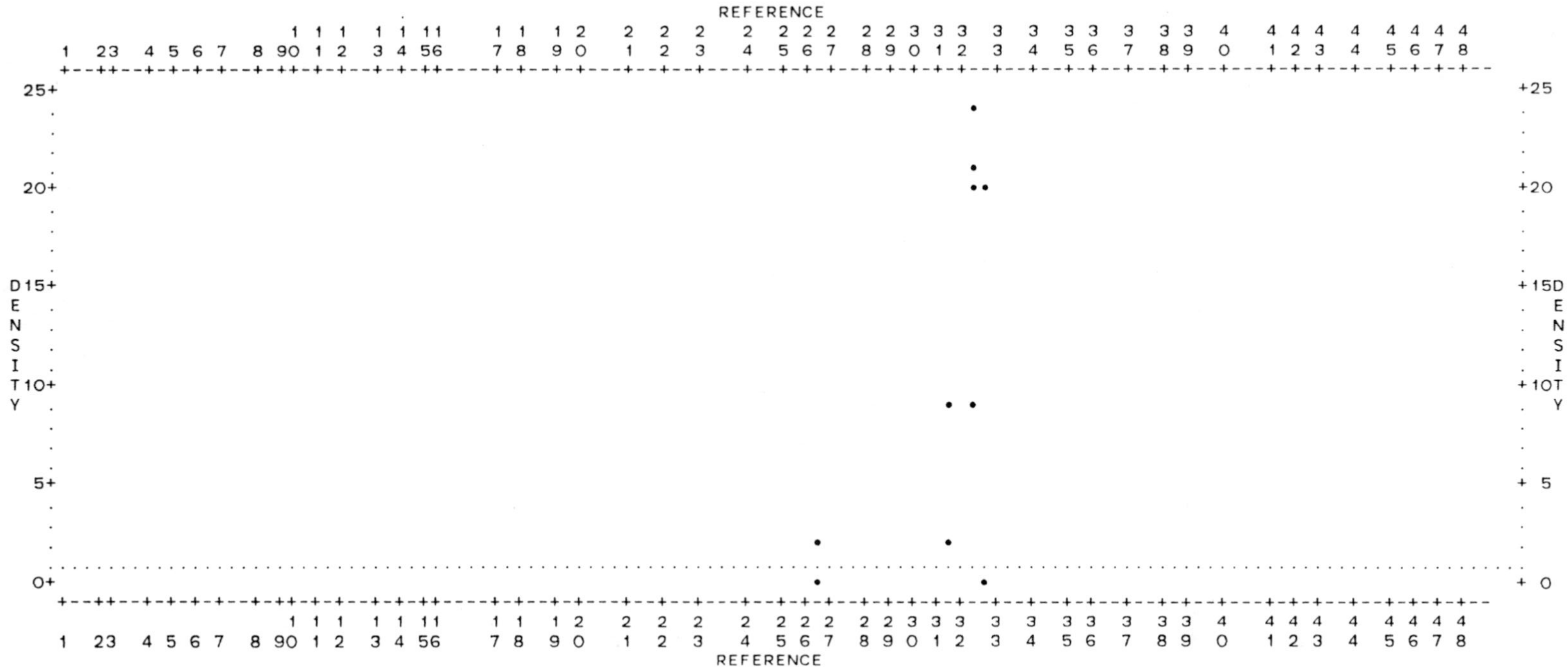

REFERENCE

CLUSTERS:

Start:	26:20	26:20	31:14	31:14	32:18	32:18	32:24	32:29
End:	32:30	26:20	31:16	32:30	32:25	32:23	32:25	32:30
Count:	10	2	8	2	6	4	2	2
Width:	3330	16	782	51	279	149	34	32
Strength:	6.27	1.08	4.38	1.07	3.09	2.07	1.06	1.08

GAPS:

Start:	1: 1	32:30
End:	26:20	48:35
Count:	2	2
Width:	14404	10235
Strength:	5.10	3.31

Linguistic Density Plot in Ezekiel 1 - 48

For baz 111 (12 times)

Each Column = 13 Verses. Separations are: Max = 9938.00, Mean = 2151.54, Min = 236.00 .

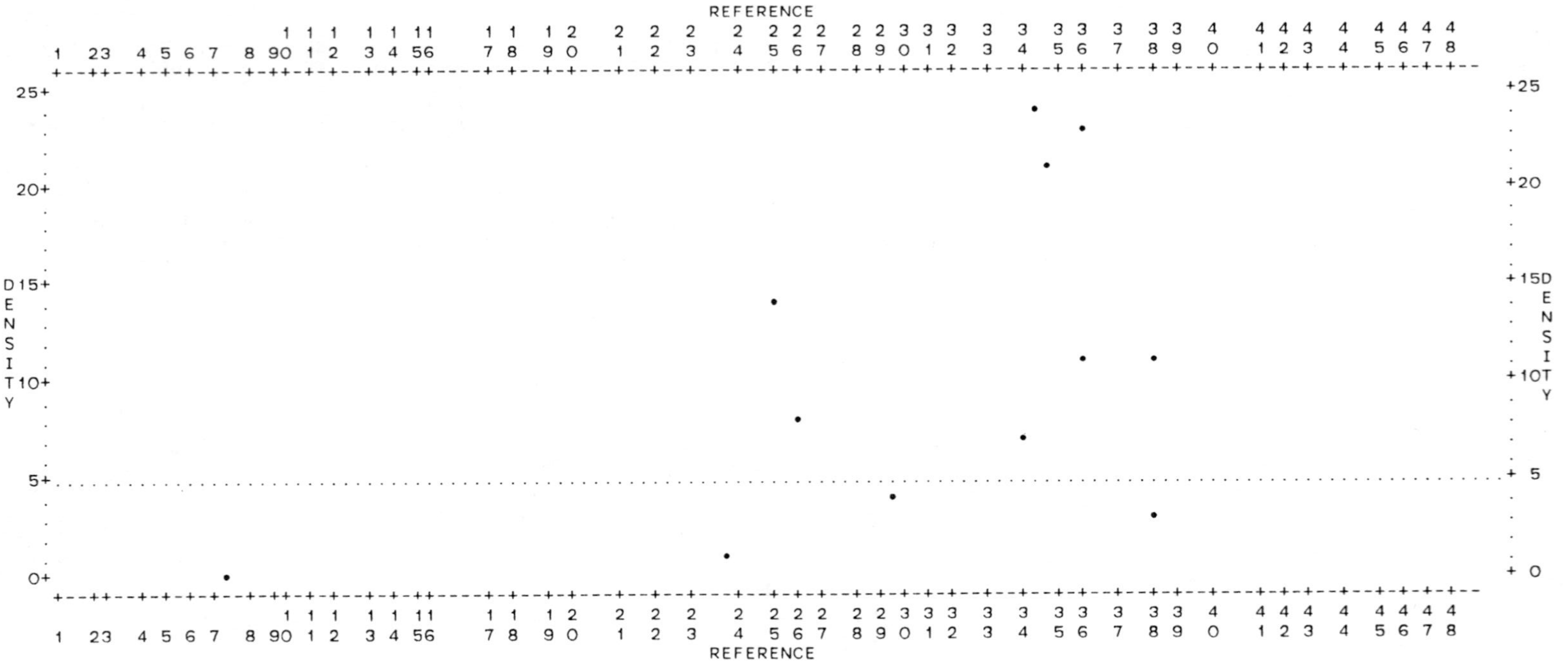

CLUSTERS:

Start:	7:21	23:46	23:46	23:46	34: 8	34: 8	34: 8	34:22	36: 4	38:12
End:	38:13	38:13	29:19	26: 5	38:13	36: 5	34:28	34:28	36: 5	38:13
Count:	12	11	4	3	7	5	3	2	2	2
Width:	18363	8425	3105	1104	2680	991	472	134	53	44
Strength:	1.96	4.15	1.06	1.18	2.74	2.20	1.42	1.01	1.05	1.05

GAPS:

Start:	1: 1	1: 1	1: 1	7:21	38:13
End:	34:22	25: 7	23:46	23:46	48:35
Count:	8	4	3	2	2
Width:	19050	13734	12967	9938	6577
Strength:	1.07	2.31	3.21	3.90	2.22

Linguistic Density Plot in Ezekiel 1 - 48

For bzh 311 (5 times)

Each Column = 13 Verses.   Separations are: Max = 9727.00, Mean = 4661.66, Min = 36.50 .

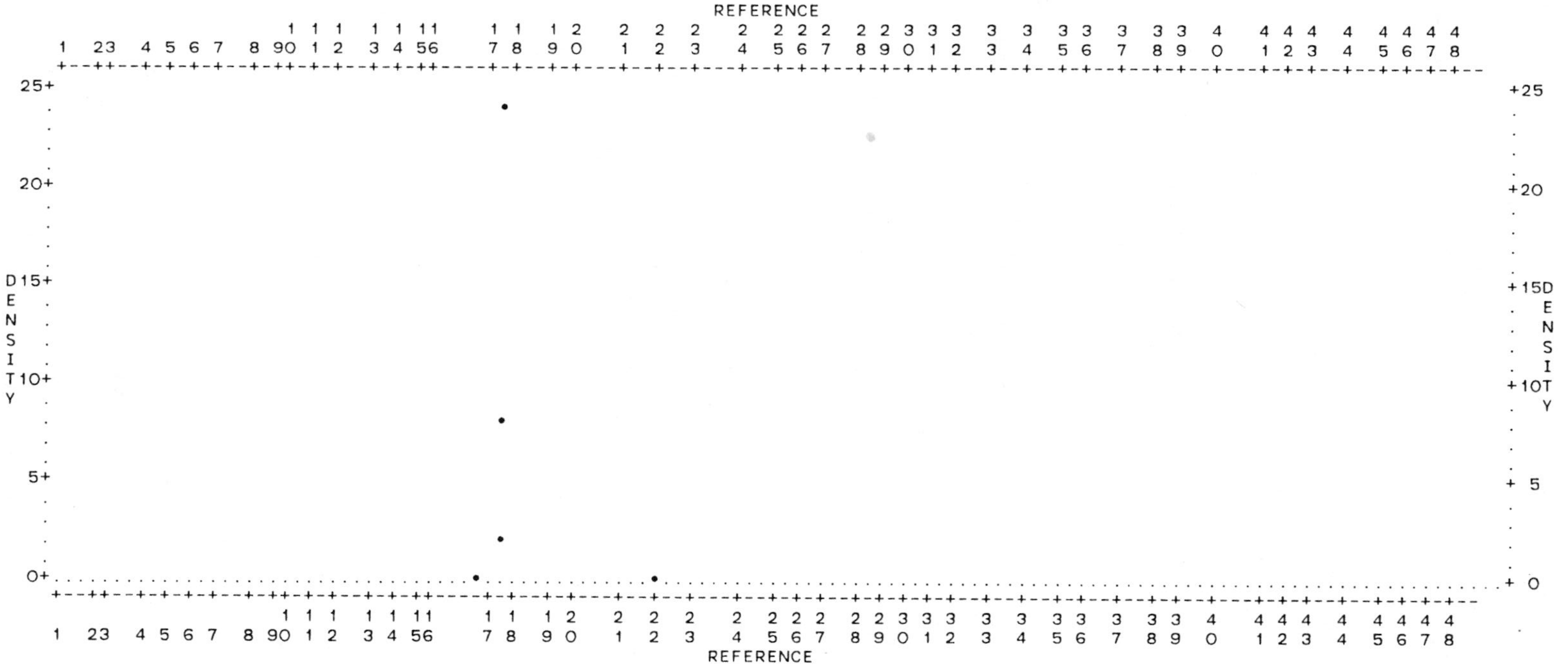

CLUSTERS:

Start:	16:59	16:59	17:16	17:18
End:	22: 8	17:19	17:19	17:19
Count:	5	4	3	2
Width:	3572	516	73	30
Strength:	3.02	2.54	1.85	1.17

GAPS:

Start:	17:19	22: 8
End:	48:35	48:35
Count:	3	2
Width:	19454	16398
Strength:	2.03	2.97

Linguistic Density Plot in Ezekiel 1 - 48

For bzz 311 (3 times)   bzz 314 (1 times)   bzz 3162 (2 times)

Each Column = 13 Verses.   Separations are: Max = 8036.00, Mean = 3995.71, Min = 245.00 .

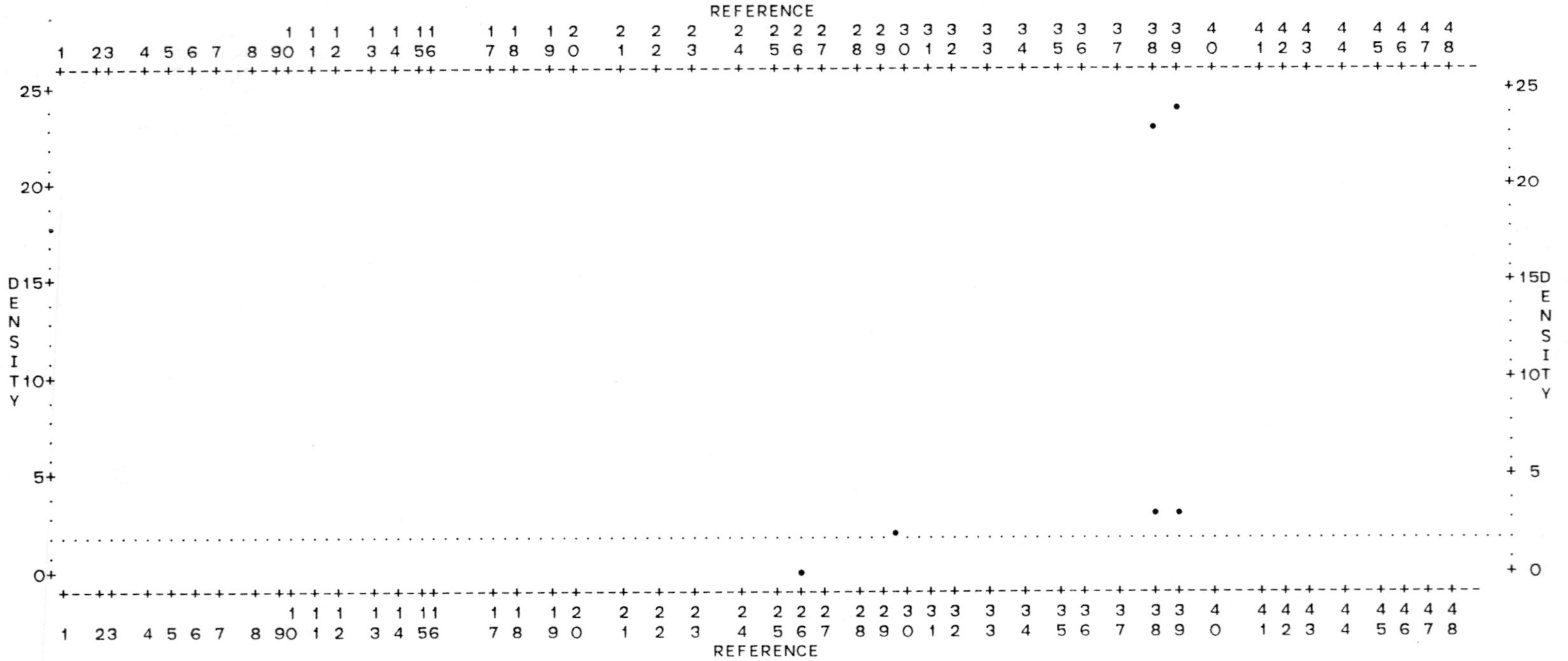

CLUSTERS:

Start:	26:12	38:12	38:12	39:10
End:	39:10	39:10	38:13	39:10
Count:	6	4	2	2
Width:	7672	534	44	2
Strength:	2.75	2.34	1.14	1.15

GAPS:

Start:	1: 1	1: 1
End:	38:12	26:12
Count:	4	2
Width:	21347	14209
Strength:	1.91	2.95

Linguistic Density Plot in Ezekiel 1 - 48

For bāḥōr 111 (5 times)

Each Column = 13 Verses.   Separations are: Max = 8381.00, Mean = 4661.66, Min = 168.50 .

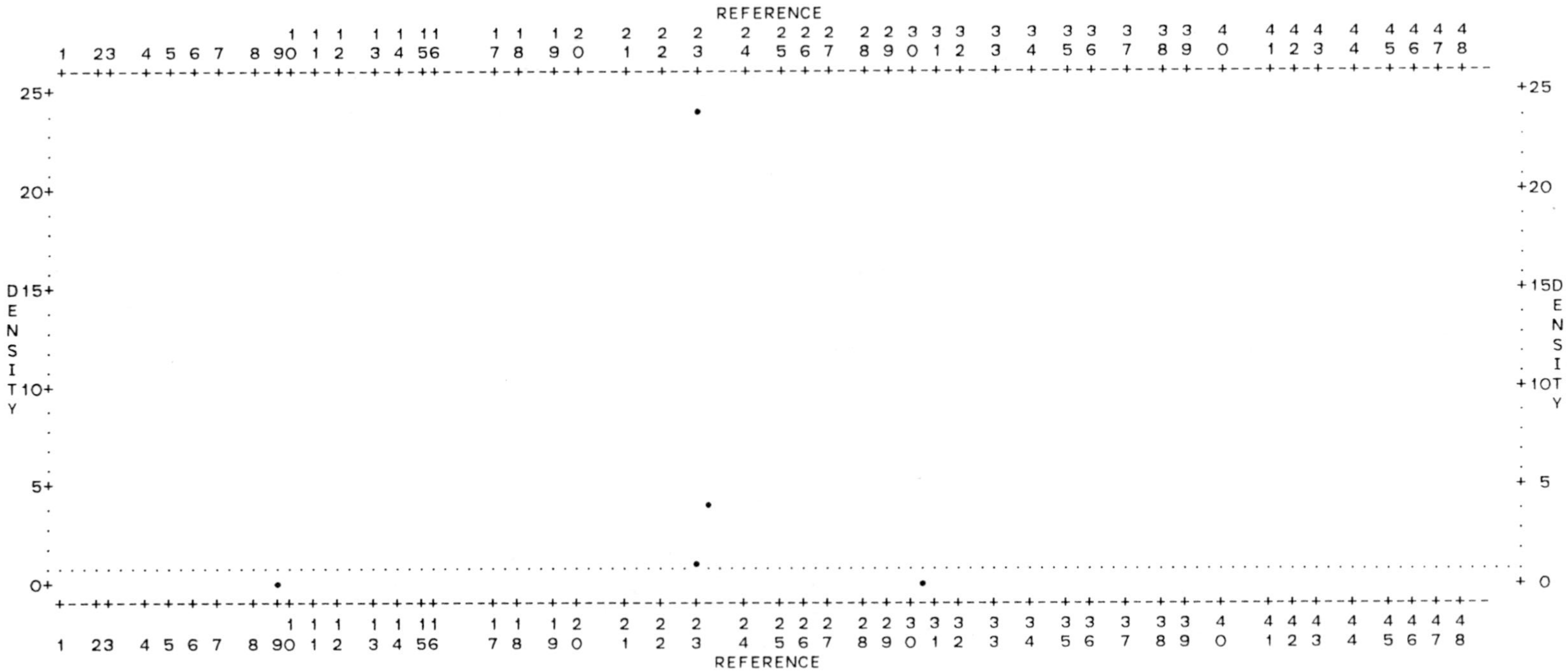

REFERENCE

DENSITY (axis labels: +25 +20 +15 +10 +5 +0)

CLUSTERS:

Start:	9: 6	23: 6	23: 6
End:	30:17	30:17	23:23	23:12
Count:	5	4	3	2
Width:	12673	4292	337	129
Strength:	1.19	1.83	1.80	1.15

GAPS:

Start:	23:23	30:17
End:	48:35	48:35
Count:	3	2
Width:	15513	11558
Strength:	1.24	1.75

For beṭaḥ 111 (11 times)

Linguistic Density Plot in Ezekiel 1 - 48

Each Column = 13 Verses.   Separations are: Max = 7799.00, Mean = 2330.83, Min = 39.00 .

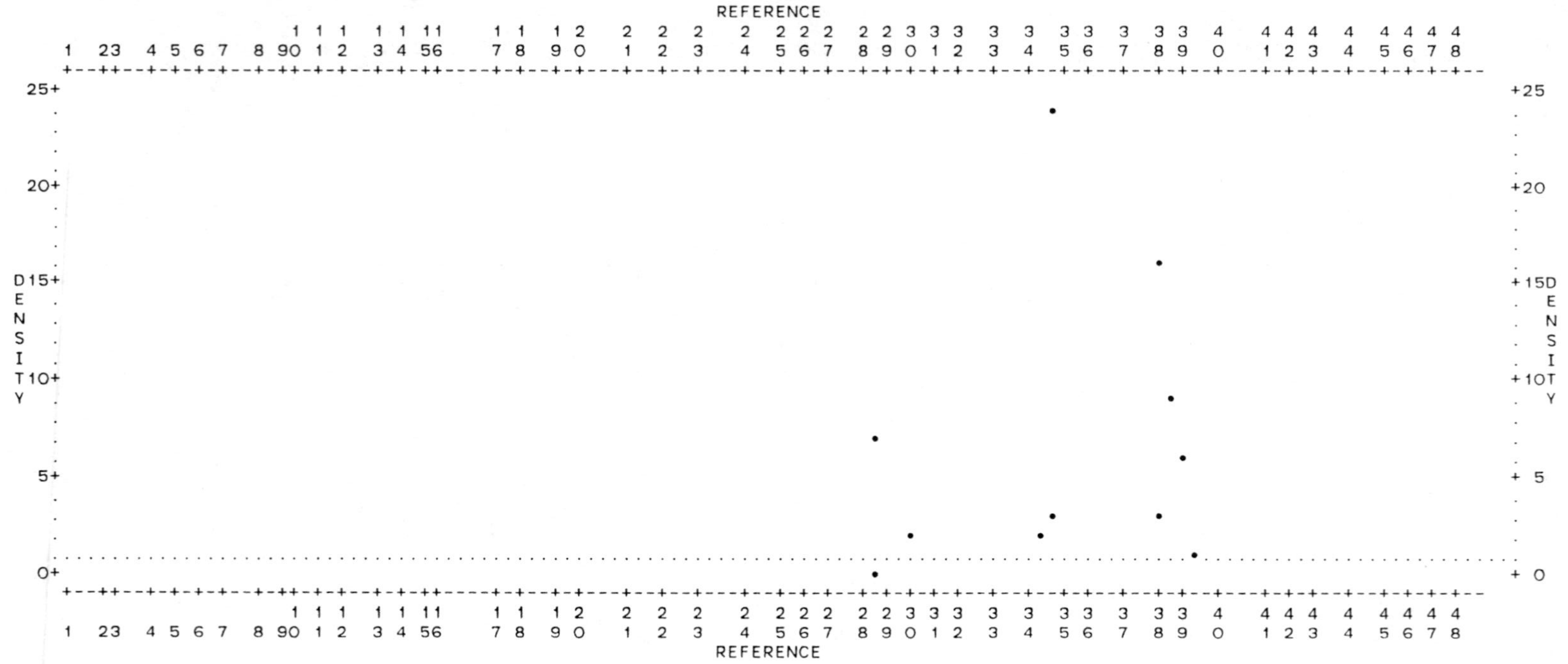

CLUSTERS:

Start:	28:26	28:26	34:25	34:27	38: 8	38: 8		
End:	39:26	30: 9	28:26	39:26	34:28	39:26	38:14	38:11
Count:	11	3	2	8	3	2	5	3
Width:	6646	681	10	3115	78	37	958	160	53
Strength:	5.76	1.37	1.08	3.45	1.58	1.06	2.28	1.55	1.06

GAPS:

Start:	1: 1	39:26
End:	28:26	48:35
Count:	2	2
Width:	15587	5736
Strength:	6.18	1.58

Linguistic Density Plot in Ezekiel 1 - 48

For bayin 111 (46 times)

Each Column = 13 Verses.   Separations are: Max = 2644.00, Mean = 595.11, Min = 4.00

```
CLUSTERS:

Start:      1:13    4: 3    8: 3    8: 3    8:16   10: 2   10: 7   18: 8   20:12   20:20   20:12   22:26   31: 3   34:17   34:20
End:       10: 7    4: 4    8:16   10: 7    8:16   10: 7   10: 7   22:26   20:20   20:20   20:12   48:22   31:14   34:22   34:22
Count:       13       2      10       2       4       6       7       8       2       3      24       3       4       3
Width:     3789      10     294     823     120      26    3119    1254     200       3   11089     250     102      41
Strength:  1.90    1.01    1.51    2.85    2.29    1.78    1.08    1.71    1.60    1.01    1.28    1.15    1.70    1.40

Start:    34:20   48:22   41:10   44:23   41:10   42:20   43: 8   44:23   47:16   47:18   47:18   47:18   47:18   48:22
End:      34:20   48:22   41:10   44:23   43: 8   43: 8   43: 8   44:23   47:18   47:16   47:18   47:18   48:22   48:22
Count:       2      15       7       5       3       8       2       6       4       4       2       4       4
Width:     4178    1895     864     175     645      12       5     175
Strength:  1.01    2.24    1.34    1.01    2.44    2.35    1.01    1.79    1.01    1.01    1.01    1.01    1.01    1.40
```

Data for bayin 111, continued.

GAPS:

Start:	1: 1	1:13	4: 3	10: 6	10: 7	10: 7	10: 7	20:20	20:20	20:20	22:26	22:26	22:26	22:26	22:26	31:14	34:22	34:22	34:22	34:22	44:23
End:	43: 8	4: 3	8: 3	20:12	20:12	19: 2	18: 8	43: 8	34:20	22:26	34:20	34:17	31:10	31: 2	34:17	43: 8	41:10	40: 7	37:21	47:16	
Count:	36	2	2	7	5	3	2	16	8	2	6	5	3	2	7	4	3	2	2		
Width:	24446	1248	1715	5830	5808	5288	4754	14395	8961	1858	7096	7035	4913	4758	2027	5393	4532	3455	1833	1638	
Strength:	2.05	1.11	1.92	1.67	3.04	5.02	7.13	2.90	3.33	2.16	3.30	4.13	4.56	7.14	2.45	1.35	2.78	2.77	2.12	1.78	

Linguistic Density Plot in Ezekiel 1 - 48

For bayit 111 (180 times)

Each Column = 13 Verses.   Separations are: Max = 1061.50, Mean = 154.53, Min = 6.00 .

REFERENCE

(vertical axis labels: +25, +20, +15 D, E, N, S, I, +10 T, Y, 5, 0)

CLUSTERS:

Start:	1:27	1:27	2: 5	3: 1	3: 1	3: 1	3: 7	3:24	3:24	3:24	4: 3	6:11	6:11	8: 6	8: 6	8: 6	8: 6	8:10
End:	48:21	3:17	2: 8	3:17	3: 9	3: 9	5: 4	4: 6	4: 4	3:27	4: 6	14:11	11:15	11:15	10: 4	8:17	8:12	8:12
Count:	180	11	3	6	6	3	3	8	7	4	4	41	24	20	14	7	4	3
Width:	27204	623	81	320	167	76	64	575	219	68	64	3706	2100	1319	676	245	126	48
Strength:	2.10	1.94	1.04	1.63	1.78	1.07	1.12	1.26	1.90	1.10	1.50	2.87	2.10	2.54	2.48	1.83	1.27	1.20

REFERENCE

Start:	8:14	8:17	9: 3	9: 3	9: 6	9: 9	10:18	10:18	11: 1	12: 2	12: 2	12: 2	12: 9	12:24	12:24	18:25
End:	8:17	14:11	10: 4	9: 9	9: 9	10: 4	11:15	11:18	11: 5	14:11	12:10	12:12	13: 9	12:27	12:24	18:31
Count:	3	7	4	3	3	5	3	5	5	2	3	7	3	4	3	5
Width:	78	303	157	61	623	1408	372	187	80	1348	713	186	54	228	200	142
Strength:	1.06	1.68	1.15	1.14	1.94	2.21	1.17	1.41	1.05	1.90	1.99	1.17	1.47	1.32	1.43	1.56

Clusters for bayit 111, continued.

```
Start:    18:29  18:29  28:24  34:30  36:10  36:17  36:21  39:12  39:22  39:12  40: 4  40: 7  40:43  40:43  40:43  40:45  41: 5  41: 5
End:      18:31  18:30  28:26  48:21  36:22  36:22  36:22  40: 9  39:29  39:21  40: 9  43:21  41:21  41:26  43:21  40:48  41:26  41:14
Count:    4      3      65     82     5      3      3      10     4      41     5      3      31     4      20     3      16     13
Width:    75     29     8507   5549   251    121    24     622    173    2857   113    28     1553   99     665    47     421    188
Strength: 1.46   1.28   1.12   3.88   1.20   1.29   1.31   1.70   1.09   3.86   1.65   1.29   3.99   1.37   3.57   1.20   3.31   3.22

Start:    41: 5  41: 6  41: 7  41: 8  42:15  42:15  43:10  43:10  43:10  43:11  43:11  44:    44:    44: 5  44: 5  44: 5  44: 6  44:11
End:      41: 8  41: 8  41:    41:    42:15  43:21  43:    43:    43:12  43:21  48:21  44:22  44:21  44:    44:    44:    44:    44:22
Count:    8      6      3      3      9      11     4      6      5      7      29     13     22     5      7      5      3      287
Width:    82     54     27     19     589    217    65     29     87     290    2769   488    1142   58     104    47     23     287
Strength: 2.49   2.11   1.29   1.33   2.01   1.31   1.50   1.28   1.74   1.41   2.07   2.21   3.16   1.83   2.21   1.20   1.31   1.42

Start:    44:11  44:14  44:30  44:30  45:    45:    45: 4  45: 6  46:24  46:17  45:20  47:    47: 1  47: 1  47: 1
End:      44:14  44:12  45:20  45:    45:    45:    45: 8  45:    45:17  45:20  45:    47:    47:    47:    47:
Count:    4      9      8      5      4      3      4      6      21     4      80     12     3      1      1
Width:    89     35     473    221    115    45     83     13     80     36     80     21     3              
Strength: 1.41   1.26   1.78   1.30   1.31   1.21   1.31   1.36   1.44   2.16   1.44   1.67   1.36
```

GAPS:

```
Start:    1: 1   1: 1   1: 1   4: 4   4: 6   4: 6   4: 6   4: 4   5: 4   5: 4   6:11   6: 7   7:15   7:24   8:    9:    12:25  13: 9
End:      2: 6   1:27   8:10   8:10   8: 7   8: 6   7:24   7:15   6:11   12:    48:35  43:10  41:    40: 4  36:21  40:47  18:29  14: 4
Count:    10     8      2      7      7      5      4      3      3      2      133    98     82     75     55     19     16
Width:    3144   3117   692    740    1713   1487   1308   952    576    435    4182   3845
Strength: 3.88   4.41   1.76   1.04   2.11   2.84   3.18   2.73   2.96   2.74   4.31   5.37   5.79   6.71   6.99   7.02   2.25   2.67   1.82

Start:    14: 6  14: 7  14: 7  14:11  14:11  14:11  17:12  18: 6  18:29  18:30  18:30  18:30  18:31  18:31  18:31  20:13  20:31  20:40  20:40
End:      18:29  18:18  18:25  18:    16:41  18: 6  18: 6  16:41  36:21  28:24  20:30  20:27  20:    20:27  20: 5  20:27  28:24  28: 8  25: 9  23:47
Count:    10     9      7      5      3      2      2      2      35     20     5      4      2      5      14     12     9      5
Width:    3050   2933   2519   1889   1346   411    10791  10774  6269   1013   916    363    351    5166   4956   3199   2419   2288
Strength: 4.92   5.40   6.23   7.28   7.74   1.66   6.57   6.81   5.24   1.29   1.70   1.35   1.27   5.89   4.60   5.90   6.89

Start:    20:44  22:18  24:    24: 3  25:12  26:12  28:25  28:26  28:26  29:21  33:11  33:11  33:11  33:20  33:30  34: 9  36:22  36:22
End:      23:39  23:39  24:21  24:21  28:24  28:24  36:21  36:21  33: 7  33: 7  36:17  36:10  36:21  36:10  35:15  34:30  40: 4  36:22
Count:    3      3      3      2      2      2      15     14     5      7      6      5      8      4      3      13     12
Width:    2123   1084   570    354    1690   1308   4475   4440   2411   2331   1746   1561   1876   1973   1332   763    2394   2381
Strength: 8.36   6.04   1.29   6.36   7.50   6.36   4.17   4.54   4.82   5.61   2.86   3.09   2.55   2.22   3.27   3.95   1.04   1.37

Start:    36:22  39:22  37:16  37:16  38: 6  40: 9  40: 9  45:20  47: 1  47: 1
End:      39:22  39:22  39:12  39:22  39:12  40:45  40:43  46:24  48:35  48:21
Count:    8      4      3      4      2      3      3      4      2
Width:    2074   1751   1358   1156   716    775    734    682    1186   949
Strength: 2.48   2.87   3.37   3.90   3.65   1.17   1.95   3.42   2.72   4.00   3.16   5.16
```

Linguistic Density Plot in Ezekiel 1 - 48

For bēlet 111 (14 times)

Each Column = 13 Verses.   Separations are: Max = 8525.00, Mean = 1864.67, Min = 77.50 .

REFERENCE

DENSITY

CLUSTERS:

Start:	3:21	13: 3	16:28	20: 9	20:14
End:	20:22	20:22	20:22	20:15	20:15
Count:	9	8	6	4	3	2
Width:	8834	4634	2826	337	155	22
Strength:	1.74	2.41	1.97	1.87	1.50	1.05

GAPS:

Start:	3:21	20:15	24: 8	33:15
End:	13: 3	48:35	46:20	46:20
Count:	2	8	7	5	4	2
Width:	4200	18031	17849	14775	13492	8525
Strength:	1.33	1.42	1.94	2.36	2.82	3.81

Linguistic Density Plot in Ezekiel 1 - 48

For bāmâ 114 (7 times)

Each Column = 13 Verses. Separations are: Max = 7060.50, Mean = 3496.25, Min = 1197.00 .

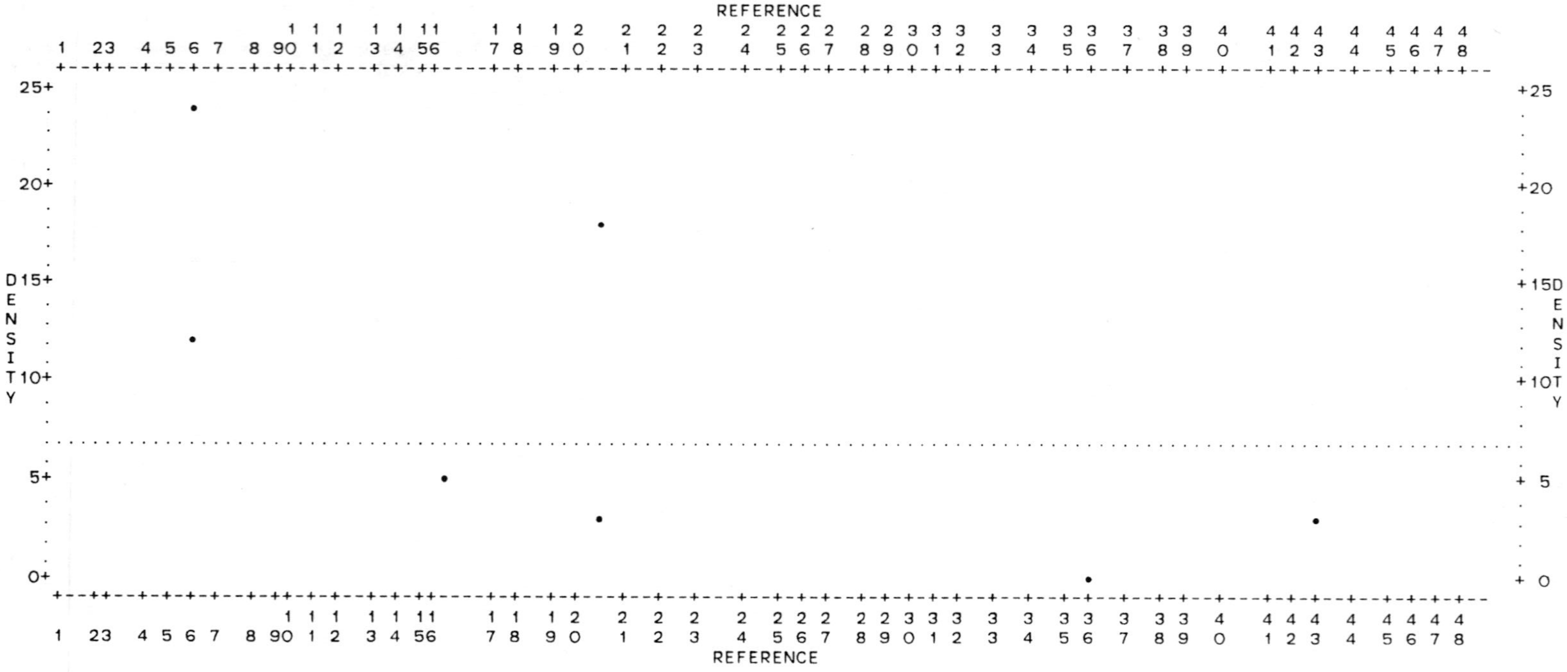

CLUSTERS:

Start:	6: 3	6: 3	20:29
End:	20:29	6: 6	20:29
Count:	5	2	2
Width:	7957	43	9
Strength:	1.29	1.11	1.13

GAPS:

Start:	20:29	20:29	20:29
End:	48:35	43: 7	36: 2
Count:	4	3	2
Width:	17662	14121	9266
Strength:	1.58	1.76	1.87

Linguistic Density Plot in Ezekiel 1 - 48

For bēn 111 (192 times)

Each Column = 13 Verses.   Separations are: Max =   643.50, Mean =   144.92, Min =   2.00

CLUSTERS:

Start:	1:3	1:3	1:3	2:3	1:11	8:11	8:5	3:1	2:1	21:14	23:2	9 23:9	1:11	14:13	14:13
End:	48:11	29:2	5:1	3:4	11:15	8:17	8:8	4:3	2:4	21:17	23:7	23:12	4:11	16:2	15:2
Count:	192	125	18	10	22	4	3	3	4	6	5	6	13	7	
Width:	27444	15592	1804	848	2340	146	76	64	28	281	1078	235	450	299	164
Strength:	1.15	2.47	1.15	1.07	1.12	1.16	1.04	1.10	1.28	1.68	1.36	1.53	1.20	1.33	1.08

Start:	16:20	18:19	20:3	21:2	21:2	8:5	8:17	1:2	2:4	21:14	23:9	2:23	23:2	24:16	24:16
End:	16:28	18:20	29:2	22:24	21:25	8:17	8:8	2:4	2:2	21:25	23:17	23:25	23:39	26:2	25:3
Count:	4	8	4	14	9	37	29	4	3	6	5	11	5	13	7
Width:	158	353	57	1148	451	3585	1943	211	60	101	132	479	84	62	672	288
Strength:	1.11	1.76	1.59	1.46	1.76	2.08	2.98	1.60	1.12	1.34	1.16	2.17	1.00	1.11	1.56	1.66

```
Clusters for bën 111, continued.

Start:     24:25  25: 2  25: 4  25: 4  25:10  33: 2  33:10  33: 2  37:    37:16  37:16  37:16  37:25  37:25  43: 7  43: 7  43:18  43:18  44: 5  44: 9
End:       25: 3  25: 3  26: 2  25:10  25:10  34: 2  33:12  33:12  38: 2  38: 2  37:21  37:18  38: 2  37:25  44:25  44: 9  43:25  44: 9  44: 9  44: 3
Count:        5      3      5      5     15     11      3      6     11      8      4      3      4      3     15     12      9      9      5      3
Width:       87    342    159     14    787    276     68    388    672    146     62    388     90   1147    753    443    154    146
Strength:  1.72   1.34   1.19   1.35   1.48   1.40   1.08   1.40   1.74   1.66   1.16   1.11   1.38   1.40   1.69   1.80   1.78   1.12   1.51   1.32

Start:     46:13  46:13  46:16
End:       47: 6  46:18  46:18
Count:        6      5      4
Width:      388    133     63
Strength:  1.05   1.55   1.49

GAPS:

Start:      1: 1   1: 3   4: 1   5:10   5:10   6: 5   7: 2   8:12   8:17  13: 2  13: 2  13: 2  15: 2  16: 2  16:45  16:45  17: 2  18: 2  18:20  18:20  20: 4
End:        2: 1   2: 1   4:13  11: 1   8: 5   8: 5   8: 2  11: 1  14:16  14:13  13:17  13:17  16: 2  16:20  18:19  18: 2  18: 2  21:14  20: 3  20:18
Count:        3      2      2     12      5      5      2      4     16      5      3      2      3      2      3     11      2      2     11      2
Width:      599    557    292   2296   1182    889    627    951    898    812    312    569    418   1318   1002    579    558    364
Strength:  1.51   2.85   1.01   1.50   2.10   2.94   3.34   2.07   1.11   1.51   1.15   1.37   1.89   1.28   3.49   3.00   1.04   2.86   1.51

Start:     20:31  25:10  25:10  25:10  25:10  25:10  25:10  26: 2  27:15  27:15  28: 2  28: 2  28:12  29: 2  29: 2  30: 5  30: 5  30: 5  31: 2  32: 2
End:       21: 2  33:30  33: 2  33: 2  27:11  30: 2  27: 2  27: 2  27:32  30: 2  30: 2  29:18  29:18  29:18  30:21  31:14  31:14  33: 2  33: 2
Count:        2     28     24     20     19     12      3      3      8      5      5      4      7      2      2      3
Width:      372   4660   4263   3991   3980   2321    809    650   1443   1050    927    754    373   1598    757    290    305    693
Strength:  1.57   1.07   1.42   2.06   2.34   1.56   1.50   1.76   1.14   1.01   1.21   1.28   1.57   2.08   1.29   1.00   1.10   1.98

Start:     32:18  33:30  33:30  33:30  34: 2  35: 5  35: 5  36: 1  36: 1  37:15  37:25  37:25  37:25  38: 2  39: 1  39:17  40: 4  40:46  44: 9  44:15
End:       33: 2  37:25  37:16  35: 9  35: 2  37: 1  37: 3  37: 3  48:35  40:46  40:46  40:46  40:46  37: 3  40:46  40:46  43: 7  46:16  46:16
Count:        2     15     14     10      5      9      5      3      3     36      7      6      4      2      3      8      6
Width:      354   2578   2575   2277   2118   1253    804    688    905    522   6930   2257   2171   1622   1287    897   1086   1428   1280
Strength:  1.44   1.05   1.37   2.29   2.93   2.52   2.35   3.76   3.02   2.61   2.40   3.97   4.53   4.77   4.90   5.21   6.52   1.10   1.73

Start:     44:15  44:25  44:25  44:18  46:18  47: 6  48:11
End:       46:13  46: 6  45:18  47:22  47:22  47:22  48:35
Count:        5      4      3      3      2      2
Width:     1210   1038    792    534    611    356    483
Strength:  2.20   2.42   2.46   2.69   1.57   1.46   2.34
```

Linguistic Density Plot in Ezekiel 1 - 48

For bnh 311 (6 times)   bnh 312 (1 times)   bnh 314 (2 times)   bnh 3162 (4 times)
                                bnh 321 (1 times)   bnh 322 (2 times)

Each Column = 13 Verses. Separations are: Max = 3805.00. Mean = 1645.29. Min = 63.50 .

REFERENCE

DENSITY

CLUSTERS:

Start:	4: 2	16:24	16:24	16:24	26:14	26:14	27: 4	36:10	36:33	
End:	39:15	17:17	16:31	16:25	39:15	28:26	27: 5	39:15	36:36	36:36
Count:	16	4	3	2	8	3	4	2		
Width:	20517	1269	127	16	7730	1333	246	2174	547	42
Strength:	1.95	1.45	1.48	1.05	1.16	1.43	1.05	1.09	1.29	1.03

GAPS:

Start:	17:17	27: 5	28:26	36:36	39:15
End:	26:14	48:35	36:10	48:35	48:35
Count:	3	7	2	3	2
Width:	5778	13467	4223	7610	5983
Strength:	1.17	1.14	1.66	2.03	2.79

Linguistic Density Plot in Ezekiel 1 - 48

For bnh 311 (6 times)

Each Column = 13 Verses. Separations are: Max = 6516.50, Mean = 3995.71, Min = 2928.50 .

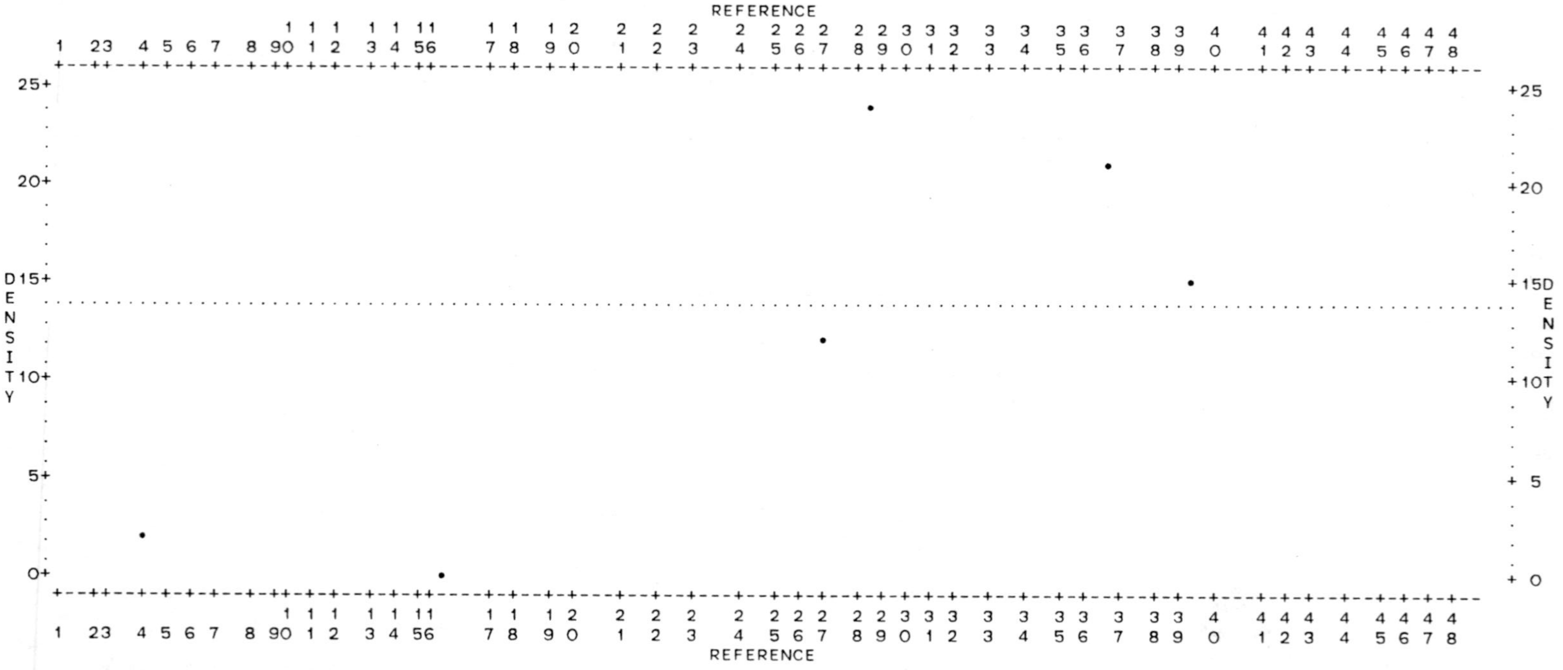

REFERENCE

REFERENCE

DENSITY

All cluster strengths are less than 1.00.

GAPS:

Start: 4: 2
End: 27: 5
Count: 3
Width: 13033
Strength: 1.12

Linguistic Density Plot in Ezekiel 1 - 48

For binyān 111 (7 times)

Each Column = 13 Verses.   Separations are: Max = 11809.50, Mean = 3496.25, Min = 27.00 .

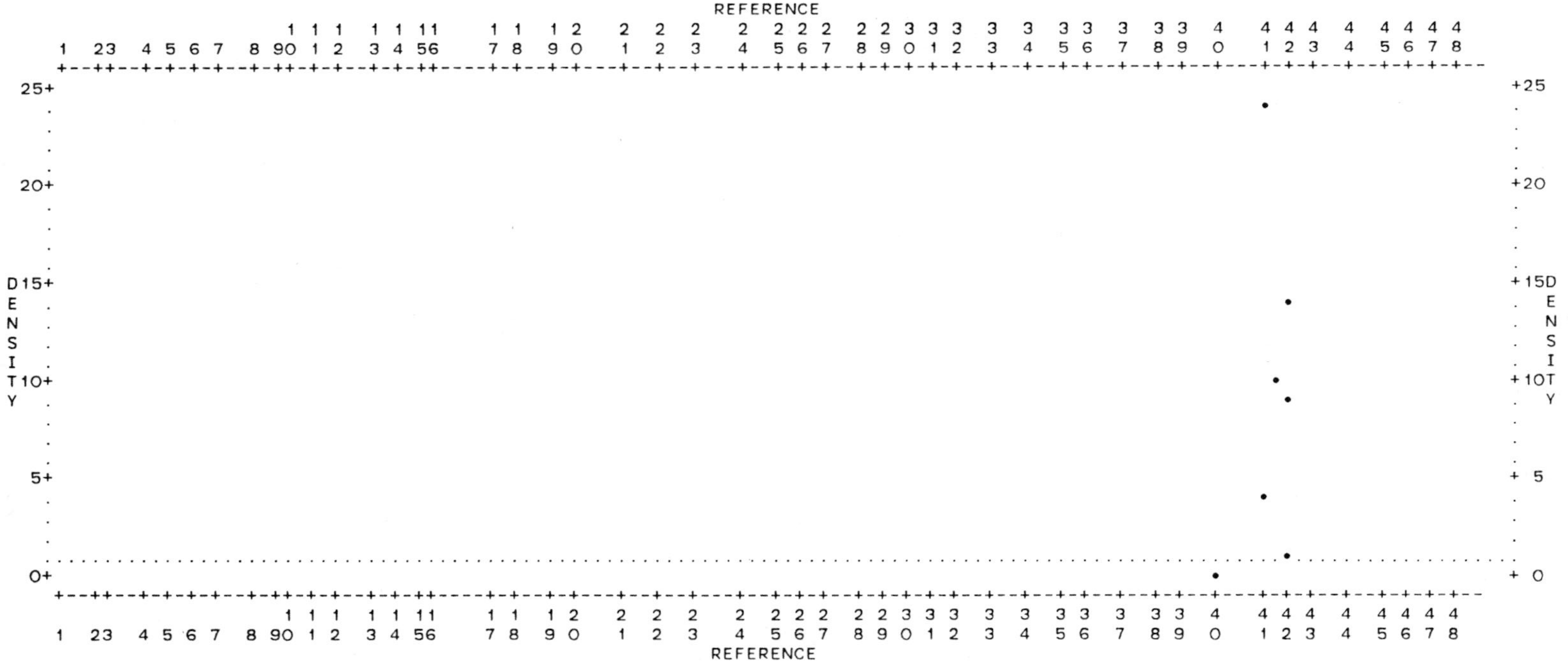

REFERENCE

CLUSTERS:

Start:	40: 5	41:12	41:12	41:12	42: 1	42: 1
End:	42:10	41:15	41:12	42:10	42:10	42: 5
Count:	7	6	3	2	3	2
Width:	1605	449	54	13	149	65
Strength:	4.79	3.77	1.71	1.12	1.69	1.11

GAPS:

Start:	1: 1	1: 1
End:	41:12	40: 5
Count:	3	2
Width:	23618	22462
Strength:	4.11	6.15

Linguistic Density Plot in Ezekiel 1 - 48

For b'r 314 (2 times)   b'r 331 (3 times)   b'r 332 (1 times)   b'r 362 (1 times)

Each Column = 13 Verses. Separations are: Max = 5524.00, Mean = 3496.25, Min = 21.00 .

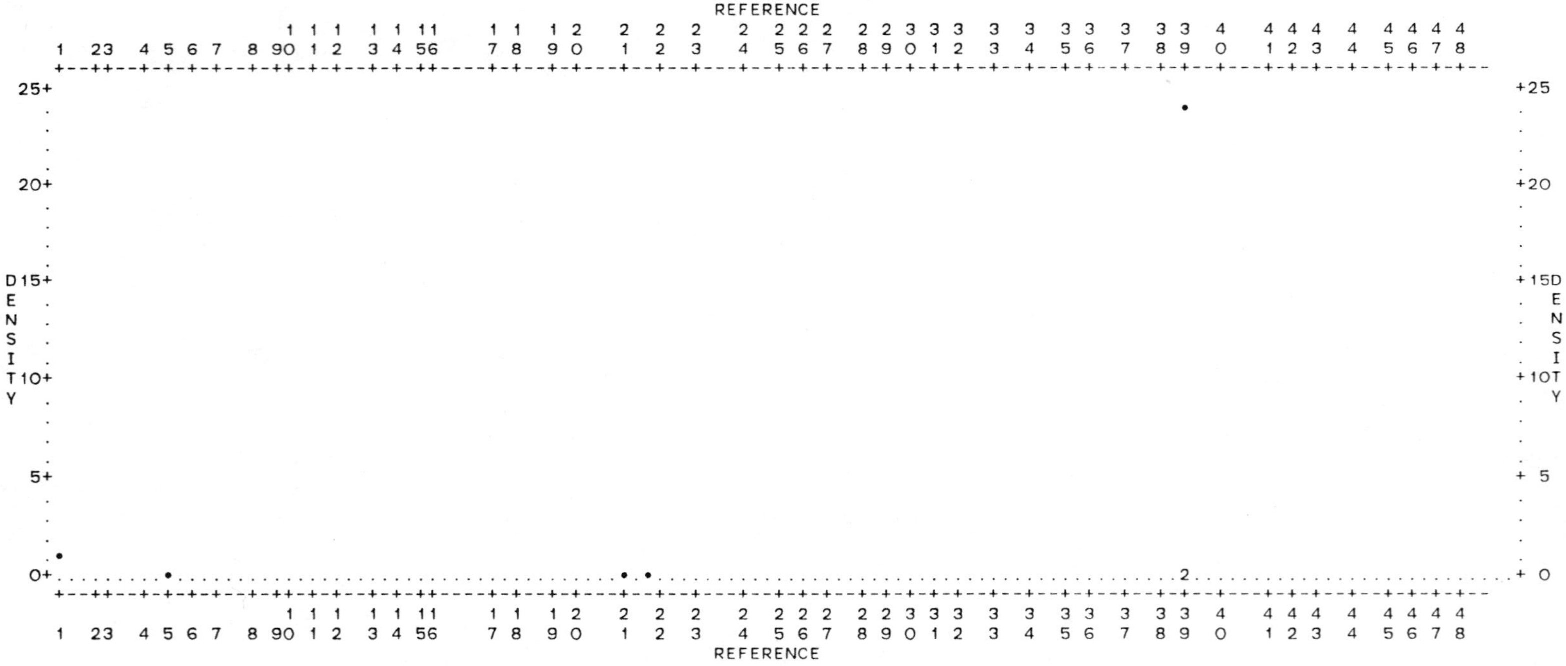

(vertical axis: DENSITY — marks at +25, +20, +15, +10, +5, +0)

CLUSTERS:

Start:	39: 9	39: 9
End:	39:10	39:10
Count:	3	
Width:	42	20
Strength:	1.72	1.12

GAPS:

Start:	1:13	5: 2	21:36
End:	39: 9	21: 4	39: 9
Count:	5		
Width:	21581	8902	10412
Strength:	1.62	1.75	2.24

Linguistic Density Plot in Ezekiel 1 - 48

For bq' 311 (1 times)   bq' 3262 (1 times)   bq' 331 (1 times)   bq' 332 (1 times)
     bq' 344 (1 times)

Each Column = 13 Verses. Separations are: Max = 6098.50, Mean = 4661.66, Min = 1112.00 .

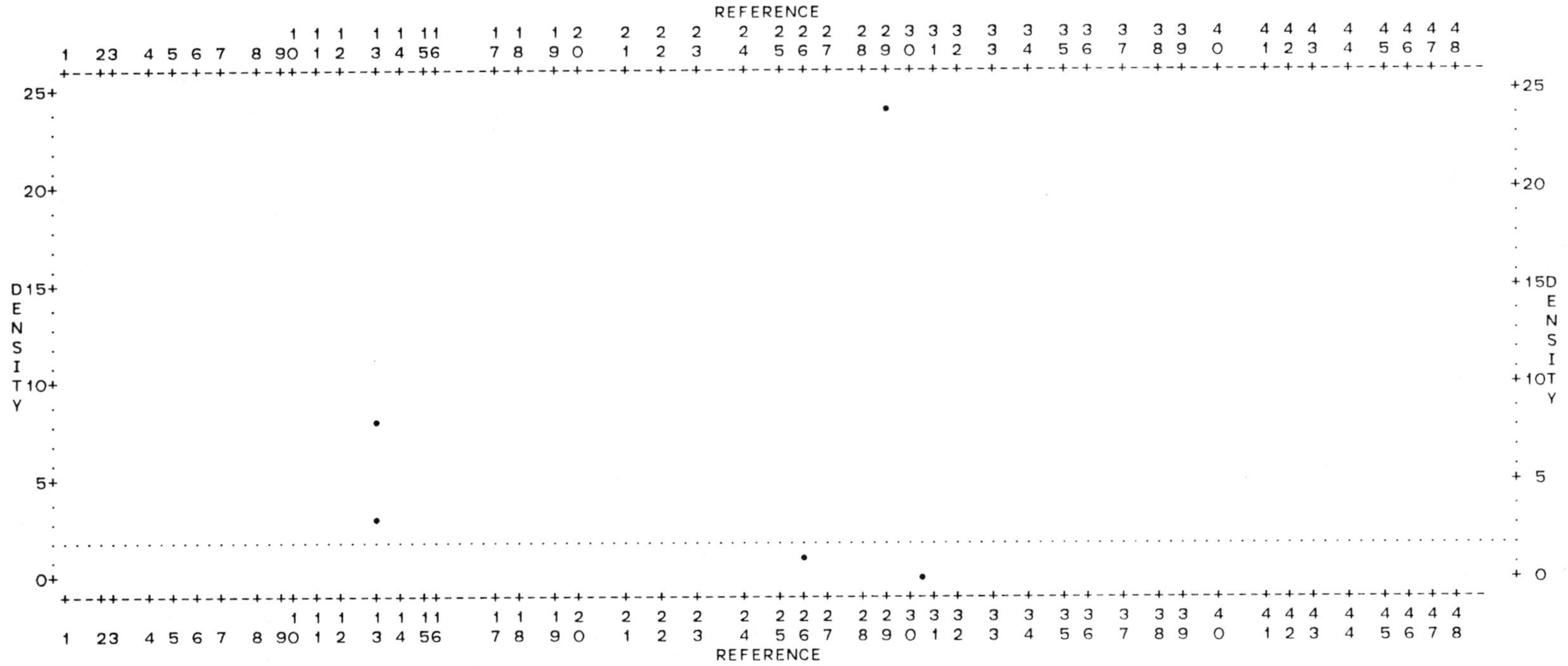

REFERENCE

REFERENCE

CLUSTERS:

Start:	13:11	13:11	26:10	29: 7
End:	30:16	13:13	30:16	30:16
Count:	5	2	3	2
Width:	10755	22	2224	634
Strength:	1.58	1.17	1.42	1.02

GAPS:

Start:	30:16
End:	48:35
Count:	2
Width:	11563
Strength:	1.75

Linguistic Density Plot in Ezekiel 1 - 48

For biq'â 114 (5 times)

Each Column = 13 Verses.   Separations are: Max = 9549.00, Mean = 4661.66, Min =   664.50 .

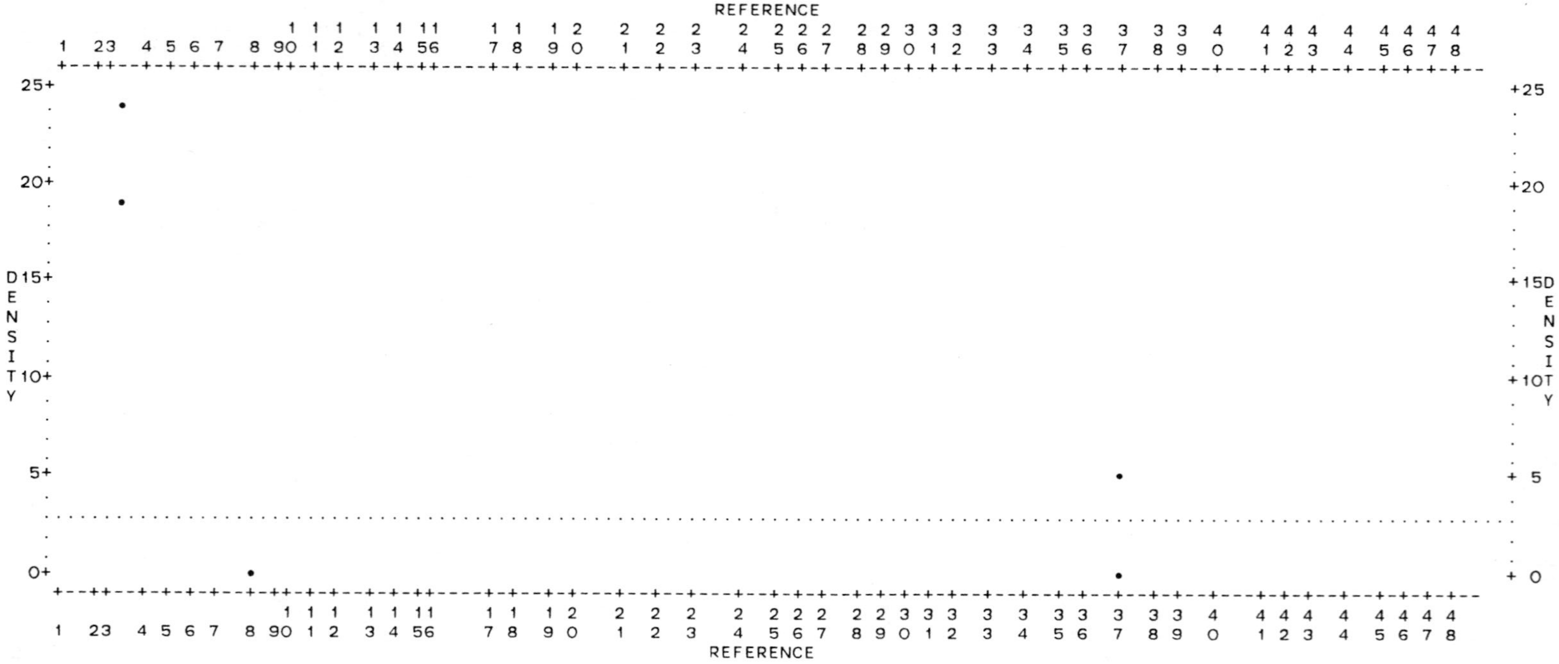

REFERENCE

DENSITY

REFERENCE

CLUSTERS:

Start:	3:22	3:22	37: 1
End:	8: 4	3:23	37: 2
Count:	3	2	2
Width:	1939	11	18
Strength:	1.48	1.18	1.17

GAPS:

Start:	3:23	3:23	8: 4
End:	48:35	37: 1	37: 1
Count:	5	3	2
Width:	26641	19098	17170
Strength:	1.60	1.96	3.17

For bōqer 111 (10 times)

Linguistic Density Plot in Ezekiel 1 - 48

Each Column = 13 Verses.   Separations are: Max = 8345.00, Mean = 2542.73, Min = 6.00 .

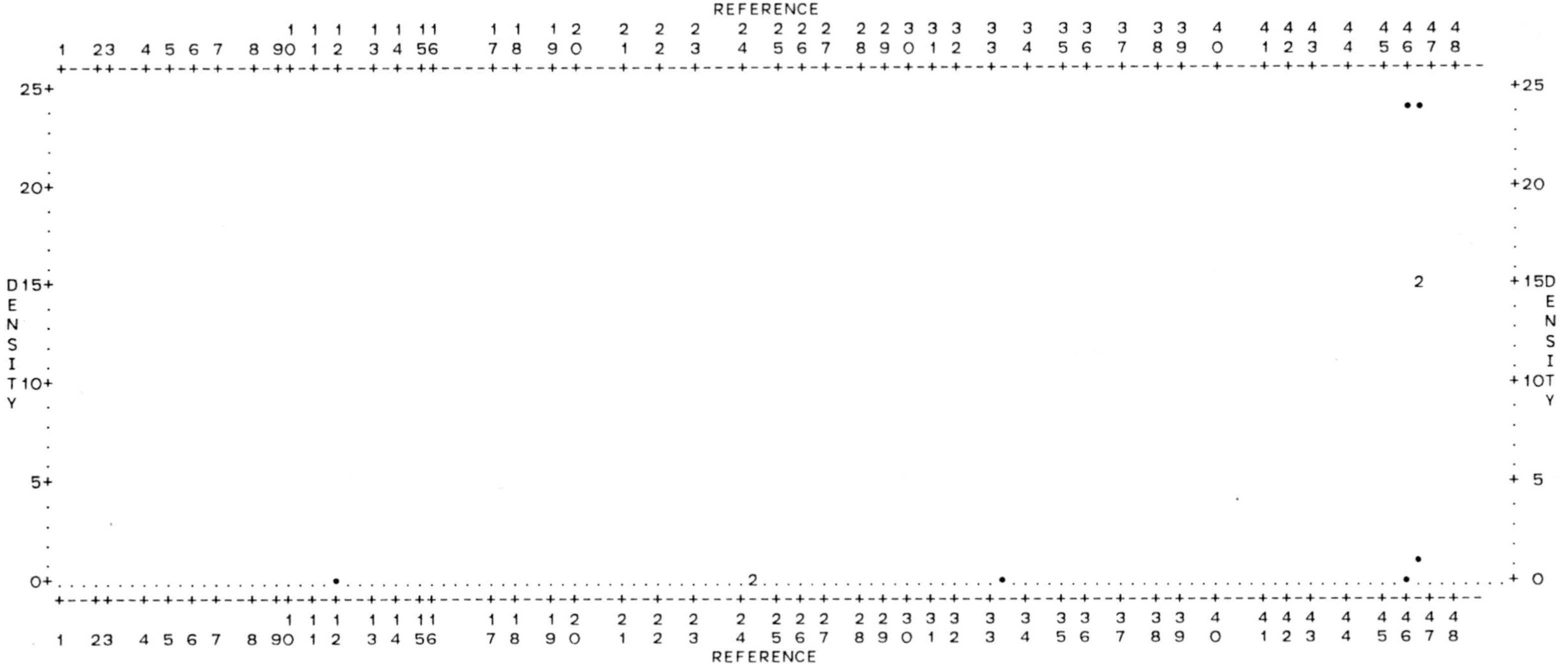

REFERENCE

DENSITY axis: +25 +20 +15 +10 +5 +0

CLUSTERS:

Start:	24:18	24:18	46:13	46:13	46:14	46:15
End:	46:15	24:18	46:15	46:14	46:14	46:15
Count:	9	2	2	6	4	2	2
Width:	13174	10	44	14	2	2	2
Strength:	1.99	1.09	3.15	2.11	1.09	1.09	1.09

GAPS:

Start:	1:1	1:1	1:1	1:1	12:8	24:18	33:22
End:	46:15	46:14	46:13	24:18	24:18	46:13	46:13
Count:	10	8	6	3	2
Width:	26550	26520	26508	13378	13120	8345	8217
Strength:	1.17	2.24	3.43	2.66	2.49	2.57	2.44

Linguistic Density Plot in Ezekiel 1 - 48

For bāqār 111 (6 times)

Each Column = 13 Verses.   Separations are: Max = 22956.00, Mean = 3995.71, Min = 54.00 .

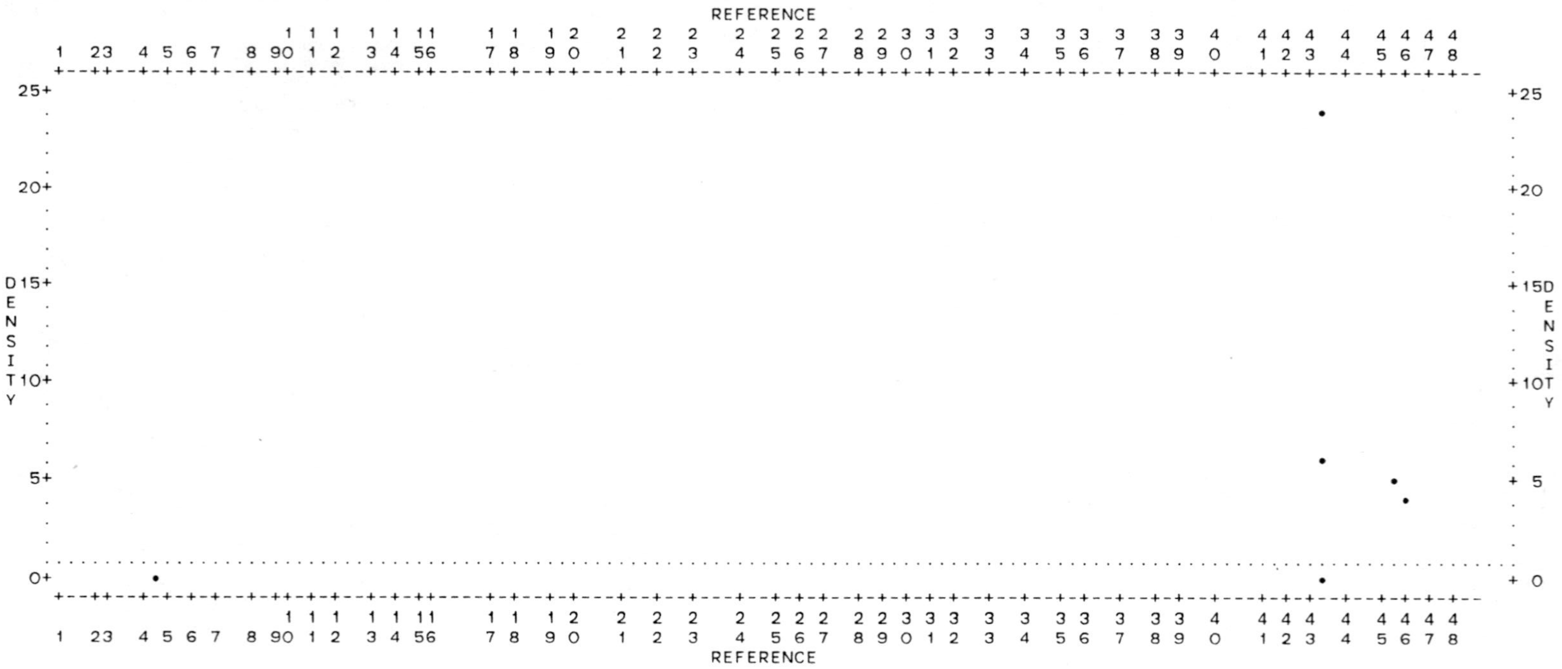

CLUSTERS:

Start:	43:19	43:19	43:23	45:18
End:	46: 6	43:25	43:25	46: 6
Count:	5	3	2	2
Width:	1583	108	36	258
Strength:	2.94	1.76	1.14	1.07

GAPS:

Start:	1: 1	1: 1	4:15
End:	43:23	43:19	43:19
Count:	4	3	2
Width:	24815	24743	22956
Strength:	2.62	3.74	5.47

Linguistic Density Plot in Ezekiel 1 - 48

For bqs 331 (3 times)   bqs 332 (5 times)   bqs 334 (1 times)   bqs 342 (1 times)

Each Column = 13 Verses. Separations are: Max = 5667.50, Mean = 2542.73, Min = 136.50 .

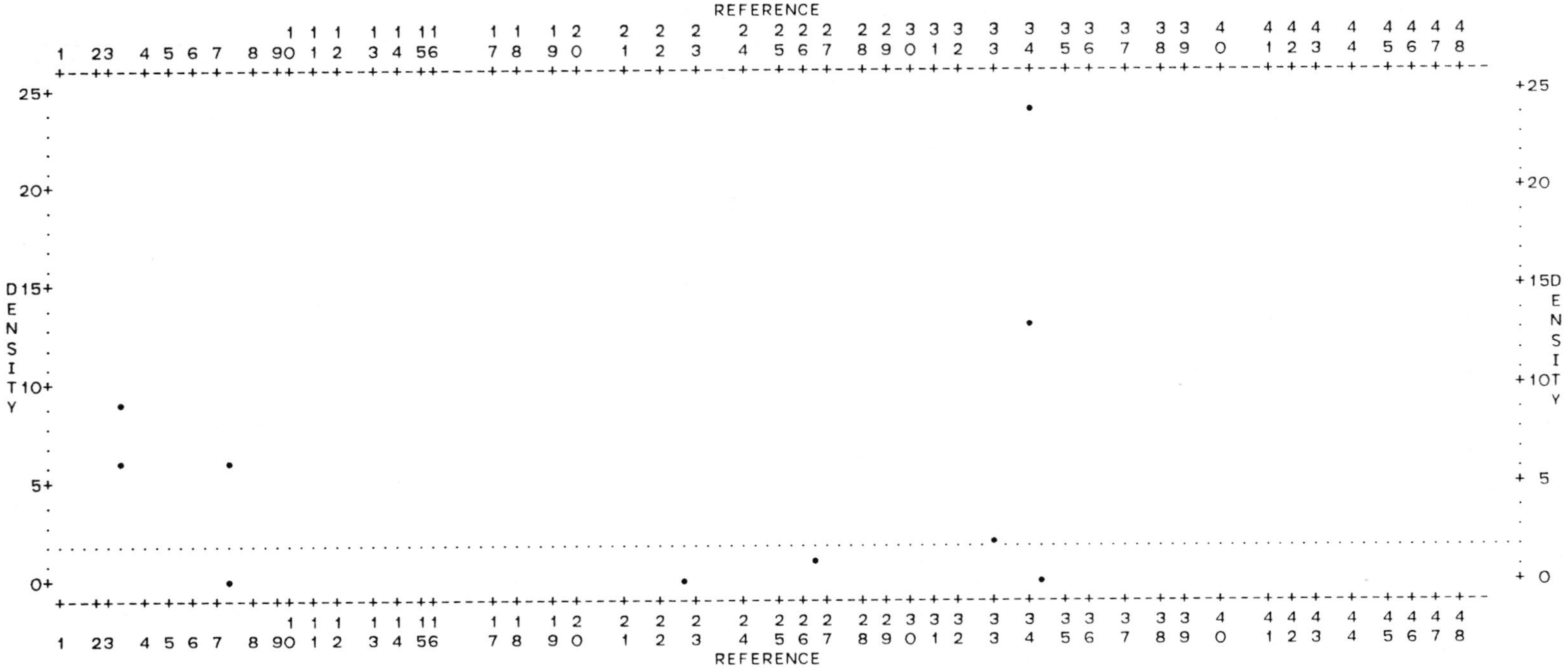

REFERENCE

CLUSTERS:

Start:	3:18	3:18	7:26	7:25	22:30	33: 8	34: 4	34: 4
End:	34:16	7:26	3:20	7:26	34:16	34:16	34:16	34: 6
Count:	10	4	2	2	4	3	2	
Width:	17704	1892	67	6918	950	273	49	
Strength:	1.66	1.59	1.06	1.08	1.44	1.85	1.54	1.07

GAPS:

Start:	7:26	7:26	7:26	34: 6	34:16
End:	48:35	34: 4	22:30	48:35	48:35
Count:	8	5	4	3	2
Width:	24866	15539	14862	9278	9054
Strength:	1.81	1.38	2.01	1.34	2.80

Linguistic Density Plot in Ezekiel 1 - 48

For bqs 332 (5 times)

Each Column = 13 Verses.   Separations are: Max = 8343.50, Mean = 4661.66, Min =   639.50 .

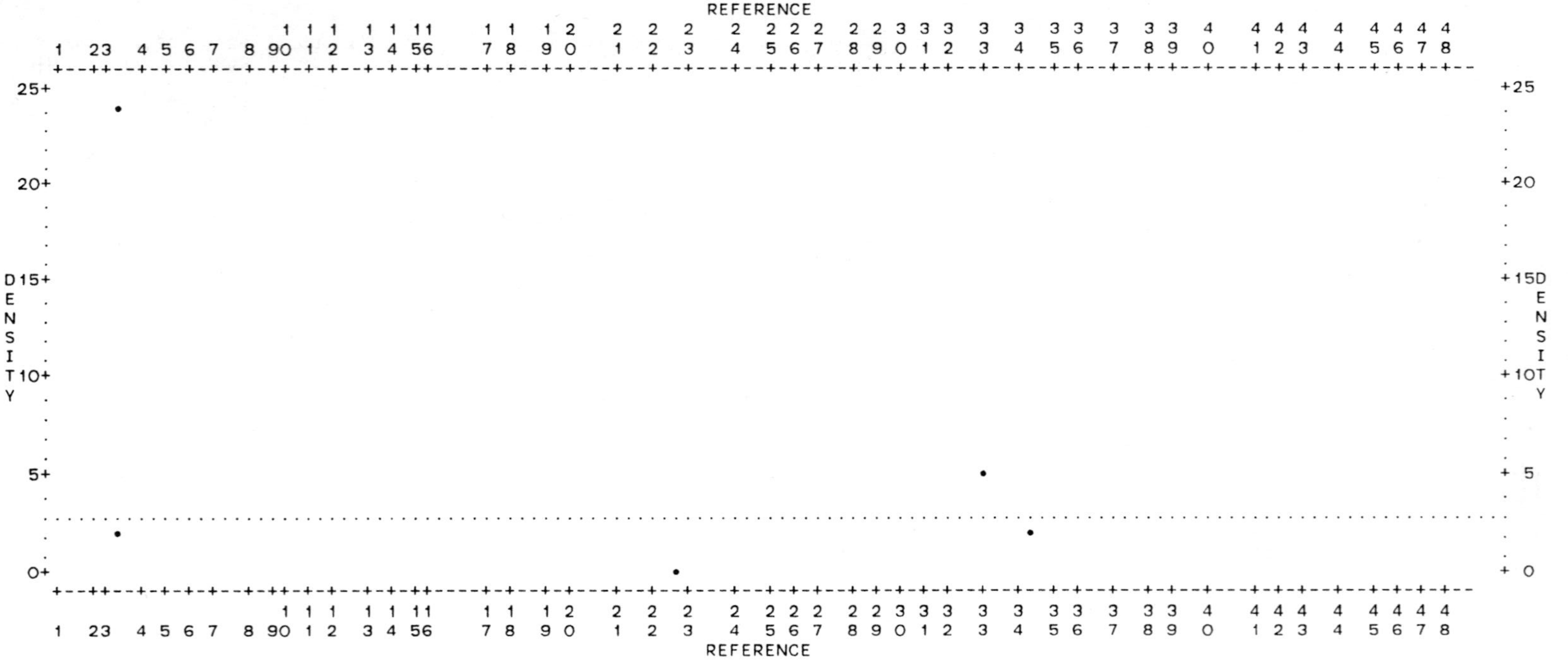

REFERENCE

(plot area)

CLUSTERS:

Start:	3:18			
End:	3:20			
Count:	2			
Width:	67			
Strength:	1.16			

GAPS:

Start:	3:20	3:20	3:20	34:16
End:	48:35	33: 8	22:30	48:35
Count:	5	3	2	2
Width:	26691	16687	10719	9054
Strength:	1.61	1.47	1.53	1.11

Linguistic Density Plot in Ezekiel 1 - 48

For br' 321 (1 times)   br' 3262 (2 times)   br' 3361 (3 times)

Each Column = 13 Verses. Separations are: Max = 6329.00, Mean = 3995.71, Min = 119.00 .

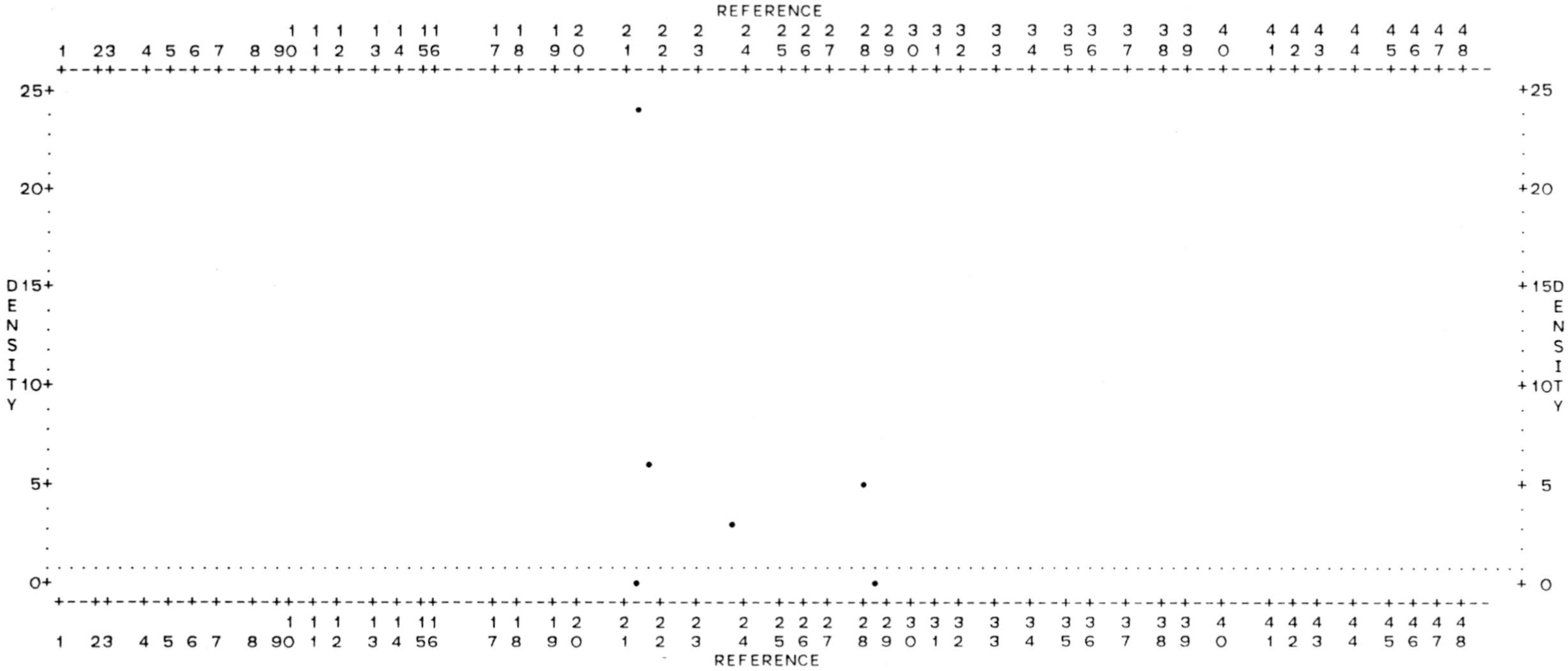

REFERENCE

CLUSTERS:

Start:	21:24	21:24	21:24	28:13
End:	28:15	23:47	21:35	21:24	28:15
Count:	6	4	3	2	2
Width:	4186	1823	238	5	27
Strength:	3.53	2.07	1.73	1.15	1.14

GAPS:

Start:	1: 1	28:15
End:	21:24	48:35
Count:	2	2
Width:	11152	12631
Strength:	2.06	2.49

Linguistic Density Plot in Ezekiel 1 - 48

For barzel 111 (6 times)

Each Column = 13 Verses.   Separations are: Max =   6658.00, Mean =   3995.71, Min =   751.00 .

REFERENCE

```
                1 1 1 1   1 1 1 1   2 2 2 2   2 2 2 2   3 3 3 3   3 3 3 3   4 4 4 4   4 4 4 4
  1 23  4 5 6 7 8 90 1 2  3 4 5 6   7 8 9 0 1 2 3  4 5 6 7 8 9 0 1 2 3  4 5 6 7 8 9 0 1 2 3  4 5 6 7 8
```

25+

+25

20+

+20

D15+   +15D
E   E
N   N
S   S
I   I
T10+   +10T
Y   Y

5+   +5

0+   +0

```
  1 23  4 5 6 7 8 90 1 2  3 4 5 6   7 8 9 0 1 2 3  4 5 6 7 8 9 0 1 2 3  4 5 6 7 8 9 0 1 2 3  4 5 6 7 8
                1 1 1 1   1 1 1 1   2 2 2 2   2 2 2 2   3 3 3 3   3 3 3 3   4 4 4 4   4 4 4 4
```

REFERENCE

CLUSTERS:

Start:	4: 3	4: 3	22:18	22:18	27:12
End:	27:19	4: 3	27:19	22:20	27:19
Count:	6	2	4	2	2
Width:	13276	6	3022	37	118
Strength:	1.50	1.15	1.83	1.14	1.12

GAPS:

Start:	4: 3	4: 3	27:19
End:	48:35	22:18	48:35
Count:	6	2	2
Width:	26468	10248	13198
Strength:	1.45	1.80	2.65

Linguistic Density Plot in Ezekiel 1 - 48

For berit 114 (18 times)

Each Column = 13 Verses.   Separations are: Max = 4309.00, Mean = 1472.11, Min = 8.50 .

CLUSTERS:

Start:	16: 8	16: 8	16: 8	16:59	16:59	16:59	16:61	17:13	17:13	17:13	17:15	17:18	37:26
End:	44: 7	20:37	17:19	17:19	16:62	16:60	16:62	17:19	17:16	17:14	17:16	17:19	37:26
Count:	18	13	12	11	5	3	2	6	4	2	2	2	2
Width:	18204	3601	1631	514	58	17	144	77	22	26	28	2	
Strength:	3.55	4.66	4.71	4.54	2.28	1.52	1.05	2.62	1.90	1.03	1.03	1.03	1.05

GAPS:

Start:	1: 1	1: 1	17:16	17:19	20:37	37:26
End:	16:59	16: 8	37:26	34:25	48:35	44: 7
Count:	3	2	7	5	4	3	5	2
Width:	8003	6886	12606	12539	10588	8618	5706	6911	4032
Strength:	2.63	3.87	1.29	2.60	2.70	2.95	3.03	2.06	1.83

For bāśār 111 (24 times)

Linguistic Density Plot in Ezekiel 1 - 48

Each Column = 13 Verses.   Separations are: Max = 3472.50,   Mean = 1118.80,   Min = 50.00 .

Linguistic density plot (DENSITY vs REFERENCE).

CLUSTERS:

Start:	4:14	4:14	10:12	11: 3	11:19	21: 4	21: 4	21: 9	23:20	36:26	36:26	36:26	39:17
End:	44: 9	11:19	11:19	11:11	11:19	24:10	21:10	21:10	23:20	44: 9	40:43	37: 8	36:26	39:18
Count:	24	7	6	5	3	2	2	2	9	7	4	2	2
Width:	23351	2971	610	335	129	2438	100	395	4966	3076	7	4
Strength:	1.59	1.59	2.27	2.05	1.41	1.43	1.43	1.03	1.55	1.55	1.66	1.03	1.03

GAPS:

Start:	1: 1	4:14	11:19	11:19	16:26	23:20	24:10	24:10	44: 9
End:	10:12	10:12	21: 9	21: 4	21: 4	36:26	36:26	32: 5	48:35
Count:	3	2	4	3	2	4	3	2	2
Width:	4136	2361	6124	6031	3523	7773	6945	3967	2843
Strength:	1.27	1.15	1.55	2.54	2.23	2.47	3.16	2.64	1.60

Linguistic Density Plot in Ezekiel 1 - 48

For bsl 311 (1 times)   bsl 332 (2 times)   bsl 334 (2 times)

Each Column = 13 Verses.   Separations are: Max = 13558.00, Mean = 4661.66, Min = 7.00

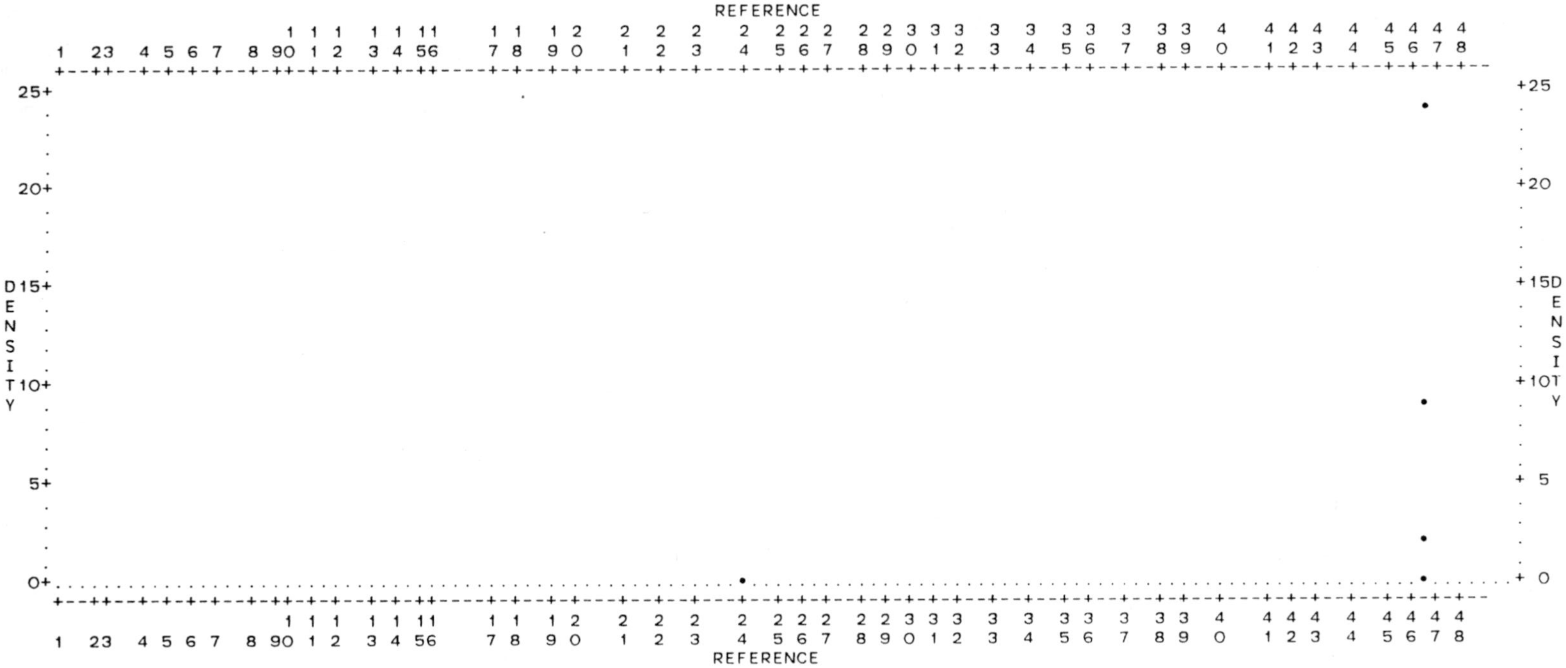

REFERENCE

CLUSTERS:

	Start	End	Count	Width	Strength
Start:	24: 5	46:20	46:23	46:24	
End:	46:24	46:24	46:24		
Count:	5	4	3	2	
Width:	13644	86	14	2	
Strength:	1.00	2.62	1.86	1.18	

GAPS:

Start:	1: 1	1: 1	1: 1	24: 5
End:	46:24	46:23	46:20	46:20
Count:	5	4	3	2
Width:	26757	26745	26673	13558
Strength:	1.62	2.41	3.48	2.25

Linguistic Density Plot in Ezekiel 1 - 48

For bat 111 (7 times)

Each Column = 13 Verses.   Separations are: Max = 12955.50, Mean = 3496.25, Min =   3.50 .

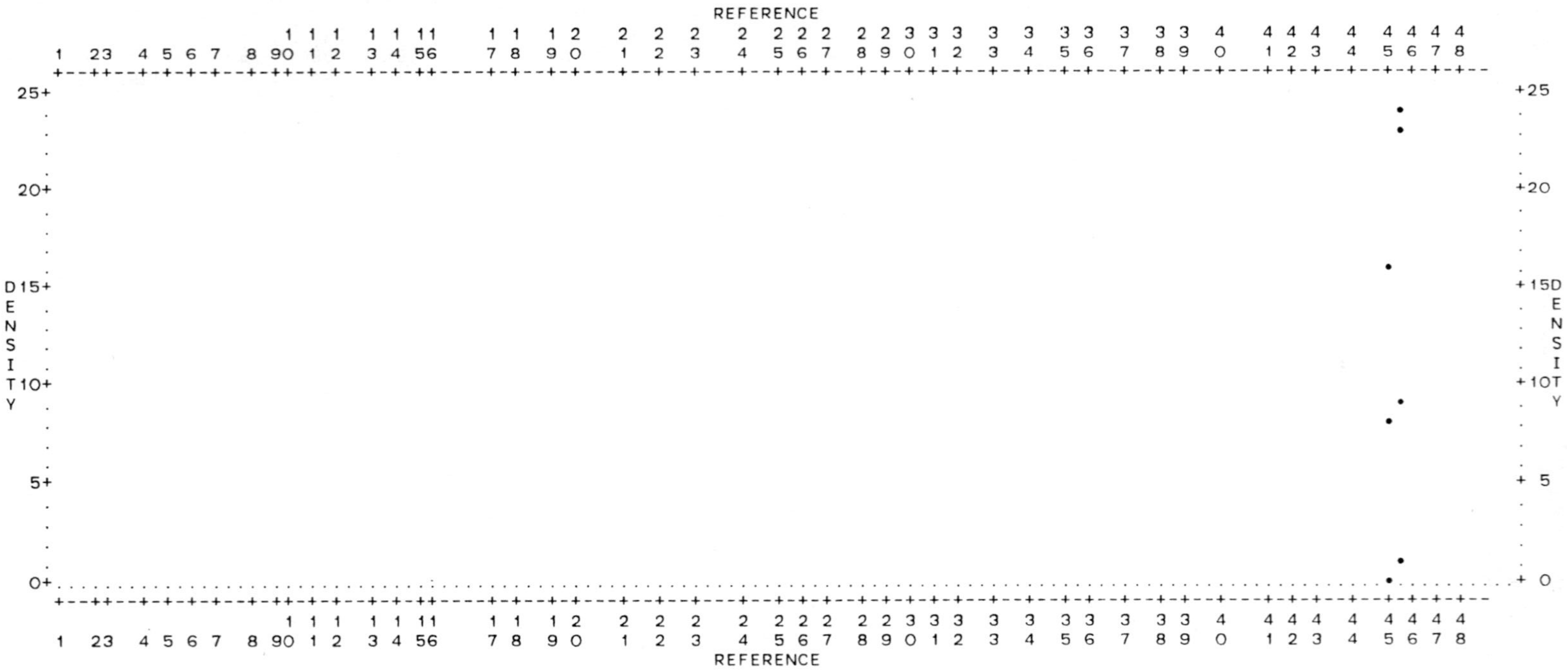

CLUSTERS:

Start:	45:10	45:10	45:10	45:14	45:14
End:	45:14	45:11	45:11	45:14	45:14
Count:	7	3	2	4	2
Width:	72	15	7	11	3	4
Strength:	5.17	1.72	1.13	2.32	1.13	1.13

GAPS:

Start:	1: 1	1: 1
End:	45:14	45:10
Count:	5	2
Width:	25964	25903
Strength:	2.56	7.26

Linguistic Density Plot in Ezekiel 1 - 48

For bat 114 (36 times)

Each Column = 13 Verses.   Separations are: Max = 8089.00, Mean = 755.95, Min = 9.00

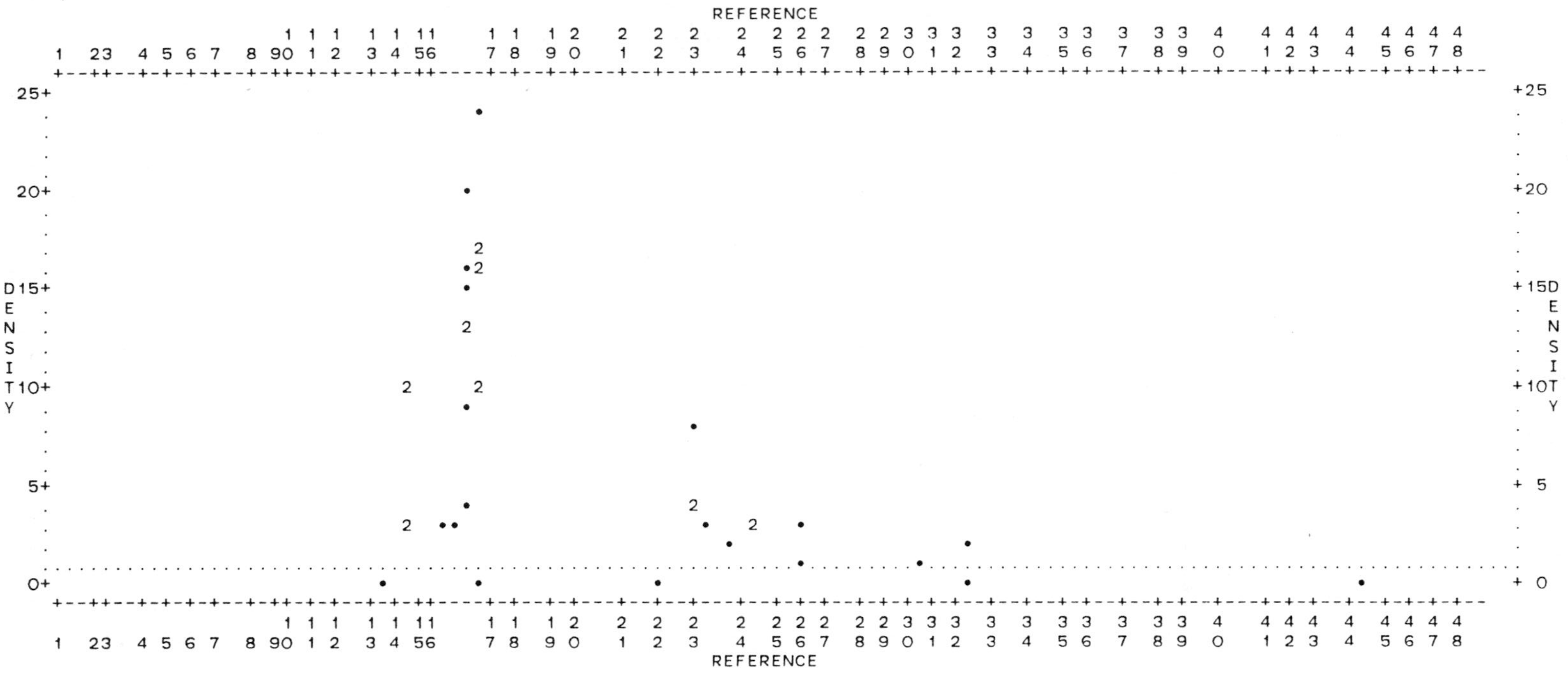

CLUSTERS:

Start:	13:17	13:17	13:17	14:16	14:16	16:20	16:44	16:44	16:44	16:46	16:46	16:48	16:48	16:48	16:53	16:53	16:53	16:55	16:55	16:55
End:	44:25	32:18	16:61	14:22	14:20	16:61	16:61	16:49	16:46	16:46	16:45	16:49	16:48	16:61	16:57	16:61	16:53	16:57	16:55	16:55
Count:	36	35	22	5	3	17	15	7	4	2	3	7	8	2	7	3	5	3	2	
Width:	19765	11676	2280	727	144	95	914	388	121	57	19	27	174	90	7	53	18	9		
Strength:	6.52	11.32	6.04	1.62	1.71	1.38	4.97	4.63	1.78	2.63	1.02	1.00	1.44	1.01	2.87	1.01	2.65	2.10	1.45	1.01

Start:	16:57	16:57	22:11	22:11	23: 2	24:21
End:	16:57	32:18	26: 8	23:47	23:10	26:21
Count:	2	13	10	6	3	4
Width:	6	5821	2493	1358	571	144	671
Strength:	1.01	1.53	2.21	1.56	1.36	1.33	1.28

Data for bat 114, continued.

GAPS:

```
Start:     1: 1    1: 1    1: 1   16:57   16:61   16:61   23: 4   26: 8   26: 8   26: 8   32:18   32:18
End:      14:18   14:16   13:17   48:35   23: 2   22:11   48:35   48:35   32:16   30:18   48:35   44:25
Count:        4       3       2      17       4       3       2      13       6       3       2       3       2
Width:     6402    6354    5771   20002    4086    4002    3575   15877   13850    3279    2328   10522    8089
Strength:  3.33    4.71    6.81    3.51    1.46    2.42    3.83    3.20    6.49    1.72    2.13    8.78    9.96
```

Linguistic Density Plot in Ezekiel 1 - 48

For gā'ôn 111 (9 times)

Each Column = 13 Verses.   Separations are: Max = 5323.00, Mean = 2797.00, Min = 557.50

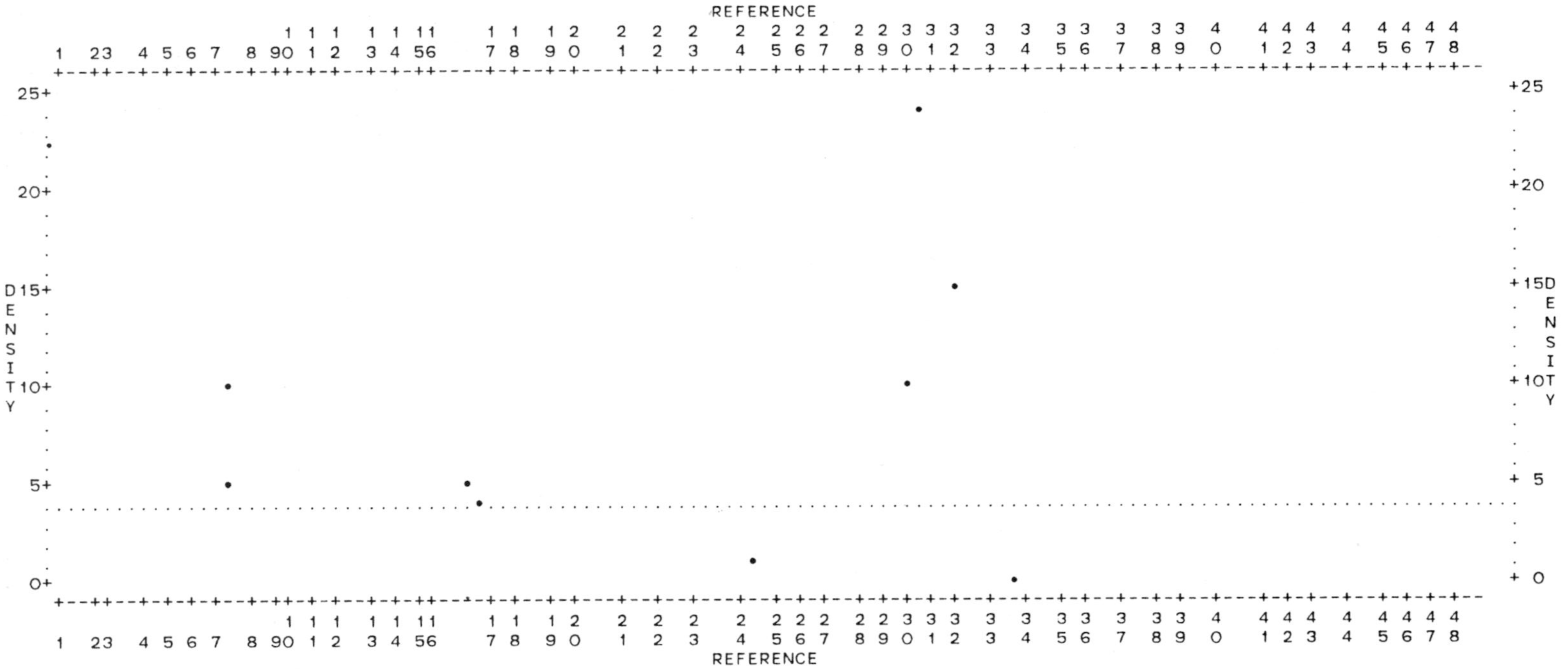

CLUSTERS:

Start:	7:20	7:20	16:49	24:21	30: 6	30: 6
End:	33:28	7:24	16:56	33:28	33:28	30:18
Count:	9	2	2	5	4	2
Width:	15425	78	178	4993	2219	231
Strength:	2.06	1.07	1.03	1.49	1.59	1.01

GAPS:

Start:	16:56	32:12	33:28
End:	24:21	48:35	48:35
Count:	2	3	2
Width:	5483	10646	9542
Strength:	1.06	1.49	2.66

Linguistic Density Plot in Ezekiel 1 - 48

For gab 111 (7 times)

Each Column = 13 Verses. Separations are: Max = 17077.00, Mean = 3496.25, Min = 159.50 .

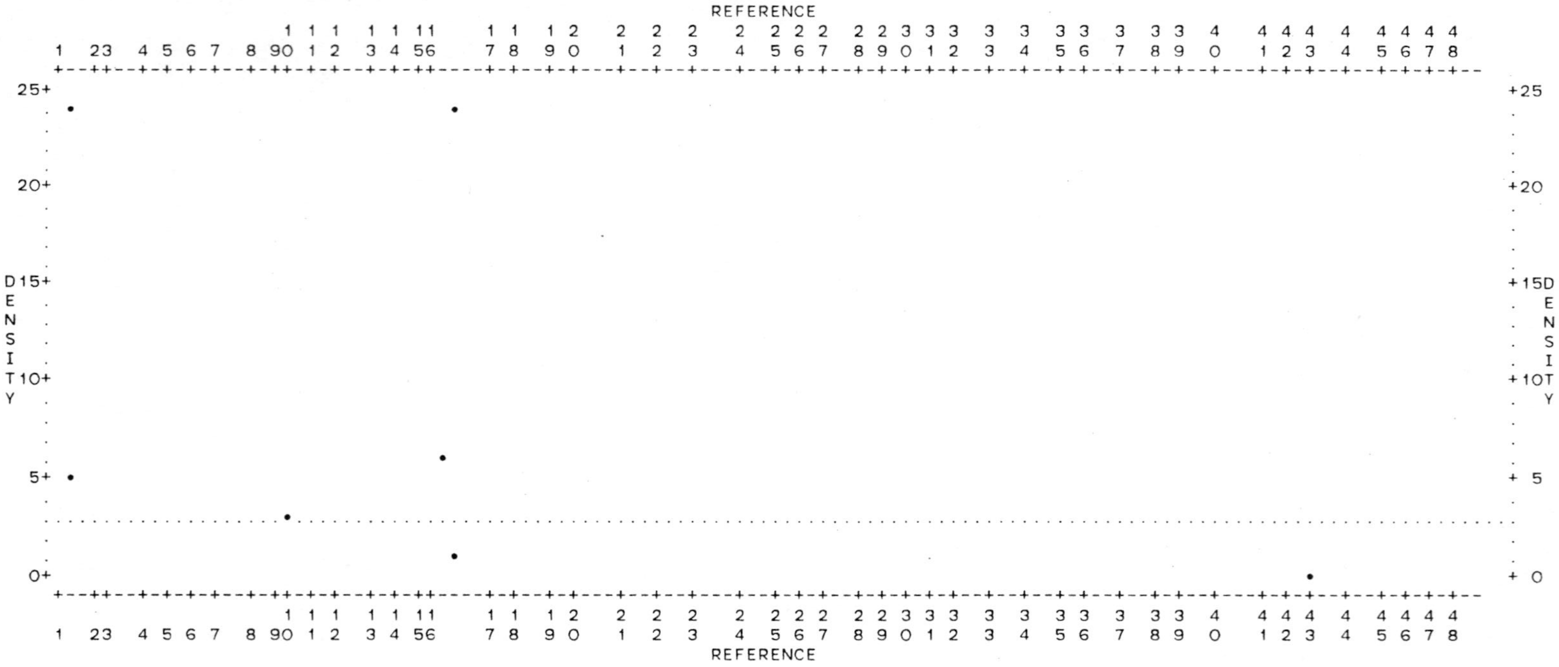

REFERENCE

CLUSTERS:

Start:	1:18	1:18	10:12	16:24	16:24
End:	16:39	1:18	16:39	16:39	16:31
Count:	6	2	4	3	2
Width:	7202	11	3392	319	126
Strength:	2.27	1.13	1.57	1.65	1.09

GAPS:

Start:	1:18	16:31	16:39	16:39
End:	48:35	48:35	48:35	43:13
Count:	7	4	3	2
Width:	27629	20631	20438	17077
Strength:	1.64	2.24	3.33	4.40

Linguistic Density Plot in Ezekiel 1 - 48

For gôbah 111 (6 times)

Each Column = 13 Verses.   Separations are: Max = 9169.00, Mean = 3995.71, Min = 2380.50 .

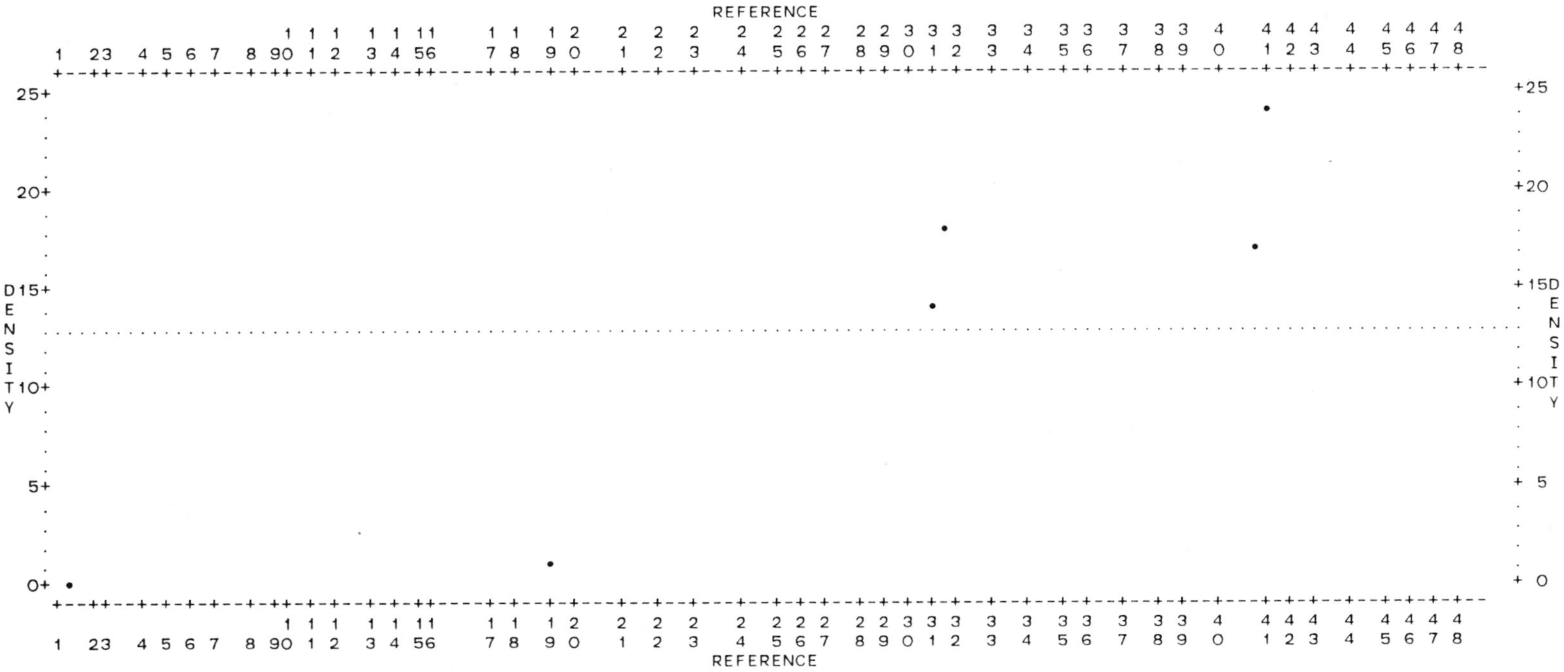

CLUSTERS:

Start:	31:10	31:10	40:42
End:	41: 8	31:14	41: 8
Count:	4	2	2
Width:	6721	96	349
Strength:	1.07	1.12	1.05

GAPS:

Start:	1:18	1:18
End:	31:10	19:11
Count:	3	2
Width:	16504	9169
Strength:	1.90	1.49

Linguistic Density Plot in Ezekiel 1 - 48

For gāḇōah 21 (6 times)

Each Column = 13 Verses. Separations are: Max = 5526.00, Mean = 3995.71, Min = 1351.50 .

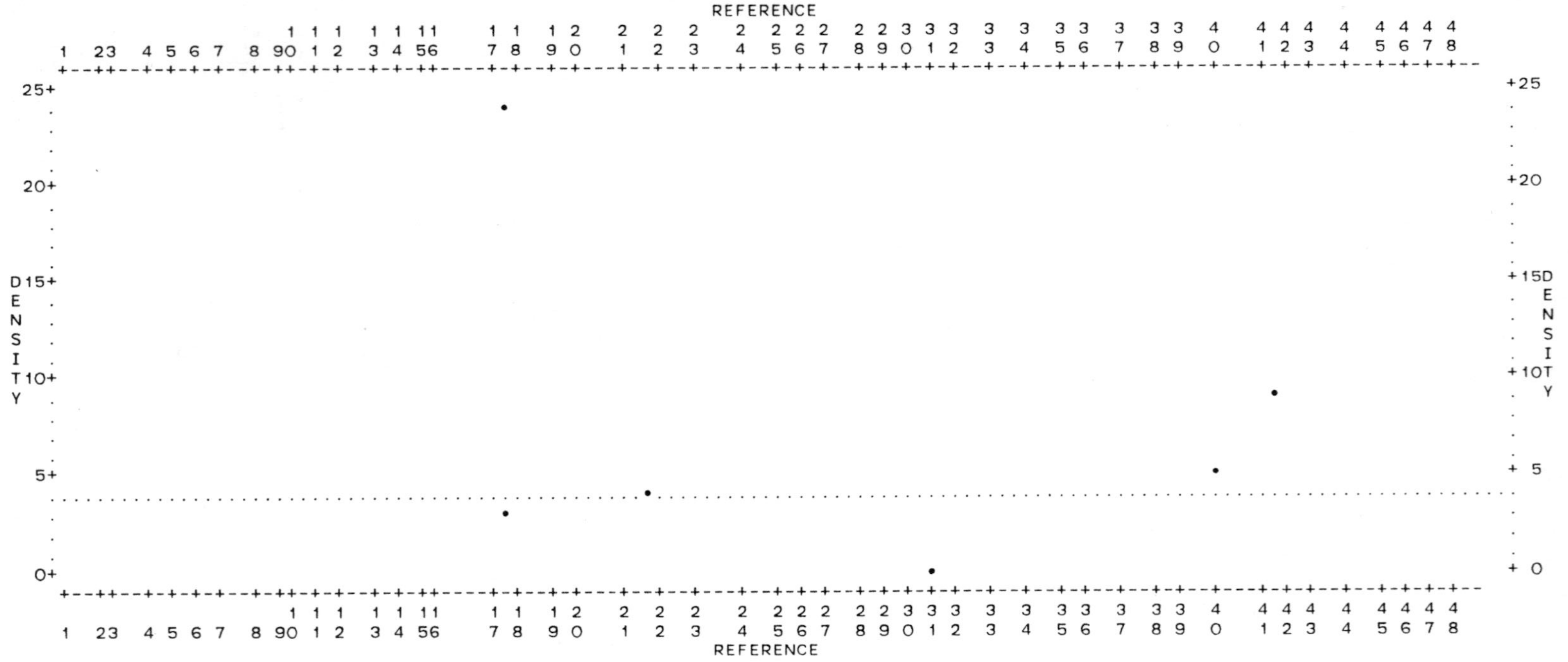

REFERENCE

CLUSTERS:

Start:	17:22	17:22	17:22
End:	41:22	21:31	17:24
Count:	6	3	2
Width:	15202	2703	43
Strength:	1.06	1.18	1.14

GAPS:

Start:	1: 1
End:	17:22
Count:	2
Width:	8602
Strength:	1.33

Linguistic Density Plot in Ezekiel 1 - 48

For gbh 311 (4 times)　　　　gbh 312 (4 times)　　　　gbh 361 (1 times)　　　　gbh 363 (1 times)

Each Column = 13 Verses. Separations are: Max = 5574.00, Mean = 2542.73, Min = 103.50 .

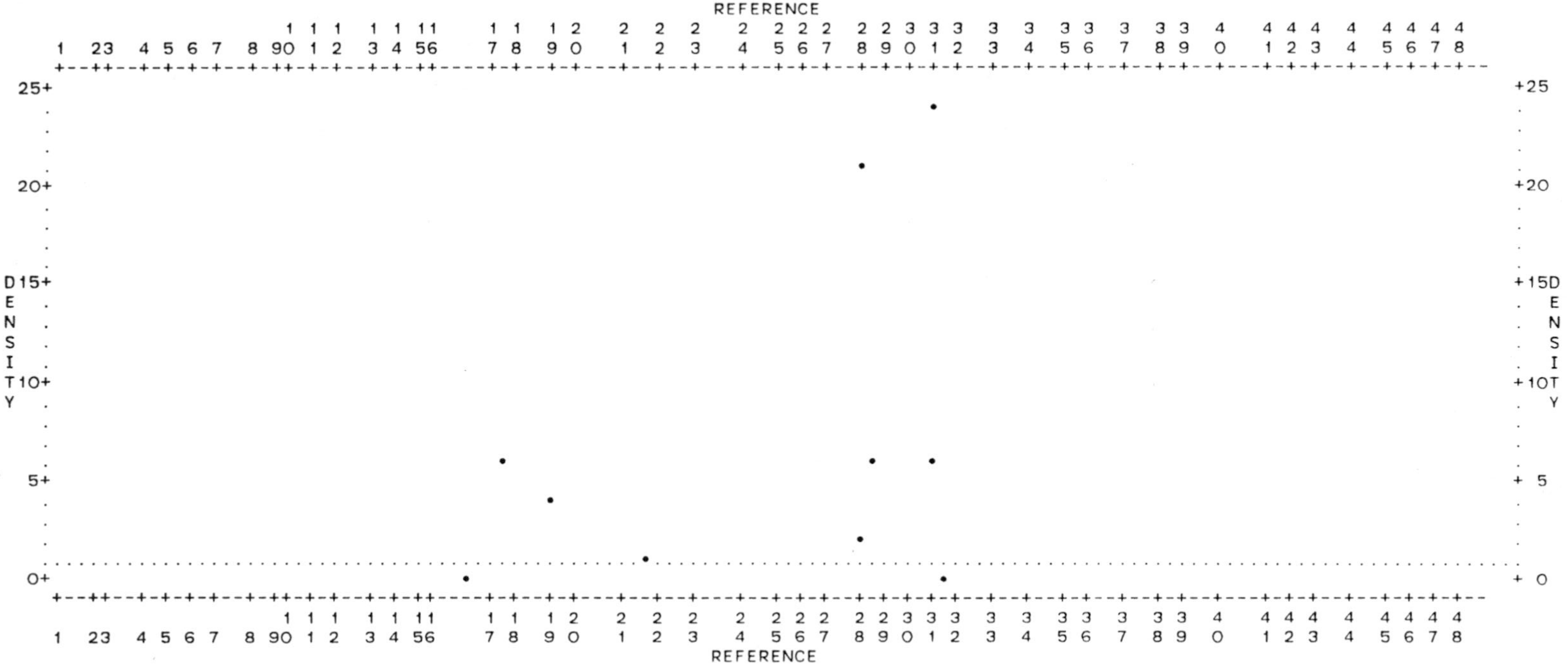

REFERENCE

(Linguistic density scatter plot with vertical axis labeled DENSITY, values 0+ through 25+, and horizontal REFERENCE axis numbered by column.)

CLUSTERS:

Start:	16:50	16:50	16:50	28:2	28:2	28:2	31:5	31:10
End:	31:14	21:31	19:11	31:14	28:17	31:14	31:14	31:14
Count:	10	4	3	6	3	2	3	2
Width:	9116	3509	1698	1818	278	66	207	89
Strength:	4.42	1.14	1.08	2.70	1.54	1.06	1.56	1.05

GAPS:

Start:	1:1	1:1	31:14
End:	17:24	16:50	48:35
Count:	3	2	2
Width:	8646	7794	11059
Strength:	1.14	2.26	3.66

Linguistic Density Plot in Ezekiel 1 - 48

For gĕbûl 111 (43 times)

Each Column = 13 Verses. Separations are: Max = 5657.00, Mean = 635.68, Min = 4.50 .

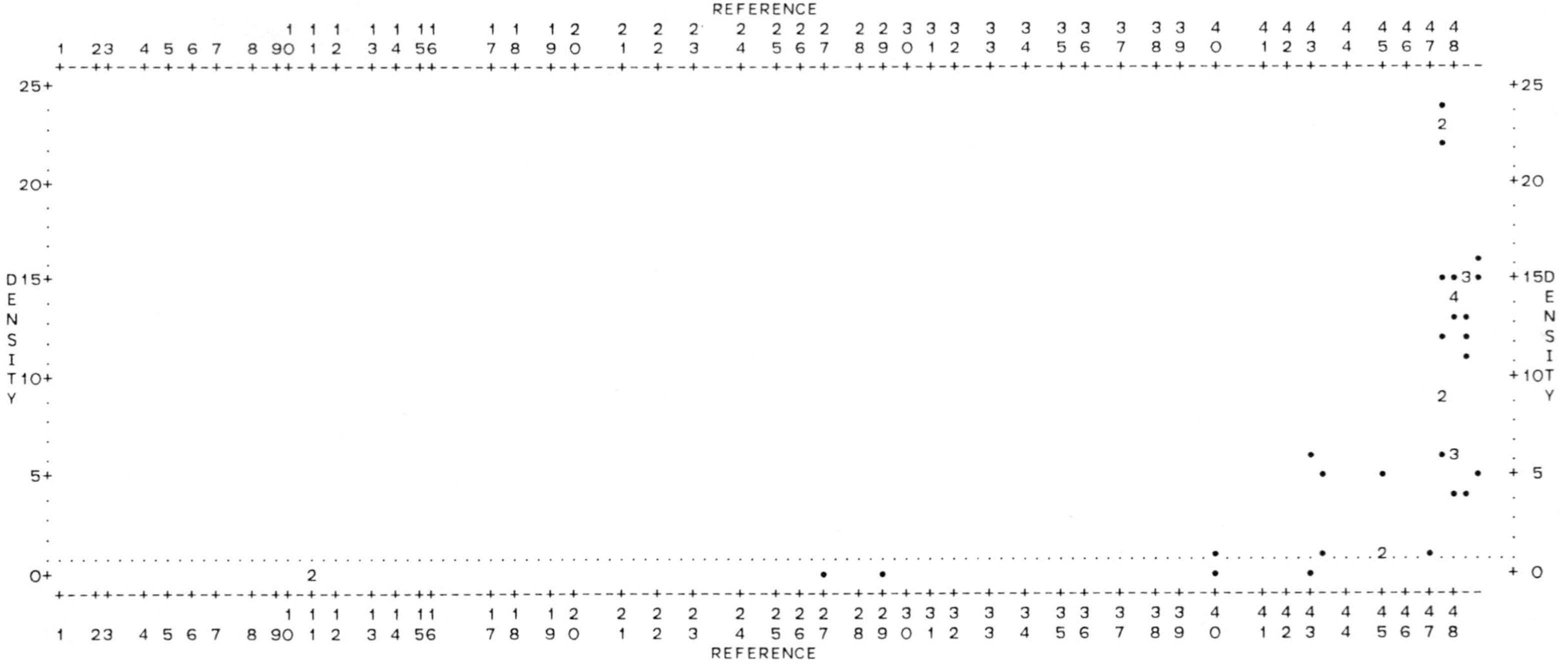

REFERENCE
DENSITY
REFERENCE

CLUSTERS:

Start:	11:10	40:12	40:12	40:12	43:12	43:12	45: 1	45: 7	47:13	47:13	47:13	47:13	47:16	47:16	47:16	47:16	47:17	48: 1	48: 1	48: 1
End:	48:28	48:28	45: 7	40:12	45: 7	43:20	45: 7	45: 7	48:28	48:13	47:20	47:17	47:17	47:17	47:16	47:17	47:17	48:13	48: 8	48: 3
Count:	43	39	9	2	7	4	3	2	30	20	10	8	6	4	2	2	2	10	8	3
Width:	23322	5248	3248	9	1267	193	154	3	778	449	145	84	25	14	4	4	6	214	91	29
Strength:	3.88	13.21	1.14	1.00	1.77	1.63	1.28	1.01	8.93	5.63	3.31	2.86	2.38	1.80	1.01	1.01	1.01	3.27	2.85	1.42

Start:	48: 2	48: 4	48: 4	48: 4	48: 7	48:12	48:21	48:21	48:21	48:22	48:22	48:24	48:26	48:26	48:28
End:	48: 3	48: 8	48: 6	48: 5	48: 8	48:13	48:28	48:25	48:21	48:25	48:22	48:25	48:28	48:27	48:28
Count:	2	5	3	2	2	2	10	6	2	4	2	2	4	2	2
Width:	12	49	24	12	12	6	121	77	11	34	4	12	32	12	8
Strength:	1.00	2.08	1.43	1.00	1.00	1.01	3.32	2.34	1.00	1.78	1.01	1.00	1.78	1.00	1.00

Data for geb01 111, continued.

GAPS:

Start:	1: 1	1: 1	1: 1	11:11	11:11	29:10	40:12
End:	45: 7	40:12	11:10	40:12	27: 4	40:12	43:12
Count:	13	6	2	4	2	2	2
Width:	25835	22590	4516	18048	9950	6734	1972
Strength:	9.80	14.66	6.24	15.35	14.98	9.81	2.14

Linguistic Density Plot in Ezekiel 1 - 48

For gibbôr 21 (6 times)

Each Column = 13 Verses. Separations are: Max = 8741.50, Mean = 3995.71, Min = 91.00 .

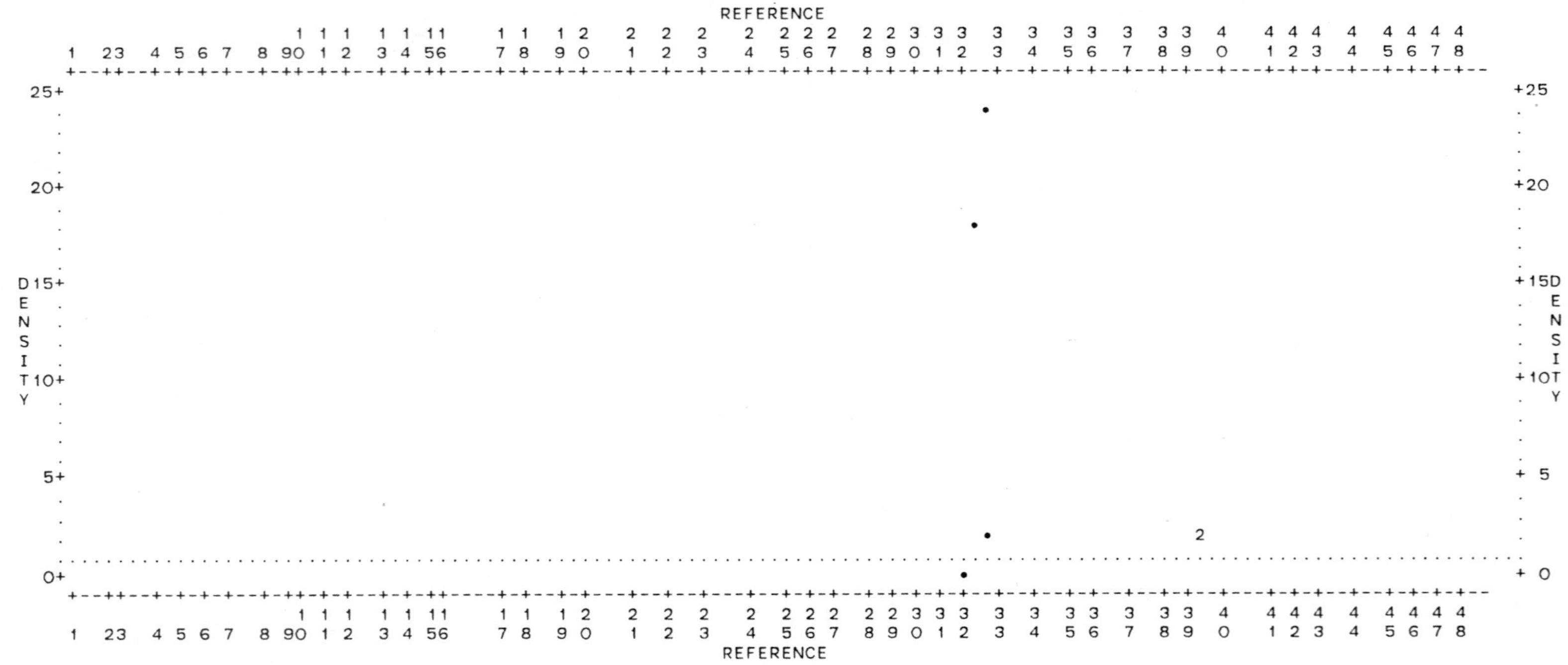

REFERENCE

CLUSTERS:

Start:	32:12	32:12	32:12	39:18
End:	39:20	32:27	32:27	39:20
Count:	6	4	2	2
Width:	4781	352	170	28	41
Strength:	3.40	2.37	1.10	1.14	1.14

GAPS:

Start:	1: 1	1: 1	1: 1
End:	32:27	32:21	32:12
Count:	4	3	2
Width:	17636	17482	17312
Strength:	1.15	2.12	3.84

Linguistic Density Plot in Ezekiel 1 - 48

For gib'â 114 (8 times)

Each Column = 13 Verses.   Separations are: Max =   8052.00, Mean =   3107.78, Min =   164.50 .

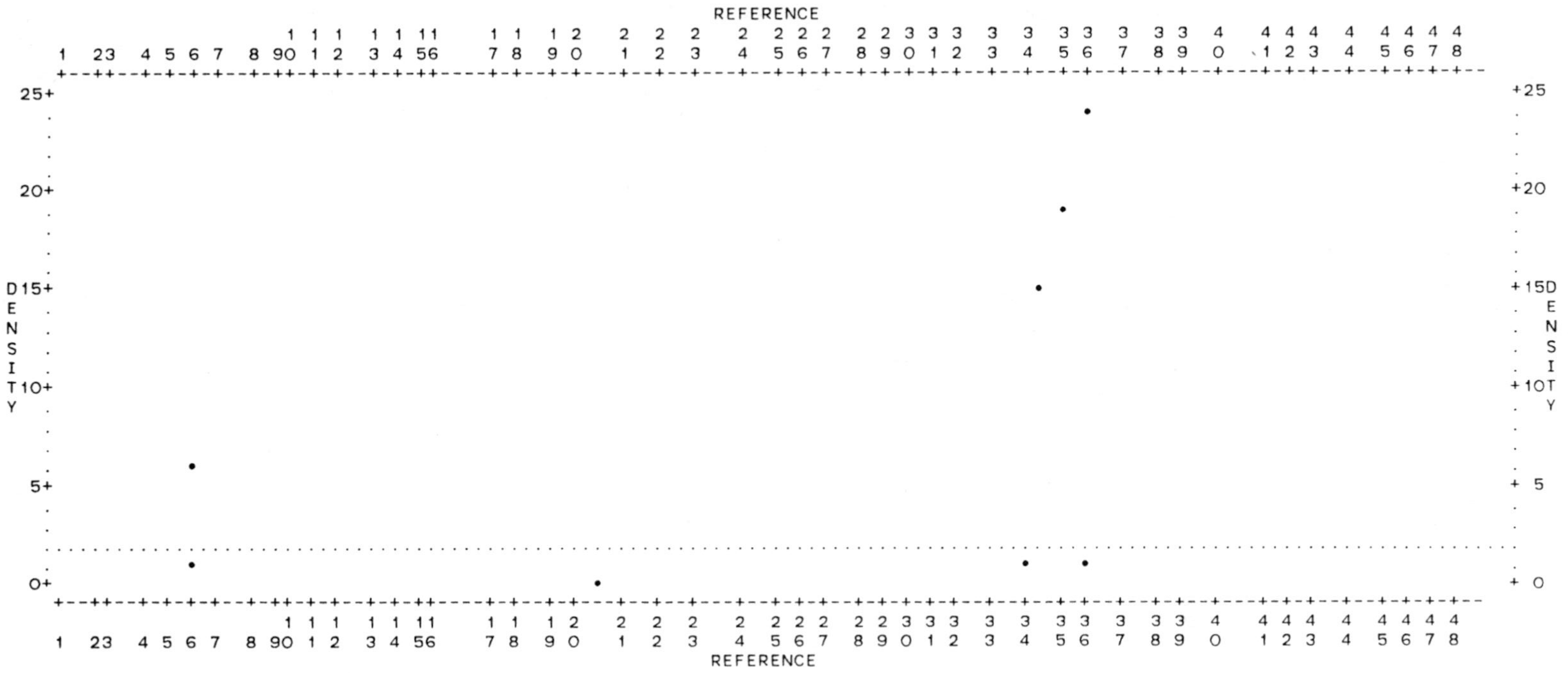

CLUSTERS:

Start:	6: 3	6: 3	34: 6	34:26	34:26	36: 4
End:	36: 6	6:13	36: 6	36: 6	35: 8	36: 6
Count:	8	2	5	4	2	
Width:	17381	237	1040	587	258	83
Strength:	1.18	1.03	2.59	2.09	1.02	1.08

GAPS:

Start:	6:13	6:13	20:28	36: 6
End:	34:26	34: 6	34: 6	48:35
Count:	4	3	2	
Width:	16557	16104	8413	8253
Strength:	1.73	2.68	1.90	1.85

Linguistic Density Plot in Ezekiel 1 - 48

For gādōl 21 (36 times)

Each Column = 13 Verses.   Separations are: Max =   2476.50, Mean =   755.95, Min =   39.00 .

CLUSTERS:

Start: 1: 4   8: 6   8: 6   8: 6   8:13   8:18   16:46   16:61   16:61   17: 7   17: 7   36:23   38:13   38:13   47:10
End: 11:13   11:13   9: 9   9: 1   9: 1   9: 1   17:17   17:17   17: 3   17:17   17: 7   39:17   39:17   38:19   48:28   47:20
Count: 11   8   7   6   4   2   10   8   3   2   3   2   6   3   5   4
Width: 4521   1289   536   306   148   12   4382   765   427   92   1   248   78   1   1967   632   155   853   209
Strength: 1.50   2.25   2.39   2.23   1.71   1.01   1.24   2.54   2.45   1.38   1.02   1.63   1.39   1.02   1.16   1.32   1.54   1.66

Start: 47:15   47:19
End: 47:20   47:20
Count: 3   2
Width: 95   10
Strength: 1.38   1.01

Data for gādōl 21, continued.

GAPS:

```
Start:     3:13   9: 9   9: 9  11:13  17: 7  17: 7  17: 7  17: 7  17: 7  17: 9  17:17  17:17  23: 4  23: 4  29:18  38:15  38:19  39:17  39:17
End:       8: 6  16:61  16:46  16:46  48:35  47:19  38:13  38:13  29: 3  38:13  21:19  29: 3  25:17  38:13  36:23  47:15  47:10  47:10  43:14
Count:        2      4      3      2     21     18     11     10      9      5      2      3      2      4      2      6      5      4      3      2
Width:     2205   4199   3861   3108  19754  18978  13194  13117  12947   7206   2610   3589   1879   5392   4057   5652   5544   5430   4953   2588
Strength:  1.96   1.55   2.28   3.19   2.04   2.70   2.79   3.24   3.69   2.96   2.51   2.02   1.52   2.52   4.48   1.20   1.78   2.55   3.35   2.48
```

Linguistic Density Plot in Ezekiel 1 - 48

For gdl 312 (1 times)   gdl 331 (1 times)   gdl 351 (1 times)   gdl 362 (2 times)

Each Column = 13 Verses. Separations are: Max = 6604.50. Mean = 4661.66. Min = 2489.00 .

REFERENCE

CLUSTERS:

Start: 24: 9
End: 38:23
Count: 4
Width: 8450
Strength: 1.04

All gap strengths are less than 1.00.

Linguistic Density Plot in Ezekiel 1 - 48

For gôg 12 (11 times)

Each Column = 13 Verses. Separations are: Max = 10577.50, Mean = 2330.83, Min = 14.50 .

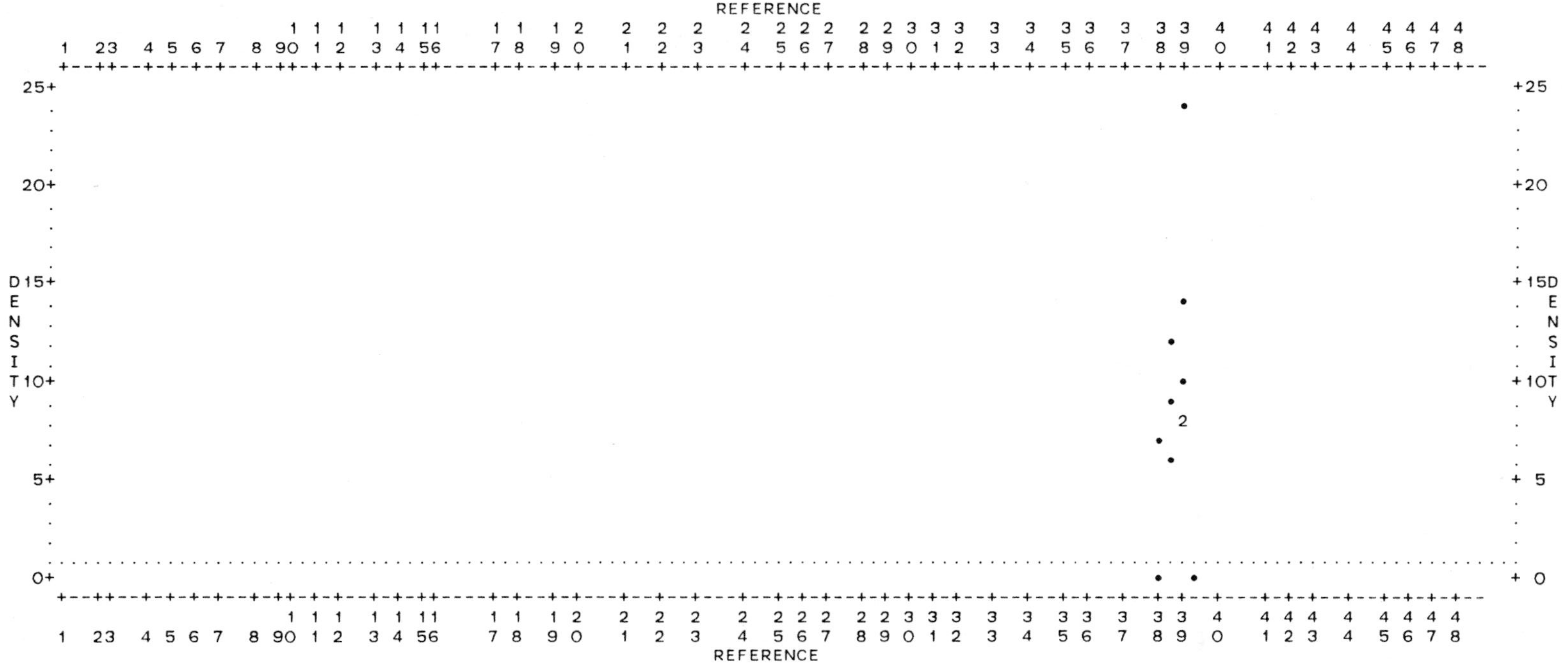

CLUSTERS:

Start:	38: 2	38: 2	38: 2	38:14	38:14	38:16	39: 1	39:11	39:11	39:11
End:	39:15	39: 1	38: 3	39: 1	38:18	38:18	39: 1	39:15	39:11	39:11
Count:	11	7	2	5	3	2	2	4	3	2
Width:	867	559	23	272	116	39	12	104	29	10
Strength:	7.76	3.46	1.07	2.47	1.57	1.06	1.08	2.05	1.60	1.08

GAPS:

Start:	1: 1	1: 1	39:15
End:	39: 1	38: 2	48:35
Count:	7	2	2
Width:	21678	21131	5971
Strength:	1.98	8.76	1.69

Linguistic Density Plot in Ezekiel 1 - 48

For gôy 111 (87 times)

Each Column = 13 Verses.   Separations are: Max = 2855.50. Mean = 317.84. Min = 10.00 .

REFERENCE

DENSITY

(plot axis labels: +25 +20 +15 +10 +5 0)

REFERENCE

CLUSTERS:

Start:	2: 3	2: 3	4:13	4:13	5: 5	5: 5	5: 7	5:14	19: 4	19: 4	20: 9	25: 7	25: 7	28: 7	28: 7	29:12	30:23
End:	39:28	7:24	7:24	6: 9	5: 8	5: 8	5: 8	6: 9	39:28	20:23	20:23	26: 5	25:10	32:18	39:28	30:11	30:11
Count:	87	12	11	10	6	3	8	4	70	6	4	5	3	19	53	7	5
Width:	21628	2427	1330	707	307	93	45	247	12914	788	360	337	76	2259	7084	1113	400
Strength:	12.91	1.08	1.96	2.39	1.86	1.90	1.33	1.31	7.39	1.16	1.10	1.51	1.26	2.89	6.47	1.06	1.41

Start:	30:23	31: 6	31:16	32: 9	34:28	34:28	36: 3	36:13	36:13	36:13	36:19	36:19	36:22	36:22	37:21	37:21
End:	31:12	31:12	32:18	32:18	39:28	36:36	36:36	36:36	36:24	36:15	36:21	36:24	36:23	36:24	37:28	37:22
Count:	5	3	7	4	21	5	5	7	4	4	11	7	13	4	13	3
Width:	315	114	454	189	3087	1165	569	149	70	226	471	124	34	51	1386	214
Strength:	1.54	1.17	1.94	1.42	5.15	4.17	2.06	1.27	1.81	3.28	3.13	1.70	1.32	1.69	2.38	1.37

Clusters for gθy 111, continued.

Start:	38:12	39:21	39:21
End:	39:28	39:28	39:23
Count:	9	5	3
Width:	912	165	34
Strength:	1.91	1.79	1.36

GAPS:

Start:	1: 1	1: 1	2: 3	6: 9	6: 9	6: 9	6: 9	6: 9	7:24	12:16	12:16	16:14	20:32	20:41	22:16	22:16	23:30	26: 5	26: 5
End:	29:15	5: 5	4:13	29:15	22:15	20:22	12:15	11:12	11:12	20:22	19: 4	19: 4	22: 4	22: 4	29:15	25: 7	25: 7	29:12	28:25
Count:	39	4	2	28	17	12	5	3	2	7	3	2	3	2	11	3	7	4	3
Width:	15955	1956	1097	13506	9252	7675	2729	2117	1494	4918	4153	2362	1132	894	4235	2016	1101	1829	1496
Strength:	2.63	1.86	2.47	3.60	3.64	4.26	2.35	3.35	3.74	4.02	7.95	6.50	1.12	1.83	1.12	3.12	2.49	1.62	1.94

Start:	1: 1	39:21	39:28	26: 5	28: 7
End:	5: 5	39:28	48:35	32:18	34:28
Count:	5	5	2	2	2
Width:	1742	5857	5696	1116	1738
Strength:	2.50	7.42	17.11	2.53	4.51

For gôlâ 114 (11 times)

Linguistic Density Plot in Ezekiel 1 - 48

Each Column = 13 Verses.   Separations are: Max = 11442.50, Mean = 2330.83, Min = 22.50 .

```
                                              REFERENCE
      1 1111111111222222222233333333334444444444
  D   2345678901234567890123456789012345678901234 5678
I 25+ ·
N     ·
S 20+ ·            •        • •        •
I     ·
T 15+ ·
Y     ·
  10+ ·
      ·
   5+ ·
      ·                                          •
   0+ +--+--+--+--+--+--+--+--+--+--+--+--+--+--+--+--+--+--+--+--+--
      1 1111111111222222222233333333334444444444
      2345678901234567890123456789012345678901234 5678
                                              REFERENCE
```

CLUSTERS:

```
Start:     1: 1   1: 1   3:11  11:24  11:24  12: 3  12: 7
End:      25: 3  12:11   3:15  12:11  11:25  12: 4  12:11
Count:      11     10      3      2      5      3      2
Width:   13627   5069   1104    242    115     82     45     17     79
Strength:  3.34   4.73   1.23   3.54   2.51   1.04   1.59   1.07   1.05
```

GAPS:

```
Start:    12: 4  12: 7  12:11  25: 3
End:      48:35  48:35  48:35  48:35
Count:      5      4      3      2
Width:   23012  22964  22885  14327
Strength:  3.74   4.75   6.30   5.59
```

Linguistic Density Plot in Ezekiel 1 - 48

For gzl 311 (4 times)   gzl 312 (1 times)

Each Column = 13 Verses. Separations are: Max = 9494.50, Mean = 4661.66, Min = 62.00

CLUSTERS:

Start:	18: 7	18: 7	18: 7	18:16
End:	22:29	18:18	18:12	18:18
Count:	5	4	2	2
Width:	3211	209	85	41
Strength:	3.09	2.60	1.16	1.17

GAPS:

Start:	1: 1	18:18	22:29
End:	18: 7	48:35	48:35
Count:	2	3	2
Width:	8771	18989	15987
Strength:	1.04	1.93	2.87

Linguistic Density Plot in Ezekiel 1 - 48

For gizrâ 114 (7 times)

Each Column = 13 Verses.   Separations are: Max = 11825.50, Mean =   3496.25, Min =   12.50

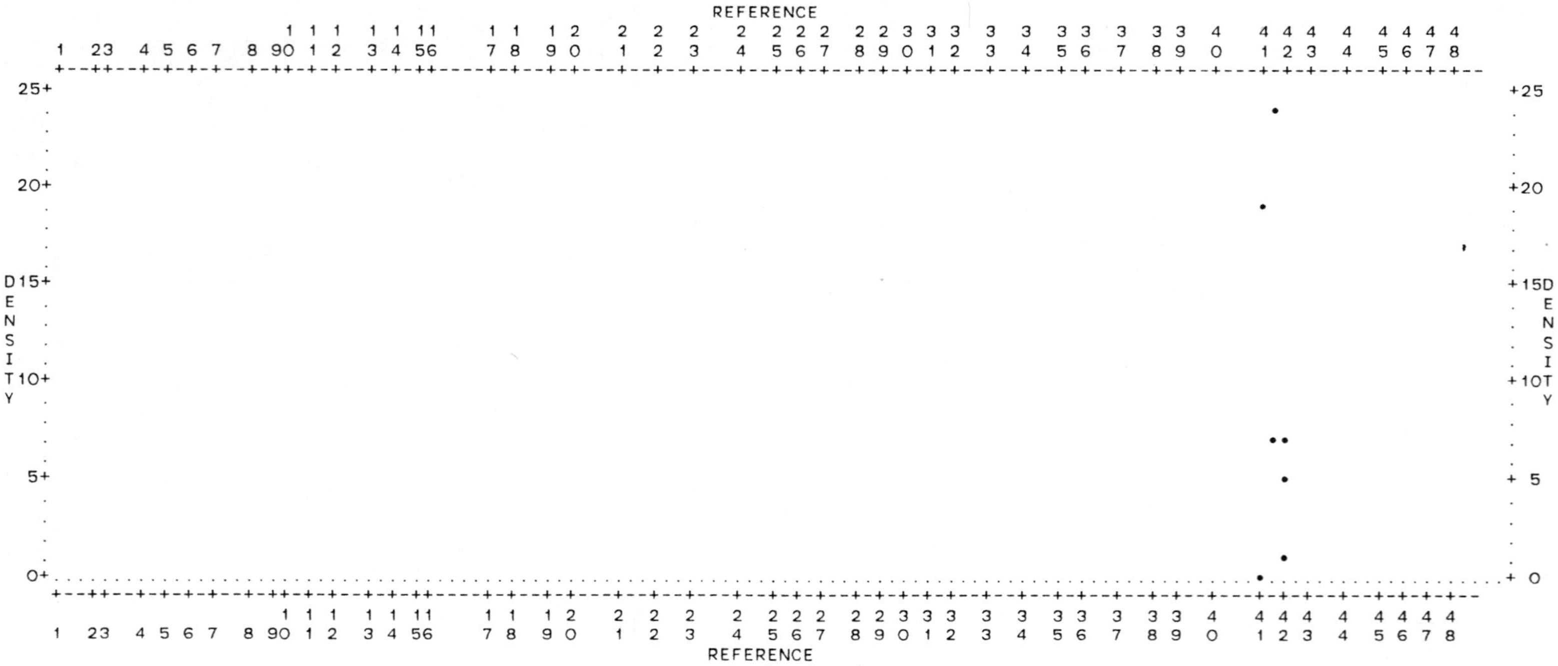

CLUSTERS:

Start:	41:12	41:12	41:13	41:14	42: 1	42:10
End:	42:13	41:15	41:15	42:13	42:13	42:13
Count:	7	4	3	2	3	2
Width:	508	53	25	11	216	67
Strength:	5.07	2.31	1.72	1.13	1.67	1.11

GAPS:

Start:	1: 1	1: 1	1: 1
End:	41:14	41:13	41:12
Count:	4	3	2
Width:	23664	23650	23622
Strength:	2.91	4.12	6.52

Linguistic Density Plot in Ezekiel 1 - 48

For gay' 111 (10 times)

Each Column = 13 Verses.   Separations are: Max = 7264.00, Mean = 2542.73, Min = 48.00 .

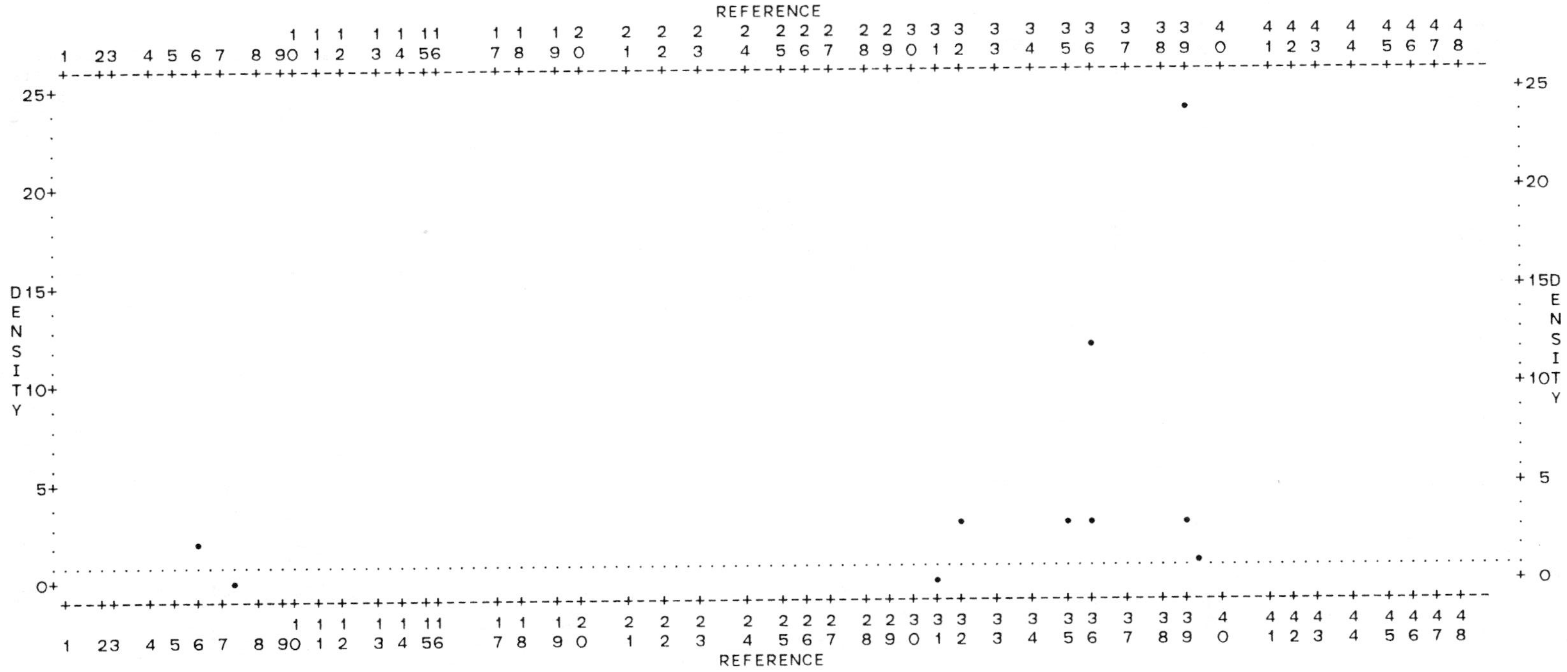

CLUSTERS:

Start:	6: 3	31:12	35: 8	35: 8	36: 4	39:11	39:11
End:	39:15	39:15	39:15	36: 6	36: 6	39:15	39:11
Count:	10	8	6	3	2	3	2
Width:	19656	5128	2606	331	96	83	21
Strength:	1.03	3.26	2.51	1.52	1.05	1.60	1.08

GAPS:

Start:	1: 1	1: 1	1: 1	7:16	39:15
End:	36: 4	35: 8	31:12	31:12	48:35
Count:	7	6	4	2	2
Width:	19638	19390	16868	13945	5973
Strength:	1.08	1.66	2.56	4.91	1.47

Linguistic Density Plot in Ezekiel 1 - 48

For galgal 111 (5 times)

Each Column = 13 Verses.   Separations are: Max = 7746.00, Mean = 4661.66, Min = 118.50 .

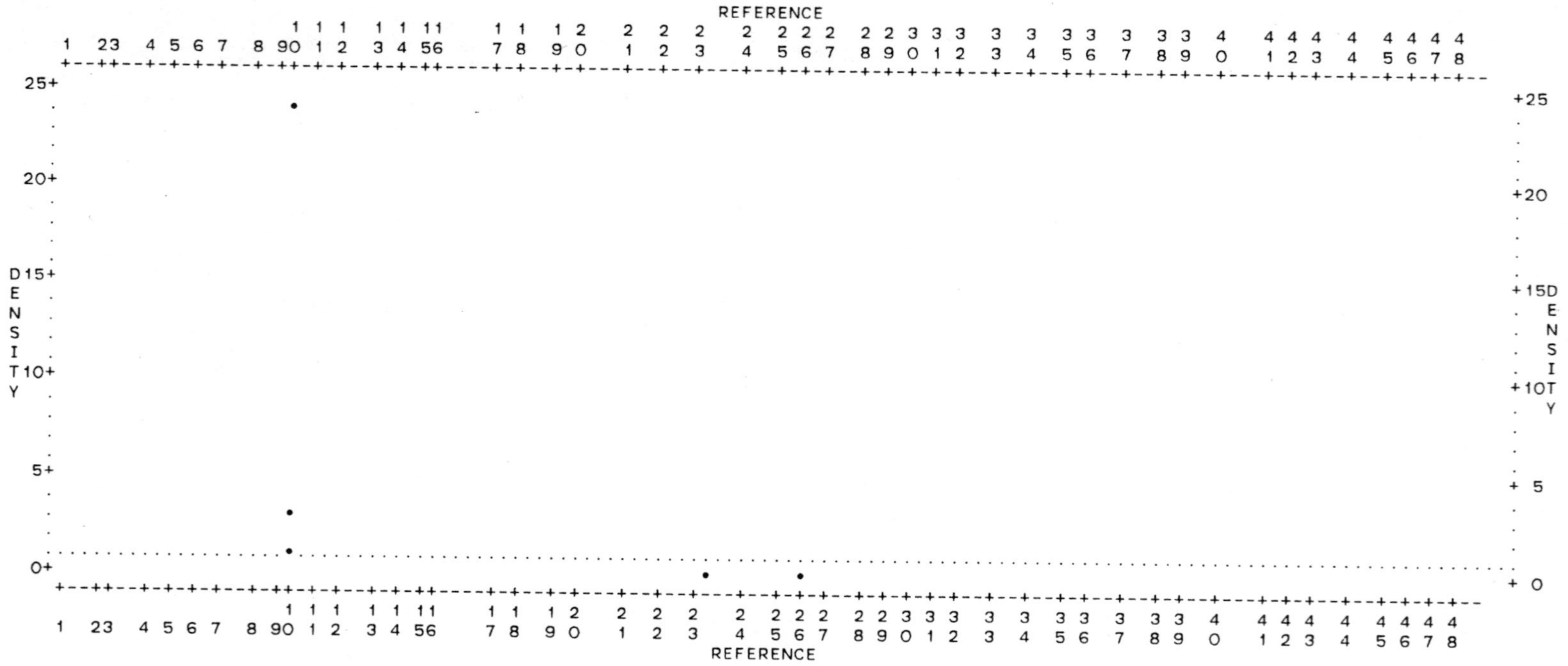

REFERENCE

REFERENCE

CLUSTERS:

Start:	10: 2	10: 2	10: 2
End:	26:10	10:13	10: 6
Count:	5	3	2
Width:	10242	237	94
Strength:	1.68	1.82	1.15

GAPS:

Start:	10: 6	10:13	26:10
End:	48:35	48:35	48:35
Count:	5	4	2
Width:	23950	23807	13802
Strength:	1.06	1.85	2.31

Linguistic Density Plot in Ezekiel 1 - 48

For glh 311 (2 times)   glh 313 (1 times)   glh 321 (2 times)   glh 322 (2 times)
     glh 3262 (1 times)   glh 331 (3 times)   glh 332 (2 times)   glh 3662 (1 times)

Each Column = 13 Verses.   Separations are: Max = 4902.00, Mean = 1864.67, Min = 76.00 .

REFERENCE

(Linguistic density scatter plot; vertical axis DENSITY marked +25, +20, +15D/E/N/S, +10T/Y, +5, 0; horizontal axis columns 1 23 4 5 6 7 8 90 1 2 3 4 56 7 8 90 1 2 3 4 5 6 7 8 90 1 2 3 4 5 6 7 89 0 1 2 3 4 5 6 7 8)

REFERENCE

CLUSTERS:

Start:	12: 3	12: 3	12: 3	12: 3	16:36	16:36	21:29	23:10	23:18
End:	39:28	23:29	16:57	13:14	16:57	16:37	23:29	23:18	23:18
Count:	14	12	6	3	3	2	6	3	2
Width:	17354	7703	3041	792	514	55	1359	426	152
Strength:	2.89	4.14	1.90	1.23	1.35	1.03	2.41	1.84	1.06

GAPS:

Start:	1: 1	23:18	23:29	39:28
End:	12: 3	48:35	39:23	48:35
Count:	2	5	3	2
Width:	4914	15626	9530	5701
Strength:	1.74	2.64	4.39	2.19

Linguistic Density Plot in Ezekiel 1 - 48

For glh 311 (2 times)
     glh 3262 (1 times)

glh 313 (1 times)   glh 321 (2 times)

glh 322 (2 times)

Each Column = 13 Verses. Separations are: Max = 9530.00, Mean = 3107.78, Min = 396.00

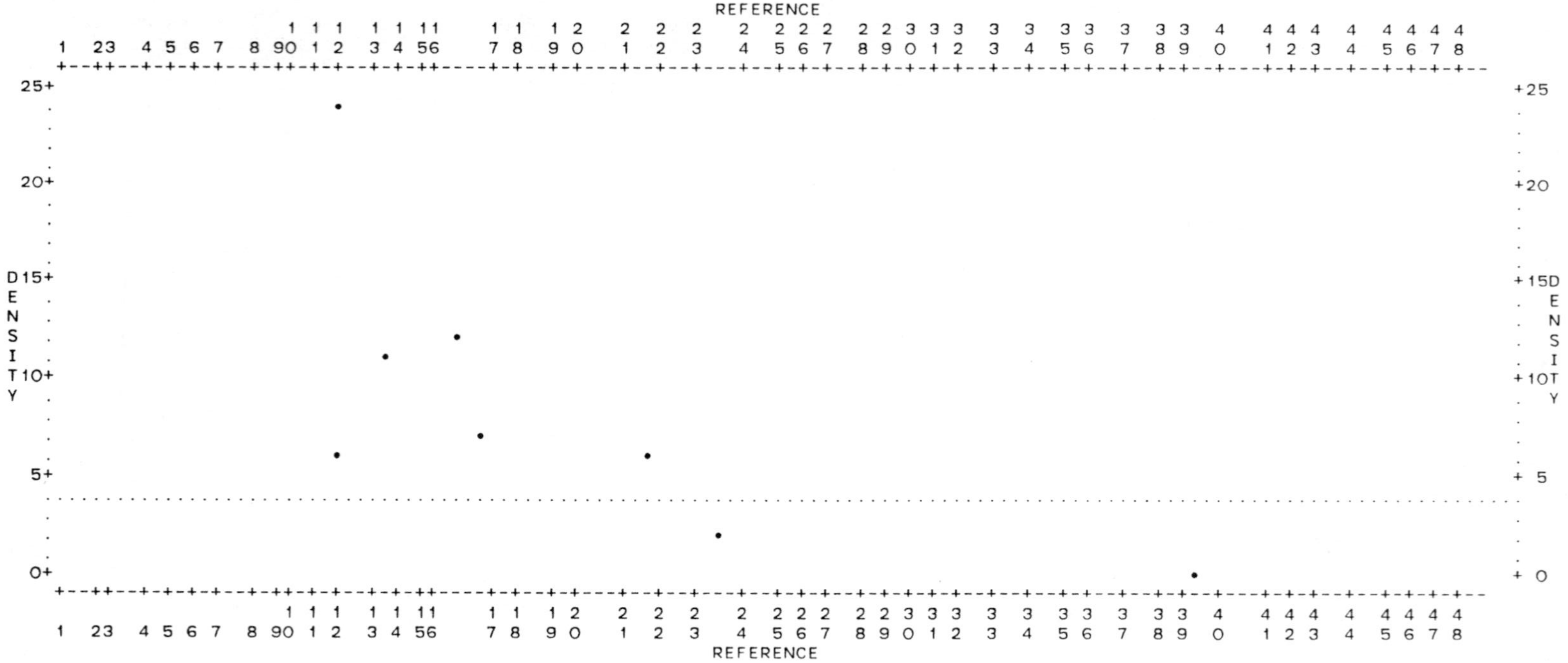

CLUSTERS:

Start:	12: 3	12: 3	12: 3	12: 3	12: 3
End:	39:23	23:29	16:57	13:14	12: 3
Count:	8	7	5	3	3
Width:	17233	7703	3041	792	6
Strength:	1.22	2.62	2.13	1.47	1.11

GAPS:

Start:	16:57	23:29	23:29
End:	48:35	48:35	39:23
Count:	5	3	2
Width:	20014	15352	9530
Strength:	1.72	2.48	2.31

Linguistic Density Plot in Ezekiel 1 - 48

For glh 331 (3 times)   glh 332 (2 times)

Each Column = 13 Verses.   Separations are: Max = 7815.00. Mean = 4661.66. Min = 76.00 .

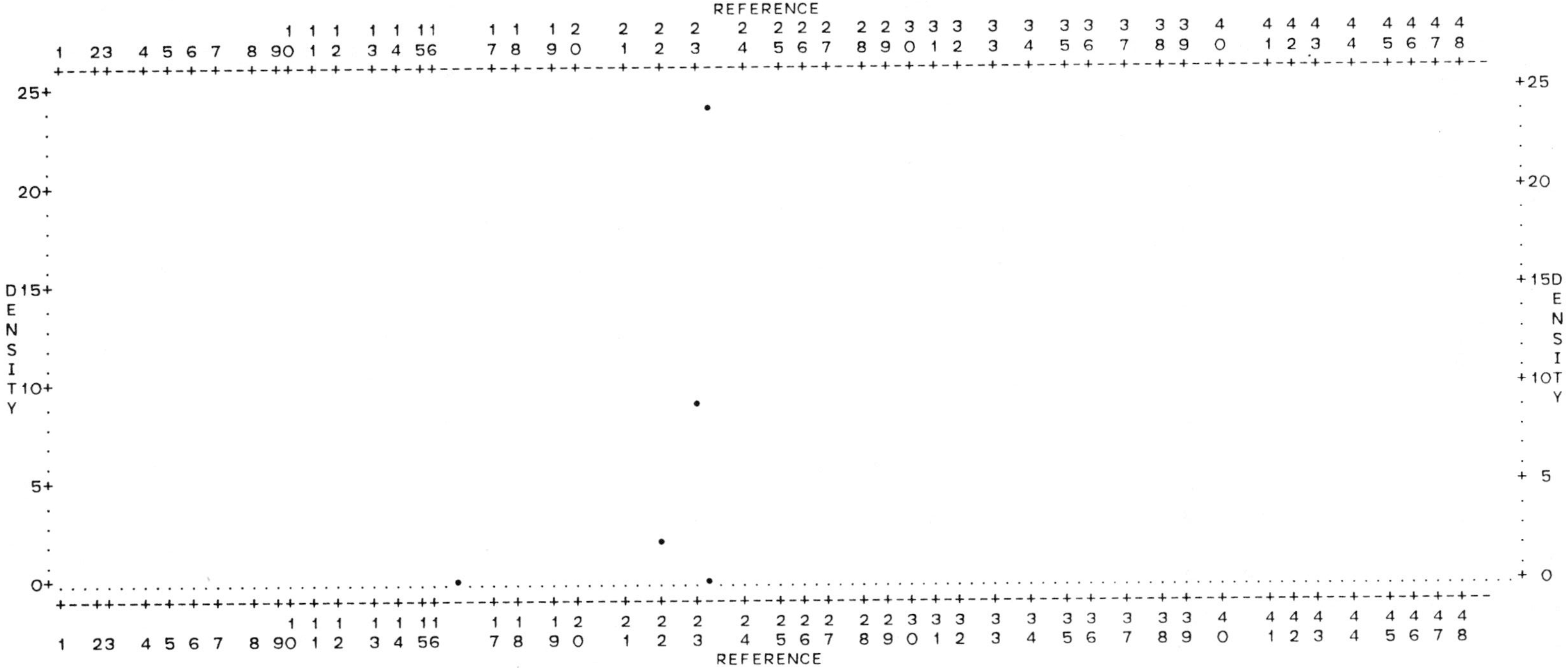

REFERENCE

CLUSTERS:

Start:	16:37	22:10	23:10	23:18
End:	23:18	23:18	23:18	
Count:	5	4	3	2
Width:	4847	746	152	4
Strength:	2.76	2.50	1.84	1.18

GAPS:

Start:	23:18
End:	48:35
Count:	2
Width:	15626
Strength:	2.78

For g1l1Q1 111 (39 times)

Linguistic Density Plot in Ezekiel 1 - 48

Each Column = 13 Verses. Separations are: Max = 2668.50, Mean = 699.25, Min = 18.50

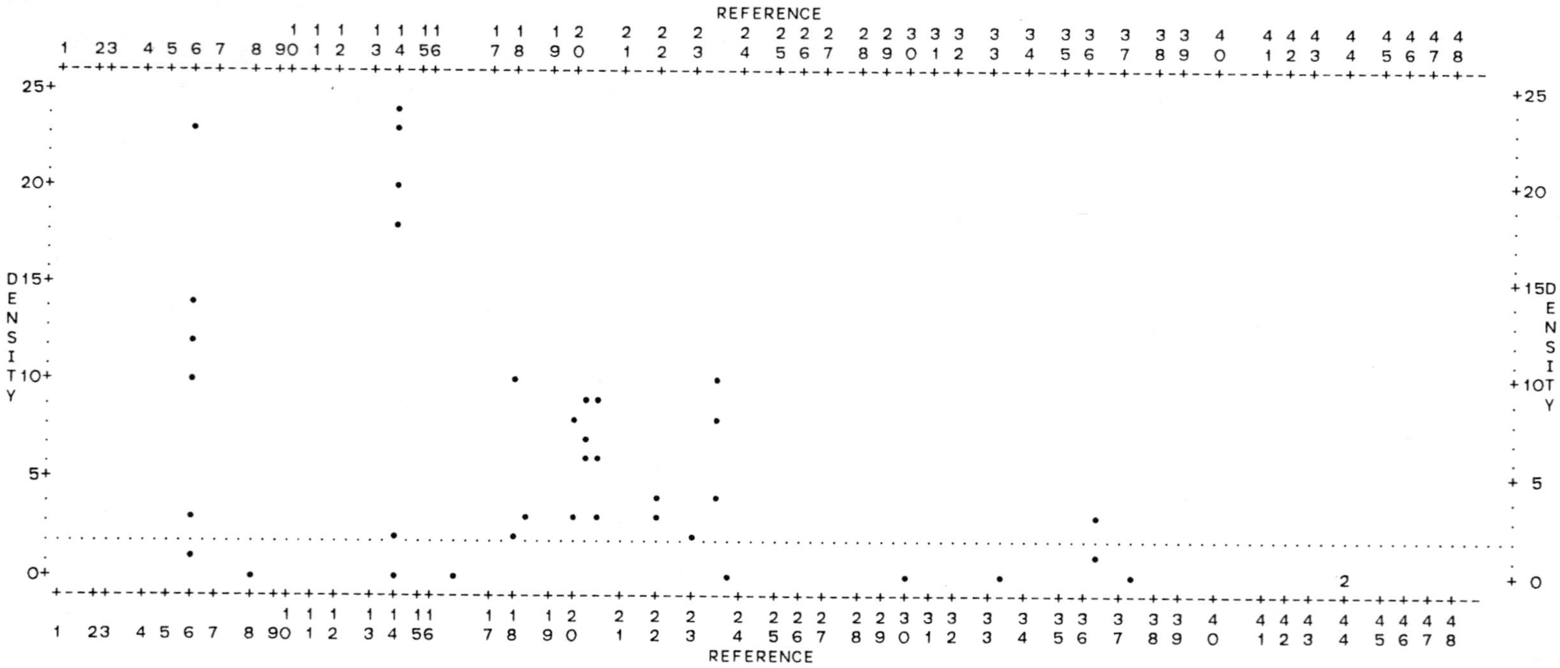

REFERENCE

(scatter/density plot — vertical axis labels: 25+, 20+, D15+, E, N, S, I, T10+, Y, 5+, 0+ ; right-hand axis labels: +25, +20, +15D, E, N, S, I, +10T, Y, +5, +0 ; horizontal axis numbered across the columns)

CLUSTERS:

Start:	6: 4	6: 4	6:13	8:10	6: 4	6: 4	6: 4	6: 4	6: 5	6: 4	14: 3	14: 3	14: 4	18: 6	18: 6	18: 6	20: 7	20:24	22: 3
End:	44:12	23:49	16:36	8:10	16:36	6:13	48:35	23:49	16:36	14: 7	14: 7	23:49	20:39	18:15	20:39	20:18	20:39	23:49	22: 4
Count:	39	32	14	7	6	14	10	3	14	4	6	18	11	3	8	4	7	14	4
Width:	22837	10650	5087	1013	230	2613	16473	2619	12354	68	1461	4271	1805	175	824	292	379	1534	376
Strength:	3.92	6.04	1.95	2.04	2.26	2.80	3.60	1.28	4.49	1.76	1.75	3.52	2.74	1.28	2.45	1.56	1.49	1.70	1.49

GAPS:

Start:	1: 1	6:13	6:13	8:10	6:13	6: 4	23:39	23:39	23:39	14: 3	14: 4	23:49	36:25	37:23	44:12
End:	6: 4	14:14	16:36	14: 3	18: 6	48:35	44:10	36:18	33:25	36:18	30:13	44:10	48:35	44:10	48:35
Count:	2	4	2	3	14	10	8	5	4	3	2				
Width:	2366	3436	3396	2613	16473	12354	7169	6957	5337	5022	4213	2766			
Strength:	2.44	1.16	2.09	2.80	4.86	4.49	3.33	4.22	4.13	3.80	5.15	3.02			

For gam 23 (29 times)

Linguistic Density Plot in Ezekiel 1 - 48

Each Column = 13 Verses.   Separations are: Max =   5475.00, Mean =   932.33, Min =   15.50

CLUSTERS:

Start:	5: 8	5: 8	5: 8	5: 8	5:11	16:28	16:28	16:28	16:41	16:52	18:11	20:12	21:14	21:14	23:35	24: 3	24: 3
End:	39:16	24: 9	10:16	5:11	5:11	16:28	20:25	16:52	16:52	16:52	20:25	20:25	21:32	24: 9	24: 9	24: 5	24: 5
Count:	29	27	6	3	2	21	11	6	2	5	4	4	10	6	9	4	3
Width:	19961	11167	2182	92	9	5906	2878	556	264	13	1337	338	2238	344	139	481	123
Strength:	4.90	7.65	1.32	1.41	1.02	5.37	2.72	2.19	1.68	1.00	1.40	1.63	2.67	1.62	1.37	2.23	1.77	1.02

GAPS:

Start:	1: 1	9:10	10:16	24: 5	24: 9	31:17	39:16
End:	5: 8	16:28	16:28	48:35	48:35	48:35	48:35
Count:	2	3	2	5	4	3	2
Width:	2039	3441	3079	14855	14763	10950	5969
Strength:	1.22	1.25	2.37	6.51	7.93	7.24	5.58

Linguistic Density Plot in Ezekiel 1 - 48

For gan 111 (5 times)

Each Column = 13 Verses.   Separations are: Max =   8384.50, Mean =   4661.66, Min =   21.00 .

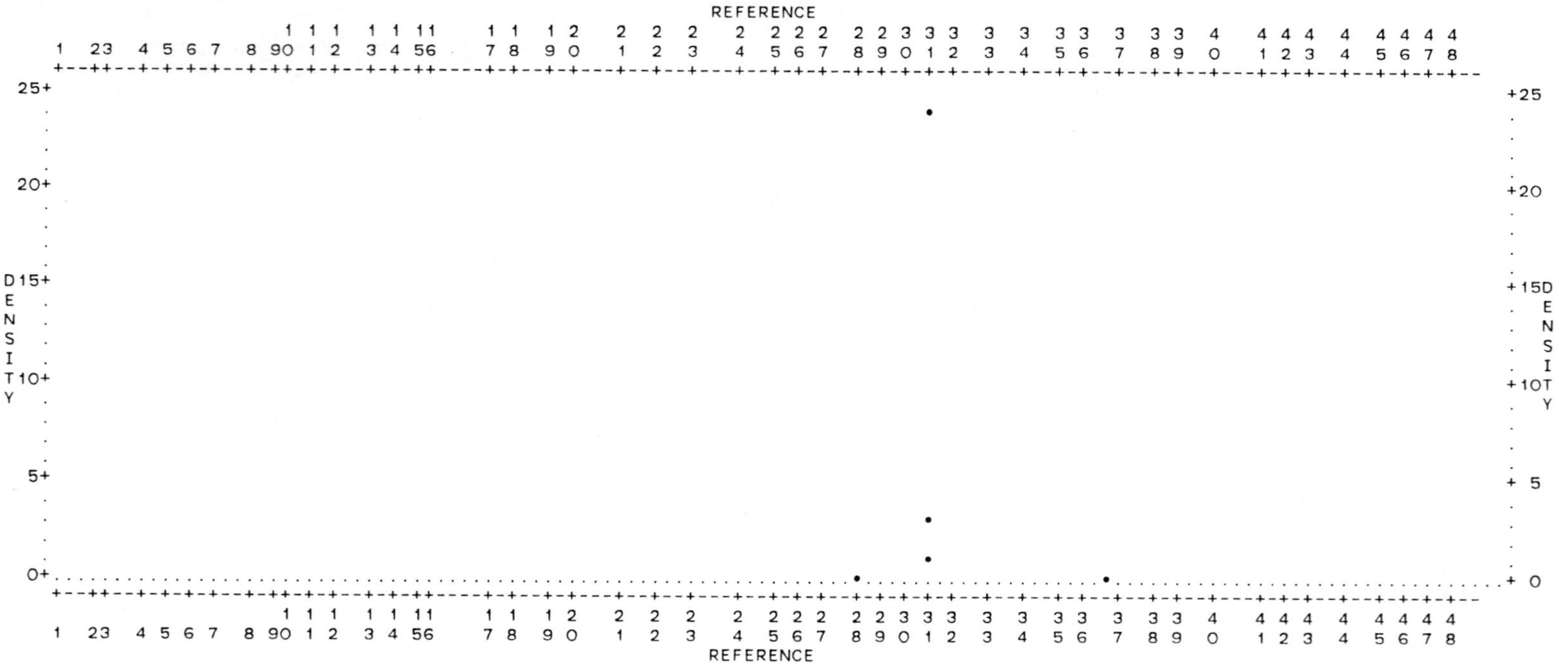

CLUSTERS:

Start:	28:13	28:13	31: 8	31: 8
End:	36:35	31: 9	31: 9	31: 8
Count:	5	4	3	2
Width:	5059	1531	42	18
Strength:	2.72	2.35	1.86	1.17

GAPS:

Start:	1: 1	1: 1
End:	31: 8	28:13
Count:	3	2
Width:	16768	15279
Strength:	1.49	2.69

Linguistic Density Plot in Ezekiel 1 - 48

For gepen 114 (7 times)

Each Column = 13 Verses.   Separations are: Max = 9854.00, Mean = 3496.25, Min = 19.00 .

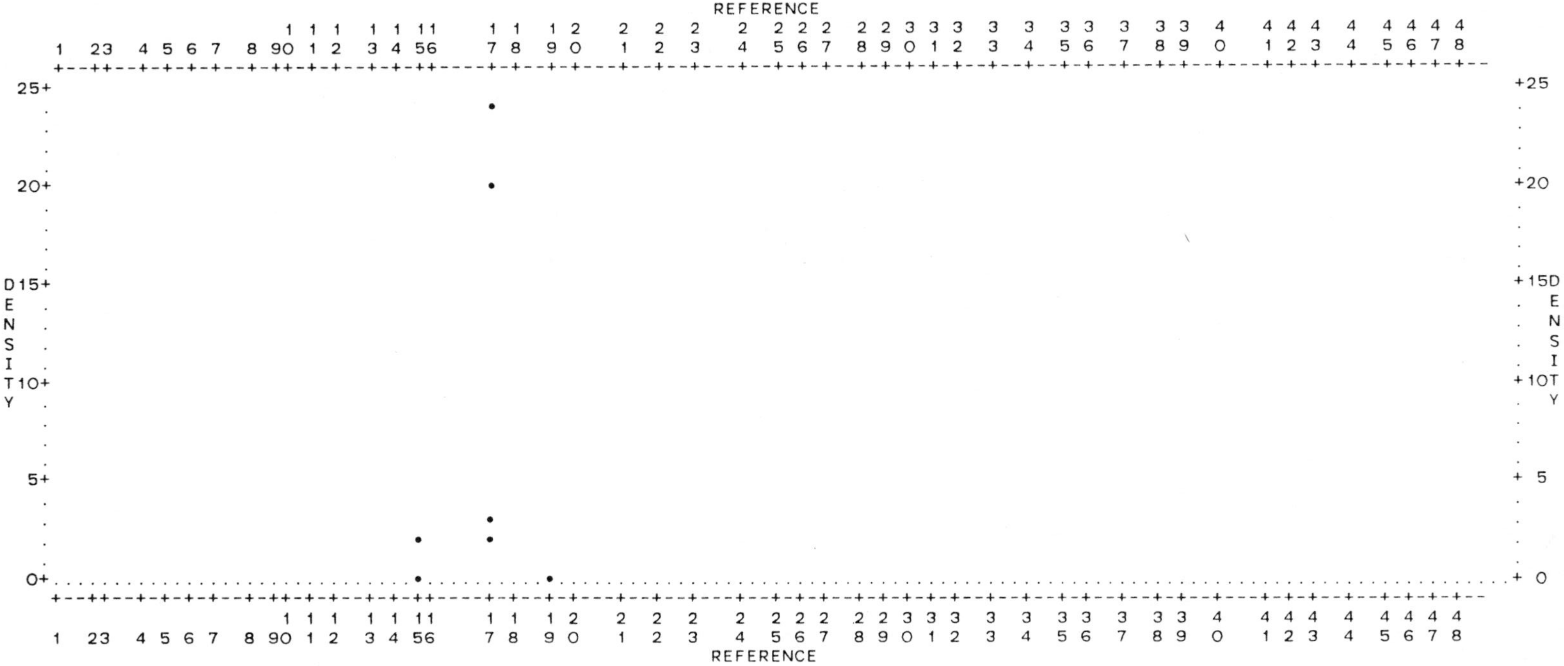

CLUSTERS:

Start:	15: 2	15: 2	17: 6	6 17:	6
End:	19:10	15: 6	19:10	17: 7	17: 6
Count:	7	2	5	4	3	2
Width:	2899	83	1284	77	38	19
Strength:	4.47	1.10	2.72	2.30	1.72	1.12

GAPS:

Start:	17: 7	17: 8	19:10
End:	48:35	48:35	48:35
Count:	4	3	2
Width:	19747	19708	18501
Strength:	2.05	3.14	4.86

Linguistic Density Plot in Ezekiel 1 - 48

For gēr 111 (5 times)

Each Column = 13 Verses.   Separations are: Max = 7839.00, Mean = 4661.66, Min = 367.50 .

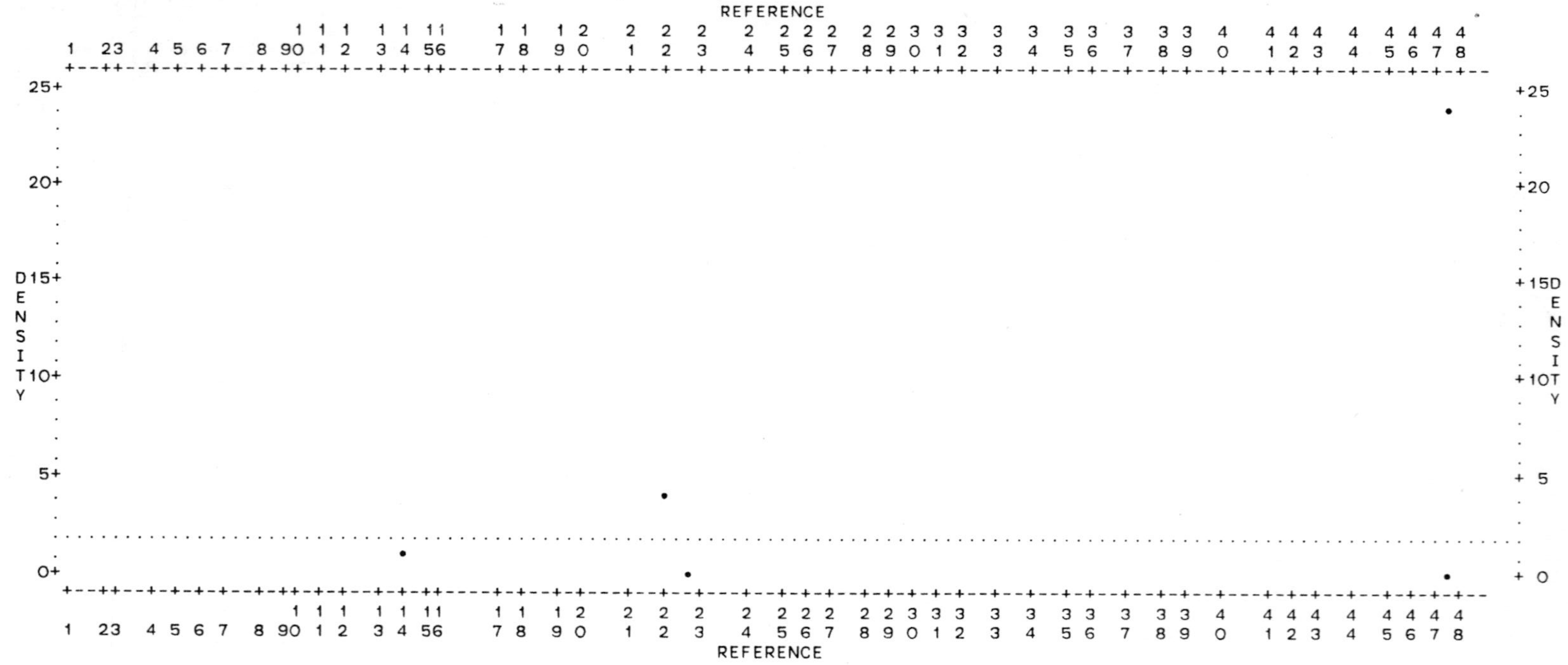

CLUSTERS:

Start:	22: 7	47:22
End:	22:29	47:23
Count:	2	2
Width:	435	35
Strength:	1.07	1.17

GAPS:

Start:	1: 1	22:29
End:	47:22	47:22
Count:	5	2
Width:	27234	15243
Strength:	1.72	2.68

Linguistic Density Plot in Ezekiel 1 - 48

For geŝem 111 (6 times)

Each Column = 13 Verses.   Separations are: Max =   6746.50, Mean =   3995.71, Min =   1250.50 .

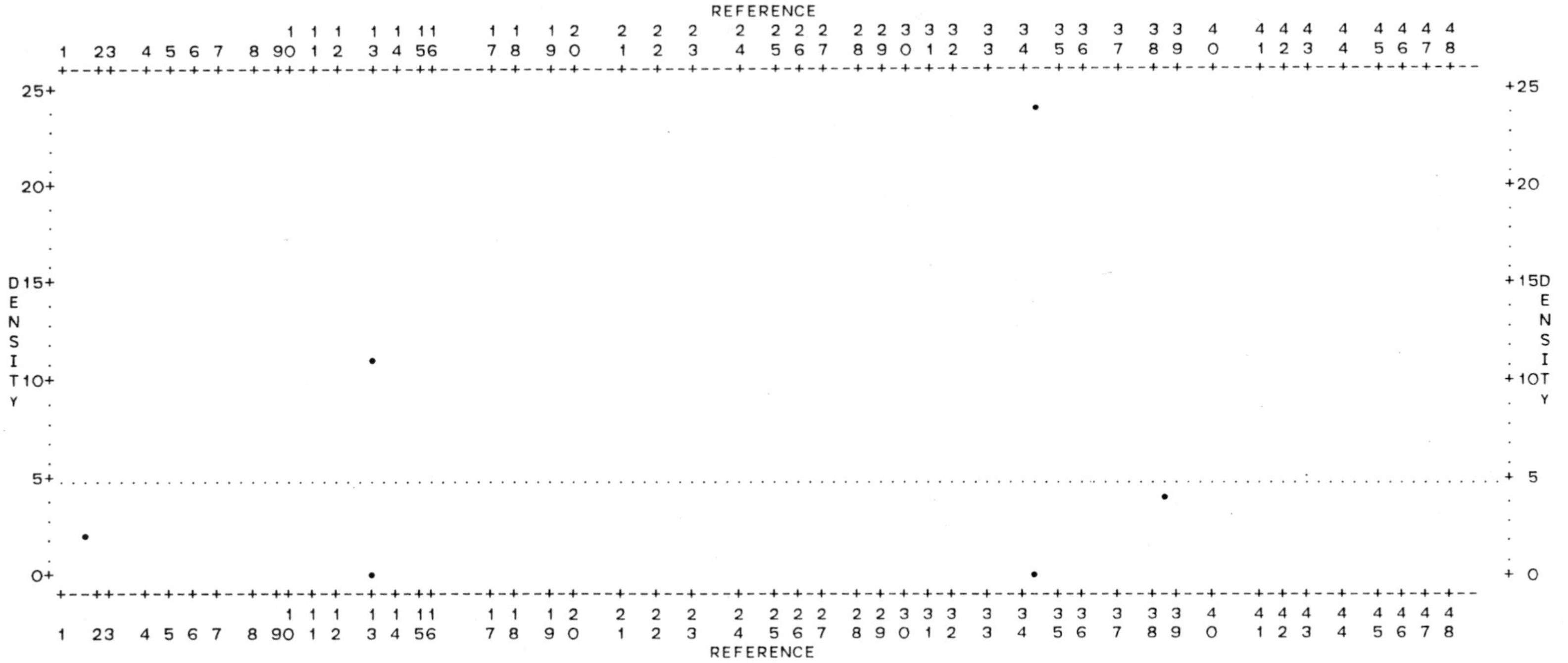

CLUSTERS:

Start:	13:11	34:26	34:26
End:	13:13	38:22	34:26
Count:	2	3	2
Width:	39	2501	4
Strength:	1.14	1.22	1.15

GAPS:

Start:	13:13
End:	34:26
Count:	2
Width:	13454
Strength:	2.73

Linguistic Density Plot in Ezekiel 1 - 48

For dābār 111 (82 times)

Each Column = 13 Verses. Separations are: Max = 3425.00, Mean = 336.99, Min = 6.50 .

Linguistic density plot. Vertical density axis labelled (reading upward): +25, +20, D15+/+15, E, N, S, I, T10+/+10, Y, 5+/+5, 0+/+0, with "DENSITY" spelled vertically at the D–Y marks. Horizontal axis runs across columns labelled 1 through 48 (in stacked digits), with "REFERENCE" marked along the axis.

CLUSTERS:

Start:	1: 3	1: 3	1: 3	2: 6	3: 4	3: 4	11:14	11:14	11:25	12:17	12:17	12:23	12:25	12:28	12:28	21: 1
End:	38:10	23: 1	3:17	2: 7	3:17	3:10	16: 1	13: 6	12: 8	13: 6	12:26	12:26	13: 2	13: 6	13: 2	23: 1
Count:	82	47	33	3	5	3	20	15	3	11	6	4	3	5	3	9
Width:	21272	12005	6671	454	267	118	2105	926	166	313	178	46	22	96	34	13 1335
Strength:	12.87	2.30	2.76	2.24	1.65	1.18	3.35	3.31	1.08	3.07	2.07	1.69	1.39	1.91	1.71	1.41 1.51

REFERENCE

Start:	21: 1	21: 1	21: 6	24: 1	24: 1	32: 1	32: 1	33:23	33:23	33:30	35: 1	35: 1
End:	21:23	21: 6	38:10	25: 3	25: 1	38:10	36:16	36:16	34: 9	34: 1	36:16	35:13 36: 4
Count:	5	3	35	5	4	16	20	12	6	7	4	5 4 3
Width:	416	94	8282	297	583	4220	2835	1623	261	447	82	667 362 119
Strength:	1.42	1.23	2.11	1.25	1.16	1.70	1.88	2.01	1.96	1.99	1.62	1.04 1.13 1.18

Data for dābār 111, continued.

GAPS:

```
Start:      1: 3   3:17   6: 1   6: 3   7: 1   7: 1   7: 1  12:28  13: 1  13: 2  13: 6  14:12  16: 1  16: 1  16: 1  16: 1  17:11  18: 1  20: 2  23: 1
End:        2: 6  11:25  11:25  11:14  11:14  11:14   9:11  48:35  48:35  48:35  21: 1  21: 1  21: 1  21: 1  17: 1  16:35  21: 1  21: 1  21: 1  24:15
Count:      2      7      2      5      4      3      2     59     58     57     13     12      9      7      3      2      3      1      2      1
Width:    675   3695   1133   2539   2281   1978   1259  22531  22522  22501   5240   5178   4449   3999   1393    720   2382   2045   1116   1271
Strength: 1.01   2.11   2.38   1.82   2.22   2.78   2.76   2.13   2.34   2.53   1.11   1.42   1.94   2.50   1.53   1.14   2.40   2.92   2.33   1.27

Start:     23: 1  33:31  34: 1  34: 9  36: 1  36: 9  38:10
End:       24: 1  48:35  48:35  48:35  48:35  48:35  48:35
Count:      2     15     13     11      8      7      2
Width:    985   9459   9399   9220   8410   8349   6659
Strength: 1.94   4.14   4.98   5.88   7.13   8.00  18.98
```

Linguistic Density Plot in Ezekiel 1 - 48

For   deber 111 (12 times)

Each Column = 13 Verses.   Separations are: Max = 5969.50, Mean = 2151.54, Min = 125.00 .

```
                              REFERENCE
        1 1   1 1 1 1   1 1 1   2 2 2 2 2 2 2 2 2 2 3 3 3 3 3 3 3 3 3 3 4 4 4 4 4 4 4 4 4
  1 23  4 5 6 7 8 90 1 2 3 4 56 7 8 90 1 2 3 4 5 6 7 8 90 1 2 3 4 5 6 7 8 90 1 2 3 4 5 6 7 8
25+                                                                                          +25

                 .                                                                           +20
20+              .  .
        .           .                                                                      +15  D
D15+                                                                                             E
E                                                                                               N
N                                                                                               S
S                                                                                               I
I                                                                                          +10  T
T10+                                                                                             Y
Y         .         .                    .                      .                          + 5
5+        .
                    .                    .       .       .
0+                                                                                         + 0
  1 23  4 5 6 7 8 90 1 2 3 4 56 7 8 90 1 2 3 4 5 6 7 8 90 1 2 3 4 5 6 7 8 90 1 2 3 4 5 6 7 8
                              REFERENCE
```

CLUSTERS:

```
Start:     5:12   5:12   5:12   6:11   6:11   7:15  12:16  14:19
End:      38:22  14:21   5:17   7:15   6:12   7:15  14:21  14:21
Count:       12      9      6      4      2      3      3      2
Width:    19492   4339    772    146    380     17   1280     67
Strength:  1.54   3.53   2.74   1.00   1.92   1.07   1.12   1.04
```

GAPS:

```
Start:     6:12   7:15  14:21  14:21  33:27  38:22
End:      48:35  48:35  48:35  28:23  48:35  48:35
Count:       10      8      5      2      3      2
Width:    25435  25059  21492   9020   9553   6339
Strength:  1.75   2.68   3.73   3.44   1.94   2.10
```

Linguistic Density Plot in Ezekiel 1 - 48

For dbr 324 (1 times)   dbr 331 (34 times)   dbr 332 (15 times)   dbr 333 (9 times)
     dbr 334 (5 times)   dbr 3361 (1 times)   dbr 3362 (2 times)

Each Column = 13 Verses.   Separations are: Max = 1799.00, Mean = 411.32, Min = 7.50 .

REFERENCE

```
                                                                                                    +25

                                                                                                    +20

                                                                                                    +15D
                                                                                                       E
                                                                                                       N
                                                                                                       S
                                                                                                       I
                                                                                                    +10T
                                                                                                       Y

                                                                                                    + 5

                                                                                                    + 0
```

REFERENCE

CLUSTERS:

Start:	1:28	1:28	1:28	1:28	2: 7	3:10	3:10	5:13	11:25	12:23	12:23	12:25	12:25
End:	44: 5	20:27	10: 5	3:27	3: 4	3:27	3:18	5:17	14: 9	13: 8	12:28	12:25	12:25
Count:	67	33	19	14	4	6	3	3	8	7	5	4	3	2
Width:	24418	9622	3407	821	304	34	22	154	394	95	167	311	115	1331	699	213	94	41	15	3
Strength:	4.79	2.10	2.69	3.41	2.51	1.73	1.40	1.56	1.89	1.27	1.15	1.33	1.24	2.07	2.13	2.36	1.95	1.72	1.41	1.00
Start:	32:21	36:36	36:36	37:14	38:17								
End:	39: 8	39: 8	37:21	37:21	39: 8								
Count:	16	8	4	3	4								
Width:	4344	1457	506	148	317								
Strength:	1.30	1.38	1.05	1.18	1.32								

Data for dbr 324, dbr 331, dbr 332, dbr 333, dbr 334, dbr 3361, dbr 3362, continued.

GAPS:

```
Start:     3:27  5:17  6:10  6:10 12:25 13: 8 13: 8 14: 9 17:24 17:24 17:24 17:24 17:24 20:27 24:18 24:27 26:14 26:14
End:      12:23 12:23 11:25 10: 5 48:35 33:30 17:21 17:21 33:30 21:37 21:22 21:22 24:14 21:22 33: 2 33: 2 33: 2 32:21
Count:        8     5     4     3     2    46    24     4     2    20     5     4     9     2     9     8     6     5
Width:     3928  3046  2850  2364  1508 22597 22413 12907  3020  2388  9805  2778  2463  4629   942   905  4417  4221  3530  3217
Strength:  1.02  1.76  2.33  2.70  2.70  2.56  3.36  2.16  2.58  4.87  1.31  1.42  1.77  1.23  1.30  1.21  1.03  1.31  1.67  1.98

Start:    26:14 29: 3 30:12 33:30 38:19 39: 8 39: 8 39: 8 40: 4 40: 4 43: 6 44: 5
End:      28:10 32:21 32:21 48:35 48:35 48:35 41:22 40:45 40:45 48:35 48:35 48:35
Count:        2     3     2    18     9     7     4     3     3     6     5
Width:      979  1826  1138  9496  6413  6147  2001  1446   873  3598  2957
Strength: 1.39  1.76  1.79  1.71  2.87  3.85  1.10  1.09  1.13  4.87  6.27
```

Linguistic Density Plot in Ezekiel 1 - 48

For dbr 331 (34 times)

Each Column = 13 Verses.   Separations are: Max =   3103.50, Mean =   799.14, Min =   57.50 .

```
CLUSTERS:

Start:     2: 2   2: 2   2: 2   3: 4   5:13   5:13  21:22  21:22  21:22  21:22  33: 8  36:36  38:17
End:      39: 8   6:10   3:18   3:18   6:10   5:17  39: 8  26:14  22:28  39: 8  39: 8  39: 8  39: 8
Count:      34      9      5      3      4      3     21      8      4     11      6      4
Width:   21206   1877    572    290    311  10701   3140    855   3876   1457    317
Strength:  4.77   2.30   1.76   1.20   1.59   1.37   2.28   1.31   1.18   1.95   1.55   1.59

GAPS:

Start:     5:17   6:10   6:10  14: 9  17:24  17:24  28:10  30:12  38:19  39: 8
End:      17:21  17:21  13: 7  17:21  21:37  21:22  33: 8  48:35  48:35
Count:      5      4      2      3      2      3      8      4      2
Width:    6279   6083   3054   2388   2778   2463   2706   1606   6413   6147
Strength:  2.07   2.82   2.90   2.04   1.08   2.14   1.02   1.03   3.07   6.88
```

For dbr 332 (15 times)

Linguistic Density Plot in Ezekiel 1 - 48

Each Column = 13 Verses.   Separations are: Max =   4412.50, Mean =   1748.13, Min =   7.50 .

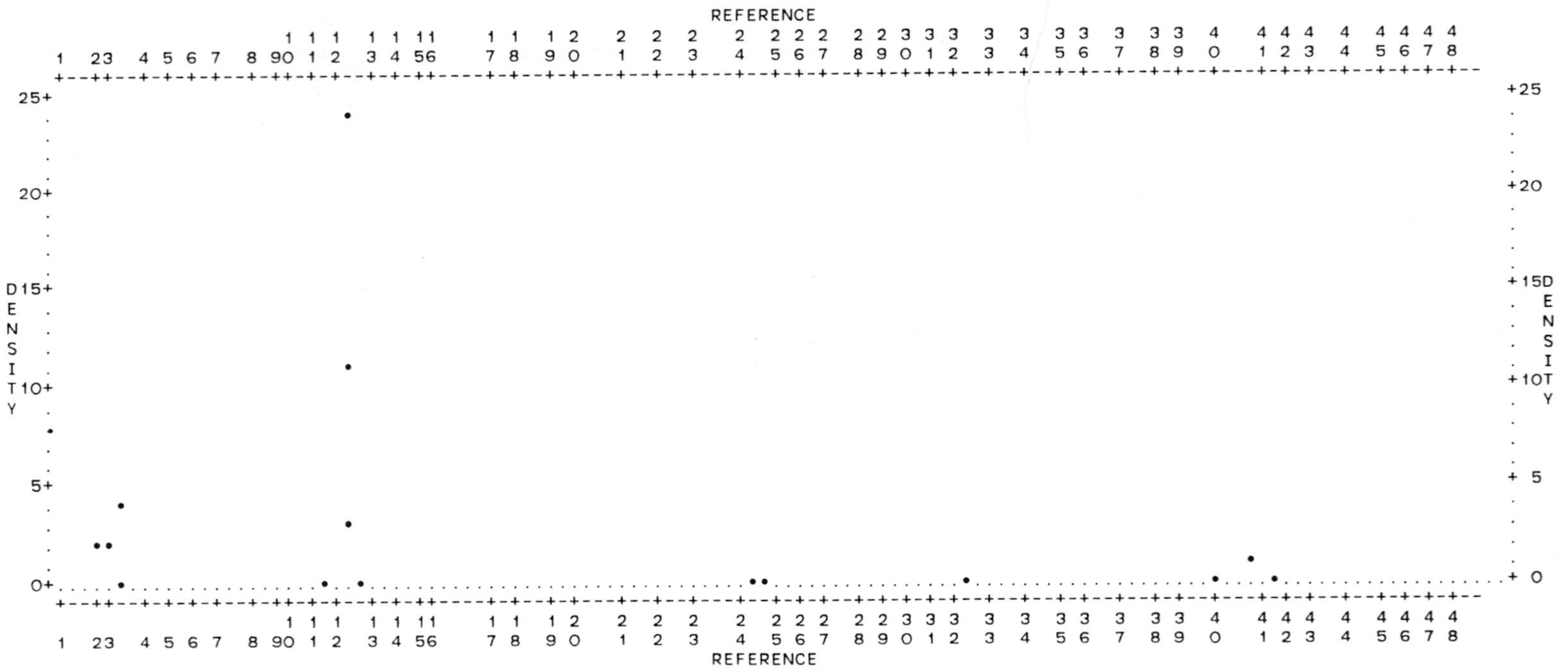

REFERENCE

(density plot — vertical axis labelled DENSITY, horizontal axis REFERENCE, markers +25, +20, +15, +10, +5, 0)

CLUSTERS:

Start:	2: 1	3:10	3:22	11:25	12:25	12:25		
End:	12:28	3:24	3:24	12:28	12:25	12:25		
Count:	9	4	3	4	3	2		
Width:	4831	753	338	580	68	15	3	
Strength:	2.69	1.69	1.40	1.04	2.18	1.95	1.55	1.06

GAPS:

Start:	3:24	12:25	12:28	12:28	24:27	24:27	32:21	41:22	
End:	11:25	48:35	48:35	24:18	48:35	40:45	40: 4	48:35	
Count:	2	10	9	8	6	4	3	2	
Width:	3498	22597	22585	22532	14399	9698	8825	4917	4146
Strength:	1.06	2.03	2.53	3.05	3.76	1.79	1.68	2.37	1.92	1.45

Linguistic Density Plot in Ezekiel 1 - 48

For dbr 333 (9 times)

Each Column = 13 Verses. Separations are: Max = 4505.00, Mean = 2797.00, Min = 1540.00 .

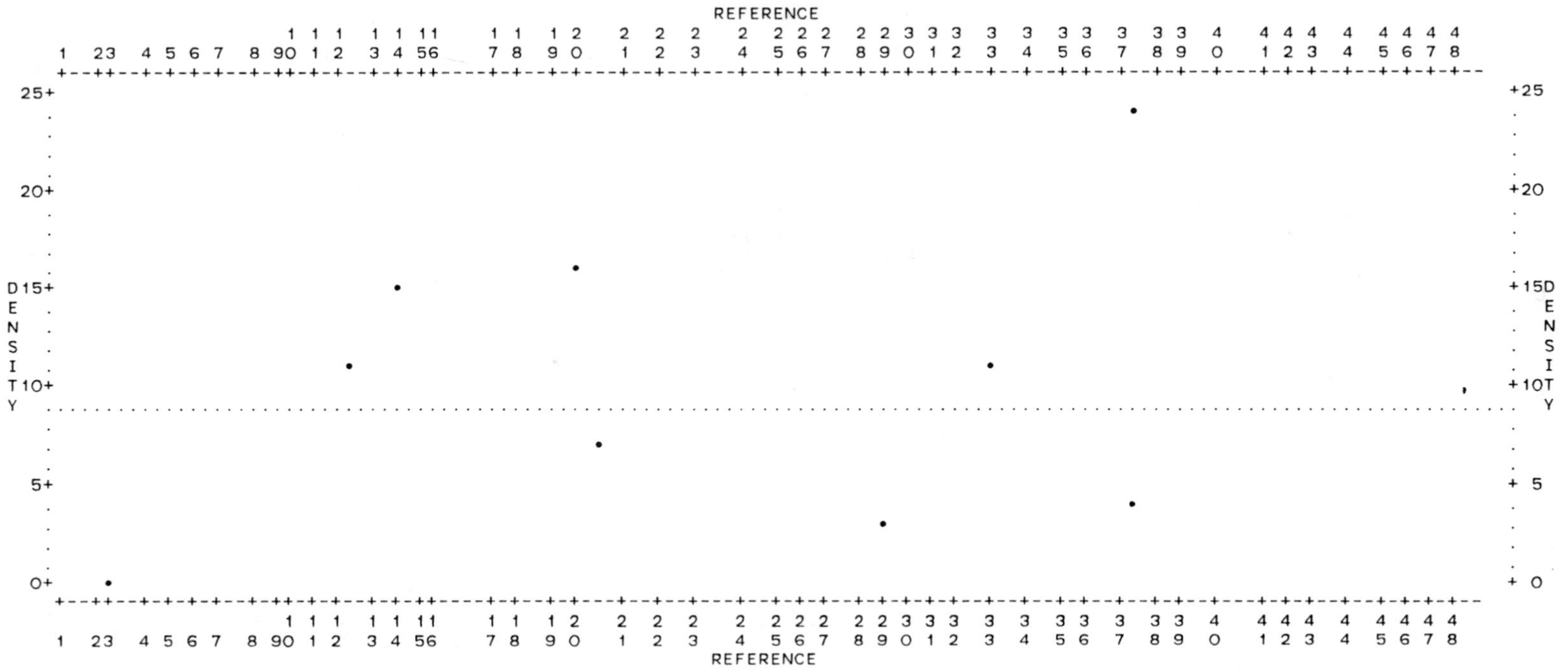

CLUSTERS:

Start:	37:19
End:	37:21
Count:	2
Width:	58
Strength:	1.08

GAPS:

Start:	20:27	37:21
End:	29: 3	48:35
Count:	2	2
Width:	5436	7098
Strength:	1.04	1.69

Linguistic Density Plot in Ezekiel 1 - 48

For dbr 334 (5 times)

Each Column = 13 Verses.   Separations are: Max = 12123.00, Mean = 4661.66, Min =   86.00 .

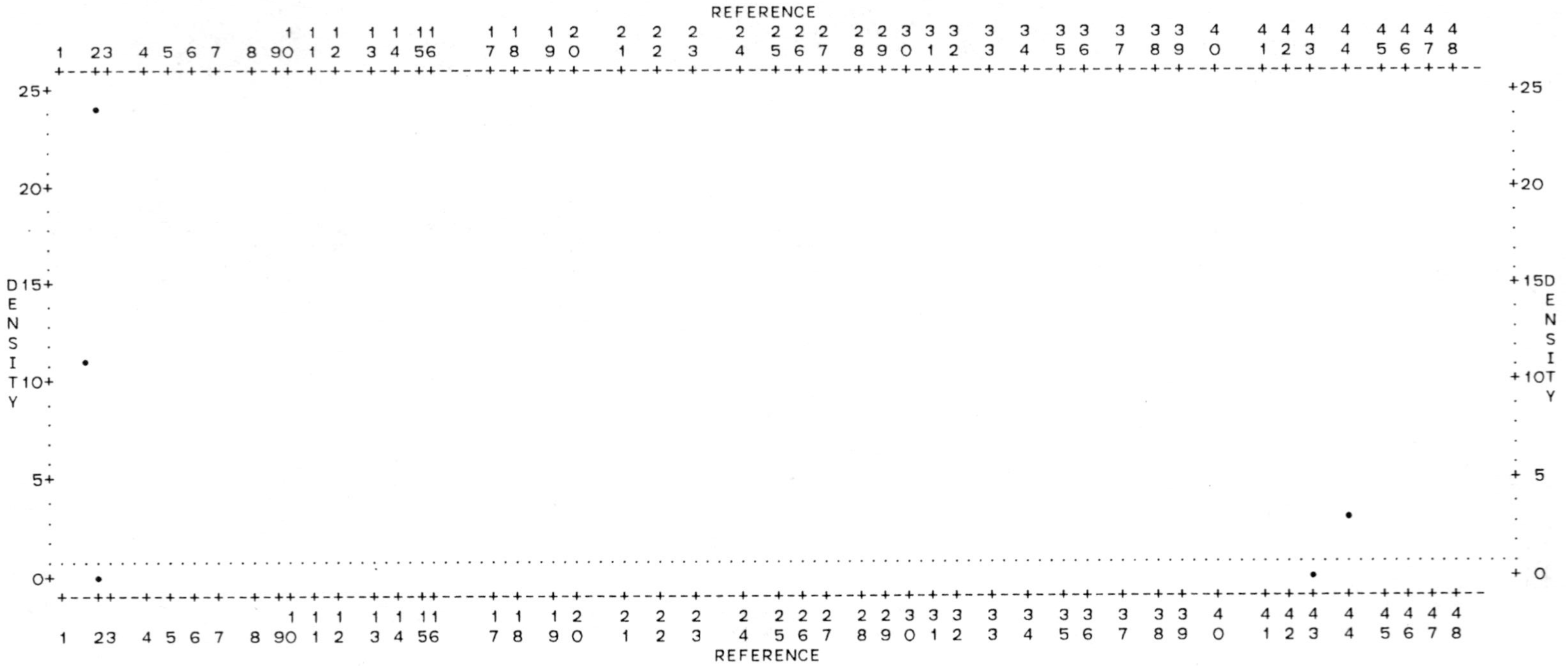

CLUSTERS:

Start:	1:28	1:28	43: 6
End:	2: 8	2: 2	44: 5
Count:	3	2	2
Width:	172	34	641
Strength:	1.83	1.17	1.02

GAPS:

Start:	2: 2	2: 8	2: 8
End:	48:35	48:35	43: 6
Count:	5	4	2
Width:	27341	27203	23605
Strength:	1.74	2.50	4.80

Linguistic Density Plot in Ezekiel 1 - 48

For débaš 111 (6 times)

Each Column = 13 Verses.   Separations are: Max =   9010.00, Mean =   3995.71, Min =   1365.50 .

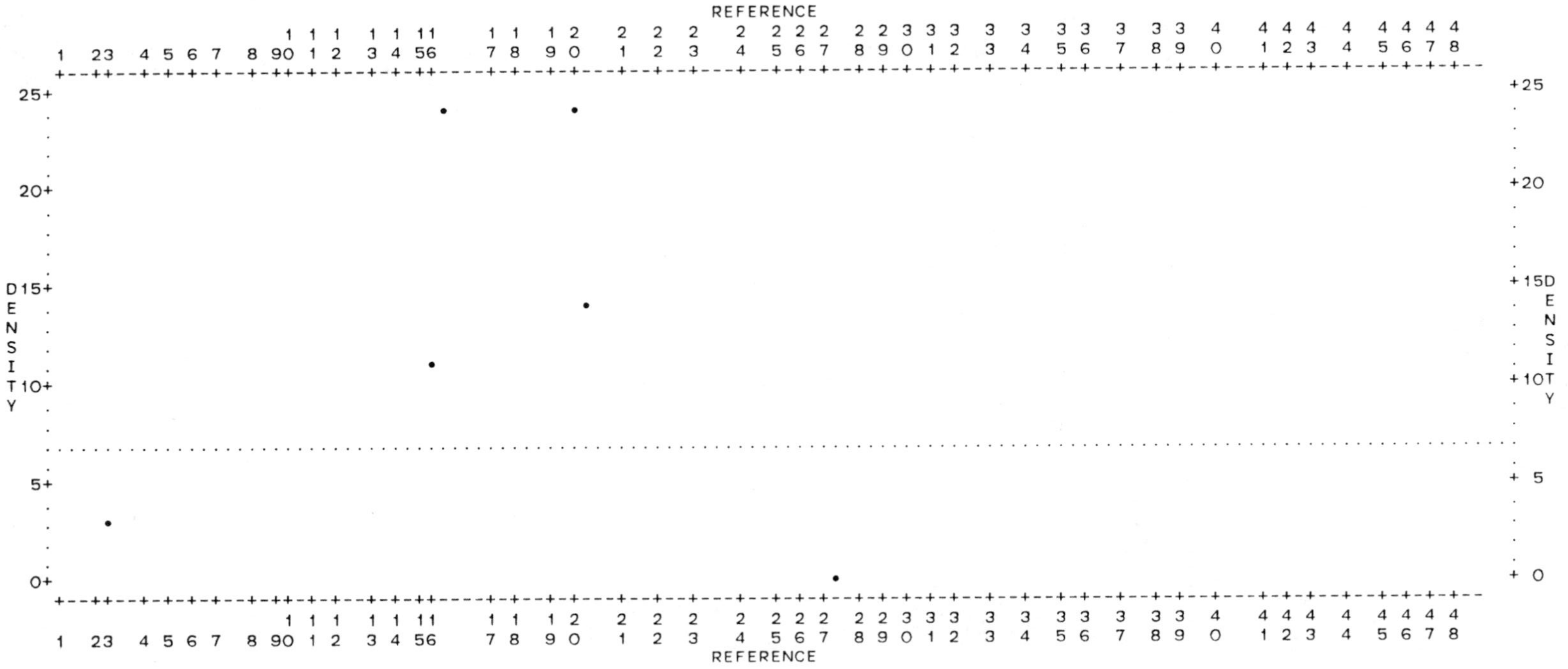

CLUSTERS:

Start:	3: 3	16:13	16:13	20: 6
End:	27:17	27:17	20:15	20:15
Count:	6	5	4	2
Width:	13854	7759	2971	134	240
Strength:	1.37	1.68	1.84	1.11	1.08

GAPS:

Start:	20:15	27:17
End:	48:35	48:35
Count:	3	2
Width:	18020	13232
Strength:	2.24	2.66

Linguistic Density Plot in Ezekiel 1 - 48

For dãgã 114 (6 times)

Each Column = 13 Verses. Separations are: Max = 7854.00. Mean = 3995.71, Min = 16.00 .

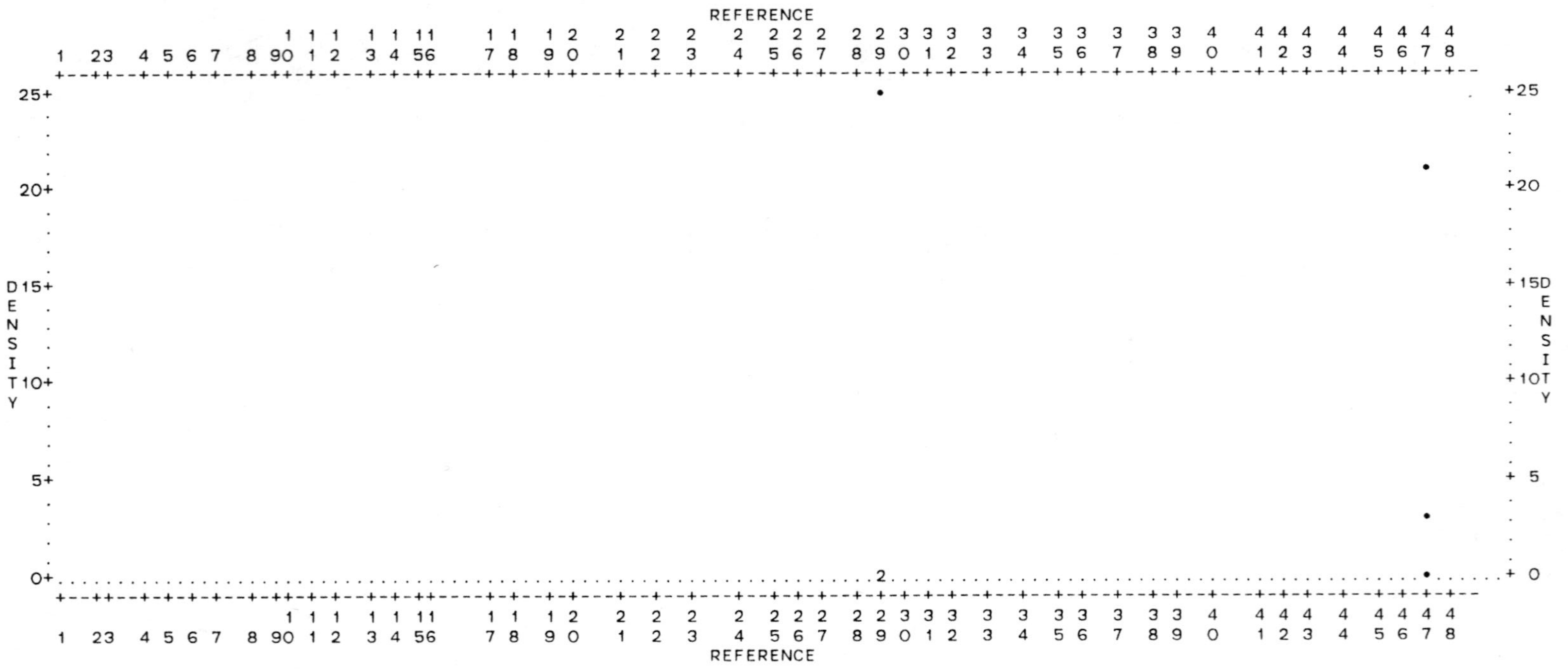

CLUSTERS:

Start:	29: 4	29: 4	29: 4	47: 9	47:10
End:	47:10	29: 5	29: 4	47:10	47:10
Count:	6	3	2	3	2
Width:	11301	32	16	42	3
Strength:	1.94	1.78	1.14	1.77	1.15

GAPS:

Start:	1: 1	1: 1	1: 1	29: 5
End:	47:10	29: 4	29: 4	47: 9
Count:	6	3	2	2
Width:	26989	15707	15691	11227
Strength:	1.56	1.72	3.37	2.08

Linguistic Density Plot in Ezekiel 1 - 48

For dālīt 114 (7 times)

Each Column = 13 Verses.   Separations are: Max = 5584.50, Mean = 3496.25, Min = 58.00 .

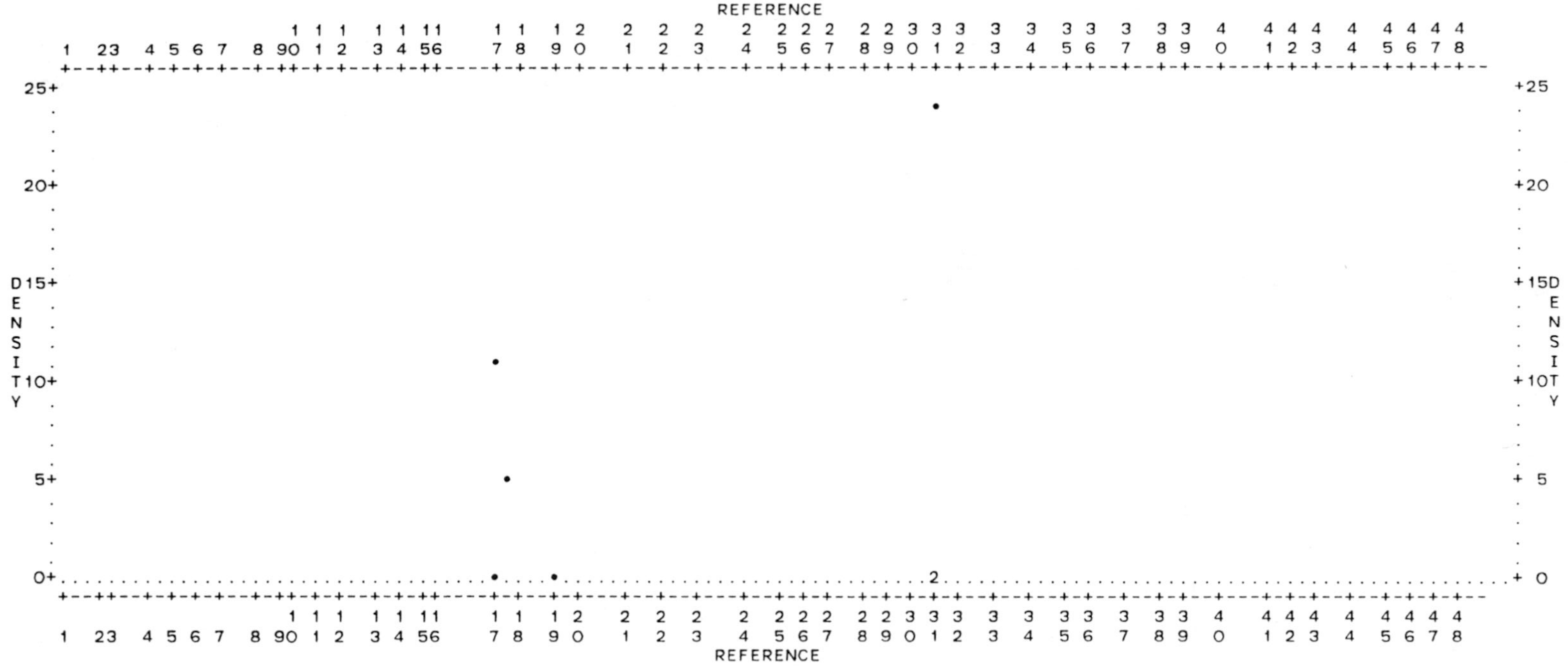

REFERENCE

CLUSTERS:

Start:	17: 6	17: 6	17: 6	31: 7	31: 7
End:	31:12	19:11	17:23	17: 7	31:12	31: 9
Count:	7	4	3	2	3	2
Width:	8680	1315	442	40	116	46
Strength:	3.04	2.03	1.62	1.12	1.70	1.11

GAPS:

Start:	1: 1	19:11	31: 9	31:12
End:	17: 6	31: 7	48:35	48:35
Count:	2	3	2	
Width:	8190	7249	11169	11099
Strength:	1.52	1.21	1.03	2.46

Linguistic Density Plot in Ezekiel 1 - 48

For delet 114 (9 times)

Each Column = 13 Verses.   Separations are: Max = 10669.50, Mean = 2797.00, Min =   2.50 .

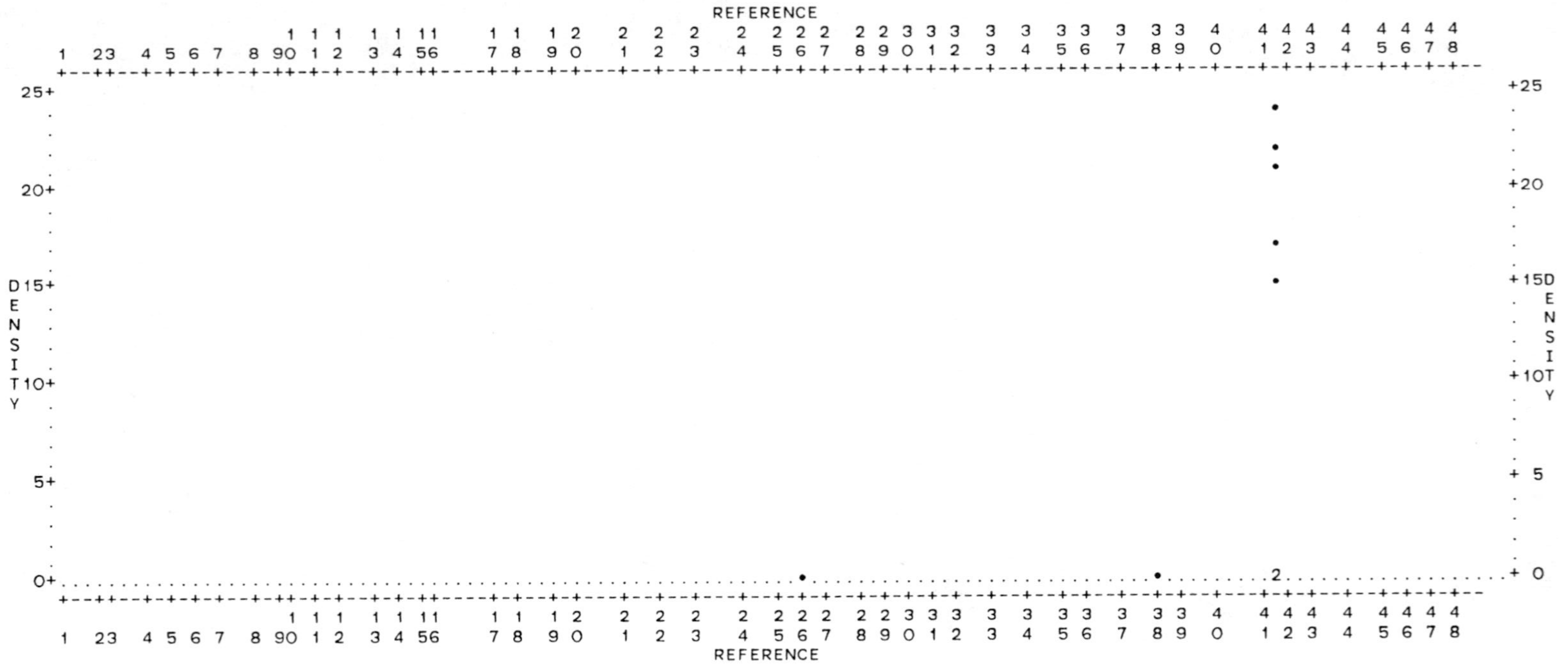

CLUSTERS:

Start:	26: 2	38:11	41:23	41:23	41:24	41:24	41:24	
End:	41:25	41:25	41:24	41:25	41:24	41:24	41:24	
Count:	9	8	7	3	2	3	2	
Width:	9860	2524	28	10	4	15	7	3
Strength:	3.71	4.41	4.05	1.65	1.10	2.16	1.65	1.10

GAPS:

Start:	1: 1	1: 1	1: 1	1: 1
End:	41:24	41:23	38:11	26: 2
Count:	5	4	3	2
Width:	23842	23834	21338	14002
Strength:	3.06	3.99	4.66	4.42

Linguistic Density Plot in Ezekiel 1 - 48

For dām 111 (55 times)

Each Column = 13 Verses.   Separations are: Max = 1996.00, Mean = 499.46, Min = 4.00 .

Linguistic density scatter plot. Vertical axis (DENSITY) labelled 0+, 5+, D15+, +20, 25+ with reference ticks +25, +20, +15, +10, +5, 0. Horizontal axis labelled by column numbers (verse references) 1 23 4 5 6 7 8 9 0 1 2 3 4 5 6 7 8 9 0 1 2 3 4 5 6 7 8 9 0 1 2 3 4 5 6 7 8 with REFERENCE baseline.

CLUSTERS:

Start:	3:18	3:18	14:19	14:19	14:19	16:36	16:22	16:38	21:37	21:37	21:37	22: 2	22: 6	23:37	23:37
End:	45:19	24: 9	24: 9	19:10	16:38	16:38	16:38	24: 9	22:13	22:27	22: 4	22:13	24: 5	23:45	
Count:	55	33	28	12	9	5	4	3	2	16	9	8	4	3	4
Width:	24872	11999	6783	3048	1096	482	91	327	60	1780	520	245	64	34	122
Strength:	3.05	2.17	3.62	1.66	2.23	1.58	1.68	1.40	1.36	3.48	2.68	2.65	1.71	1.40	1.64

Start:	23:45	23:45	38:22	39:17	39:19	35: 8	36:18	35:25	33: 8	33:25	32: 6	33: 4
End:	23:45	23:45	39:19	39:18	39:19	36:18	35:18	35: 4	35: 2	33:25	33: 8	35: 4
Count:	5	2	4	3								
Width:	75	590	442	107	618	503	1159					
Strength:	1.00	1.08	1.01	1.26	1.78	1.66	1.44	1.88	1.60	1.70		

```
Data for dam 111, continued.

GAPS:

Start:     1: 1   1: 1   3:20   3:20   7:23   9: 9  16:38  16:38  16:38  18:13  19:10  23:45  24: 9  24: 9  33:25  35: 6  35: 6  35: 6
End:      16: 6   3:18  16: 6  14:19   5:17  14:19  22: 2  21:37  18:10  21:37  21:37  33: 4  32: 6  28:23  35: 6  48:35  39:17  38:22
Count:       8      2      6      5      2      3      6      5      2      3      2      8      4      3      2      4     12      3
Width:    6813   1206   5540   5149   1013   2579   3937   3907   1307   2540   1955   4908   4648   3992   2294    992   8609   2690   2273
Strength: 2.70   1.43   2.87   3.30   1.04   4.23   1.36   2.00   1.64   2.24   2.96   1.15   3.77   4.35   3.65   1.00   2.11   1.42   1.85

Start:    36:18  39:18  39:19  43:20  44:15  45:19
End:      38:22  48:35  43:18  48:35  48:35  48:35
Count:       2      8      7      2      5      3
Width:    1667   5914   2645   3220   2659   1891
Strength: 2.37   1.97   4.37   1.28   2.41   2.83
```

Linguistic Density Plot in Ezekiel 1 - 48

For dmh 311 (4 times)   dmh 321 (1 times)

Each Column = 13 Verses. Separations are: Max = 8386.50, Mean = 4661.66, Min = 66.50 .

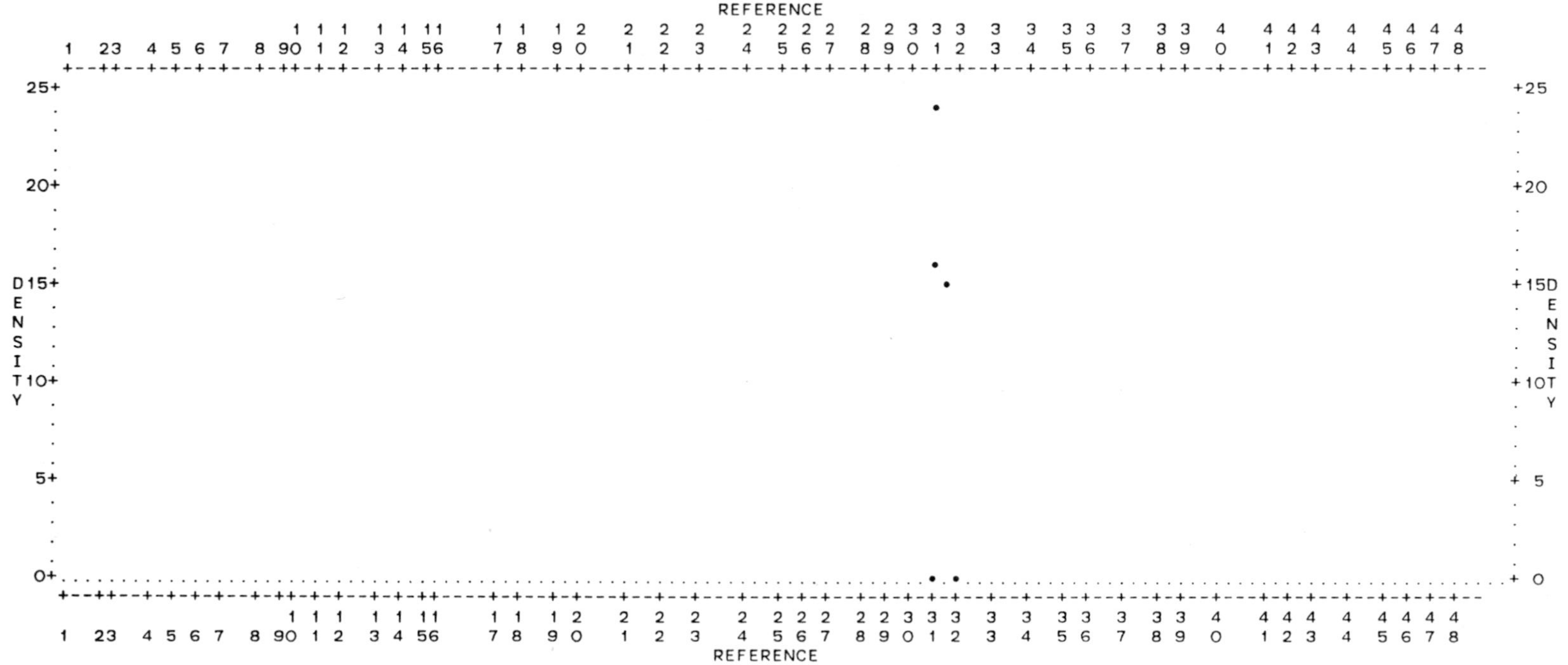

CLUSTERS:

Start:	31: 2	31: 2	31: 8	31:18
End:	32: 2	31: 8	32: 2	
Count:	5	3	2	2
Width:	454	133	17	70
Strength:	3.65	1.84	1.17	1.16

GAPS:

Start:	1: 1	1: 1	32: 2
End:	31: 8	31: 2	48:35
Count:	3	2	2
Width:	16772	16656	10859
Strength:	1.49	3.04	1.57

Linguistic Density Plot in Ezekiel 1 - 48

For dĕmût 114 (16 times)

Each Column = 13 Verses. Separations are: Max = 11822.50, Mean = 1645.29, Min = 3.00 .

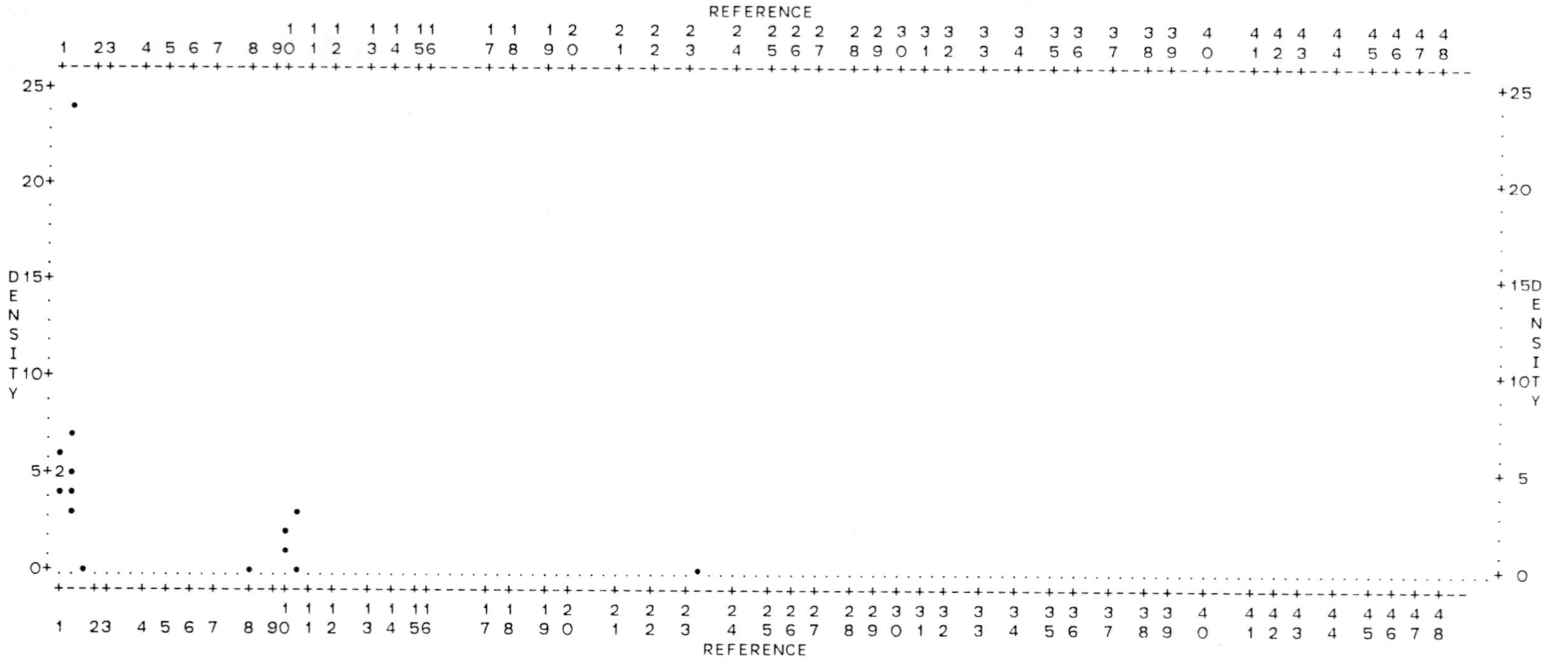

CLUSTERS:

Start:	1: 5	1: 5	1: 5	1: 5	1: 5	1: 5	1:13	1:22	1:26	1:26	1:26	8: 2	10: 1	10:21
End:	23:15	10:22	1:28	1:16	1:10	1: 5	1:16	1:28	1:28	1:26	1:26	10:22	10:22	10:22
Count:	16	15	10	5	3	2	2	5	4	3	2	5	4	2
Width:	12200	4233	490	206	81	7	56	166	67	6	2	1145	416	7
Strength:	5.87	7.48	4.35	2.27	1.51	1.05	1.02	2.29	1.93	1.54	1.05	1.94	1.79	1.05

GAPS:

Start:	1:26	10:22	23:15
End:	48:35	48:35	48:35
Count:	9	3	2
Width:	27449	23645	15678
Strength:	4.34	9.58	9.04

Linguistic Density Plot in Ezekiel 1 - 48

For damméséq 12   (5 times)

Each Column = 13 Verses.   Separations are: Max = 13560.50, Mean = 4661.66, Min =   19.50 .

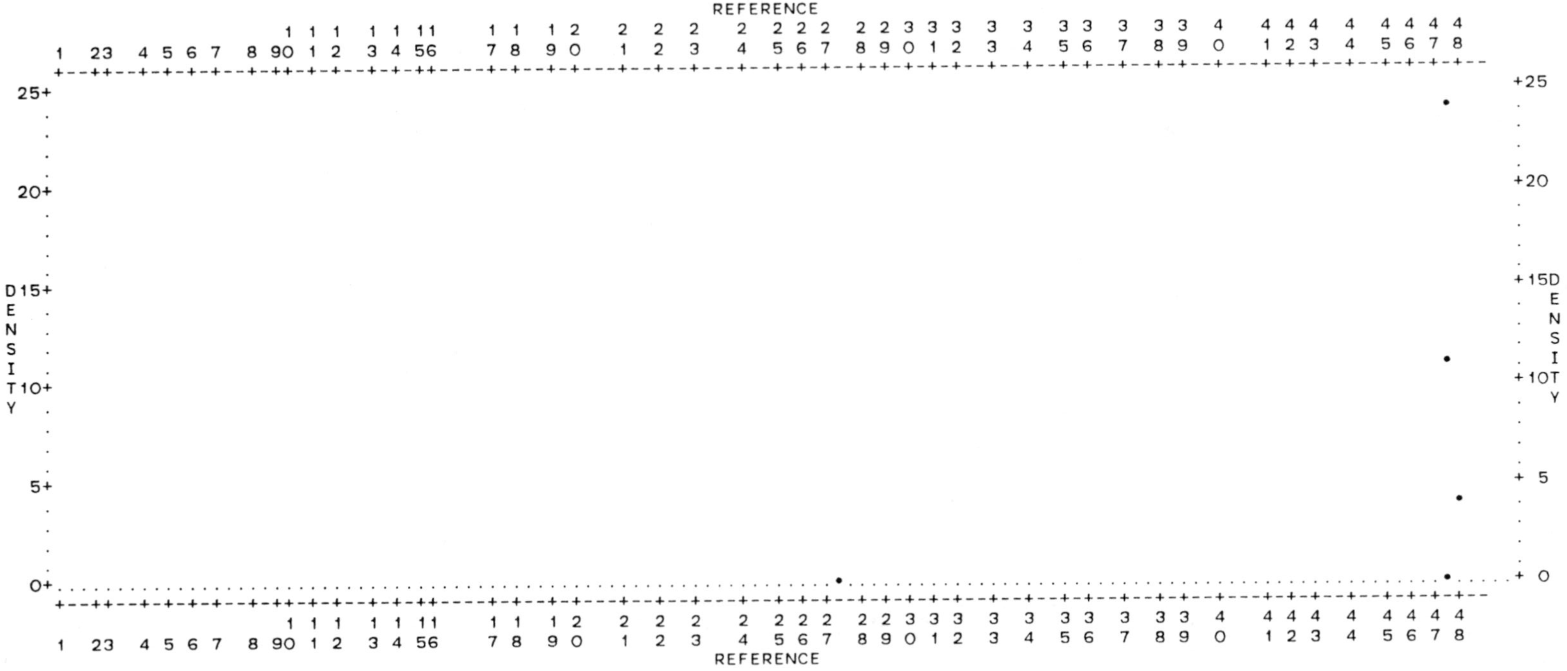

CLUSTERS:

Start:	27:18	47:16	47:16	47:16
End:	48: 1	48: 1	47:18	47:17
Count:	5	4	3	2
Width:	12551	176	39	19
Strength:	1.22	2.61	1.86	1.17

GAPS:

Start:	1: 1	1: 1
End:	47:16	27:18
Count:	3	2
Width:	27120	14745
Strength:	3.57	2.55

Linguistic Density Plot in Ezekiel 1 - 48

For dārôm 111 (13 times)

Each Column = 13 Verses.   Separations are: Max = 12114.00. Mean = 1997.86. Min =   8.00 .

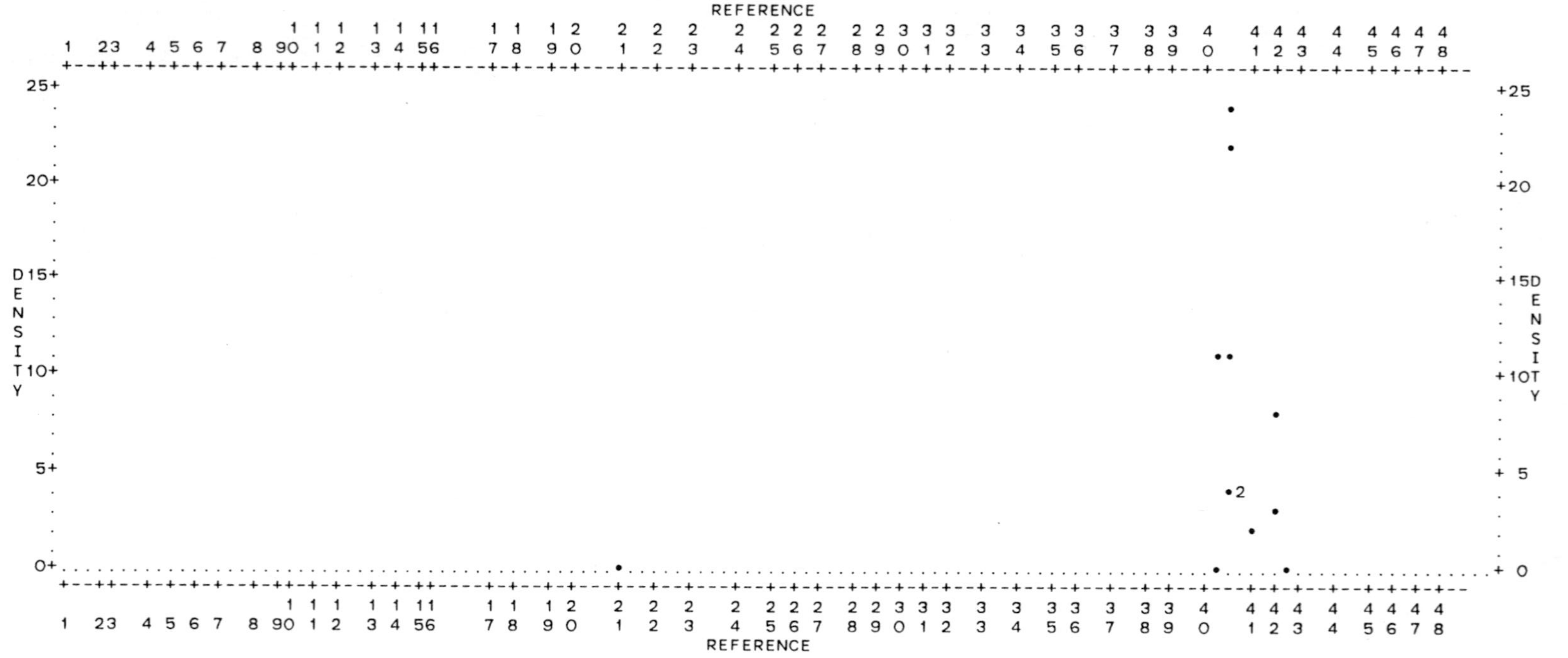

REFERENCE

(density plot, vertical axis labelled DENSITY: +25, +20, +15, +10, +5, 0)

REFERENCE

CLUSTERS:

Start:	21: 2	40:24	40:24	40:24	40:27	40:27	40:28	40:44	42:12	42:12
End:	42:18	42:18	41:11	40:28	40:28	40:27	40:28	40:45	42:18	42:13
Count:	13	12	9	6	2	2	4	2	3	2
Width:	13512	1398	770	93	5	8	24	350	19	132	22
Strength:	4.13	6.94	4.25	2.85	1.07	1.06	2.01	1.07	1.44	1.06	1.52	1.06

GAPS:

Start:	1:: 1	1:: 1	21:: 2
End:	40:28	40:24	40:24
Count:	7	3	2
Width:	22926	22838	12114
Strength:	3.06	7.45	5.43

For derek 111 (107 times)

Each Column = 13 Verses. Separations are: Max = 2325.50, Mean = 258.98, Min = 3.00 .

Linguistic Density Plot in Ezekiel 1 - 48

REFERENCE

```
25+

20+

D15+
E
N
S
I
T10+
Y

 5+

 O+
```

REFERENCE

CLUSTERS:

Start:	3:18	7: 3	7: 3	7:27	16:25	16:25	16:43	16:43	18:29	18:23	18:25	20:30	20:43	21:24	21:24	28:15	33: 8	33: 8
End:	48: 1	8: 5	7: 9	8: 5	18:30	16:31	16:47	16:31	18:30	18:23	18:25	21:26	21: 5	21:26	21:25	48: 1	36:32	33:20
Count:	107	7	4	3	15	3	3	8	4	4	3	3	9	5	3	20	64	14
Width:	26096	608	109	146	2027	119	107	144	20	62	14	859	45	65	20	11955	2342	286
Strength:	3.75	1.54	1.51	1.02	1.77	1.10	1.13	2.52	1.71	1.62	1.39	1.72	1.95	1.25	1.37	3.30	1.17	2.54

Start:	33: 8	33: 8
End:	33:11	...
Count:	5	
Width:	99	
Strength:	1.85	

Start:	33: 8	33: 9	33: 8	36:17	36:17	36:32	40: 6	40: 6	40: 6	40:20	40:22	40:27	40:44	40:44	41:12	42: 1	42: 1	42:10
End:	48: 1	33:20	33: 4	36:17	36:19	36:32	40: 6	48: 1	40:32	40:24	40:32	40:32	40:44	41:12	40:46	42: 7	43: 4	42:15
Count:	32	3	4	5	3	3	9	15	9	7	6	4	4	4	21	4	2	13
Width:	349	47	349	44	49	36	524	2491	259	101	43	94	367	1063	31	448	109	293
Strength:	1.34	1.65	1.35	1.31	5.72	5.24	2.20	2.75	2.10	1.53	1.31	1.17	1.69	3.95	3.88	1.51	1.00	3.34

Start:	42:10
End:	42:15
Count:	9
Width:	145
Strength:	2.74

Clusters for derek 111, continued.

```
Start:     42:10 42:12 42:12 42:12 42:12 43: 1 44: 1 44: 3 46: 2 46: 2 46: 8 46: 9 46: 9 47: 2 47: 2
End:       42:12 42:11 42:12 42:12 42:12 43: 4 44: 4 44: 4 48: 1 46: 1 46: 9 46: 9 46: 9 47: 1 47: 3
Count:         7     3     4     3     2     4     4     3     8     5     7     5     3           3
Width:        55    19    11     6     1    66    62    12  1050   163    40    20     9   488    11
Strength:   2.44  1.38  1.73  1.41  1.00  1.61  1.62  1.39  2.44  2.50  2.46  2.00  1.40  1.08  1.40
```

GAPS:

```
Start:      1: 1 42: 1 21:24 18:29 18:25  1: 1  7: 8  1: 1  3:19  7: 3 18: 7 18:25 16:47 14:22 13:22  9:10 11:21 14:23 16:47 16:47
End:       42: 1 21:24 18:29 18:25  8: 5  7: 8  3:18  7: 3 18:25 16:47 14:22 13:22  9:10 11:21 16:47 13:22 16:25 18:23
Count:        83    75    37    28    26     9     6     2    17    16    12     6     4     3     2     4     2     3
Width:     24108 23904 11155  9231  9163  3267  2755  2665  1193  1440  5890  5882  4452  3234  2639  2070  1152   690  1413  1365
Strength:   2.50  3.80  1.44  1.92  2.37  1.70  2.59  4.28  3.63  4.60  1.83  2.15  1.97  3.44  4.22  4.29  3.47  1.67  1.44  2.34
```

```
Start:     16:61 18:23 21:26 18:30 18:30 21:25 21:26 21:26 21:26 21:26 21:26 21:26 23:31 23:13 24:14 28:15 33:20 33:20
End:       18:23 21:24 20:44 20:43 20:30 42: 1 42: 1 40:24 33:20 33:17 33:11 33: 9 33: 8 33: 8 33: 8 33: 8 40:24 36:17
Count:         2     6     4     3     2    38    36    25    14    12    10     8     7     5     4     3     2    11     2
Width:      1082  1887  1441  1403  1073 12746 12721 11654  7049  7007  6860  6789  6768  5695  5308  4651  2617  4600   848  1707
Strength:   3.20  1.05  1.50  2.44  3.17  2.48  2.91  4.88  4.22  5.13  6.11  7.54  8.49  9.20 10.29 11.44  9.18  2.58  2.29  5.64
```

```
Start:     36:17 36:19 36:19 36:32 36:32 36:32 43:32 44: 4 44: 4 48: 1
End:       40:24 40:24 40:22 40:20 40: 6 40: 6 44: 6 44: 8 46: 2 48:35
Count:         9     8     7     5     4     2     3     2
Width:      2883  2849  2811  2506  2448  2183   553  1395  1272   680
Strength:   1.15  1.57  2.04  2.90  3.79  7.49  1.14  2.42  3.94  1.63
```

Linguistic Density Plot in Ezekiel 1 - 48

For drs 311 (3 times)   drs 312 (2 times)   drs 314 (2 times)   drs 3162 (3 times)
     drs 322 (5 times)   drs 3261 (1 times)

Each Column = 13 Verses.   Separations are: Max = 4582.00, Mean = 1645.29, Min = 20.50

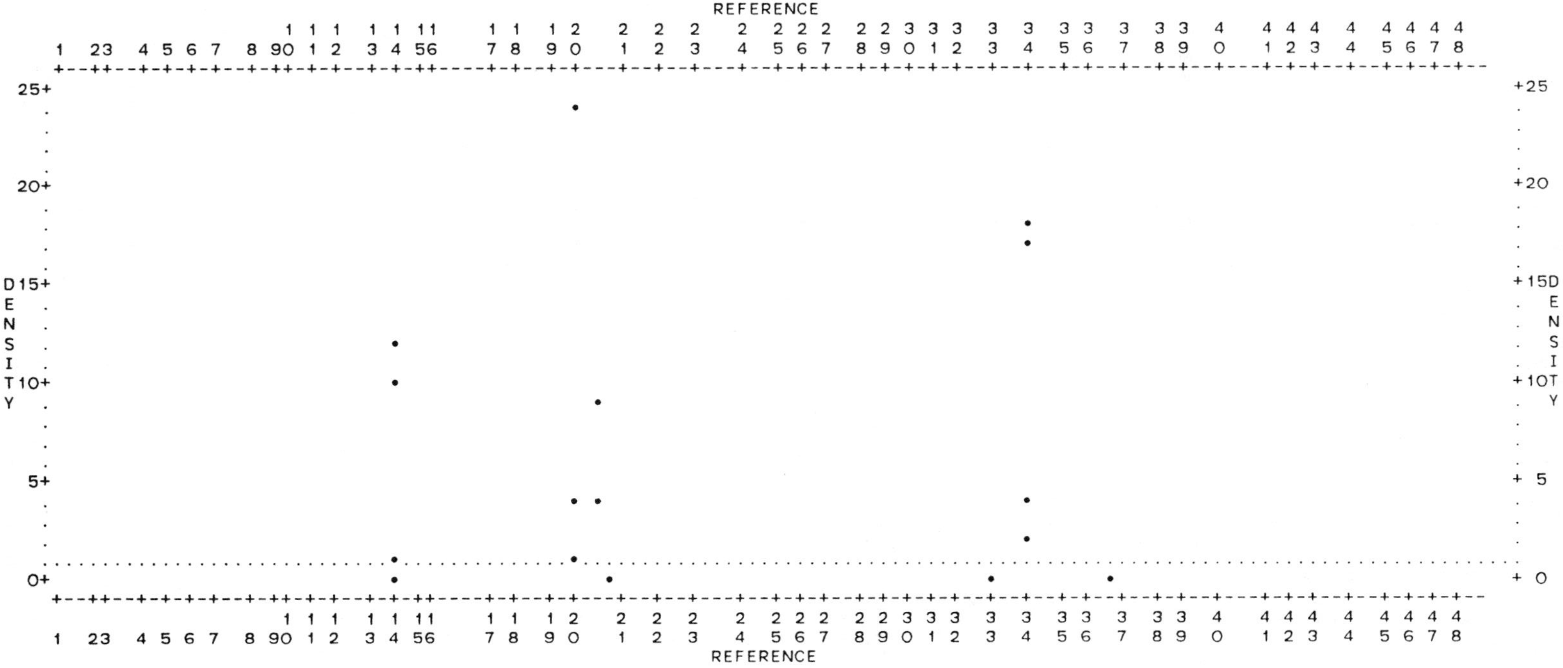

Scatter / density plot. Vertical axis (DENSITY) ticks: 25+, 20+, 15 (D15+), 10 (T10+), 5+, 0+ (left side) and +25, +20, +15 D, +10 T, +5, +0 (right side, with DENSITY lettered vertically: D E N S I T Y). Horizontal axis labelled REFERENCE (top and bottom), column indices 1 through 48.

CLUSTERS:

Start	14: 3	14: 3	14: 7	14:10	20: 1	20: 3	20:31	20:31	20:40	33: 6	34: 6	34: 8
End	36:37	20:40	14:10	14:10	20:40	20:40	20:31	20:40	20:40	34:11	34:10	34:10
Count	16	10	2	4	6	3	2	5	2	6	3	2
Width	14369	4574	211	73	998	224	2463	893	12	117	73	33
Strength	4.85	3.10	1.87	1.05	2.40	1.52	1.91	1.91	1.05	2.03	1.51	1.03

GAPS:

Start	1: 1	14:10	20:31	20:40	34:10	34:11	36:37
End	14: 3	20: 1	48:35	34: 6	48:35	48:35	
Count	2	9	6	4	3	2	
Width	6006	3365	17601	8320	9208	9164	7594
Strength	2.81	1.10	1.34	1.34	1.69	2.76	3.83

Linguistic Density Plot in Ezekiel 1 - 48

For drs 311 (3 times)   drs 312 (2 times)   drs 314 (2 times)   drs 3162 (3 times)

Each Column = 13 Verses. Separations are: Max = 4604.00, Mean = 2542.73, Min = 36.50 .

CLUSTERS:

Start:	14: 7	14: 7	14: 7	20: 1	20: 1	33: 6	34: 6	34: 6	34: 8
End:	34:11	20:40	14:10	20:40	20: 3	34:11	34:11	34:10	34:10
Count:	10	5	2	3	4	5	3	3	2
Width:	12661	4436	73	998	33	893	117	73	33
Strength:	3.28	1.47	1.06	1.31	1.08	2.38	2.08	1.60	1.08

GAPS:

Start:	1: 1	20: 3	34:10	34:11	
End:	14: 7	33: 6	48:35	48:35	
Count:	2	3	2		
Width:	6144	8297	7332	9208	9164
Strength:	1.55	1.03	2.06	1.32	2.85

Linguistic Density Plot in Ezekiel 1 - 48

For drs 322 (5 times)   drs 3261 (1 times)

Each Column = 13 Verses.   Separations are: Max = 10007.00, Mean = 3995.71, Min = 372.50 .

REFERENCE

```
25+                                                                              +25
                                                                                 .
                              •                                                  .
20+                                                                              +20
                                                                                 .
                                                                                 .
D15+                                                                             +15D
E                                                                                   E
N                                                                                   N
S                                                                                   S
I                                                          •                      +10T
T10+                      •                                                           I
Y                                                                                   Y
                                            •           •
5+                                                                               +5
                                                                                 .
                                                            •
0+                                                                               +0
     1 23 4 5 6 7  8 90 1 2 3 4 56  7 8 9 0  1 2 3 4 5 6 7 8 9 0  1 2 3 4 5 6 7 8
```

REFERENCE

CLUSTERS:

Start:	14: 3	14: 3	20: 3	20:31
End:	36:37	20:31	14:	20:31	20:31
Count:	6	5	2	3	2
Width:	14369	4362	1	745	12
Strength:	1.25	2.37	1.15	1.62	1.15

GAPS:

Start:	20:31	20:31
End:	48:35	36:37
Count:	3	2
Width:	17601	10007
Strength:	2.15	1.73

Linguistic Density Plot in Ezekiel 1 - 48

For drs 322 (5 times)

Each Column = 13 Verses. Separations are: Max = 10007.00, Mean = 4661.66, Min = 372.50 .

DENSITY

REFERENCE

CLUSTERS:

Start:	14: 3	20:31	20:31
End:	20:31	20:31	
Count:	4	3	2
Width:	4361	745	12
Strength:	1.82	1.72	1.18

GAPS:

Start:	20:31	20:31
End:	48:35	36:37
Count:	3	2
Width:	17601	10007
Strength:	1.66	1.35

Linguistic Density Plot in Ezekiel 1 - 48

For ha 51 (5 times)   ha- 51 (42 times)

Each Column = 13 Verses.   Separations are: Max = 5382.00, Mean =   582.71, Min =   10.50

REFERENCE

(vertical axis, right: DENSITY)

+25
+20
+15
+10
+5
+0

(vertical axis, left)
25+
20+
D15+
E
N
S
I
T10+
Y
5+
0+

REFERENCE

CLUSTERS:

Start:	8: 6	8: 6	8: 6	8:12	8:15	8:17	8:17	9:17	9:17:	9:17:	9:17:	9:17:	17:10	17:10	17:15	18:23	18:23 18:23
End:	47: 6	28: 9	16:20	9: 8	8:17	8:17	16:20	22:14	28: 9	22: 9	20: 4	17:12	17:10	17:12	20: 4	18:29	18:23 18:25
Count:	47	38	13	6	5	3	2	4	25	20	15	9	3	2	9	6	4
Width:	23590	11920	3857	519	251	122	58	4	6943	3406	1364	148	67	542	149	75	
Strength:	4.02	5.74	1.81	1.96	1.88	1.68	1.38	1.04	3.52	3.92	3.74	2.26	1.73	2.76	1.01	1.42	1.01 1.72

Start:	18:23	18:25	18:29	20: 3	22: 2	37: 3	38:13	38:13
End:	18:23	18:25	18:29	20: 4	22: 2	38:17	38:13	38:14
Count:	2	2	2	3	2	6	3	3
Width:	9	5	7	21	227	1046	118	41
Strength:	1.00	1.01	1.00	1.43	1.17	1.52	1.40	1.00

Data for ha 51, ha- 51, continued.

GAPS:

Start:	1: 1	1: 1	1: 1	1: 1	9: 8	22: 2	22: 2	24:25	24:25	24:25	26:15	28: 9	34:18	38:13	38:14	38:17	38:17
End:	8:17	8:15	8:12	8: 6	12: 9	48:35	38:13	38:13	37: 3	34: 2	34: 2	34: 2	37: 3	48:35	48:35	48:35	47: 6
Count:	5	4	3	2	2	17	12	8	6	4	3	2	2	5	4	3	2
Width:	3540	3486	3422	3293	1226	16518	9932	7860	6932	5079	4329	3389	1495	6580	6545	6468	5382
Strength:	1.09	1.79	2.82	4.74	1.12	3.81	2.09	2.68	3.29	3.44	3.96	4.91	1.59	3.84	4.95	6.64	8.40

Linguistic Density Plot in Ezekiel 1 - 48

For ha 51 (5 times)

Each Column = 13 Verses.   Separations are: Max = 6079.00, Mean = 4661.66, Min = 3214.00 .

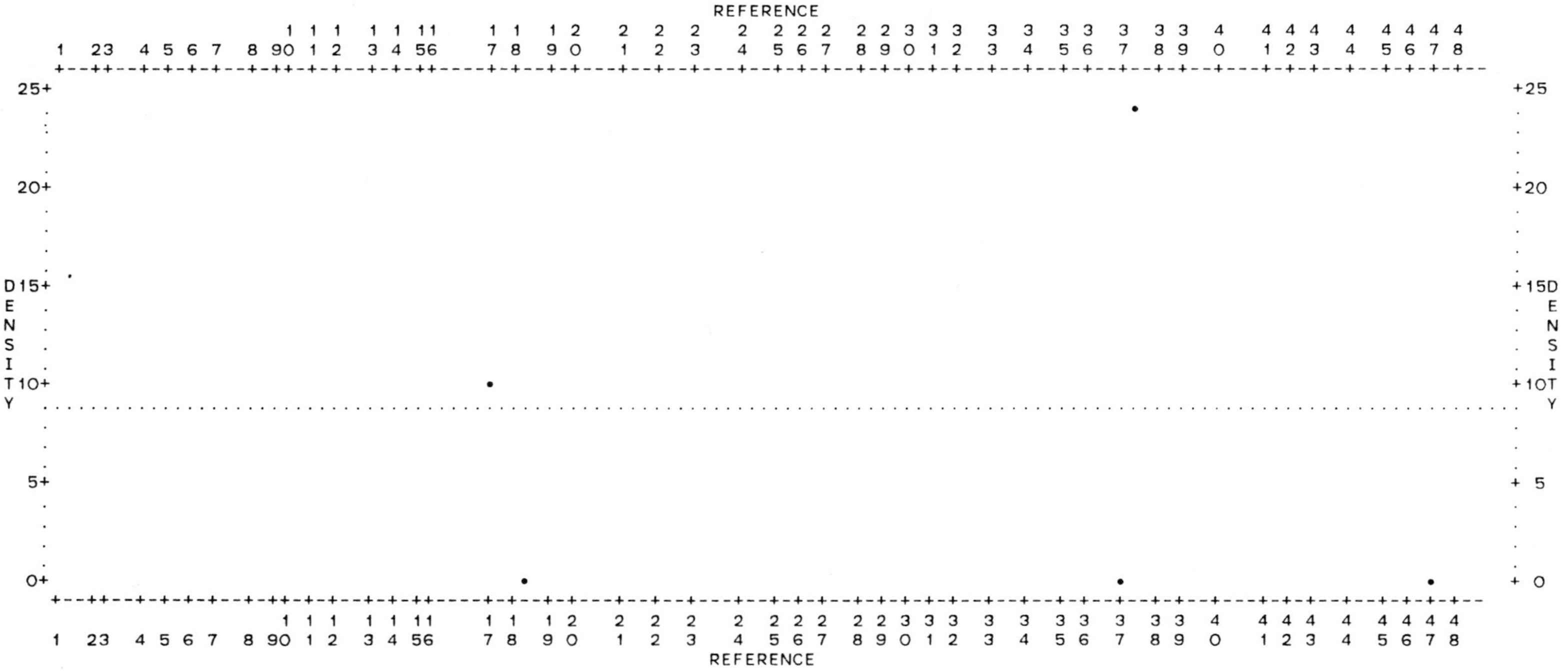

REFERENCE

CLUSTERS:

Start:	37: 3
End:	37:18
Count:	2
Width:	349
Strength:	1.09

GAPS:

Start:	1: 1	18:23
End:	37: 3	37: 3
Count:	4	2
Width:	20455	11354
Strength:	1.22	1.69

Linguistic Density Plot in Ezekiel 1 - 48

For ha- 51 (42 times)

Each Column = 13 Verses.   Separations are: Max = 3272.50, Mean = 650.47, Min = 10.50 .

REFERENCE

DENSITY

REFERENCE

CLUSTERS:

Start:	8: 6	8: 6	8: 6	8:12	8:15	8:17	8:17	12: 9	17: 9	17: 9	17:10	17:15	18:23	18:23	18:25
End:	38:17	28: 9	16:20	9: 8	8:17	8:17	8:17	16:20	28: 9	22:14	20: 4	17:10	17:15	20: 4	18:23	18:29	18:25
Count:	42	36	13	6	4	3	2	5	7	23	18	13	8	5	3	2
Width:	18208	11920	3857	519	251	122	58	2112	3406	6943	1364	148	542	149	75
Strength:	9.52	6.60	2.08	2.02	1.91	1.70	1.39	1.01	1.22	3.49	3.71	3.40	1.42	2.00	2.57	2.00	1.38	1.01

Start:	18:29	20: 3	20: 4	20:30	22: 2	22: 2	38:13	38:13
End:	18:29	20: 4	20: 4	22:14	22:14	38:17	38:14	38:13
Count:	2	3	2	5	3	4	3	2
Width:	7	21	4	1354	227	118	41	6
Strength:	1.01	1.44	1.01	1.20	1.70	1.41	1.01

Data for ha- 51, continued.

GAPS:

```
Start:      1: 1   1: 1   22: 2  22: 2  24:25  26:15  28: 9  34:18  38:13  38:14  38:17
End:        8:15   8:12   8: 6   48:35  38:13  38:13  34: 2  34: 2  38:13  38:13  48:35  48:35
Count:      4      3      2      14     10     6      4      3      2      4      3      2
Width:      3486   3422   3293   16518  9932   7860   5079   4329   3389   2423   6580   6545   6468
Strength:   1.42   2.38   4.15   4.16   2.37   3.40   2.91   3.40   4.30   2.78   4.30   5.90   9.15
```

Linguistic Density Plot in Ezekiel 1 - 48

For hŌ' 6113 (52 times)

Each Column = 13 Verses.   Separations are: Max = 2059.50, Mean = 527.74, Min = 28.00 .

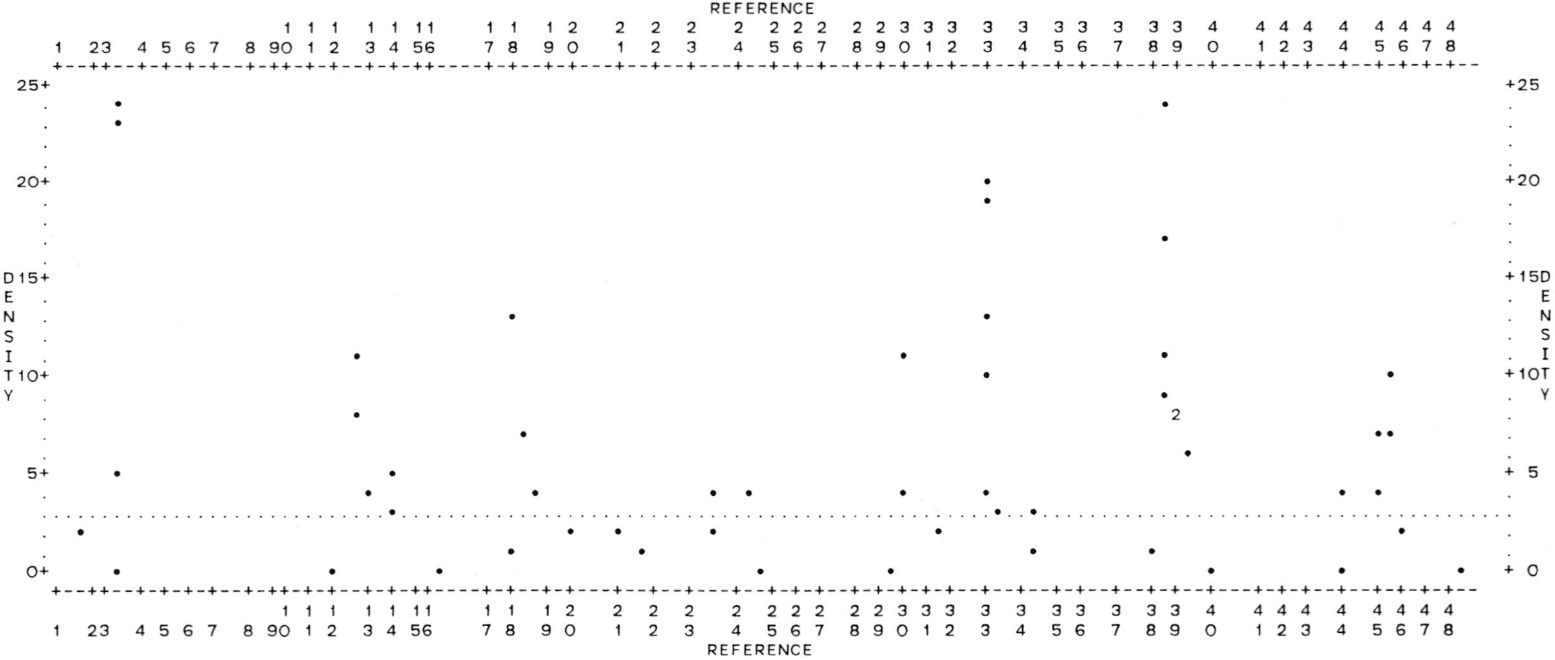

REFERENCE

(plot axis values, top) 25+ … +25 20+ … +20 D15+ … +15D E … E N … N S … S I … I T10+ … +10T Y … Y 5+ … +5 0+ … +0

DENSITY (vertical axis letters): D E N S I T Y

Column header reference (verse references):
1 23 4 5 6 7 8 9 0 1 2 3 4 5 6 … 1 2 3 4 5 6 7 8

REFERENCE

CLUSTERS:

Start:	1:28	3:18	12:12	12:12	12:27	12:27	18: 9	18: 9	18: 9	29:21	29:21	33: 5	33: 5	34:23	38:10	38:10	38:17
End:	3:21	3:20	16:14	13:10	13:10	12:27	18:27	18:17	34:23	30:11	34:23	33:19	34:23	48:15	40: 3	38:19	38:19
Count:	5	4	7	3	3	2	5	4	3	12	6	8	2	17	9	5	3
Width:	711	56	1886	507	215	9	875	393	153	2974	193	1204	113	6253	1082	253	58
Strength:	1.39	1.69	1.06	1.22	1.15	1.00	1.22	1.35	1.24	1.83	1.18	1.93	1.67	1.25	2.30	1.84	1.37

Start:	39: 8	44: 1	45: 1	45:17
End:	40: 3	46: 3	46: 3	46: 3
Count:	4	7	5	3
Width:	571	1366	597	242
Strength:	1.15	1.49	1.50	1.12

Data for h0' 6113, continued.

GAPS:

Start:	1: 1	3:20	3:21	3:21	14: 9	16:14	18:17	18:27	20: 6	21:28	24:27	24:27	24:27	34:23	34:23	39:11	39:22	40:	46: 3
End:	12:27	12:27	12:27	12:12	18:	18: 9	23:38	23:38	21: 5	23:38	33: 5	30: 9	29:21	38:14	38:10	44: 1	44: 1	44: 1	48:15
Count:	8	4	3	2	3	2	6	5	2	6	6	3	2	2	3	4	3	2	2
Width:	5409	4154	4119	3827	2618	1810	3824	3584	1111	1549	4309	2692	2539	2352	2232	3021	2775	2522	1283
Strength:	1.33	2.92	4.22	6.36	2.15	2.47	1.06	1.46	1.12	1.97	1.50	2.25	3.88	1.78	3.28	1.63	2.37	3.84	1.45

Linguistic Density Plot in Ezekiel 1 - 48

For -hQ 6113 (530 times)

Each Column = 13 Verses.   Separations are: Max = 730.00, Mean = 52.67, Min = 2.50

REFERENCE

+25

+20

D +15
E
N
S
I +10 T
Y

+ 5

0 +

REFERENCE

CLUSTERS:

Start:	1:3	1:26	1:27	3:12	3:12	3:18	3:18	3:19	3:19	3:19	3:20	3:20	3:20	4:9	7:13	7:13	7:13	7:20	7:20	7:20
End:	48:21	1:27	1:27	3:21	5:9	3:18	3:21	3:19	3:20	3:21	3:20	3:21	4:10	8:12	7:21	7:16	7:21	7:21	7:21	7:21
Count:	530	4	3	16	25	5	15	3	5	10	4	4	3	18	16	4	10	6	5	3
Width:	27690	38	19	207	988	22	98	61	32	172	14	28	16	583	64	24	38	24	11	
Strength:	2.34	1.31	1.15	2.89	1.09	1.79	3.28	2.63	1.69	1.92	1.57	1.42	1.02	1.02	1.16	1.02	1.92	1.77	1.26	

Start:	8:11	9:1	9:1	8:11	9:1	9:1	9:2	9:2	9:2	12:5	12:12	12:12	12:14	13:14	13:22	13:22	14:4	14:4	14:4	14:9
End:	8:12	10:11	9:6	8:12	9:9	9:4	9:9	9:9	9:4	12:14	12:14	12:14	12:13	13:15	13:22	13:22	14:14	14:14	14:9	14:14
Count:	4	16	10	40	37	8	3	5	3	7	4	4	3	4	9	3	4	6	9	10
Width:	40	511	138	76	37	20	17	50	28	188	42	50	6	29	19	277	131	15	26	78
Strength:	1.29	1.38	2.14	2.11	1.65	1.14	1.18	1.30	2.07	1.42	1.27	1.33	1.05	3.05	1.96	1.20	2.02	1.61	1.77	1.26

```
Start:    14: 7   14: 7
End:      14: 7   14: 7
Count:       4       4
Width:      40      11
Strength:  1.29    1.61
```

```
Start:    17:16  17:16  17:19  17:19  17:20  17:19  17:20  17:22  17:23  17:22  18:17  18:18  18:15  18:15  18:13  18:14  18:11  18:14   18: 8  18: 7   18: 6  18: 5  18: 6   18: 6   18: 6   18:30
End:      17:18  17:17  17:19  17:20  17:21  17:20  17:21  17:23  17:23  17:23  18:18  18:18  18:17  18:15  18:14  18:18  18:14  18:11   18:     18: 8  18: 8  18: 8   18:18   18:30   18:18   18:30
Count:       54      4     110      5      21      3      8     52      39      36    256     81     37     8     14     256    51      148    27     5      13     52     36      981     256     36
Width:       13     13     38      7       5       7      8     27      8      36     81    148     81     81     14      52    51      148    27    13      13     52     36      981     256     511
Strength:  1.78   1.59   2.71   1.80   1.31   1.31   1.30  1.04   1.30   4.42  2.07  2.07  1.32  1.51  1.22  2.99  1.51   2.68  1.04  1.33   2.68   1.50   4.42    4.77    2.99    4.42
```

```
Start:    18:20  18:24  18:22  18:22  18:22  18:23  18:24  18:24  18:26  18:27  18:26  18:28  19:11  19:11  19:11  19:12  19: 9  19: 9   19: 4  19: 9   19: 4  19: 7   19: 4   18:26   18:26   18:30
End:      18:24  18:21  18:24  18:22  18:22  18:22  18:24  18:24  18:27  18:28  18:30  18:30  19:11  19:11  19:12  19:11  19: 9  19: 7   19: 9  19: 7   19:12  19:20   19:19   18:26   18:30   18:30
Count:       54    110     38     6       7       3      3      13     16     5      5      40     81     34     4      13     41     47      11    4      170     16      364     40      74      18
Width:      101     66     38     9      12       9      3      12     16     20     5      20     12     34     21     13     47    102      11   41      170    364     364     74      74     208
Strength:  2.76   1.20   1.92   1.29   1.80   1.31   2.38  1.23  2.11  1.14  1.62   1.14  1.24  1.35   1.50  1.23  2.14   2.57  2.57  1.21  2.91   2.11   2.91   1.61    1.61    3.21
```

```
Start:    22:11  22:11  26:11  26:11  28:12  28:12  28:12  28:12  29:    29:18  29:20  29:18  30:22  30:24  31: 6  31: 2  31: 3  31: 6   31:11  31:     31: 2  31: 8   31: 2   31: 2   31: 3   22:11
End:      22:11  22:11  26:10  26:11  48:21  40:37  48:21  29:18  31: 6  29:20  29:18  29:20  30:24  31: 6  31:    29:18  31:13  31:13   31:    31:     29:    31:     31: 6   31: 6   31: 9   22:11
Count:      101     18      42    302  12481   7851   4123   1638    54    216     41     50    216     49     15    126     27     89     375    886     73    1638     27     54     50      87
Width:      101     18     302   302  12481   7851   4123   1638   126    216     41     50    216     49    216    126     27     89     375    886    886    1638     27     54     50      87
Strength:  2.76   1.53   1.60   1.20   5.61   4.31   4.78   3.17  4.78   2.68   5.41   4.82  5.41   1.19  2.68   4.78   1.04   2.65   5.41   4.82  1.62   3.17   1.04   4.78   4.82   1.17
```

```
Start:    31: 5  31: 5  31: 5  31: 5  31: 7  31: 7  31: 7  31: 8  31: 9  31: 9  31: 9  31: 9  31:10  31:11  31:11  31:11  31:11  31:11   31:11  31:11   31:10  31:13   31:13   31:13   31:13   31:15
End:      31: 6  31: 6  31: 3  31:13  31:13  31:    31:    31: 9  31: 3  31:    31:    31:    31:13  31:11  31:11  31:12  31:13  31:     31:12  31:11   31:10  31:13   31:13   31:13   35: 8   31:15
Count:       12     12     26    150    150     53     15     7      3      6      5      5     48    14      9      17     74      5      9     375    17    2425   1277   72      58      22
Width:       12     19    150    150     15     53     15     13     6      13     14      5     74    48      9      9      74      5      9    2425   17    2425   1277   72      58     656
Strength:  1.24   1.52   4.54   2.87   2.87   1.56   1.56   1.88  1.88   1.33   1.87   1.34   2.90   1.87   1.33   1.54   3.41  2.25  1.29   3.18  1.54   3.18   4.59   3.18    3.32    1.90
```

```
Start:    31:15  32:10  31:15  31:17  31:15  31:15  31:15  31:13  32:18  32:22  32:21  32:18  32:31  32:31  32:32  32:32  32:31  32:31   33:     33: 6  33: 9  33: 4   33: 9   33: 4   33: 8   32:26
End:      31:15  32: 2  31:16  31:16  31:16  31:15  31:16  31:17  32:26  32:26  32:21  32:22  32:32  32:32  32:32  33:    33: 9  33:      33: 9  33:    33: 5  33:     33: 9   33: 8   33: 3   32:26
Count:      333    15     73     10     19     4       60    174     74     4      60    494     244      32     16    136     56     23      14     8       5     74     16      56     23     656
Width:      333   146     73     12     19     4      60    174    494    244     60    494     244      32     16    136     56     23      14    74       5     74     16      56     23     1277
Strength:  2.07   2.50   2.55   2.50   1.52   1.24  1.43  1.10  4.48   3.20  1.43  4.48   3.20   1.38   1.19   2.92  2.25  2.04   1.19   2.25  1.29   3.20  1.38    2.25    2.04    1.90
```

```
Start:    33: 8  33: 9  33: 8  33: 8  33:10  33:12  33:12  33:13  33:13  33:16  33:13  33:20  33:14  33:13  33:16  34:12  35:    35:     36:10   37:16  37:16   37:19  37:16   37:37   38:21   38:22
End:      33: 9  33: 9  33: 8  33: 8  33:12  33:12  33:12  33:16  33:20  33:16  33:14  33:14  34:12  33:13  34:12  34:12  35:    35:     40:37   37:16  37:19   37:16  37:16   37:37   38:22   38:22
Count:       36     15     6     36    221     85      30    15     61     7      10     16      8      72     30     94     6      10     3308    59     26      94     136     16     1505     3
Width:       36     15      6     30    221     85     123    30    123    15      30     16     72     72     30     94    72      10    3308    59     26      94     136     32     1505    656
Strength:  1.93   1.20   1.79  1.79  2.99   1.71   1.20  1.55  1.98  1.20  1.27   1.55  1.44   1.04  1.30  1.44  1.27   1.27    1.04  4.09  1.44    1.44   2.92    1.19    4.09    1.30
```

```
Start:    40: 2  40:    40:20  40:37  40:26  40:22  40:20  40:21  40:21  40:20  40:21  40:21  40:22  40:25  40:26  40:26  40:24  40:25   40:24  40:26   40:22  40:22   40:26   40:29   40:29   40:29
End:      40:37  40:    40:26  40:37  40:26  40:22  40:21  40:21  40:21  40:21  40:21  40:22  40:22  40:26  40:25  40:26  40:24  40:26   40:26  40:33   40:22  40:22   40:33   40:29   40:33   40:29
Count:       50    753     43    374    160     70     36      7     12     24     4      6      24     53     10     177    20     3       91     177     3     22      12      10     17     208
Width:      753    753    374    374    160     70     36     15     12     24     4      6      53     53     10     177    20    14       91     177    53     22      12     91      17      208
Strength:  5.20   5.20   3.86  5.61  3.86   3.11  2.18  1.57  1.24  2.03  1.60  1.33  2.27   2.27   1.27   3.92  1.51  1.57    2.82   3.92  1.33   1.60   2.03   2.82    1.84    3.21
```

```
Start:    40:31  40:33  40:33  40:37  40:34  40:34  40:36  40:21  40:20  40:36  40:37  40:37  40:46  40:37  41:22  42:15  42:20  42:20   41:22  40:46   40:37  41:22   41:22   41:22   43:11   43:11
End:      40:33  40:33  40:37  40:37  40:36  40:34  40:34  40:21  40:21  40:36  40:37  40:37  48:21  40:37  41:22  42:15  42:20  41:22   42:20  40:46   40:37  41:22   41:22   41:22   43:11   43:11
Count:       50     24    753    374    160     70     36     12     36    160     24     53    1768    104    13     24     177     92      177   4438    50     7       14      91      91     263
Width:      753    374    753    374    160     70     36     12     36    160     24     53    1768    104    13     24     177     92      177   4438    50    13       14      91      55     263
Strength:  5.20   1.08  5.61  5.61  3.86   3.11  2.18  1.24  2.18  3.86  2.03  2.27   1.78  2.05  1.88  2.27   3.92  1.12   3.92   2.05  1.18  1.31    1.57    2.82    2.28    3.11
```

```
Start:    40:33  40:33  40:34  40:36  40:34  40:36  40:    40:    41:    42: 2  43: 2  44: 7  42:15  44:21  43:    43:12  43:11  43:11   43:12  43:21   43:21  43:11   43:11   43:11   43:11   43:11
End:      40:33  40:37  40:37  40:37  40:34  40:36  40:    40:    44: 7  44: 3  43: 4  41:22  42:20  43:    43:    43:12  43:12  43:11   43:12  43:11   43:21  43:11   43:12   43:11   43:11   43:11
Count:       47     17      5      3     10     40     18      9    104     27     46     7      5      148    27     13     10     557     47     263    92     148     55      91     23     10
Width:       47     17      5      6     10     72     18      9    104     27     46     5      5      148    27    104     10     557     47     263    92     148     263     91     23     10
Strength:  2.09   1.84  1.33  1.33  1.16  2.14  1.16  1.63  1.30  1.31  1.88  1.30  1.30   1.16  1.88  1.12  1.30   3.10   1.30   3.11  1.18   1.30   2.67    2.82    2.28    1.62
```

Clusters for -h0 6113, continued.

Clusters

Start	End	Count	Width	Strength
43:11	43:11	3	8	1.30
43:17	43:17	3	18	1.16
43:17	43:17	9	91	2.23
43:18	43:18	4	30	1.40
43:18	43:18	3	10	1.27
43:20	43:20	5	30	1.71
43:20	43:21	11	208	1.26
43:26	43:26	8	96	1.15
43:26	44:	6	208	1.42
44:2	44:3	4	32	1.20
44:14	48:21	58	2478	1.38
44:14	46:18	38	1376	1.39
44:14	44:27	5	76	1.85
44:24	44:27	4	22	1.27
44:26	44:27	6	10	1.49
44:26	44:27	22	235	1.31
45:22	46:18	27	503	3.30
46:9	46:18	21	235	3.54
46:9	46:18	10	111	2.31
46:9	46:12	6	72	1.62
46:11	46:12	4	33	1.37
46:12	46:12	3	13	1.23
46:14	46:14	4	24	1.46
46:12	46:18	11	74	2.74
46:16	46:16	8	40	2.37
46:16	46:16	3	6	1.33
46:16	46:17	5	21	1.80
46:17	46:17	3	9	1.29
46:17	46:18	9	15	1.20
46:18	46:18	5	11	1.42
47:3	47:14	12	249	1.91
47:10	47:12	11	54	1.48
47:12	47:12	6	5	
47:12	47:12	5	28	1.42
47:12	47:12	20	48	1.83
47:12	47:12	7	20	1.81

GAPS:

Start	End	Count	Width	Strength
1:1	1:1	434	23812	2.13
41:22	40:36	421	23073	1.92
1:1	35:8	354	19384	1.37
33:8	33:4	314	17867	3.51
32:22	32:22	311	17852	2.54
31:11	31:11	302	17501	2.73
30:11	30:11	274	16859	4.07
29:19	29:19	241	16259	6.05
18:13	18:13	237	16079	6.05
17:6	17:16	159	8886	3.46
12:14	12:14	136	8451	2.53
12:12	12:12	123	8196	3.46
7:13	17:6	121	8191	3.68
1:1	1:26	5	450	2.27
1:1	1:27	7	525	1.62
1:4	1:26	5	300	2.61
1:12	1:26	6	238	3.51
1:26	3:18	642	622	3.22
3:18	3:18	513	633	4.02
7:20	7:21	6	392	1.09
8:11	8:11	5	385	1.65
8:2	8:12	2	148	1.80
8:11	9:1	2	167	2.16
9:6	9:2	1100	1468	3.01
10:6	10:11	980	1072	6.90
12:25	12:25	3	314	2.80
13:14	13:22	244	184	2.48
13:10	13:22	385	148	1.65
14:9	15:4	1514	1477	12.30
15:5	16:15	1524	1501	9.42
18:23	18:30	2517	106	2.03
22:11	21:32	2212	1814	10.44
19:12	21:32	1986	1943	7.27
20:7	20:40	1458	1541	14.29
25:9	25:9	2247	359	2.32
29:18	26:9	370	247	3.68
26:11	29:18	1460	1873	9.82
30:11	30:24	342	263	1.40
33:20	33:27	134	868	1.53
33:26	35:8	977	413	2.72
34:12	34:12	451	409	4.08
35:8	40:20	3628	3461	5.81

```
Gaps for -hQ 6113, continued.

Start:    35: 8 35: 8 35: 8 35: 8 35: 8 35: 8 35: 8 36:21 36:29 36:29 37:19 37:19 37:19 38: 6 38:22 38:22 38:22 38:22 39:15
End:      40:20 38:22 38:21 37:19 37:16 37:16 36:20 37:16 37:16 37: 7 38: 2 38:21 38:21 38:21 40:20 39:15 39:11 39:15 40:20
Count:       32    18    16    11     8     3     2     4     2     3     2     4     5     2    14     3     2    10
Width:     3362  2259  2237  1449  1369  1361   633   420   718   520   319   782   768   391  1099   339   332   262   755
Strength:  6.07  6.38  7.19  5.59  7.22  8.14  7.09  6.97  6.15  5.57  5.05  5.44  6.70  6.42  2.20  1.98  3.04  3.97  1.79

  .

Start:    39:15 40: 6 40: 6 40: 3 40: 2 40: 9 40:13 40:36 40:36 40:37 40:37 40:37 40:37 40:37 41: 4 41: 4 41:22 41:22 42: 7 42: 9
End:      40: 3 40:40 40:40 40:40 40:20 40:20 40:20 41:22 41:22 41:22 41: 2 40:49 40:46 41:12 41:22 42:20 42:15 42: 7 42:15 43:11
Count:        5     3     2     4     3     2    11    10     7     8     3     2     4     2     6     2     2     2     9     2
Width:      482   383   368   258   199   118   730   725   703   693   310   256   192   185   439   383   200   154   208
Strength:  2.58  3.73  5.98  1.09  1.25  1.23  1.23  1.59  2.41  2.93  1.66  2.02  2.64  2.50  1.49  2.46  2.79  1.91  1.37

Start:    43: 4 43:11 43:12 43:20 43:26 44: 3 44: 3 44: 7 44:14 44:14 44:27 44:27 45: 3 45: 3 45: 8 45:11 45:11 45:22 46: 2 46:18
End:      43:11 43:17 43:20 46: 2 46: 2 44:14 44:14 44:14 44:26 44:24 45: 2 46: 2 45: 2 45: 2 46: 2 45:11 47:11 47:11 45:22 47:10
Count:        2     2     2    23    20     5     3     7     2     8     5     7     2     8     3     3     4     5     2     3
Width:      166   117  1482  1384   319   304   192   166   278   224   693   681   131   122   532   327   212   367   356   330
Strength:  2.14  1.21  1.33  1.69  1.02  1.60  2.64  2.31  3.24  2.34  1.48  2.84  1.30  2.97  3.05  1.48  3.02  2.17  3.01

Start:    47:12 47:12 47:23 47:23 48:10 48: 1 48: 1 48:14 48:21
End:      48:35 47:23 47:23 48:35 48:35 48:35 48: 8 48:19 48:35
Count:       14     3     2     8     5     2     7     2     2
Width:      935   220   192   694   665   499   115   134   225
Strength:  1.33  1.53  2.64  2.34  2.71  2.74  1.17  1.53  3.26
```

Linguistic Density Plot in Ezekiel 1 - 48

For hî' 6143 (37 times)

Each Column = 13 Verses.   Separations are: Max = 2651.50, Mean = 736.05, Min = 8.50 .

CLUSTERS:

Start:	1: 2	1: 2	10:15	11: 3	14:17	18: 4	19:14	21:16	21:16	21:16	21:17	46:16
End:	20:15	11:15	11:15	11:11	20:15	20:15	23:43	22:24	21:19	21:17	21:17	46:16
Count:	21	11	6	4	3	10	5	7	6	5	2	2
Width:	9922	4608	446	230	119	3581	1228	391	1909	871	69	22
Strength:	2.14	1.39	2.13	1.63	1.35	1.59	1.24	1.08	1.53	1.85	2.09	1.80	1.02	1.01

GAPS:

Start:	4:12	10:15	21:16	21:17	21:19	21:19	22:24	22:24	22:24	23:43	32:16	39:11
End:	10:15	14:17	48:35	46:16	21:17	38: 8	38: 1	30:18	28:18	37: 1	46:16	39:11
Count:	2	2	16	14	11	8	9	8	4	3	2	
Width:	2471	1733	16966	15549	15502	10199	9397	8557	4571	3541	2503	3034	4665
Strength:	2.41	1.38	2.70	3.47	3.66	4.12	2.36	2.44	2.53	1.18	1.10	1.03	3.20	5.47

Linguistic Density Plot in Ezekiel 1 - 48

For -hā 6143 (304 times)

Each Column = 13 Verses. Separations are: Max = 1151.50, Mean = 91.70, Min = 2.50 .

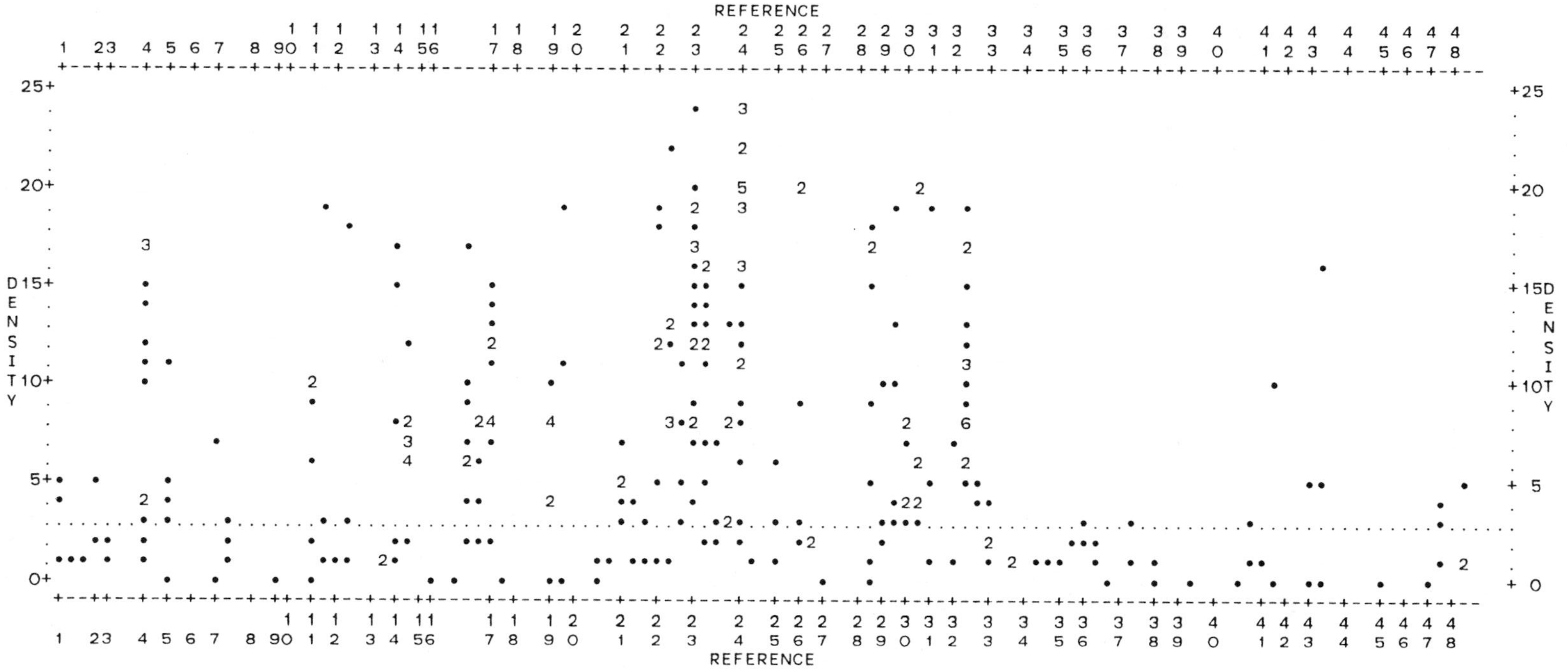

REFERENCE
DENSITY
25+
20+
D15+
T10+
5+
0+
+25
+20
+15D
+10T
+ 5
+ 0

CLUSTERS:

Start:	1: 4	1: 4	1: 4	4: 1	4: 1	4: 1	4: 1	4: 1	4: 2	4: 3	5: 1	5: 5	7:12	11: 5	11: 5	11: 5	11: 5	11: 5	11: 7	11:18
End:	48:18	27: 9	5: 6	5: 6	4:12	4: 3	4: 2	4: 2	4: 2	4: 3	5: 6	5: 6	7:14	17:14	16: 2	11:18	11:11	11: 9	11: 9	11:18
Count:	304	209	27	18	13	10	7	4	3	3	5	3	3	59	32	9	6	5	3	3
Width:	27579	14496	1900	528	274	69	34	19	10	22	124	22	47	3955	2278	276	94	55	30	8
Strength:	1.60	6.14	1.08	2.80	2.65	2.79	2.32	1.61	1.33	1.24	1.33	1.24	1.05	2.17	1.16	1.78	1.79	1.71	1.18	1.35

Start:	12:19	13:14	14:13	14:13	14:13	14:13	14:17	14:19	14:21	16:32	16:32	16:44	16:44	16:44	16:44	16:48	16:53	16:53	17: 7	17: 7
End:	12:19	16: 2	16: 2	14:20	14:16	14:13	14:20	14:20	14:23	17:14	16:57	16:57	16:49	16:46	16:45	16:49	16:57	16:55	17:14	17:10
Count:	3	19	16	11	6	4	5	3	4	27	14	13	8	5	3	3	5	4	13	10
Width:	9	1007	442	158	63	16	57	18	66	1036	603	302	121	57	10	27	88	46	173	96
Strength:	1.34	1.70	2.69	2.66	1.94	1.63	1.70	1.27	1.32	3.01	1.82	2.56	2.17	1.70	1.33	1.20	1.53	1.44	2.98	2.69

Clusters for -hã 6143, continued.

```
Start:     17: 7  17: 9  17: 9  17: 9  17:12  19: 2  19: 2  19: 2  19: 2  21: 3  21: 8  21:32  21:32  22: 2
End:       17: 7  17:10  17:10  17:14  17:14  23:19  19:14  19:14  23:19  21:10  21:10  23:19  22: 3  22: 3
Count:        3      7      3      4     47     117     11      5      3     50      5      3      8      6
Width:       16     48     12     22    5237   3034     71     37     44   1062    225    176     29
Strength:   1.29   2.25   1.32   1.60   6.95   5.03   1.59   1.13   1.07   5.84   1.46   1.94   2.11

Start:     22: 3  22:21  22:21  22:21  22:24  22:24  22:25  22:27  22:27  23: 8  23: 8  23: 8  23: 8  23:10
End:       22:21  23:19  22:30  22:26  22:26  22:25  22:26  22:28  22:30  23:23  23:23  23:10  23: 9  23:14
Count:        4     42     12      8      6      3      3      7      4     10      3      9      6
Width:       12    541    183     69     35     16      6     20     46    182    115     52     17
Strength:   1.66   5.90   2.76   2.39   2.08   1.29   1.37   1.26   1.06   4.03   3.79   3.03   1.63   2.34

Start:     23:10  23:11  23:11  23:16  23:17  23:17  23:17  23:18  23:18  23:31  23:31  23:41  23:41  24: 4
End:       23:11  23:11  23:11  23:17  23:19  23:18  23:17  23:19  23:19  23:44  23:34  23:44  23:42  24:24
Count:        5      5      3     10      7      4      3      8      5     46      35      5     15     27
Width:       19     10     68     38     18     11     10     11   1926    861     52     46    421
Strength:   1.90   1.33   2.79   1.27   2.30   1.62   1.33   1.33   3.88   4.48   1.06   1.72   1.06   4.83

Start:     24: 6  24: 6  24: 6  24: 6  24:24  24:11  24:11  24:11  24:11  25:10  26: 4  26: 4  28:21  28:22
End:       24:24  24: 8  24: 7  24: 7  24:11  24:11  24:11  24:12  24:12  26: 6  26: 4  26: 4  28:23  28:23
Count:        8      8      5     12      6      6      9      7      3      8      4      7      6      9
Width:       45     19     12    224     27     36     21      5    274     11      7    125     52     25
Strength:   1.37   2.49   1.94   1.74   1.20   1.37   2.72   2.15   1.67   1.53   1.67   1.36   2.15   2.24   2.13   1.34

Start:     28:23  29:11  29:11  29:11  29:11  29:18  29:19  29:19  30: 4  30: 6  30:18  30:18  32:12  32:12  32:12
End:       28:23  31: 4  30:12  29:20  29:12  29:20  29:20  29:19  30:12  30: 8  30:21  30:18  33: 3  32:24  32:16
Count:        3     24     14      8      5      3      4      3      6      5      6      4      3     17     83
Width:       10    834    473    224     27     41     20      8     10     42     66     92   1228    475
Strength:   1.33   3.01   2.22   1.74   1.20   1.78   1.61   1.35   1.67   1.35   1.93   1.15   3.05   3.51   2.33

Start:     32:15  32:16  32:16  32:18  32:18  32:22  32:22  32:23  32:25  32:25  32:25  32:25  41:13  43:13  43:17
End:       32:16  32:16  32:24  32:20  32:18  32:22  32:23  32:33  33: 2  32:26  32:25  32:25  41:15  43:17  43:17
Count:        6      4     15      9     32      4      6      3      8      7      5      3      3      5     11
Width:       33     15     99     32     45     24     10    227    109     42     27     85
Strength:   2.09   1.64   2.48   1.16   2.03   1.58   1.33   1.73   1.98   1.78   1.20   1.54   1.33

GAPS:

Start:     1: 1   1: 1   1: 1   1: 1   1: 1   1: 5   1: 1   1: 5   1: 9   1:27   1: 9   2:10   3: 3   3: 3   3:13
End:      16:45  12:19  11:18   4: 2   4: 1   1: 4   4: 1   2:10   1:23   2:10   2:10   4: 1   4: 1   4: 1
Count:       69     45     42     13     11      5      9      4      5      2      4     11      9      3
Width:     7671   5270   4717   1466   1459   1362    713    646    283    264    636    576    367
Strength:  2.15   2.19   1.75   1.17   1.50   1.87   2.45   1.90   2.34   2.08   1.87   2.28   3.03   3.00   3.60

Start:     7:22   9: 4  11: 5  11:18  11:18  12:19  12:19  13:16  13:16  14:22  14:23  16: 2  16:44  17:12  17:14  19:14
End:      11: 5  11: 7  12:13  12:13  12:13  14:13  13:14  14:13  13:14  16:44  16:44  16:32  17: 7  19:12  19: 2
Count:        3      2      2      3      5      5     11      6      5      6      9      7      3      5      2     17
Width:     1387    729    550    421   1007   1001    436    527    302   1237   1171   1113    641    983    940   1928
Strength:  9.32   6.96   2.83   3.59   2.69   3.48   3.76   2.65   2.29   1.96   3.50   5.30   6.00   1.67   3.59   9.27   1.29

Start:     19:14  22: 2  24:11  24:12  24:12  20:29  20:29  21:16  21:16  22: 3  22: 3  24:11  24:12  24:12  24:12  24:12
End:      22: 2  22: 1  21: 3  25:13  24:26  21: 3  20:42  21:35  21:16  22:21  23:31  43:13  48:35  41:11  26: 4  25:13
Count:       15     14     10      6      7      3      4      2      4      3      2    100    113     98     10    542
Width:     1911   1905   1426   1215    704    465    340    393    318    345    277  11357  14727  10437    780    601
Strength:  1.87   2.20   2.21   4.66   6.69   1.20   2.71   1.62   2.47   2.76   2.02   3.04   5.78   2.06   1.58   2.06   2.77
```

Gaps for -hā 6143. continued.

```
Start:     24:24  26: 4  26: 4  26: 4  26: 6  26:17  26:17  27: 9  28:23  28:26  31: 4  32:24  32:29  33:12  33:12  33:12  33:12
End:       25:10  28:23  28:22  28:22  26:17  28:22  28:21  29:11  29:11  29:11  32:12  41:15  37:25  37:25  36: 5  35:10  33:28
Count:         2     12      9      8      2      4      3      3      2      6      2     33     17     13      8      6      2
Width:       291   1461   1445   1441   1436    271   1132   1105    884    349    276    702    634   6135   5993   3340   2928   1583   1332    331
Strength:   2.17   1.51   2.78   3.33   3.98   1.95   5.42   7.13   8.66   1.27   2.01   1.19   5.92   6.53   8.43   5.25   5.87   3.92   4.29   2.61
```

```
Start:     33:33  33:33  34:27  36: 5  36: 5  36:18  36:38  37:25  37:25  38:13  39:14  40:46  41:15  43:13  43:13  43:13  43:17  43:17  43:17
End:       35:10  34:16  35:10  37:25  36:17  37:25  37:25  40:45  41:15  40:38  41:15  41:13  43:13  48:35  48:15  48:15  48:15  47:14
Count:         4      2      2      5      2      3      6      5      9      3      2     13     10      8      7      4
Width:       873    379    278   1325    241   1050    629   2243   2647   1740   1149    392    368    917   3367   2972   2896   2890   2391
Strength:   3.78   3.13   2.03   5.26   1.62   6.71   5.87   8.78   7.48  12.05  11.56   1.61   3.01   9.02   7.28   7.93   9.41  10.53  13.40
```

```
Start:     43:17  45: 1  47:14  47:22  48:16  48:18
End:       47:10  47:10  48:15  48:15  48:35  48:35
Count:         3      2      3      2      3      2
Width:      2303   1302    487    347    391    310
Strength:  16.42  13.23   2.34   2.78   1.60   2.38
```

Linguistic Density Plot in Ezekiel 1 - 48

For hyh 311 (130 times)   hyh 312 (182 times)   hyh 313 (1 times)   hyh 3161 (2 times)
     hyh 3162 (18 times)   hyh 321 (2 times)

Each Column = 13 Verses. Separations are: Max = 682.00. Mean = 83.24, Min = 3.00 .

REFERENCE

D E N S I T Y

REFERENCE

CLUSTERS:

Start:	1: 1	1: 3	11:11	11:11	12:17	14:10	14:10	14:10	14:11	15: 1	15: 1	16: 1	16:22	16:49	16:49	17: 6
End:	1: 3	1: 3	11:16	11:14	13:	16:34	16:	16:16	14:14	15: 5	15:	16:23	16:23	16:49	23:10	17:14
Count:	4	3	5	4	7	22	12	7	3	3	4	5	3	12	62	7
Width:	51	16	134	75	279	1201	487	142	37	18	66	151	70	163	4439	204
Strength:	1.38	1.27	1.20	1.21	1.09	1.48	1.57	1.76	1.27	1.26	1.27	1.09	1.25	1.38	1.08	1.46

Start:	17: 6	17: 8	18:30	19:10	19:14	19:14	20:32	20:32	20:32	21:12	21:12	21:12	21:17	21:37	22:13	22:17
End:	17: 7	17: 7	20: 2	20: 2	20: 1	23: 1	20:32	22: 9	23:10	21:28	21:15	21:18	21:18	22:	22:23	22:19
Count:	5	4	3	9	6	4	3	3	31	10	7	3	3	6	5	4
Width:	77	29	12	320	113	40	15	16	1831	321	142	71	36	183	94	39
Strength:	1.54	1.53	1.31	1.48	1.64	1.45	1.28	1.53	1.73	1.27	1.76	1.24	1.10	1.26	1.44	1.46

Clusters for hyh 311, hyh 312, hyh 313, hyh 3161, hyh 3162, hyh 321, continued.

```
Start:     23: 1  23:32  26: 1  26: 1  27: 1  27: 1  27: 7  27: 8  27: 8  29:12  29:12  29:12  29:12  29:12  29:12  29:14  29:17  29:17  29:17  29:17  30: 1
End:       23: 4  36:17  27:19  26: 5  27:19  27:10  27: 8  27:10  27: 8  29:13  30:20  31:13  30:20  30:20  29:13  29:16  29:16  29:19  29:19  29:18  30:20
Count:        3    101     17      4     10      9      8      4      4     23     65     17     32     35     22      3      4      3      3      9
Width:       43   7287    803     93    329    182     64     35     95   1009   4060   1977    581   2977   2011    182     73     87     42    351
Strength:  1.04   1.48   1.62   1.09   1.94   2.30   2.38   1.58   2.45   2.18   2.11   1.36   2.31   2.36   2.31   1.83   1.22   1.21   1.13   1.05   1.35
```

```
Start:     30: 1  30: 9  33:21  33:21  33:33  33:33  34:22  34:26  34:22  34:22  34:14  34:29  36:12  36:28  37:15  37:15  37:15  37:24  37:24
End:       30: 9  30: 4  33:21  34:14  33:33  34: 1  36:17  34:29  35:10  36:17  33:24  34:29  36:17  36:28  38:10  38:10  37: 4  37:24  37:24
Count:        5      3     13      4      6      3     20     12     34      7      9      4     26      4     19      9
Width:      147     40   1708    641    322    150    906    387    162     34     75     99   1105    266    576    143
Strength:  1.12   1.07   2.13   1.26   1.47   1.44   1.91   1.94   1.66   1.12   1.21   1.04   2.43   1.71   2.68   1.76
```

```
Start:     37:19  37:22  37:23  37:24  37:26  37:26  37:27  38: 7  38: 7  44:17  44:17  44:17  44:30  45: 8  45: 2  45: 2  45: 3  45:10  45:10  45:12  46:16
End:       37:22  37:24  37:26  38:10  37:27  37:27  37:27  38:10  38:10  44:17  44:18  44:30  44:18  44:18  45: 4  45: 4  45: 4  45:16  45:12  46:16  46:17
Count:       75     22     10      3      4      6      4      4     34     27     15      8      4      4      5      3     19     55     38
Width:     2233   2245    245     58     34     13     58     68    507   1276    294     85     36     55    101     38     36
Strength:  1.21   1.22   2.04   1.93   1.30   1.50   1.93   1.26   2.16   2.18   1.32   1.14   1.35   1.70   1.40   1.47   1.10
```

```
Start:     47: 9  48:28  47: 9  47: 9  47:22  47:22  48: 8  48: 8  48:15  48:18  48:21  48:21
End:       47:17  48: 1  47:10  47:10  47:23  48: 1  48:18  48:28  48:18  48:12  48:28  48:22
Count:       24     11      7      5      4      8      9      4      3
Width:      902    367    197     53     20     78    443    263     99     87    101     32
Strength:  2.63   1.79   1.49   1.69   1.24   1.19   1.96   1.73   1.41   1.13   1.03   1.14
```

GAPS:

```
Start:      1: 3   1: 3   1: 3   1: 3   1: 3   1: 3   1: 3   1: 3   2: 8   2: 3   3: 3   3:16   3:16   3:16   3:16   3:16   3:16   3:16   3:16   3:26   4: 3   7:19
End:       48:35  20:32  17: 7   1: 3   3:16   3:16   3:16   3:16   3:16   3:16   3:16  16:22  14:12  12:20  11:11   7:19   5:15   5:15   5:15  11:11
Count:      334    107     82     71     10     10      5      3      3      3     60     44     31     21     14      7     21      5      3      7
Width:    27932  10339   8162   7156   1104   1089    774    371    263   6046   5094   4140   3616   3381   1821   1064    808    696   1532
Strength:  1.47   2.13   2.17   2.14   1.04   1.37   1.35   1.74   2.15   1.95   2.97   3.77   3.83   4.75   2.51   5.46   7.37   5.11
```

```
Start:      8: 1   8: 1   8: 1  10: 6   8:13   9:13   9:13   9     12: 8  12: 1  11:20  11:20  12: 1  14:16  14:10  14: 2  15: 5  16: 1  16: 8  16:15  16:49  16:63  17:14  17:23
End:       11:11  10: 6   9: 8  11:11  14:10  13:21  14:10         12:17  12:17  12:17  12:20  16: 8  14:16  15: 1  16: 1  16: 4  16:23  16:49  16: 2  16: 2
Count:        5      3      2      5      6      2      2             8      1      4      4      2     16     15      4      5      2      5      2
Width:     1384    860    648    425    536    222    241    412    189    348    446    517    194    327    186    346    298    232
Strength:  6.35   5.91   6.79   4.11   1.99   1.66   1.89   1.12   1.26   1.54   1.36   1.11   1.32   1.36   1.23   3.15   1.11   1.78
```

```
Start:     18: 5  18:20  18:20  19: 3  20: 1  20:24  20:32  20: 2  20: 2  20:12  20:20  20:32  21:37  21:37  21:12  22:19  22:23  23: 2  23: 2  23: 4  23: 4  24:20
End:       18:20  18:30  19:19  20:32  20:32  21:12  20:20  20:32  21: 1  22:23  24:27  23: 1  24:27  24:24
Count:        3      6      3      2      2      5     13      2      2     23     10      2      4      9      7
Width:      317    296    220    810    785    454    524    325    202    559    187   1809   2210   1490   1413   1329
Strength:  1.27   1.10   1.64   2.13   2.73   2.44   1.91   2.90   1.42   1.36   1.24   2.86   3.42   3.54   3.81   4.10
```

```
Start:     23: 4  23:10  23:10  24: 1  23:10  25: 1  26: 5  27:11  27:10  27:36  27:36  28:11  31: 8  32: 1  32: 1  33: 5  33: 5  33:21  33:24  36: 4  36:17  36:28
End:       24:15  24: 1  23:32  24: 2  23:32  26: 1  26:14  27:19  27:36  27:36  28:11  31:32  32: 1  32:17  33:23  33:33  33:33  33:21  36:12  36:28
Count:        6      5      2      6      2      5      2      3      4      2      3     11      8      2      6      4      2
Width:     1228   1106    820    459    390    185    434    465    297    173    174    329   1136    694    431    375    244    206    247
Strength:  4.39   4.67   5.57   4.52   3.68   1.21   1.49   2.27   2.44   1.07   1.08   2.95   1.17   1.50   1.26   3.50   1.93   1.47   1.96
```

```
Start:     37: 1  37:15  37:15  41: 6  40:21  40:21  39:13  38:19  38:10  41: 6  41: 6  43:27  44:18  45: 2  46:17  47: 9
End:       37:27  41: 6  41: 6  41: 6  41: 6  44:18  41: 6  38:21  38:16  41: 2  44: 3  43:27  44: 2  45: 2  47: 9
Count:        3      2     18     17     11     10     19      4      8      4      3      2      2     10
Width:      319    197   2421   2414   2390   2203   1946    169   1567   1174    740    866   1364   1410   1852   2223
Strength:  1.29   1.36   3.01   3.33   4.02   5.29   6.26   1.02   9.18   8.59   7.90   9.42  10.21   8.09   8.48   2.11
```

Linguistic Density Plot in Ezekiel 1 - 48

For hyh 311 (130 times)

Each Column = 13 Verses.   Separations are: Max = 1288.50. Mean =   213.51, Min =   7.00 .

REFERENCE

REFERENCE

CLUSTERS:

```
Start:    14:11  19: 3  21:12  21:12  21:27  22: 6  22:13  24: 7  24: 7  24: 7  26: 1  27: 7  27: 7  27: 7
End:      14:15  23: 2  21:32  21:17  21:32  22:18  22:18  24: 7  30: 9  34: 2  27:36  27:36  27:19  27:11  27:10  27: 7
Count:    3      18     6      3      6      5      3      9      30     41     13     10     9      8      7      3
Width:    89     2709   1150   409    116    124    215    514    85     3106   5434   1081   1902   529    242    95     64     22
Strength: 1.13   1.12   1.77   1.41   1.04   1.01   1.18   1.52   1.14   2.87   2.77   2.10   1.89   2.26   2.51   2.55   2.39   1.35

Start:    27: 8  28:13  29: 9  29:17  30: 3  30:20  31: 1  34:27  36:12  36:28  37:17  37:17  37:17  37:23
End:      27:10  30: 9  29:19  29:19  30: 9  30: 9  31: 8  48:28  36:17  36:34  40:21  39:13  37:20  37:27
Count:    4      12     8      9      3      3      4      52     11     3      14     12     6      3
Width:    35     989    458    263    114    75     305    8683   1256   85     1981   1154   300    71     114
Strength: 1.66   2.01   1.89   1.40   1.04   1.17   1.30   1.85   1.35   1.14   1.09   1.76   1.64   1.19   1.04
```

Clusters for hyh 311, continued.

```
Start:    38: 7  43: 6  43:27  44:11  46:17  47: 9  47:22  47:22  47:22  48:15  48:15  48:18
End:      38:10  48:28  44:18  44:18  47:17  47:10  48:28  48:12  48:28  48:28  48:21  48:21
Count:       3     27      6     17      6      3     11      5      5      6      3      5
Width:      68   3459    488   1243    538     33    613    269     40    267    166     85
Strength: 1.20   2.15   1.24   2.72   1.13   1.31   2.35   1.39   1.29   1.71   1.64   1.14
```

GAPS:

```
Start:     1: 1   1: 1   1: 1   1: 1   1: 1   1: 1   1: 3   2: 5   5: 5   5:16   5:16   5:16   5:16   5:16   5:16   7:19  13:11  14:15  15: 2
End:      48:18  37:19  30: 3  27: 8  27: 7  16:49  14:14   5:15   4: 3  14:14  14:11  13: 9  13: 4   7:16  13: 4  13:11  14:11  16:49  16:49
Count:      128     92     65     48     47     17     13      5      3      8      7      5      4      2      4      3      2      3      2
Width:    27651  20852  16156  14559  14552   7768   6301   1512    816   4050   3990   3322   3244   2499    667   2499   1438    601   1193
Strength:  1.27   1.26   2.04   3.87   4.07   5.45   5.79   3.63   2.84   4.66   5.32   5.89   7.14  10.78   2.13   4.20   2.18   1.82   2.56
```

```
Start:    15: 2  16:22  16:49  16:49  16:56  17:23  19:14  19:14  19:14  20:24  21:12  22:18  22:18  22:18  22:18  23: 2  31: 8  31:13  32: 1  32:17  34: 2  34: 2
End:      16:49  21:17  19: 3  19: 3  19: 3  21:17  20:20  21:17  21:12  21:12  27: 7  24:20  24: 7  24: 4  27: 7  33:22  33:22  33:22  33:22  33:10  34:27  35:10
Count:       2     11      4      3      2      5      4      2      5     10      4      5      4      3      5      4      3      3      2      2      2      3
Width:     618   3239   1568   1407   1467   1355   1467    732   2780   1741   1657   1407   1108   1493   1370   1183    844    836    556
Strength:  1.90   1.70   2.54   3.28   1.46   1.96   1.32   2.44   1.39   2.11   2.78   3.28   4.21   1.52   2.00   2.53   2.97   1.36   1.61
```

```
Start:    37:27  38: 8  38: 8  38:10  39:13  39:13  40: 1  40:21  40:21  43: 6  43:27  44:11  44:18  44:28  45: 4  45: 4
End:      47: 9  47: 9  44:17  44:11  44:11  43:27  43:27  43:27  43: 6  47: 9  44:17  44:11  46:17  47: 9  46:17  47: 9
Count:      21     19     13     11     10      7      6      4      3      4      3      2      4      6      3      2
Width:    5848   5672   4072   3902   3860   3224   2935   2542   2108   1610   1571   1356   1193    852
Strength:  1.80   2.18   2.14   2.73   3.14   3.81   4.96   5.22   5.62   6.58   1.07   1.96   2.56   3.01
```

Linguistic Density Plot in Ezekiel 1 - 48

For hyh 312 (182 times)

Each Column = 13 Verses.   Separations are: Max = 1649.00, Mean = 152.84, Min = 6.00 .

REFERENCE

REFERENCE

CLUSTERS:

Start:	1: 1	9: 8	9: 8	11:11	11:11	11:11	12:17	12:17	12:17	14:10	14:10	14:10	14:10	16: 8	16:15	16:31	16:63
End:	20: 2	20: 2	14: 2	11:16	11:14	11:16	14: 1	12:21	13: 1	14:34	14:12	16: 1	16:34	16:23	16:23	16:34	20: 2	17:11
Count:	74	55	22	9	5	4	10	6	3	33	15	7	8	5	4	3	18	7
Width:	9590	5799	2188	499	134	75	764	230	78	3370	1201	487	528	301	160	69	1514	248
Strength:	1.55	2.60	1.55	1.71	1.58	1.46	1.37	1.58	1.05	1.94	1.71	1.16	1.36	1.02	1.13	1.10	1.81	1.82

Start:	16:63	17: 7	17: 7	6	18: 1	18: 1	19:11	19:14	21:37	29:12	29:12	29:12	29:15	33: 1	33:21	34:22	34:22
End:	17: 7	17: 7	20: 2	18:20	20: 2	22: 1	20: 2	22: 1	38:21	30: 7	31: 1	29:17	33: 7	38:21	35:15	35: 4	34:29
Count:	6	4	3	11	6	3	4	3	16	3	6	10	3	50	10	17	8	6
Width:	134	29	12	929	389	66	108	29	732	343	95	40	88	5731	1288	486	263	162
Strength:	1.87	1.63	1.36	1.27	1.11	1.11	1.33	1.28	1.34	1.25	1.38	1.23	1.01	1.92	1.98	1.99	2.03	1.79

```
Clusters for hyh 312, continued.

Start:    34:22  34:26  36:16  37:22  37:22  37:26  44: 2  44:18  44:18  44:29  44:29  45: 2  45: 5  45:10  45:10  45:10  48: 1  48: 8
End:      34:24  34:29  38:21  38: 1  37:24  38: 1  46: 1  45: 8  45: 1  45: 8  45: 4  45: 4  45: 8  45:16  45:16  45:12  48:10  48:10
Count:        3      3     16      7     11      4      3     18     17     10      8      5      8      3      7      5      4      3
Width:       38     69   1700    705    199     76     58   1299    850    471    229    122     48     80    316    101     38    163    71
Strength:  1.24   1.10   1.04   1.75   1.95   1.45   1.15   2.16   2.73   2.02   2.12   1.62   1.19   1.05   1.63   1.69   1.60   1.12   1.09

GAPS:

Start:     1:28   3:16   3:16   3:16   3:16   3:26   3:26   8: 1   8: 1   8: 1  10:10  16:34  17: 6  17: 6  17:11  20: 1  20: 2  20:32
End:       3:16   3: 3  11:20  11:11   7:26   7: 1   6: 1  11:11  10: 6   9: 8  11:11  16:63  47:10  48:35  18: 1  20:32  20:32  21: 1
Count:        3      2     19     14      9      5      2      3      5      2      2      2    115    123      2      3      2    100      1
Width:      572    309   3616   3381   1954   1478   1222    896   1384    860    648    425    655  19768  18783    337    812    787  16602    325
Strength:  1.23   1.02   1.40   2.63   1.73   2.87   4.27   4.88   2.56   2.58   3.25   1.78   3.30   1.15   1.35   1.20   2.35   4.16   1.43   1.12

Start:    21:37  21:37  22: 1  22: 1  23: 4  23: 4  23: 4  23:10  23:10  23:10  23: 4  25: 1  26: 5  27: 1  28:24  30:20
End:      47:10  34:23  34:23  33: 4  29:15  29:15  28:20  26: 1  24: 1  23:32  26: 1  28: 1  28: 1  29:12  33: 1
Count:       93     82     45     34     20     16     15     13      7      6      3      2      2      2      2      1
Width:    15557  14478   7650   6420   4510   3863   3358   1891   1769   1106    820    459    390   1386   1016    623   1319
Strength:  1.45   2.04   1.04   1.73   2.55   2.77   2.98   2.65   2.98   2.47   2.39   2.01   1.55   1.84   2.12   3.08   1.09

Start:    30:20  31: 1  31: 1  33: 5  33: 1  35:15  35:15  35:15  37:22  37:24  37:24  38: 1  38:21  38:21  46:17  47:10
End:      32:17  32:17  32: 1  33:21  33:21  37:22  36:38  36:16  45:10  45: 3  44:29  38: 1  44:18  44: 2  47:10  48: 1
Count:        4      3      2      2      7      3      4     23     18     16     13      6      4      3      6      2
Width:      955    793    451    375   1386    866    674    391   4978   4796   4728   4618   3989   3747   3298   1888    373    314
Strength:  1.89   2.27   1.95   1.45   1.27   1.55   1.71   1.56   2.40   3.67   4.30   5.45   6.99   9.59  12.55  13.95   1.44   1.05
```

Linguistic Density Plot in Ezekiel 1 - 48

For hyh 3162 (18 times)

Each Column = 13 Verses.   Separations are: Max =   2312.00, Mean =   1472.11, Min =   304.50

CLUSTERS:

Start:	6: 8	15: 5	34: 8	34: 8
End:	44: 7	20:12	37:28	36: 3
Count:	18	5	5	4
Width:	22638	3225	2401	893
Strength:	1.24	1.04	1.36	1.54

GAPS:

Start:	6:13	22:19	29: 6	37:28	44: 7
End:	15: 5	34: 8	34: 8	48:35	48:35
Count:	2	4	2	4	2
Width:	4063	6942	2953	6860	2901
Strength:	1.85	1.10	1.06	1.07	1.02

Linguistic Density Plot in Ezekiel 1 - 48

For hêkāl 111 (10 times)

Each Column = 13 Verses.   Separations are: Max = 9969.50, Mean = 2542.73, Min = 23.00 .

REFERENCE

+25

+20

+15 D
   E
   N
   S
+10 I
   T
   Y

+5

+0

REFERENCE

CLUSTERS:

Start:	8:16	41: 1	41: 1	41:15	41:20	41:20	41:23
End:	8:16	42: 8	41: 4	41:25	41:25	41:21	41:25
Count:	2	8	2	6	5	4	2
Width:	15	650	77	345	172	73	1	27
Strength:	1.08	4.41	1.06	3.07	2.57	2.10	1.09	1.08

GAPS:

Start:	1: 1	8:16	8:16
End:	41:20	41:20	41: 1
Count:	7	5	2
Width:	23790	20266	19862
Strength:	2.12	2.59	7.46

Linguistic Density Plot in Ezekiel 1 - 48

For hin 111 (6 times)

Each Column = 13 Verses.   Separations are: Max = 24475.00, Mean = 3995.71, Min = 66.00 .

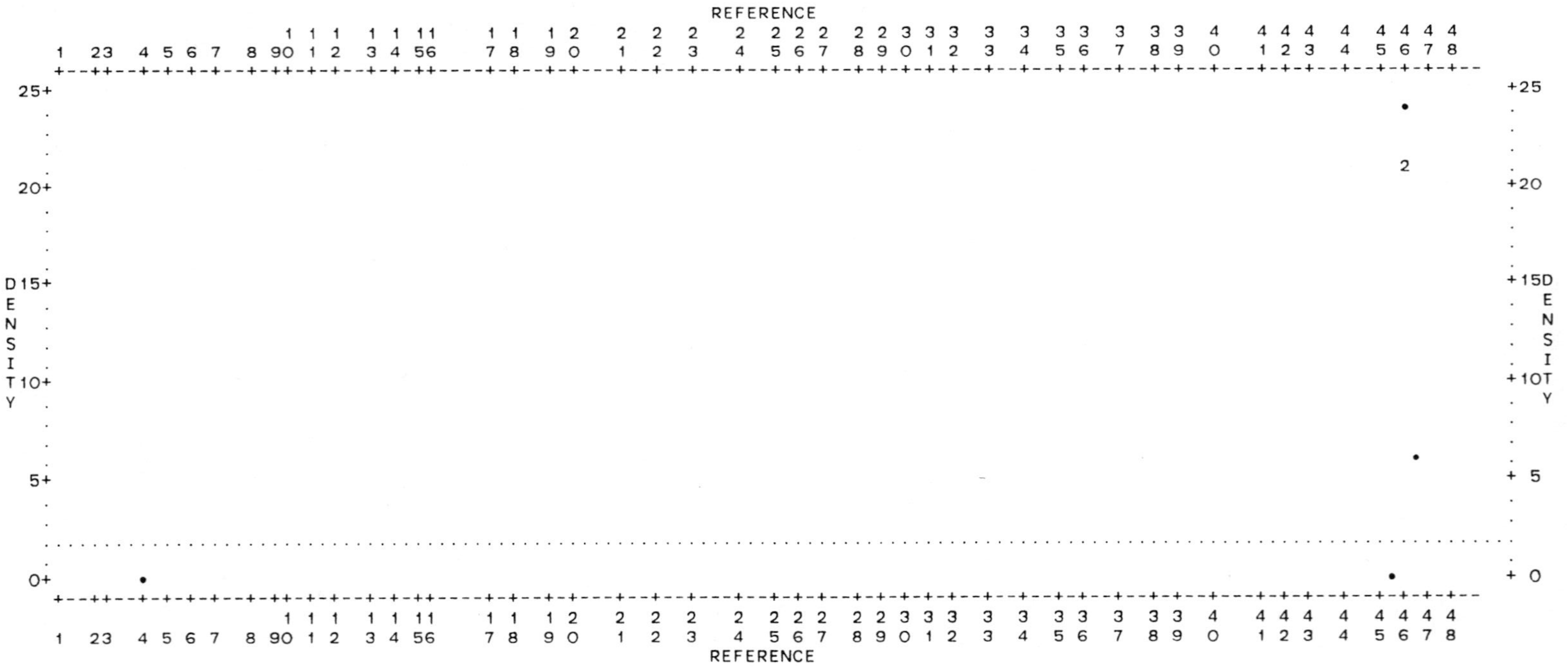

CLUSTERS:

Start:	45:24	45:24	46: 5	46:11
End:	46:14	46: 7	46:14	
Count:	5	3	2	2
Width:	345	172	38	79
Strength:	3.19	1.75	1.14	1.13

GAPS:

Start:	1: 1	1: 1	4:11
End:	46: 5	45:24	45:24
Count:	4	3	2
Width:	26317	26183	24475
Strength:	2.92	4.07	5.91

Linguistic Density Plot in Ezekiel 1 - 48

For hlk 311 (12 times)   hlk 312 (21 times)   hlk 313 (5 times)   hlk 314 (6 times)
     hlk 315 (1 times)   hlk 3161 (9 times)   hlk 3162 (4 times)   hlk 332 (1 times)
     hlk 351 (1 times)   hlk 352 (1 times)   hlk 354 (1 times)   hlk 361 (1 times)
     hlk 362 (4 times)

Each Column = 13 Verses.   Separations are: Max = 2609.00, Mean = 411.32, Min = 2.50 .

REFERENCE

D E N S I T Y

+25
+20
+15
+10
+5
0

REFERENCE

CLUSTERS:

Start:	1: 9	1: 9	1: 9	10:11	10:11	10:11	1:12	1:12	1:12	1:12	1:12	1:17	1:17	1:17	1:17	1:17	1:17	1:19	1:20	1:20	1:20	1:20	1:21
End:	21:12	13: 3	7:17	10:11	11:12	10:16	1:24	1:13	1:12	1:12	1:12	1:24	1:21	1:19	1:21	1:17	1:17	1:21	1:19	1:20	1:21	1:20	1:21
Count:	51	39	26	22	90	308	18	90	27	5	3	11	151	71	32	10	5	3	6	5	5	2
Width:	10773	5317	2774	941	308	2774	308	308	27	5	3	151	151	71	32	10	5	3	194	194	104	60
Strength:	6.59	6.16	4.62	4.94	2.48	4.58	2.04	2.48	1.76	1.43	1.01	3.18	3.32	3.18	2.03	1.43	1.00	1.00	2.05	1.43	1.01	1.00

Start:	3: 1	3:14	10:11	10:11	10:11	10:16	16:47	20:13	20:13	20:21
End:	3:14	13: 3	11:12	10:11	10:11	21:12	21:12	20:13	20:16	20:21
Count:	4	13	9	7	5	6	2	6	3	3
Width:	267	1371	448	93	23	194	3209	1061	194	104	60
Strength:	1.39	2.77	2.61	2.48	2.04	2.11	1.06	1.77	2.11	1.26	1.33

```
Data for hlk 311, hlk 312, hlk 313, hlk 314, hlk 315, hlk 3161, hlk 3162, hlk 332, hlk 351, hlk 352, hlk 354, hlk 361,
         hlk 362, continued.

GAPS:

Start:     1:20   3:14   5: 7   5: 7   7:17  10:16  11:21  11:21  12:11  13: 3  13: 3  20:16  20:19  20:19  20:21  21:12  21:12  25: 3  25: 3
End:      48:35   5: 6  10:11   7:14  10:11  48:35  20:16  20:13  18: 9  18: 9  16:47  48:35  48:35  30:17  30:17  30:17  23:31  30:17  28:14
Count:       55      2      4      2      2     36      9      8      4      3      2     23     21      8      7      5      3      3      2
Width:    27597    886   2097    867   1172  23767   5180   5090   4019   3717   3324   2247  17940   6393   6353   5486   1710   2782   1690
Strength:  3.95   1.16   1.24   1.12   1.87   5.56   1.74   2.16   2.99   3.59   4.39   4.52   5.67   6.33   4.06   4.84   3.43   3.20   3.44   3.15

Start:    30:18  31: 4  31: 4  30:18  37:21  33:31  37:24  37:24  43: 1
End:      48:35  37:21  36:12  33:15  36:12  48:35  47: 6  40:24  47: 6
Count:       13      8      7      5      3      2      5      4      2
Width:    11518   4438   4201   3154   1471   1313   6966   5885   1832   2609
Strength:  5.12   1.52   1.81   1.90   1.13   2.22   6.71   6.72   3.50   5.42
```

Linguistic Density Plot in Ezekiel 1 - 48

For hlk 311 (12 times)   hlk 312 (21 times)   hlk 313 (5 times)   hlk 314 (6 times)
     hlk 315 (1 times)   hlk 3161 (9 times)   hlk 3162 (4 times)

Each Column = 13 Verses.   Separations are: Max = 3540.00, Mean = 474.07, Min = 2.50

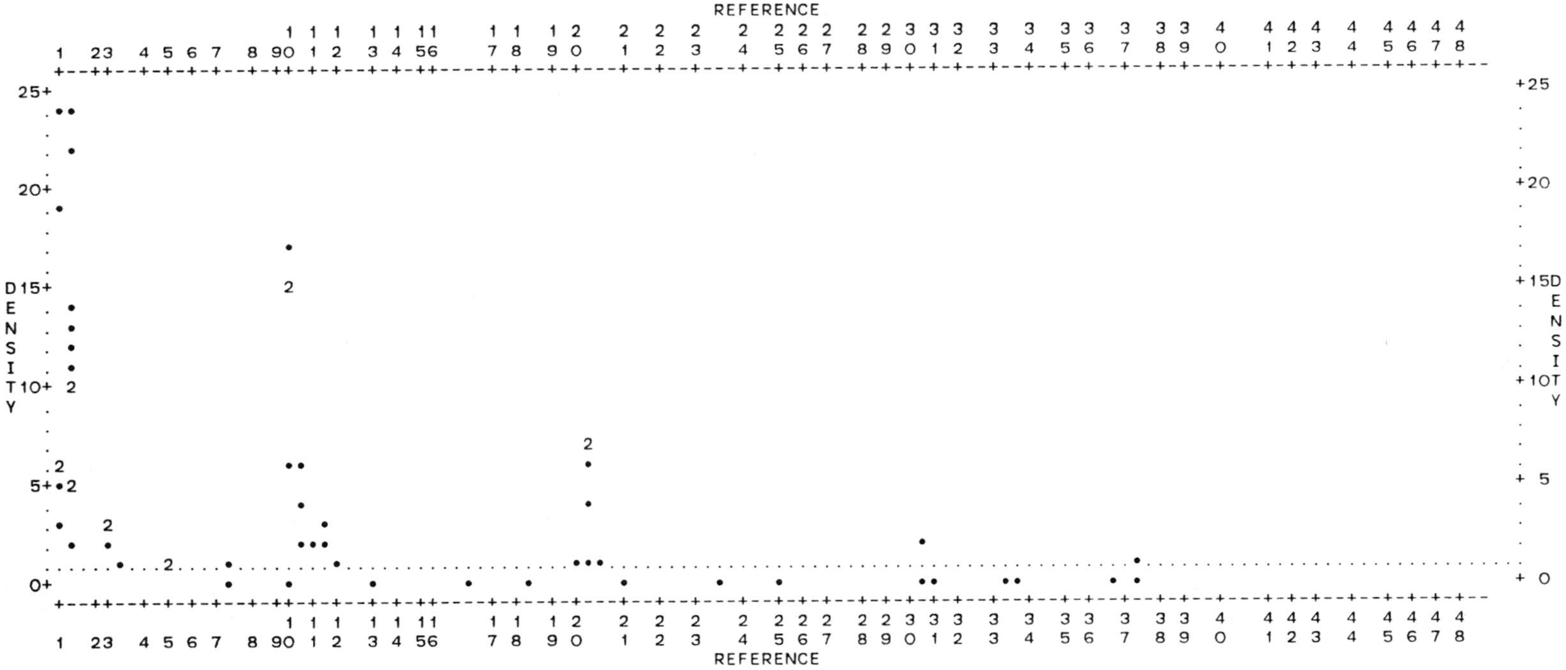

(Density plot. The y-axis is labelled vertically "DENSITY" with scale markings +25, +20, +15, +10, +5, 0. The word "REFERENCE" appears within the plot area. X-axis columns run 1 23 4 5 6 7 8 9 0 1 2 … through 4 5 6 7 8.)

CLUSTERS:

Start:	1: 9	1: 9	1: 9	1: 9	1: 9	1: 9	1:12	1:12	1:12	1:12	1:12	1:17	1:17	1:17	1:17	1:17	1:19	1:19	1:20	1:20	1:21
End:	37:24	13: 3	7:17	3:14	1:24	1:12	1:12	1:12	1:24	1:21	1:11	1:17	1:19	1:21	1:17	1:24	1:19	1:17	1:20	1:21	1:21
Count:	58	38	25	21	17	6	4	3	3	2	10	5	2	2	3	6	5	2	5	2	2
Width:	20840	5317	2774	941	308	75	12	5	4	3	71	32	2	6	2	151	20	5	1	2
Strength:	9.45	7.00	4.85	4.99	4.53	2.28	1.77	1.00	1.44	1.01	3.23	2.05	1.01	1.44	1.01	3.38	2.06	1.44	1.01	1.01	1.01

Start:	3: 1	3:14	10:11	10:11	10:11	10:11	10:11	10:13	20:13	20:18	30:17
End:	3:14	13: 3	11:12	10:16	10:11	10:11	10:16	20:21	20:16	20:21	31: 4
Count:	4	13	9	7	5	3	6	8	6	3	3
Width:	267	1371	448	93	23	10	104	194	1061	60	266
Strength:	1.45	2.97	2.70	2.52	2.06	1.43	1.29	1.93	2.16	1.35	1.04

Data for hlk 311, hlk 312, hlk 313, hlk 314, hlk 315, hlk 3161, hlk 3162, continued.

GAPS:

Start:	1:20	7:17	10:16	11:21	12:11	13: 3	13: 3	20:16	20:19	20:21	21:12	21:12	25: 3	30:18	31: 4	31: 4		
End:	48:35	10:11	48:35	20:16	20:13	18:17	16:47	48:35	48:35	30:17	30:17	23:31	30:17	48:35	37:21	37:21	33:15	
Count:	47	2	28	7	6	5	4	3	3	17	15	6	4	2	8	6	5	2
Width:	27597	1172	23767	5180	5090	4788	4395	3485	2247	17990	6393	6353	5486	1710	2782	11518	4438	4201	1471
Strength:	3.86	1.49	6.09	2.13	2.70	3.18	3.74	3.88	3.80	7.35	3.25	3.95	5.12	2.65	4.95	7.02	2.05	2.53	2.13

Start:	33:31	33:31	37:24
End:	37:21	36:27	48:35
Count:	3	2	2
Width:	2360	1654	6966
Strength:	2.15	2.53	13.92

Linguistic Density Plot in Ezekiel 1 - 48

For hlk 311 (12 times)

Each Column = 13 Verses.   Separations are: Max = 4905.00, Mean = 2151.54, Min = 97.00 .

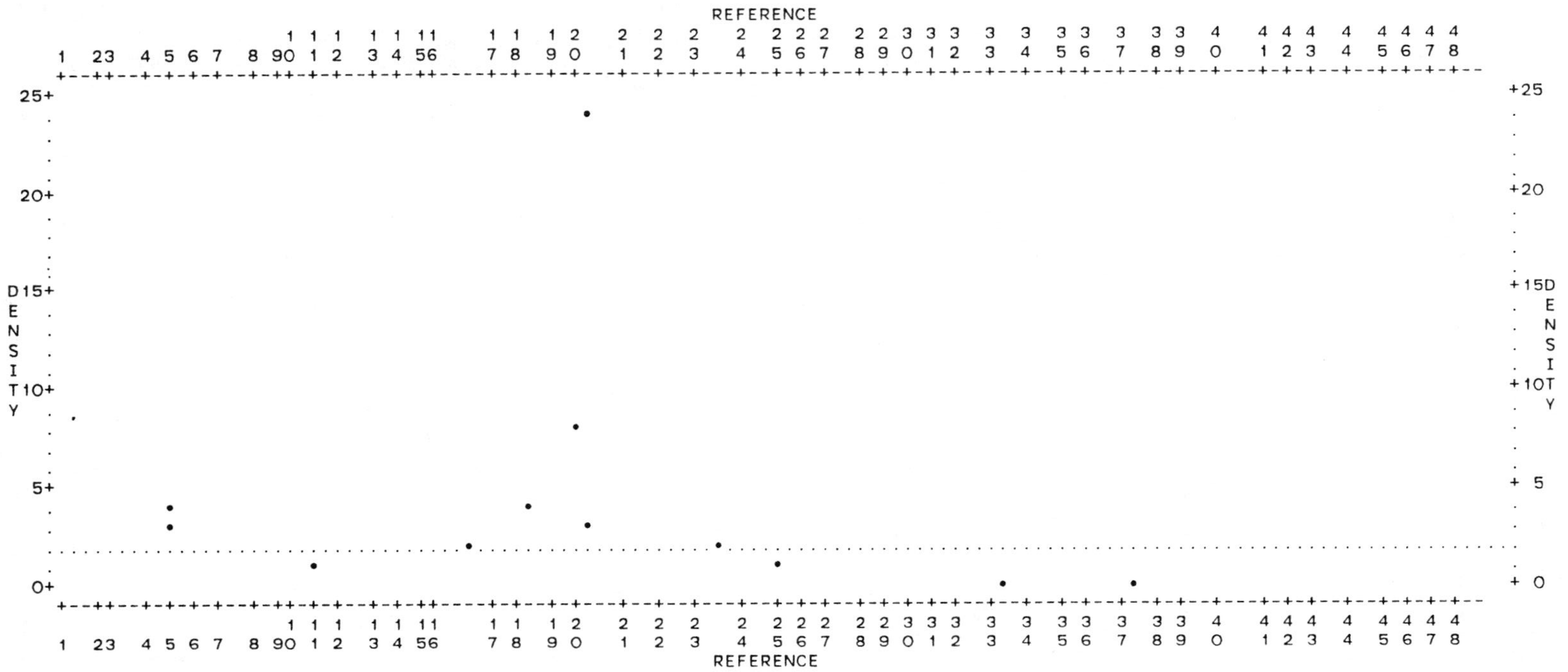

CLUSTERS:

Start:	5: 6	5: 6	5: 6	16:47	16:47	18:17	20:13	20:13
End:	37:21	25: 3	5: 7	25: 3	20:21	20:21	20:21	20:16
Count:	12	10	2	7	5	4	3	2
Width:	18899	11650	22	5913	2342	1104	194	90
Strength:	1.76	2.23	1.06	1.87	1.81	1.69	1.52	1.03

GAPS:

Start:	20:16	20:21	25: 3	37:21
End:	48:35	48:35	33:15	48:35
Count:	7	6	4	2
Width:	18004	17900	14329	7080
Strength:	1.36	1.96	1.18	2.47

Linguistic Density Plot in Ezekiel 1 - 48

For hlk 312 (21 times)

Each Column = 13 Verses.   Separations are: Max = 3893.00, Mean = 1271.36, Min = 19.50 .

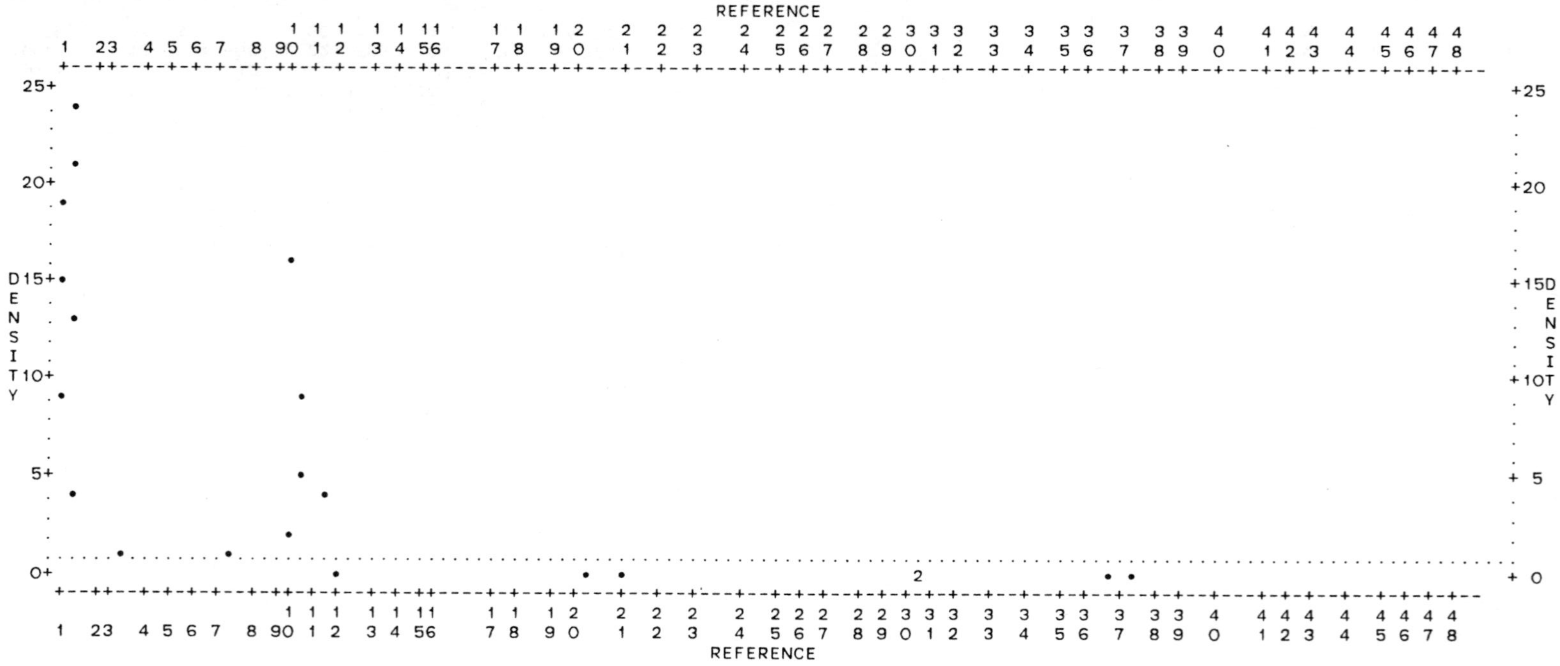

REFERENCE

(Linguistic density plot, vertical axis labelled DENSITY, gridline labels +25, +20, +15, +10, +5, +0; horizontal axis verse columns 1–48.)

```
CLUSTERS:

Start:      1:9    1:9    1:9    1:9    1:9    1:12   1:12   1:17   1:17   1:20   7:17   10:11  10:11  10:11  10:11  30:17
End:       37:24  21:12  12:11   3:14   1:21   1:12   1:12   1:19   1:21   1:21  12:11  12:11  10:22  10:16  10:11  30:18
Count:       21     17     15      8      7      3      2      2      2      2      7      6      4      3      2      2
Width:    20833  10766   4917    934    221     64      8     69     30     19   2150    972    229     87     13     29
Strength:  2.73   3.68   4.59   2.93   2.85   1.47   1.03   1.87   1.02   1.03   2.20   2.10   1.79   1.46   1.03   1.02

GAPS:

Start:      1:12  10:11  10:16  10:22  12:11  12:11  21:12  30:18  30:18  37:24
End:       48:35  30:17  30:17  30:17  30:17  20:18  30:17  48:35  36:27  48:35
Count:       20     12      8      7      6      4      2      4      2      2
Width:    27735  23841  12294  12220  12078  11335   4922   5486  11518   3732   6966
Strength:  1.78   3.37   1.24   2.34   1.76   3.75   3.00   3.46   3.84   2.02   4.68
```

Linguistic Density Plot in Ezekiel 1 - 48

For hlk 313 (5 times)

Each Column = 13 Verses.   Separations are: Max = 8970.00, Mean = 4661.66, Min = 98.50 .

REFERENCE

(density plot)

CLUSTERS:

Start:	3:1	3:1	20:19
End:	20:39	3:11	20:39
Count:	5	3	2
Width:	9690	197	498
Strength:	1.79	1.83	1.05

GAPS:

Start:	3:4	3:11	20:39	
End:	48:35	48:35	20:19	48:35
Count:	5	4	2	
Width:	27077	26935	8995	17442
Strength:	1.69	2.44	1.09	3.24

Linguistic Density Plot in Ezekiel 1 - 48

For hlk 314 (6 times)

Each Column = 13 Verses. Separations are: Max = 5640.50, Mean = 3995.71, Min = 1300.50 .

REFERENCE

DENSITY

REFERENCE

CLUSTERS:

Start: 7:14
End: 13:3
Count: 3
Width: 2601
Strength: 1.20

GAPS:

Start: 13:3   33:31
End: 48:35 48:35
Count: 5   2
Width: 22489 9440
Strength: 1.32   1.57

Linguistic Density Plot in Ezekiel 1 - 48

For hlk 3161 (9 times)

Each Column = 13 Verses.   Separations are: Max = 13790.00, Mean = 2797.00, Min = 9.00 .

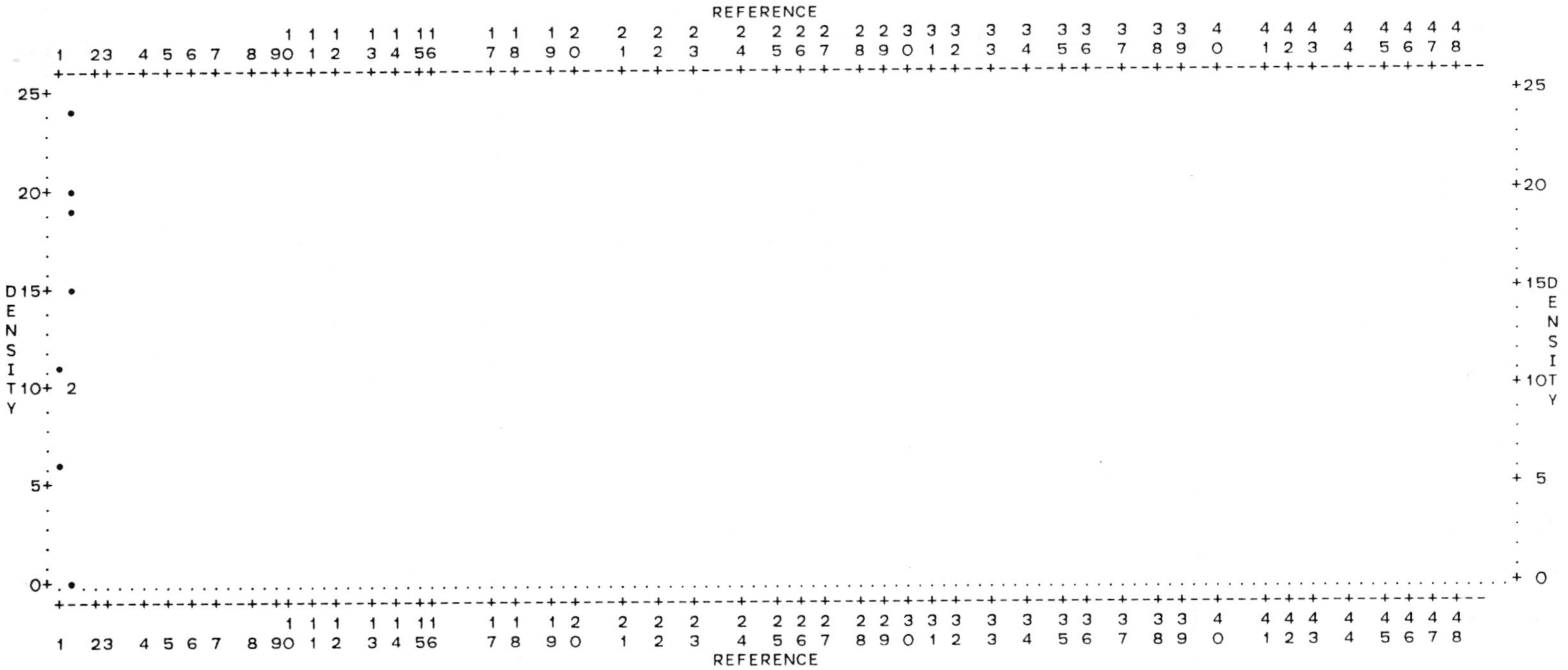

(Linguistic density plot — vertical axis labelled DENSITY with gridlines at +25, +20, +15, +10, +5, +0 / 0; horizontal axis labelled REFERENCE, columns numbered 1 through 48.)

CLUSTERS:

Start:	1:12	1:12	1:17	1:17	1:17	1:17	1:20	1:20
End:	1:24	1:12	1:24	1:21	1:19	1:17	1:21	1:20
Count:	9	2	7	6	3	2	3	2
Width:	238	5	151	69	30	6	18	5
Strength:	6.56	1.10	4.02	3.30	1.64	1.10	1.65	1.10

GAPS:

Start:	1:20	1:21	1:24
End:	48:35	48:35	48:35
Count:	4	3	2
Width:	27593	27580	27498
Strength:	4.96	6.51	9.76

Linguistic Density Plot in Ezekiel 1 - 48

For hlk 361 (1 times)   hlk 362 (4 times)

Each Column = 13 Verses. Separations are: Max = 9921.50, Mean = 4661.66, Min = 2026.50 .

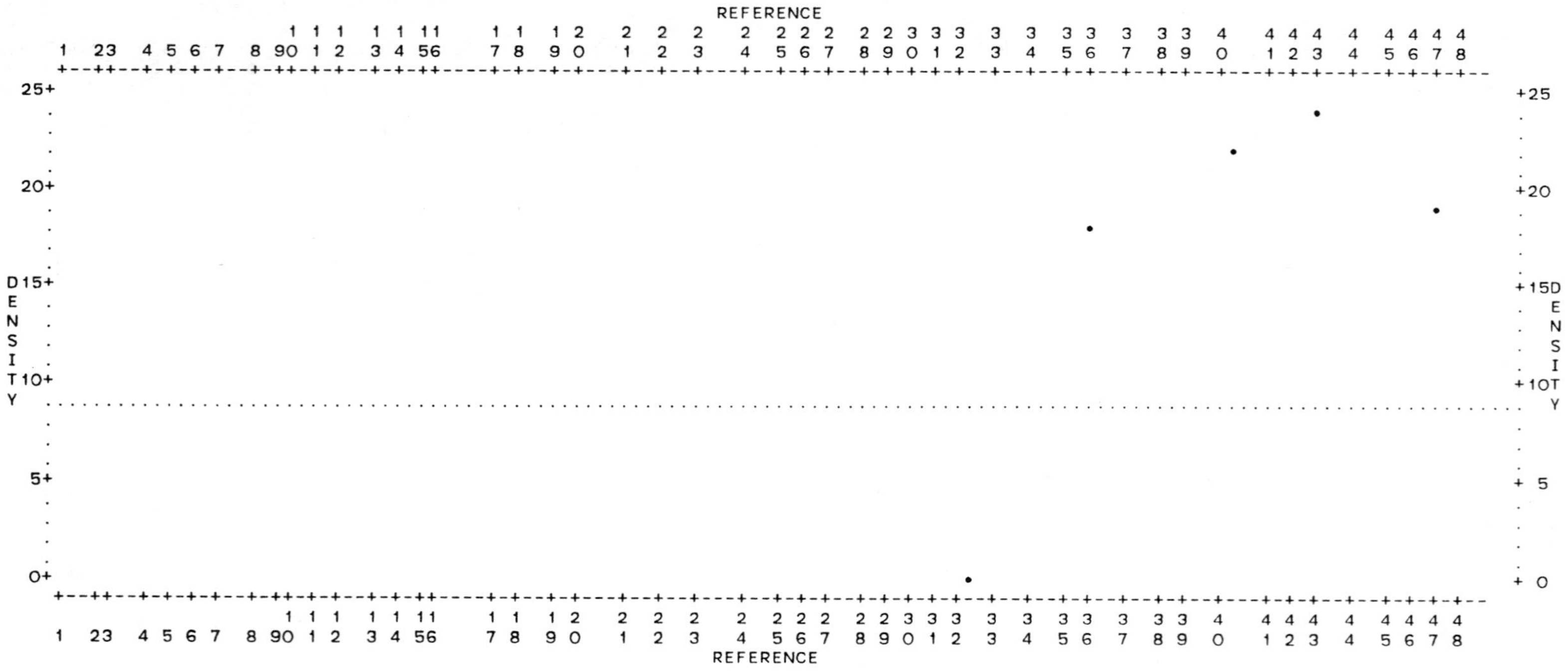

CLUSTERS:

Start:	32:14	40:24
End:	47: 6	47: 6
Count:	5	3
Width:	9526	4053
Strength:	1.83	1.05

GAPS:

Start:	1: 1	1: 1
End:	40:24	32:14
Count:	4	2
Width:	22835	17362
Strength:	1.67	3.22

Linguistic Density Plot in Ezekiel 1 - 48

For hêm 6133 (67 times)

Each Column = 13 Verses.   Separations are: Max = 2170.00, Mean = 411.32, Min = 14.50

REFERENCE

REFERENCE

(vertical axis label: D E N S I T Y)

CLUSTERS:

Start:	2:3	2:3	2:3	2:3	2:3	2:3	2:3	2:3	3:6	3:6	3:6	8:6	8:6	10:13	10:20	12:2	14:14	20:9	23:8	23:8
End:	47:12	27:24	14:20	3:27	14:20	2:7	2:5	3:15	3:9	14:20	3:15	8:16	12:10	12:11	11:7	12:10	14:14	14:20	27:24	25:4
Count:	67	44	27	11	9	5	3	3	3	16	4	4	12	5	8	3	4	17	15	7
Width:	26390	14188	5800	789	477	106	43	190	71	3154	1771	234	908	310	165	165	142	5050	2676	1508
Strength:	1.33	2.15	2.99	2.78	2.59	1.94	1.36	1.50	1.32	2.15	2.22	1.44	1.92	1.68	1.15	1.15	1.57	1.07	2.26	1.00

Start:	23:8	23:8	25:4	27:8	27:8	40:46	43:7	44:15	44:19
End:	23:25	23:16	25:4	27:24	27:17	44:29	44:29	44:16	44:29
Count:	4	3	2	5	3	11	10	5	3	3
Width:	364	138	5	270	160	2308	1187	425	143	29	207
Strength:	1.25	1.20	1.00	2.54	1.87	1.51	2.20	2.39	1.89	1.39	1.08

Data for hẻm 6133, continued.

GAPS:

```
Start:     3:27 10:22 10:22 12: 3 12:10 14:20 14:20 21: 5 25: 4 25: 4 27:22 27:24 27:24 27:24 27:24 27:24 27:24 34:30 36: 7 37:27
End:       8: 6 25: 4 23: 8 23: 8 14:14 23: 8 20: 9 23: 8 44:11 27: 8 44:11 44:11 34:24 33:17 32:29 31:17 37:25 37:11 37:11 44:11
Count:        2    17    12     9     2     4     2     8    24     2    17    16    10     6     3     4     2     3     2     6
Width:     1857  9339  7836  7228  1241  5712  3338  1372 11507   898 10367 10339  6194  4258  3355  2856  2181  1403   873  4085
Strength:  3.56  1.93  2.67  3.62  2.04  6.47  7.21  2.36  1.28  1.19  2.65  2.98  2.18  2.50  3.06  3.57  4.36  1.01  1.13  2.30

Start:    37:27 38:17 43: 7 44:19 44:24 44:29 44:29
End:      43: 7 40:46 48:35 48:35 48:35 47:12 44:29
Count:        4     3     2     5     4     3     2
Width:     3323  2898  1777  2573  2480  2366  1438
Strength:  3.02  3.64  3.36  1.17  1.80  2.71  2.53
```

Linguistic Density Plot in Ezekiel 1 - 48

For -hem 6133 (739 times)

Each Column = 13 Verses.   Separations are: Max =   725.50. Mean =   37.80. Min =   2.50 .

Vertical axis (left, top to bottom): 25+, 20+, D15+, E, N, S, I, T10+2, Y, 5+, O+
Vertical axis (right, top to bottom): +25, +20, +15D, E, N, S, I, +10T, Y, 5, O
Center label: REFERENCE

CLUSTERS:

Start:	1: 6	1: 6	1: 6	1: 6	1: 6	1: 6	1: 6	1: 6	1: 8	1: 8	1: 8	1:10	1: 8	1:13	1:16	1:17	1:17	1:18	1:20
End:	48:34	33:11	15: 7	7:27	3:17	2: 7	1: 9	1:11	1: 9	1: 9	1:11	1:11	1: 9	1:19	1:16	1:19	1:18	1:18	2: 7
Count:	739	501	243	127	59	46	22	13	9	6	10	30	4	111	3	34	20	3	367
Width:	27835	17912	6581	3024	1058	636	242	91	20	47	10	30	4	111	15	34	20	7	367
Strength:	1.10	2.05	5.32	4.50	4.10	4.33	3.23	2.78	2.40	1.68	2.00	1.27	1.26	1.79	1.12	1.54	1.42	1.27	2.81

Start:	1:20	1:26	1:20	1:20	1:20	1:23	1:25	1:25	1:23	1:20	2: 3	2: 5	2: 6	3: 4	3: 8	3:25	3:25	4:12	4:12
End:	1:23	1:26	1:21	1:21	1:21	1:24	1:26	1:25	1:25	1:21	2: 7	2: 6	2: 7	3: 9	3: 9	3:27	3:26	5: 6	4:13
Count:	15	15	7	26	53	8	4	4	6	47	9	3	3	9	68	41	68	263	3
Width:	127	127	53	26	53	24	15	6	12	47	19	13	4	102	1752	41	1752	263	16
Strength:	2.86	1.88	1.65	1.16	2.12	1.36	1.49	1.29	1.94	1.68	1.05	1.18	1.42	1.62	2.64	1.10	1.31	1.22	1.10

Clusters for -hem 6133, continued.

```
Start:     5: 6   5: 2   5: 2   5: 2   5: 4   6: 9   6: 9   6:10   6: 9   6: 9   6:10   6:12   6:12   6:13   6:13   6:14   6:14   7:16   7:18
End:       5: 6   5: 4   5: 4   7:27   7:27   6: 9   6:10   6:10   6: 9   6: 9   6:10   6:13   6:13   6:13   6:13   6:14   6:14   7:19   7:19
Count:     6      30     3      17     48     13     6      40     14     3      21     4      65     3      7      3      21     16     10
Width:     87     36     17     1055   536    161    40     79     28     15     21     16     65     7      21     65     221    128    50
Strength:  1.20   1.60   1.08   2.87   1.31   2.25   1.76   1.76   1.14   1.30   1.01   1.48   1.75   1.27   1.01   1.75   3.35   3.02   2.57

Start:     7:18   7:19   7:19   7:19   7:19   7:27   7:24   7:20   7:20   7:27   7:27   8:11   8:11   10: 8  10: 8  8:11   8:11   10:11  10:16
End:       7:19   7:19   7:19   7:19   7:19   7:27   7:27   7:20   7:22   7:27   7:27  15: 1   11: 4  10:12  10:12  11: 4  15: 1  10:12  10:16
Count:     6      3      3      4      3      28     4      11     36     9      6      30     43     13     6      30     116    5      4
Width:     28     14     8      17     4      519    24     70     161    60     54     318    1015   90     350    3293   116    13     211
Strength:  1.90   1.14   1.25   1.46   1.20   2.60   1.68   2.59   1.17   1.52   1.59   1.65   2.40   2.79   3.73   2.82   1.48   1.82   2.63

Start:     10:16  10:17  10:16  10:17  10:17  10:19  10:19  10:19  10:21  11:15  11:15  11:15  11:15  11:15  11:16  11:19  11:20  11:21  11:21
End:       10:22  10:17  10:17  10:17  10:22  10:19  10:19  10:22  10:22  15: 7  13: 7  11:22  11:19  11:15  11:16  11:19  11:22  11:21  11:21
Count:     15     7      16     5      8      4      3      3      7      3      18     36     8      3      7      3      10     11     3
Width:     133    7      36     43     79     26     28     15     73     818    184    576    116    45     36     25     51     29     5
Strength:  2.82   2.06   1.78   1.07   1.86   1.33   1.30   1.12   2.15   1.04   2.97   3.42   1.48   1.48   1.17   2.18   2.56   1.85   1.31

Start:     11:22  12: 2  12: 2  12: 2  12: 4  12: 7  12: 7  12:14  12:14  12:14  12:15  12:16  13:20  13:20  13:20  14: 3  14: 3  14:18  14:22
End:       11:23  12:16  12:12  12:12  12:12  12:16  12:12  12:16  12:14  12:14  12:16  12: 4  15: 7  15: 4  14: 5  14:14  14:14  14:23  14:23
Count:     3      18     8      4      26     10     12     38     22     12     4      3      28     11     7      5      3      10     5
Width:     11     318    86     26     14     179    68     22     202    818    12     28     85     7      25     16     9      132    39
Strength:  1.20   2.10   1.79   1.33   1.14   1.42   1.09   1.49   1.39   1.04   1.18   1.18   2.26   1.47   2.18   1.78   1.23   1.32   1.48

Start:     14:22  15: 7  15: 7  16:16  16:16  16:17  16:17  16:20  16:21  16:36  16:37  18:19  20:15  20:15  21:34  20:43  20:30  20:19  20: 8
End:       14:22  15: 7  15: 1  16:21  16:19  16:19  16:18  16:21  16:21  16:37  20:15  21:34  20:15  20:15  21:34  20:30  20:30  20:26  20:15
Count:     11     7      3      10     5      4      3      5      6      4      36     43     94     35     111    42     36     26     14
Width:     12     20     118    5      70     39     19     23     6      36     334    920    94     40     334    111    365    231    192
Strength:  1.18   1.03   1.96   1.07   1.07   1.13   1.05   1.69   1.29   1.17   2.80   3.39   2.80   1.51   2.24   4.41   4.38   3.84   3.79

Start:     20: 8  20: 9  20: 9  20: 9  20: 9  20:11  20:11  20:11  20:13  20:13  20:14  20:27  20:16  20:16  20:16  20:16  20:16  20:17  20:17
End:       20:11  20: 7  20: 7  20: 7  20: 7  20:15  20:12  20:11  20:15  20:13  20:13  20:28  20:30  20:43  20:19  20:18  20:18  20:17  20:17
Count:     10     7      4      3      9      14     4      8      17     8      4      10     36     42     7      3      6      4      3
Width:     70     28     10     6      57     112    17     57     33     38     18     107    365    697    71     34     48     16     8
Strength:  2.39   2.15   1.57   1.29   2.08   2.80   1.46   2.08   1.84   1.49   1.45   2.06   4.38   3.62   2.38   2.08   1.66   1.48   1.25

Start:     20:21  20: 9  20: 9  20:22  20:21  20:23  20:24  20:24  20:25  20:26  20:30  20:28  20:28  20:28  20:28  20:16  20:16  22:18  22:26
End:       20:21  20:11  20: 7  20:23  20:23  20:23  20:24  20:25  20:26  20:19  20:28  20:28  20:29  20:29  20:19  20:19  20:19  23:30  23:28
Count:     16     26     10     11     13     3      13     9      7      6      5      3      10     10     26     58     61     897    38
Width:     119    26     70     11     70     25     25     25     3      25     22     19     34     10     231    58     1921   107    38
Strength:  3.09   1.65   2.59   1.94   1.16   1.16   1.23   1.94   1.27   1.23   1.05   1.05   1.20   1.22   3.84   1.55   1.23   1.83   2.23

Start:     22:30  22:31  22:31  23: 6  23: 6  23: 6  23: 6  23:12  23:15  23:15  23:15  23:15  23:17  23:20  23:20  23:20  23:20  23:22  23:37
End:       22:31  22:31  22:31  23:30  23:17  23:23  23:23  23:17  23:16  23:15  23:15  23:16  23:17  23:24  23:19  23:11  23:20  23:23  23:23
Count:     36     4      13     28     15     67     6      9      8      3      13     5      3      10     26     10     10     9      107
Width:     36     5      13     215    519    67     86     86     56     9      258    29     10     119    231    71     34     897    107
Strength:  1.52   1.52   1.31   2.24   2.60   1.44   1.94   2.03   1.61   1.23   1.50   1.61   1.22   1.95   3.84   2.38   1.20   1.83   1.16

Start:     23:37  23:39  23:45  23:47  24:20  24:25  24:25  24:25  24:25  24:24  26:16  26:16  28:24  28:24  28:24  26:16  26:16  29:16  29:12
End:       23:39  23:39  23:47  23:47  25:    24: 5  24: 5  24: 2  24:25  24:25  26:16  26:16  28:26  29:16  28:26  26:16  26:16  29:16  29:16
Count:     27     6      5      12     11     74     4      2      5      4      3      5      3      19     5      3      11     31     3
Width:     27     51     5      254    135    74     20     9      29     5      13     29     39     444    39     3      223    31     74
Strength:  1.31   1.29   1.32   1.31   2.04   2.14   2.23   1.37   1.57   1.31   1.16   1.61   1.48   1.48   1.22   1.30   1.58   1.16   1.36
```

```
Start:     29:15  31:14  31:14  31:14  32: 7  32: 7  32: 9  32:12  32:13  32:13  32:22  32:22  32:24  32:24  32:25  32:26  32:26  32:26  32:27
End:       29:16  33:11  31:14  31:14  32:14  32:10  32:10  32:14  32:13  32:14  32: 2  33: 2  32:25  32:25  32:25  33: 2  32:31  32:27  32:27
Count:        13     43      5     10      5     21     40     16     24      8     27    520     55     21    199    115     40     15
Width:        21   1112     26    142     69     21    199    115     40     15    520    315     96     55     14     16    199     40
Strength:   1.01   1.99   1.65   1.23   1.75   1.08   1.01   1.48   1.27   1.46   2.44   3.10   1.68   1.58   1.14   2.53   2.60   2.02   1.80

Start:     32:27  32:27  32:29  32:29  32:30  32:30  33:   33: 2  33:17  33:17  33:17  33:29  33:31  33:31  33:32  33:32  33:32  34: 8  34:10
End:       32:27  32:31  34:10  34:10
Count:         3      6      4     29     13      3      3     17     12      5      8     20     81      8     50     97     16     54    170
Width:         8     45     29     13                     68    195    452    712   1904   4098    153
Strength:   1.25   1.70   1.28   1.16   1.16   1.01   3.96   1.98   1.01   1.77   2.12   2.37   1.73   1.25   1.27   1.33   1.08   1.10   2.73   1.59   1.66   1.18

Start:     34:11  34:11  34:13  34:13  34:13  34:13  34:20  34:20  34:23  34:26  34:27  34:27  34:27  34:28  34:30  36:   36: 5  36:12  36:17  36:18  36:19
End:       34:15  34:13  34:13  35:11  34:13  34:13  34:30  34:30
Count:        10      7      5     16      6     17     34      7     66     72      8     22      4     37    244    412    156     74     26     38     21
Width:        97     53     16    101    337    456    223     96     58     10    220    117     28     13     15      4    413
Strength:   2.15   1.88   1.78   1.03   1.08   4.28   1.20   1.98   1.12   1.93   1.39   1.25   3.10   1.52   1.62   2.03   1.28   1.16   2.55   2.28   2.63   2.18   1.65   1.52   1.25   1.20   1.78   1.72   1.29

Start:     36:37  36:37  37:   37:   37: 8  37:17  37:17  37:19  37:20  37:21  37:21  37:21  37:21  37:21  37:21  37:22  37:23  37:23  37:23  37:23  37:24  37:25
End:       39:29  37:28  37:12  37: 8  37:28  37:21  37:21  37:21  37:21  37:22  37:22  37:24  37:28  37:23  37:23  37:23  37:23  37:23  37:24  37:24  37:28
Count:        85     44      6      3     34      7     96     58      6     28     13      5     16     27    117    121    227     63     11      7      4     29     16     11     78
Width:      1912    732    101     17
Strength:   3.87   3.71   1.03   1.08   4.28   1.41   1.98   1.55   1.22   1.62   1.52   3.10   4.02   2.36   3.86   2.65   2.63   2.18   1.27   1.28   1.10   2.52

Start:     37:25  37:26  38:   38:   38: 4  38: 4  38: 4  38: 5  38: 8  38:11  38:11  38:11  39:   39:18  39:18  39:21  39:21  39:23  39:23  39:23  39:24  39:24  39:24  39:26
End:       37:26  37:27  37:26  37:26  38:29  38:11  38:   39:24  39:24  39:23  39:29  39:23  39:23  39:24  39:24  39:26  39:29
Count:         4      7      6     27     12      8      6      4      8      6      3     41     30     26    441    227    121     63     21      3      7     15      8     78
Width:        19     52      7     12   1110    157     93      8     17
Strength:   1.43   1.89   1.91   1.27   1.18   1.72   1.07   1.13   1.46   1.25   3.86   3.28   2.36   2.65   1.01   2.37   1.80   1.25   3.05

Start:     39:26  39:27  39:27  39:28  39:27  39:28  39:28  39:28  39:29  43:   43: 7  43: 7  43: 7  43: 8  43: 8  43: 8  43: 9  43: 9  43:10  43:11  43:11  43:24  44:10
End:       39:27  39:29  39:28  39:27  39:27  39:29  39:28  39:29  43:24  43:16  43:10  43:24  43:   43:10  43:    43:   43:10  43:   45:15  44:29
Count:         5     13      9     47     24      8      4     18      9    418    241     82     46     15      9     10     18      4      4     25     28      3      4     12
Width:        25    732     52     27    274    147     83      9
Strength:   1.66   1.16   2.39   1.68   1.25   1.23   1.45   1.23   2.88   2.72   1.07   2.48   2.02   2.60   3.02   2.60   2.06   1.62   1.23   1.64   1.12   1.23   1.03   1.34   1.30   1.18   1.48   1.16   1.03   2.21   3.48

Start:     44:10  44:11  44:11  44:11  44:11  44:11  44:13  44:17  44:17  44:18  44:19  44:19  44:19  44:19  44:20  44:20  44:23  44:23  44:28  44:28  44:28  44:29  45:15  46:10  46:16  46:17  46:18  46:22
End:       44:14  44:14  44:14  44:12  44:12  44:14  44:29  44:17  44:23  44:19  44:19  44:20  44:20  44:29  44:28
Count:        11      9      6     35     12      9     21      3     15      6     16     27      9      3     20     31      4     16      8     28      4      3    453     22     23     10
Width:       100     67     35     12    274    295    147    201    176    130    223    194    154    320    290    314    256      8     47
Strength:   2.33   2.21   1.82   1.54   1.23   2.88   1.72   2.48   1.71   1.10   1.64   1.12   1.23   1.23   1.03   1.87   1.48   1.25   1.00   1.14   1.25   3.48   2.21   2.41   4.04

GAPS:

Start:      1: 1   1: 1   1: 6   2:   2:   2: 6   2: 7   2: 7   3:11   3:11   3:13   3:17   3:17   3:25   3:25   3:26   3:27   4:   4:   5:   5:   5:   5: 4   5: 6   5: 6   5:10   5:12   6:   6:   6: 5   6: 9   6:13   6:14   6:14
End:        1: 6   2:   3:   3:   3: 6   3:   4:   4:13   4:13   3:25   3:25   4:    5:10   5:12   5:12   5:12   5:12   6:10   6:   6:   7:11   7:11   7:11
Count:         2      3      4      2      6      3      7      2      5      3      2      2      5      4      3      4      2      2      2      2      4      9      5      6      2      9      5      3      3      2      2      5      3      3
Width:       113    165    145    195    182    154    690    336    214    146    336    229    200    172    125     90     97    240    205    191
Strength:   1.97   1.66   2.82   1.24   1.98   3.06   1.46   3.06   1.31   4.65   2.44   1.55   2.44   2.29   1.76   1.79   1.36   1.31   1.17   1.55   2.29   1.10   1.36   1.55   1.10   1.04   4.04

Start:      7:27  10:12  10:22  10:22  11:   11: 1  11:15  11:15  12:19  12:23  13:   14: 3
End:       10:12   8:11  11:15  11:16  10: 8  10:10  11:15  11:15  12:28  14: 3
Count:        22      6      4      6      3      4      2     10      3      3      5
Width:      1000    314    290    256    194    320    223    154    212    731    510
Strength:   1.20   2.53   2.69   3.37   1.48   1.00   2.21   1.22   3.46   1.07   4.75
```

Gaps for -hem 6133, continued.

```
Start:     13: 6  13:10  13:10  14: 3  14:23  14:23  14:20  14: 5  14: 5  14: 5  14: 5  15: 7  15: 7  15: 7  15: 7  16:21  16:21  16:21  16:21  16:21  16:21  16:21
End:       14: 3  13:20  14: 3  16:20  16:20  15: 2  16:20  14:10  14:11  14:11  16:20  16:16  16:17  16:17  16:20  16:21  20: 4  19: 8  16:37  16:37  16:36  16:33
Count:         4      3             24     15     10     15      2      5      4     24      4      3      5      4     20      4     16      5      4      4      3
Width:       468    364    247   1067    606    135    688    136    234    161   1067    356    387    400    464   2265   2473   2265    322    309    296    217
Strength:   5.42   5.39   5.52   1.10   2.35   2.56   1.13   2.58   1.09   1.59   1.10   8.41   5.82   4.38   1.99  11.72  10.79  11.72   2.26   2.98   4.12   4.73

Start:     16:37  16:37  16:39  16:39  16:39  16:40  16:40  16:40  18:26  18:26  18:26  18:26  19: 7  19: 8  19: 8  19: 8  19: 8  19: 8  20:29  20:30  20:30  20:30  20:38  20:38  20:38  20:38  20:38  20:38
End:       19: 8  19: 7  19: 7  18:24  18:24  18:24  18:19  17:12  18:31  19: 4  19: 7  18:31  19: 4  20: 3  20: 4  20: 4  20: 3  19: 4  20:38  20:38  20:34  20:38  22:31  21:28  21:28  21:28  21:28  21:19
Count:        11     10      9      5               2      2                                 3      4      3      3      4      3              2      4                                                   6
Width:      1933   1908   1880   1621   1579   1451    790    689    103    177    223    205    171    204    197    168     98    732    726    572
Strength:  13.10  13.91  14.84  19.50  22.44  25.77  19.91   7.13   1.71   1.89   1.67   1.39   3.51   1.38   2.26   1.72   1.58   3.47   3.98   4.54

Start:     20:41  20:43  20:43  21:20  21:24  21:24  21:28  21:28  21:28  21:33  21:34  21:34  22:31  22:26  22:18  23:28  23:24  23:24  23:30  23:40  23:47  23:47  23:47  23:47  23:47
End:       21:19  21:11  21:11  21:28  21:28  28:24  22:31  22:26  21:33  22:26  22:18  23: 6  23: 6  23:23  23: 6  23:37  23:37  23:39  23:37  23:45  24:25  24:25  24:25  24:25  24:25
Count:         4      2      3      3      2             5     11     10      3      2             6      5      2      7      5      9      6      9
Width:       460    411    240    142     80    791    689    104    550    366    297    276    180    188    178    321    297    137     96    563    551    548    545
Strength:   5.30   6.27   5.34   1.23   1.10   3.47   7.13   1.74   8.88   8.68   1.27   1.65   2.61   3.96   3.70   4.59   1.29   2.61   1.52   5.87   4.29   5.26   6.60

Start:     24: 3  24: 3  24:25  24:25  24:25  24:25  24:25  25: 4  25: 4  25: 4  25:17  25:17  25:17  26:16  26:16  26:16  26:16  26:16  26:17  26:17  27:11  27:11  27:21  27:21
End:       24:25  24:20  29:16  28:26  28:24  28:24  26:16  26:16  25:17  25:12  26:10  26:16  25:17  28:24  27:30  27:29  27:29  28:24  27: 9  27: 2  27:21  27:29  27:21  27:21
Count:         3      2             8      6     24     11     10      6      7      6     12      9      7      5      6      2      5
Width:       457    338   2430   1988   1985    753    745    630    291    178    321    188   1227    654    637    594    237    311    170
Strength:   7.14   7.93   3.94   6.27   6.60   3.15   3.59   5.23   4.02   3.70   4.59   3.96   6.52   4.63   5.31   5.87   4.40   5.26   3.48

Start:     27:30  27:32  27:35  28: 7  28:26  29: 7  29: 7  29:12  29:16  29:16  29:16  29:16  29:16  29:16  29:16  29:16  29:16  29:16  30: 9  30: 5  30: 3  30:11  30:11  30:23  30:26
End:       28:24  28:24  28:24  28:24  29: 6  29:14  29:12  29:14  32:27  32:14  33:31  31:14  31:14  30: 9  30: 5  30: 3  30: 4  30:11  30: 5  30: 3  31:14  30:23  31:14
Count:         5      4      2                            10      8      9      37     35     59     22     10      4      3      2
Width:       564    538    481    342    140    147    118   2547   1679   1672   1377    951    934    294    216    137    603    237    297
Strength:   5.47   6.49   7.59   8.04   2.69   1.32   2.11   1.28   1.43   1.79   3.41   5.41   6.72   2.75   2.62   2.61   7.49   5.26   6.85

Start:     31:14  32: 7  31:14  32:14  32:14  32:30  32:30  33: 2  33: 2  33: 2  33: 7  33: 7  33:11  33:19  33:19  33:27  33:31  33:31  34: 2  34: 3  34: 4  34: 8
End:       32: 9  32: 7  32: 2  32:22  32:24  33:31  33:31  33:31  33:31  33:31  33:17  33:17  33:17  33:25  33:19  33:31  33:31  33:31  34: 3  34: 3  34: 4  34: 8
Count:         5      2      2      6      4     18     17     15     12     11      6      5      6      5      2      3      3
Width:       326    278    192    187    146    806    801    785    701    694    376    264    289    171    137     90
Strength:   2.31   3.78   4.07   1.11   2.85   1.05   1.30   1.82   2.28   2.65   2.97   3.52   1.82   3.51   1.08   1.14   1.36   2.00

Start:     34:15  34:23  34:15  34:30  34:30  34:30  34:30  35:11  35:11  35:11  35:11  36: 7  36:12  36:19  36:20  36:23  37:10  37:12  37:12  37:17  38: 5  38: 5  38: 5
End:       34:20  34:34  36:19  36:17  35:11  35: 8  34:30  36: 4  36:17  36: 6  36: 5  36:12  36:37  36:37  36:37  36:37  37:19  37:17  43: 7  43: 7  38: 5  43: 7  43: 7
Count:        22     20     17     11      4      7      8      6      5      4      5      4     18     55     53
Width:       979    972    959    716    229    171    104    476    483    394    387    370    282    197    162    124   3226   3218
Strength:   1.08   1.55   2.36   2.84   1.76   1.77   1.74   2.77   3.40   4.29   3.12   3.92   6.45   1.27   1.61   2.27   4.43   4.76

Start:     38: 5  39:24  40:16  40:26  40:39  40:42  40:42  40:44  40:44  40:44  40:44  43:11  43:11  43:11  43:16  43:24  43:11  43:24  43:24  44:10  44:14  44:17  44:14  44:20  44:23  44:28
End:       39:23  39:21  40:22  43: 7  40:39  40:42  42:14  42:14  42:11  42: 4  41:16  43:24  43:24  43:24  43:16  44:10  43:24  44:10  44:17  44:17  44:17  44:14  44:17  40:39  40:22  46:10
Count:        20     18      2      8      2      6                5      4     11      9      2      4      2      2
Width:       959    243    148    257   1198    938    903    817    710    449    246    276    261    284    164    322    893    849    519    271
Strength:   2.36   1.97   2.90   5.79   9.37   8.89   9.97  10.76  11.88  10.88   5.50   3.55   2.48   3.46   1.75   3.33   7.22   7.83   6.20   6.16
```

Gaps for -hem 6133, continued.

Start:	44:29	44:29	45: 5	45: 8	45:15	46:10	46:10	46:10	46:18	46:18	46:23	46:23	46:23	47:10	47:10
End:	46:10	45: 4	46:10	46:10	46:18	46:17	46:16	46:18	48:35	46:22	48:35	48:34	48:29	48:29	48:12
Count:	6	2	4	3	4	3	2	6	9	2	6	5	4	3	2
Width:	804	132	648	550	418	197	186	153	1345	109	1226	1205	1117	870	505
Strength:	7.30	2.48	8.18	8.88	10.05	1.27	2.06	3.03	9.80	1.87	12.31	13.98	15.36	14.88	12.36

Linguistic Density Plot in Ezekiel 1 - 48

For hāmōn 111 (26 times)

Each Column = 13 Verses.   Separations are: Max =   5674.50.   Mean =   1035.93.   Min =   22.50 .

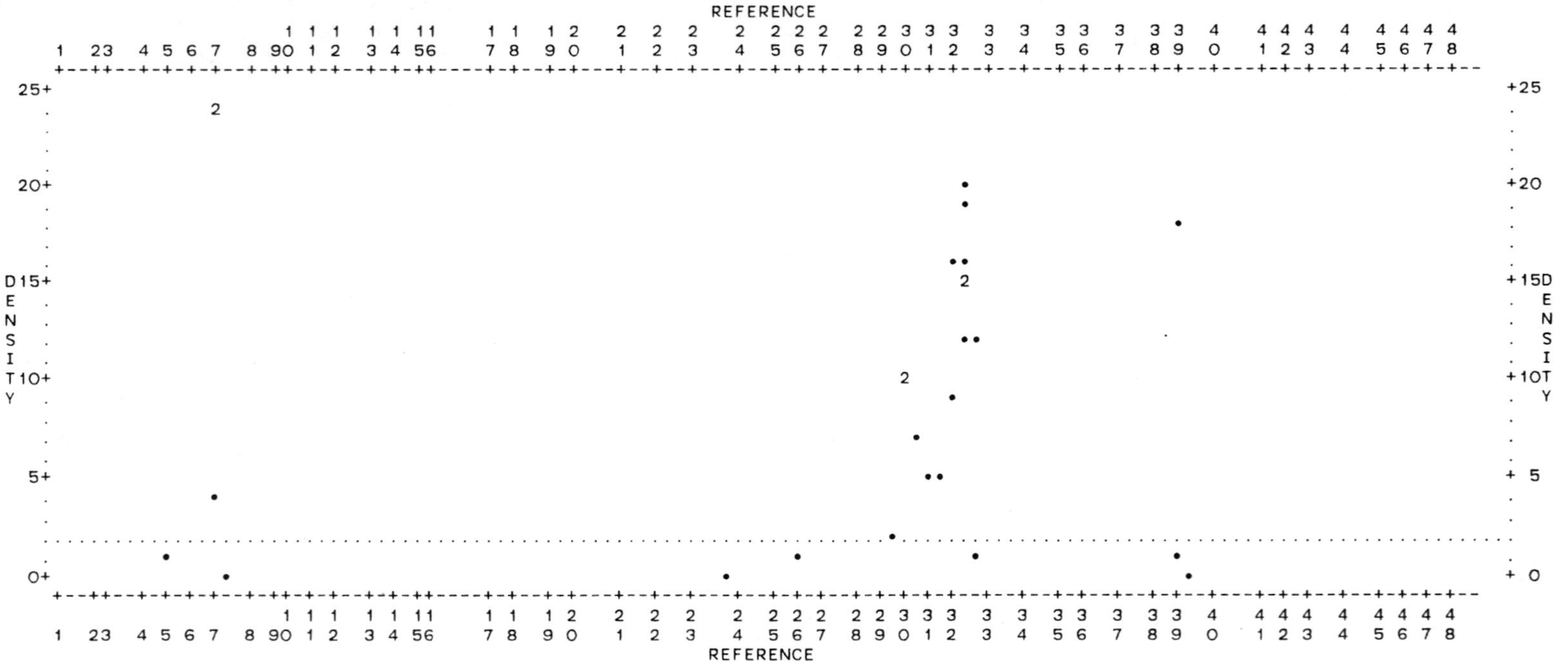

(ASCII linguistic density scatter plot; vertical axis "DENSITY" marked +25, +20, +15, +10, +5, 0; horizontal axis gives verse-reference tick labels; "REFERENCE" axis labels at center.)

```
CLUSTERS:

Start:     5: 7   5: 7   7:11   7:11   7:12  23:42  29:19  29:19  31:18  32:12  32:12  32:16  32:20  32:25  39:11
End:      39:15   7:14   7:14   7:13   7:13  39:15  32:32  30:15  32:32  32:18  32:18  32:18  32:32  32:26  39:15
Count:       26      5      4      3      2     21     16      4     11      5      4      6      4      2      3
Width:    19996    886     74     45     18   9124   1711    328    706    125     11    299    138     34     80
Strength:  4.26   1.73   1.82   1.46   1.01   5.00   4.97   1.89   5.26   1.79   1.02   2.37   1.78   1.00   1.43
```

```
GAPS:

Start:     1: 1   7:13   7:14   7:14   7:14  32:32  39:11
End:      32:12  32:12  30:10  29:19  23:42  39:11  48:35
Count:       15     11     10      6      4      2      3      2
Width:    17314  14456  14427  13401   9986  13177   6047   5972
Strength:  1.06   1.60   2.04   4.00   6.06   8.96   3.11   2.87   4.94
```

Linguistic Density Plot in Ezekiel 1 - 48

For hēn 6163 (8 times)

Each Column = 13 Verses. Separations are: Max = 5517.00, Mean = 3107.78, Min = 77.00 .

REFERENCE

```
                                                                 +25

                                                                 +20

                                                                 +15 D
                                                                     E
                                                                     N
                                                                     S
                                                                     I
                                                                 +10 T
                                                                     Y

                                                                 +5

                                                                 +0
```

REFERENCE

CLUSTERS:

Start:	18: 4	18: 4	42: 5	42: 5	42:13
End:	42:14	18: 4	42:14	42: 6	42:14
Count:	8	2	4	2	2
Width:	15470	10	203	9	49
Strength:	1.70	1.11	2.18	1.11	1.10

GAPS:

Start:	1: 1	1: 1	18: 4	30:17
End:	42: 5	18: 4	42: 5	42: 5
Count:	6	2	4	2
Width:	23977	8710	15257	7558
Strength:	1.91	2.01	1.42	1.60

Linguistic Density Plot in Ezekiel 1 - 48

For -hen 6163 (64 times)

Each Column = 13 Verses.   Separations are: Max = 3038.50, Mean = 430.31, Min = 3.50 .

REFERENCE (vertical axis: D E N S I T Y)

CLUSTERS:

```
Start:     1: 5   1: 5   1: 5   1: 9   1: 9   1:10   1:16   1:16   1:17   1:17   1:23  13:17  13:17  16:45  16:45
End:      44: 8  23:47   1:24   1:12   1:10   1:10   1:24   1:18   1:18   1:18   1:24  23:47  18:14  13:17  16:61  16:47
Count:      64     50     15      7      5      2      8      5      4      3      2      2     35     17      2     15     14      5
Width:   25007  12892    386    142     75     34      6    182     46     29     12     37   7212   3132   1226    364     56
Strength: 3.53   5.52   3.98   2.44   1.98   1.38   1.00   2.65   2.02   1.74   1.42   1.00   1.38   4.31   2.53   1.00   3.38   3.79   2.01
```

```
Start:    16:45  16:47  16:50  16:50  16:53  16:53  16:55  23:13  23: 3  23: 3  23: 3  23:36  23:36  23:37  23:42  23:42
End:      16:45  16:47  16:61  16:50  16:55  16:53  16:61  23:47  23: 4  23: 4  23: 4  23:37  23:36  23:37  23:47  23:42
Count:       2      3      9      8      4      4      5     18      6      5      2      3      2      5      3      2
Width:      13    124    243     68     36    197    926      4     32     20    238     12      4    364     97      6
Strength: 1.42   2.70   2.82   1.69   1.73   2.12   4.22   1.00   2.04   2.05   3.48   1.00   1.76   1.00   2.49   1.00
```

```
Clusters for -hen 6163, continued.

Start:     23:45 23:47 23:47 34:21 41:25 42: 6 42:11 42:11 42:11 42:11 42:11
End:       23:47 23:47 23:47 34:23 44: 8 42:14 42:14 42:12 42:11 42:11 42:11 42:11
Count:         5     3     2     3    11     9     7     6     5     2     3
Width:        41    18     6    42  1244   187    95    36    15     3     8
Strength:   2.03  1.41  1.00  1.37  2.46  2.98  2.87  2.49  2.30  2.06  1.00  1.43  1.00

GAPS:

Start:      1:18  1:23  1:24 13:17 16:55 16:61 18:14 23:36 23:37 23:47 23:47 23:47 34:23 34:23 34:23 34:23 42:11 42:11 42:12
End:       16:45 13:17 13:17 16:45 23: 3 23: 3 23: 3 23:47 42:11 42:11 42:11 34:21 42:11 42: 9 42: 6 41:25 48:35
Count:         8     6     3     2     4     3     2    18    16     9     8     3     2     5     4     3     2     5     4
Width:      7353  5447  5294  1902  4135  4016  3154 11328 11317 11105 11093  6077  6048  5003  4972  4911  4781  3872  3851
Strength:   4.06  3.59  7.50 11.47  3.93  5.30  6.42  2.65  3.35  6.77  7.57  8.77 13.25  3.96  5.09  6.81 10.26  2.59  3.54

Start:     42:14 44: 8
End:       48:35 48:35
Count:         3     2
Width:      3792  2865
Strength:   4.92  5.74
```

Linguistic Density Plot in Ezekiel 1 - 48

For hēn 84 (1 times)   hinnēh 84 (104 times)   hinnēh 84- (11 times)

Each Column = 13 Verses.   Separations are: Max = 1041.50. Mean = 239.06. Min = 21.00

CLUSTERS:

Start:	1: 4	1: 4	1: 4	3:23	7: 5	8: 2	8: 2	8: 2	8: 7	8:14	12:27	13: 8	14:22	17: 7	17: 7
End:	47: 7	18:18	11: 1	4:16	7:10	11: 1	9: 2	8: 5	8:10	9: 2	18:18	13:12	16: 8	15: 5	18:18
Count:	116	51	30	11	4	14	6	3	3	5	21	3	5	4	5
Width:	26838	8932	4301	1464	474	1184	443	192	146	3590	374	89	131	772	484
Strength:	1.95	2.37	2.36	1.28	1.02	2.37	2.48	1.92	1.13	1.40	1.22	1.16	1.24	1.43	1.16

Start:	17: 7	17:12	23:22	24:16	25: 4	25: 9	28: 3	31: 3	33:32	34:10	37: 2	37: 2	37: 2	46:19	47: 7
End:	21: 3	26: 7	26: 7	26: 7	26: 7	25: 7	31: 9	40:24	36: 9	33:32	34:20	38: 3	37:12	37: 5	47: 7
Count:	19	13	9	7	4	3	11	25	6	4	16	10	7	5	3
Width:	772	3350	1675	1542	772	449	127	1254	4309	476	2401	711	220	111	52
Strength:	1.06	1.02	1.52	1.75	1.73	1.44	1.17	1.28	1.01	1.37	1.38	1.37	2.09	2.13	1.80

Data for hēn 84, hinnēh 84, hinnēh 84-, continued.

GAPS:

```
Start:     1:15   7:10  10: 1  10: 1  10: 1  10: 9  11: 1  13:12  13:20  15: 5  17:12  17:12  18:18  21:12  22:19  23:40  26: 7  30:22  30:22
End:       2: 9  48:35  14:22  13:10  12:27  12:27  12:27  14:22  14:22  23:39  23:39  21: 3  21: 3  22: 6  23:22  24:16  28: 3  37: 2  33:32
Count:        2    102      9      6      5      4      3      2      2     22     14      6      2      2      2      2      3      2     12      3
Width:      512  25175   2594   1732   1668   1507   1333   1041    837    630   6197   4475   2401   1751    597    646    482   1024   3923   2015
Strength:  1.14   1.16   1.04   1.02   1.52   1.93   2.55   3.38   1.07   1.64   1.19   1.68   2.31   6.37   1.50   1.71   1.02   3.30   1.72   4.60

Start:    31: 3  33:32  36: 9  37: 2  37: 2  37: 8  37:12  37:12  37:12  37:21  37:21  38: 3  39: 8  40: 5  40: 5  40:24  40:24  43:12  44: 4  47: 2  47: 7
End:      37: 2  48:35  48:35  47: 1  48:35  46:19  46:19  46:19  40: 3  40: 3  39: 1  46:19  43: 2  43: 2  42: 8  46:19  46:19  48:35  48:35
Count:        2     26     23     21     18     16     14      5      2      5      9      2      9      8      5      2      3      3      2
Width:     1871    654   7523   7419   7310   6114   6001   5781   1494    536    562   4222   1851   1193   2296   2083   1684   1153   1070
Strength:  6.88   1.74   1.46   2.14   2.60   2.25   2.80   3.30   1.14   1.25   1.36   3.55   1.91   4.02   3.87   4.80   6.09   2.02   3.50
```

Linguistic Density Plot in Ezekiel 1 - 48

For hinnēh 84 (104 times)

Each Column = 13 Verses. Separations are: Max = 1271.00, Mean = 266.38, Min = 21.00 .

REFERENCE

Vertical axis (density): +25 +20 +15 D E N S I +10 T Y +5 +0 O

```
CLUSTERS:

Start:      1: 4   1: 4   1: 4   7: 5   7:10   8: 2   8: 7   8:14  14:22  17: 7  17: 7  21:12  23:22  24:16  25: 4
End:       47: 7  18:18  11: 1   9: 2   7:10   9: 2   8:10   9:15  15: 5  17:18  17:12  26: 7  26: 7  26: 7  26: 7
Count:       104     41     26     17     13      9      3      3      3      4      3     17     13      9      7
Width:     26838   8932   4301   1651    910    443    192    146    131    270    122   3156   1675    772    449
Strength:   1.61   1.30   2.03   2.67   2.64   1.58   1.00   2.34   1.96   1.16   1.04   1.08   1.10   1.16   1.13   1.75   1.88   1.82

Start:     25: 4  25: 7  25:16  28: 3  28: 3  29:10  33:32  33:32  34:10  37: 2  37: 2  37: 2  46:19  47: 1
End:       25: 9  25: 9  26: 7  31: 3  29: 6  36: 9  40:24  34:20  34:24  37: 5  37: 8  37:12  47: 5  47: 7  47: 7
Count:       127      4      3      6     11     25      9      6      4     16     10      7      5      3      3
Width:       127     50    158   1542    716   4309   1254    476    251   2401    711    220    111     52    239    126
Strength:   1.48   1.29   1.00   1.40   1.06   1.82   1.21   1.47   1.21   1.67   2.21   2.18   1.83   1.29   1.58   1.09
```

Data for hinnēh 84, continued.

GAPS:

Start	End	Count	Width	Strength
3:25	7: 5	4	1335	1.18
4:14	7: 5	2	958	2.61
10: 1	15: 4	7	2705	1.75
10: 1	14:22	6	2594	2.18
10: 1	12:27	5	2420	2.60
11: 1	14:22	2	1333	2.15
11: 1	12:27	3	1041	2.93
13:12	14:22	2	837	2.16
15: 5	23:39	18	6197	1.66
17:12	23:39	11	4475	2.27
18:18	23:39	8	3825	2.89
18:18	22:13	4	2666	4.12
18:18	22: 6	3	2542	5.40
18:18	21:12	2	1945	6.35
22:19	23:22	2	646	1.43
26: 7	28: 3	12	1024	2.86
30:22	33:32	3	3923	1.19
30:22	33:32	2	2015	3.99
31: 3	33:32	3	1871	6.07
36: 9	37: 2	2	654	1.46

Start	End	Count	Width	Strength
37: 8	48:35	23	7419	1.40
37:12	48:35	21	7310	1.85
37:12	47: 1	18	6114	1.58
37:21	46:19	16	6001	2.10
38: 3	46:19	14	5781	2.59
38: 3	39: 1	3	536	1.01
39: 8	40: 3	2	562	1.11
40: 5	46:19	9	4222	2.90
40: 5	43: 2	5	1851	1.50
40:24	42: 8	3	1449	2.46
40:24	43: 2	4	1193	3.50
43: 5	46:19	5	2296	3.30
43:12	46:19	5	1684	5.37
44: 4	46:19	3	2083	4.17
47: 2	48:35	2	1153	1.66
47: 7	48:35	2	1070	3.04

Linguistic Density Plot in Ezekiel 1 - 48

For hinnēh 84- (11 times)

Each Column = 13 Verses. Separations are: Max = 8612.50, Mean = 2330.83, Min = 148.00 .

CLUSTERS:

Start:	4:16	4:16		13: 8	13: 8	13: 8	13: 8		21: 3
End:	21: 8	8:17	6: 3	21: 8	16:37	14:22	13:20	13:10	21: 8
Count:	11	4	3	7	5	4	3	2	
Width:	9028	1763	537	5268	1903	935	296	64	88
Strength:	4.93	1.55	1.42	2.24	2.02	1.80	1.50	1.05	1.04

GAPS:

Start:	13:10	21: 8
End:	48:35	48:35
Count:	7	2
Width:	22341	17137
Strength:	2.15	6.90

Linguistic Density Plot in Ezekiel 1 - 48

For har 111 (47 times)

Each Column = 13 Verses.   Separations are: Max = 2840.50, Mean = 582.71, Min = 10.00 .

REFERENCE

DENSITY scale markings: +25, +20, +15, +10, +5, 0

CLUSTERS:

Start	End	Count	Width	Strength
6: 2	43:12	47	22257	5.69
6: 2	7:16	6	608	1.88
6: 2	6: 3	3	20	1.43
6:13	7:16	3	343	1.02
17:22	22: 9	9	2985	1.12
17:22	19: 9	6	862	1.68
17:22	18:15	5	310	1.82
17:22	17:23	5	135	1.28
17:22	17:23	2	135	1.01
20:40	20:40	2		1.01
28:14	43:12	31	9247	4.25
28:14	36: 8	22	4445	3.93
31:12	32: 6	3	336	1.03
33:28	36: 8	17	1335	4.24
33:28	34:14	5	467	1.68
34: 6	34:14	4	227	1.57
34:13	34:14	3	33	1.41
35: 2	35:13	12	497	3.52
35: 2	35: 8		113	1.69

Start	End	Count	Width	Strength
35:12	36: 8	8	287	2.68
35:12	36: 4	6	150	2.26
35:15	36: 1	4	76	1.72
36: 1	36: 1	3	22	1.43
37:22	40: 2	8	1442	1.86
38:20	39: 4	6	760	1.76
38:20		4	135	1.66

Data for har 111, continued.

GAPS:

Start:	1: 1	1: 1	6: 2	6: 3	7: 7	7:16	11:23	20:40	20:40	22: 9	28:16	32: 6	38:21	39: 4	39:17	40: 2	43:12	
End:	20:40	17:22	17:22	17:22	17:22	17:22	17:22	32: 5	28:14	28:14	31:12	33:28	48:35	48:35	48:35	48:35	48:35	48:35
Count:	15	9	7	6	4	3	2	6	3	2	2	7	6	5	4	3	2	
Width:	10554	8601	2312	6281	6269	5865	5681	3774	6627	4764	3736	1505	1232	6357	6238	5926	5613	3400
Strength:	1.31	2.64	3.02	2.10	2.74	4.25	5.65	5.59	3.04	4.50	5.52	1.61	1.13	2.16	3.53	4.31	5.56	4.93

Linguistic Density Plot in Ezekiel 1 - 48

For hrg 311 (2 times)   hrg 312 (3 times)   hrg 314 (2 times)   hrg 315 (1 times)
     hrg 322 (1 times)   hrg 3262 (1 times)

Each Column = 13 Verses.   Separations are: Max = 7265.00. Mean = 2542.73, Min = 57.00 .

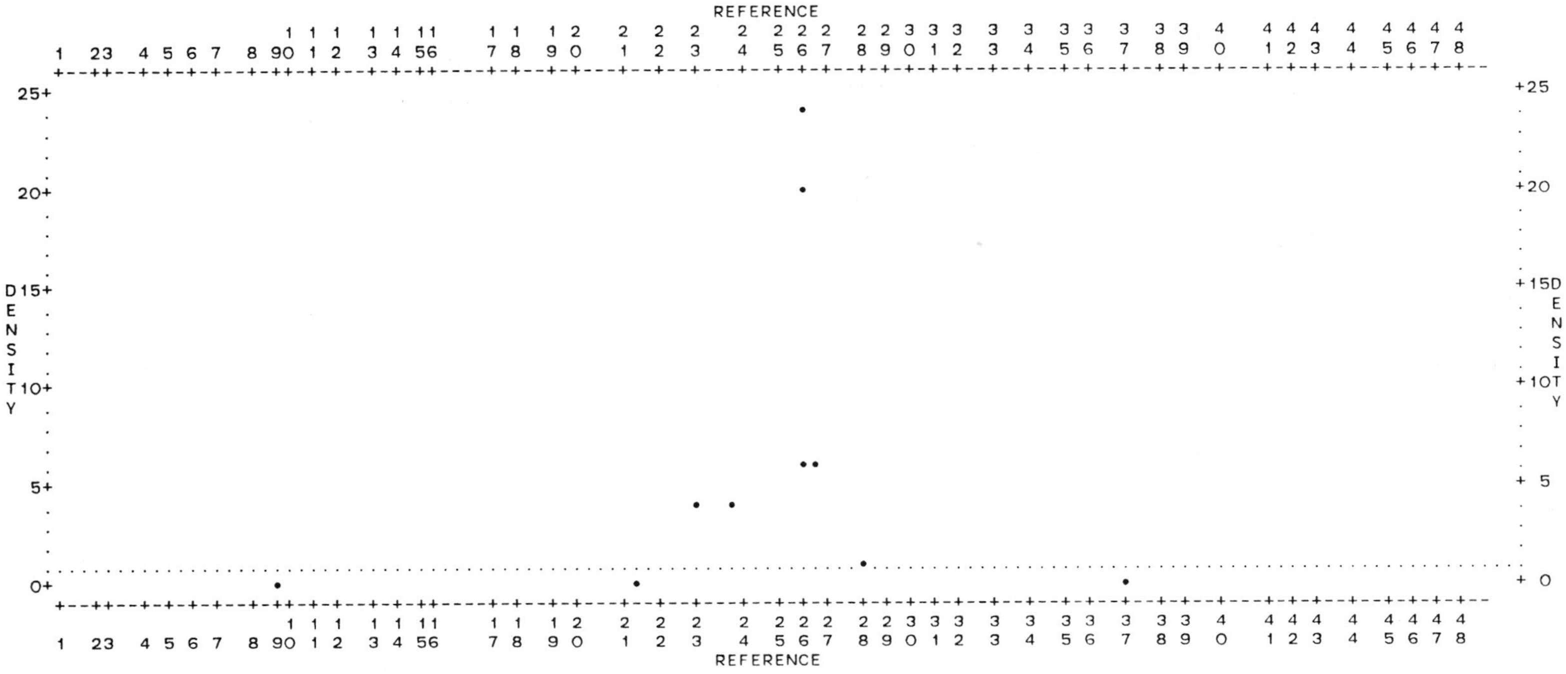

CLUSTERS:

Start:	9: 6	21:16	26: 6	26: 6	26: 6	26:11
End:	37: 9	37: 9	28: 9	26:15	26: 8	26:15
Count:	10	9	8	5	4	2	2
Width:	16852	9587	4210	1138	201	43	87
Strength:	1.93	2.99	3.49	2.32	2.06	1.07	1.05

GAPS:

Start:	1: 1	1: 1	9: 6	26:15	28: 9	37: 9
End:	23:10	21:16	21:16	48:35	48:35	48:35
Count:	4	3	2	4	3	2
Width:	12205	11010	7265	13686	12749	7372
Strength:	1.27	1.90	2.03	1.68	2.46	2.08

Linguistic Density Plot in Ezekiel 1 - 48

For hrs 311 (4 times)   hrs 321 (2 times)

Each Column = 13 Verses. Separations are: Max = 4172.00, Mean = 3107.78, Min = 624.50 .

hrs 324 (2 times)

REFERENCE (vertical, along plot): DENSITY

+25
+20
+15D
  E
  N
  S
  I
+10T
  Y
 +5
 +0

REFERENCE

CLUSTERS:

Start:	13:14	26: 4	26: 4	36:35	36:35
End:	38:20	30: 4	26:12	38:20	36:36
Count:	8	6	3	3	2
Width:	15901	7557	2139	175	1249	14
Strength:	1.59	1.81	1.10	1.05	1.35	1.11

GAPS:

Start:	1: 1	16:39	38:20
End:	26: 4	26: 4	48:35
Count:	4	2	2
Width:	14038	6508	6374
Strength:	1.13	1.22	1.17

Linguistic Density Plot in Ezekiel 1 - 29

For wĕ- 531- (924 times)

Each Column = 7 Verses.   Separations are: Max = 156.00, Mean = 17.43, Min = 2.00

REFERENCE

(Density axis labels, top to bottom: +25, +20, +15 D, E, N, S, I, +10 T, Y, +5, 0 — spelling "DENSITY")

Reference axis (columns): 1 2 3 4 5 6 7 8 9 10 11 12 13 14 15 16 17 18 19 20 21 22 23 24 25 26 27 28 29

REFERENCE

CLUSTERS:

Start:	1: 1	1: 1	1: 1	1: 1	1: 1	1: 1	1: 4	1: 4	1: 4	1: 4	1: 4	1: 5	1: 6	1: 7	1: 8	1:10	1:10	1:10	1:10	1:10	1:10	1:13
End:	29: 9	19:14	9: 3	5:12	3:15	1:23	1: 7	1: 4	1: 1	1: 1	1: 4	1: 7	1: 7	1: 8	1: 8	1:23	1:16	1:12	1:11	1:11	1:11	1:16
Count:	924	594	262	161	89	45	10	4	14	3	6	4	4	4	20	30	18	8	6	4	17	10
Width:	15806	9538	3650	2149	1115	436	59	17	87	8	32	17	20	59	276	276	134	134	31	49	65	65
Strength:	11.40	3.13	3.76	3.18	2.69	2.92	1.87	1.15	2.23	1.07	1.40	1.15	1.05	1.15	1.73	2.47	2.27	1.43	1.15	1.57	1.43	1.75

Start:	1:13	1:15	1:16	1:16	1:18	1:19	1:18	1:21	1:18	1:23	2:10	2:10
End:	1:15	1:16	1:23	1:16	1:21	1:18	1:19	1: 3	1: 8	2:10	3: 3	2:10
Count:	6	4	12	9	6	28	69	119	361	84	59	10
Width:	36	15	69	28	44	11	210	119	625	84	59	84
Strength:	1.30	1.22	1.42	1.25	1.50	1.35	1.97	1.25	1.11	1.39	1.05	1.73

Clusters for we- 531-, continued.

Start: 3:18 3:18 3:20 3:20 4:7   4:7   4:7   4:7   4:16 4:16 4:16 4:16 4:16 4:16 5:9   5:11 5:11 5:11
End: 3:20 3:19 3:21 3:21 4:14 4:9   4:4   4:4   5:1   5:1   5:4   5:4   5:1   4:16 5:12 5:12 5:11 5:11
Count: 6   4   5   44   19   10   20   29   6   7   10   104   48   7   10   102   14   3
Width: 34   18   32   557   166   49   166   317   28   48   104   48   44   28   10   102   14   3
Strength: 1.35 1.12 1.07 1.72 2.01 2.06 1.05 1.87 1.50 1.11 1.00 1.31 1.68 1.11 1.04 1.68 1.25 1.03

Start: 5:12 5:12 5:14 5:14 5:14 5:14 5:15 5:15 5:16 5:17 5:17 5:17 7:13 7:13 7:13 7:15 7:15 7:17
End: 5:12 9:3   6:12 6:3   5:14 5:15 5:15 5:17 5:17 5:17 5:17 5:17 7:20 7:20 7:15 7:15 7:15 7:20
Count: 4   101   58   350   14   6   5   4   5   3   3   31   16   3   61   4   17   8
Width: 20   1468 812 145   27   41   21   29   18   13   13   427   157   31   61   17   17   71
Strength: 1.05 1.66 1.42 1.30 1.17 1.02 1.15 1.28 1.11 1.11 1.01 1.55 1.31 1.23 1.15 1.15 1.09

Start: 7:25 7:25 8:2   8:6   8:6   8:10 8:10 8:10 8:11 8:14 8:16 8:17 9:3   9:4   9:4   9:6   9:6   9:7
End: 7:27 7:26 8:2   9:3   8:11 8:11 8:10 8:11 8:10 9:3   8:16 9:3   10:17 9:4   9:4   9:6   9:6   9:7
Count: 6   4   3   27   11   7   3   5   16   5   5   10   41   24   51   26   19   4
Width: 41   21   349   27   44   25   11   44   187   16   24   95   523   281   89   51   50
Strength: 1.17 1.02 1.07 1.18 1.32 1.27 1.07 1.41 1.10 1.30 1.17 1.61 1.99 1.79 1.44 1.23 1.27 1.07

Start: 9:9   9:9   9:9   10:12 10:12 10:12 12:13 13:7 13:12 13:13 13:12 13:10 13:10 13:11 13:15 13:15 14:7
End: 9:11 9:11 10:17 10:12 10:12 10:14 12:14 13:13 13:13 13:12 13:10 13:10 13:11 13:17 13:17 14:7
Count: 6   15   150   7   4   5   17   8   3   3   11   4   4   7   50   48
Width: 40   20   96   13   18   72   168   29   8   8   26   14   48   6
Strength: 1.20 1.05 1.44 1.11 1.12 1.61 1.59 1.07 1.85 1.15 1.99 1.73 1.15 1.11 1.27 1.31

Start: 14:7 14:16 14:16 14:19 14:19 14:21 14:21 16:7 16:8 16:13 16:11 16:13 16:13 16:16 16:18 16:19 16:36
End: 14:23 14:16 14:20 14:23 14:20 14:22 14:21 16:58 16:16 13:13 16:11 16:13 16:20 16:16 16:20 16:19 16:58
Count: 18   10   95   18   65   7   38   83   36   15   38   9   24   82   44   6   43
Width: 184   41   95   18   65   8   38   1243 83   13   38   7   24   82   44   24   527
Strength: 1.57 1.17 1.17 1.12 1.23 1.55 1.23 1.30 1.22 2.05 1.89 1.16 1.61 1.41 1.15 1.85

Start: 16:45 16:45 16:46 16:46 16:48 16:49 16:49 16:52 16:52 16:53 16:55 16:55 16:55 16:55 17:16 17:17 18:4 18:4
End: 16:58 16:47 16:47 16:51 16:51 16:49 16:53 16:53 16:58 16:55 16:56 16:56 16:55 17:19 17:18 18:9 18:7
Count: 32   10   22   3   32   13   4   31   9   29   13   9   19   70   4   9   4   7
Width: 305   56   28   7   52   13   122 31   15   29   9   68   13   70   10   91   47
Strength: 2.46 1.92 1.35 1.18 1.22 1.28 1.43 1.87 1.28 1.76 1.03 1.44 1.28 1.12 1.08 1.25 1.34

Start: 18:11 18:11 18:31 20:19 20:19 20:23 22:18 22:18 22:20 22:20 22:25 22:25 22:28 22:28 22:29 22:29 23:3   23:3
End: 18:21 18:13 18:31 20:20 20:20 20:25 22:20 22:18 22:20 22:4 22:30 23:12 22:30 22:29 22:29 23:3   23:12 23:3
Count: 21   13   3   20   3   8   60   4   5   27   12   9   36   16   5   8   10   3
Width: 238   122   41   20   9   38   349 23   36   349 125   27   63   36   24   171   45
Strength: 1.42 1.44 1.03 1.05 1.03 1.25 1.33 1.52 1.32 1.18 1.15 1.54 1.60 1.53 1.19 1.12 1.25 1.08

Start: 23:3 23:20 23:20 23:20 23:23 23:23 23:24 23:25 23:25 23:29 23:29 23:32 23:35 23:36 23:38 23:38
End: 24:17 23:37 23:27 23:24 23:24 23:23 23:24 23:27 23:25 23:37 23:34 23:33 23:37 23:37 24:17 23:49
Count: 7   78   17   10   9   5   6   9   4   16   9   4   7   5   45   25
Width: 979   378   183   96   42   21   55   9   17   153   84   34   43   22   577   223
Strength: 2.47 1.85 1.38 1.16 1.97 1.38 1.02 1.15 1.15 1.61 1.11 1.15 1.35 1.43 1.19 1.35 1.67 1.12 2.31

Start: 23:38 23:40 23:40 23:41 23:42 23:44 23:46 23:46 24:10 24:10 24:11 24:14 24:14 24:14 24:16 24:16 24:21 24:21 24:22 26:7
End: 23:42 23:41 23:41 23:42 23:49 23:45 23:49 24:17 24:11 24:17 24:14 24:14 24:17 24:16 24:16 24:21 24:21 24:23 26:7
Count: 12   4   8   4   13   4   7   55   15   3   10   79   3   6   3   5   7   3   19   8
Width: 86   17   38   15   121   7   28   152   28   6   79   13   7   34   43   22   19
Strength: 1.83 1.15 1.81 1.22 1.46 1.02 1.18 1.41 1.15 1.15 1.15 1.48 1.28 1.11 1.15 1.35 1.43 1.11 1.08 1.45

Clusters for wē-531-, continued.

```
Start:     26:11  26:12  26:12  26:12  27:12  27:12  27:12  27:15  27:16  27:16  27:16  27:17  27:18  27:18  27:18
End:       26:13  26:13  26:12  26:12  27:17  27:24  27:14  27:17  27:17  27:16  27:16  27:17  27:24  27:22  27:19
Count:         6      5      3      6     15     30     15     10      9      9      5      6      8     50      4
Width:        42     23     58    708     85    201     42     97     27     13     10      6     50     97     15
Strength:   1.14   1.32   1.15   2.23   2.45   3.29   2.19   2.26   2.28   1.61   1.52   1.52   2.26   1.55   1.22
```

```
Start:     27:18  27:21  27:22  27:22  27:24  28:13  28:13
End:       27:19  27:22  27:23  27:24  27:27  28:13  28:13
Count:         3      4      7      4      5      5      7
Width:         5     20     38     13     25     15      7
Strength:   1.19   1.05   1.55   1.28   1.27   1.55   1.11
```

GAPS:

```
Start:      1: 1   1: 1   1:21   1:23   1:26   1:27   1:27   2: 1   2: 3   2:10   3: 1   3: 3   3: 5   3:14   3:18   3:14   3:15   3:18   3:23   3:25   4: 1   4: 2   4: 4   4: 5   4:12   4:14   4:14   4:16   5: 2   5:11
End:        1: 4   1: 4   1:23   1:26   1:27   1:27   1:27   2: 3   2: 5   2:10   3: 3   3: 5   3: 3   3:18   3:25   3:15   3:18   3:23   3:25   3:25   4: 2   4: 4   4: 5   4: 5   4:14   4:16   4:16   4:16   5: 2   5:11
Count:         2      4      2      5      2      4      1      1      3      5      3      5      2      3      3      2      2      2     10      2      2      2      2      5      2      2      2     10      5      2
Width:        60     49     54    109    102     92     47     37     42     90     86     48     56     72     43     38     56     74    212     69     42     37     38     47     47     38     47    215     37    215
Strength:   1.00   1.78   2.07   1.11   1.63   2.30   1.66   1.09   1.38   1.23   1.10   1.72   2.18   1.48   1.43   1.15   2.18   1.57   1.05   1.36   1.38   1.09   1.15   1.66   1.66   1.15   1.66   1.10   1.09   1.10
```

```
Start:      5: 4   5: 5   5: 7   5: 7   5:10   5:11   6: 3   6: 6   6: 6   6: 9   6:11   6:12   6:13   6:13   7: 4   7: 7   7:20   7:21   7:25   8: 2   8: 2   8: 4   8: 8   8: 8   8: 8
End:        5: 5   5: 5   5: 9   5: 9   5:11   5:11   6: 6   6: 6   6: 6   6:11   6:11   6:12   6:13   6:13   7: 7   7: 7   7:25   7:25   7:25   8: 8   8: 8   8: 7   8: 8   8: 8   8: 6
Count:         7      4      7      9      7      9      3      6      3      2      3      2     13      4      7      9      5      4      2      8      8      7      5      3      3
Width:        39     97     39     39     38     60     97     54      2     10    222     92     83     86     92     74     52     61     42    152    117     67
Strength:   1.21   1.46   1.21   1.15   1.15   1.00   1.46   2.07   1.00   2.50   1.24   1.30   1.00   1.10   1.95   1.57   1.95   1.04   1.10   1.10   1.34   1.28
```

```
Start:      8: 5   8: 6   8:11   8:11   8:11   8:16   8:16   9: 3   9: 3   9: 4   9: 8   9: 9   9:11   9:12   10:10  10:10  10:12  10:16  10:16  10:17  10:19  10:21  11: 7  11: 7  11: 7  11:11  11:11  11:12  11:12  11:13  11:16
End:        8: 6   8:16   8:14   8:11   8:14   8:17   8:17   9: 4   9: 4   9: 4   9: 9   9: 9   11:7   11:7   10:12  10:12  10:21  10:19  10:19  10:19  10:21          11:7   11:11  11:21  11:21  11:13          11:12  11:13  11:16
Count:         2      3      4      3      2      2     13      3      4      5      9      8      2      5     10     10      5      2     28     29      2     30      3      3     13     29      3      7     10     11     16
Width:        61     93     36     92     28     64    300     46     28     92     41     38    105     92    105     64    212    664    669    327     40     41    300     58    105    669    212    105     10    212      3
Strength:   2.47   2.34   1.03   2.25   2.30   1.16   1.50   1.61   1.15   4.25   1.32   1.15   1.00   4.25   1.00   1.32   1.00   2.16   1.98   1.27   1.26   1.98   2.30   2.30   1.00   1.98   1.05   1.05   1.05   1.30   1.77
```

```
Start:     11:16  11:18  11:20  11:22  11:22  12: 2  12: 2  12:12  12:13  12:13  12: 2  12:10  12: 3  12: 3  12: 7  12:10  12:14  12:18  12:14  12:13  13: 7  12:14  12:18  12:20  12:20  12:20  12:20  12:23  12:23  12:20
End:       11:18  11:20  11:22  11:22  12: 2  12: 2  12:13  12:13  12:15  12:13  12:12  12:12  12:10  12:13  12:10  12:12  12:18  12:13  12:18  13: 7          12:14  12:18  12:20  13: 6  13: 7  12:23  12:23          12:23
Count:         5      5      2      2      4     13      8      2      2      6      5      8      6      3      2      5      3      3     19     11      9     68    252    389     58    231     83     64     92     79
Width:       107     52    332     90     82    175    235    226    175     56     69    150    226     40    150    226     19     11    389    252     56     68    252    389    300    231     83    212     92    212
Strength:   1.05   1.95   2.04   1.23   1.89   2.24   1.93   2.18   1.93   2.18   1.36   2.29   2.25   1.26   2.29   2.18   1.02   1.40   1.02   1.40   2.18   1.32   1.40   1.02   2.30   1.85   1.93   1.16   1.30   1.77
```

```
Start:     12:24  12:25  12:25  12:27  12:28  12:28  13:     13:     13:     13:12  13:13  13:15  13:19  13:19  13:21  13:23  13:22  13:23  13:22  13:22  14: 4  14: 7  14: 6  14: 7  14:17  14:13  14: 7  14:16  14:14  14: 7
End:       13: 6  13:    12:27  13:     13: 3  13:     13:     13: 9  14:17  14:17  13:15  13:22  13:21  13:22  14:     14:     14:     14:     14: 7  14:     14: 6  14:    14:17  14:    14:16  14:13  14:    14:16  14:11  14: 7
Count:         6      5      2      3      3      6     13      9      2     37     42     86    190     86    162    731    142     54     48    244    162    213    244    213    159     93
Width:       156    141     76     45     36     36    731    162     37    731    162    213    190    222    162    731    142    142    162    244    190    213    244    213    159     93
Strength:   1.75   2.03   1.26   1.65   1.55   1.03   1.00   1.38   1.38   1.00   1.38   2.05   1.47   1.72   2.64   1.00   2.96   2.07   1.72   1.26   2.07   1.97   1.26   1.83   1.83   1.33
```

```
Start:     14: 9  14:11  14:11  14:13  14:13  14:14  14:22  14:22  14:22  14:22  14:22  14:22  14:23  14:23  14:23  14:23  14:23  15: 7  16: 3  16: 4  16: 3  16: 4  16: 7  16: 8  16:11  16:13  16:11  16:16  16:16  16:13
End:       14:11  14:11  14:13  16:     16:     16:     16: 7  16:31  16:34  16:     16:     16:     16:     15: 4  15: 7  15:     16:     16:     16: 3  16:    16: 4  16: 3  16:    16:12  16:12  16:18  16:16  16:16  16:16  16:16
Count:         2      2      2     12     20     14    359    277    363    246    254    237    198    142    225    389     19     11    198    237     77     97    252    244    213    159    112     78     64     92
Width:        52     45    477    363    170    231    359    277    363    246    254    237    198    142    225    389     77     89     78     97    252    231     78     64     74     92
Strength:   1.95   1.55   1.93   2.17   2.11   1.85   2.49   1.86   2.17   3.31   2.86   3.84   4.82   2.96   4.45   4.82   3.39   3.45   3.45   1.46   2.17   1.85   3.45   1.16   1.96   1.83   3.22   1.78   1.30   1.77
```

```
Start:     16:19  16:19  16:34  16:19  16:34  16:22  16:22  16:22  16:34  16:22  16:22  16:22  16:22  16:39  16:39  16:41  16:51  16:49  16:52  16:55  16:55  16:56  16:58  17:17  17: 7
End:       16:38  16:38  16:34  16:41  16:31  16:34  16:28  16:27  16:31  16:28  16:45  16:43  16:42  16:43  16:41  16:41  16:52  16:52  13:      16:     22:18  17: 7  16:58  17: 7
Count:        20     19     13     69    231     66    112    109    125    150    225    109     90    109     76     39      3      3     47    178     66    279    286    240      8
Width:       409    405    290    290    231     66    112    109    125    150    225    109     90    109     76     39     47   3815    286    279      6
Strength:   1.02   1.24   1.42   1.70   1.85   2.39   3.11   3.33   2.39   1.05   3.84   4.45   1.23   1.11   1.36   1.21   1.66   3.50   2.17   2.97   3.40   3.40   2.97   3.92   1.96
```

Gaps for we- 531-, continued.

```
Start:    16:58  16:58  16:63  17:    17:    17:10  17:10  17:10  17:10  17:18  17:18  17:19  17:21  17:22  18:19  18:19  18:21  18:21  18:21  18:24  18:27
End:      17: 6  16:61  17: 6  17: 6  17: 2  17:15  17:15  17:13  17:12  17:24  17:24  17:21  17:24  17:24  18:31  18:30  18:30  18:24  18:24  18:27  18:30
Count:    5      5      3      6      2      5      4      3      2      5      6      3      5      2      13     11     8      6      2      2      2
Width:    217    75     119    82     109    96     76     49     49     238    157    37     87     49     279    253    211    140    40     50     59
Strength: 4.22   3.27   3.39   3.68   1.11   1.43   1.65   1.78   1.78   1.15   1.78   1.09   2.09   1.78   1.15   1.42   1.92   1.34   1.26   1.84   2.35

Start:    18:31  18:31  18:31  18:31  18:31  18:31  19:    19:    19:12  19:13  19:13  19:14  19:14  19:14  20:11  20:11  20:11  20:11
End:      22:18  21: 7  21: 2  20:34  20:33  20:19  19: 7  19:12  19:11  20:11  20: 7  20: 8  20: 7  20: 4  20: 3  20: 2  20: 4  20: 7
Count:    102    62     59     47     45     34     29     16     6      3      2      3      8      7      6      4      3      2
Width:    2448   1517   1423   1136   862    737    537    216    108    88     101    63     314    286    274    189    175    159
Strength: 4.15   3.44   3.20   2.89   2.91   2.73   4.11   3.30   2.95   4.02   2.66   2.58   3.82   4.25   4.79   4.52   5.67   8.10

Start:    20: 8  20:11  20:13  20:15  20:20  20:20  20:21  20:23  20:24  20:24  20:24  20:25  20:25  20:25  20:28  20:30  20:34  20:34  20:38  20:40  20:40  20:40  20:43
End:      20:11  20:15  20:24  20:24  20:20  20:24  20:23  20:33  20:30  20:30  20:30  20:28  20:30  20:34  20:34  20:38  20:38  20:38  20:44  20:44  20:43  21:    21:
Count:    2      2      2      5      4      2      2      11     4      2      5      4      3      2      12     3      2      3      3      3      2      3
Width:    71     37     121    110    98     78     240    235    160    152    143    79     283    66     55     137    111    72     90
Strength: 3.04   1.09   1.46   1.89   2.54   3.45   1.19   1.49   2.58   3.29   4.37   3.50   1.58   1.24   2.12   2.79   3.07   3.10   2.22   2.30

Start:    21: 7  21:19  21:19  21:11  21:11  21:14  21:17  21:19  21:18  21:17  21:25  21:30  21:28  21:22  21:22  21:31  21:33  21:33  22:13  22:13  22:14  22:18
End:      21: 7  21:19  21:18  21:17  21:17  21:17  21:31  21:30  21:28  22:    22: 4  22:18  22:    22: 4  22: 2  22:18  22:13  22:14  22:18
Count:    40     11     10     6      5      4      15     9      9      3      4      6      2      2      3      4      3      2      ...
Width:    927    239    234    155    143    114    45     683    454    233    129    108    73     213    177    154    105    88     78     52
Strength: 2.31   1.17   1.47   1.73   2.09   2.03   1.55   3.23   1.89   2.53   2.95   3.16   3.22   4.12   4.82   5.00   1.16   1.73   1.95

Start:    22:20  22:20  22:26  22:26  22:25  23:    23:    23:    23:10  23:12  23:12  23:23  23:23  23:27  23:29  23:29  23:32  23:47  23:49  24:    24:    24: 5  24: 6
End:      22:20  22:20  22:26  22:25  23: 2  23:23  23:23  23:23  23:23  23:20  23:20  23:23  23:29  23:29  23:32  24:10  24: 3  24: 4  24: 3  24:10  24:21  24:17
Count:    9      192    126    109    85     53     350    354    243    232    203    149    42     40     229    68     83     50     111    79     78     72
Width:    192    126    109    85     53     354    350    243    232    203    149    42     40     229    83     68     50     111    79     78     72
Strength: 1.06   2.43   2.99   3.85   2.01   2.03   2.34   3.99   4.65   6.81   7.52   1.38   1.26   1.81   1.00   1.32   1.84   3.07   3.50   3.10

Start:    24:23  24:25  24:27  24:27  25:    25: 3  25: 3  25: 5  25: 6  25: 6  25:13  25:13  25:14  25:14  26:    26: 6  26: 7  26: 7  26: 8  26:10  26:10  26:12  26:13  26:13  26:16  26:17  26:21
End:      24:25  26:    26: 7  26: 7  26: 7  25:13  25:13  25:    25:    26: 8  25:    26: 7  25:14  26: 6  26:21  26:21  26:21  26:21  26:12  26:21  26:21  26:21  26:16  26:17  26:21  27:10
Count:    2      19     18     17     13     3      9      5      9      9      4      2      6      2      11     10     9      5      4      2      7      5      9      4      7      7
Width:    36     543    540    537    473    228    181    110    88     58     237    179    266    269    195    207    65     89     158
Strength: 1.03   3.12   3.41   3.72   4.39   1.79   1.78   1.89   2.13   2.30   6.11   7.21   9.25   6.52   2.08   3.93   4.72   2.70   4.08   2.60   4.05   1.24

Start:    26:21  27:    27:24  27:24  27:24  27:27  27:30  27:30  27:30  27:33  27:36  28:    28: 2  28: 2  28: 4  28: 9  28: 9  28: 9  28:13  28:13  28:13  28:13  28:14  28:14  28:19
End:      27:    27:27  28: 9  27:27  27:27  27:30  27:34  27:33  28:    28:    28: 2  28:    28: 9  28: 9  28: 9  28:12  28:13  28:    29: 2  29: 2  28:24  28:22  28:22  28:19
Count:    3      2      18     36     9      2      72     57     38     114    64     49     80     216    339    344    822    185    171    119
Width:    108    90     373    46     139    57     72     38     114    64     49     80     216    339    344    822    185    171    119
Strength: 2.95   4.13   1.07   1.03   1.61   1.32   1.48   2.24   1.15   2.03   3.56   1.16   1.78   2.60   4.05   3.58   6.52   3.30   3.92   5.80

Start:    28:24  29: 2  29: 2  29: 5  29: 5  29: 7  29: 8  29: 9
End:      29: 2  29:21  29:21  29:21  29: 7  29:21  29: 7  29:21
Count:    2      10     5      3      2      304
Width:    114    474    383    71     39     304
Strength: 5.51   6.08   8.99   1.44   1.21   16.43
```

Linguistic Density Plot in Ezekiel 29 - 48

For wĕ- 531- (924 times)

Each Column = 5 Verses.   Separations are: Max = 111.00.   Mean = 13.35, Min = 2.00 .

CLUSTERS:

Start:	29: 9	30: 5	30: 5	30:16	31: 5	30:18	31: 5	33: 3	33: 3	33:13	33:16	33:16	33:18	33:18	33:25	33:25	33:29	33:32	34: 3	34: 3	34: 4
End:	48:35	30: 5	30: 5	30:18	31: 5	30:18	33: 6	33: 3	33: 3	33:33	33:19	33:33	33:19	33:19	33:33	33:26	33:33	33:33	34: 6	34: 4	34: 4
Count:	924	5	3	5	3	5	5	7	3	7	35	8	23	5	10	5	13	24	11	7	6
Width:	12134	9	4	21	6	26	39	39	26	69	376	44	206	17	77	106	24	79	39	39	26
Strength:	10.17	1.64	1.17	1.19	1.07	1.01	1.24	1.27	1.02	1.42	1.39	1.01	1.41	1.34	1.07	1.17	1.08	1.28	1.24	1.28	1.35

Start:	34: 4	34: 4	34:13	34:16	34:16	34:17	34:17	34:16	34:19	34:20	34:21	35: 6	36: 4	36: 4	36:35	37: 9	37:10	37:16	37:16	37:22	37:23
End:	34: 4	34: 4	34:17	34:17	34:16	34:16	34:17	34:16	34:21	35:11	35:11	36: 1	36: 4	36: 4	36:35	37:16	37:18	37:16	37:24	37:23	37:24
Count:	4	10	6	5	3	8	5	3	6	6	13	5	4	3	4	9	7	4	11	6	5
Width:	16	69	23	15	10	3	7	8	36	108	16	69	12	8	49	7	5	16	88	35	26
Strength:	1.02	1.27	1.45	1.42	1.01	1.01	1.12	1.01	1.01	1.12	1.02	1.27	1.23	1.19	1.25	1.12	1.01	1.08	1.07	1.05	1.01

Clusters for we- 531-, continued.

Start	End	Count	Width	Strength
38: 2	38: 7	12	92	1.23
38: 4	38: 7	56	8	1.33
38: 5	38:13	26	5	1.01
38:11	38:13	41	20	1.47
38:12	38:13	20	5	1.23
38:13	38:13	5		1.12
38:19	38:19	167	1735	3.09
38:20	38:20	25		1.04
38:20	38:20	12	6	1.19
38:20	38:22	6	3	1.07
38:22	38:22	19	10	1.58
38:22	38:22	10		1.28
39: 9	39: 9	7	29	1.55
39: 9	39: 9	5	13	1.49
39:10	39:10	3	7	1.01
40: 6	40: 7	5	21	1.19
40: 6	40:46	103	744	4.85
40: 9	40:23	284		2.49
40: 9	40:15	37	105	1.19
40: 9	40:10	13	34	1.08
40: 9	40:10	9	9	9

Start	End	Count	Width	Strength
40:16	40:16	49	89	2.16
40:16	40:18	8	25	1.04
40:16	40:19	24	16	1.25
40:18	40:21	31	13	2.22
40:19	40:21	166	151	1.38
40:20	40:21	46	69	1.49
40:21	40:22	5	3	1.60
40:21	40:23	13	6	1.07
40:22	40:26	3	5	1.56
40:24	40:27	43	26	1.97
40:24	40:31	8	11	2.28
40:25	40:29	4	16	1.23
40:26	40:29	13	55	1.38
40:27	40:29	5	16	1.07
40:31	40:29	3	3	1.27
40:37	40:37	255	444	3.61
40:46	40:42	66	107	2.77
40:37	40:40	11	62	1.69

Start	End	Count	Width	Strength
40:29	40:30	30	85	1.79
40:30	40:31	8	5	1.07
40:31	40:37	6	18	1.31
40:33	40:34	17	47	2.04
40:33	40:33	16	16	1.38
40:34	40:33	6	27	1.31
40:35	40:36	6	53	1.07
40:37	40:37	183	201	1.78
40:40	40:42	23	35	2.00
40:42	40:42	42	50	1.97
40:41	40:42	31	20	1.18
40:40	40:40	4	8	1.36

Start	End	Count	Width	Strength
40:42	40:47	136	214	3.91
40:44	44:27	655	1241	3.99
41: 2	41: 8	57	19	1.02
41: 7	41:22	182	92	1.03
41:11	41:17	102	113	1.25
41: 5	41:12	295	182	1.62
41:11	41:15	8	21	1.73
41:12	41:17	16	52	1.38
41:13	41:17	4	11	1.17
41:15	41:15	20	50	1.97
41:15	41:16	6		1.55

Start	End	Count	Width	Strength
41:16	41:17	80	137	1.76
41:17	41:22	27	64	1.94
41:17	41:18	9	16	1.32
41:17	41:19	7	18	1.61
41:11	41:18	134	248	1.88
42: 5	42:12	575	287	1.00
42:10	42:13	6	11	1.08
42:12	42:14	34	31	1.63
42:11	42:13	14	21	1.19
42:13	42:13	12	4	1.17
42:13	43: 7	163	1462	1.93

Start	End	Count	Width	Strength
43: 8	43:11	81	248	1.92
43:11	44:25	40	95	1.10
43:11	43:16	5	8	1.36
43:16	43:13	9	54	1.25
43:13	44:27	41	36	1.23
43:13	44:25	16	11	1.19
43:18	44:27	66	29	1.57
43:11	44:25	14	6	1.28
43:11	44:28	137	222	4.28
43:16	47:12	127	2376	3.32
43:16	44:35	287	163	1.58

Start	End	Count	Width	Strength
44:28	44:29	70	644	2.59
45: 7	45: 3	30	241	2.06
45: 7	45: 3	17	133	1.51
44:30	45: 3	7	43	1.12
44:29	45: 5	10	382	1.69
45: 9	45: 5	75	143	1.32
45: 4	45:11	21	94	1.19
45: 4	45: 1	8	217	1.23
45: 5	45: 2	32		1.73
45:17	45:17	1.23	1.17	

Start	End	Count	Width	Strength
45:17	45:22	91	291	1.98
45:17	46: 1	7	41	1.18
45: 3	46: 9	11	24	1.08
45:24	46: 4	19	136	1.85
45: 6	46:12	34	76	1.59
46: 9	46:15	12	30	1.52
46: 7	46:15	8	16	1.02
46: 4	47:20	95	362	1.05
46:15	47:20	3	100	1.03
46:12	47:17	7	59	1.50
47:17	47:17	864	2376	3.18

Start	End	Count	Width	Strength
47:17	48: 2	6	91	1.00
47:18	48:10	151	458	1.58
48:10	48:10	34	207	1.67
48:13	48:21	17	103	1.34
48:13	48:14	60	34	1.74
48:13	48:16	11	25	1.67
48:13	48:16	7	16	1.23
48:13	48:18	17	28	2.15
48:17	48:18	94	362	2.06
48:17	48:17	7	100	1.30
48:17	48:21	4	47	1.41
48:19	48:21	7	47	1.00

```
Start:     48:21   48:21   48:32   48:32   48:32   48:32
End:       48:35   48:31   48:35   48:32   48:33   48:32   48:32
Count:     26      17      9       66      31      12      6
Width:     244     159
Strength:  1.35    1.02    1.07    1.07    1.49    1.19    1.07
```

GAPS:

```
Start:     29:1    29:1    29:1    29:1    29:1    29:1    29:1    29:1    29:1    29:1    29:1    29:1    29:1    29:1    29:1    29:1    29:1    29:1    29:1    29:1
End:       48:17   48:17   48:17   45:17   45:9    45:5    44:29   44:22   44:17   43:13   42:13   42:13   42:13   41:18   41:13   41:13   41:7    40:42   40:42   40:42
Count:     890     888     886     884     752     737     722     705     688     680     627     588     587     545     527     526     513     484     482     480
Width:     12016   12011   12006   12001   10402   10264   10135   9982    9828    9742    8972    8533    8531    8128    8034    8032    7900    7605    7588    7582
Strength:  1.82    2.04    2.26    2.46    2.34    2.65    3.00    3.34    3.67    3.75    3.22    3.54    3.60    4.31    5.01    5.07    5.26    5.69    5.73    5.84
```

```
Start:     29:1    29:1    29:1    29:1    29:1    29:1    29:1    29:1    29:1    29:1    29:1    29:1    29:1    29:1    29:1    29:1    29:1    29:1    29:1    29:1
End:       40:39   40:38   40:38   40:19   39:9    38:13   38:11   38:2    37:9    36:35   33:28   30:5    30:5    30:17   30:17   30:10   30:16   30:11   30:16   29:15
Count:     475     474     470     408     344     316     311     295     266     254     128     19      17      18      10      134     92      95      79      3
Width:     7530    7528    7498    7117    6217    5754    5718    5520    4982    4726    2806    571     566     564     406     247     212     152     106     64
Strength:  5.91    5.96    6.08    8.34    8.34    8.04    8.23    8.42    7.85    7.44    7.94    5.88    6.64    7.08    6.47    7.24    2.84    2.74    2.83    3.75
```

```
Start:     29:16   29:18   29:17   29:18   29:18   29:18   29:18   29:18   29:18   30:     30:5    30:5    30:5    30:5    30:5    30:5    30:7    30:10   30:10   30:11   30:11
End:       29:18   29:18   29:18   30:     30:5    30:5    29:21   29:21   30:     30:     31:     31:3    33:14   33:18   33:19   33:25   30:10   30:16   30:16   30:12   30:11
Count:     3       3       2       3       5       4       5       3       3       4       9       17      92      87      95      102     7       95      56      9       2
Width:     59      32      154     148     114     75      227     204     223     109     92      477     1956    2015    2029    2165    2233    106     95      56      36
Strength:  1.68    1.36    3.75    4.65    4.60    4.58    5.36    5.63    4.96    4.63    3.07    2.69    6.84    6.30    6.44    6.06    3.59    2.83    3.15    1.66
```

```
Start:     30:13   30:16   30:18   30:18   30:18   31:     30:18   30:21   30:22   30:25   31:     31:     31:     31:     31:     31:     31:     31:     31:     31:     31:     31:     31:     31:10   31:10
End:       30:16   31:     31:     31:2    31:2    30:21   30:21   30:21   31:     31:     33:14   33:10   33:9    33:6    33:     32:18   32:18   32:18   32:13   31:     31:     31:     31:10   31:10   31:8
Count:     2       7       3       5       2       3       2       2       3       2       69      57      54      46      26      21      6       58      158     667     768     1211    1337    1468    1342
Width:     48      244     227     204     68      121     43      114     75      68      1473    1468    1337    1211    768     667     158     95      58      39      92
Strength:  2.55    5.01    5.36    5.63    2.18    4.97    4.05    4.60    4.58    4.05    5.32    5.44    6.27    6.97    6.58    6.76    3.04    1.50    1.88    1.63    3.59    3.43    3.08
```

```
Start:     31:11   31:11   31:11   31:12   31:13   31:14   31:14   31:15   31:18   31:18   32:     32:     32:     32:     32:7    32:10   32:13   32:15   32:16   32:18   32:18
End:       32:13   31:14   31:13   31:13   31:16   31:14   31:16   31:15   32:     32:     32:6    32:6    32:6    32:     32:13   32:13   32:18   32:18   32:18   33:     33:
Count:     15      4       3       2       11      87      3       56      87      7       4       5       3       3       117     90      68      94      84      67      36      20
Width:     502     79      60      33      414     296     157     312     157     134     48      65      40      29      117     90      68      158     84      67      36
Strength:  6.34    1.66    1.73    1.43    6.66    6.60    3.17    6.19    5.04    5.66    2.55    2.00    1.95    1.13    4.76    5.70    4.05    1.50    2.11    1.66    3.62
```

```
Start:     32:18   32:20   32:22   32:22   32:24   32:27   32:28   32:28   32:30   32:30   32:30   33:     33:     33:     33:2    33:7    33:     33:19   33:19   33:22   33:23   33:25   33:28
End:       32:28   32:26   32:26   32:26   32:26   32:28   32:28   33:     32:30   32:32   32:32   33:     33:     33:     33:4    33:     33:16   33:19   33:22   33:25   33:28   33:25   33:28
Count:     8       194     138     116     74      36      10      197     189     155     136     65      40      48      90      134     29      74      47      36      48
Width:     222     194     138     116     74      36      10      197     189     155     136     65      40      48      90      134     29      133     74      47      48
Strength:  3.63    4.25    4.22    4.70    4.50    1.66    1.91    2.17    2.94    3.08    2.00    2.55    1.95    1.73    5.70    5.66    1.13    1.60    2.48    1.66    1.10
```

```
Start:     33:28   33:32   33:33   34:     34:     34:     34:8    34:10   34:10   34:12   34:13   34:13   34:14   34:15   34:16   34:16   34:16   34:     34:22   34:24   34:24   34:24   34:24
End:       36:35   34:     34:     34:     34:     34:     34:10   34:12   34:12   34:13   34:14   34:16   34:16   34:16   34:16   34:16   34:27   34:28   34:     34:27   34:27   34:24   34:26
Count:     125     4       4       3       2       6       29      92      43      98      74      47      133     181     205     216     231     239     235     227     98      82      37
Width:     1915    69      56      44      32      181     29      92      43      98      47      63      133     181     205     216     231     239     235     227     90      82      37
Strength:  1.86    2.21    3.15    2.25    1.36    2.22    1.58    1.03    2.18    1.03    2.48    1.89    1.60    2.47    2.11    1.95    1.52    1.30    1.27    1.80    1.35    1.79    1.73
```

```
Start:     34:29   34:31   34:31   35:     35:     35:10   35:10   35:11   35:11   35:13   35:15   36:     36:     36:     36:     36:     36:     36:     36:     36:     36:     36:     36:6    36:11
End:       35:5    35:     35:     35:     36:     35:10   36:     35:11   35:15   35:15   35:15   36:     36:     36:     36:     36:     36:     36:     36:     36:35   36:35   36:35   36:8    36:15
Count:     5       3       2       2       12      200     183     88      77      39      48      34      4       5       37      71      63      85      98      701     697     621     33      5
Width:     86      61      32      44      205     200     183     88      77      39      48      34      4       5       37      71      63      90      82      701     697     621     81
Strength:  1.20    1.79    1.36    2.25    1.30    1.57    2.01    2.05    2.64    1.88    1.10    2.64    1.16    2.47    1.88    1.31    1.89    1.35    1.79    3.45    3.62    3.54    1.01
```

```
Start:    36:11 36:11 36:11 36:15 36:15 36:15 36:19 36:20 36:26 36:30 36:31 36:32 36:32 36:35 36:35 37: 2 37: 2 37:
End:      36:14 36:13 36:12 36:35 36:29 36:18 36:25 36:25 36:29 36:35 36:35 36:35 36:34 36:35 37: 1 37: 9 37: 9 37:
Count:        4     3     2    17    11     6     3     5     5     6     4     3    12     9     1    10     9     8
Width:       71    60    41   427   315    58   143   117    81   101    68    50    29   254    82   168   163   118
Strength:  1.31  1.73  2.03  4.02  4.31  1.63  6.14  7.73  1.01  1.13  1.18  1.20  1.13  2.42  5.10  1.18  1.48  1.70

Start:    37: 2 37: 7 37: 8 37:10 37:10 37:10 37:10 37:11 37:11 37:17 37:17 37:17 37:18 37:19 37:21 37:24 37:25
End:      37: 7 37: 7 38: 2 37:25 37:23 37:16 37:16 37:16 37:13 37:23 37:22 37:22 37:22 37:22 37:22 37:25 38: 2
Count:        2     2     9    25    18     5     4     2    10     9     7     5     3     4     2     2     4
Width:       81    29   536   433   346   155   149   104    52   166   173   151   132   123    85    46    30   100
Strength:  5.03  1.13  2.32  1.73  2.17  2.94  3.56  4.43  2.85  1.56  1.31  2.15  2.93  3.06  3.57  2.40  1.21  2.57

Start:    37:25 38: 7 38: 9 38:13 38:13 38:13 38:13 38:13 38:13 38:15 38:15 38:20 38:22 38:22 39: 1 39: 4 39: 7
End:      38: 2 38: 8 38:11 38:22 38:22 38:20 38:20 38:20 38:20 38:19 38:20 38:22 39: 4 39: 3 39: 3 39: 9 39: 9
Count:        3     2     2    14    13     9     8     7     5     2     3     2     4     3     5     4     2
Width:       94    49    38   461   261   205   202   199   171   118    91    31    85    72    28    85    40
Strength:  3.54  2.63  1.80  1.46  1.81  2.59  3.07  3.63  4.39  5.78  4.81  1.28  1.36  1.06  1.16  1.16  1.95

Start:    39: 9 39: 9 39: 9 39: 9 39:10 39:10 39:11 39:14 39:17 39:18 39:20 39:20 39:21 39:21 39:22 39:24 39:26
End:      39:20 39:20 39:17 39:17 39:17 39:11 39:16 39:16 39:20 39:20 40: 3 39:28 39:28 39:26 39:26 39:26 39:28
Count:       30    16    13     9     7     5     3     2     4     2     3     6     8     4     3     3     2
Width:      550   255   248   174   158   136    85    46    64    30   292   286   162    99    79    40    46
Strength:  2.29  1.05  1.54  1.81  1.77  3.08  3.06  2.40  1.01  1.21  2.46  2.72  3.18  2.53  2.74  1.95  2.40

Start:    39:29 40: 1 40: 1 40: 2 40:18 40:44 40:44 42:12 42:15 42:15 42:15 42:15 43:15 43:17 43:18 43:22 43:27
End:      40: 3 40: 2 40: 2 40:19 40:47 40:47 40:47 42:13 43: 2 43: 2 43: 3 43:20 43:20 43:20 44:17 44:17 44:11
Count:        5     4     2     2     4     3     2     6     5     4     3     2     3     2     2    27    16
Width:       93    85    72    50    28    76    60   108   101    92    82    62    70    42    29   488   311
Strength:  1.46  1.92  2.37  2.70  1.06  1.53  1.73  1.36  2.70  1.76  2.22  2.90  3.60  2.26  2.10  1.13  2.09  2.14

Start:    43:27 44: 2 44: 2 44: 5 44: 5 44: 5 44: 5 44: 8 44: 9 44:15 44:15 44:15 44:27 45: 3 45: 4 46:15 46:15
End:      44: 5 44: 5 44: 4 44:11 44:11 44: 7 44: 7 44: 7 44:11 44:15 44:15 44:28 45: 4 45: 2 45: 2 46:23 46:22
Count:        6     4     2     8     7     4     3     5     7     3     2     2     2     2     2     7     7
Width:      109    73    34   179   171    82    78    65    50    39    35    30    28    19     8   189   180
Strength:  1.40  1.40  1.51  2.41  2.77  1.79  2.00  2.25  2.70  2.69  1.16  1.58  1.36  1.21  1.06  1.88  3.78  3.04

Start:    46:15 46:15 46:17 46:18 46:19 46:20 46:21 46:23 46:23 46:23 47: 1 47: 2 47: 3 47: 7 47: 7 47:12 47:12
End:      46:21 46:19 46:17 46:19 46:21 47:11 47:11 47:47 47:47 47: 2 47: 2 47: 1 47: 7 47: 9 47: 5 47:16 47:15
Count:        6     4     2     2     4     5     7     4     6     2     4     2     5     3     7     3     2
Width:      162   113    35    47    30   255   154    71    28    72    91   138   132   123    94    72    50
Strength:  3.18  3.13  1.58  2.48  1.21  2.88  2.91  1.31  1.06  1.21  1.39  4.35  1.20  1.25  1.57  2.31  2.37  2.70

Start:    47:20 47:20 47:20 47:22 48:10 48:10
End:      48: 6 48: 3 48: 2 48: 1 48:13 48:13
Count:       10     6     5     4     3     2
Width:      167   130   123   111    81    51    48    44
Strength:  1.16  2.10  2.59  3.05  2.85  2.55  1.26  2.25
```

Linguistic Density Plot in Ezekiel 1 - 48

For wĕ- 532- (1265 times)

Each Column = 13 Verses.   Separations are: Max = 246.00, Mean =   22.09, Min =   2.00 .

REFERENCE

CLUSTERS:

Start:	1: 1	1: 1	1:28	1:28	1:28	1: 1	2: 2	3: 3	3:10	3:10	3:10	3:10	3:10	3:11	3:14	3:20	3:22	3:22
End:	48:21	33: 7	14: 4	2: 3	2: 5	1: 1	2: 3	3: 4	3: 4	7: 9	5: 6	3:24	3:17	3:12	3:17	3:24	3:23	3:24
Count:	1265	896	293	8	10	75	4	23	102	1776	62	953	158	22	68	11	9	59
Width:	27735	17929	6045	47	111	75	12	23	102	953	62	352	158	22	68	116	59	22
Strength:	6.09	5.15	1.22	1.83	1.32	1.35	1.01	1.11	2.13	2.34	2.34	1.48	1.40	1.14	1.47	1.50	1.88	1.14

REFERENCE

Start:	3:23	3:23	3:25	3:25	4:13	4:17	4:17	4: 5	4: 1	4: 2	4: 3	5:13	5:13	6: 3	6: 3	6: 3	6: 7
End:	3:24	3:24	4: 9	4: 4	5: 1	5: 6	5: 6	4: 6	4: 4	4: 4	4: 4	5:13	6: 1	6: 5	6: 4	6: 9	6: 8
Count:	5	3	38	14	17	11	5	6	11	4	5	40	12	11	4	12	7
Width:	20	10	582	280	233	130	40	16	38	15	30	112	112	30	12	26	11
Strength:	1.53	1.07	1.77	1.68	1.36	1.30	1.08	1.30	1.13	1.32	1.62	1.55	1.40	1.40	1.04	1.04	1.04

```
Start:     6:14   7: 3   7: 8   7: 8   7:16   7:16   7:16   7:16   7:21   7:21   7:22   7:22   7:24   7:24   7:24   7:27   7:27   8: 3   8: 7   8: 8   8:10   8:17   9: 6
End:       7: 1   7: 3   7: 8   7: 8   7:15   7:16   7:16   7:26   7:22   7:26   7:22   7:22   7:25   7:25   7:26   8: 1   8: 6   8: 8   8:10   8:10   8:10   9: 9   9: 9
Count:        4      3      3      3    145     73     16     39     80     12     10      6     19      5     33     11     23     21     49     24     34    533     77
Width:       26     12    176    513   3132   1156     41    584    189     33     80    134    201     41   1043    149    363     21   1147     24    173     55     34
Strength:  1.04   1.01   2.01   4.57   2.38   1.90   1.68   1.66   2.22   1.07   2.22   2.97   3.60   1.56   1.56   1.02   3.05   1.17   3.98   1.09   2.05   1.70   1.32

Start:     9: 6   9: 8   9: 9  10: 1  10: 6  10: 7  10: 7  10: 9  10:10  10:15  10:18  10:18  10:18  10:20  11: 8  11: 8  11:13  11:13  11:13  11:13  11:13  11:13  11:17
End:       9: 8   9: 9  10: 1  10: 7  10: 7  10:10  10:10  10: 9  10:19  10:15  10:20  10:19  10:19  10:18  11: 9  11:11  11:14  11:14  11:13  11:13  11:13  11:12  11:13
Count:        8      4      3      9      7      5      4      9     59     46      6      3      18     18      9      4    118     31     19      4     22
Width:       26     15      7     17     11     27     66      5    838     46      4     10     59     18    363     31    118     31     19      9    345
Strength:  1.11   1.32   1.17   2.01   1.72   2.00   1.20   1.22   1.03   1.07   1.27   1.07   1.25   1.25   1.47   1.28   1.47   1.28   1.22   1.11   1.18

Start:    11:17  11:17  11:17  11:19  11:22  12:13  12:13  13:13  13:14  13:14  13:14  13:20  13:21  13:23  14: 8  14: 8  14: 8  14: 8  14:10
End:      11:17  11:20  11:18  11:20  12: 1  12:13  12:13  13:13  13:14  13:14  13:14  13:21  13:14  13:14  18:29  24: 7  24:33  16:29  14:14
Count:       17     10      5      5      7     17     12      5      3      5     11     41     26      5    182    603    363   3069    182
Width:      186     81     10     41     71     28     18     11     26     12      8     41   6914  11773   3069    363    182   1147      89
Strength:  1.90   1.77   1.40   1.06   1.13   1.92   1.58   1.43   1.70   1.14   1.01   1.06   1.40   1.40   3.37   3.89   3.05   3.98   2.05

Start:    14:11  14:15  14:13  14:14  16: 5  16:29  16: 5  16:14  16: 7  16: 8  16: 8  16: 8  16: 8  16: 8  16: 8  16: 8  16: 8  16: 8  16:13  16:14  16:15  16:13  16:15
End:      14:14  14:14  14:13  14:14  16: 4  16:29  16:14  16: 7  16: 7  16: 8  16:11  16:11  16:10  16:11  16:10  16:11  16:16  16:16  16:15  16:14  16:15  16:13  16:29
Count:        9     54     25     58    201     51      8     26    134      5      6     16     21      8      6      3      8      9    363      9    288      29      8
Width:       89     54     25     58    201     51     78     26    134      4     21     16     42      8      9      3      8     21      9      9    288
Strength:  1.40   1.44   1.42   4.57   3.60   1.77   1.40   1.13   3.13   1.27   1.80   1.30   2.36   1.14   1.14   1.14   1.14   1.11   1.70   1.11   2.85

Start:    16:15  16:21  16:15  16:15  16:16  16:17  16:17  16:18  16:23  16:23  16:19  16:21  16:23  16:25  16:27  16:27  16:33  16:33  16:37  16:39  16:39  16:39  16:39
End:      16:16  16:18  16:17  16:15  16:17  16:18  16:18  16:18  16:26  16:29  16:21  16:29  16:26  16:26  16:29  16:29  16:54  16:43  16:38  16:39  16:41  16:40  16:40
Count:       16     11      7      4      4      3      3      3      8      5     36     13     27      5      5      8    516    242     28     15     11      7
Width:      145     73     41     10     20     16      4     10     61    109     36     13     27     33      5      8    516    242     28     95     11     30
Strength:  2.18   2.11   1.68   1.07   1.19   1.07   1.30   1.07   1.59   2.04   1.17   1.34   1.38   1.24   1.38   1.14   1.38   2.53   1.35   2.60   2.34   1.89   1.14

Start:    16:39  16:40  16:42  16:50  16:50  16:59  16:59  16:59  16:61  16:60  16: 8  16: 9  16:10  16:10  16:10  16:10  16:13  16:13  16:14  16:15
End:      16:40  16:41  16:51  16:51  16:50  16:59  17: 7  17: 3  16:61  16:60  16: 9  16:10  16:11  16:10  16:11  16:13  16:14  16:15  16:14  16:29
Count:        4      4     27     30      3     28    127     21     11      3      4      5      6     10     57     21     17      8
Width:       16     21     30     30      8    434    219     28     11     11     42     26     10     57    173     17      8      9
Strength:  1.30   1.17   1.01   1.31   1.14   1.42   2.26   1.34   1.15   1.04   1.30   1.21   1.40   1.07   2.34   1.80   1.14   1.11

Start:    17:19  17:20  17:21  17:23  17:23  16:59  16:59  18:27  18:27  18:28  17: 3  17: 3  17: 5  17: 7  17: 7  17:11  17:12  17:13  17:19  17:19
End:      17:20  17:20  17:22  17:24  17:23  17:15  17: 7  18:28  18:28  18:28  17: 7  16:61  17: 7  17: 7  17: 7  17:13  17:13  17:13  17:19  17:22
Count:        5      3      4      6     24    219     21      4     53    127      6      3     10      3      6     50      3      5      7
Width:       21      5      4     24     11    434     28     24    127     53     70     10     41      6     26     50      3     16    209     76
Strength:  1.51   1.11   1.04   1.44   1.43   1.42   2.26   1.09   1.15   1.34   1.94   1.27   1.39   1.20   1.40   1.21   1.40   1.07   1.43   1.60

Start:    20:10  20:11  20:28  20:28  20:34  20:41  21: 8  21:16  22:15  22:16  22:15  21:12  21:12  18:32  18:32  22:20  22:20  22:20  22:30  19: 6  19: 8  19: 9  19:11
End:      20:26  20:20  20:28  20:38  20:38  21:16  21:16  21:16  22:15  22:17  22:15  21:12  21:12  20:38  19: 2  22:21  22:21  22:23  23:27  19: 7  19: 7  19: 9  19:12
Count:        3     10      7      8     74     13     85     26    193     17      7     17      8     33    119     17     57     37     22     25
Width:      111     57      4     95    384    166     85     24    193     30     44    119     68    420   1196     57   1074    555     25      4
Strength:  1.32   1.69   1.04   1.01   1.53   1.29   1.46   1.04   2.53   1.01   1.04   1.62   1.63   2.32   1.69   1.45   1.58   1.66   1.14   1.83   1.06   1.06

Start:    23:13  23:27  23:13  23:16  23:17  23:18  23:18  23:24  23:24  23:26  23:29  23:29  23:47  23:48  24: 1  24:11  24:11  24:18  24:18  24:23
End:      23:27  23:21  23:17  23:17  23:17  23:19  23:21  23:25  23:27  23:27  23:29  23:29  24: 1  24: 7  24:33  24:27  24:24  24:20  24:19  24:24
Count:      299    142     80     34     11     25     56     18     60     11     17     11     58     33    240     68     37      5     35     19     26
Width:      299    142     80     34     11     25     56     18     60     11     17     11     58     33   4697   1233   1074      5      5     42     19
Strength:  1.98   2.02   1.54   1.54   1.04   1.06   1.09   1.25   1.33   1.27   1.04   1.04   1.05   1.24   1.89   1.40   1.00   1.45   1.19   1.04   1.22   1.04
```

Clusters for we- 532-, continued.

```
Start:    24:23  25: 4  25: 7  25: 7  25:10  25:10  25:10  25:12  25:16  26: 4  26: 3  26: 8  26: 7  26: 4  26: 3  26:12  26:12
End:      24:24  25: 7  25: 7  27: 3  26: 1  25:14  25:14  25:14  25:17  26: 4  26: 6  26: 8  26: 6  26: 4  26: 3  26:17  26:14
Count:    3      9      4      43     15     7      87     5      4      10     6      3      5      4      18     11     5
Width:    11     95     19     665    175    76     32     39     19     115    62     27     10     18     261    124    42
Strength: 1.04   1.30   1.22   1.86   1.62   1.03   1.15   1.10   1.22   1.26   1.29   1.38   1.07   1.38   1.26   1.38   1.04

Start:    26:12  26:16  26:16  27:25  27:29  27:31  27:31  28:26  28:26  28:26  28:26  28:26  28:24  28:22  29: 3  29:17  29:12
End:      26:12  26:17  26:17  29:17  27:32  27:32  28:26  28:26  28:26  28:26  28:26  28:26  28:26  28:23  29:17  29:17  29:17
Count:    3      6      8      60     7      3      20     257    41     5      3      8      8      6      6      21     9
Width:    8      38     172    1120   57     23     244    634    257    28     12     149    71     54     334    111
Strength: 1.14   1.46   1.38   1.10   1.39   1.47   1.81   1.69   1.14   1.35   1.40   1.73   1.42   1.13   1.20   1.09   1.04

Start:    29:19  29:19  29:19  29:21  30:    30:    30:    30:    30:    30:19  30:20  30:16  30:14  30:13  30:13  30:22  30:23
End:      31: 1  30:    30:    30:    31:    30:    30:16  30:16  30:20  30:20  30:20  30:16  30:16  30:14  30:13  30:22  30:24
Count:    50     17     11     4      4      4      3      3      3      3      3      4      4      5      3      6      
Width:    562    207    114    59     33     18     11     87     48     10     25     27     9      18     15     34
Strength: 3.43   1.66   1.53   1.35   3.15   2.43   2.52   2.05   1.42   1.07   1.01   1.25   1.42   1.11   1.54   1.04

Start:    30:24  30:25  31: 1  31:12  31:15  31:15  32:    32:    32:    32:    32:12  32:13  33: 4  33: 3  33: 3  33:20
End:      31: 1  30:25  32:17  31:17  32: 17 31:15  32:    32:    32:    32:    32:13  33: 7  33: 4  33: 3  41: 5
Count:    9      4      40     5      5      20     16     9      3      4      3      12     3      5      3      259
Width:    60     22     707    34     30     244    163    65     16     23     10     123    12     20     8      5243
Strength: 1.86   1.14   1.13   1.22   1.63   1.83   1.97   1.78   1.24   1.11   1.07   1.63   1.01   1.53   1.14   1.44

Start:    34:10  34:13  34:22  34:25  34:25  34:25  36:    36:    36:    36:    36:10  36:11  36:11  36:23  36:23  36:23
End:      34:13  34:13  34:27  34:27  34:26  34:27  36:    36:    36:    36:    36:11  36:12  41: 5  36:39  37:15  36:23
Count:    4      20     11     5      3      22     14     22     8      4      5      3      181    59     181    32
Width:    102    282    120    59     22     10     143    311    64     35     17     22     109    1645   181    405
Strength: 1.19   1.43   1.44   1.88   1.49   1.07   1.81   1.51   2.63   2.04   1.60   1.14   1.27   1.49   2.09   3.37   2.30

Start:    36:23  36:24  36:26  36:26  36:27  36:29  36:29  36:29  36:33  36:38  37:    37:    37:    37:10  37:10  37:10
End:      36:26  36:26  36:31  36:28  36:28  36:31  36:30  36:29  37: 4  37: 4  37:    37:    37:    37:13  37:15  37:13
Count:    8      6      12     6      3      4      4      12     12     4      3      3      6      14     8      
Width:    72     40     110    11     6      52     22     162    69     25     231    83     49     121    74
Strength: 1.40   1.41   1.81   1.04   1.04   1.17   1.14   1.01   1.10   1.16   3.07   2.38   1.40   1.23   2.09   1.37

Start:    37:10  37:10  37:14  37:14  37:15  39:    38:    37:19  37:19  37:20  38:    38:    38:    38:18  38:20  38:23
End:      37:11  37:10  37:14  37:15  39:    38:    37:22  37:22  37:20  38:    38:    38:    38:    38: 3  38:21  39: 3
Count:    4      3      6      3      8      50     25     7      4      3      16     9      3      26     3      10
Width:    16     7      25     8      10     878    333    68     21     12     188    34     16     188    12     57
Strength: 1.30   1.17   1.72   1.14   1.07   1.34   1.83   1.18   1.17   1.72   1.53   1.54   1.25   1.68   1.01   2.14

Start:    38:23  38:23  39:    39:    39:    39:    39:21  39:11  39:11  39: 9  39:11  39:13  39:15  39:22  39:22  39:22
End:      38:23  38:23  39:    40:19  40:19  39:28  39:11  39:11  39:    39:    39:13  39:15  39:21  39:28  39:26  39:23
Count:    4      3      2      3      3      39     26     11     7      3      5      6      3      13     9      5
Width:    10     18     54     54     507    335    64     120    7      4      31     14     57     148    86     42
Strength: 1.45   1.58   1.20   1.40   2.47   1.98   1.26   1.44   1.17   1.01   1.28   1.30   1.07   1.53   1.44   1.04

Start:    39:25  40:    43:20  44:    45:18  46: 3  46:12  46:12  46:24  47: 5  47: 4  47: 4  47:10  47: 6  47: 9  47:10
End:      39:26  40:    43:21  44: 5  45:19  46: 1  46:12  46:12  47: 5  47: 5  47: 4  47:10  47: 4  47: 6  47:10  47:10
Count:    3      4      3      5      4      6      2      11     22     7      4      3      5      9      9      3
Width:    11     25     7      27     10     36     32     110    218    30     11     8      90     55     23     21
Strength: 1.04   1.06   1.17   1.38   1.07   1.50   1.06   1.44   2.44   1.89   1.04   1.32   1.87   1.42   1.11   1.11
```

Data for we- 532-, continued.

GAPS:

```
Start:     1:1    1:1    1:4    1:4    1:4    1:4    1:25   1:27   2:3    2:3    2:5    3:3    3:3    3:4    3:4    3:4    3:17   3:20   4:9    4:9    4:9    5:4    5:4
End:       3:23   1:28   1:24   1:15   1:15   1:15   1:28   1:28   2:9    2:9    2:7    3:11   3:11   3:11   3:10   3:11   3:20   3:22   4:15   4:13   4:15   5:10   5:8
Count:     47     6      3      2      2      3      3      2      3      2      5      3      3      4      3      3      2      3      9      9      4      5      8
Width:     1323   584    526    399    215    100    55     155    155    48     91     165    165    156    145    113    78     54     116    69     151    151    109
Strength:  2.08   6.53   8.42   11.35  8.71   1.77   1.46   1.49   1.48   1.15   1.48   1.72   1.72   2.33   3.21   4.09   2.50   1.42   1.28   2.10   1.40   1.40   2.06

Start:     5:6    5:8    5:13   5:13   5:15   5:16   6:10   6:12   7:1    7:16   7:3    7:4    7:8    7:9    7:16   7:18   7:21   8:10   8:12   8:13   9:1    9:2    9:9    9:9    9:1    10:1   10:18  10:18  10:15
End:       5:10   5:13   5:16   5:16   5:16   5:16   6:12   6:12   7:16   7:16   7:7    7:8    7:16   7:16   7:16   7:21   7:21   8:12   8:13   8:13   9:2    9:2    9:18   9:18   10:1   10:18  10:18  10:15  10:15
Count:     2      2      4      2      2      2      8      8      10     2      3      3      3      3      3      3      3      4      2      2      9      9      4      4      2      53     119
Width:     78     77     89     56     63     289    10     156    127    47     94     94     80     175    306    111    177    78     94     83     54     53     181    173    119
Strength:  2.50   2.46   1.41   1.51   1.83   1.35   1.02   2.55   4.72   1.10   3.56   2.60   2.60   3.23   2.06   4.00   2.88   1.83   1.58   1.22   1.42   1.37   2.98   4.11   4.36

Start:     11:5   11:8   11:13  11:13  11:14  11:17  11:20  11:25  12:1   12:1   12:4   12:7   12:8   12:9   12:13  12:13  12:13  12:13  12:21  12:21  12:21  12:22  12:25  12:26  12:26  13:1   13:9   13:13
End:       11:8   11:17  11:17  11:21  11:17  11:17  13:14  12:13  12:13  12:13  12:13  12:13  12:13  12:20  12:20  13:14  13:14  12:25  12:25  13:14  13:14  12:26  13:13  13:14  13:13
Count:     2      2      6      4      2      2      8      7      3      3      5      2      8      2      2      13     14     2      2      14     13     2      2      6      2
Width:     58     70     91     171    152    79     938    264    253    52     184    126    175    48     89     95     93     83     71     166    192    52     121    79     47
Strength:  1.60   2.14   1.48   1.21   2.23   2.55   1.08   1.86   2.22   1.33   2.15   2.60   2.83   1.15   3.00   1.61   1.54   1.22   1.52   1.11   1.33   1.41   1.41   1.48   1.10

Start:     13:9   13:13  13:15  13:15  13:19  13:20  14:2   14:2   14:4   14:14  14:15  14:15  14:15  14:19  14:22  14:23  15:5   15:3   15:5   16:1   16:5   16:29  16:29  16:33  16:37  16:36
End:       13:13  13:21  13:20  13:18  13:20  13:18  14:14  14:8   14:8   14:15  14:22  14:17  14:22  15:5   15:5   16:16  16:16  16:37  16:37  16:37  16:36
Count:     2      4      2      6      14     14     2      8      4      5      5      3      5      3      5      3      6      2      7      5      5      9      2      2      2
Width:     70     171    152    4      192    55     177    111    306    175    48     89     95     147    323    138    192    79     184    67     159    153    173    119    47
Strength:  2.14   1.21   2.23   2.23   1.64   1.46   2.88   4.00   2.06   3.00   2.83   1.15   1.61   1.46   3.18   2.99   1.09   1.22   1.48   2.01   1.59   2.25   1.41   4.36   1.10

Start:     16:42  16:42  16:43  16:43  16:47  16:50  16:50  16:50  16:51  16:51  16:51  16:51  16:53  16:54  16:59  16:59  16:60  16:60  17:4   17:5   17:7   17:7   17:11  17:12  17:13  17:13  17:13  17:19  17:13
End:       16:50  16:50  16:47  16:47  16:60  16:60  16:51  16:60  16:53  16:59  17:20  17:12  17:20  17:19  17:13  17:13
Count:     5      5      3      8      6      5      4      2      2      40     4      11     5      2      3      5      4      3      2      2
Width:     190    183    169    112    215    193    181    168    175    45     93     154    138    159    153    147    323    114    192    135    128    45     95     269    101    89     67
Strength:  2.29   3.04   3.98   4.05   1.02   1.66   2.08   2.64   3.18   1.01   3.18   1.47   2.99   1.59   2.25   3.27   1.46   4.14   1.09   1.04   1.60   1.01   3.27   1.05   1.80   3.00   2.01

Start:     17:15  17:19  17:23  17:23  17:23  17:24  18:   18:1   18:5   18:10  18:10  18:10  18:14  18:14  18:19  18:21  18:26  18:28  18:29  18:32  18:32  20:11  20:13  20:14  20:14  20:17  20:20  20:14
End:       17:19  18:26  18:21  18:10  18:10  18:4   18:4   18:10  18:21  18:14  18:19  18:32  18:32  20:13  20:13  20:21  20:21  20:24  20:17
Count:     2      2      16     11     4      4      3      6      5      2      4      3      2      19     5      2      4      2      7      6      2      6      2
Width:     96     562    557    440    198    185    159    90     236    68     159    95     101    89     47     189    176    135    135    71
Strength:  3.32   2.36   2.64   3.14   2.47   3.09   3.66   3.05   2.53   2.05   2.41   3.27   1.80   3.00   1.10   1.03   1.31   1.78   2.55   2.19

Start:     20:18  20:20  20:22  20:22  20:22  20:22  20:26  20:28  20:29  20:29  20:34  20:34  20:37  20:38  20:38  20:38  20:41  20:41  21:12  21:13  21:13  21:14  21:16  21:22  21:23  21:23  21:23  21:28  21:23
End:       20:20  20:28  20:28  20:27  20:26  20:22  20:34  20:34  20:41  20:41  21:22  21:22  21:22  21:23  21:32  21:42
Count:     47     147    131    109    79     122    112    135    128    118    96     93     45     510    555    158    125    334    200    104
Width:     47     147    131    109    79     122    112    135    128    118    96     572    510    555    169    158    125    334    200    104
Strength:  1.10   1.31   1.68   2.06   2.55   2.47   4.05   1.04   1.60   2.34   3.32   2.16   3.20   2.62   2.67   3.63   4.63   2.51   4.97   3.68

Start:     21:33  21:36  22:4   22:4   22:4   22:4   22:12  22:15  22:17  22:20  23:    23:1   23:4   23:7   23:10  23:21  23:24  23:27  23:29  23:34  23:34  23:43  23:42  23:34  23:42
End:       21:36  22:20  22:16  22:15  22:15  22:12  22:30  22:30  22:26  22:23  23:24  23:10  23:42  23:48
Count:     2      9      7      4      4      8      5      2      4      2      3      2      15     6      5      196
Width:     54     305    216    197    191    139    84     230    187    142    165    76     48     80     541    189    200    208    196
Strength:  1.42   2.05   1.53   3.40   4.68   5.27   2.78   1.54   1.96   2.41   1.06   1.13   1.00   2.81   2.00   1.96   2.42

Start:     23:36  23:42  23:44  23:44  23:48  24:1   24:3   24:11  24:11  24:11  24:11  24:11  24:18  24:23  24:22  24:23  24:24  24:24  24:27  25:4   25:7   25:10  26:3   26:8   26:6   26:12  27:25
End:       23:42  23:48  23:48  24:11  24:11  24:23  24:11  24:18  24:11  24:23  24:27  24:20  24:24  24:27  25:    25:2   26:    26:20
Count:     3      2      3      2      6      3      9      4      250    162    143    137    77     78     62     49     51     47     76
Width:     153    81     83     58     234    206    162    250    143    137    77     78     62     51     47     76     208
Strength:  3.47   2.64   1.22   1.60   2.49   5.16   6.31   1.16   1.99   2.95   2.41   1.06   1.03   1.78   1.19   1.28   1.10   2.41   7.24
```

Gaps for we- 532-, continued.

Block 1

Start	End	Count	Width	Strength
26:20	27:25	5	459	8.39
27: 3	27:25	2	402	17.18
27:25	27:31	4	106	1.02
27:25	27:29	2	72	2.23
27:32	28:16	12	370	1.03
27:32	28: 7	3	355	1.52
27:32	28: 1		192	1.09
27:32	28: 2		97	1.67
28: 8	28:16	4	147	2.09
28:12	28:16	2	93	3.18
28:16	28:18	2	45	1.01
29:17	29:19		75	2.37
30:20	30:22		60	1.69
31: 1	31: 5	5	86	2.87
31: 5	31: 9	3	140	1.15
31: 7	31: 9	7	88	1.38
31:12	31:15		81	1.46
31:16	31:18	2	46	2.64

Block 2

Start	End	Count	Width	Strength
32:13	33: 3	18	500	1.37
32:13	32:30	10	392	2.91
32:13	32:15	2	58	1.60
32:16	32:30	8	327	2.94
32:16	32:27	5	252	2.86
32:16	32:27	2	230	3.20
32:17	32:24	3	147	3.27
32:25	32:27	2	100	3.50
32:30	32:23	2	49	1.19
33: 3	36:11	66	1924	2.81
33: 6	36: 9	62	1897	3.26
33: 6	34:25	35	1223	3.71
33: 6	34:13	27	950	3.63
33: 6	34:11	24	908	3.80
33: 6	34: 5	16	756	4.98
33: 7	33: 5	14	723	5.49
33: 8	33:28	8	501	5.93

Block 3

Start	End	Count	Width	Strength
33: 7	33: 7	7	352	7.46
33:22	33:20	28	299	12.52
33:22	33:28	4	138	1.86
33:24	33:28	3	96	3.32
33:29	34: 6	6	215	2.11
33:29	34: 5	3	123	2.50
33:31	34: 5	3	84	1.25
33:33	34: 8	2	70	2.14
34: 1	34: 5	2	69	2.10
34: 5	34: 8	2	48	1.15
34:25	34:26	2	263	1.85
34:22	34:25	6	257	2.29
34:13	34:25	4	251	2.84
34:13	34:13		245	3.54
34:13	34:13		239	4.50
34:26	34:26		178	1.03
35: 3	35: 3	3	666	2.21
36: 9	36:15		492	3.17
36:10	36:10	10	409	

Block 4

Start	End	Count	Width	Strength
35: 8	35: 9	9	161	1.63
35:15	35:12	2	87	1.35
36: 1	36: 5	5	57	1.55
36: 3	36: 2	2	51	1.28
36: 9	36: 9		235	3.31
36: 6	36: 6	2	182	4.40
36:12	36:16		103	3.64
36:16	36:23		70	2.14
36:21	36:23		48	1.15
36:31	36:33	6	163	1.05
36:33	37:21	4	123	1.47
37:23	37:23	3	117	2.31
37:19	37:19	3	108	3.86
37:15	37:23	4	52	1.33
38: 4	38:10	9	145	1.27
38:10	38:10	8	135	1.78
38: 4	38: 7	2	109	2.06
38: 9	38: 3	67	2.01

Block 5

Start	End	Count	Width	Strength
38:11	38:11	130	276	2.07
38:20	38:16	86	142	1.96
38:16	38:20	74	97	3.37
38:18	38: 2	59	93	1.54
39: 3	39: 9	45	119	1.36
39: 2	39:20	9	106	1.48
39: 9	39:28	9	91	1.87
39: 9	39:28	5	65	1.92
39:17	40: 1	2	64	1.09
39:17	40: 5	7	79	1.20
43: 1	40: 5	7	198	2.51
43: 5	40: 1		1334	4.97
46:12	40: 2	53	2306	6.23
40: 3	40: 3		2524	5.14
40: 5	40: 4		2940	5.01
40: 6	40: 6		4656	7.59
841			2524	

Block 6

Start	End	Count	Width	Strength
40: 6	40: 6	13	511	3.22
40:32	40:23	9	343	2.66
40:32	40:23	7	294	2.98
40:17	40:13	3	81	1.16
40:14	40:23	4	195	3.35
40:19	40:17	2	55	1.46
40:24	40:23	4	109	3.91
40:24	40:28	2	84	2.78
40:28	40:32		160	2.43
40:32	40:48	5	322	5.28
40:32	40:45	3	265	7.05
40:35	40:45	2	206	8.30
40:32	40:48	14	883	11.33
40:28	40:32	67	967	8.57
40:32	40:32	84	305	6.23
41: 1	41: 5	9	427	12.25
41: 5	42: 1	5	351	14.87
42:43	447	6.81		

Block 7

Start	End	Count	Width	Strength
42: 1	42: 1	5	429	7.71
43: 3	43: 1	4	371	7.96
42: 1	42:14	2	212	8.57
42:13	43: 1	2	94	3.23
43: 5	43:20	12	413	2.32
43: 7	43:20	11	409	2.69
43:19	43:20	8	132	4.95
43:18	43:18	6	190	4.65
43:19	43:21	2	1297	5.30
45:18	45:18	44	1713	5.35
43:20	46:12	31	172	1.23
43:20	44:10	4	124	1.49
43:18	44: 7	6	51	1.28
44: 5	44: 6	58	1.60	
339	310	80	79	
3.40	3.80	4.27	4.62	5.01

Block 8

Start	End	Count	Width	Strength
44:11	45:18	12	906	9.08
44:16	44:13	6	165	1.09
44:11	44:12	3	83	1.22
44:13	45:18	2	60	1.69
44:17	44:19	6	736	12.68
44:19	45:18	2	66	1.96
44:19	44:28	13	663	15.60
44:19	45:14	5	329	13.87
45:18	46: 2	4	412	1.92
46:12	46:12	6	170	1.19
46: 2	46: 2	5	164	1.70
46:12	46:12	4	310	5.01
46:12	46:12	3	190	4.62
46: 3	47: 2	132	124	4.27
46:12	47: 5	171	172	1.28
46:12	46:21	207	51	1.94

Block 9

Start	End	Count	Width	Strength
46:12	48:21	2	105	3.73
46:17	48:35	19	50	1.24
47:10	48:18	16	1000	6.46
47:21	47:21	4	681	4.10
47:10	47:12	6	244	2.69
47:14	47:21	3	103	1.86
47:17	47:21	2	122	2.47
47:22	48:18	10	82	2.69
47:23	48:10	8	427	3.44
48:10	48:10	4	387	3.97
48:18	48:17	3	201	3.51
48:12	48: 6	2	163	3.79
48: 1	48: 8	113	4.09	
48: 8	48:12	158	2.38	
48:18	48:35	119	313	2.46
48:15	48:35	77	234	8.59
48:21	343	310	207	
48:35	199	191	1.67	9.57
7.62	4.94	3.68	3.01	

Linguistic Density Plot in Ezekiel 1 - 48

For zō't 6243 (23 times)

Each Column = 13 Verses.   Separations are: Max =   5891.00, Mean =   1165.42, Min =   7.00 .

```
CLUSTERS:

Start:      3: 1    3: 1    3: 1    3: 2   20:27   20:27   21:31   21:31   21:31   36:37   43:12   43:12   43:12   45: 3   47:14   47:20
End:       11: 6    6:10    3: 3    3: 3   23:38   21:32   21:32   21:31   21:31   48:29   48:29   45:16   43:12   45:16   48:29   47:21   47:21
Count:      7       5       3       2       4       5       3       4       9      10       5       3       2       4       3       2
Width:      3615    1664    33      16      2550    1081    1445    14      7474    3284    1445    14      300     754     123
Strength:   1.39    1.43    1.48    1.02    1.01    1.30    1.49    1.04    1.11    2.29    1.54    1.02    1.31    1.48    1.42    1.03

GAPS:

Start:     11: 6   11: 6   11: 6   21:31   21:32   23:38   23:38
End:       21:31   20:27   17: 7   47:20   43:12   36:37
Count:      4       3       2      11      10       4       3       2
Width:      6849    5782    3773    15909   15897   13251   11782   7592
Strength:   1.81    2.23    2.33    1.54    1.99    5.27    6.11    5.74
```

Linguistic Density Plot in Ezekiel 1 - 48

For zebaḥ 111 (7 times)

Each Column = 13 Verses.   Separations are: Max = 11760.00, Mean = 3496.25, Min =   23.00 .

REFERENCE

DENSITY (vertical axis)

REFERENCE

CLUSTERS:

```
Start:     20:28  39:17  39:17  39:17
End:       46:24  46:24  40:42  39:19  39:17
Count:       7      6      4      3      2
Width:     16491   4731   1190    46      7
Strength:   1.11   2.82   2.06   1.72   1.13
```

GAPS:

```
Start:      1: 1  20:28
End:       39:17  39:17
Count:       3      2
Width:     22033  11760
Strength:   3.72   2.67
```

Linguistic Density Plot in Ezekiel 1 - 48

For zbḥ 311 (1 times)   zbḥ 312 (3 times)   zbḥ 314 (1 times)

Each Column = 13 Verses. Separations are: Max = 5883.50, Mean = 4661.66, Min = 1733.50 .

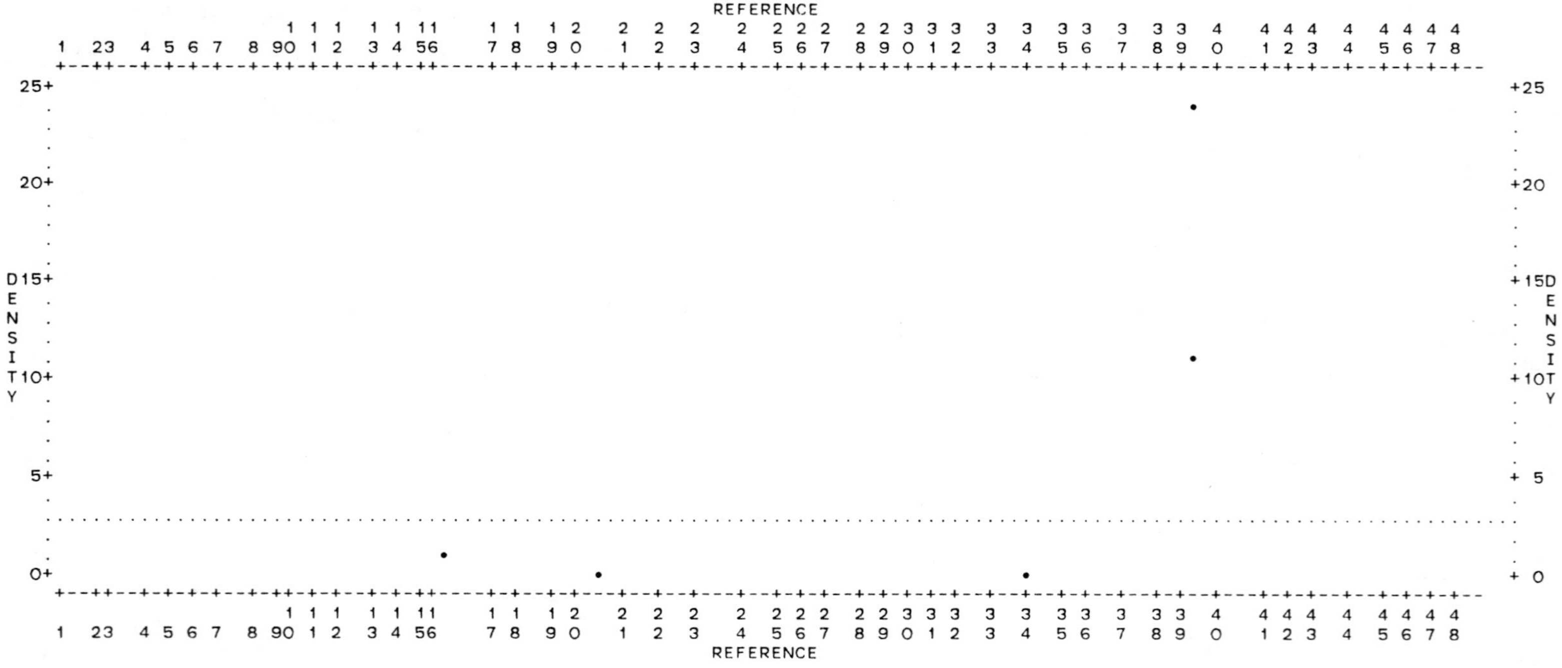

REFERENCE

CLUSTERS:

Start:	34: 3	39:17
End:	39:19	39:19
Count:	3	2
Width:	3467	45
Strength:	1.17	1.17

All gap strengths are less than 1.00.

Linguistic Density Plot in Ezekiel 1 - 48

For zeh 6213 (30 times)

Each Column = 13 Verses.   Separations are: Max = 5104.00, Mean =   902.26, Min =   21.50 .

CLUSTERS:

```
Start:     12:10  12:22  18: 2  24: 2  40: 1  40:45  43:13  43:13  45: 2  45: 7  46:20  46:20  47: 7  47: 7  47:12  47:12  48:21
End:       12:23  12:23  18: 3  24: 2  48:21  41:22  48:21  45: 7  45: 7  45: 7  48:21  47:15  47: 7  47:15  47:12  47:12  48:21
Count:         3      2      2     18      2     14      5      3      2      9      7      6      2      4      2      3
Width:       272     27     26      9   5368    555   3094   1195    113    430   1031    193     84      3
Strength:   1.26   1.00   1.02   4.05   1.02   3.53   1.45   1.39   2.37   2.55   2.85   1.02   2.55   1.79   1.02   1.02
```

GAPS:

```
Start:      1: 1   1: 1   1: 1   1: 5   2: 3   2: 3  12:23  18: 3  20:29  24: 2  24: 2
End:       48:21  47:12  47: 7  45: 7  24: 2  12:10  12:10   8: 5  18: 2  16:49  12:23  24: 2  45: 2  40:45  40: 1
Count:        30     26     24     21     12      4      3      3      2      3      2      9      8      3      2
Width:     27698  27016  26907  25799  13054   4965   4399   2623   3344   2435   4352  12736   2744  10208   9270
Strength:   1.26   2.28   2.84   3.27   1.32   1.54   2.13   1.96   1.26   1.75   2.09   2.55   2.10   3.05   6.91   9.57
```

Linguistic Density Plot in Ezekiel 1 - 48

For zāhāb 111 (8 times)

Each Column = 13 Verses.   Separations are: Max =   6334.50, Mean =   3107.78, Min =   238.00 .

CLUSTERS:

Start:	7:19	7:19	16:13	27:22	28:4
End:	16:17	16:17	28:13	28:13	
Count:	4	2	3	2	
Width:	4098	8	97	476	159
Strength:	1.25	1.11	1.08	1.56	1.06

GAPS:

Start:	16:17	16:17	28:13	38:13
End:	48:35	27:22	48:35	48:35
Count:	6	2	3	2
Width:	20907	7762	12669	6569
Strength:	1.22	1.67	1.75	1.24

Linguistic Density Plot in Ezekiel 1 - 48

For zhr 321 (5 times)   zhr 361 (8 times)   zhr 3662 (2 times)

Each Column = 13 Verses. Separations are: Max = 8276.50, Mean = 1748.13, Min = 10.50 .

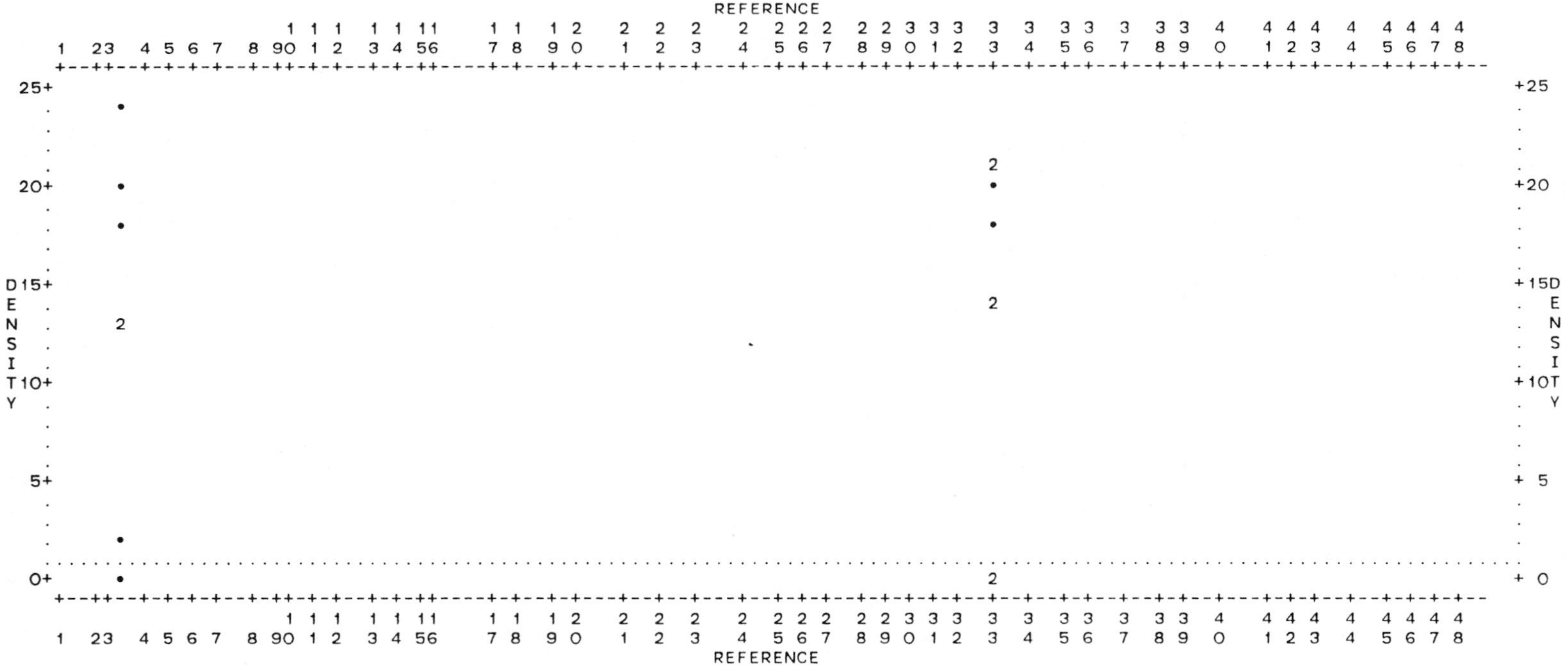

CLUSTERS:

Start:	3:17	3:17	3:17	3:18	3:18	3:20	3:21	3:21	33: 3	33: 3	33: 3	33: 5	33: 7
End:	33: 9	3:21	3:19	3:18	3:18	3:21	3:21	3:21	33: 9	33: 4	33: 6	33: 9	33: 9
Count:	15	7	4	3	2	3	2	8	5	2	3	2	
Width:	16800	127	46	21	6	37	14	134	57	11	27	8	39	18
Strength:	3.42	3.15	1.96	1.54	1.06	1.54	1.05	3.59	2.36	1.05	1.54	1.05	1.54	1.05

GAPS:

Start:	3:18	3:18	3:21	33: 8	33: 9
End:	48:35	33: 5	33: 3	48:35	48:35
Count:	14	8	6	3	2
Width:	26779	16675	16645	16539	10021	10000
Strength:	1.53	1.31	2.51	9.00	2.90	5.02

Linguistic Density Plot in Ezekiel 1 - 48

For zhr 321 (5 times)

Each Column = 13 Verses. Separations are: Max = 16550.00, Mean = 4661.66, Min =   13.50 .

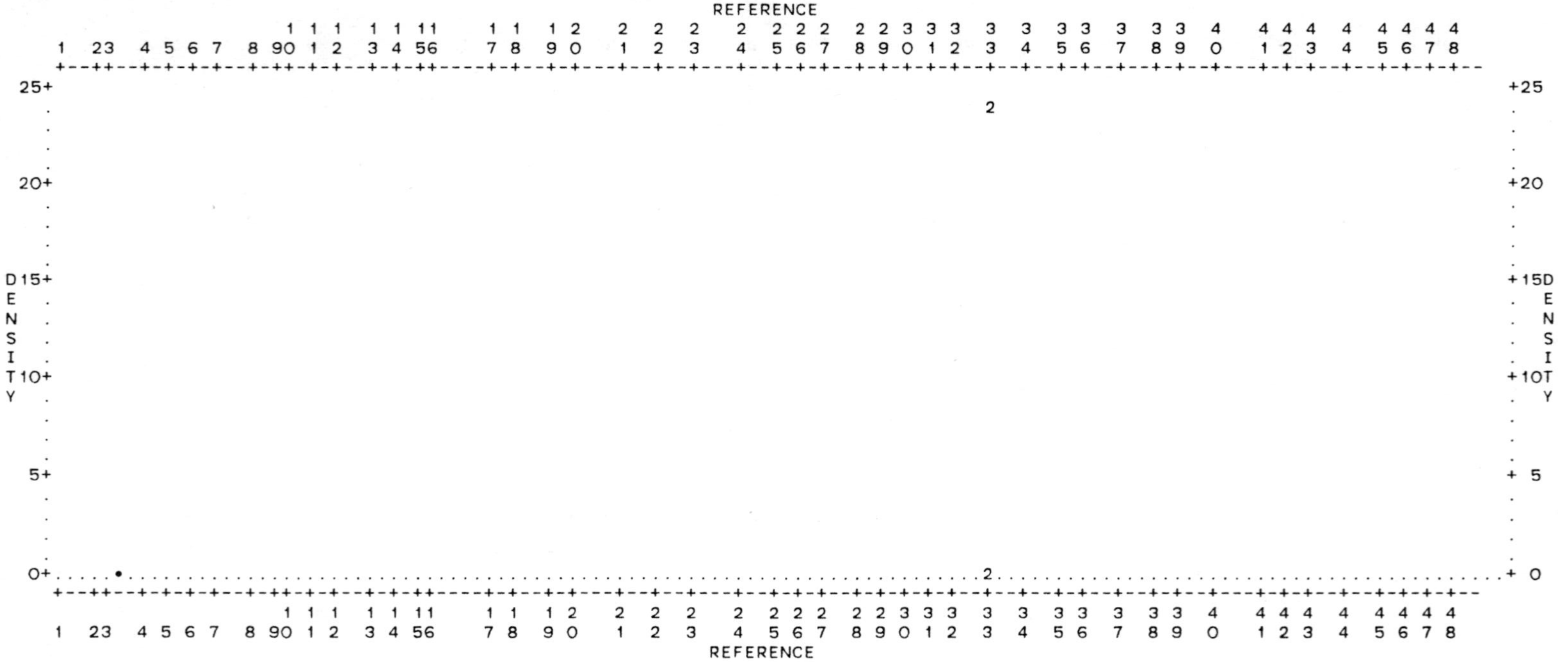

CLUSTERS:

Start:	33: 4	33: 4	33: 5
End:	33: 6	33: 5	33: 5
Count:	4	3	2
Width:	46	27	8
Strength:	2.63	1.86	1.18

GAPS:

Start:	1: 1	3:21	33: 6
End:	33: 4	33: 4	48:35
Count:	3	2	
Width:	17846	16550	10077
Strength:	1.71	3.01	1.37

Linguistic Density Plot in Ezekiel 1 - 48

For zhr 361 (8 times)   zhr 3662 (2 times)

Each Column = 13 Verses.   Separations are: Max = 8324.00, Mean = 2542.73, Min = 10.50 .

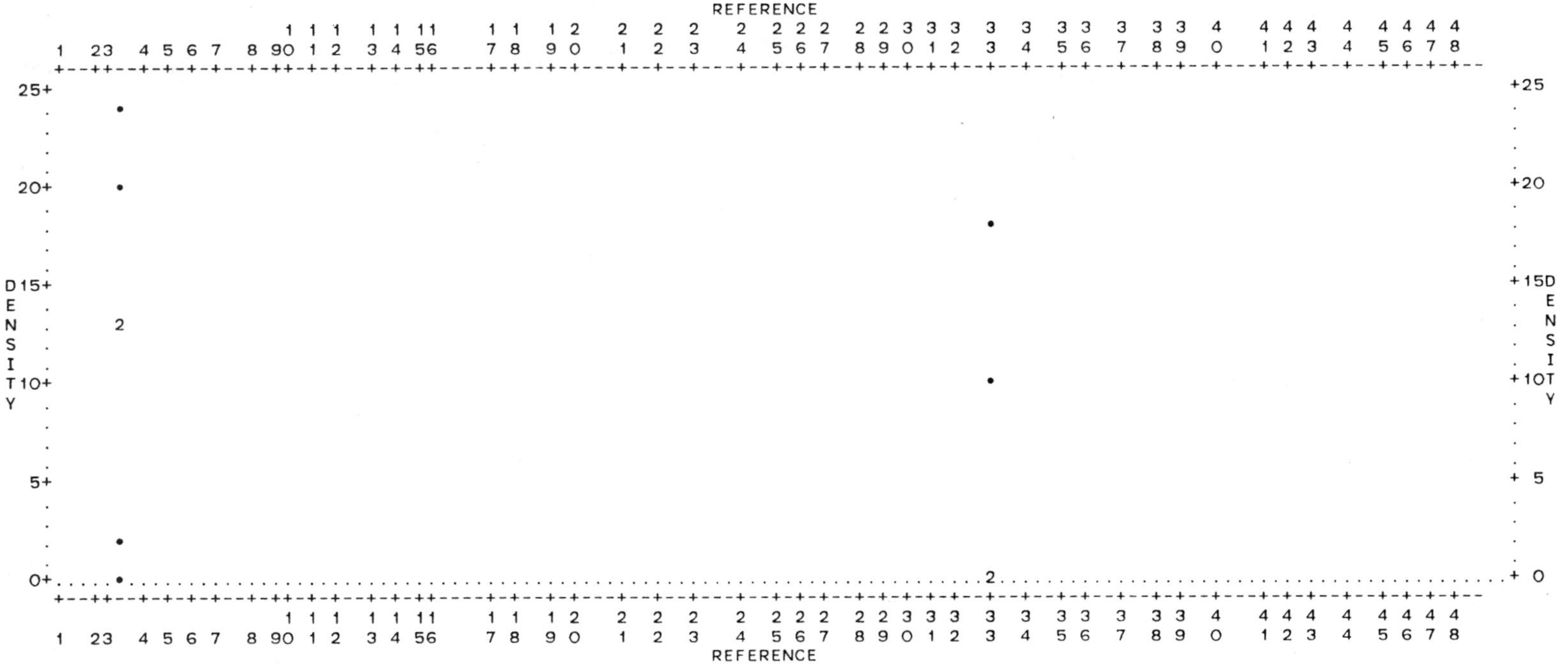

REFERENCE

CLUSTERS:

Start:	3:17	3:17	3:17	3:18	3:20	33: 3	33: 7	33: 7
End:	33: 9	3:21	3:19	3:18	3:21	33: 9	33: 9	33: 8
Count:	10	6	4	3	2	4	3	2
Width:	16800	113	46	21	6	23	134	39	18
Strength:	1.95	3.13	2.10	1.62	1.09	1.08	2.08	1.62	1.08

GAPS:

Start:	3:18	3:18	3:21	3:21	33: 8	33: 9
End:	48:35	33: 7	33: 3	48:35	48:35
Count:	9	6	3	2
Width:	26779	16648	16553	10021	10000
Strength:	1.78	1.00	3.71	1.58	3.21

Linguistic Density Plot in Ezekiel 1 - 48

For zhr 361 (8 times)

Each Column = 13 Verses.   Separations are: Max = 8324.00. Mean = 3107.78, Min = 23.00 .

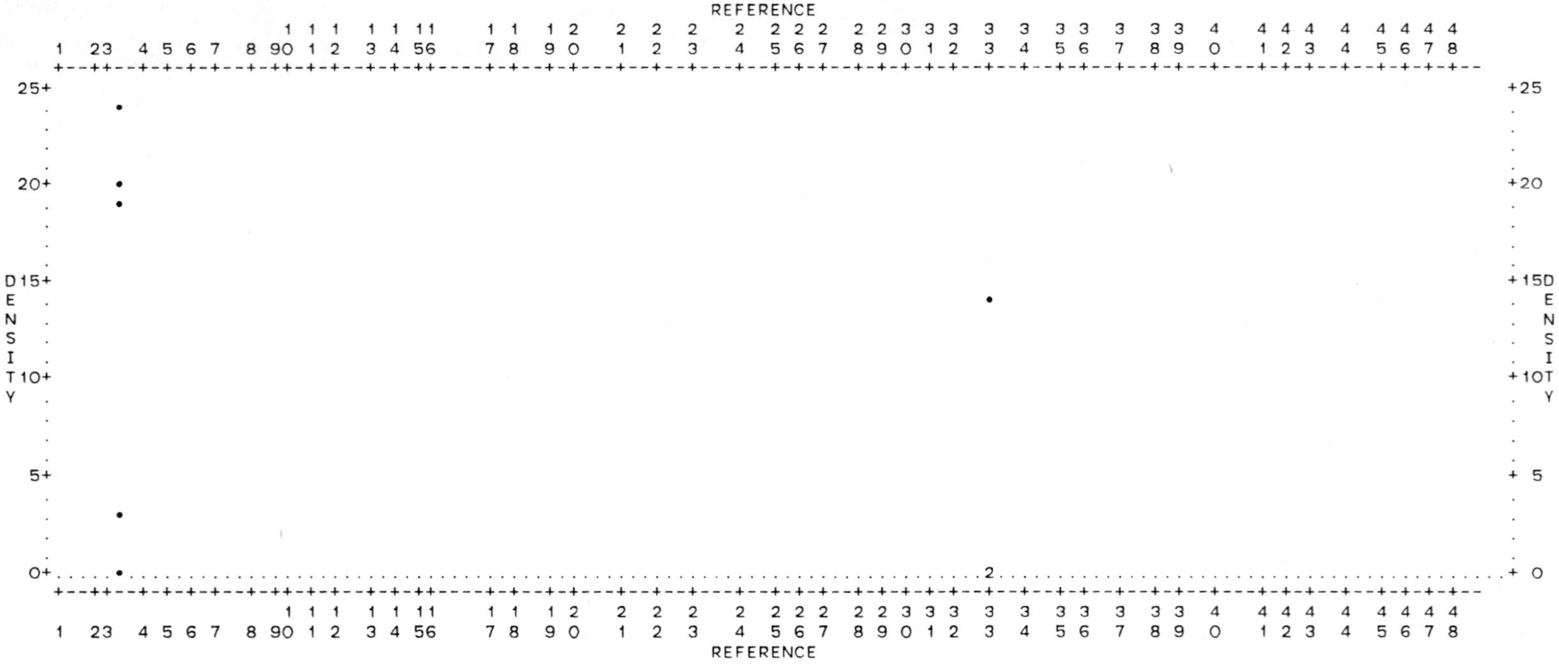

CLUSTERS:

Start:	3:17	3:17	3:17	3:20	33: 3	33: 7
End:	33: 9	3:21	3:18	3:21	33: 9	33: 9
Count:	8	5	3	2	3	2
Width:	16800	113	46	15	134	39
Strength:	1.34	2.80	1.67	1.11	1.65	1.10

GAPS:

Start:	3:18	3:21	3:21	33: 9	
End:	48:35	48:35	33: 7	33: 3	48:35
Count:	8	5	3	2	
Width:	26785	26687	16648	16553	10000
Strength:	1.36	3.24	2.83	4.83	2.47

Linguistic Density Plot in Ezekiel 1 - 48

For zkr 311 (7 times)   zkr 312 (2 times)   zkr 3162 (1 times)   zkr 322 (7 times)
     zkr 3262 (1 times)   zkr 361 (1 times)   zkr 364 (2 times)

Each Column = 13 Verses. Separations are: Max = 4897.50, Mean = 1271.36, Min = 14.00

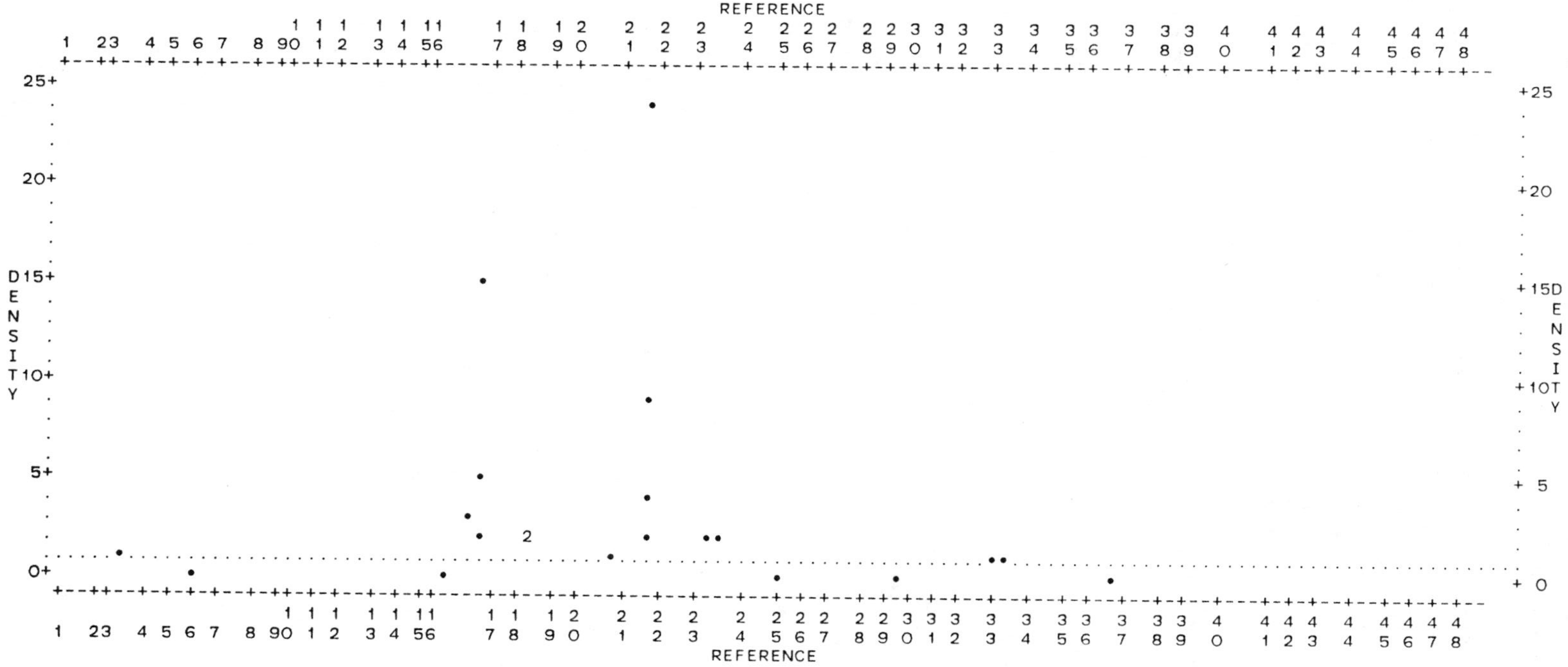

CLUSTERS:

Start:	3:20	3:20	16:22	16:22	16:60	16:22	18:22	20:43	21:28	21:28	21:28	33:13
End:	36:31	25:10	25:10	18:24	16:61	16:63	18:24	25:10	21:37	21:29	21:29	33:16
Count:	21	17	15	7	3	5	2	8	3	2	2	2
Width:	18986	12541	6630	1958	894	67	18	3157	781	190	12	51
Strength:	3.84	3.00	3.98	2.18	1.86	1.47	1.03	2.11	1.91	1.81	1.49	1.03

GAPS:

Start:	1:1	1:1	6:9	21:29	25:10	33:16	36:31
End:	16:43	16:22	16:22	48:35	33:13	48:35	48:35
Count:	5	4	2	11	3	3	2
Width:	7619	7178	4735	16715	16699	9795	7716
Strength:	1.12	1.68	2.85	1.83	1.05	4.32	5.30

Linguistic Density Plot in Ezekiel 1 - 48

For zkr 311 (7 times)   zkr 312 (2 times)   zkr 3162 (1 times)

Each Column = 13 Verses.   Separations are: Max = 7697.00, Mean = 2542.73, Min = 33.50

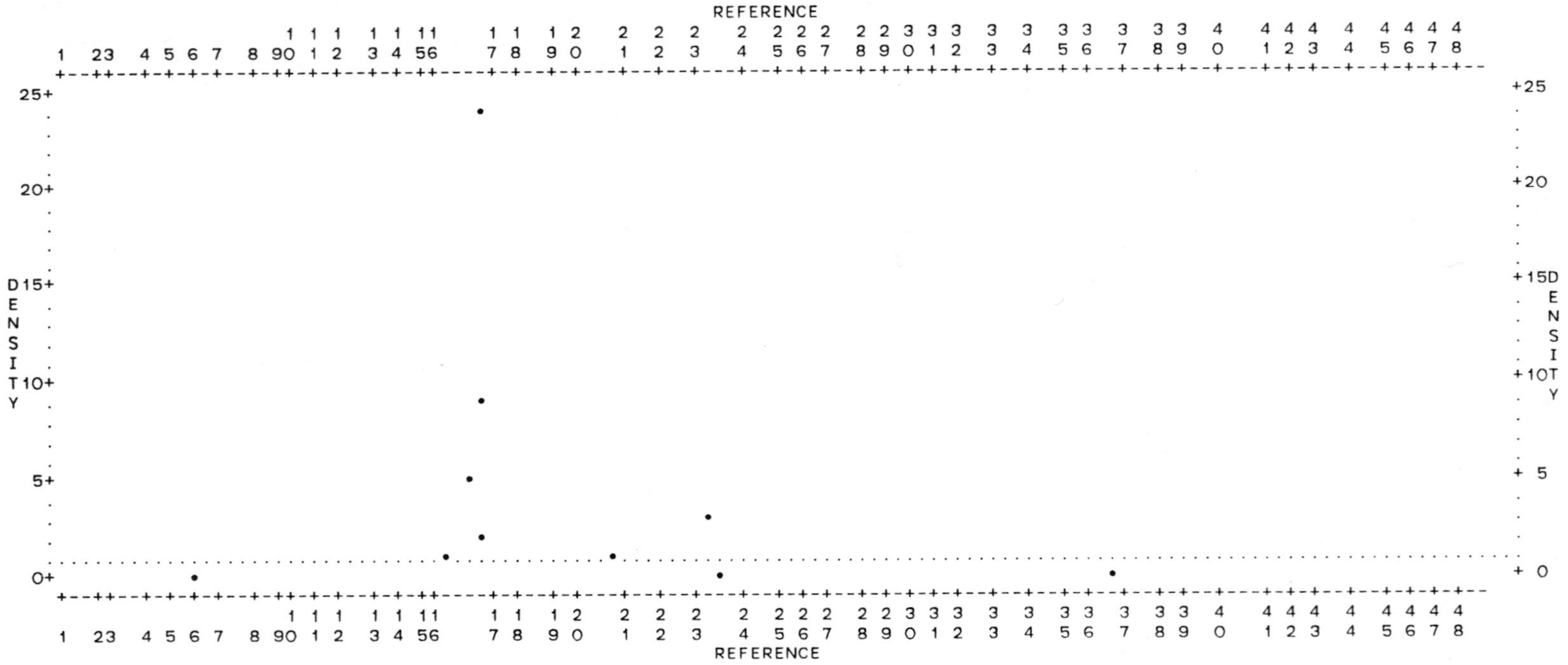

(Plot — vertical axis: DENSITY, scale +25, +20, +15, +10, +5, 0; horizontal axis: REFERENCE)

CLUSTERS:

Start:	6: 9	6: 9	16:22	16:60	16:60	20:43	23:19
End:	36:31	23:27	16:63	16:63	16:61	23:27	23:27
Count:	10	9	8	5	3	2	3	2
Width:	17810	10132	5397	894	67	18	1924	206
Strength:	1.62	2.83	3.19	2.38	1.61	1.08	1.01	1.00

GAPS:

Start:	16:61	16:63	23:27	36:31
End:	48:35	48:35	48:35
Count:	7	6	3	2
Width:	19946	19897	15394	7716
Strength:	1.16	1.78	3.31	2.22

For zkr 311 (7 times)

Linguistic Density Plot in Ezekiel 1 - 48

Each Column = 13 Verses.   Separations are: Max = 9602.00, Mean = 3496.25, Min = 202.00 .

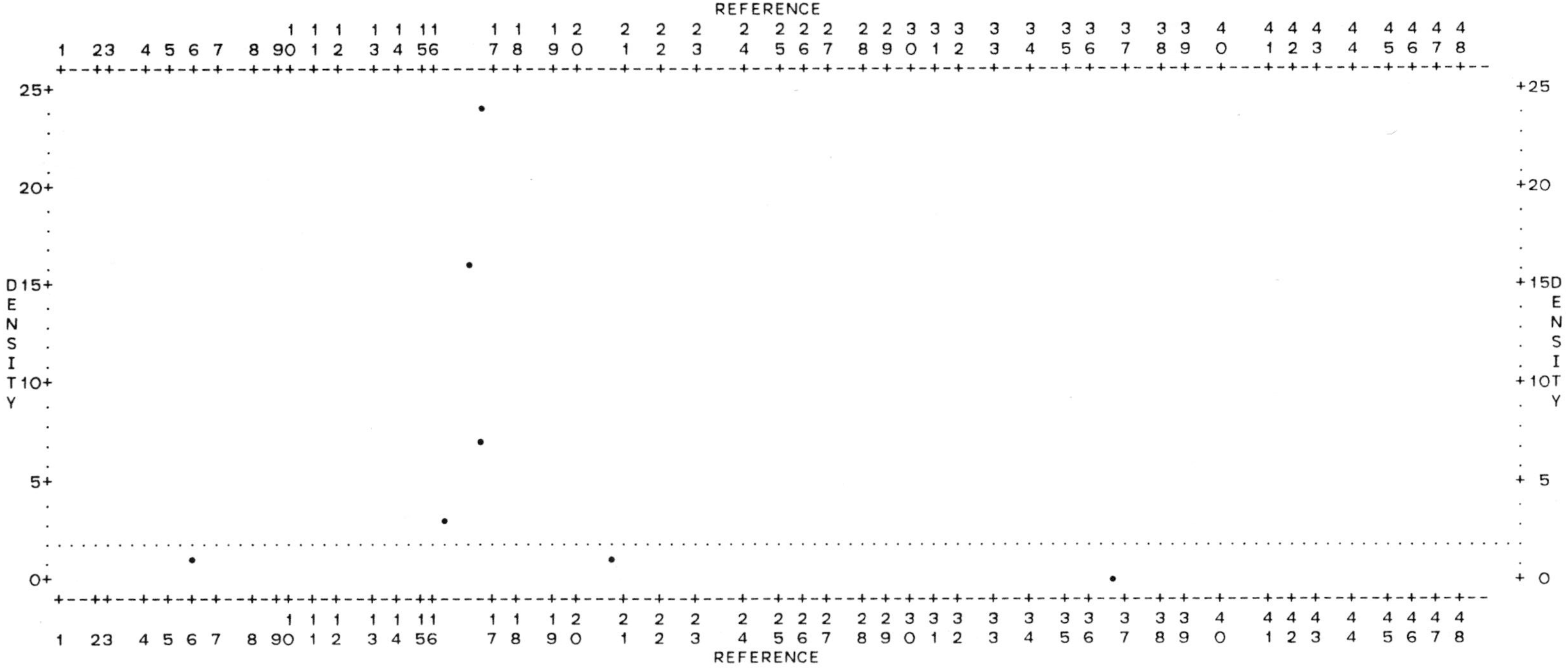

CLUSTERS:

Start:	6: 9	16:22	16:43	16:60	
End:	20:43	20:43	16:61	16:61	
Count:	6	5	4	3	2
Width:	8208	3473	845	404	18
Strength:	2.05	2.25	2.13	1.63	1.12

GAPS:

Start:	16:61	20:43	
End:	48:35	48:35	36:31
Count:	4	3	2
Width:	19946	17318	9602
Strength:	2.09	2.55	1.98

Linguistic Density Plot in Ezekiel 1 - 48

For zkr 322 (7 times)   zkr 3262 (1 times)

Each Column = 13 Verses. Separations are: Max = 7816.00, Mean = 3107.78, Min = 1093.50 .

REFERENCE

REFERENCE

CLUSTERS:

```
Start:      3:20  18:22  18:22  21:29  33:13
End:       33:16  33:16  21:37  21:37  33:16
Count:         8      7      4      2      2
Width:     16907   9091   2349     53    162     51
Strength:   1.31   2.29   1.67   1.09   1.05   1.09
```

GAPS:

```
Start:      3:20  33:16
End:       18:22  48:35
Count:         2      2
Width:      7816   9795
Strength:   1.69   2.40
```

Linguistic Density Plot in Ezekiel 1 - 48

For zkr 322 (7 times)

Each Column = 13 Verses. Separations are: Max = 7816.00, Mean = 3496.25, Min = 1174.50 .

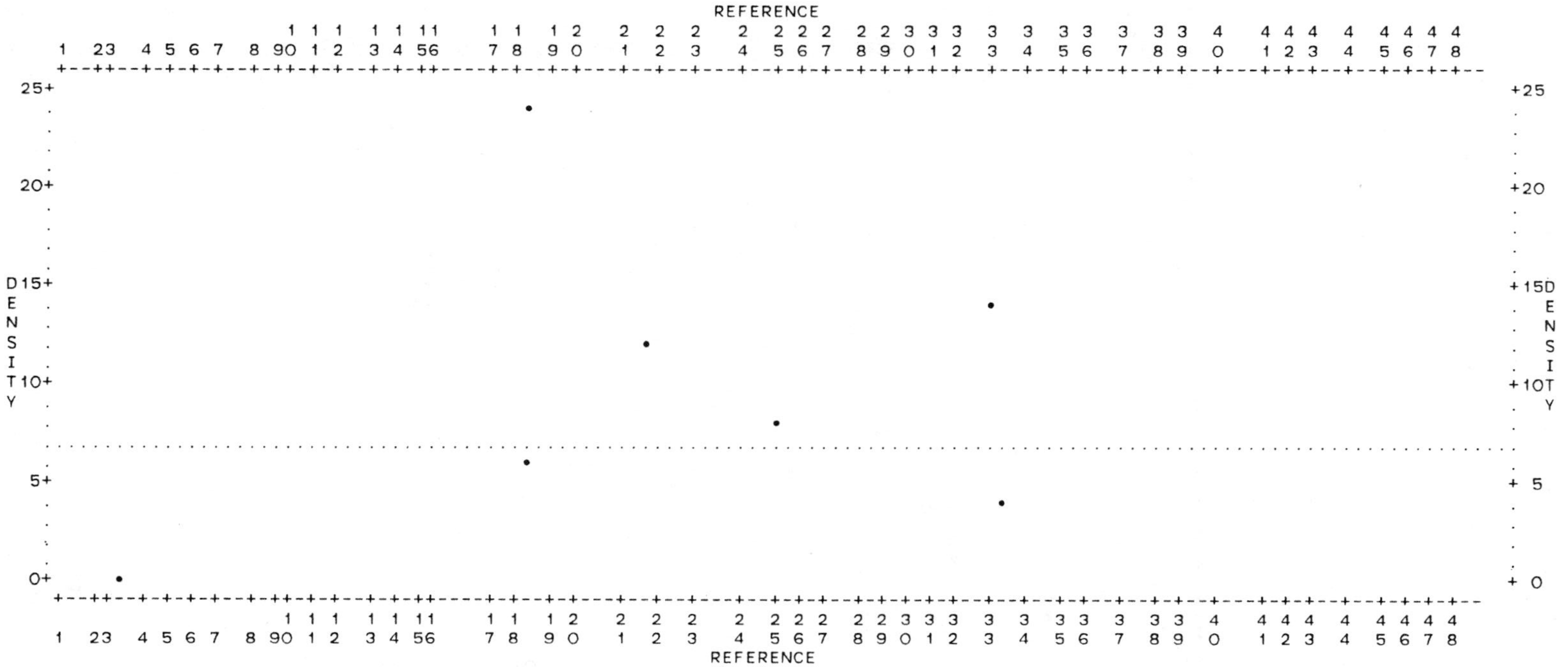

CLUSTERS:

Start:	3:20	18:22	18:22	18:22	33:13
End:	33:16	33:16	21:37	18:24	33:16
Count:	7	6	3	2	2
Width:	16907	9091	2349	53	51
Strength:	1.00	1.85	1.15	1.11	1.11

GAPS:

Start:	3:20	33:16
End:	18:22	48:35
Count:	2	2
Width:	7816	9795
Strength:	1.40	2.04

For zimmâ 114 (14 times)

Linguistic Density Plot in Ezekiel 1 - 48

Each Column = 13 Verses.   Separations are: Max = 7479.50, Mean = 1864.67, Min =   7.50 .

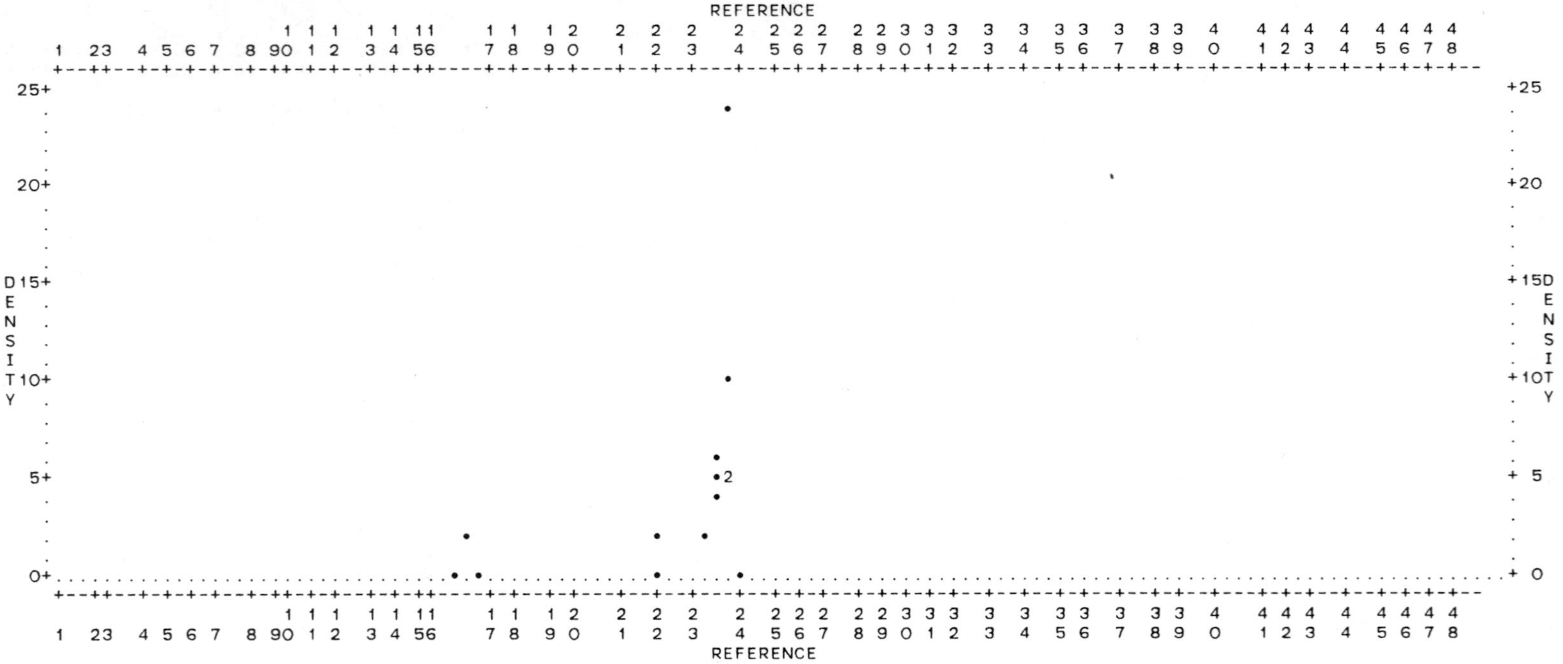

CLUSTERS:

Start:	16:27	16:58	22: 9	22:11	23:21	23:27	23:27	23:35	23:44	23:44	23:48	23:48
End:	24:13	16:58	24:13	22:11	23:35	23:29	23:35	23:29	23:49	23:49	23:49	23:49
Count:	14	3	11	9	4	5	3	5	4	3	15	2
Width:	5977	688	1674	30	867	175	331	69	337	83	56	4
Strength:	7.68	1.27	5.14	1.05	4.02	1.49	1.88	1.02	2.30	1.97	1.56	1.06

GAPS:

Start:	1: 1	1: 1	16:58	23:49	24:13	
End:	22: 9	16:43	16:27	22: 9	48:35	48:35
Count:	5	3	2	3	2	
Width:	11590	7648	7287	3615	14959	14705
Strength:	1.33	1.64	3.10	1.00	4.72	7.36

Linguistic Density Plot in Ezekiel 1 - 48

For znh 311 (2 times)   znh 312 (9 times)   znh 314 (9 times)   znh 3162 (1 times)
     znh 341 (1 times)

Each Column = 13 Verses.   Separations are: Max = 7532.00, Mean = 1216.09, Min =   18.00 .

CLUSTERS:

Start:	6: 9	6: 9	16:15	16:15	16:26	16:26	16:28	16:30	16:31	16:34	20:30	23: 3	23:19	23:43
End:	23:44	16:41	16:41	16:16	16:41	16:28	16:28	16:35	16:33	16:35	23:44	23:44	23:44	23:44
Count:	22	14	2	3	9	8	3	2	2	8	7	3	5	3
Width:	10460	5132	10	569	58	343	180	51	94	36	14	18	2584	860
Strength:	9.37	3.77	1.03	4.49	1.47	3.45	3.17	1.47	2.20	1.48	1.03	1.02	2.25	1.48

GAPS:

Start:	1: 1	6: 9	16:41	16:41	23: 3	23:44
End:	6: 9	16:15	23: 3	20:30	48:35	48:35
Count:	2	2	3	2	7	2
Width:	2458	4553	4468	2744	15905	15051
Strength:	1.06	2.86	1.26	1.31	3.43	11.88

Linguistic Density Plot in Ezekiel 1 - 48

For znh 312 (9 times)

Each Column = 13 Verses. Separations are: Max = 7933.50, Mean = 2797.00, Min = 25.50 .

CLUSTERS:

Start:	16:15	16:15	16:15	16:26	16:28	23: 3	23: 3	
End:	23:43	16:17	16:16	16:28	23:43	23: 5		
Count:	9	6	3	2	3	5		
Width:	5884	277	58	27	51	9	847	44
Strength:	4.88	3.25	1.64	1.09	1.64	1.10	1.40	1.08

GAPS:

Start:	1: 1	16:28	23: 5	
End:	16:15	48:35	48:35	
Count:	2	5	3	
Width:	7021	20671	15867	15064
Strength:	1.66	2.29	3.04	4.84

Linguistic Density Plot in Ezekiel 1 - 48

For znh 314 (9 times)

Each Column = 13 Verses.   Separations are: Max =   8817.50, Mean =   2797.00, Min =   18.00

REFERENCE

```
25+

20+

D15+
E
N
S
I
T10+
Y

 5+

 0+
    +-+-+-+-+-+-+-+-+-+-+-+-+-+-+-+-+-+-+-+-+-+-+-+-+-+-+-+-+-+-+-+-+-+-+-+-+-+-+-+-+-+-+-+-+-+-+-+-+
    1 2 3 4 5 6 7 8 9 1 1 1 1 1 1 1 1 1 1 2 2 2 2 2 2 2 2 2 2 3 3 3 3 3 3 3 3 3 3 4 4 4 4 4 4 4 4
                      0 1 2 3 4 5 6 7 8 9 0 1 2 3 4 5 6 7 8 9 0 1 2 3 4 5 6 7 8 9 0 1 2 3 4 5 6 7 8
```

REFERENCE

CLUSTERS:

```
Start:      6: 9    6: 9   16:30   16:30   16:31
End:       23:44   16:41   16:41   16:35   16:33   16:33
Count:       9       7       2       5       3       2
Width:     10460    5132    10      257     94      36      14
Strength:   3.53    2.81    1.10    2.64    2.14    1.64    1.09
```

GAPS:

```
Start:     16:33   16:35   16:41   23:44
End:       48:35   48:35   48:35   48:35
Count:       6       5       4       2
Width:     20600   20542   20379   15051
Strength:   1.56    2.26    3.10    4.84
```

For zāqēn 21 (10 times)

Linguistic Density Plot in Ezekiel 1 - 48

Each Column = 13 Verses.   Separations are: Max = 9183.50, Mean = 2542.73, Min = 133.50 .

REFERENCE

CLUSTERS:

Start:	7:26	7:26	7:26	7:26	8:11	9: 6	20: 1
End:	27: 9	14: 1	9: 6	8: 1	8:12	9: 6	20: 3
Count:	10	7	6	4	2	2	2
Width:	11457	2857	652	312	45	36	30	23
Strength:	3.66	3.08	2.99	2.03	1.07	1.07	1.08	1.08

GAPS:

Start:	20: 3	27: 9
End:	48:35	48:35
Count:	3	2
Width:	18367	13397
Strength:	4.26	4.67

Linguistic Density Plot in Ezekiel 1 - 48

For zār 111 (7 times)

Each Column = 13 Verses.   Separations are: Max = 5816.00,   Mean = 3496.25,   Min = 575.00 .

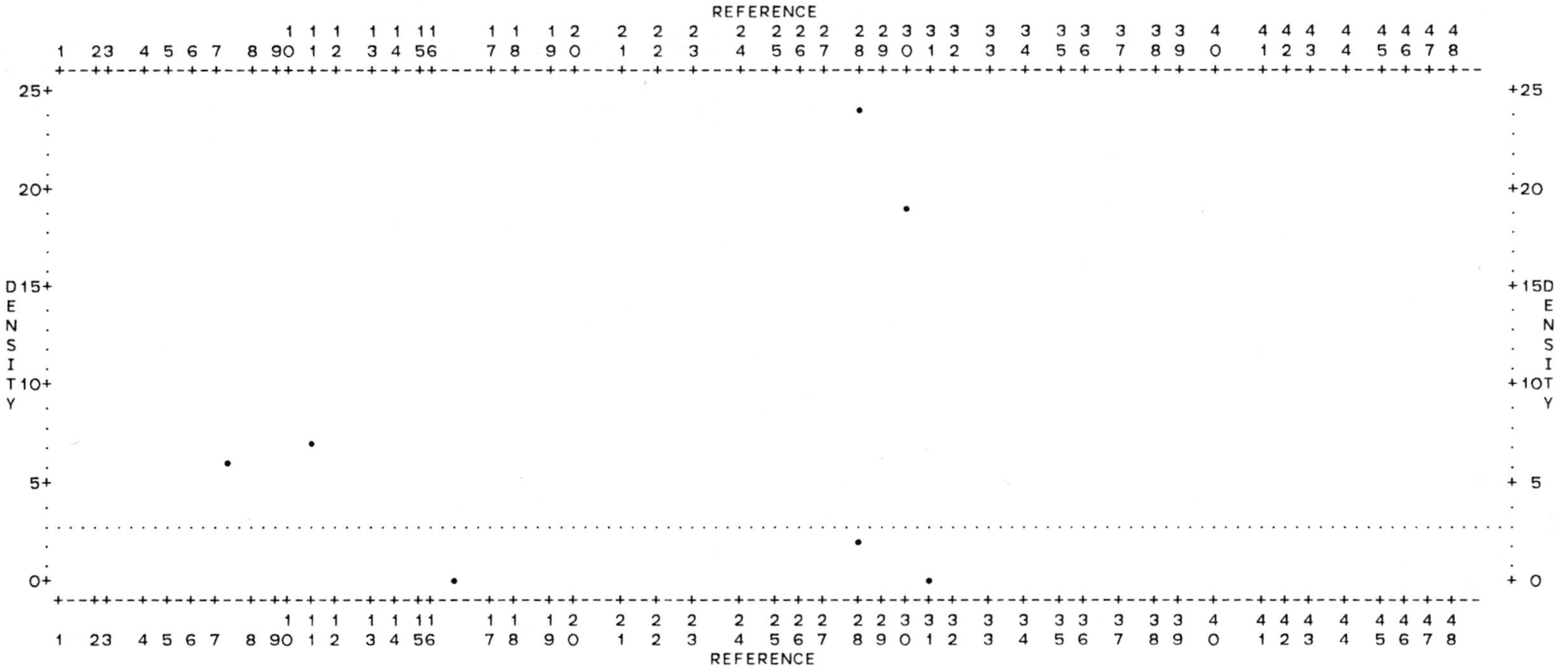

CLUSTERS:

Start:	7:21	28: 7	28: 7
End:	31:12	31:12	28:10
Count:	7	4	2
Width:	13830	1670	50
Strength:	1.77	1.95	1.11

GAPS:

Start:	16:32	31:12
End:	28: 7	48:35
Count:	2	2
Width:	7821	11112
Strength:	1.40	2.46

Linguistic Density Plot in Ezekiel 1 - 48

```
For  zrh 312 (1 times)        zrh 322 (1 times)        zrh 3262 (1 times)        zrh 331 (8 times)
     zrh 332 (1 times)        zrh 3362 (1 times)

Each Column = 13 Verses.   Separations are:   Max =  5677.50,  Mean =  1997.86,  Min =   130.50 .
```

```
                                                REFERENCE
      1   1 1   1 1   1 1   1 1   2 2   2 2   2 2   2 2   3 3   3 3   3 3   4 4   4 4   4 4
 1 23 4 5 6 7 8 90 1 2 3 4 56 7 8 90 1 2 3 4 56 7 8 90 1 2 3 4 56 7 8 90 1 2 3 4 56 7 8
+--+-+-+-+-+-+-+-+-+-+-+-+-++-+-+-+-+-+-+-+-+-++-+-+-+-+-+-+-+-+-++-+-+-+-+-+-+-+-+-++-+-
25+                                                                                        . +25
  .                                                                                        .
  .                                                                                        .
20+                                                                                        . +20
  .                                                                                        .
  .                                                                                        .
D15+                                                                                       . +15 D
E .                                                                                         .     E
N .                                                                                         .     N
S .                                                                                         .     S
I .                                                                                         .     I
T10+                                                                                       . +10 T
Y .                                                                                         .     Y
  .                                                                                         .
5+                                                                                          . +5
  .                                                                                         .
  .                                                                                         .
0+                                                                                          . +0
+--+-+-+-+-+-+-+-+-+-+-+-+-++-+-+-+-+-+-+-+-+-++-+-+-+-+-+-+-+-+-++-+-+-+-+-+-+-+-+-++-+-+-
 1 23 4 5 6 7 8 90 1 2 3 4 56 7 8 90 1 2 3 4 56 7 8 90 1 2 3 4 56 7 8 90 1 2 3 4 56 7 8
      1   1 1   1 1   1 1   1 1   2 2   2 2   2 2   2 2   3 3   3 3   3 3   4 4   4 4   4 4
                                                REFERENCE
```

```
CLUSTERS:
Start:     5: 2    5: 2    5: 2    5:10    6: 5   12:14   29:12   30:23
End:      36:19   22:15   12:15    5:12    6: 8   12:15   30:26   30:26
Count:      13       9       7       5       2       2       3       2
Width:   18086    9805    3282     540     261      70      59      22     710     68
Strength: 2.32    1.72    2.43    2.28    1.47    1.04    1.06    1.29    1.03

GAPS:
Start:    12:15   12:15   12:15   22:15   30:26   36:19
End:      48:35   30:23   29:12   29:12   48:35   48:35
Count:       8       5       4       2       3       2
Width:   22789   11366   10724    4970    4201   11355    7985
Strength: 2.43    1.03    1.59    1.59    1.18    2.91    3.21
```

Linguistic Density Plot in Ezekiel 1 - 48

For zrh 331 (8 times)   zrh 332 (1 times)   zrh 3362 (1 times)

Each Column = 13 Verses. Separations are: Max = 5711.50, Mean = 2542.73, Min = 145.00 .

REFERENCE

CLUSTERS:

Start:	5:10	5:10	5:10	5:10	12:14	29:12	30:23
End:	30:26	12:15	6:5	5:12	12:15	30:26	30:26
Count:	10	5	3	2	3	3	2
Width:	14525	3091	290	70	22	710	68
Strength:	2.68	1.82	1.53	1.08	1.06	1.40	1.06

GAPS:

Start:	12:15	12:15	30:26
End:	48:35	20:23	48:35
Count:	7	2	2
Width:	22789	4970	11355
Strength:	1.87	1.04	3.79

Linguistic Density Plot in Ezekiel 1 - 48

For zrh 331 (8 times)

Each Column = 13 Verses.   Separations are: Max = 5711.50, Mean = 3107.78, Min = 145.00 .

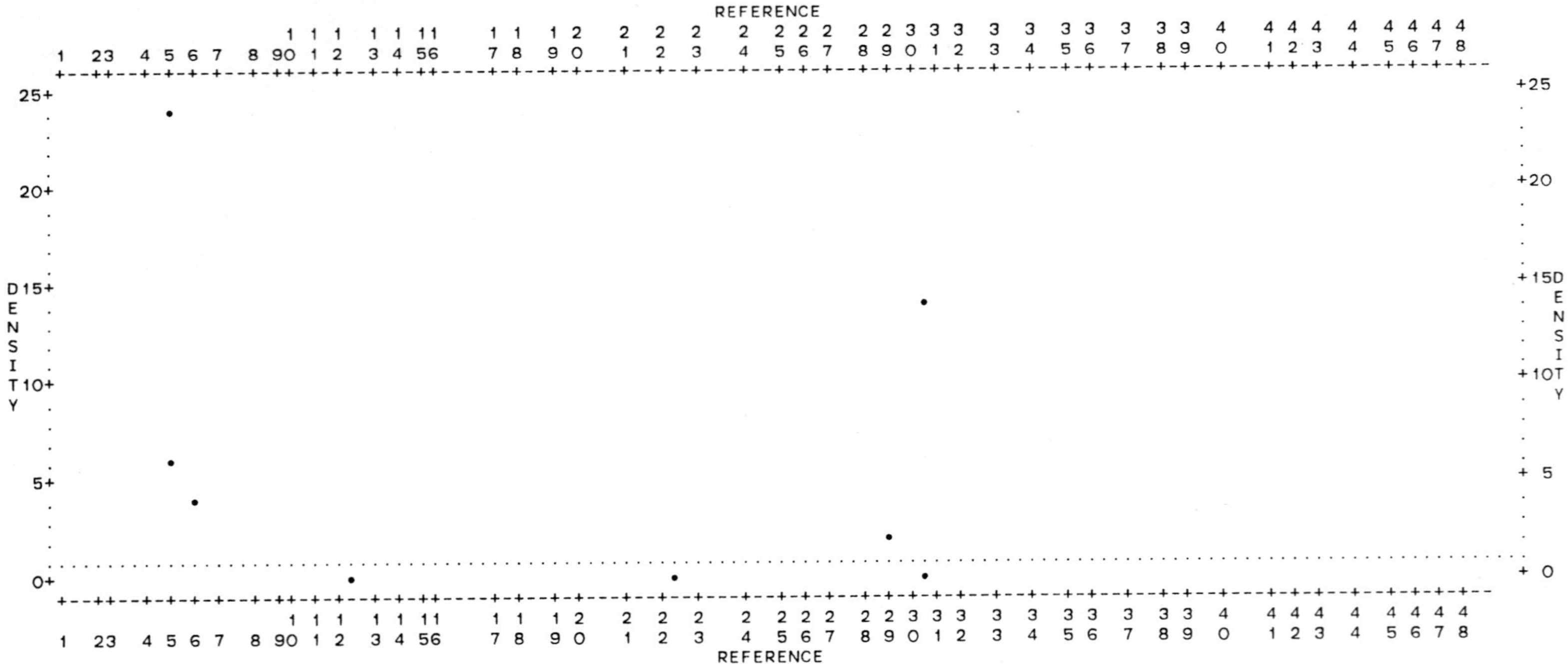

CLUSTERS:

Start:	5:10	5:10	5:10	22:15	29:12	30:23
End:	30:26	12:15	5:12	30:26	30:26	30:26
Count:	8	4	3	2	4	3
Width:	14525	3091	290	4911	710	68
Strength:	1.96	1.49	1.61	1.09	1.05	1.49

GAPS:

Start:	6: 5	12:15	12:15	30:26
End:	29:12	29:12	22:15	48:35
Count:	4	3	2	2
Width:	13525	10724	6523	11355
Strength:	1.00	1.22	1.22	2.96

Linguistic Density Plot in Ezekiel 1 - 48

For zĕrôa' 114 (13 times)

Each Column = 13 Verses. Separations are: Max = 5693.00, Mean = 1997.86, Min = 8.00 .

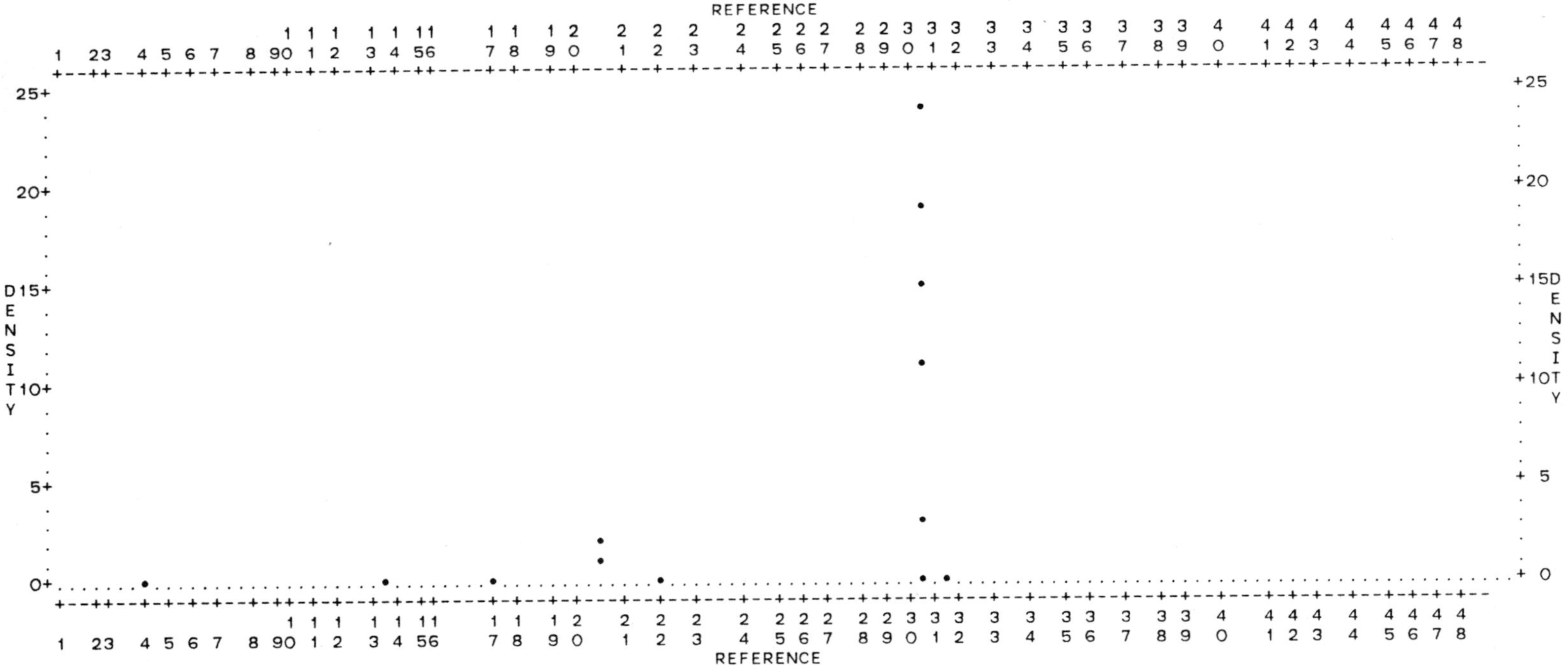

CLUSTERS:

Start:	4: 7	20:33	20:33	30:21	30:21	30:21	30:24	30:24	30:25
End:	31:17	22: 6	20:34	31:17	30:25	30:22	30:25	30:24	30:25
Count:	13	3	2	7	6	2	4	2	2
Width:	15418	1134	30	545	99	41	30	14	4
Strength:	3.38	1.13	1.05	3.20	2.85	1.05	2.01	1.06	1.07

GAPS:

Start:	4: 7	4: 7	22: 6	30:25	31:17
End:	17: 9	13:20	30:21	48:35	48:35
Count:	3	2	2	3	2
Width:	6680	4268	4944	11386	10940
Strength:	1.06	1.22	1.58	2.92	4.80

Linguistic Density Plot in Ezekiel 1 - 48

For zera' 111 (6 times)

Each Column = 13 Verses.   Separations are: Max = 8181.00, Mean = 3995.71, Min = 101.50 .

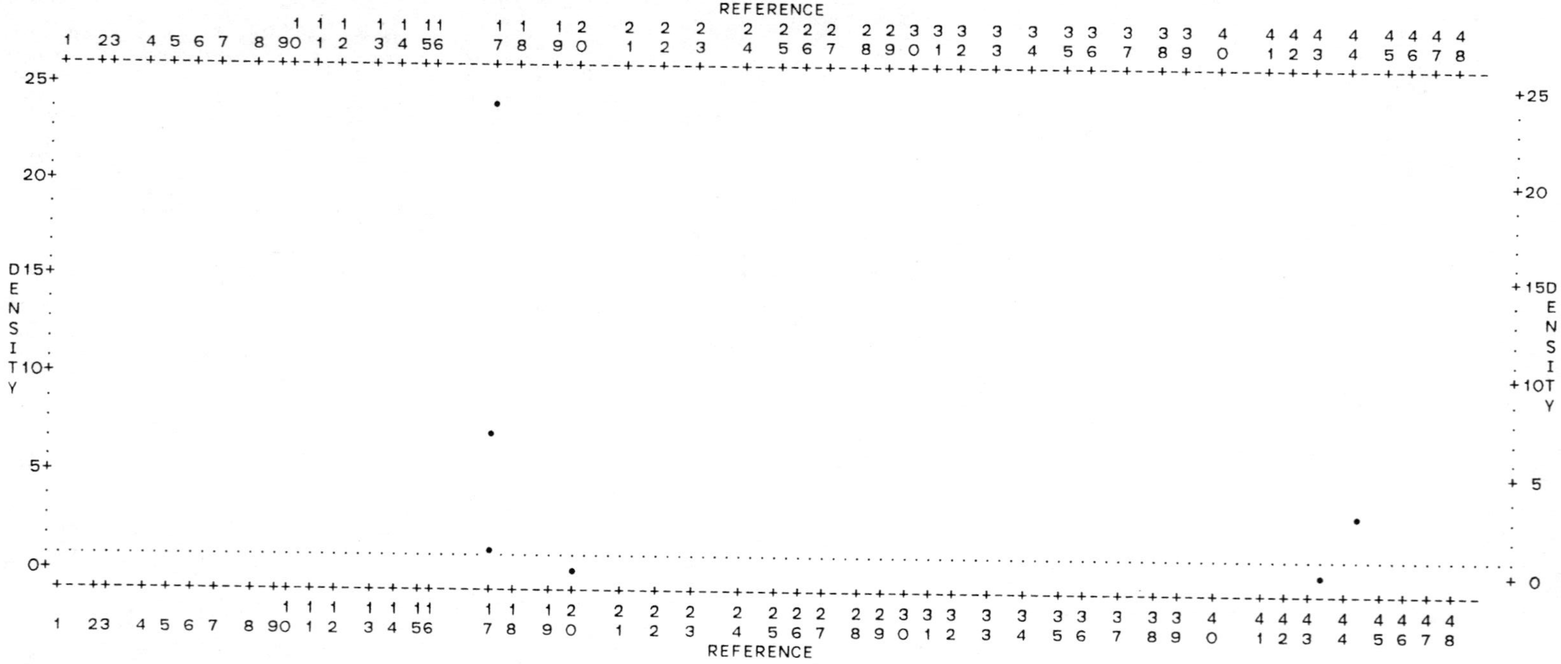

REFERENCE

REFERENCE

CLUSTERS:

Start:	17: 5	17: 5	17: 5
End:	20: 5	17:13	17: 5
Count:	4	3	2
Width:	1500	203	7
Strength:	2.14	1.74	1.15

GAPS:

Start:	1: 1	17:13	20: 5
End:	17: 5	43:19	43:19
Count:	2	3	2
Width:	8164	16362	15065
Strength:	1.20	1.87	3.19

Linguistic Density Plot in Ezekiel 1 - 48

For ḥbl 311 (1 times)   ḥbl 314 (4 times)

Each Column = 13 Verses.   Separations are: Max = 7285.50, Mean = 4661.66, Min = 25.50 .

REFERENCE

REFERENCE

DENSITY

25+
20+
D15+
E
N
S
I
T10+
Y
5+
0+

+25
+20
+15
+10
+5
+0

CLUSTERS:

Start:	18:16	27: 8	27:27	27:28
End:	27:29	27:29	27:29	27:29
Count:	5	4	3	2
Width:	6016	381	51	·14
Strength:	2.53	2.57	1.86	1.17

GAPS:

Start:	1: 1	1: 1	27:29
End:	27: 8	18:16	48:35
Count:	3	2	2
Width:	14570	8935	13018
Strength:	1.05	1.08	2.12

Linguistic Density Plot in Ezekiel 1 - 48

For ḥbš 311 (1 times) ḥbš 312 (2 times) ḥbš 315 (1 times) ḥbš 3161 (1 times)
ḥbš 3162 (1 times) ḥbš 341 (1 times)

Each Column = 13 Verses. Separations are: Max = 6677.00, Mean = 3496.25, Min = 822.50 .

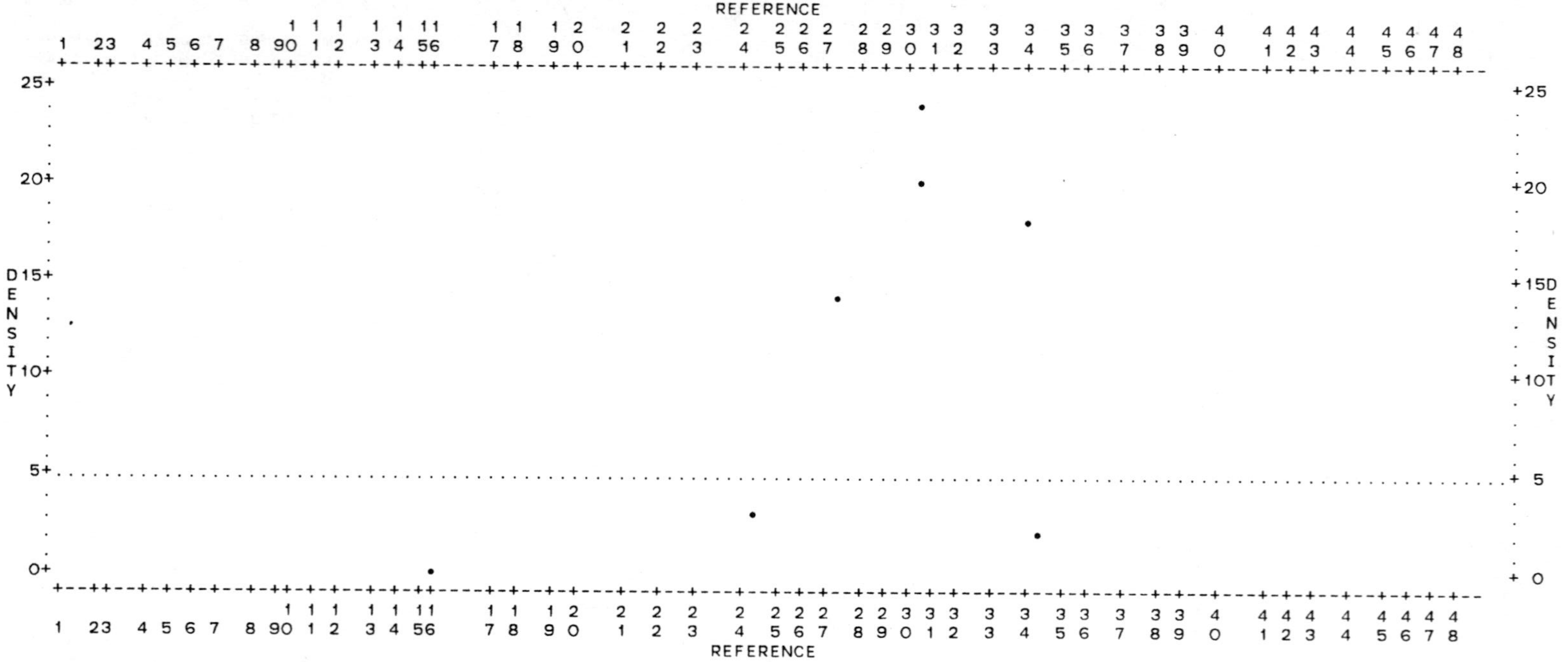

CLUSTERS:

Start:	16:10	24:17	30:21	30:21	34: 4
End:	34:16	34:16	34:16	30:21	34:16
Count:	7	6	4	2	2
Width:	12000	5570	2431	8	291
Strength:	2.22	2.63	1.78	1.13	1.03

GAPS:

Start:	1: 1	1: 1	34:16
End:	24:17	16:10	48:35
Count:	3	2	2
Width:	13353	6923	9046
Strength:	1.57	1.11	1.79

Linguistic Density Plot in Ezekiel 1 - 48

For hag 111 (5 times)

Each Column = 13 Verses. Separations are: Max = 13064.00, Mean = 4661.66, Min = 34.00 .

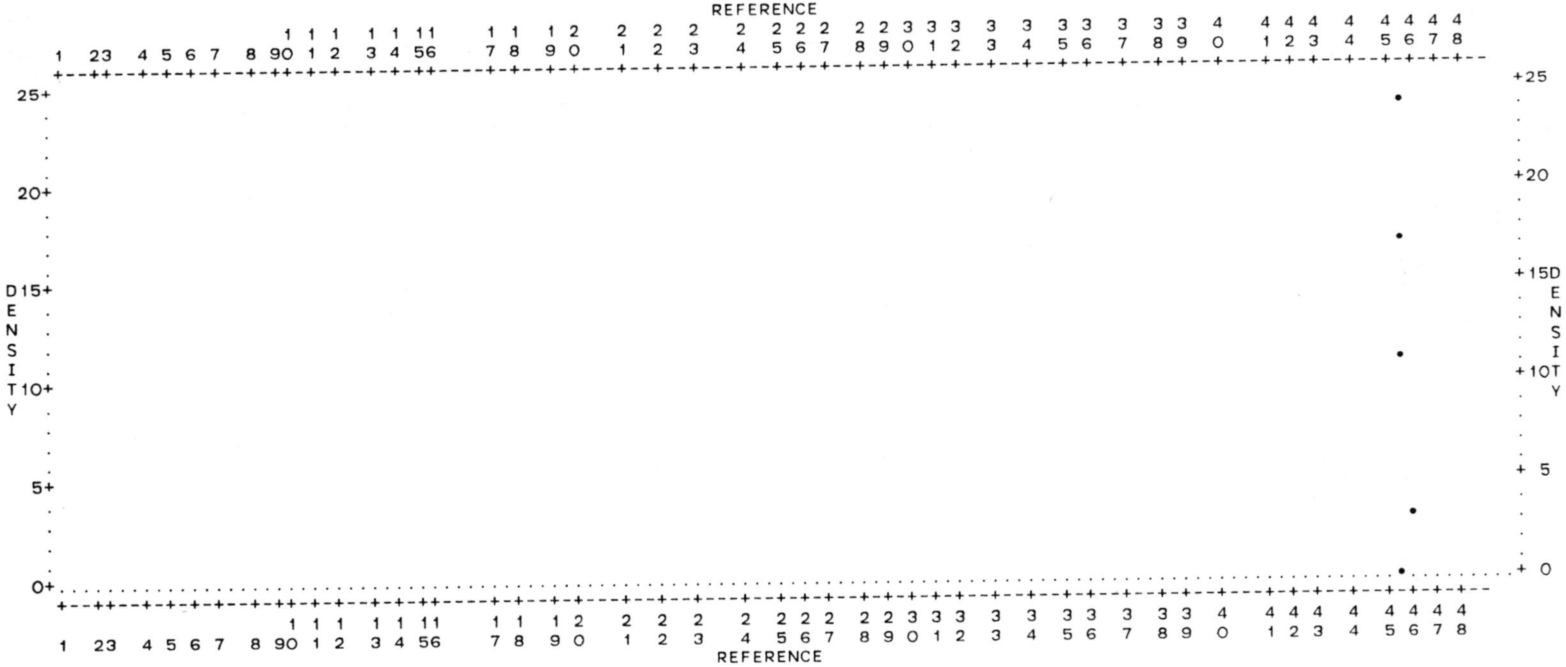

CLUSTERS:

Start:	45:17	45:21	45:21	
End:	46:11	45:25	45:23	
Count:	5	4	3	2
Width:	404	171	68	23
Strength:	3.66	2.61	1.85	1.17

GAPS:

Start:	1:1	1:1
End:	45:21	45:17
Count:	3	2
Width:	26127	26024
Strength:	3.37	5.42

Linguistic Density Plot in Ezekiel 1 - 48

For hōdeš 111 (27 times)

Each Column = 13 Verses. Separations are: Max = 4941.50, Mean = 998.93, Min = 18.00 .

CLUSTERS:

Start:	1: 1	20: 1	24: 1	29: 1	30:20	32: 1	39:12	45:17	45:17	45:20	45:25
End:	1: 2	47:12	24: 1	33:21	32:17	32: 1	47:12	40: 1	47:12	46: 1	45:21	46: 6
Count:	2	24	8	6	5	3	2	12	3	9	8	4	4	6
Width:	18	17458	5	2629	1782	954	343	5099	387	1006	296	95	18	130
Strength:	1.01	2.77	1.03	1.93	1.61	1.67	1.23	2.32	1.20	2.97	2.97	1.80	1.01	1.78

GAPS:

Start:	1: 1	1: 1	1: 2	8: 1	32: 1	32:17	33:21	39:14	40: 1
End:	32: 1	24: 1	24: 1	20: 1	45:17	39:12	45:17	45:17
Count:	13	6	5	4	3	7	4	3	2
Width:	17084	13036	13026	13008	9883	6422	8939	4846	4507	3679	4053	3706
Strength:	1.98	4.04	4.96	6.23	5.89	5.62	1.38	1.15	1.87	2.78	1.53	2.80

Linguistic Density Plot in Ezekiel 1 - 48

For ḥādāš 21 (5 times)

Each Column = 13 Verses.   Separations are: Max = 5426.00, Mean = 4661.66, Min = 2284.00 .

CLUSTERS:

Start: 18:31 36:26
End: 18:31 36:26
Count: 2   2
Width: 3   3
Strength: 1.18   1.18

GAPS:

Start: 18:31
End: 36:26
Count: 2
Width: 10849
Strength: 1.57

Linguistic Density Plot in Ezekiel 1 - 48

For ḥōmā 114 (10 times)

Each Column = 13 Verses.   Separations are: Max = 7074.00, Mean = 2542.73, Min = 33.50

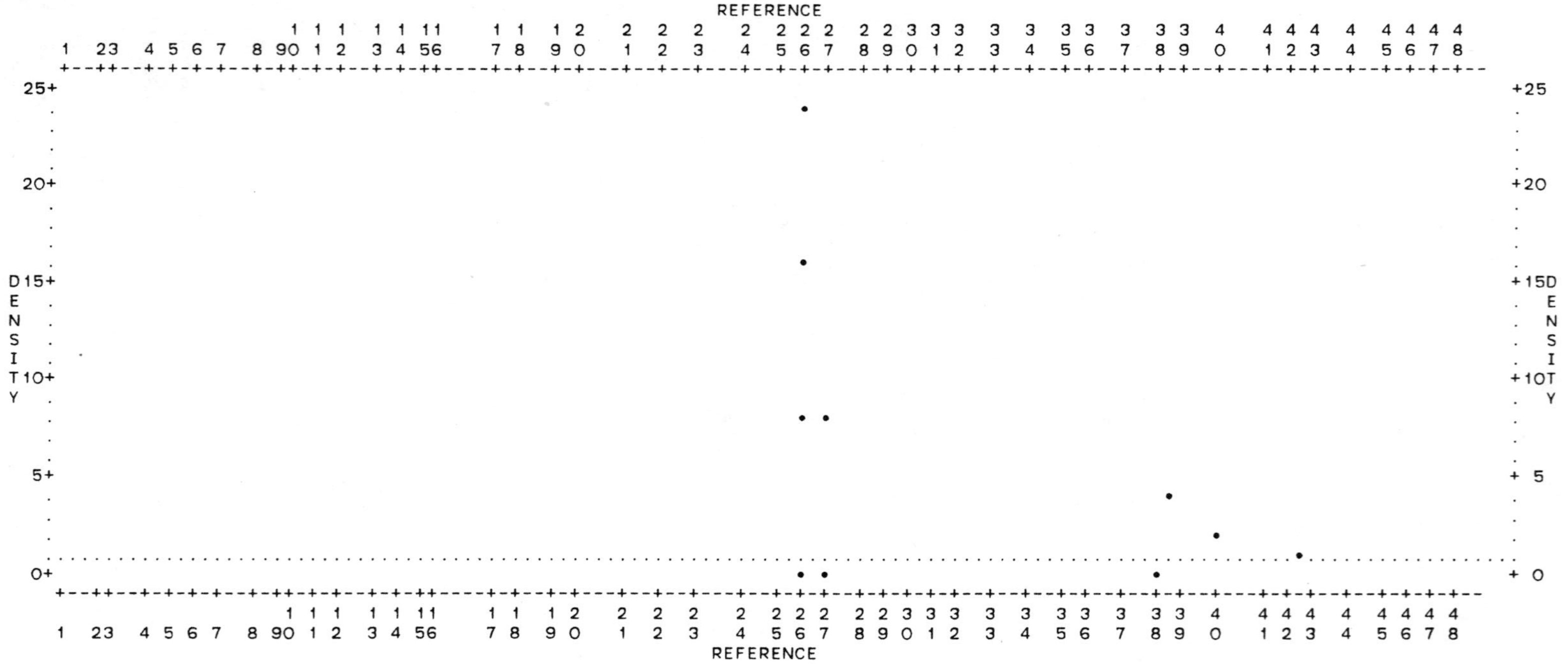

REFERENCE

DENSITY

CLUSTERS:

Start:	26: 4	26: 4	26: 9	26: 9	26:12	27:11	38:11	38:11
End:	42:20	27:11	26:12	26:10	27:11	27:11	42:20	40: 5
Count:	10	6	4	3	2	4	4	3
Width:	10225	602	179	67	24	13	2926	1105
Strength:	4.06	3.01	2.07	1.61	1.08	1.08	1.30	1.27

GAPS:

Start:	1: 1	1: 1	27:11
End:	26: 9	26: 4	38:11
Count:	3	2	2
Width:	14147	14035	6697
Strength:	2.90	4.95	1.78

Linguistic Density Plot in Ezekiel 1 - 48

For hws 311 (1 times)   hws 312 (8 times)

Each Column = 13 Verses. Separations are: Max = 8994.00, Mean = 2797.00, Min = 140.00 .

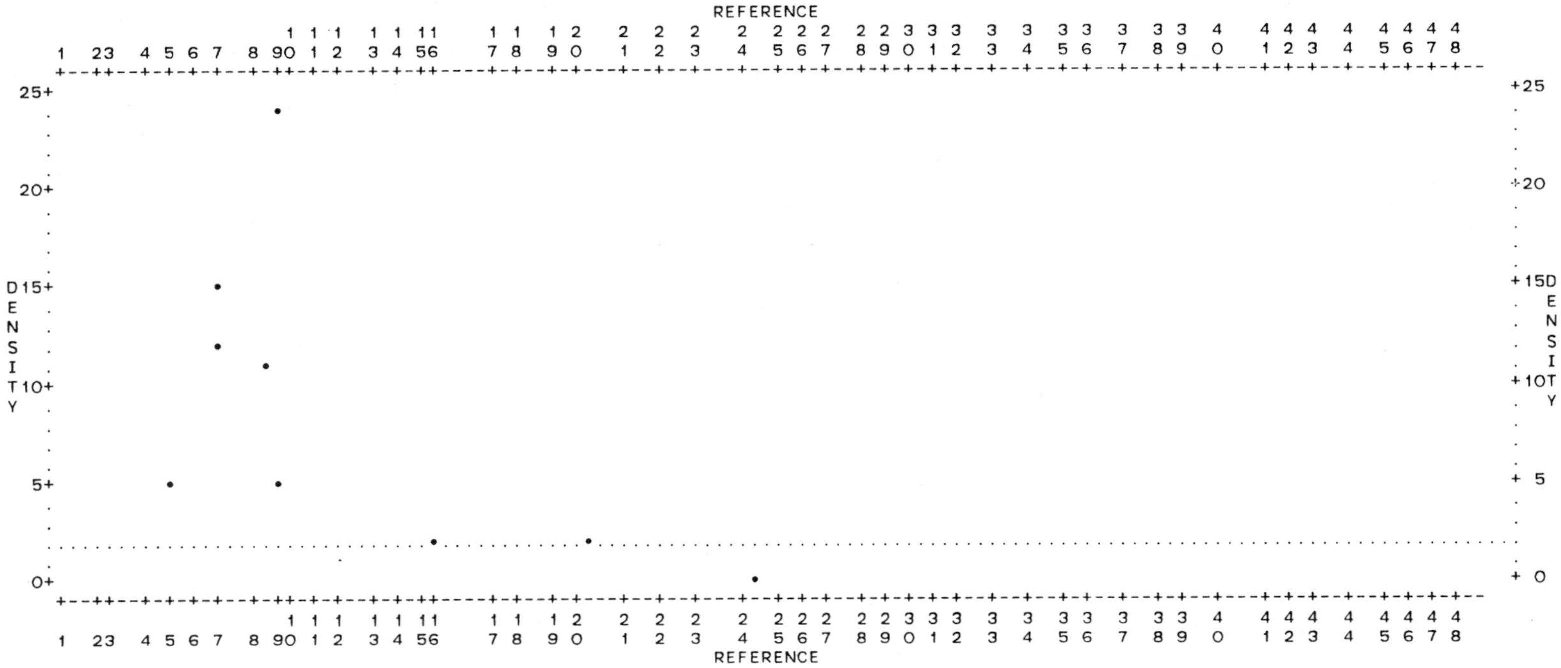

CLUSTERS:

Start:	5:11	5:11	7: 4	8:18	9: 5
End:	24:14	9:10	7: 9	9:10	9:10
Count:	9	6	2	3	2
Width:	11168	1735	640	280	131
Strength:	3.32	2.90	1.46	1.06	1.57	1.05

GAPS:

Start:	7: 9	9:10	16: 5	20:17	24:14
End:	48:35	48:35	48:35	48:35	48:35
Count:	8	5	4	3	2
Width:	25202	24107	21194	17988	14674
Strength:	1.45	3.12	3.31	3.67	4.69

Linguistic Density Plot in Ezekiel 1 - 48

For hws 312 (8 times)

Each Column = 13 Verses.   Separations are: Max =   8994.00, Mean =   3107.78, Min =   140.00 .

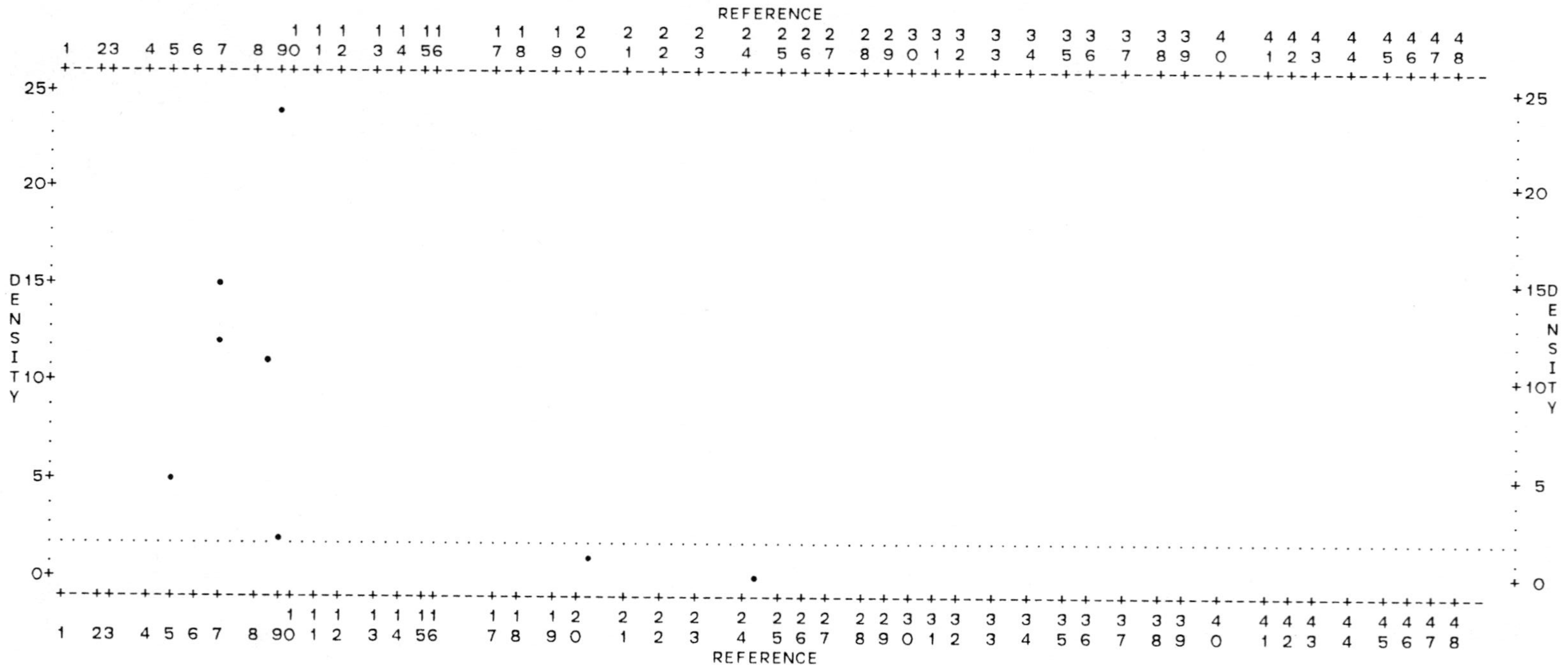

REFERENCE

(density plot)

CLUSTERS:

Start:	5:11	5:11	7: 4	8:18	9: 5	
End:	24:14	9:10	7: 9	9:10	9:10	
Count:	8	6	2	3	2	
Width:	11168	1735	640	90	280	131
Strength:	2.87	3.14	1.51	1.08	1.61	1.07

GAPS:

Start:	7: 9	9:10	24:14	
End:	48:35	48:35	20:17	48:35
Count:	7	4	2	
Width:	25202	24107	6119	14674
Strength:	1.57	3.54	1.08	4.16

Linguistic Density Plot in Ezekiel 1 - 48

For hûc 111 (18 times)

Each Column = 13 Verses.   Separations are: Max = 5614.50, Mean = 1472.11, Min = 140.00 .

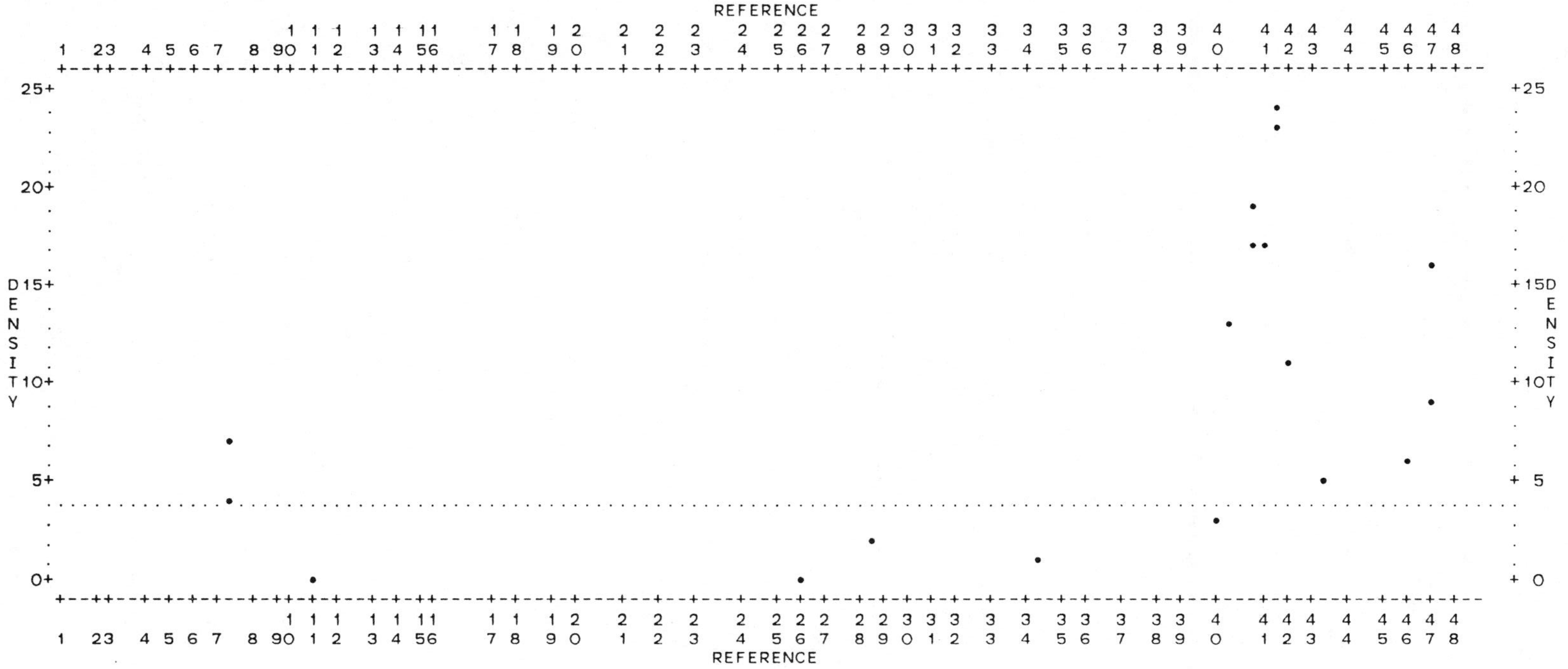

CLUSTERS:

Start:	7:15	26:11	40: 5	40: 5	40: 5	41: 9	41: 9	46: 2	47: 2
End:	7:19	47: 2	47: 2	43:21	40:44	43:21	42: 7	47: 2	47: 2
Count:	2	15	12	9	4	5	4	3	2
Width:	70	12621	4370	2344	799	1212	436	568	3
Strength:	1.00	2.90	3.82	3.05	1.58	1.83	1.74	1.23	1.05

GAPS:

Start:	1: 1	7:19	7:19	7:19	11: 6	28:23	28:23
End:	7:15	40:40	40: 5	26:11	26:11	40: 5	34:21
Count:	2	8	6	3	2	3	2
Width:	2891	20192	19480	11229	9737	6940	3538
Strength:	1.01	3.27	4.40	4.31	5.91	2.08	1.47

Linguistic Density Plot in Ezekiel 1 - 48

For ḥzh 311 (3 times)   ḥzh 312 (1 times)   ḥzh 314 (4 times)   ḥzh 3162 (1 times)

Each Column = 13 Verses. Separations are: Max = 8305.50, Mean = 2797.00, Min = 21.50 .

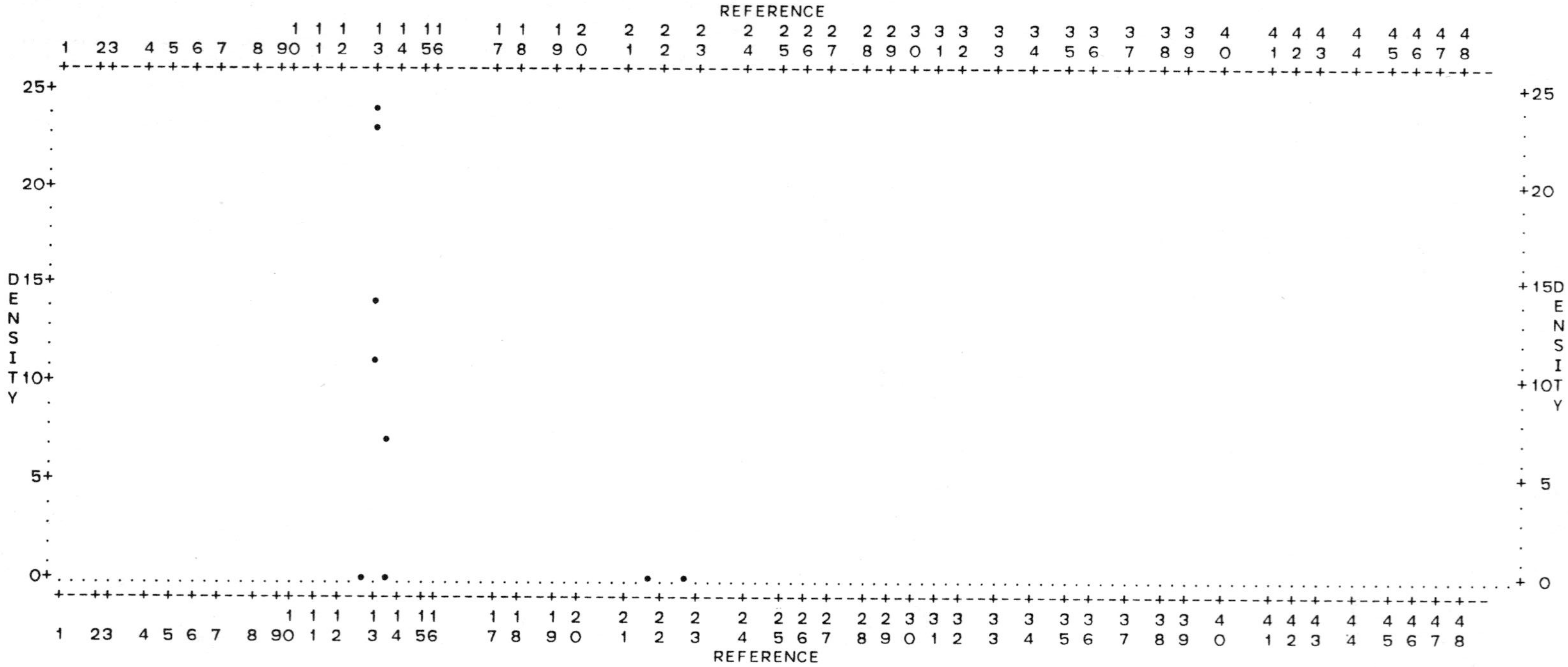

CLUSTERS:

Start:	12:27	12:27	12:27	13: 6	13: 6	13: 8	13:16
End:	22:28	13:23	13: 9	13: 9	13: 7	13: 9	13:23
Count:	9		7	5	4	2	2
Width:	6550	538	168	65	22	18	197
Strength:	4.69	3.93	2.66	2.15	1.09	1.09	1.02

GAPS:

Start:	1: 1	13: 9	13:16	13:23	13:23	22:28
End:	12:27	48:35	48:35	21:34	48:35
Count:	2	6	5	4	2
Width:	5410	22391	22218	22021	5410	16009
Strength:	1.03	1.99	2.66	3.52	1.03	5.22

Linguistic Density Plot in Ezekiel 1 - 48

For ḥāzôn 111 (7 times)

Each Column = 13 Verses. Separations are: Max = 11281.00, Mean = 3496.25, Min = 19.50 .

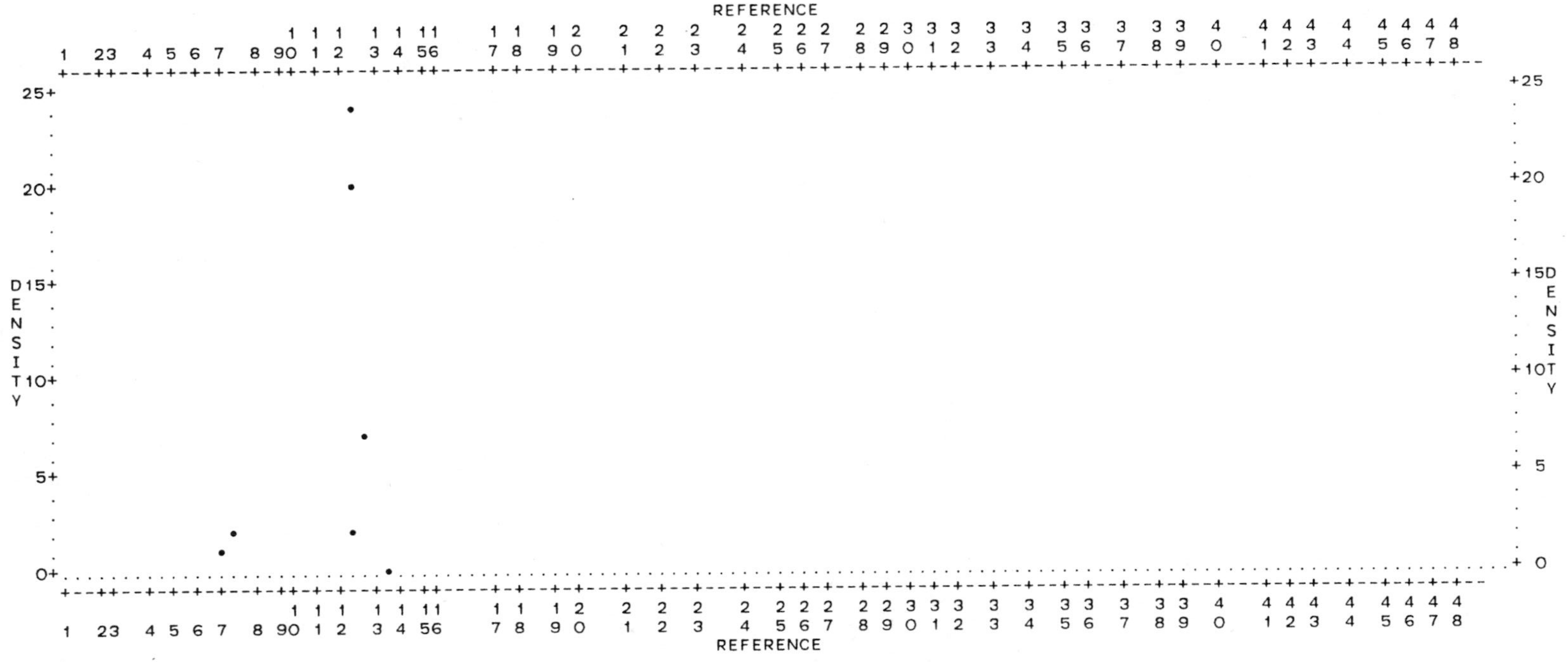

(DENSITY vs. REFERENCE scatter/density plot; vertical axis labelled "DENSITY" from 0+ to 25+ in steps of 5; horizontal axis labelled "REFERENCE" with column indices 1–48.)

CLUSTERS:

Start:	7:13	7:26	12:22	12:22	12:23
End:	13:16	13:16	12:27	12:24	12:24
Count:	7	2	5	3	2
Width:	2899	249	436	89	39	6
Strength:	4.47	1.05	2.90	2.30	1.72	1.13

GAPS:

Start:	12:24	12:27	13:16
End:	48:35	48:35	48:35
Count:	4	3	2
Width:	22612	22562	22215
Strength:	2.68	3.85	6.07

Linguistic Density Plot in Ezekiel 1 - 48

For ḥāzāq 21 (10 times)

Each Column = 13 Verses.   Separations are: Max = 5720.50, Mean = 2542.73, Min = 8.00 .

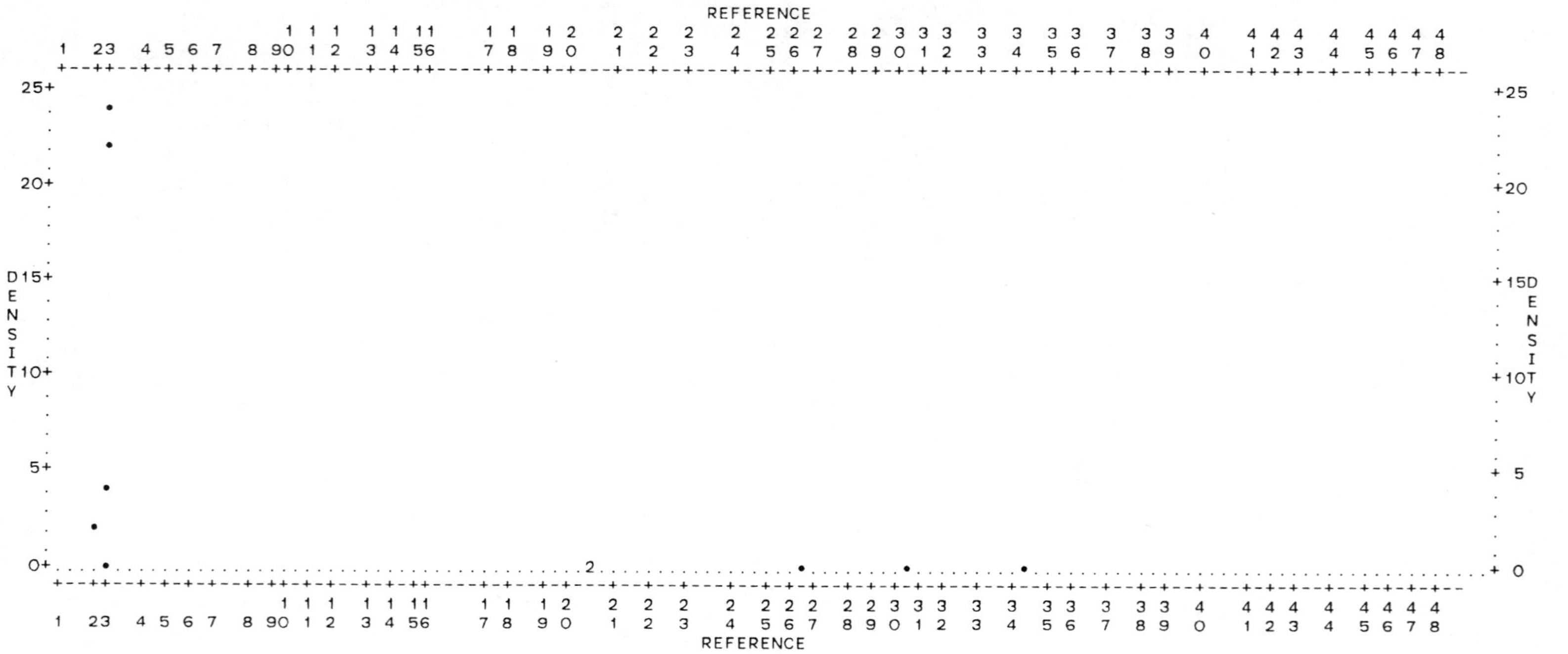

CLUSTERS:

Start:	2: 4	2: 4	3: 7	3: 7	3: 8	20:33
End:	34:16	3: 9	3: 9	3: 8	3: 9	20:34
Count:	10	5	4	2	2	2
Width:	18266	323	27	11	7	30
Strength:	1.48	2.53	2.11	1.09	1.09	1.08

GAPS:

Start:	3: 9	3: 9	20:34	30:22	34:16
End:	48:35	20:33	48:35	48:35	34:16
Count:	7	2	5	3	2
Width:	26979	9413	17536	11441	9036
Strength:	2.91	2.95	1.89	2.04	2.79

Linguistic Density Plot in Ezekiel 1 - 48

For ḥzq 311 (1 times)   ḥzq 312 (1 times)   ḥzq 3162 (1 times)   ḥzq 331 (2 times)
    ḥzq 332 (1 times)   ḥzq 3362 (1 times)   ḥzq 352 (1 times)   ḥzq 361 (2 times)
    ḥzq 364 (2 times)

Each Column = 13 Verses.   Separations are: Max = 4673.50, Mean = 2151.54, Min = 37.00 .

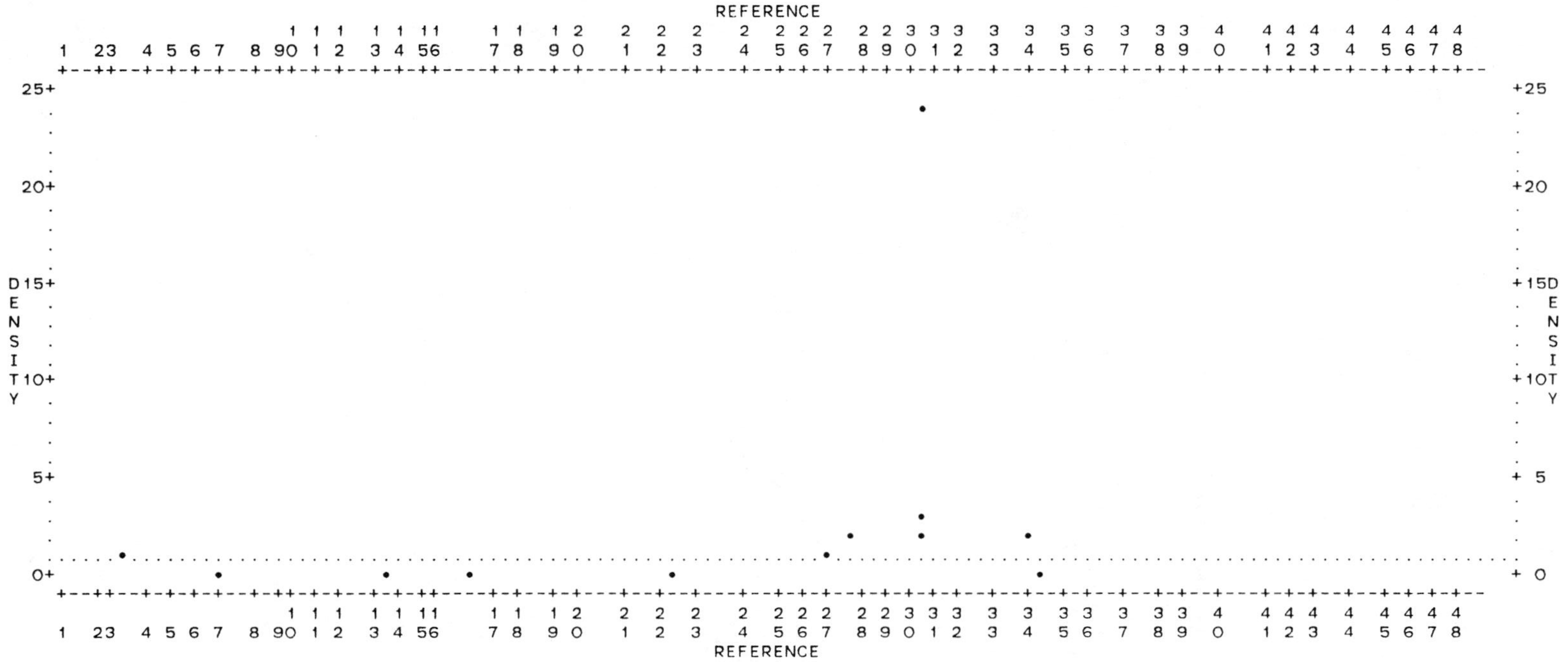

DENSITY vs REFERENCE plot (+25, +20, +15, +10, +5, 0)

CLUSTERS:

Start:	3:14	27: 9	27: 9	30:21	30:24
End:	34:16	34:16	30:25	30:25	30:25
Count:	12	7	5	3	2
Width:	17812	4347	1997	74	26
Strength:	2.17	2.29	1.56	1.91	1.06

GAPS:

Start:	30:25	34:16
End:	34:16	48:35
Count:	4	2
Width:	11392	9042
Strength:	1.56	3.45

Linguistic Density Plot in Ezekiel 1 - 48

For ḥṭ' 311 (5 times)   ḥṭ' 312 (2 times)   ḥṭ' 314 (2 times)   ḥṭ' 3162 (2 times)
     ḥṭ' 331 (4 times)   ḥṭ' 3362 (1 times)

Each Column = 13 Verses. Separations are: Max = 4477.00, Mean = 1645.29, Min = 6.00

CLUSTERS:

Start:	3:21	14:13	16:51	18: 4	33:12	37:23	43:20	43:22	43:22
End:	3:21	18:24	18:24	18:24	33:16	45:18	43:23	43:23	43:22
Count:	2	5	4	3	6	5	3	2	
Width:	5	2878	1332	425	71	5106	1304	44	12	5
Strength:	1.05	1.32	1.43	1.34	1.01	1.03	1.88	1.94	1.54	1.05

GAPS:

Start:	1: 1	3:21	3:21	3:21	3:21	18:24	33:16	37:23
End:	43:22	43:22	43:20	33:12	16:51	14:13	28:16	43:20	43:20
Count:	14	12	11	8	3	2	3	2
Width:	24799	23507	23475	16809	6523	4977	8954	6595	3802
Strength:	1.21	1.71	2.16	1.63	1.52	2.14	2.66	2.94	1.55	1.39

Linguistic Density Plot in Ezekiel 1 - 48

For ḥṭ' 311 (5 times)   ḥṭ' 312 (2 times)   ḥṭ' 314 (2 times)   ḥṭ' 3162 (2 times)

Each Column = 13 Verses.   Separations are: Max = 4898.50, Mean = 2330.83, Min = 212.50

CLUSTERS:

Start:	3:21	3:21	14:13	16:51	18: 4	18:20	33:12
End:	37:23	18:24	18:24	18:24	18:24	18:24	33:16
Count:	11	7	2	4	3	2	2
Width:	19678	7860	2878	1332	425	122	71
Strength:	1.25	1.57	1.08	1.76	1.68	1.46	1.02	1.05

GAPS:

Start:	3:21	14:13	18:24	33:16	37:23
End:	48:35	33:12	28:16	48:35	48:35
Count:	11	2	3	3	2
Width:	26677	4977	8954	6207	7004
Strength:	1.16	1.23	1.48	1.80	1.77	2.17

Linguistic Density Plot in Ezekiel 1 - 48

For hf' 311 (5 times)

Each Column = 13 Verses.   Separations are: Max = 6523.00, Mean = 4661.66, Min = 3927.50 .

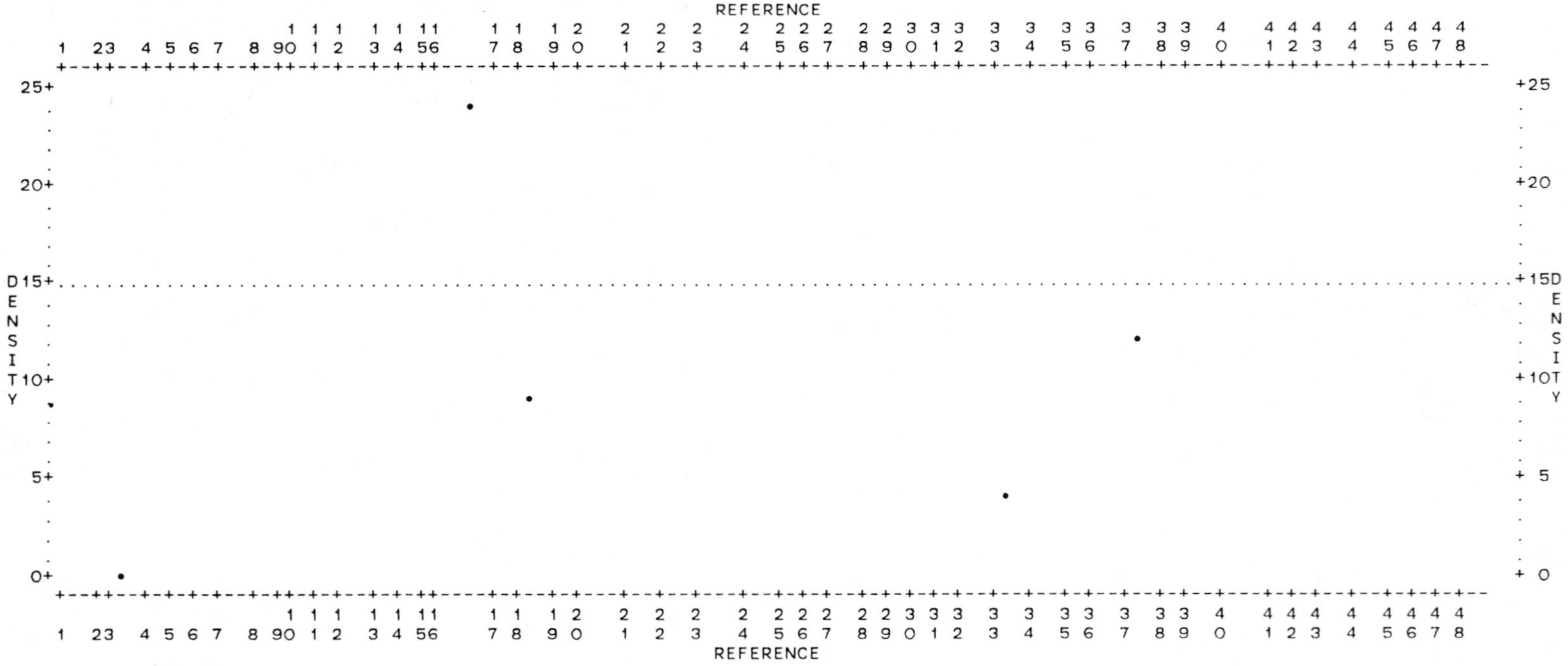

REFERENCE

All cluster strengths are less than 1.00.

GAPS:

Start: 18:24
End: 33:16
Count: 9025
Width: 2
Strength: 1.10

Linguistic Density Plot in Ezekiel 1 - 48

For ḥṭ' 331 (4 times)   ḥṭ' 3362 (1 times)

Each Column = 13 Verses.   Separations are: Max = 12400.00, Mean = 4661.66, Min =   6.00

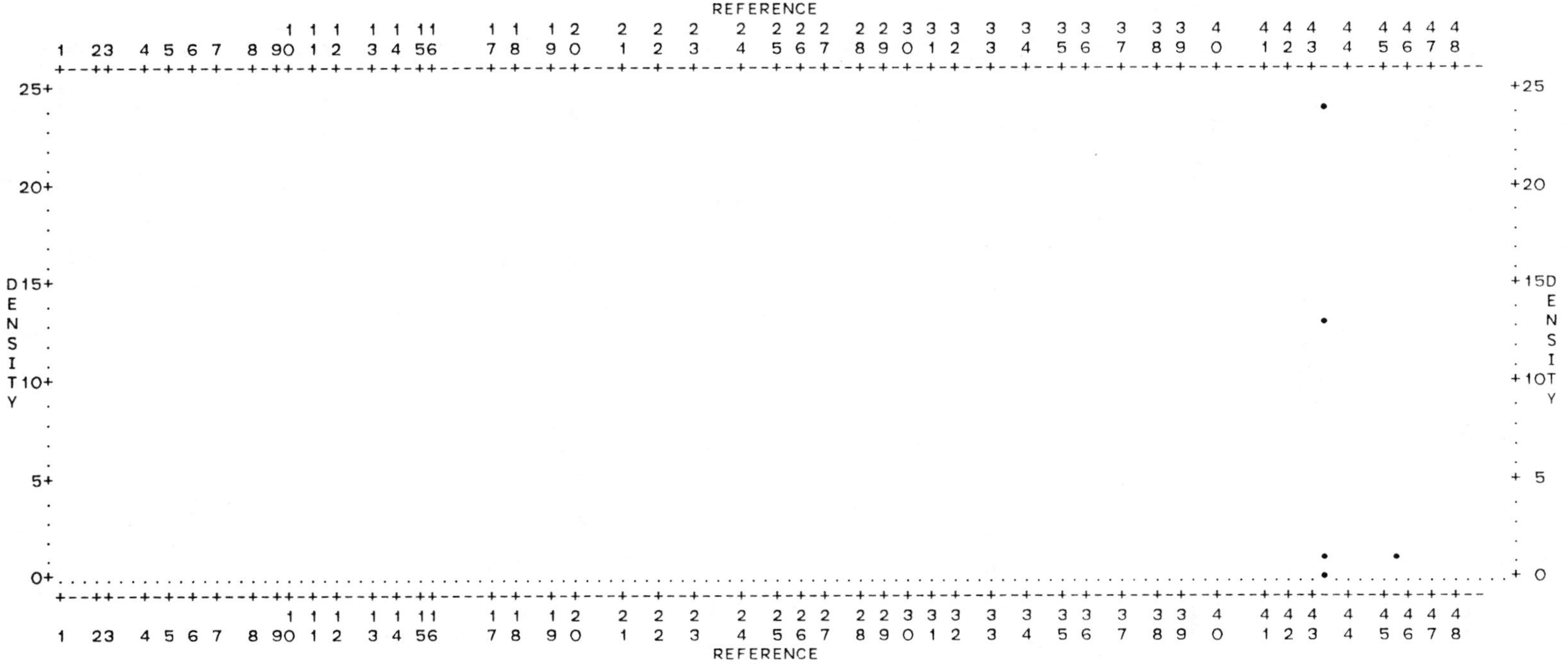

CLUSTERS:

Start:	43:20	43:20	43:22
End:	45:18	43:23	43:22
Count:	5	4	3	2
Width:	1304	44	12	5
Strength:	3.47	2.63	1.86	1.18

GAPS:

Start:	1: 1	1: 1
End:	43:22	43:20
Count:	3	2
Width:	24799	24767
Strength:	3.10	5.10

Linguistic Density Plot in Ezekiel 1 - 48

For ḫaṭṭā't 114 (24 times)

Each Column = 13 Verses. Separations are: Max = 6550.00, Mean = 1118.80, Min = 26.00 .

```
                                            REFERENCE
        1  23 4 5 6 7  8 90 1  2  3 4 56   7 8 9 0 1 2  3 4 5 6 7  8 90 1 2  3 4 5 6 7  8 9 0 1 2  3 4 5 6 7  8
    +--+-+-+-+-+-+-+--+-+-+--+--+-+-+--+---+-+-+-+-+-+--+-+-+-+-+--+-+-+-+--+-+-+-+-+--+-+-+-+-+-+--+  +25
25+ .
    .                                                                          .             .     .      +20
20+ .
    .                                                                                              .    +15  D
D15+.                                                                                                          E
 E  .                                               .                          .                       .       N
 S  .                                                                                                          S
 I  .                                                             .                                            I
T10+.                          .                           .                                           .     +10  T
 Y  .                                                                                                          Y
    .                                                            .             .                       .    + 5
 5+ .                                                      .                                           .
    .  .                                 .      .                                                .
 0+ .
    +--+-+-+-+-+-+-+--+-+-+--+--+-+-+--+---+-+-+-+-+-+--+-+-+-+-+--+-+-+-+--+-+-+-+-+--+-+-+-+-+-+--+  + 0
        1  23 4 5 6 7  8 90 1  2  3 4 56   7 8 9 0 1 2  3 4 5 6 7  8 90 1 2  3 4 5 6 7  8 9 0 1 2  3 4 5 6 7  8
                                            REFERENCE
```

CLUSTERS:

```
Start:     16:51  16:51  18:14  33:10  33:14  40:39  42:13  43:19  43:21  44:27  45:17  45:22  45:22
End:       18:24  16:52  18:24  33:16  33:16  46:20  43:25  43:25  43:22  44:29  45:19  45:25  45:23
Count:         5      2      3     17      2     14      5      4      2      2      5      2      2
Width:      1332     33    246   8669    158   3534   1699    694    100     52    630    163     56     20
Strength:   1.56   1.00   1.33   3.50   1.39   4.01   1.77   1.82   1.46   1.01   2.59   2.14   1.46   1.02
```

GAPS:

```
Start:      1:1   1:1    1:1   3:20  16:52  18:24  21:29  33:16  33:16
End:      45:22 43:21  33:14 16:51  16:51  33:14  33:10  42:13  40:39
Count:       22    15     10      3      2      7      4      3      2
Width:    26146 24777  18144   7812   6550  10299   9000   8867   6748   6608   6576   5982   4977
Strength:  1.31  3.34   3.06   3.74   5.05   1.53   3.16   4.45   5.23   1.06   1.80   2.51   3.58
```

Linguistic Density Plot in Ezekiel 1 - 48

For hay 21 (26 times)

Each Column = 13 Verses.   Separations are: Max = 7501.00, Mean = 1035.93, Min = 31.00 .

```
CLUSTERS:

Start:     5:11  14:16  14:16  16:48  17:16  20:31  26:20  32:23  32:23  32:23  32:23  32:23  32:25  33:27
End:      20:33  20:33  18: 3  14:20  18: 3  20:33  35:11  33:15  32:32  32:27  32:24  32:26  35:11
Count:       12     10      7      3      4      3     13     32     12      6      5      2      3      2      4
Width:     8294   4049   2345     95    945    262   5007   1902    623    228    132     70     34   1051
Strength:  1.19   2.11   1.76   1.42   1.30   1.30   2.82   3.65   2.86   2.41   2.13   1.00   1.44   1.00   1.23

GAPS:

Start:     1: 1   1: 1   1: 1   1: 1   7:13  20:33  20:33  35:11
End:      32:23  14:18  14:16   5:11  14:16  32:23  26:20  48:35  47: 9
Count:       15      5      4      2      2      3      2      3
Width:    17535   6392   6344   2099   3493   7142   4037   8532   7501
Strength:  1.14   1.19   1.94   1.06   2.46   3.66   3.00   4.66   6.47
```

Linguistic Density Plot in Ezekiel 1 - 48

For ḥayyâ 114 (33 times)

Each Column = 13 Verses.   Separations are: Max = 5131.50, Mean = 822.65, Min = 8.50 .

REFERENCE

CLUSTERS:

Start:	1: 5	1: 5	1:13	1:13	1:13	1:13	1:13	1:15	1:19	1:19	1:20	1:21	5:17	5:17	7:13	10:15	14:15	14:15	29: 5
End:	39:17	14:21	3:13	1:22	1:15	1:14	1:14	1:15	1:22	1:19	1:22	1:22	14:21	10:20	7:13	10:20	14:21	14:15	39:17
Count:	33	21	12	11	10	5	2	2	5	2	5	9	3	6	9	2	3	2	12
Width:	21931	6381	987	176	325	325	41	24	8	67	33	8	7	4196	2014	15	100	153	6288
Strength:	3.94	4.32	3.64	3.46	3.66	2.13	2.13	1.45	1.01	1.01	1.44	1.02	1.02	1.18	1.25	1.01	1.38	1.34	1.24

Start:	29: 5	31: 6	33:27	33:27	38:20
End:	34:28	32: 4	34:28	34: 8	39:17
Count:	9	3	5	3	3
Width:	3452	439	786	319	445
Strength:	1.56	1.08	1.64	1.19	1.07

Data for ḥayyā 114, continued.

GAPS:

Start:	1:22	7:13	10:20	14:15	14:15	14:21	14:21	14:21	14:21	34: 8	34:28	39: 4	39:17
End:	48:35	48:35	14:15	48:35	34: 5	34: 5	31: 6	29: 5	48:35	48:35	38:20	48:35	48:35
Count:	24	20	2	15	8	7	3	2	7	5	2	3	2
Width:	27551	25102	2029	21632	12326	12189	10263	9262	9248	8781	2391	6219	5945
Strength:	3.90	4.03	1.50	4.34	3.43	4.02	7.74	10.56	2.39	3.60	1.96	4.11	6.41

Linguistic Density Plot in Ezekiel 1 - 48

For hyh 311 (13 times)   hyh 312 (18 times)   hyh 314 (2 times)   hyh 3161 (9 times)
    hyh 3162 (1 times)   hyh 332 (2 times)   hyh 3362 (2 times)   hyh 3662 (1 times)

Each Column = 13 Verses. Separations are: Max = 3968.00, Mean = 570.82, Min = 6.00

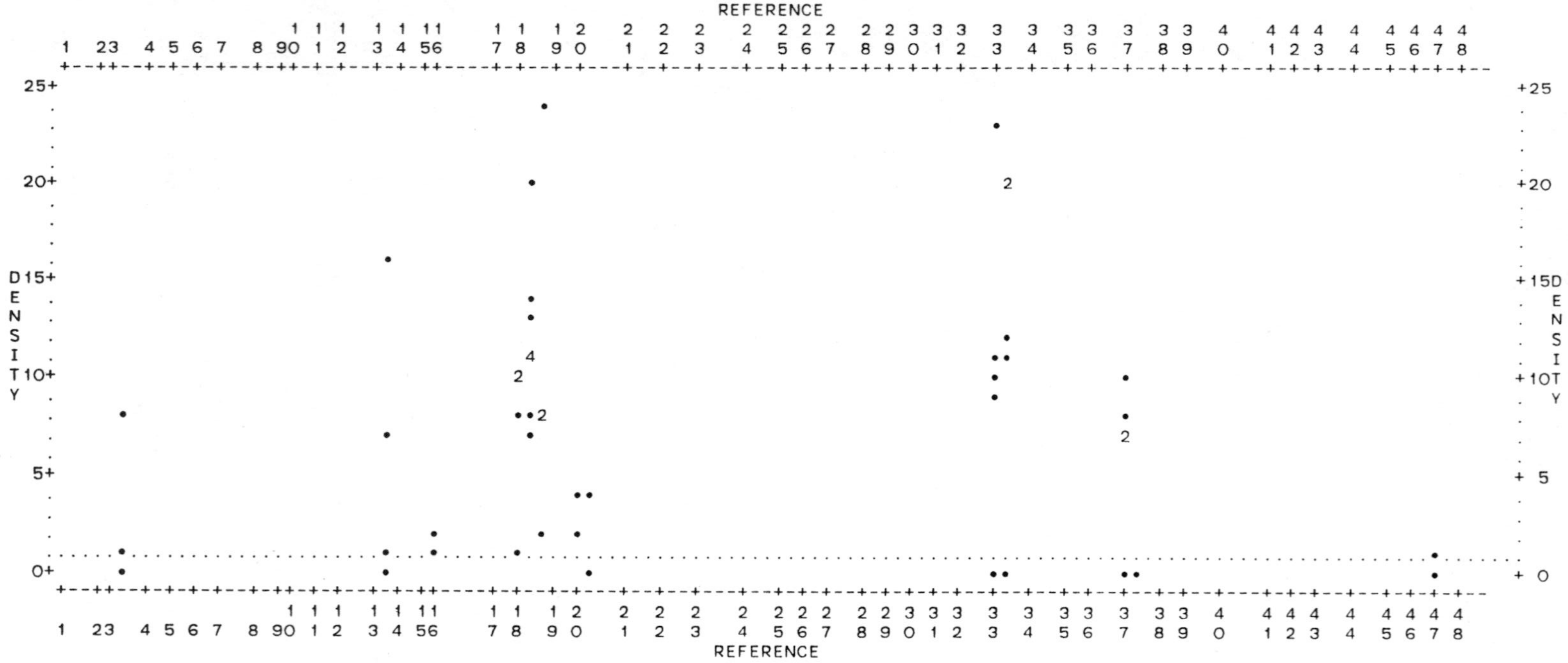

REFERENCE

(Linguistic density scatter plot. Vertical axis labelled DENSITY with scale markers 0+, 5+, +10, +15, +20, +25. Horizontal axis REFERENCE columns numbered 1 through 48.)

CLUSTERS:

Start:	3:18	3:18	3:21	13:18	13:18	13:18	18:21	18:27	20:11	33:10	33:15	33:12	33:13	33:16	37: 3	37: 3	18:17	18:19
End:	47: 9	20:25	3:21	20:25	16:	13:22	18:22	18:32	20:25	33:19	33:16	33:19	33:13	33:16	37:14	37: 6	18:19	18:19
Count:	48	30	2	27	3	6	4	9	4	10	4	5	13	2	6	3	2	2
Width:	25764	8992	97	4372	1013	125	107	315	353	205	63	63	1	254	64	110	50	1
Strength:	1.35	3.88	1.33	5.30	1.53	1.67	1.69	3.84	1.43	3.21	1.78	1.44	1.01	2.17	1.37	1.31	1.75	1.01

Start:	18:21	18:24	3:18	3:21	13:18	13:18	13:19	16:	18:	18:	9	9	18:17	18:17	18:19
End:	18:24	18:22	18:21	18:21	18:28	18:28	13:19	16:	18:32	18:24	18:13	18:	18:24	18:19	18:19
Count:	5	3	4	3	4	3	5	87	17	21	4	2	9	4	2
Width:	56	18	107	12	1375	2688	13	503	315	156	63	50	1
Strength:	2.05	1.43	1.69	1.44	3.21	3.22	2.02	1.01	1.44	4.65	3.84	5.16	1.73	3.01	1.75	1.01

Data for hyh 311, hyh 312, hyh 314, hyh 3161, hyh 3162, hyh 332, hyh 3362, hyh 3662, continued.

GAPS:

Start:	1: 1	3:21	3:21	16: 6	18:28	18:28	20:13	33:16	33:19	37:10	37:10					
End:	18: 9	3:18	13:19	13:18	18: 9	33:13	33:12	33:10	33:10	48:35	37: 3	37: 3	48:35	47: 9	47: 9	47:14
Count:	11	2	8	3	2	10	9	7	4	11	3	2	5	3	2	9
Width:	8814	1197	7520	4546	4523	1984	8886	8800	8135	7833	9787	2274	2229	7356	6334	6237
Strength:	1.94	1.11	2.54	4.34	7.06	2.52	2.44	2.94	4.14	6.77	12.98	2.55	1.44	2.96	4.68	6.63	10.13

Linguistic Density Plot in Ezekiel 1 - 48

For hyh 311 (13 times)   hyh 312 (18 times)   hyh 314 (2 times)   hyh 3161 (9 times)
     hyh 3162 (1 times)

Each Column = 13 Verses.   Separations are: Max = 3968.00, Mean = 635.68, Min = 6.50 .

```
REFERENCE
                                            (density plot — values plotted against REFERENCE verse axis)
```

CLUSTERS:

```
Start:     3:21   3:21  13:19  16: 6  18: 6  18: 9  18: 9  18: 9  18:13  18:17  18:17  18:19  18:21  18:21  18:21  18:28  18:28
End:      47: 9  20:25   3:21  20:25  16: 6  20:25  18:32  18:24  18:    18:13  18:24  18:19  18:17  18:19  18:22  18:24  18:21  18:28  18:32
Count:      43     25     2     23     2     20     16     13     9      2      9      5      2      2      3      3      1
Width:    25668   8896   4345   503   315    156    50     56     18            96            1
Strength:  1.18   3.06   1.02  4.62  1.00   4.56   3.93   3.06   1.75   1.01   1.02   1.76   2.07   1.02   1.76   1.02   1.44   1.02   1.35   1.02

Start:    20:11  33:10  33:10  33:12  33:13  33:13  33:15  33:15  33:15  33:16  37: 3  37: 3  37: 9  37:10
End:      20:25  37:14  33:13  33:13  33:13  33:13  33:16  33:15  33:19  33:16  37:14  37: 6  37:14  37:10
Count:      4     16     5      2      2      6      3      4      2      3      3      2
Width:     353   2688    205    87     63     18     254    64     110    13
Strength:  1.47   3.46   3.27   2.04   1.44   1.02   2.06   1.79   1.02   2.20   1.38   1.02   1.02   1.33   1.00
```

Data for hyh 311, hyh 312, hyh 314, hyh 3161, hyh 3162, continued.

GAPS:

```
Start:     1: 1   1: 1   3:21   3:21  16: 6  18:28  18:28  20:13  20:25  33:16  33:16  33:19  37:10  37:10  37:14
End:      18:17  18: 9   3:21  13:19  16: 9  18: 9  33:13  33:12  33:10  33:10  48:35  37: 3  37: 3  48:35  47: 9  47: 9
Count:       11     7      2      2     10      9      7      4      2     11      3      2      5      3      2
Width:     8973   8814   1293   7520   5528   4550   1984   8886   8874   8800   8135   7833   9787   2274   2229   7356   6334   6237
Strength:  1.49   3.49   1.05   4.15   4.90   6.29   2.16   1.88   2.35   3.48   5.92  11.58   1.96   1.15   2.56   4.01   5.82   9.01
```

Linguistic Density Plot in Ezekiel 1 - 48

For hyh 311 (13 times)

Each Column = 13 Verses.   Separations are: Max =   6251.00, Mean =   1997.86, Min =   103.50 .

CLUSTERS:

Start:	18:13	18:13	18:13	18:13	18:23	20:11	20:11	33:11	37: 5	37: 5
End:	47: 9	20:21	18:32	18:13	18:32	18:24	20:21	37:14	37:14	37: 6
Count:	13	8	5	2	3	2	4	3	2	
Width:	18086	1211	442	2	207	19	250	2664	212	22
Strength:	2.32	3.53	2.31	1.07	1.49	1.06	1.48	1.12	1.49	1.06

GAPS:

Start:	1: 1	20:13	20:21	37:14	37:14	
End:	18:13	37: 5	33:11	48:35	47: 9	
Count:	2	4	3	2		
Width:	8875	10611	10412	7960	7259	6251
Strength:	3.69	1.55	2.53	3.20	1.29	2.28

Linguistic Density Plot in Ezekiel 1 - 48

For hyh 312 (18 times)

Each Column = 13 Verses. Separations are: Max = 6334.00, Mean = 1472.11, Min =   31.00 .

REFERENCE

(Vertical axis labels, top to bottom): +25 +20 +15 D E N S I +10 T Y +5 +0 O

(Plot grid with density points plotted against reference columns 1–48)

REFERENCE

CLUSTERS:

Start:	13:19	18: 9	18:17	18:17	18:17	18:21	33:10	33:15	37: 3	37: 9
End:	20:25	20:25	18:28	18:28	18:22	18:19	33:10	33:16	37:10	37:10
Count:	8	7	6	5	4	2	8	5	3	2
Width:	4345	1374	407	248	117	49	17	2591	205	62	157	13
Strength:	1.97	2.56	2.52	2.21	1.88	1.01	1.04	2.55	2.22	1.50	1.45	1.04

GAPS:

Start:	1: 1	1: 1	3:21	18:22	18:28	20:25	37:10
End:	18:17	18: 9	13:19	33:13	33:10	33:10	48:35	47: 9
Count:	5	4	3	2	5	4	3	2
Width:	8974	8815	7521	9018	8931	8800	7833	7356	6334
Strength:	1.20	1.92	2.38	1.22	1.97	3.05	4.55	2.29	3.48

Linguistic Density Plot in Ezekiel 1 - 48

For hyh 3161 (9 times)

Each Column = 13 Verses.   Separations are: Max = 7521.00, Mean = 2797.00, Min = 36.50

REFERENCE

CLUSTERS:

Start:	3:21	3:21	18: 9	18:17	18:17	33:13	33:15	
End:	33:16	18:28	18:28	18:21	18:19	33:16	33:16	
Count:	9	6	5	4	3	3	2	
Width:	16888	7928	407	248	100	49	73	17
Strength:	1.62	1.43	2.60	2.10	1.62	1.08	1.63	1.09

GAPS:

Start:	3:21	18:21	18:28	33:16
End:	18: 9	33:13	48:35	
Count:	2	3	2	2
Width:	7521	9035	8887	9788
Strength:	1.86	1.01	2.40	2.76

Linguistic Density Plot in Ezekiel 1 - 48

For hayil 111 (14 times)

Each Column = 13 Verses.   Separations are: Max = 7103.50, Mean = 1864.67, Min =   12.00 .

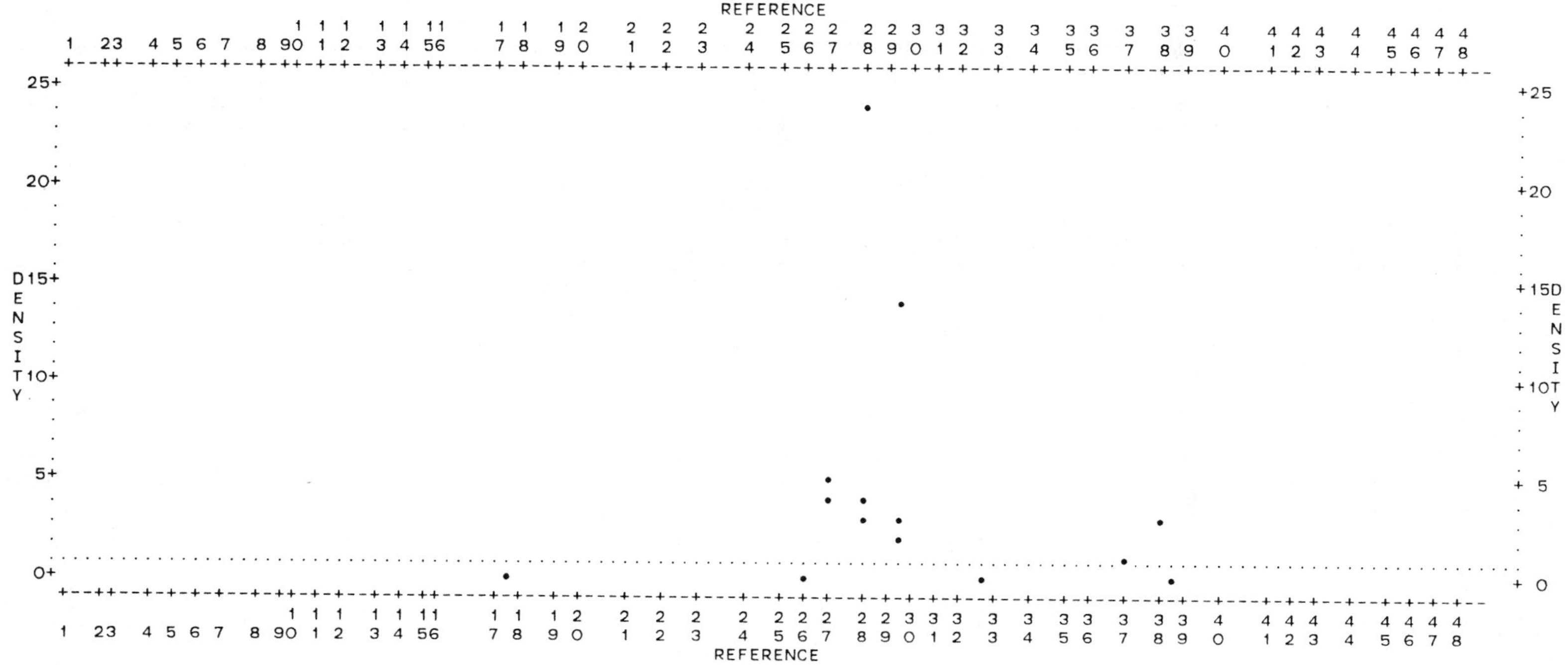

CLUSTERS:

Start:	17:17	26:12	26:12	27:10	28: 4	28: 5	29:18	29:18	37:10
End:	38:15	32:31	29:19	27:11	29:19	28: 5	29:19	29:18	38:15
Count:	14	13	10	9	2	6	3	2	3
Width:	12997	7252	3544	1872	415	940	18	64	21	839
Strength:	4.72	5.40	3.86	3.73	1.39	1.05	2.54	1.55	1.06	1.54	1.05	1.21

GAPS:

Start:	1: 1	1: 1	1: 1	1: 1	38:15
End:	28: 5	28: 4	27:10	26:12	17:17	48:35
Count:	7	6	4	3	2	2
Width:	15155	15138	14603	14206	8461	6511
Strength:	1.15	1.76	3.22	4.40	3.78	2.66

For ḥîcôn 21 (18 times)

Linguistic Density Plot in Ezekiel 1 - 48

Each Column = 13 Verses.   Separations are: Max = 18696.00.   Mean = 1472.11.   Min = 19.50 .

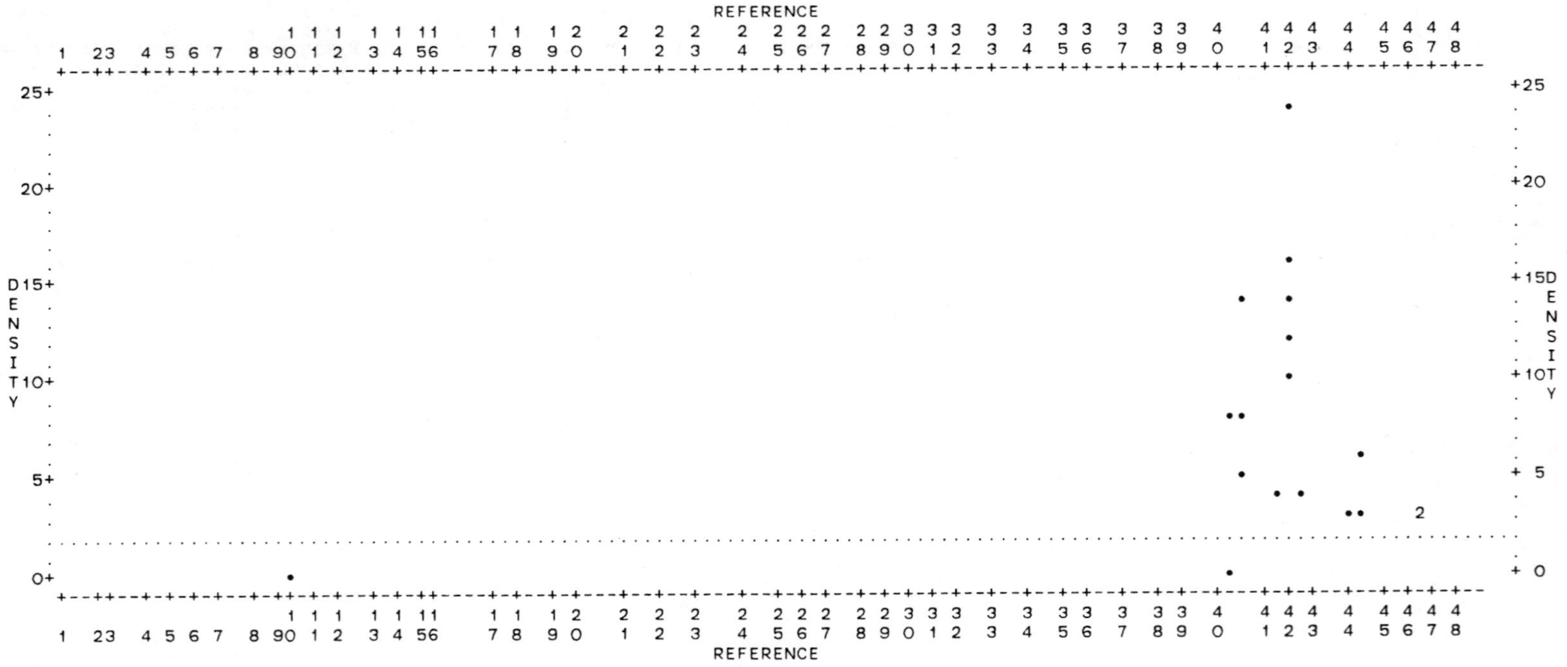

REFERENCE

(Vertical axis: DENSITY, with scale markers +25, +20, +15, +10, +5, +0)

(Horizontal axis columns numbered 1–48; marker "2" near the +5 level)

CLUSTERS:

Start:	10: 5	40:17	40:17	40:17	40:31	40:34	41:17	42: 1	42: 7	42: 7	44: 1	44:19	46:20
End:	46:21	42:14	40:20	40:37	40:37	40:37	42:14	42: 3	42: 9	42: 8	46:21	44:19	46:21
Count:	18	17	2	5	2	6	7	6	5	3	2	3	2
Width:	22705	4009	54	115	54	408	428	265	151	41	1792	480	10
Strength:	1.20	8.56	1.01	1.47	1.01	2.14	2.89	2.57	2.24	1.02	1.60	1.28	1.04

GAPS:

Start:	1: 1	1: 1	1: 1	1: 1	1: 1	10: 5
End:	44:19	42: 7	42: 1	40:34	40:17	40:17
Count:	16	11	9	6	3	2
Width:	25385	24015	23903	23045	22691	18696
Strength:	1.29	2.97	3.92	5.69	10.28	12.33

Linguistic Density Plot in Ezekiel 1 - 48

For ḥokmâ 114 (5 times)

Each Column = 13 Verses.   Separations are: Max =   7575.00, Mean =   4661.66, Min =   33.50 .

REFERENCE

CLUSTERS:

Start:	28: 4	28: 4	28:12	
End:	28:17	28: 7	28: 5	28:17
Count:	5	3	2	2
Width:	248	67	20	104
Strength:	3.69	1.85	1.17	1.15

GAPS:

Start:	1: 1	28:17
End:	28: 4	48:35
Count:	2	2
Width:	15129	12592
Strength:	2.65	2.01

Linguistic Density Plot in Ezekiel 1 - 48

For hel'â 114 (5 times)

Each Column = 13 Verses. Separations are: Max = 7357.00, Mean = 4661.66, Min = 7.50 .

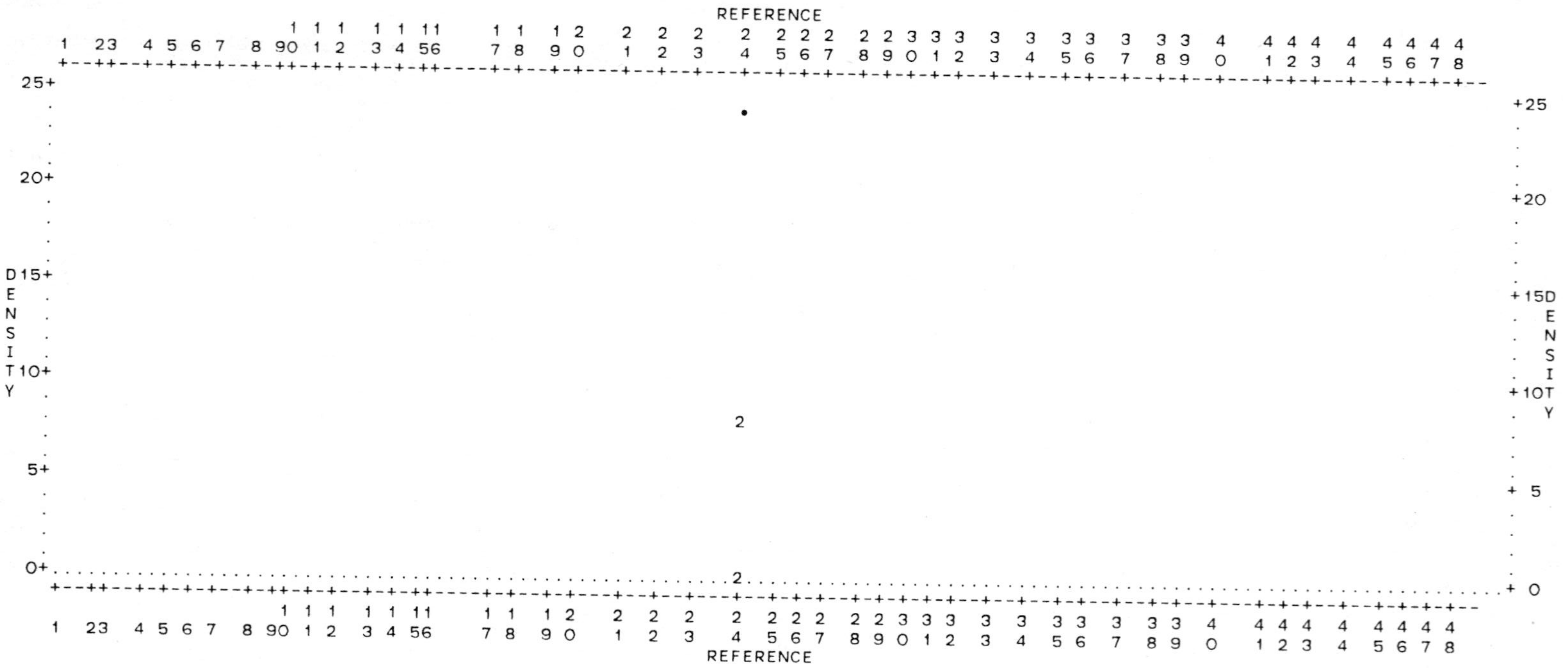

CLUSTERS:

Start:	24: 6	24: 6	24:11	24:12
End:	24:12	24: 6	24:12	24:12
Count:	5	2	3	2
Width:	126	5	15	4
Strength:	3.71	1.18	1.86	1.18

GAPS:

Start:	1: 1	24:12
End:	24: 6	48:35
Count:	2	2
Width:	13133	14710
Strength:	2.15	2.55

Linguistic Density Plot in Ezekiel 1 - 48

For ḥallôn 114 (12 times)

Each Column = 13 Verses. Separations are: Max = 11339.00, Mean = 2151.54, Min = 9.50 .

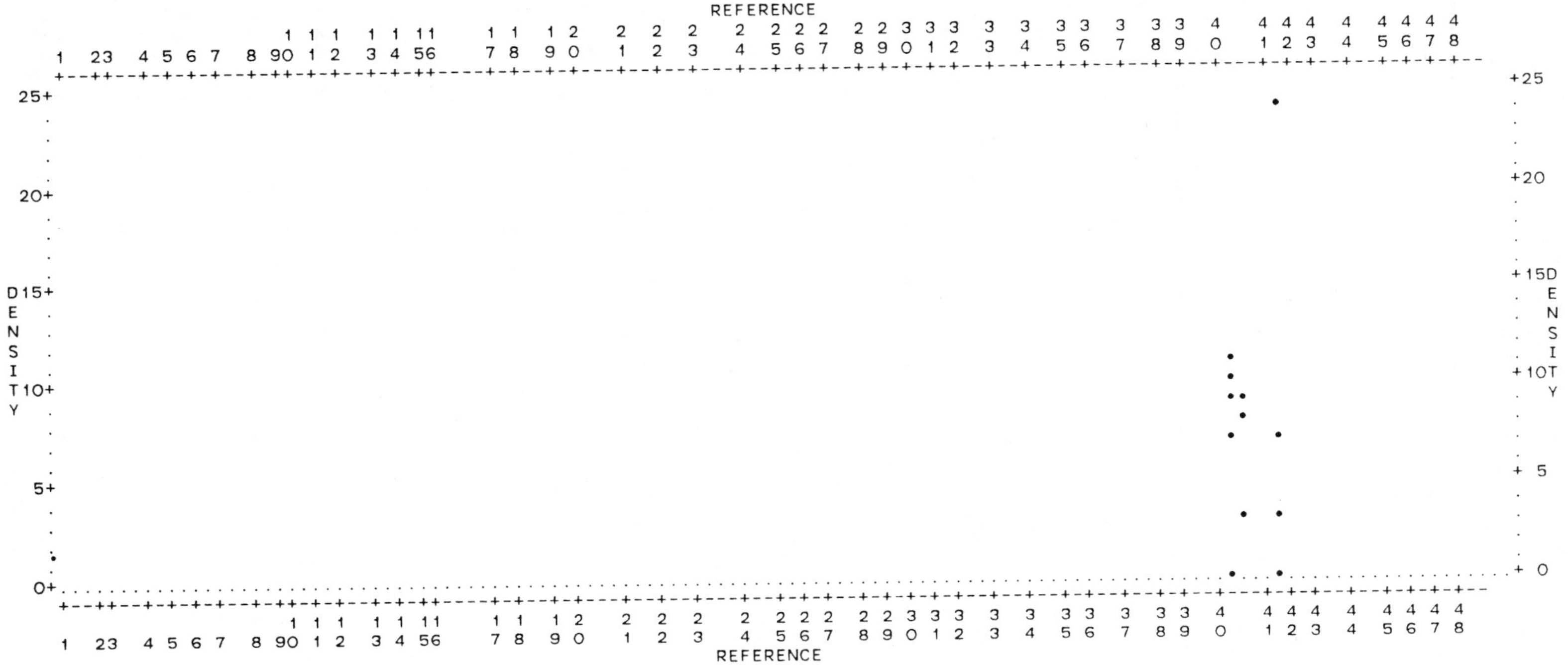

CLUSTERS:

Start:	40:16	40:16	40:16	40:16	40:22	40:25	40:29	40:33	41:16	41:16	41:16
End:	41:26	40:36	40:25	40:16	40:25	40:25	40:36	40:36	41:26	41:16	41:16
Count:	12	8	5	2	3	2	3	2	4	3	2
Width:	1223	422	207	19	80	10	132	58	183	19	2
Strength:	8.32	3.92	2.43	1.07	1.56	1.07	1.54	1.05	1.99	1.58	1.07

GAPS:

Start:	1: 1	1: 1
End:	40:16	40:25
Count:	2	5
Width:	22658	22855
Strength:	10.29	4.12

For ḥālāl 111 (35 times)

Linguistic Density Plot in Ezekiel 1 - 48

Each Column = 13 Verses.   Separations are: Max = 4292.00, Mean = 776.94, Min =   8.50 .

REFERENCE

DENSITY (vertical axis labels: +25, +20, +15, +10, +5, 0)

REFERENCE

CLUSTERS:

Start:	6: 4	6: 4	6: 4	9: 7	11: 6	11: 6	21:19	21:19	30: 4	30: 4	31:17	32:20	32:20	32:20	32:21	32:25
End:	35: 8	11: 7	6:13	11: 7	11: 7	11: 7	35: 8	21:34	21:19	35: 8	32:32	32:32	32:25	32:24	32:22	32:25
Count:	35	7	3	4	3	2	4	2	21	19	3	16	14	8	5	2
Width:	17034	2101	199	680	17	8328	305	3227	1601	403	744	304	141	81	40	34	16
Strength:	8.90	1.49	1.28	1.29	1.45	1.01	6.35	1.59	1.02	5.38	5.38	4.81	4.43	2.91	2.09	1.43	1.44	1.00

Start:	32:28	32:32	32:28	32:30	35: 8
End:	32:32	32:30	32:29	32:30	35: 8
Count:	6	4	2	2	
Width:	93	49	16	12	11
Strength:	2.38	1.79	1.00	1.01	1.01	1.01	1.00

Data for ḥālāl 111, continued.

GAPS:

Start:	1: 1	1: 1	11: 7	21:34	21:34	21:34	32:32	35: 8
End:	21:19	6: 4	21:19	30: 4	28: 8	26:15	35: 8	48:35
Count:	9		2	2	5	3	2	2
Width:	11068	2362	6605	4796	3836	2908	1615	8573
Strength:	2.53	2.09	7.71	1.16	2.16	2.81	1.10	10.31

Linguistic Density Plot in Ezekiel 1 - 48

For hll 321 (3 times)   hll 322 (1 times)   hll 331 (14 times)
     hll 332 (5 times)   hll 334 (1 times)   hll 344 (1 times)
     hll 362 (3 times)

     hll 3262 (3 times)
     hll 3362 (2 times)

Each Column = 13 Verses.   Separations are: Max = 3277.00, Mean = 822.65, Min = 8.00.

CLUSTERS:

Start:	7:21	7:21	7:21	7:21	7:21	9: 6	20: 9	20: 9	20:13	20:13	20:21	22: 8	23:38	23:38
End:	44: 7	28:18	13:19	9: 6	7:24	28:18	20:39	20:24	20:16	20:14	20:24	28:18	22:26	25: 3	23:39
Count:	33	26	7	6	4	7	8	7	4	3	3	11	8	4	2
Width:	22036	12366	2782	727	46	5619	384	188	78	76	3827	2052	354	833	20
Strength:	3.85	3.93	1.19	2.02	1.80	3.89	2.61	2.52	1.69	1.40	1.00	2.04	1.93	1.57	1.21

Start:	28: 7	28:18	36:20	36:20	36:23
End:	28:18	39: 7	36:23	36:22	36:23
Count:	3	6	5	3	2
Width:	204	1792	75	16	4
Strength:	1.29	1.38	2.11	1.46	1.02

Data for h11 321   h11 322, h11 3262, h11 331, h11 332, h11 334, h11 3362, h11 344, h11 362, continued.

GAPS:

```
Start:     1: 1   9: 6   9:: 6  13:19  23:39  28:18  36:23  39: 7  39: 7
End:       7:21  20:13  20: 9         36:20  36:20  48:35  48:35  44: 7
Count:        2      4      3      2      7      2      4      3      2
Width:     3037   6130   6020   3965   7189   4601   7890   6173   3277
Strength:  2.77   2.73   3.93   3.93   1.24   4.72   4.04   4.06   3.07
```

Linguistic Density Plot in Ezekiel 1 - 48

For ḥll 321 (3 times)   ḥll 322 (1 times)   ḥll 3262 (3 times)

Each Column = 13 Verses. Separations are: Max = 8019.50, Mean = 3496.25, Min = 168.50 .

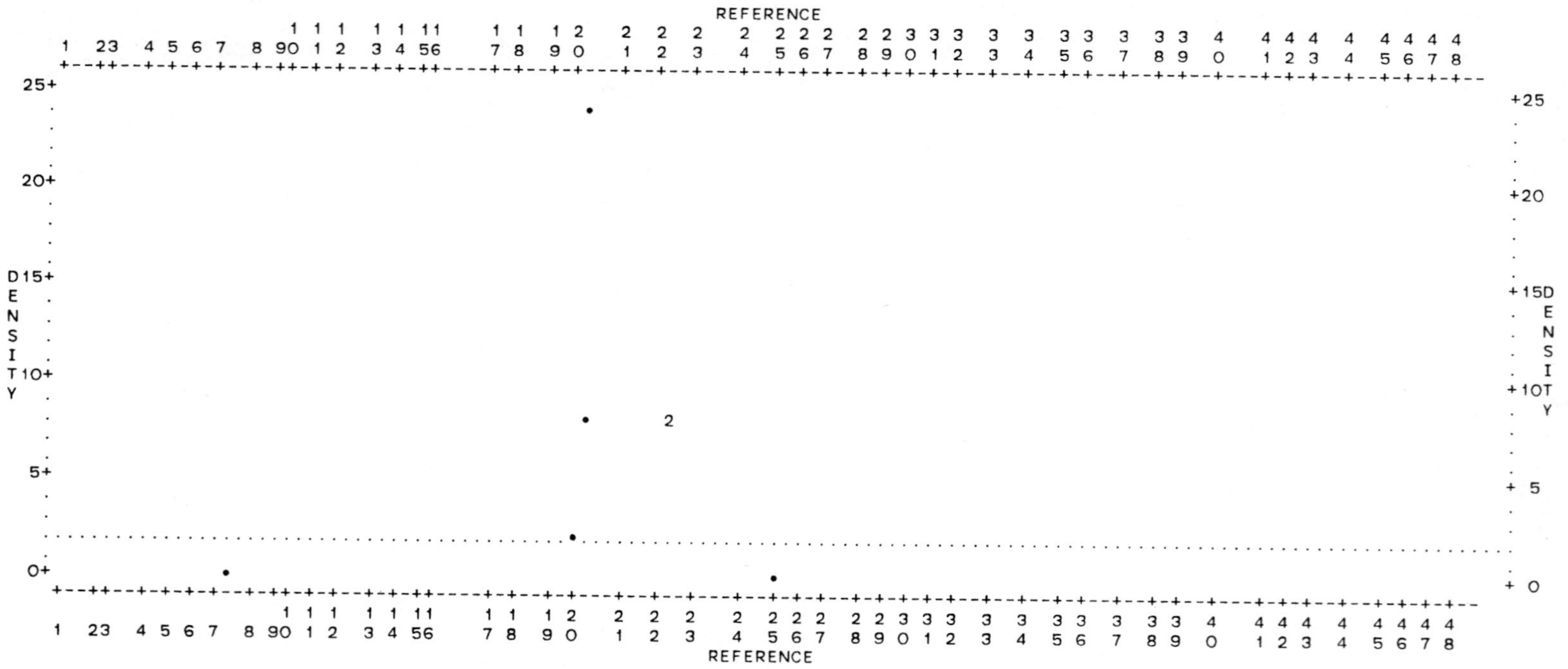

CLUSTERS:

Start:	7:24	20: 9	20: 9	22:16	22:16
End:	25: 3	25: 3	20:22	20:14	25: 3	22:26
Count:	7	6	2	3	2
Width:	10545	3844	337	133	1913	215
Strength:	2.58	3.02	1.64	1.09	1.25	1.06

GAPS:

Start:	7:24	22:26	25: 3
End:	20: 9	48:35	48:35
Count:	2	3	2
Width:	6701	16039	14341
Strength:	1.03	2.24	3.51

Linguistic Density Plot in Ezekiel 1 - 48

For hll 331 (14 times)   hll 332 (5 times)   hll 334 (1 times)   hll 3362 (2 times)
    hll 344 (1 times)

Each Column = 13 Verses.   Separations are: Max = 4994.00. Mean = 1165.42, Min = 8.00 .

CLUSTERS:

```
Start:      7:21    7:21    7:21   20:13   20:13   22: 8   23:38   28: 7   28:16   36:20   36:22   36:23
End:       44: 7   24:21    7:22   24:21   20:39   24:21   23:39   28:18   36:23   36:21   36:23   36:23
Count:        23      14       3       2      10       5       3       8       2       5       3       2
Width:     22036   10393      19       9    3536    1854     635      20    4880     204      75      24      16
Strength:   2.33    1.70    1.49    1.03    2.56    1.92    1.74    1.34    1.09    1.02    1.28    1.37    1.00    2.19    1.02    1.49    1.03
```

GAPS:

```
Start:      1: 1    7:21    7:22   13:19   28:18   36:23   36:23
End:        7:21   20:21   20:13   36:20   48:35   44: 7
Count:         2       2       5       3       2       3       2
Width:      3037    7036    6838    4075    4601    7890    4994
Strength:   1.67    1.13    2.91    2.60    3.07    3.59    3.42
```

For h11 331 (14 times)

Linguistic Density Plot in Ezekiel 1 - 48

Each Column = 13 Verses.   Separations are: Max = 3953.00, Mean = 1864.67, Min = 9.50 .

(Density plot. Vertical axis labeled DENSITY: 25+, 20+, D15+, E, N, S, I, T10+, Y, 5+, 0+. Right reference axis: +25, +20, +15D, E, N, S, I, +10T, Y, 5, O. Horizontal axis labeled REFERENCE, columns numbered 1 through 48.)

CLUSTERS:

Start:	7:21	7:21	7:21	20:13	20:13	20:21	36:21	36:22
End:	36:23	23:38	7:22	23:38	20:16	20:24	36:23	36:23
Count:	14	9	3	6	2	3	2	
Width:	17042	9758	19	9	2901	274	78	76	51	16
Strength:	3.02	1.47	1.56	1.06	1.94	1.90	1.02	1.02	1.54	1.05

GAPS:

Start:	7:22	28:18	36:23
End:	20:13	36:21	48:35
Count:	2	2	2
Width:	6838	4625	7890
Strength:	2.85	1.58	3.45

Linguistic Density Plot in Ezekiel 1 - 48

For hll 332 (5 times)

Each Column = 13 Verses.   Separations are: Max = 6306.50, Mean = 4661.66, Min = 2406.50 .

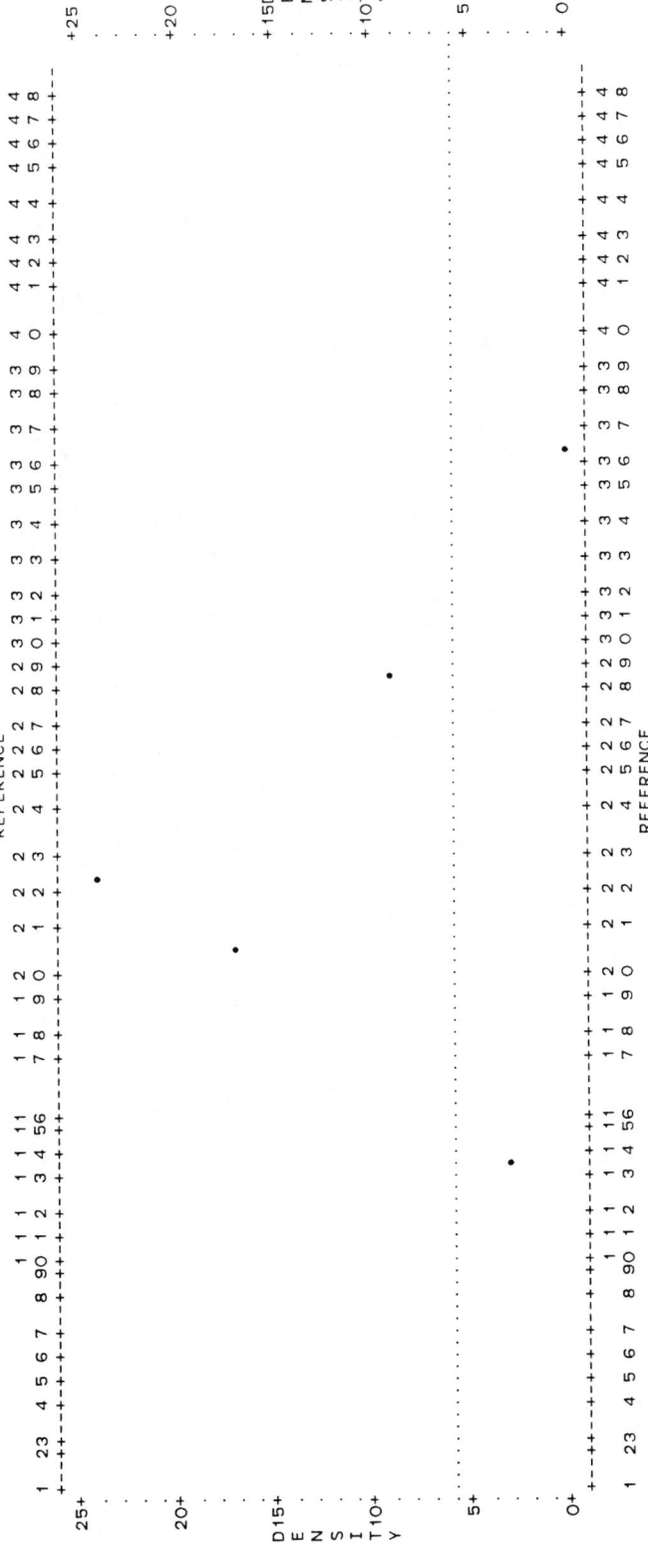

All cluster strengths are less than 1.00.

All gap strengths are less than 1.00.

Linguistic Density Plot in Ezekiel 1 - 48

For ḥēmâ 114 (33 times)

Each Column = 13 Verses.   Separations are: Max =   4004.00, Mean =   822.65, Min =   23.50

CLUSTERS:

Start:	3:14	3:14	3:14	5:13	5:13	5:15	13:13	13:13	13:13	19:12	19:12	22:20	24: 8
End:	38:18	16:42	9: 8	7: 8	7: 8	5:15	16:42	14:19	13:15	13:13	25:17	20:21	25:17
Count:	33	15	9	7	6	4	3	4	3	7	14	3	7	4
Width:	20436	6492	2716	1634	570	66	18	1922	740	47	4451	1607	587	335	2153	779
Strength:	5.29	2.15	1.92	1.83	2.11	1.79	1.00	1.02	1.30	1.28	1.43	1.01	2.71	1.84	1.40	1.17	1.54	1.25

GAPS:

Start:	5:15	9: 8	13:13	16:42	20:34	22:22	25:17	30:15	36:18	38:18
End:	48:35	13:13	48:35	19:12	48:35	48:35	48:35	36: 6	48:35	48:35
Count:	30	2	24	14	11	6	3	2
Width:	25732	1854	22279	1911	17529	16119	14008	5773	3351	8008	6426
Strength:	1.11	1.29	1.51	1.36	2.97	3.66	5.90	3.71	3.16	5.71	7.01

Linguistic Density Plot in Ezekiel 1 - 48

For hml 312 (7 times)   hml 3162 (1 times)

Each Column = 13 Verses.   Separations are: Max = 13235.00, Mean = 3107.78, Min = 140.00 .

CLUSTERS:

Start:	5:11	5:11	5:11	7: 4	8:18	9: 5
End:	36:21	16: 5	9:10	7: 9	9:10	9:10
Count:	8	5	7	3	2	
Width:	17888	4653	1733	638	280	131
Strength:	1.05	3.35	3.14	1.51	1.08	1.61	1.07

GAPS:

Start:	7: 9	9:10	16: 5	16: 5
End:	48:35	48:35	48:35	36:21
Count:	7	4	3	2
Width:	25197	24102	21182	13235
Strength:	1.57	3.54	4.06	3.64

Linguistic Density Plot in Ezekiel 1 - 48

For hml 312 (7 times)

Each Column = 13 Verses.   Separations are: Max = 16155.00, Mean = 3496.25, Min = 140.00 .

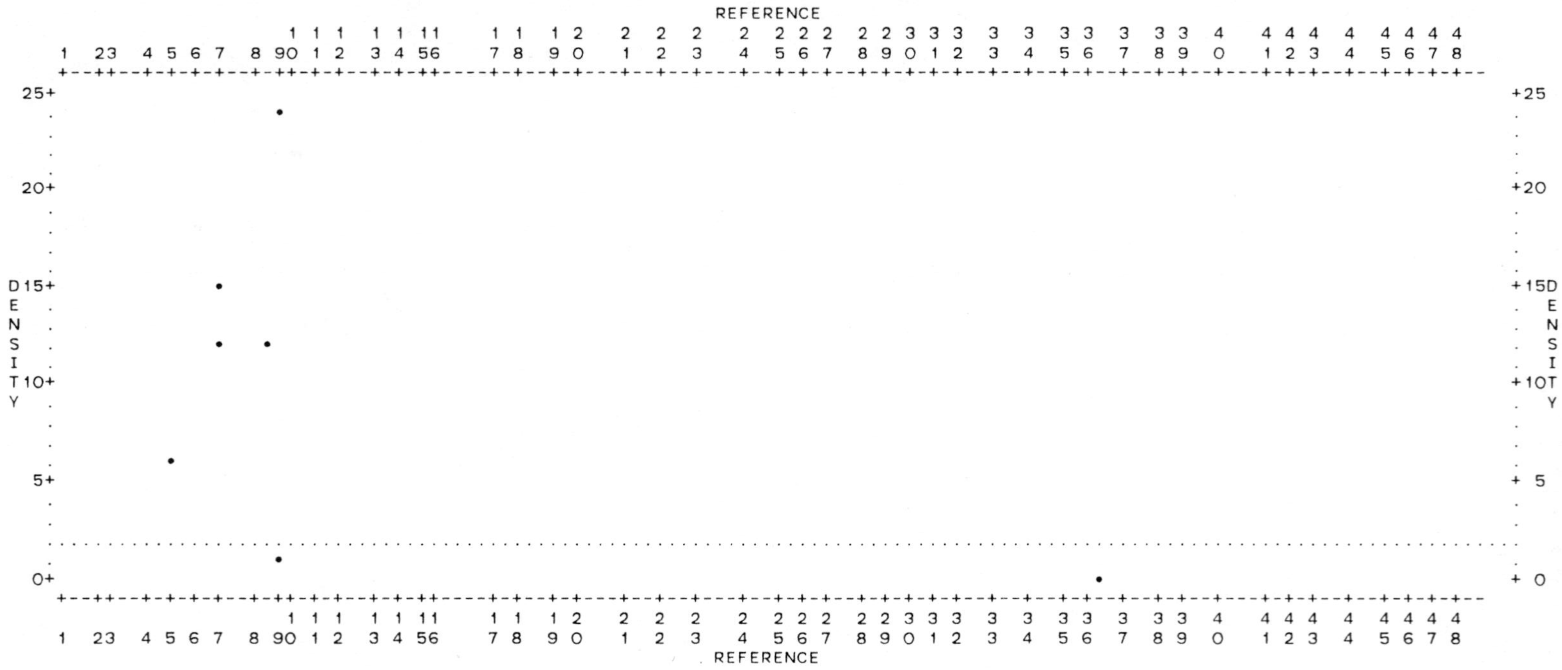

CLUSTERS:

Start:	5:11	5:11	7: 4	8:18	9: 5
End:	9:10	7: 9	7: 9	9:10	9:10
Count:	6	3	2	3	2
Width:	1733	638	88	280	131
Strength:	3.48	1.57	1.10	1.66	1.09

GAPS:

Start:	7: 9	9:10	9:10
End:	48:35	48:35	36:21
Count:	6	3	2
Width:	25197	24102	16155
Strength:	1.70	4.23	4.10

Linguistic Density Plot in Ezekiel 1 - 48

For ḥāmās 111 (6 times)

Each Column = 13 Verses.   Separations are: Max = 10525.00, Mean = 3995.71, Min = 379.00 .

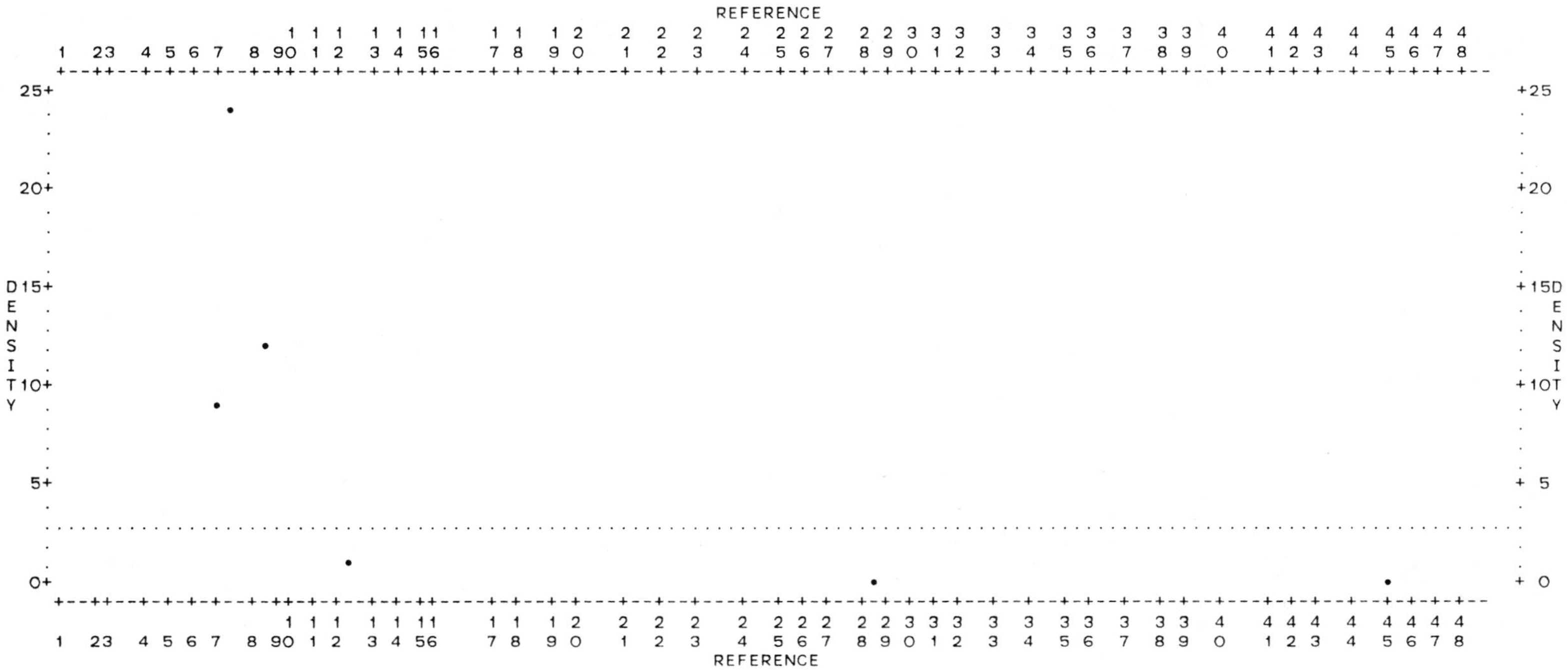

CLUSTERS:

Start:	7:11	7:11	
End:	12:19	8:17	7:23
Count:	4	3	2
Width:	2473	758	266
Strength:	1.94	1.61	1.07

GAPS:

Start:	7:23	8:17	12:19	12:19	28:16
End:	48:35	48:35	48:35	45:9	45:9
Count:	6	5	4	3	2
Width:	24901	24409	22694	20602	10525
Strength:	1.10	1.72	1.18	2.82	1.88

Linguistic Density Plot in Ezekiel 1 - 48

For ḥōmer 111 (7 times)

Each Column = 13 Verses.   Separations are: Max = 12961.00, Mean = 3496.25, Min =   3.50 .

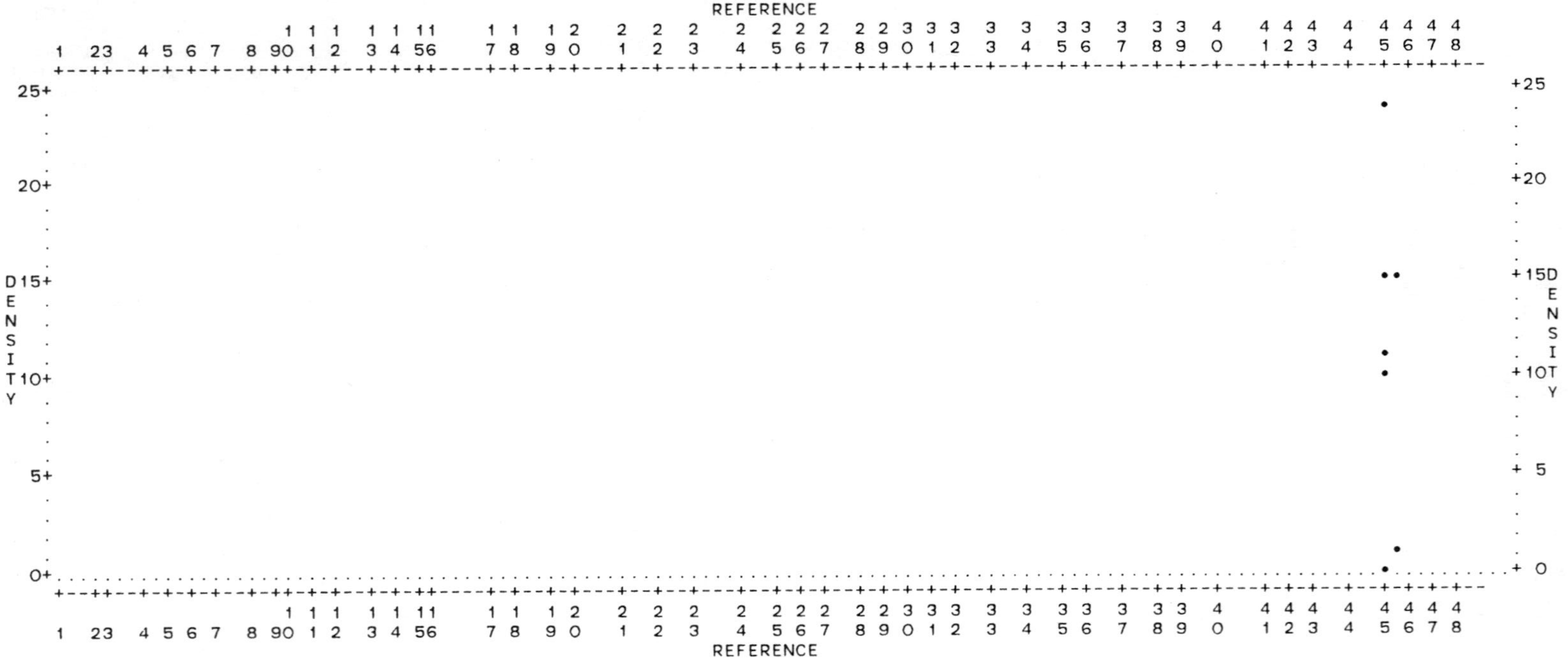

CLUSTERS:

Start:	45:11	45:11	45:11	45:13	45:14
End:	45:14	45:11	45:11	45:13 45:14	45:13	45:14
Count:	7	3	2	4	2
Width:	59	7	3	23	6	4
Strength:	5.18	1.73	1.13	2.31	1.13	1.13

GAPS:

Start:	1: 1	1: 1
End:	45:11	45:11
Count:	3	2
Width:	25921	25917
Strength:	4.68	7.27

Linguistic Density Plot in Ezekiel 1 - 48

For ḥamiššā 711 (38 times)   ḥāmēš 714 (35 times)   ḥamišî 721 (1 times)   ḥamišit 724 (1 times)

Each Column = 13 Verses.   Separations are: Max = 6952.50, Mean = 368.03, Min = 4.00

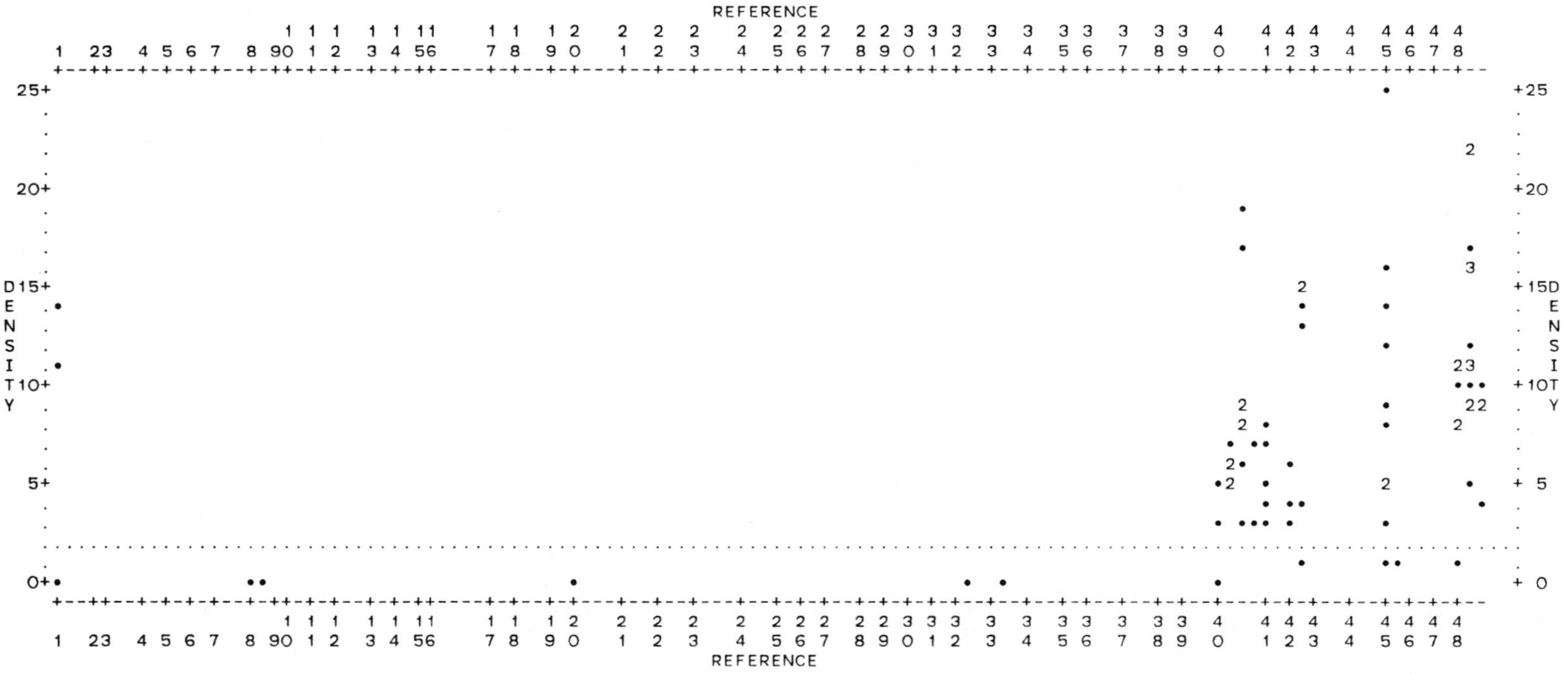

(Scatter / density plot. Vertical axis labelled DENSITY with gridlines at +25, +20, +15, +10, +5, +0 / O. Horizontal axis labelled REFERENCE, columns numbered 1 through 48.)

CLUSTERS:

```
Start:     1: 1  40: 1  40: 1  40: 1  40: 7  40:21  40:21  40:29  40:29  40:30  40:30  40:33  40:33  40:33  40:36  40:48  40:48  40:48  41: 9  42: 2  42: 2
End:       1: 2  48:34  42:20  40:36  40:15  40:36  40:25  40:36  40:30  40:30  40:36  40:33  40:36  40:36  40:36  41:12  41: 2  41:12  42:12  42:20  42:20
Count:        3     67     32     16      3     12      4      8      8      2      4      2      4     16      2      7      4      3      3      8      2
Width:       23   5632   1960    780    345    317     99    133     20      4     58      4     58    936     16    298     83     58    340    340    100
Strength:  1.39  17.31   6.03   3.73   1.15   3.32   1.61   2.65   1.74   1.00   1.68   1.00   1.32   3.61   1.00   2.22   1.64   1.32   2.66   2.66   1.24

Start:     42:16  42:20  45: 1  45: 1  45: 1  45: 2  45: 2  45: 5  48: 8  48: 8  48: 9  48:13  48:13  48:13  48:16  48:16  48:16
End:       42:20  42:19  48:34  45:25  45: 1  45: 6  45: 3  45: 6  48:21  48:34  48:10  48:21  48:17  48:15  48:13  48:17  48:17
Count:         6      4     11     16      8      8      5      4      3      4      3     20     16     12      4      8      4
Width:        53     32   2271    518    111     41    ...     20      2     35     24    544    325    212     34    121     45     51     25
Strength:   2.26   1.72   1.00   6.46   2.67   2.00   1.74   1.42   1.38   4.83   1.37   4.18   3.50   1.70   2.73   1.73
```

```
Clusters for ḥamissā 711, ḥāmēs 714, ḥāmîšî 721, ḥāmîšî 724, continued.

Start:     48:17 48:20 48:30
End:       48:17 48:21 48:34
Count:         4     4     4
Width:        15    47    70
Strength:   1.75  1.70  1.66

GAPS:
  .

Start:     1: 1  1: 1  1: 1  1: 1  1: 1  1: 2  1: 2  1: 2  1: 2  1: 2  8:16  8:16 20: 1 33:21 42:20 45:12 45:25
End:      45: 2 42:20 40:36 40:33 40:30 40:25 40:21 40:13 40: 7 40: 1  8: 1 40: 1 32:17 40: 1 45: 3 48: 8 48: 8
Count:       43    40    24    22    20    16    13    11     9     8     7     5     3     2     3     8     2
Width:    25692 24266 23086 23032 22973 22867 22836 22742 22595 22479 22279 18791 13905  7853  4057  1458  1209
Strength:  6.45  6.22  9.98 10.73 11.57 13.67 15.84 17.69 20.08 21.59 23.35 24.33 25.80 20.60 10.15  1.41  2.31
```

Linguistic Density Plot in Ezekiel 1 - 48

For ḥamiššā 711 (38 times)

Each Column = 13 Verses.   Separations are: Max =   7367.00, Mean =   717.18, Min =   5.00 .

REFERENCE

CLUSTERS:

Start:	8: 1	32:17	40:15	40:15	40:25	42: 2	42: 7	45: 1	45: 1	45: 1	45: 2	45: 5	45: 6	45:12	45:12	48: 8	48: 8
End:	48:21	48:21	48:21	40:36	40:36	42: 8	48:21	45:25	45: 6	45: 3	45: 3	45: 6	45: 6	45:25	45:12	48:21	48:15
Count:	38	34	9	6	4	3	2	25	9	6	3	2	2	3	2	16	8
Width:	24572	10299	5068	1375	431	219	100	2052	518	111	41	29	12	5	6	325	158
Strength:	2.01	11.03	11.65	2.44	2.13	1.63	1.36	1.01	7.04	2.92	2.34	1.42	1.00	1.44	1.01	1.20	4.84

Start:	48: 9	48: 9	48:13	48:13	48:15	48:17	48:17	48:20	48:21
End:	48:10	48:10	48:13	48:15	48:21	48:17	48:17	48:20	48:21
Count:	3	4	2	2	4	2	2	2	2
Width:	34	45	11	7	106	8	4	47	12
Strength:	1.43	1.00	1.78	1.00	2.89	1.81	1.01	1.78	1.01

Data for hämissä 711. continued.

GAPS:

Start:	1: 1	1: 1	1: 1	1: 1	1: 1	1: 1	1: 1	1: 1	1: 1	1: 1	1: 1	1: 1	1: 1	1: 1	1: 1
End:	48:20	48:17	48:17	45: 6	42: 7	40:33	40:29	40:25	40:21	40:15	8: 1	40:15	8:16	33:21	42: 8
										40:15	32:17	40:15	45: 1		
Count:	36	34	33	32	19	13	10	9	8	7	6	2	4	2	2	1
Width:	27676	27627	27622	27617	25777	24021	23032	22957	22867	22773	22655	3151	19136	13905	4402	1641
Strength:	1.91	2.48	2.75	3.01	5.83	7.55	8.89	9.64	10.51	11.57	12.89	3.48	14.41	18.86	5.27	1.32

Linguistic Density Plot in Ezekiel 1 - 48

For ḥāmēš 714 (35 times)

Each Column = 13 Verses.   Separations are: Max = 11242.00, Mean =   776.94, Min =   6.50

CLUSTERS:

Start:	1: 1	40: 1	40: 1	40:21	40:29	40:29	40:30	40:30	40:48	40:48	41: 2	41: 2	41: 9	41:11	42:16	42:16	42:16	42:18
End:	1: 2	48:34	42:20	40:36	40:36	40:30	40:30	42:20	40:48	41:12	40:48	41:12	41:11	41:12	42:16	42:19	42:17	42:19
Count:	2	33	23	7	5	3	2	13	2	7	2	3	2	6	4	2	2	
Width:	18	5632	1960	311	126	13	4	936	5	298	5	83	19	53	32	10	11	
Strength:	1.00	13.30	6.75	2.53	2.06	1.46	1.02	3.86	1.02	2.54	1.02	1.76	1.00	1.41	1.00	2.40	1.80	1.01

Start:	42:20	45: 2	48:16	48:16	48:16	48:30	48:33
End:	42:20	48:34	48:34	48:16	48:16	48:34	48:34
Count:	2	10	8	4	2	4	2
Width:	2250	361	25	8	8	70	20
Strength:	1.02	2.38	1.81	1.01	1.01	1.77	1.00

```
Data for hâmês 714, continued.

GAPS:

Start:      1: 1   1: 1   1: 1   1: 1   1: 1   1: 2   1: 2   1: 2   1: 2   45: 2
End:       45: 2  42:20  40:30  40:29  40:25  40:21  40: 7  40: 1  48:16
Count:             27     25     10      9      8      7      6      5      3      2
Width:    25692  24266  22973  22965  22938  22846  22753  22484  22284   1886
Strength:  2.66   2.59   8.02   8.76   9.62  10.66  11.92  13.59  19.87  28.46   1.46
```

Linguistic Density Plot in Ezekiel 1 - 48

For ḥamāṭ 12 (6 times)

Each Column = 13 Verses.   Separations are: Max = 13562.50, Mean = 3995.71, Min =   15.50 .

REFERENCE

```
25+                                                                    .        +25
                                                   .                            
20+                                                                             +20
                                                                                
D15+                                                                            +15D
E                                                                                 E
N                                                                                 N
S                                                                                 S
I                                                                                 I
T10+                                                                            +10T
Y                                                                                 Y
                                                                                
5+                                                                              + 5
                                                                                
0+                                                                              + 0
```

REFERENCE

CLUSTERS:

Start:	47:16	47:16	47:20	48: 1
End:	48: 1	47:17	47:16	48: 1
Count:	6	3	2	
Width:	186	31	10	91
Strength:	4.43	1.78	1.15	1.76

GAPS:

Start:	1: 1	1: 1
End:	48: 1	47:16
Count:	6	2
Width:	27292	27114
Strength:	1.63	6.68

Linguistic Density Plot in Ezekiel 1 - 48

For hācēr 114 (48 times)

Each Column = 13 Verses.   Separations are: Max = 9348.00, Mean = 570.82, Min = 2.00

CLUSTERS:

Start:	8: 7	8: 7	9: 7	10: 3	40:14	40:14	40:14	40:14	40:17	40:17	40:17	40:27	40:27	40:27	41:15	41:15	42: 1	42: 1	42: 3	42: 3
End:	46:22	10: 5	10: 5	10: 5	40:14	43: 5	40:47	46:22	40:17	40:20	40:23	40:32	40:37	40:47	43: 5	42:10	42:10	42:10	42: 3	42:10
Count:	48	6	4	3	42	25	6	14	4	5	9	9	11	8	4	11	8	9	2	5
Width:	23398	670	212	30	4082	1721	177	670	104	54	406	194	666	363	94	177	156	363	64	41
Strength:	4.38	1.82	1.58	1.41	13.21	6.05	2.23	3.86	1.74	2.01	2.59	1.70	3.16	2.87	1.00	2.23	2.77	1.40	1.00	2.04

Start:	42: 6	42: 8	44:17	44:17	44:17	44:19	44:19	45:19	46:20	46:21	46:21	46:21	46:21	46:21	46:21
End:	42:10	46:22	44:27	44:21	44:19	44:19	44:19	46:22	46:22	46:21	46:22	46:21	46:21	46:21	46:22
Count:	3	2	6	6	4	9	11	3	33	10	2	5	3	4	2
Width:	34	5	17	224	102	626	46	15	626	33	9	3	2	41	1
Strength:	1.41	1.01	4.17	2.19	2.01	3.18	1.75	1.00	3.10	1.00	2.09	1.45	1.01	1.40	1.01

```
Data for hacer 114, continued.

GAPS:

Start:     1: 1    1: 1    1: 1    1: 1    1: 1    1: 1    1: 1    1: 1    1: 1    1: 1    1: 1
End:      46:21   46:21   46:21   44:19   42: 9   42: 3   40:17   10: 3    8: 7   40:17   10: 5   10: 5   46:22
                                                                                                  40:14   48:35
Count:      45      44      43      35      29      24       9       5       2       3       2               2
Width:    26713   26710   26707   25384   24053   23936   22690    3964    3324   18696   18646           1247
Strength:  1.33    1.66    1.97    3.27    4.12    5.47   12.39    1.55    4.92   22.42   32.31           1.20
```

Linguistic Density Plot in Ezekiel 1 - 48

For ḥōq 111 (6 times)

Each Column = 13 Verses. Separations are: Max = 7889.50, Mean = 3995.71, Min = 1455.50 .

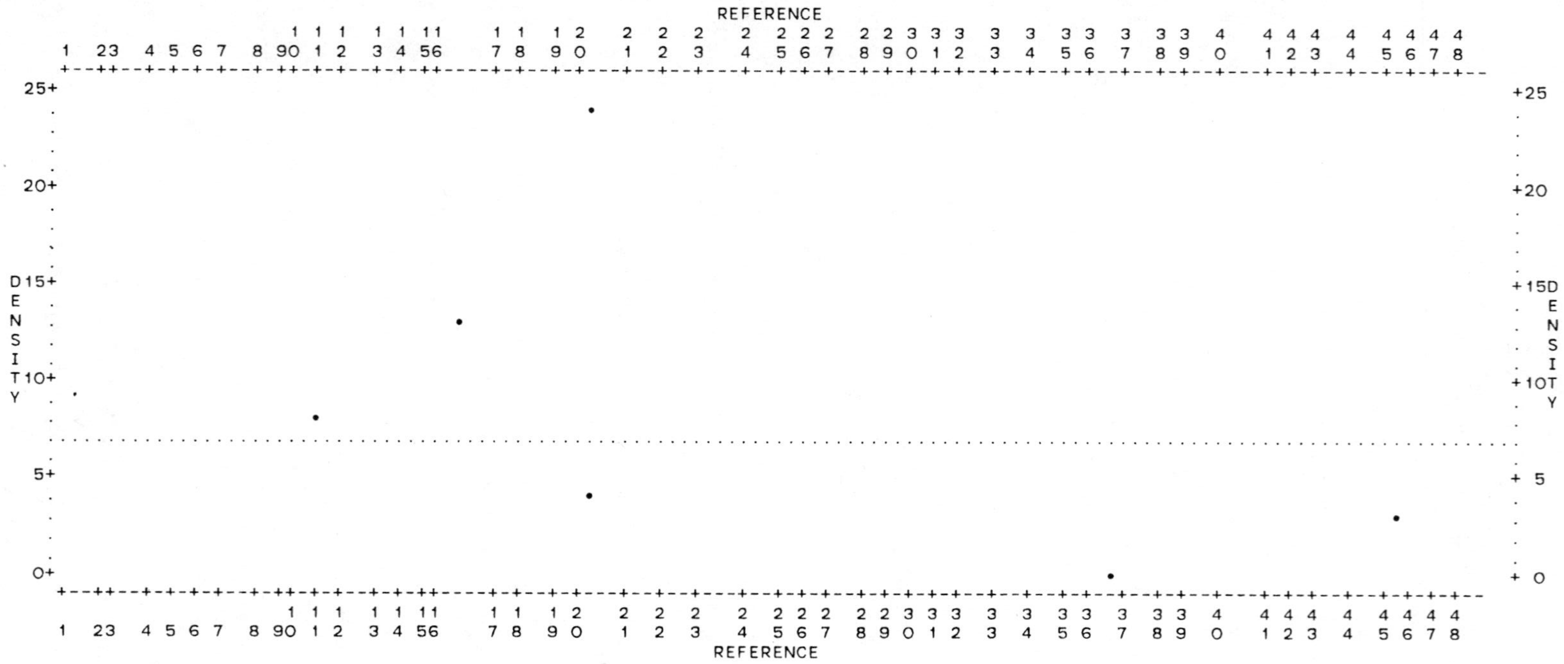

CLUSTERS:

Start:	11:12	20:18
End:	20:25	20:25
Count:	4	2
Width:	5629	178
Strength:	1.29	1.10

GAPS:

Start:	20:25	20:25	20:25
End:	48:35	45:14	36:27
Count:	4	3	2
Width:	17786	15779	9998
Strength:	1.18	1.74	1.73

Linguistic Density Plot in Ezekiel 1 - 48

For ḥuqqâ 114 (22 times)

Each Column = 13 Verses.   Separations are: Max = 5422.00, Mean = 1216.09, Min = 17.50 .

Linguistic density plot with REFERENCE axes, vertical scale from 0+ through D15+, +20, +25, and DENSITY labels.

CLUSTERS:

```
Start:     5: 6   5: 6   5: 6   6  18: 9  18:17  18:19  20:11  20:16  20:11  43:11  43:11  43:11
End:      20:24   5: 7   5: 7  20:24 18:21  18:21  20:24  20:13  20:21  20:24  44: 5  43:18  43:11
Count:      14     3      2     10     4      2      6      2      3      4      3
Width:     8187    35     13   1359   264    103    340     51    199    104     39   2005    973    486    173
Strength:  2.69   1.48   1.03  3.44  1.75   1.44   2.43   1.00   1.79   1.44   1.01   1.73   1.79   1.64   1.40   1.02
```

GAPS:

```
Start:     5: 7   5: 7  11:20  20:21  20:24  37:24
End:      43:11  18:17 18: 9  43:11  33:15  43:11
Count:      15     4      3      2      5      2
Width:    22522  6954  6793   4052  14465  14370   7996   3526
Strength:  1.97   1.71  2.71   2.43   4.43   5.57   5.82   1.98
```

Linguistic Density Plot in Ezekiel 1 - 48

For hereb 114 (91 times)

Each Column = 13 Verses.   Separations are: Max =   3175.00, Mean =   304.02, Min =   2.50

REFERENCE

CLUSTERS:

Start:	5: 1	5: 1	5: 1	5:12	5:12	6: 8	11: 8	14:17	21: 8	21: 8	21: 8	21: 8	21: 8	21:14	21:14	21:19	21:19
End:	39:23	7:15	6:12	6:12	6:12	6:12	11:10	14:21	21:33	26:11	21:17	21:10	21:17	21:14	21:17	21:33	21:20
Count:	91	12	10	7	4	3	3	3	15	24	7	3	4	2	8	6	4
Width:	20320	1051	688	389	197	105	31	104	1687	3357	509	191	44	1	65	282	97
Strength:	16.64	2.43	2.37	2.00	1.38	1.18	1.36	1.19	2.88	2.89	2.27	1.33	1.64	1.00	1.64	2.40	2.16

Start:	21:19	21:19	25:13	26: 6	28: 7	30: 4	30: 4	30: 6	30: 4	30: 4	31:17	32:10	32:20
End:	21:19	21:19	26:11	26:11	39:23	30:25	30:17	30:25	30:24	33:27	31:17	32:24	32:20
Count:	3	5	2	4	45	12	5	3	9	4	26	9	6
Width:	321	1	114	71	6979	1402	257	56	435	28	1367	268	83
Strength:	1.51	1.00	1.54	1.26	4.41	2.06	1.62	1.31	2.44	1.60	4.83	2.64	2.18

REFERENCE

Clusters for hereb 114, continued.

Start:	32:20	32:20	32:25	32:25	32:25	32:28	32:30	33: 2	33: 2
End:	32:22	32:20	33:27	33: 6	32:32	32:32	32:32	33: 6	33: 4
Count:	4	2	15	13	8	5	3	6	5
Width:	42	2	804	305	181	93	44	90	44
Strength:	1.68	1.00	3.31	3.42	2.53	1.89	1.33	1.90	1.33

GAPS:

Start:	1: 1	1: 1	7:15	11: 8	11: 8	11:10	12:16	14:17	14:17	14:17	14:21	17:21	21:33	21:33	21:33	26:11	26:11
End:	21:14	5: 2	11: 8	21:14	14:17	12:14	14:17	21:14	14:17	21: 8	21:14	21: 8	26: 6	25:13	23:10	30: 4	28:23
Count:	27	3	2	13	5	4	2	8	5	6	2	7	6	6	5	5	3
Width:	10964	1851	1580	6479	1881	1853	1174	4591	4490	4465	4368	1099	2275	2734	2527	857	1964	1315
Strength:	2.34	5.14	4.24	2.89	1.12	1.82	2.89	3.20	4.51	5.49	6.70	2.64	6.55	1.26	1.53	1.83	1.26	1.67

Start:	26:11	32:20	33: 6	33:27	33:27	35: 8	38:21	39:23	
End:	28: 7	48:35	38:21	38: 4	35: 5	38: 4	48:35	48:35	
Count:	2	28	8	6	4	2	3	2	
Width:	997	10500	3719	3220	2797	935	1794	6350	5798
Strength:	2.30	1.73	2.06	2.58	3.65	2.09	4.95	13.57	18.26

Linguistic Density Plot in Ezekiel 1 - 48

For ḥrb 311 (1 times)   ḥrb 312 (2 times)   ḥrb 324 (2 times)   ḥrb 361 (1 times)
    ḥrb 371 (1 times)   ḥrb 374 (1 times)

Each Column = 13 Verses. Separations are: Max = 6038.50, Mean = 3107.78, Min = 926.00

REFERENCE

CLUSTERS:

Start:	6: 6	6: 6	19: 7	26: 2
End:	30: 7	6: 6	30: 7	30: 7
Count:	8	2	5	4
Width:	13844	6	6826	2227
Strength:	2.15	1.11	1.27	1.70

GAPS:

Start:	6: 6	30: 7
End:	48:35	48:35
Count:	8	2
Width:	25572	11734
Strength:	1.03	3.10

Linguistic Density Plot in Ezekiel 1 - 48

For ḥŏrbâ 114 (14 times)

Each Column = 13 Verses. Separations are: Max = 5835.50, Mean = 1864.67, Min = 253.00 .

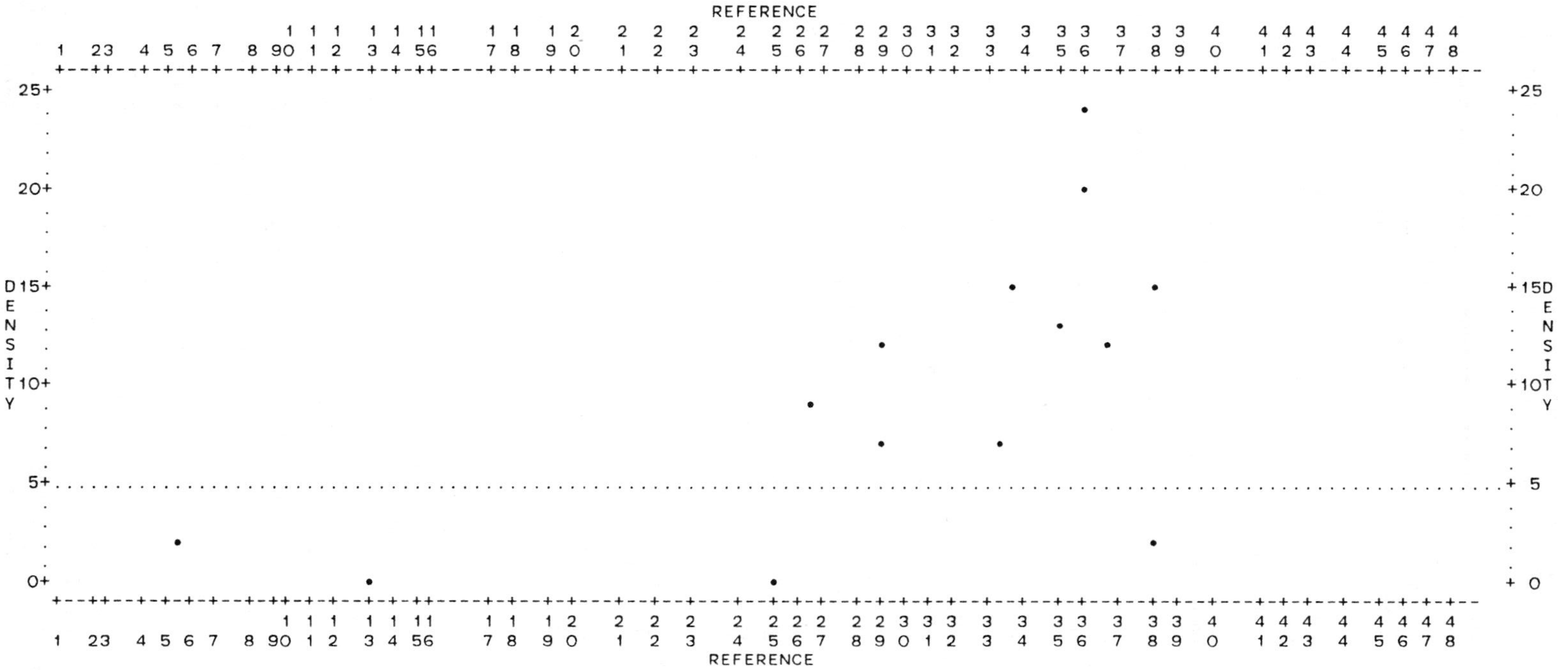

CLUSTERS:

Start:	5:14	25:13	25:13	29: 9	33:24	33:24	33:24	35: 4	35: 4	38: 8
End:	38:12	38:12	29:10	29:10	38:12	36:33	33:27	36:33	36:10	38:12
Count:	14	12	4	2	8	6	2	4	3	2
Width:	19157	7486	1980	30	3043	2007	81	1013	506	89
Strength:	2.13	4.21	1.29	1.05	2.86	2.21	1.02	1.63	1.35	1.01

GAPS:

Start:	1: 1	1: 1	5:14	13: 4	38:12
End:	29: 9	25:13	25:13	25:13	48:35
Count:	6	4	3	2	2
Width:	15818	13868	11671	8377	6615
Strength:	1.97	2.95	3.34	3.73	2.72

For hrd 311 (2 times)　　　　hrd 312 (1 times)　　　　hrd 364 (2 times)　　　　hrd 3662 (1 times)

Linguistic Density Plot in Ezekiel 1 - 48

Each Column = 13 Verses. Separations are: Max = 7179.00, Mean = 3995.71, Min = 974.50

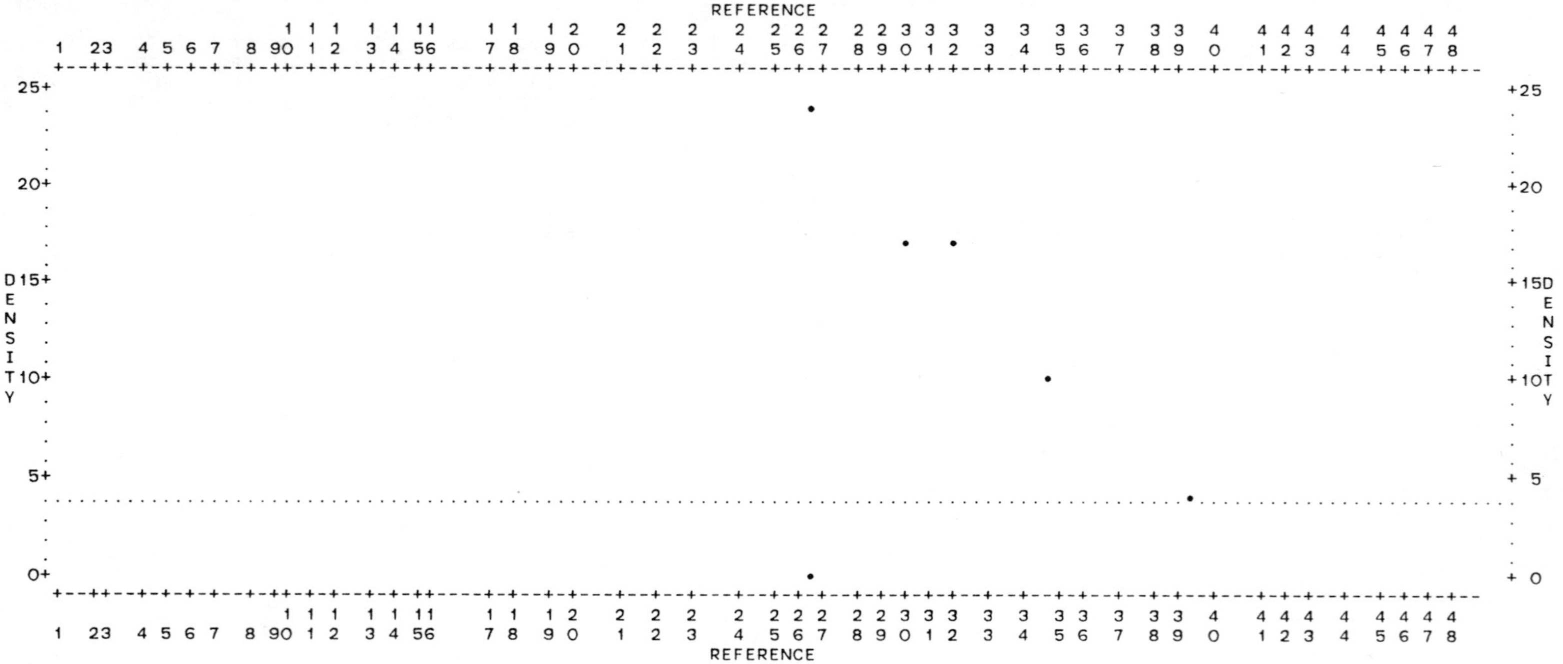

CLUSTERS:

Start:	26:16	26:16	26:16	30: 9
End:	39:26	34:28	26:18	34:28
Count:	6	5	2	3
Width:	7920	4883	41	2934
Strength:	2.69	2.26	1.14	1.13

GAPS:

Start:	1: 1
End:	26:16
Count:	2
Width:	14316
Strength:	2.98

Linguistic Density Plot in Ezekiel 1 - 48

For herpâ 114 (7 times)

Each Column = 13 Verses. Separations are: Max = 4565.00, Mean = 3496.25, Min = 1106.50 .

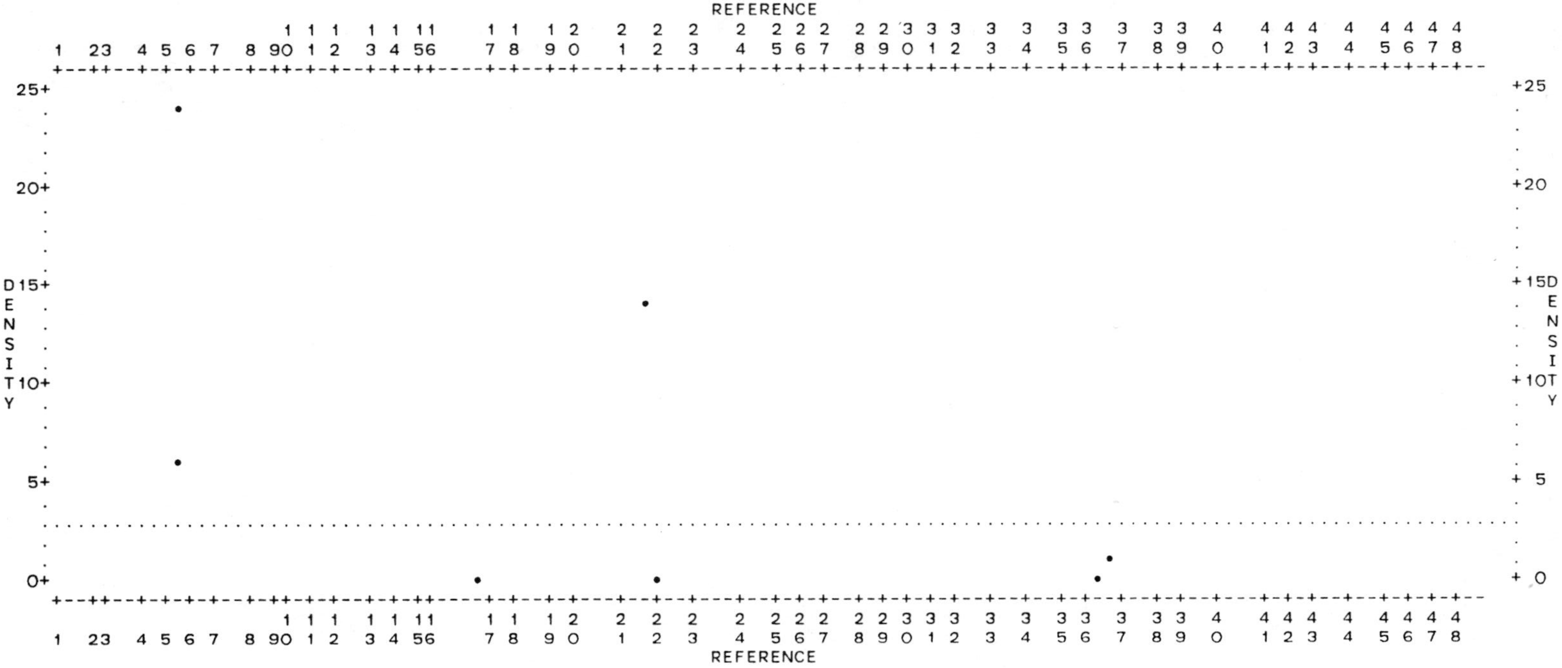

CLUSTERS:

Start:	5:14	5:14	21:33	36:15
End:	22: 4	5:15	22: 4	36:30
Count:	5	2	2	2
Width:	9314	12	172	340
Strength:	1.00	1.12	1.07	1.02

GAPS:

Start:	5:15	22: 4	22: 4	36:30
End:	48:35	48:35	36:15	48:35
Count:	7	4	2	2
Width:	25757	16455	8394	7721
Strength:	1.18	1.32	1.58	1.36

Linguistic Density Plot in Ezekiel 1 - 48

For hittit 114 (8 times)

Each Column = 13 Verses.   Separations are: Max = 8766.50, Mean = 3107.78, Min = 30.50 .

```
                                                                                       REFERENCE
          1  23   4 5 6 7  8 90 1 2  1 1 1 1  1 1 1  1 1  2  2  2 2  2 2  2 2 2  2 2 2 2  2 2 3 3  3 3 3  3 3 3 3  4 4 4 4  4 4 4 4
                             3 4 56   7 8   9 0 1 2  3   1  2 3  4 5  6 7  8 9 0 1 2 3  4 5  6 7 8 9  0 1  2 3 4  5 6 7 8
25+
20+                                                                         • 2               • •
D15+
E
N
S
I
T10+
Y
5+                                                                    •    •            •
0+
          1  23   4 5 6 7  8 90 1 2  1 1 1 1  1 1 1  1 1  2  2  2 2  2 2  2 2 2  2 2 2 2  2 2 3 3  3 3 3  3 3 3 3  4 4 4 4  4 4 4 4
                             3 4 56   7 8   9 0 1 2  3   1  2 3  4 5  6 7  8 9 0 1 2 3  4 5  6 7 8 9  0 1  2 3 4  5 6 7 8
                                                                                       REFERENCE
```

+25
+20
+15
+10
+5
+0

CLUSTERS:

Start:	26:17	32:23	32:23	32:23	32:25	32:30
End:	32:32	32:32	32:27	32:27	32:26	32:32
Count:	8	7	5	2	3	2
Width:	3409	227	131	27	70	43
Strength:	4.98	4.41	2.79	1.10	1.67	1.10

GAPS:

Start:	1: 1	1: 1	32:32
End:	32:23	26:17	48:35
Count:	3	2
Width:	17532	14350	10210
Strength:	3.07	4.04	2.55

Linguistic Density Plot in Ezekiel 1 - 48

For ḥtr 311 (1 times)   ḥtr 312 (2 times)   ḥtr 313 (2 times)

Each Column = 13 Verses.   Separations are: Max = 11479.50, Mean = 4661.66, Min = 71.00 .

CLUSTERS:

Start:	8: 8	8: 8	12: 5	12: 5
End:	12:12	12: 8	12:12	12: 7
Count:	5	2	3	2
Width:	1764	5	142	49
Strength:	3.38	1.18	1.84	1.17

GAPS:

Start:	8: 8	12: 7	12:12
End:	48:35	48:35	48:35
Count:	5	3	2
Width:	24625	22959	22866
Strength:	1.19	2.73	4.62

Linguistic Density Plot in Ezekiel 1 - 48

For thr 311 (2 times)   thr 312 (1 times)   thr 331 (4 times)   thr 332 (1 times)
     thr 3362 (3 times)   thr 344 (1 times)

Each Column = 13 Verses.   Separations are: Max = 6633.50. Mean = 2151.54, Min = 4.50 .

REFERENCE

REFERENCE

CLUSTERS:

Start:	22:24	22:24	24:13	24:13	36:25	36:25	36:25	39:12	39:14
End:	43:26	24:13	24:13	43:26	39:16	37:23	36:33	39:16	39:16
Count:	12	4	3	2	8	7	3	2	
Width:	12994	1405	9	4	4736	1877	841	176	75	36
Strength:	3.95	1.60	1.07	1.59	2.77	2.96	1.78	1.53	1.07	1.56	1.06

GAPS:

Start:	1: 1	1: 1	24:13
End:	24:13	22:24	36:25
Count:	3	2	
Width:	13266	11870	6853
Strength:	3.32	4.87	2.35

Linguistic Density Plot in Ezekiel 1 - 48

For thr 331 (4 times)   thr 332 (1 times)   thr 3362 (3 times)   thr 344 (1 times)

Each Column = 13 Verses.   Separations are: Max = 6633.50, Mean = 2797.00, Min = 37.50

CLUSTERS:

Start:	22:24	36:25	36:25	36:25	39:12	39:14
End:	43:26	43:26	39:16	37:23	36:33	39:16
Count:	9	7	6	3	3	2
Width:	12994	4726	1867	831	166	75	36
Strength:	2.78	2.91	2.87	1.41	1.03	1.63	1.09

GAPS:

Start:	1: 1	1: 1	1: 1	24:13
End:	39:12	36:25	22:24	36:25
Count:	7	4	2	2
Width:	21930	20138	11870	6872
Strength:	1.24	3.03	3.58	1.61

Linguistic Density Plot in Ezekiel 1 - 48

For ṭôb 21 (9 times)

Each Column = 13 Verses. Separations are: Max = 4502.00. Mean = 2797.00. Min = 44.00 .

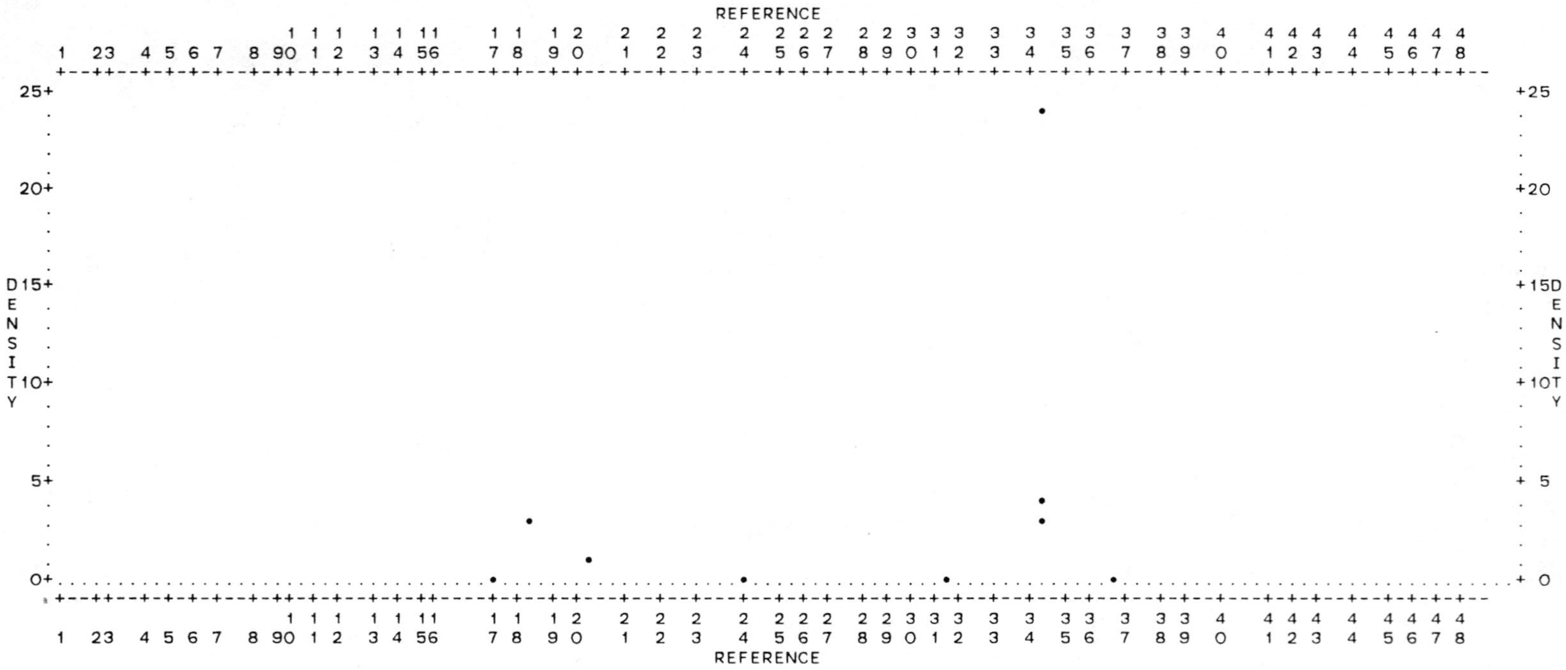

CLUSTERS:

Start:	17: 8	17: 8	31:16	34:14	34:14	34:14
End:	36:31	20:25	36:31	36:31	34:18	34:14
Count:	9	3	5	4	3	2
Width:	12018	1940	3249	1386	88	16
Strength:	3.07	1.08	1.92	1.81	1.63	1.09

GAPS:

Start:	1: 1	34:18	36:31
End:	17: 8	48:35	48:35
Count:	2	3	2
Width:	8245	9004	7706
Strength:	2.15	1.01	1.94

Linguistic Density Plot in Ezekiel 1 - 48

For ṭāmē' 21 (5 times)

Each Column = 13 Verses.   Separations are: Max = 13564.00, Mean =   4661.66, Min = 193.00 .

REFERENCE

DENSITY

CLUSTERS:

Start:	22: 5	22: 5
End:	22:26	22:10
Count:	3	2
Width:	386	69
Strength:	1.79	1.16

GAPS:

Start:	4:13	22:26	22:26
End:	22: 5	48:35	44:23
Count:	2	3	2
Width:	9791	16052	13564
Strength:	1.30	1.35	2.25

Linguistic Density Plot in Ezekiel 1 - 48

For ṭm' 311 (1 times)   ṭm' 312 (1 times)   ṭm' 3162 (2 times)   ṭm' 321 (4 times)
     ṭm' 324 (2 times)   ṭm' 331 (9 times)   ṭm' 332 (4 times)   ṭm' 333 (1 times)
     ṭm' 352 (5 times)

Each Column = 13 Verses.   Separations are: Max = 3578.00.   Mean = 932.33, Min = 37.00 .

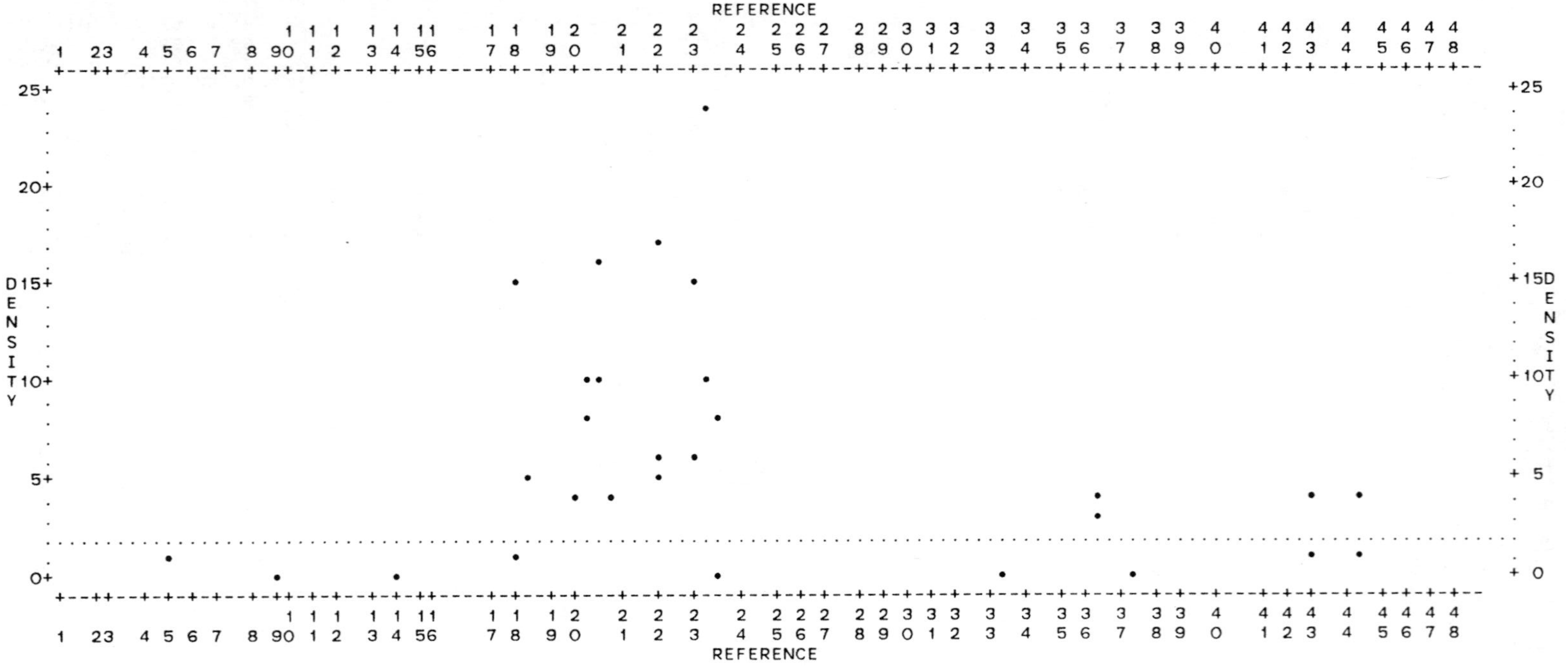

(Vertical axis label: DENSITY, with scale marks +25, +20, +15D, +10T, +5, +0)
(Horizontal axis label: REFERENCE)

CLUSTERS:

Start:	5:11	5:11	18: 6	18: 6	18: 6	20: 7	20:26	20:30	22: 3	22: 3	23: 7	23:13	43: 7	44:25
End:	44:25	23:38	23:38	20:43	18:15	20:43	20:31	20:31	23:38	22:11	23:17	23:17	44:25	44:25
Count:	29	21	18	9	6	4	3	2	9	2	6	4	4	2
Width:	23436	10673	4030	1908	174	469	933	154	1298	132	638	183	1138	24
Strength:	2.12	3.36	4.74	2.49	1.34	1.54	1.99	1.36	2.77	1.38	2.14	1.73	1.42	1.10

GAPS:

Start:	1: 1	18:11	1: 1	9: 7	14:11	23:17	23:17	23:38	36:18	36:18	37:23	44:25	48:35
End:	18:11	18: 6	5:11	18: 6	18: 6	48:35	44:25	36:17	33:26	43: 7	44:25	48:35	48:35
Count:	6	5	2	3	2	12	10	3	2	2	3	2	2
Width:	8850	8754	2111	4978	2520	15640	13194	7611	5589	5548	4434	3467	2422
Strength:	2.23	2.94	1.30	2.48	1.76	2.22	2.08	2.27	5.16	1.06	2.04	2.81	1.65

Linguistic Density Plot in Ezekiel 1 - 48

For ṭm' 311 (1 times)   ṭm' 312 (1 times)   ṭm' 3162 (2 times)   ṭm' 321 (4 times)
     ṭm' 324 (2 times)

Each Column = 13 Verses.   Separations are: Max = 12885.00, Mean = 2542.73, Min = 91.50.

```
                                              REFERENCE
                                                                                                    +25

                                                                                                    +20

                                                                                                    +15  D
                                                                                                         E
                                                                                                         N
                                                                                                         S
                                                                                                         I
                                                                                                    +10  T
                                                                                                         Y

                                                                                                    + 5

                                                                                                    + 0
                                              REFERENCE
```

CLUSTERS:

Start:	20:30	20:30	20:30	22: 3	23: 7	23:13	
End:	44:25	23:30	20:31	23:30	23:17	23:17	
Count:	10	9	3	2	6	4	3	2
Width:	15195	2310	334	19	1152	492	183	74
Strength:	2.46	5.01	1.52	1.08	2.87	1.98	1.57	1.06

GAPS:

Start:	1: 1	23:17	23:30	23:30
End:	20:30	48:35	48:35	44:25
Count:	2	4	3	2
Width:	10328	15640	15331	12885
Strength:	3.35	2.22	3.28	4.45

Linguistic Density Plot in Ezekiel 1 - 48

For ṭm' 331 (9 times)   ṭm' 332 (4 times)   ṭm' 333 (1 times)

Each Column = 13 Verses. Separations are: Max = 3578.00, Mean = 1864.67, Min = 87.00 .

CLUSTERS:

Start:	5:11	18: 6	18: 6	18:11	22:11	36:17	43: 7
End:	23:38	20:26	18:15	18:15	23:38	36:18	43: 8
Count:	9	7	4	3	2	3	2
Width:	10673	4030	1439	174	78	1166	35	43
Strength:	1.21	2.08	1.48	1.49	1.02	1.07	1.04	1.04

GAPS:

Start:	1: 1	9: 7	23:38	23:38	36:18
End:	18: 6	18: 6	36:17	33:26	43: 7
Count:	4	2	3	2
Width:	8754	4978	7156	5589	4434
Strength:	1.12	1.78	1.44	2.13	1.47

Linguistic Density Plot in Ezekiel 1 - 48

For ṭm' 331 (9 times)

Each Column = 13 Verses.   Separations are: Max = 6643.00. Mean = 2797.00. Min = 87.00 .

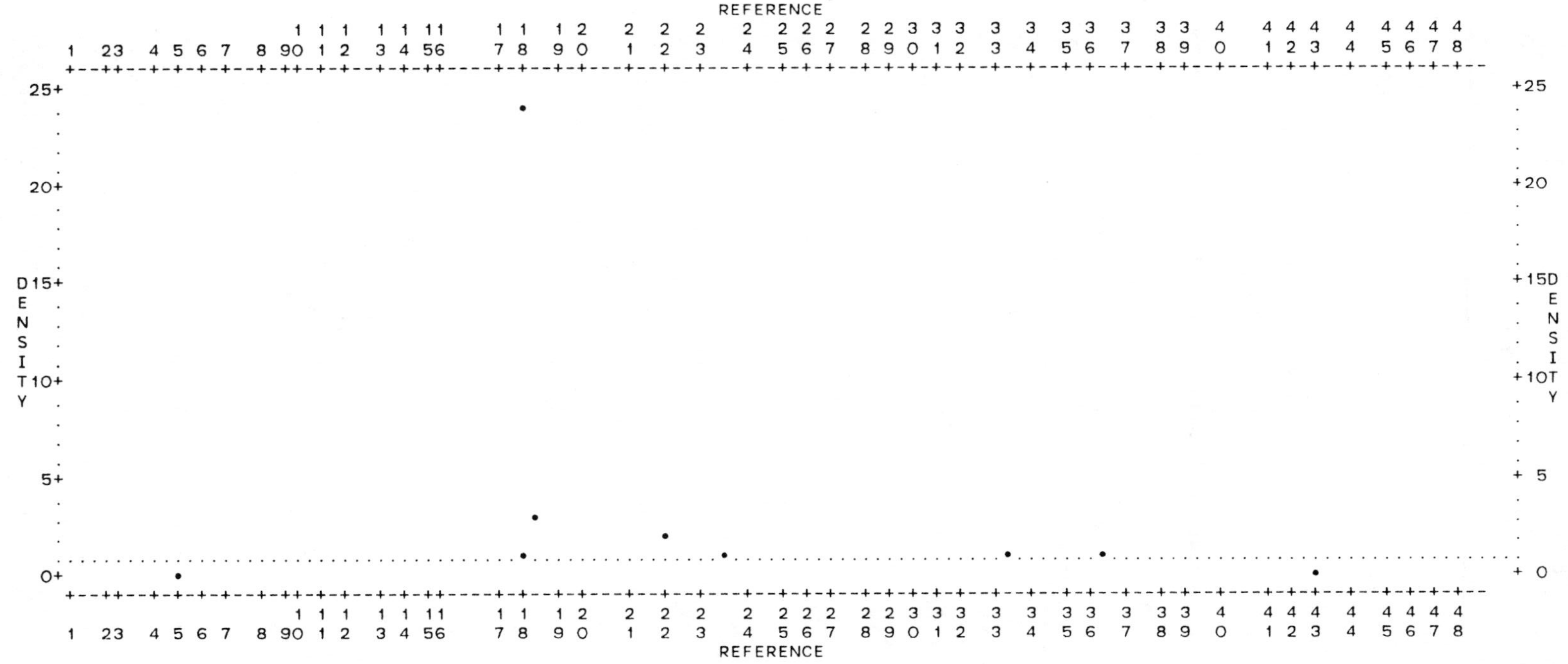

CLUSTERS:

Start:	18: 6	18:11	
End:	23:38	18:15	
Count:	5	3	2
Width:	4030	174	78
Strength:	1.73	1.60	1.07

GAPS:

Start:	5:11	23:38
End:	18: 6	33:26
Count:	2	2
Width:	6643	5589
Strength:	1.51	1.10

Linguistic Density Plot in Ezekiel 1 - 48

For ṭm' 352 (5 times)

Each Column = 13 Verses.   Separations are: Max = 7763.00, Mean = 4661.66, Min = 1893.50 .

REFERENCE

CLUSTERS:

Start:	14:11	20: 7
End:	20:18	20:18
Count:	3	2
Width:	3787	292
Strength:	1.11	1.10

GAPS:

Start:	20:18	20:18
End:	44:25	37:23
Count:	3	2
Width:	15526	10921
Strength:	1.24	1.58

Linguistic Density Plot in Ezekiel 1 - 48

For ṭum'â 114 (8 times)

Each Column = 13 Verses.   Separations are: Max = 6621.00, Mean = 3107.78, Min = 15.50 .

REFERENCE

REFERENCE

CLUSTERS:

```
Start:    22:15  22:15  24:11  24:13  36:17  36:25
End:      39:24  24:13  24:13  39:24  36:29  36:29
Count:        8      4      3      2      4      2
Width:    10466   1563     31     10   2224     87
Strength:  3.06   1.86   1.68   1.11   1.70   1.61   1.08
```

GAPS:

```
Start:     1: 1   1: 1  24:13
End:      24:11  22:15  36:17
Count:        3      2      2
Width:    13241  11709   6679
Strength:  1.91   3.09   1.28
```

Linguistic Density Plot in Ezekiel 1 - 48

For ʔerep 111 (5 times)

Each Column = 13 Verses.   Separations are: Max = 8041.00, Mean = 4661.66, Min = 557.50 .

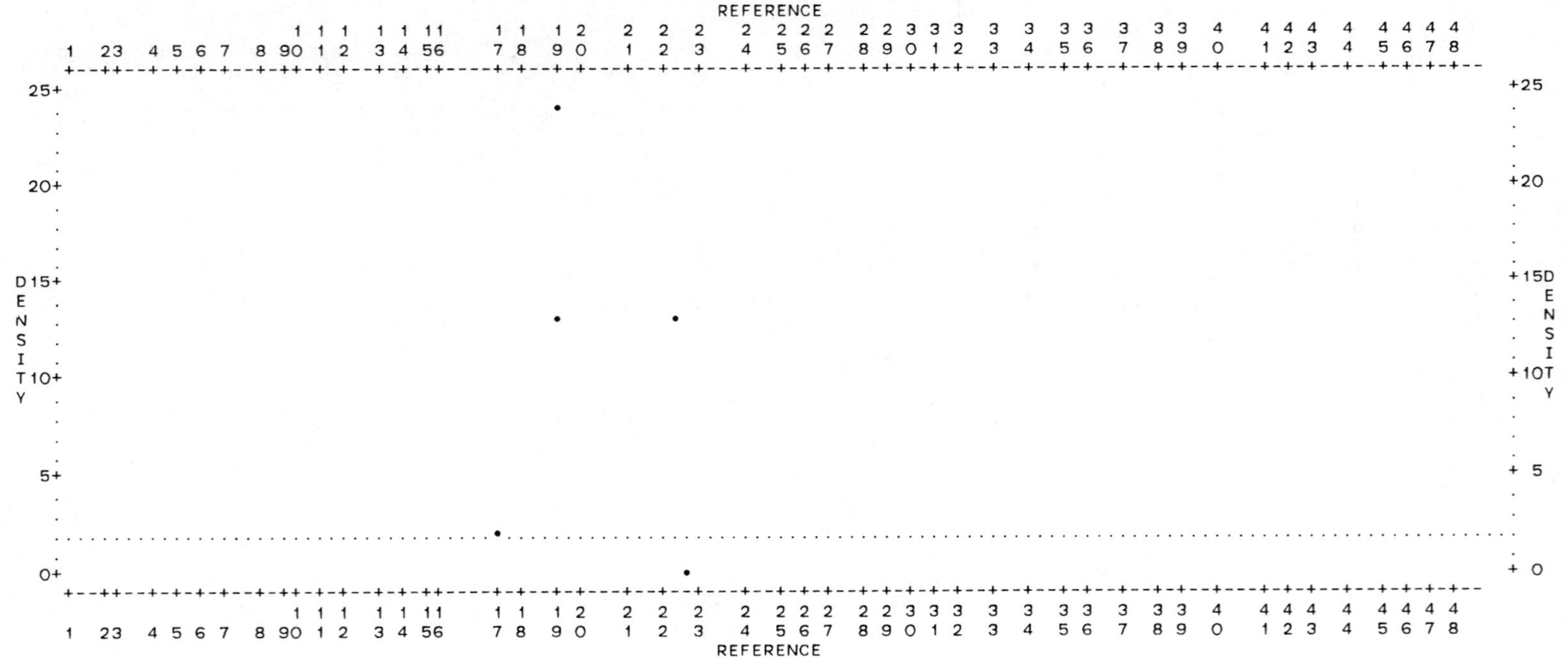

CLUSTERS:

Start:	17: 9	17: 9	19: 3	22:25
End:	22:27	19: 6	19: 6	22:27
Count:	5	3	2	2
Width:	3658	1115	47	55
Strength:	3.00	1.64	1.17	1.16

GAPS:

Start:	22:27
End:	48:35
Count:	2
Width:	16027
Strength:	2.88

Linguistic Density Plot in Ezekiel 1 - 48

For ye·ôr 111 (9 times)

Each Column = 13 Verses.   Separations are: Max =   7839.00, Mean =   2797.00, Min =   8.00 .

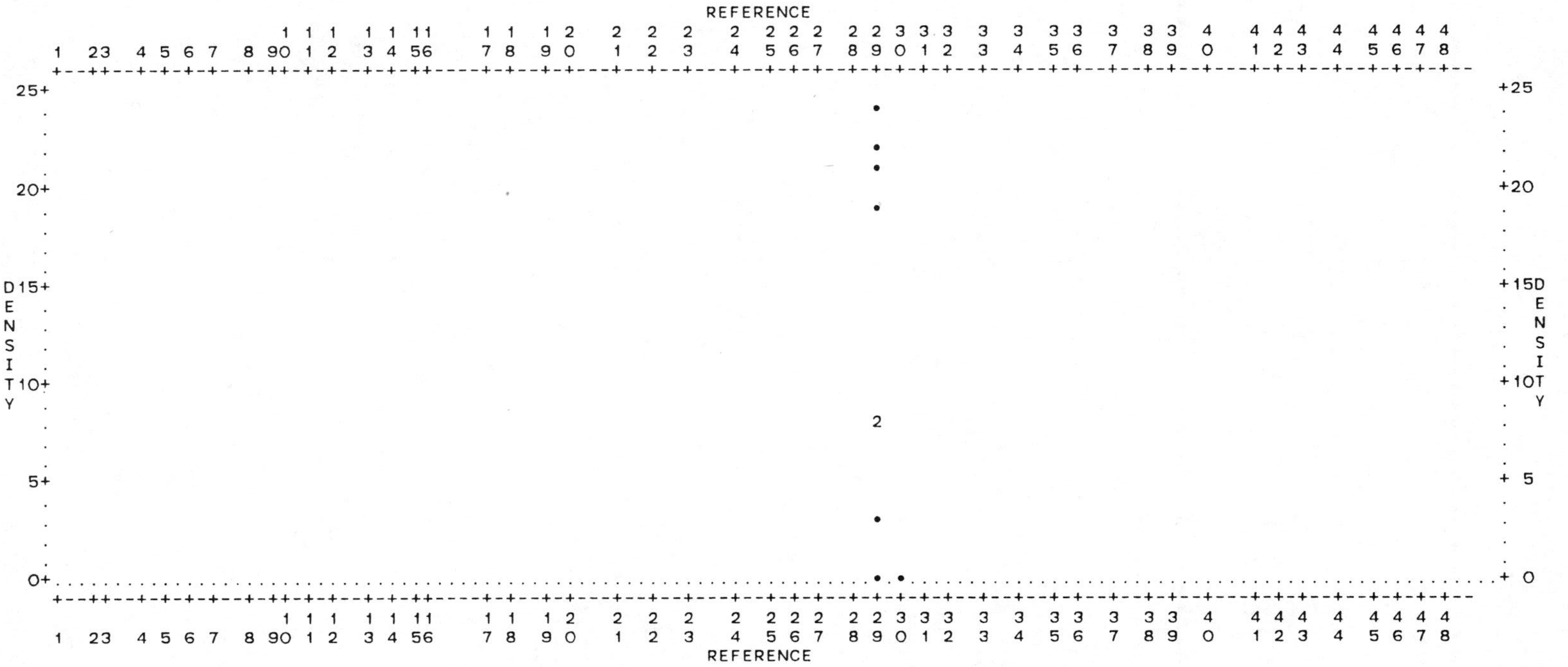

REFERENCE

(density plot chart, vertical axis labeled DENSITY with markers +25, +20, +15, +10, +5, 0; horizontal axis REFERENCE)

CLUSTERS:

Start:	29: 3	29: 3	29: 3	29: 3	4 29:	4 29:	4 29: 9
End:	30:12	29:10	29: 5	29: 3	5 29:	4 29:	4 29:10
Count:	9	8	6	2	4	3	2	2
Width:	648	168	52	5	32	16	6	14
Strength:	6.44	5.02	3.30	1.10	2.16	1.65	1.10	1.09

GAPS:

Start:	1: 1	29:10	30:12
End:	29: 3	48:35	48:35
Count:	2	3	2
Width:	15672	12129	11649
Strength:	5.08	1.93	3.49

Linguistic Density Plot in Ezekiel 1 - 48

For ybs 311 (3 times)   ybs 312 (3 times)   ybs 3161 (1 times)   ybs 361 (2 times)

Each Column = 13 Verses.   Separations are: Max = 11115.00, Mean = 2797.00, Min = 3.00 .

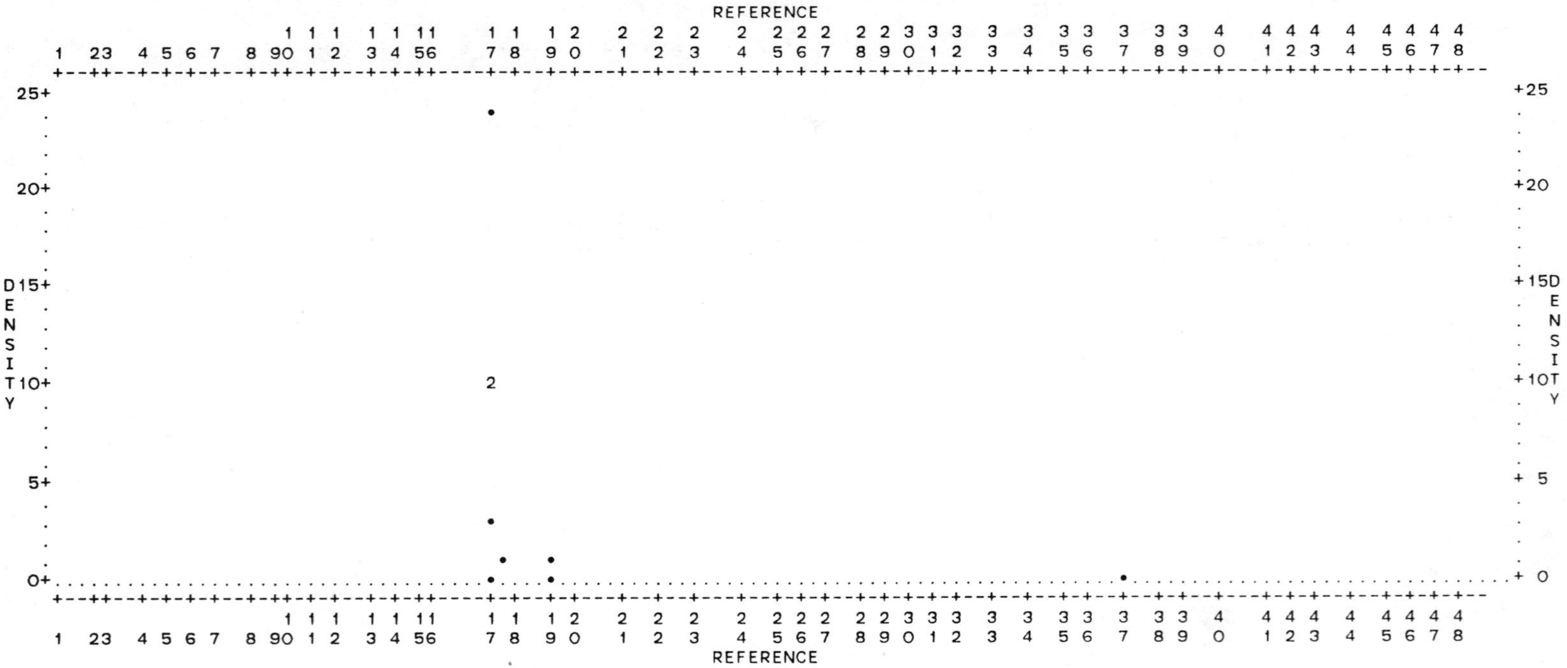

REFERENCE

CLUSTERS:

Start:	17: 9	17: 9	17: 9	17: 9	17:10	17:10	19:12
End:	37:11	19:12	17:24	17:10	17: 9	17:10	19:12
Count:	9	8	6	5	2	3	2
Width:	12355	1240	367	41	5	6	1	5
Strength:	2.97	4.74	3.22	2.69	1.10	1.65	1.10	1.10

GAPS:

Start:	1: 1	19:12	19:12
End:	17: 9	48:35	37:11
Count:	2	3	2
Width:	8282	18447	11115
Strength:	2.16	3.81	3.28

Linguistic Density Plot in Ezekiel 1 - 48

For ybs 311 (3 times)   ybs 312 (3 times)   ybs 3161 (1 times)

Each Column = 13 Verses.   Separations are: Max = 11115.00, Mean = 3496.25, Min = 3.00 .

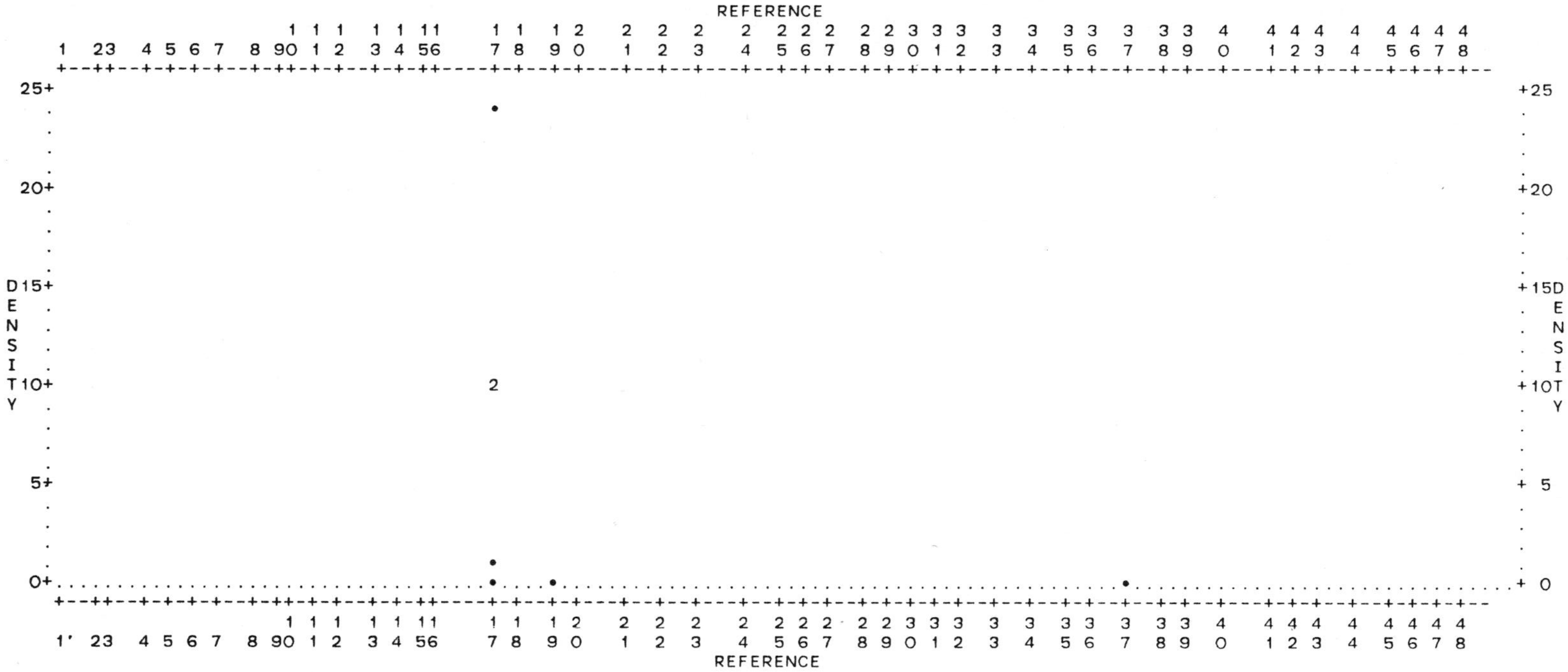

CLUSTERS:

Start:	17: 9	17: 9	17: 9	17:10	17:10	17:10
End:	37:11	19:12	17:10	17:10	17:10	17:10
Count:	7	6	5	2	3	2
Width:	12355	1240	41	5	6	1
Strength:	2.13	3.59	2.99	1.13	1.73	1.13

GAPS:

Start:	1: 1	17:10	17:10	19:12	19:12
End:	17: 9	48:35	48:35	37:11	37:11
Count:	2	5	4	3	2
Width:	8282	19651	19646	18447	11115
Strength:	1.55	1.21	2.02	2.83	2.47

Linguistic Density Plot in Ezekiel 1 - 48

For yād 114 (108 times)

Each Column = 13 Verses.   Separations are: Max = 1384.00, Mean = 256.61, Min =   14.50 .

CLUSTERS:

Start:	1: 3	2: 9	3:14	6:14	6:14	7:17	7:27	10: 7	10: 7	13: 9	13:18	13:21	20: 5	20: 5	20: 5
End:	31:11	3:22	3:22	9: 2	8: 3	8: 1	10: 7	8: 3	11: 9	13:23	13:23	13:23	20:42	20:15	20: 6
Count:	76	5	4	9	6	5	14	3	5	8	5	6	10	4	3
Width:	16786	518	197	1037	606	275	2243	85	471	703	163	56	980	270	530
Strength:	1.99	1.01	1.31	1.45	1.21	1.49	1.26	1.19	1.10	1.67	1.72	1.63	1.81	1.14	1.34

Start:	20:22	21:12	23: 9	23:28	23:28	25:13	25: 6	30:10	30:22	33: 6	34:27	37: 1	37:17	37:19	38:12
End:	20:28	23:45	23:45	23:37	23:31	25:16	25:16	30:12	31:11	40: 5	35: 5	37:20	37:20	37:20	38:12
Count:	3	13	8	6	4	3	5	3	7	23	5	4	3	5	10
Width:	141	2019	768	359	172	64	236	86	551	4538	452	74	36	1097	495
Strength:	1.03	1.26	1.57	1.65	1.36	1.25	1.57	1.30	1.62	1.03	1.14	1.59	1.33	1.65	1.05

Clusters for yåd 114, continued.

Start:	39: 3	39:21	40: 1	46: 5
End:	39: 9	40: 5		46:11
Count:	3	5	3	3
Width:	127	328	111	132
Strength:	1.07	1.39	1.12	1.06

GAPS:

Start:	1: 8	3:22	3:22	3:22	11: 9	11: 9	12: 7	13:22	13:23	14:13	14:13	14:13	14:13	14:13	14:13	16:49	16:49	18:17	23:28
End:	2: 9	8: 1	7:27	7:17	6:14	13:18	13: 9	13: 9	20: 5	20: 5	20: 5	18: 8	16:39	16:27	16:11	16:49	17:18	20: 5	48:35
Count:	3	2	6	5	3	4	3	2	12	11	9	7	3	3	2	2	3	2	54
Width:	977	656	1863	1624	1293	1291	1069	558	3729	3702	3384	2515	1250	989	662	1005	706	709	15377
Strength:	1.29	1.56	1.03	3.10	4.07	1.19	1.55	1.18	1.12	1.47	1.91	1.60	1.09	1.32	1.59	1.37	1.76	1.77	1.33

Start:	23:45	25:16	25:16	28:10	28:10	30:24	30:25	30:25	31:11	33: 8	33:22	35: 5	35: 5	36: 7	39: 3	39: 3	39:23	40: 3
End:	25: 6	28: 9	27:15	30:12	30:10	37:19	35: 3	33: 3	34:27	33: 6	34:27	37:17	37: 1	36: 1	39: 3	48: 1	46: 5	46: 5
Count:	2	4	2	3	14	8	3	6	4	17	15	3	7	10	5	5	4	4
Width:	756	1290	1091	1055	4267	2696	1313	1068	1213	906	1463	1085	662	6243	5562	4587	4148	3929
Strength:	1.96	1.19	1.61	3.13	1.07	1.37	2.23	3.18	1.01	1.09	1.58	1.59	1.59	2.26	2.20	3.10	4.28	5.78

Start:	40: 5	44:12	48: 1
End:	43:26	46: 5	48:35
Count:	2	2	2
Width:	2421	1097	670
Strength:	8.51	3.30	1.62

Linguistic Density Plot in Ezekiel 1 - 48

<pre>
For yd' 311 (78 times)   yd' 312 (4 times)   yd' 314 (1 times)   yd' 3162 (3 times)
     yd' 321 (3 times)   yd' 322 (2 times)   yd' 361 (3 times)   yd' 362 (2 times)
     yd' 363 (3 times)
</pre>

Each Column = 13 Verses. Separations are: Max = 1714.00, Mean = 279.70, Min = 12.00 .

Linguistic density scatter plot. Vertical axis (DENSITY): +25, +20, +15 D, +10 T, +5, +0, with the word DENSITY spelled vertically (D E N S I T Y). Horizontal axis labelled in 13-verse columns across Ezekiel 1–48, with two REFERENCE baselines.

CLUSTERS:

<pre>
Start: 2: 5   5:13   5:13   6: 7 10:20 10:20 10:20 11: 5 12:15 12:15 16:62 19: 7 20: 4 20: 9 23:49 24:24
End: 44:23   7:27   7: 9   6:14 20:26 16: 2 13:14 11:12 13:14 12:20 20:26 20:12 20:12 20:44 26: 6 26: 6
Count: 99   8   7   4   27   15   9   3   5   12   6   3   5   3   9   8
Width: 24788   961   609   197   5908   2415   1415   105   549   2144   807   454   166   1064   571
Strength: 6.72   1.40   1.61   1.35   1.11   1.55   1.08   1.16   1.04   1.07   1.62   1.70   1.00   1.27   1.65   1.95

Start: 24:24 25: 5 25:11 28:19 28:19 28:19 29: 6 30:19 33:29 34:27 35: 9 36:11 36:11 36:32
End: 25:11 28:19 44:23 28:19 32:15 39:28 30: 8 30:26 35:15 35: 4 35:15 39:28 37:28 37: 6
Count: 5   3   46   9   44   10   8   5   9   3   4   20   6   5
Width: 306   129 10056   1961   6833   810   183   491   162   3823   1104   57   1263   685   236
Strength: 1.48   1.10   1.82   2.02   3.76   2.14   1.71   1.15   1.01   3.20   1.50   1.96   1.04   1.49   1.57   1.61
</pre>

```
Clusters for yd' 311, yd' 312, yd' 314, yd' 3162, yd' 321, yd' 322, yd' 361, yd' 362, yd' 363, continued.

Start:    36:32  38:14  38:23  39:    39:22
End:      36:38  39:28  39:    39: 7  39:28
Count:        3     10      7      5      3
Width:      120    825    367    141     24   134
Strength:  1.12   2.12   1.98   1.79   1.37  1.09

GAPS:

Start:     1: 1   1: 1   2: 5   7: 4   7: 9   7:27  11:12  16: 2  16: 2  16: 2  17:24  20:44  21:10  22:26  22:26  25:17
End:      11:10   5:13   5:13  11: 5  10:20  10:20  12:15  20: 4  17:21  17:12  16:62  20: 4  24:24  22:    24:24  23:49  28:19
Count:       13      7      4      5      4      3      2      7      4      3      2      8      2      3      2      3
Width:     4522   2423   2178   1482   1744   1656   1515   1163    620   2925   1855   1622   1006    767   2836    582   1099   1465
Strength:  1.28   3.33   4.15   4.33   1.14   1.71   2.45   3.18   1.22   1.88   2.13   2.72   3.85   1.14   1.75   1.23   1.08   2.95   2.32

Start:    26: 6  30:26  30:26  32:15  33:33  38:23  39: 7  39:23  39:28  39:28  44:23
End:      28:19  34:27  33:29  33:29  34:27  48:35  48:35  48:35  43:11  48:35
Count:        2      6      4      2      2     10      8      5      4      2
Width:     1344   2541   1818    644   1049    600   6301   5828   2280   5708   2485
Strength:  3.84   1.88   2.06   1.31   2.77   1.15   4.74   5.94   8.63   7.22  10.25   7.96
```

Linguistic Density Plot in Ezekiel 1 - 48

For yd' 311 (78 times)   yd' 312 (4 times)   yd' 314 (1 times)   yd' 3162 (3 times)

Each Column = 13 Verses. Separations are: Max = 2914.00, Mean = 321.49, Min = 30.50 .

CLUSTERS:

Start:	2: 5	5:13	6: 7	10:20	11: 5	12:15	12:15	20:38	20:38	23:49	24:24	24:24	25: 5	25:14	28:19
End:	39:28	7:27	6:14	15: 7	11:12	13:14	12:20	21:10	39:28	26: 6	25:11	26: 6	25:11	26: 6	39:28
Count:	86	8	4	14	3	5	3	4	55	9	8	6	3	3	40
Width:	21565	961	197	2381	105	549	121	364	11750	1064	571	306	129	184	6833
Strength:	12.89	1.58	1.40	1.69	1.20	1.17	1.16	1.10	3.87	1.74	2.07	1.56	1.14	1.02	3.84

Start:	28:19	28:23	29: 6	30:19	33:29	33:29	34:27	36:11	36:36	36:36	37:28	38:14	39:22
End:	32:15	28:26	30: 8	30:26	37:14	35:15	35: 4	37:14	37: 6	39:28	39: 7	39: 7	39:28
Count:	15	3	5	3	16	8	3	8	4	9	5	3	3
Width:	1961	95	491	162	2281	1104	151	882	172	1161	703	135	134
Strength:	2.31	1.22	1.27	1.07	2.25	1.41	1.09	1.68	1.45	1.63	1.47	1.13	1.13

Data for yd' 311, yd' 312, yd' 314, yd' 3162, continued.

GAPS:

Start:	1: 1	2: 5	7: 9	7: 9	7:27	15: 7	15: 7	15: 7	17:24	20:44	21:10	22:22	22:22	25:17	26: 6	30:26	30:26	30:26
End:	5:13	11: 5	10:20	10:20	17:21	17:12	16:62	20:12	19: 7	24:24	22:16	24:24	23:49	28:19	28:19	34:27	33:29	32: 9
Count:	3	4	3	2	4	3	3	2	2	6	2	3	2	3	2	6	4	2
Width:	2178	1656	1515	1163	1889	1656	1383	1221	767	2836	847	1668	1175	1465	1344	2541	1818	644
Strength:	3.43	1.27	1.95	2.64	1.69	2.26	3.33	1.29	1.40	1.76	1.65	2.29	2.68	1.83	3.21	1.34	1.56	1.01

Start:	32:15	39:23	39:28
End:	33:29	48:35	48:35
Count:	2	3	2
Width:	1049	5828	5708
Strength:	2.28	11.60	16.94

Linguistic Density Plot in Ezekiel 1 - 48

For yd' 311 (78 times)

Each Column = 13 Verses.   Separations are: Max = 2914.00, Mean = 354.05, Min = 30.50 .

REFERENCE

(axis labels, right side: +25, +20, +15D, E, N, S, I, +10T, Y, +5, 0)

(axis labels, left side: 25+, 20+, D15+, E, N, S, I, T10+, Y, 5+, 0+)

REFERENCE

CLUSTERS:

Start:	2: 5	5:13	5:13	6: 7	6: 7	11: 5	11: 5	12:15	13:14	13:14	20:38	20:38	20:26	23:49	23:49	23:49	24:24	24:24	25: 5
End:	39:28	7:27	7: 9	6:14	7: 9	15: 7	12:20	12:20	13:14	15: 7	20:44	21:10	21:10	32:15	39:28	26: 6	26: 6	25:11	25:11
Count:	78	8	8	4	6	12	6	3	4	5	3	4	5	46	23	9	8	5	3
Width:	21565	961	609	197	364	2240	846	121	462	966	166	364	665	9241	4369	1064	571	306	129
Strength:	11.59	1.70	1.82	1.44	1.84	1.52	1.21	1.19	1.00	1.05	1.10	1.16	1.09	4.32	2.43	1.87	2.14	1.61	1.17

Start:	25:14	28:22	28:22	28:22	29: 6	30:19	33:29	33:29	34:27	34:27	35: 9	36:36	36:36	36:36	38:23	39:22
End:	26: 6	32:15	30: 8	28:24	30: 8	30:26	39:28	36:23	34:27	35:15	36:36	37:28	37:14	39: 7	39:28	
Count:	3	14	8	4	5	8	23	10	6	4	9	13	7	6	3	
Width:	184	1910	759	132	491	162	3823	1646	923	381	1911	750	369	593	135	134
Strength:	1.06	2.32	2.19	1.55	1.34	1.11	2.82	1.54	1.74	1.82	1.13	1.17	2.08	1.65	1.83	1.48

Data for yd' 311, continued.

GAPS:

Start	End	Count	Width	Strength
1: 1	6: 7	4	2423	2.27
1: 1	5:13	3	2178	2.99
2: 5	5:13	2	1482	3.22
7: 4	11: 5	4	1744	1.13
7: 9	11: 5	3	1656	1.92
7:27	11: 5	2	1304	2.71
13:23	20:42	11	4662	1.07
15: 7	17:21	4	1889	1.38
15: 7	17:12	3	1656	1.92
15: 7	16:62	2	1383	2.94
17:24	20:42	4	1988	1.54
17:24	20:38	3	1875	2.37
17:24	20:26	3	1574	3.48
20:44	24:24	6	2836	1.39
21:10	22:16	2	847	1.40
22:22	24:24	3	1668	1.95
22:22	23:49	2	1175	2.34
25:17	28:22	3	1516	1.64
26: 6	28:22	2	1395	2.97
30:26	34:27	6	2541	1.01

Start	End	Count	Width	Strength
30:26	33:29	4	1818	1.26
32:15	33:29	3	1049	1.98
39:23	48:35	2	5828	10.42
39:28	48:35	2	5708	15.31

Linguistic Density Plot in Ezekiel 1 - 48

For yd' 321 (3 times)   yd' 322 (2 times)

Each Column = 13 Verses. Separations are: Max = 5246.50, Mean = 4661.66, Min = 1101.00 .

REFERENCE

REFERENCE

CLUSTERS:

Start:	20: 5	20: 5	35:11
End:	38:23	20: 9	38:23
Count:	5	2	3
Width:	11994	125	2202
Strength:	1.33	1.15	1.42

GAPS:

Start:	1: 1	20: 9
End:	20: 5	35:11
Count:	2	2
Width:	9668	9667
Strength:	1.27	1.27

Linguistic Density Plot in Ezekiel 1 - 48

For yd' 361 (3 times)   yd' 362 (2 times)   yd' 363 (3 times)

Each Column = 13 Verses.   Separations are: Max = 6310.00, Mean = 3107.78, Min = 907.50 .

REFERENCE

REFERENCE

CLUSTERS:

Start:	16: 2	20: 4	20: 4
End:	22:26	22:26	20:11
Count:	5	4	2
Width:	5204	2279	185
Strength:	1.64	1.68	1.05

GAPS:

Start:	1: 1	22:26	22:26
End:	16: 2	43:11	39: 7
Count:	2	3	2
Width:	6717	12620	9867
Strength:	1.29	1.74	2.43

For yəhûdâ 12 (15 times)

Linguistic Density Plot in Ezekiel 1 - 48

Each Column = 13 Verses. Separations are: Max = 4901.50, Mean = 1748.13, Min = 99.00 .

REFERENCE

(density plot with vertical axis labelled D E N S I T Y and gridlines 25+, 20+, D15+, 10+, 5+, 0+)

REFERENCE

CLUSTERS:

Start:	4: 6	8: 1	21:25	25: 3	25: 8	37:16	48: 7
End:	9: 9	9: 9	27:17	25:12	37:19	48:31	48: 8
Count:	4	3	5	4	3	4	2
Width:	2245	674	3556	1087	198	95	510
Strength:	1.13	1.25	1.16	1.56	1.46	1.00	1.78	1.06

GAPS:

Start:	1: 1	9: 9	9: 9	25:12	25:12	27:17	37:19
End:	48: 7	25: 3	21:25	48: 7	37:16	37:16	48: 7
Count:	13	3	2	5	3	2	2
Width:	27382	9803	7334	13546	6913	6024	6538
Strength:	2.18	2.81	3.40	2.23	1.52	2.60	2.91

Linguistic Density Plot in Ezekiel 1 - 48

For yhwh 121 (432 times)

Each Column = 13 Verses.   Separations are: Max = 746.50, Mean = 64.60, Min = 4.50 .

CLUSTERS:

Start:	1: 3	27: 3	5:17	6:14	6:14	6:14	8:12	8:12	8:16	11:	11: 5	11:10	11:10	11:10	11:21	12: 8	12: 8	12: 8	12: 8	12:15
End:	27: 3	7: 9	6: 3	7: 9	7: 5	7: 2	8:14	8:16	12: 1	11: 1	8: 1	11:17	11:14	11:12	12: 1	18: 9	16:14	14: 9	13: 9	12:19
Count:	242	13	30	6	5	4	29	6	3	4	11	7	80	4	1	54	38	24		
Width:	14443	494	167	84	84	625	345	155	80	75	1985	1162	579	77						
Strength:	1.68	1.27	1.08	1.08	1.35	1.22	1.09	1.66	1.18	1.81	1.13	1.48	1.47	1.01	1.06	3.26	3.27	3.00	1.04	

Start:	12:16	12:16	12:19	12:20	12:20	12:25	12:28	12:28	13:	13: 5	13: 5	13: 7	14: 4	14:11	15: 6	16: 8	16:58	16:62	16:63
End:	12:19	13: 9	12:26	12:23	12:26	12:28	13: 1	13: 1	13: 9	13: 6	13: 8	13:13	14: 9	14: 9	15: 1	16: 3	17: 3	17: 3	17: 3
Count:	3	18	6	3	3	12	5	3	9	6	8	14	9	5	9	6	4	3	25
Width:	34	316	104	36	28	179	45	19	96	10	28	520	168	59	303	81	23	140	55
Strength:	1.04	2.99	1.52	1.01	1.10	2.51	1.65	1.20	1.85	1.30	1.10	1.39	1.07	1.83	1.17	1.37	1.16	1.27	1.13

```
Clusters for yhwh 121, continued.

Start:     17:24  17:24  18:23  18:23  20: 1  20:26  20:36  20:44  20:44  20:26  20: 1  21: 4  21: 4  21: 4  21: 3  21:10  21: 6  21:37  22:12  22:12
End:       18: 3  18: 1  27: 3  22: 3  20: 7  22: 3  21: 1  21: 1  21: 5  21: 3  20: 3  21:23  21:13  21:23  21:13  21:21  22: 3  22: 3  23: 1  22:19
Count:         4     99     44      7      1     31     10      7      5     15      3     16      7     10      3      5      3     34     11      5
Width:        52   5382   2369    147     45   1256    269     63     29    530     45    689    169    100     23    345     34   2825    387    107
Strength:   1.26   1.68   1.01   1.52   1.33   1.99   1.62   1.51   1.09   1.57   1.33   1.13   1.38   1.22   1.16   1.23   1.04   1.49   1.28   1.17

Start:     22:28  23: 1  23:46  23:46  24:14  24:20  24:24  24:27  25: 1  25:13  25:13  25:14  25:16  25:14  25:14  26: 1  26: 7  26:14  26:21  28: 1
End:       23: 1  27: 3  25: 3  24:15  24:15  25: 3  24:24  25: 3  25: 3  25:13  25: 8  25:16  26: 7  26: 3  26: 7  26: 3  27: 3  26:15  27: 3  40: 1
Count:         4     39     16      3      5      7      5      4      5      8      4     28      3      6      3      3      3     10      3    146
Width:        72   1528    665     29    206    101    789     35    157     65     28    186    108     28     26    222     10     34          7263
Strength:   1.08   2.43   1.23   1.09   1.15   1.22   2.14   1.42   1.46   1.15   1.10   1.82   1.49   1.10   1.12   1.05   1.30   1.04          3.31

Start:     28: 1  28:10  28:20  28:20  28:23  28:25  29:13  29:13  29:13  29:20  29:20  29:20  29:20  30:19  32:14  32:31  32:31  33:22
End:       29: 9  28:12  29: 9  28:22  28:25  31: 1  31: 1  30:13  30:13  30: 8  30:13  30: 3  30: 1  32: 1  32:17  40: 1  33: 1  34:11
Count:        50     18      9     12      3      3     32     15     21     11      5      6      4     96     73     13
Width:      2355    748    665    378    105     37   1517    432    725    246    142     26     64     96   3123    529
Strength:   1.90   1.34   1.23   1.57   1.51   1.00   1.40   1.98   2.00   1.98   1.82   1.12   1.16   2.79   3.05   1.11

Start:     34: 7  34:15  34:15  34:15  34:30  34:31  35: 9  35: 9  35: 9  35:12  35:15  36: 3  36: 3  36: 7  36: 5  36:11  36:13  36:20  36:32
End:       34:11  36:23  37:21  34:15  35: 6  35: 3  36:23  36: 7  35:11  36: 2  36: 2  36: 7  36: 6  36:36  36:23  36:16  36:16  36:23  37:21
Count:         5     56     36     13      5      9      9      3     11     12      3      6      9      4      5     20
Width:       102   1966   1180    433    120     29    678    333    151     94     20    158     77     26     86    593
Strength:   1.21   3.54   2.95   1.55   1.70   1.09   2.51   2.20   1.77   1.27   1.19   1.14   1.04   1.12   1.23   2.30

Start:     36:32  36:36  36:36  37: 9  37: 9  37:12  37:12  37:14  37:15  39: 5  39: 8  43:18  43:27  43:27  43:27  44: 2  44: 5  44: 4
End:       37: 9  37: 1  36:38  37: 1  37: 6  37: 2  37:15  37:15  37:15  39: 8  39: 4  44:15  44: 9  44: 2  44: 9  44: 3  44: 5  44: 5
Count:        13      8      3      5      3      5      7      5      9     16     12      9      2      3     10      3     13
Width:       303    135     62     11    125     24    220     73    120    612    414    218     92     32     39
Strength:   2.14   1.87   1.81   1.29   1.03   1.15   1.06   1.31   1.07   1.45   1.40   1.89   1.88   1.06   1.38   1.27

GAPS:

Start:      1: 1   1: 1   1: 1   1: 1   1: 1   2: 4   3: 11  3: 12  3: 12  3: 16  3: 16  3: 23  3: 27  4: 14  7: 1   7: 5   7: 5   7: 9   7: 9
End:       12:20  6:14   5:17   5:17   1:28   3:11   5:17   5:17   4:13   3:22   4:13   4:13   4:13   5: 5   8:12   7:27   7:27   7:19   7:19
Count:        73     70     28     21     19      2     15      7      2      3      9      9      6      6      2
Width:      5292   2623   2296    997    526    371   1223    659    160    399    199    814    734    352    192
Strength:   1.28   2.70   3.56   7.20   7.15   4.74   1.33   1.72   1.47   2.95   2.07   1.64   2.86   2.44   1.96

Start:      8: 1   8:16   8:16   8:16   9: 1   9:10   10: 4  10:18  12: 1  16: 1  16: 3  16: 3  16: 3  16:23  16:36  16:36  16:48  17: 3
End:        8:12   9: 1   9: 4   9:16  11: 5  11: 5  10:18  12: 8  16:63  16:35  16:19  16:14  16: 8  16:35  16:63  16:58  16:58  17: 9
Count:         2      4      3      7      5      5      7      2      8      3      4      3      7      3      2
Width:       267    326    286    165    569    438    258    159    720    701    400    163    223    549    208    235
Strength:   3.13   1.18   1.71   1.55   1.15   1.39   2.99   1.45   1.57   1.99   1.84   1.51   1.02   3.18   2.21   2.63   1.22

Start:     18: 1  18: 1  18: 1  18: 9  18: 9  18:32  20: 5  20: 5  20: 5  20: 7  20:12  20:20  22: 3  22:28  22:28  22:28  23: 1
End:       20: 1  18:30  18:30  18:30  18:23  20: 1  20:26  20:26  20:19  20:19  20:26  20:19  22:14  24:27  24:14  23:49
Count:        23      7      6      4      2      7      6      3      7      4      3     10      1
Width:      1850    920    890    567    442    281    530    340    292    156    163    237   1337   1051    981
Strength:   1.45   3.38   3.94   3.34   3.43   3.35   3.19   1.43   1.30   1.78   1.51   1.41   1.90   1.02   1.12   1.49   2.44   3.12

Start:     23:35  23: 1  23: 1  23:28  26: 7  26:14  27: 1  27: 3  28:12  28:20  31: 1  31:15  31:18  32:17  32:31  33: 1  33: 1
End:       23:32  23:22  23:28  23:46  28:10  28: 2  28: 2  31:10  31:18  31:15  32:32  32:31  34: 7  33:22  33:11
Count:         5      4      3      9     11      6      3      2      9
Width:       668    614    538    374    289    218    167    792    623    593    177    319    350    180    436    325    914    787    487    247
Strength:   3.18   3.76   4.48   4.79   1.74   2.37   1.58   3.26   5.41   8.19   1.73   2.07   2.42   1.78   2.17   4.03   1.32   1.49   3.92   2.82
```

Gaps for yhwh 121, continued.

Start:	36:23	37:15	37:15	37:21	38: 3	38: 3	38: 3	39: 8	39: 8	39: 8	39:22	40: 1	40: 1	40: 1	40: 1	43: 5	43: 5	44: 4	44: 4
End:	36:32	44: 4	38:23	37:28	38:17	38:14	38:10	43:24	43: 4	43: 4	43: 4	43: 4	42:13	41:22	40:46	43:24	43:18	48:35	46: 3
Count:	2	40	12	2	4	3	2	24	18	14	9	5	4	3	2	4	2	30	17
Width:	193	4248	940	373	351	274	154	3161	3009	2525	2211	2005	1803	1493	965	460	335	2986	1304
Strength:	1.98	4.49	1.08	1.60	1.40	1.58	1.37	5.56	7.32	7.35	9.36	13.59	14.44	14.97	13.96	2.38	4.18	3.31	1.06

Start:	44: 5	44: 5	44: 5	44: 6	44: 9	44: 9	44: 9	45: 4	45: 4	46: 4	46: 4	46:16	46:16	46:16	46:16	46:16	48:10	48:14	48:14
End:	46: 3	45: 9	45: 9	44: 9	45: 1	44:27	44:27	45: 9	45: 9	48:35	48:35	48: 9	47:23	47:13	48:35	48:29	48:35	48:14	48:29
Count:	16	10	9	8	7	5	4	2	13	8	4	9	5	2	3	4	3	3	2
Width:	1294	879	852	824	753	548	459	263	1675	1409	865	720	499	131	501	421	317
Strength:	1.32	1.55	1.85	2.19	2.32	2.25	2.37	3.07	4.08	5.64	6.02	6.48	6.73	1.02	2.75	3.19	3.90

Linguistic Density Plot in Ezekiel 1 - 48

For yôm 111 (112 times)

Each Column = 13 Verses.   Separations are: Max = 1463.00, Mean =   247.52, Min =   2.00 .

DENSITY axis (vertical): +25, +20, +15, +10, +5, 0

REFERENCE (horizontal axis): verses 1 – 48

Linguistic density scatter plot with DENSITY on the vertical axis and verse REFERENCE on the horizontal axis.

CLUSTERS:

Start:	1:28	7:19	12: 3	12:22	23:19	23:38	24: 2	24:25
End:	1:28	7:19	12: 7	12:27	24: 2	24: 2	24: 2	24:27
Count:	15	3	3	5	4	6	3	3
Width:	197	596	91	98	691	273	171	36
Strength:	1.63	1.79	1.16	1.52	1.01	1.48	2.23	1.32

Start:	7: 7	7: 7	12: 3	12: 5	38:17	38:18	43:18	43:27
End:	7:19	7:12	12: 7	12: 5	38:19	38:19	43:27	43:27
Count:	8	3	3	7	8	7	25	5
Width:	249	97	196	133	317	133	852	36
Strength:	1.17	1.15	1.79	2.30	2.47	2.30	1.67	1.96

Start:	4: 9	4: 6	4: 4	4: 6	4: 6	4: 4	4: 4	4: 4
End:	4:10	4: 4	4: 1	4: 8	4: 4	4: 5	4: 8	4:10
Count:	3	3	4	3	3	3	4	4
Width:	25	1	25	43	7664	25	92	152
Strength:	1.35	1.00	1.35	1.65	1.78	1.35	2.37	2.92

Start:	4: 4	4: 4	1:28	5: 2
End:	4:10	4: 4	1:28	5: 2
Count:	10	11	15	11
Width:	342	2407	1312	342
Strength:	2.86	2.13	2.49	2.86

Start:	29:21	29:21	30: 2	30: 9	33:12	36:33	38:	38: 8	38:17	39:	39: 8	43:18	43:18	43:25
End:	29:21	30:18	30: 3	30:18	33:12	36:35	40: 1	38:19	38:18	40: 1	39:13	48:35	44:27	43:25
Count:	8	3	4	9	2	41	14	8	39: 8	25	26	9	43:18	43:25
Width:	691	317	173	2029	1089	7664	1089	596	2741	1195	3260	1797	852	171
Strength:	1.01	2.47	1.35	1.78	2.54	1.78	2.54	2.30	1.09	1.72	2.69	3.86	1.67	2.23

Start:	29:21	32:10	30:18	30: 3
End:	29:21	30:18	30: 3	30: 3
Count:	16	11	9	5
Width:	2741	1195	326	51
Strength:	1.09	1.72	2.46	1.93

Clusters for yôm 111, continued.

Start:	43:25	45:21	45:21	45:21	45:21	45:23	45:23	45:23	45:25	46: 1
End:	43:26	46:13	46: 6	46: 1	45:23	45:23	45:23	45:23	46: 1	46: 1
Count:	3	16	14	12	7	3	4	3	5	3
Width:	17	384	202	113	50	16	21	8	42	9
Strength:	1.38	3.74	3.60	3.36	2.44	1.38	1.71	1.40	1.95	1.40

GAPS:

Start:	1: 1	4: 6	4: 6	4: 6	4: 6	4: 6	4: 6	4: 6	4: 9	4:10	4:10	4:10	4:10	4:10	5: 2	7:12	7:19	12: 4	12:27	12:27
End:	1:28	48:35	45:23	38:18	30: 3	30: 3	30: 2	24: 2	24: 2	23:38	24: 2	23:38	12: 3	7: 7	7: 7	12: 3	12: 3	23:38	23:38	20: 5
Count:	2	104	92	71	51	50	49	38	37	34	33	31	7	3	2	3	2	24	19	9
Width:	573	26374	24569	19936	14556	14553	14550	11457	11454	11369	11355	11094	3220	1036	846	2087	1935	7846	7377	4242
Strength:	1.32	1.18	1.97	2.05	1.67	1.86	2.06	1.86	2.08	2.68	2.90	3.17	2.95	1.56	2.43	4.60	6.87	2.04	3.04	3.36

Start:	12:27	13: 5	16: 5	16: 4	16:60	20: 5	20: 6	20: 6	20:29	20:31	20:31	22:24	22:24	24: 2	24: 2	24:27	24:27	24:27	28:15	30: 3	30:18	30:18	32:10
End:	16: 4	16: 4	20: 5	20: 5	20:29	23:38	20:29	21:30	23:19	21:30	23:38	30: 2	30: 2	30: 2	27:27	28:13	29:21	33:12	33:12	38:17	33:12	31:15	33:12
Count:	3	2	6	10	2	2	10	2	3	7	4	3	18	2	4	2	2	2					
Width:	1339	1240	2854	1641	3102	622	930	2436	2581	3081	1748	1369	797	764	5355	1647	532	778					
Strength:	2.44	4.04	2.99	5.67	1.23	1.52	2.77	1.11	1.21	1.20	1.86	2.38	2.52	2.10	2.23	2.14	1.22	2.16					

Start:	33:12	33:12	34: 2	34:12	34:12	34:12	34:12	34:12	38:18	38:19	38:19	38:19	39:13	39:13	39:22	40: 1	43:18	43:27	44:27	46:13
End:	38:17	34:17	38: 2	38:17	38:16	38:14	38: 8	36:33	43:25	43:22	43:25	39:25	39:25	43:18	43:18	43:18	44:26	45:21	45:21	48:35
Count:	10	9	2	6	5	3	6	8	5	2	10	7	9	4	3	2	8			
Width:	3422	3407	718	2665	2631	2585	2401	3310	3282	3230	2844	2761	2571	2375	561	675	1463			
Strength:	1.68	2.12	1.91	2.00	2.58	3.29	5.51	1.52	1.93	2.37	3.82	4.79	6.00	8.66	1.27	1.74	4.95			

Linguistic Density Plot in Ezekiel 1 - 48

For yld 311 (3 times)   yld 312 (1 times)   yld 361 (3 times)   yld 3761 (2 times)

Each Column = 13 Verses. Separations are: Max = 10505.00, Mean = 2797.00, Min = 194.00

CLUSTERS:

Start:	16: 4	16: 4	16: 4	16: 4	18:10
End:	31: 6	18:14	16:20	16: 5	18:14
Count:	8	5	3	2	2
Width:	9983	2140	388	49	71
Strength:	2.48	2.18	1.54	1.08	1.07

GAPS:

Start:	1: 1	18:14	23:37	23:37	31: 6
End:	16: 4	48:35	48:35	47:22	47:22
Count:	2	6	4	3	2
Width:	6752	19077	15196	14467	10505
Strength:	1.56	1.20	1.76	2.63	3.04

For yām 111 (60 times)

Linguistic Density Plot in Ezekiel 1 - 48

Each Column = 13 Verses.   Separations are: Max = 7015.00, Mean = 458.52, Min = 5.00

REFERENCE

CLUSTERS:

Start:	25:16	25:16	25:16	26:17	26:16	26:16	27: 3	27:25	27:32	27:32	27:32	38:20	45: 7	45: 7	46:19
End:	48:34	32: 2	28: 8	26:18	26:18	27: 9	27: 9	27:29	28: 2	27:33	27:34	48:34	48:34	45: 7	48:34
Count:	60	20	19	4	9	7	3	9	8	5	3	40	36	3	33
Width:	13989	3164	1260	338	287	69	113	78	203	95	6	6367	2120	15	1276
Strength:	20.65	3.37	4.31	2.77	2.32	1.70	1.27	1.68	1.85	1.66	1.00	6.75	7.92	1.42	7.55

Start:	46:19	47: 8	47: 8	47: 8	47:15	47:18	47:19	47:19	47:20	48: 1	48: 6	48: 6	48:16	48:16	48:23
End:	48:10	48:10	47:20	47:10	47:20	47:20	47:20	47:20	48:10	48: 8	48: 5	48: 8	48:21	48:18	48:34
Count:	21	20	10	3	7	5	20	3	10	4	3	4	5	44	164
Width:	783	521	285	66	105	39	141	10	336	12	79	44	124	336	69
Strength:	5.02	4.97	3.04	1.34	2.50	2.04	3.16	1.43	3.44	1.01	1.99	1.73	1.94	2.44	2.28

REFERENCE

Data for yām 111, continued.

GAPS:

Start:	1: 1	1: 1	1: 1	1: 1	1: 1	1: 1	27:33	27:34	28: 8	28: 2	28: 8	32: 2	39:11	39:11	42:19
End:	47:20	45: 7	27:32	26:17	26: 3	25:16	45: 7	45: 7	45: 7	45: 7	38:20	38:20	45: 7	41:12	45: 7
Count:	37	26	16	6	3	2	10	9	8	7	3	7	4	2	7
Width:	27201	25821	15009	14336	14029	13952	10806	10789	10717	10609	6362	4458	3918	1722	1574
Strength:	6.12	8.21	5.31	12.35	20.72	29.91	5.30	5.93	7.42	8.60	8.86	3.30	2.79	2.47

Linguistic Density Plot in Ezekiel 1 - 48

For yāmîn 114 (5 times)

Each Column = 13 Verses.   Separations are: Max = 10530.00, Mean = 4661.66, Min = 3622.00 .

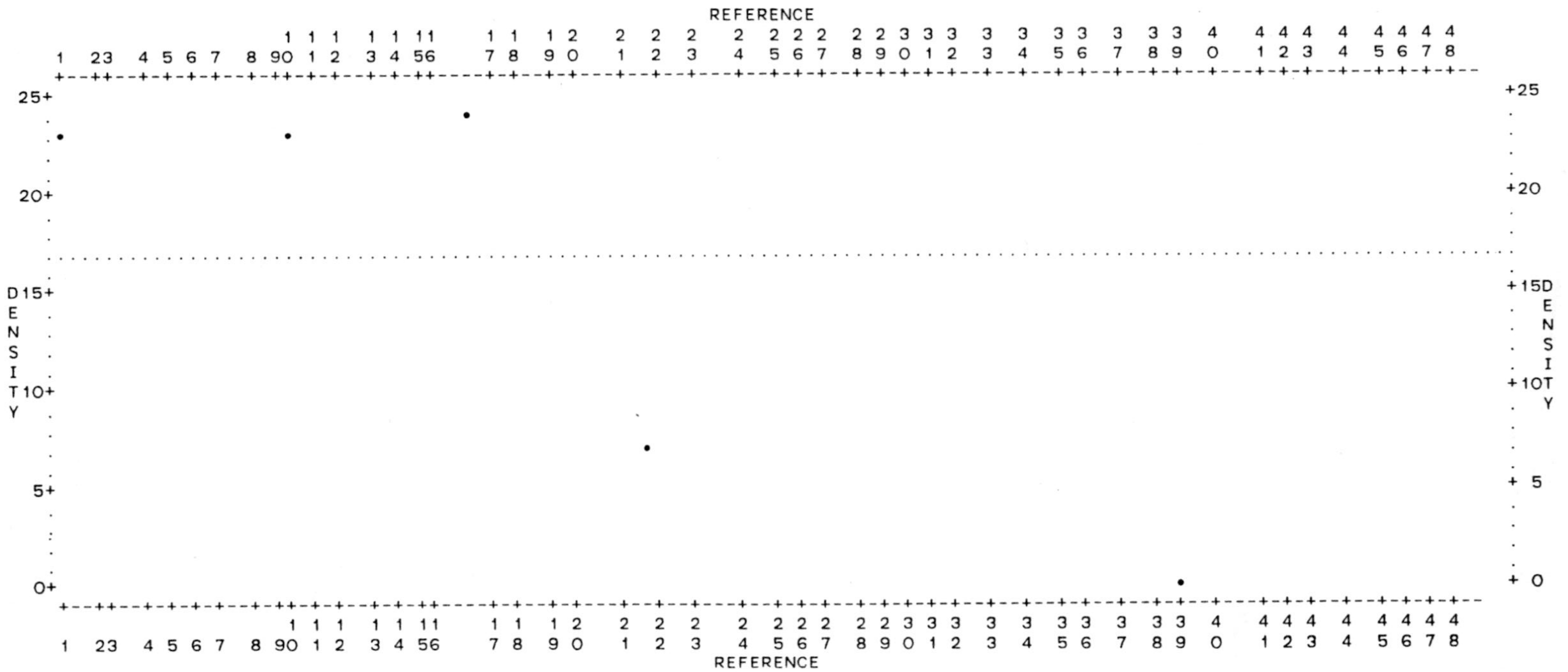

All cluster strengths are less than 1.00.

GAPS:

Start:	21:27	21:27
End:	48:35	39: 3
Count:	3	2
Width:	16772	10530
Strength:	1.49	1.48

Linguistic Density Plot in Ezekiel 1 - 48

For ynh 361 (4 times)   ynh 362 (2 times)   ynh 3662 (1 times)

Each Column = 13 Verses. Separations are: Max = 7316.00, Mean = 3496.25, Min =   84.00 .

REFERENCE

CLUSTERS:

Start:	18: 7	18: 7	18:12
End:	22:29	18:16	18:16
Count:	5	3	2
Width:	3224	168	78
Strength:	2.30	1.69	1.10

GAPS:

Start:	1: 1	22:29	22:29
End:	18: 7	48:35	45: 8
Count:	2	4	2
Width:	8764	15981	13863
Strength:	1.70	1.21	3.36

For ya'an 111 (40 times)

Linguistic Density Plot in Ezekiel 1 - 48

Each Column = 13 Verses.   Separations are: Max =   5325.00, Mean =   682.20, Min =   13.00 .

REFERENCE

CLUSTERS:

Start:	5: 7	5: 7	12:12	12:12	13: 8	13:10	20:16	20:16	20:16	21: 9	23:35	25: 3	25: 3	28: 2	34: 8
End:	44:12	5:11	16:43	13:22	13:10	13:10	44:12	36:13	20:16	21:29	21:29	25:12	25:12	36:13	29: 9	36:13
Count:	40	3	8	4	2	29	28	14	6	8	3	6	3	2	9
Width:	23196	107	2505	808	364	57	15241	9916	4039	1810	914	418	1281	374	208	128	4780	733	1164
Strength:	3.66	1.35	1.39	1.49	1.49	1.40	1.01	1.92	4.15	2.40	1.13	1.00	1.01	2.15	2.15	1.63	1.32	2.03	1.16	2.51

Start:	35: 5	35: 5	36: 2	36: 3
End:	36:13	36: 3	36: 3	36: 3
Count:	7	5	3	2
Width:	555	276	26	2
Strength:	2.31	1.91	1.43	1.02

Data for ya'an 111, continued.

GAPS:

Start:	1: 1	5:11	5:11	5:11	16:43	29: 9	29: 9	31:10	36: 3	36:13	36:13
End:	5: 7	13:10	13: 8	12:12	20:16	34:21	34: 8	34: 8	48:35	48:35	44:12
Count:	2	4	3	2	2	4	3	2	5	3	2
Width:	2000	3502	3448	3004	2339	3195	2883	1888	8377	8098	5325
Strength:	1.97	1.29	2.24	3.48	2.48	1.02	1.63	1.81	4.41	7.24	6.97

Linguistic Density Plot in Ezekiel 1 - 48

For ya'ar 111 (6 times)

Each Column = 13 Verses.   Separations are: Max = 5566.50, Mean = 3995.71, Min = 2039.50 .

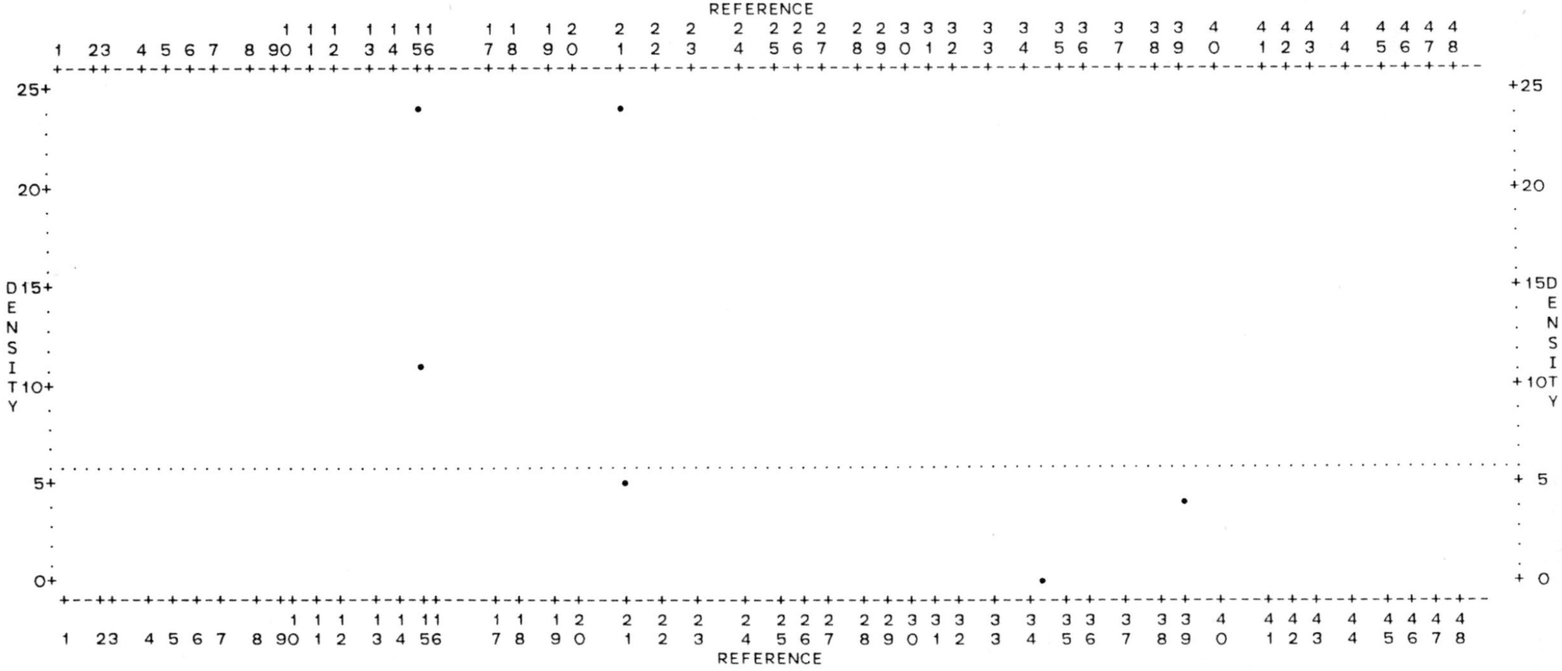

CLUSTERS:

Start:	15: 2	15: 2	21: 2	
End:	39:10	21: 3	15: 6	21: 3
Count:	6	4	2	
Width:	15289	4156	77	6
Strength:	1.04	1.60	1.13	1.15

GAPS:

Start:	21: 3	21: 3
End:	48:35	34:25
Count:	4	2
Width:	17235	8388
Strength:	1.07	1.26

Linguistic Density Plot in Ezekiel 1 - 48

For yōpî 111 (10 times)

Each Column = 13 Verses.   Separations are: Max = 6297.50, Mean = 2542.73, Min = 77.00 .

CLUSTERS:

Start:	16:14	16:14	16:14	27: 3	27: 3	28: 7	28: 7		
End:	31: 8	16:25	16:15	31: 8	28:17	27:11	27: 4	28:17	28:12
Count:	10	3	2	7	6	3	2		
Width:	9794	232	19	2305	886	154	9	179	81
Strength:	4.20	1.55	1.08	3.22	2.94	1.58	1.09	1.57	1.06

GAPS:

Start:	1: 1	1: 1	16:25	28:12	28:17	31: 8
End:	27: 3	16:14	27: 3	48:35	48:35	
Count:	5	2	2	4	3	2
Width:	14488	6999	7257	12693	12595	11176
Strength:	1.11	1.91	2.03	1.40	2.41	3.71

Linguistic Density Plot in Ezekiel 1 - 48

For yc' 311 (8 times)   yc' 312 (20 times)   yc' 313 (2 times)   yc' 314 (6 times)
     yc' 3162 (1 times)   yc' 361 (14 times)   yc' 362 (8 times)   yc' 363 (1 times)
     yc' 364 (1 times)   yc' 3662 (5 times)   yc' 371 (1 times)   yc' 374 (1 times)

Each Column = 13 Verses. Separations are: Max = 1541.00, Mean = 372.93, Min = 7.00

(Density plot with REFERENCE axis along the bottom and DENSITY axis (0+, 5+, 10+, 15+, 20+, 25+) along the side)

CLUSTERS:

Start:	1:13	3:22	9: 7	9: 7	9: 7	10: 7	10: 7	12: 4	12: 4	14:22	19:14	19:14	20: 6	20:34	21: 8
End:	16:14	3:25	16:14	11: 9	12:12	9:10	11: 9	12:12	15: 7	12: 6	21:24	20:10	20:10	20:41	21:24	21:10
Count:	25	3	19	15	7	5	3	8	4	13	6	4	3	4
Width:	6729	73	3208	1321	710	438	212	168	41	182	1607	586	266	111	731	184	310
Strength:	1.48	1.30	2.55	3.11	1.75	1.46	1.03	1.71	2.22	1.08	2.43	1.59	1.35	1.22	1.73	1.08	1.35

Start:	24: 6	33:30	42: 1	46: 2	46:10	46:10	46: 9	46:20	46:20	47: 1
End:	24:12	47:12	47:12	47:12	46:12	46:10	46:12	47:12	46:20	47: 3	47: 3
Count:	3	29	22	17	9	8	6	5	3	8	2
Width:	109	8553	3143	777	228	123	55	26	14	355	136	48	125
Strength:	1.23	1.21	3.25	3.94	2.78	2.66	2.26	1.39	1.00	1.41	1.87	1.34	1.20

```
Data for yc' 311, yc' 312, yc' 313, yc' 314, yc' 3162, yc' 361, yc' 362, yc' 363, yc' 364, yc' 3662, yc' 371, yc' 374.   continued.

GAPS:

Start:     1: 1   1: 1   1:13   3:23   3:25   5: 4   7:10   9: 7  12:12  12:12  12:12  14:22  14:22  14:22  15: 7  16:14  20:10  20:10  21:10
End:      46:10   9: 7   3:22   9: 7   9: 7   9: 7   9: 7  46:10  20: 9  14:22  20: 6  19:14  19:14  19:14  46:10  46: 9                       24: 6
Count:       64      8      3      5      4      3      2     56     43      8      2      6      5      4      3      2     35     32      3
Width:    26423   3784   1052   2458   2396   1843    988  22637  21318   4695   1390   3299   3194   3039   2863   2548  16617  16581   2260
Strength:  2.48   1.25   1.84   1.33   2.03   2.12   1.67   1.49   3.55   2.23   2.76   1.79   2.36   3.05   4.09   5.90   2.46   3.17   2.92

Start:    21:24  24: 6  24: 6  24: 6  24:12  24:12  24:12  24:12  28:18  30: 9  34:13  34:13  37: 1  38: 8  38: 8  39: 9  42:15  42:15  44:19
End:      24: 6  46: 9  46: 8  42:14  42:14  33:30  38: 1  27:33  33:30  33:30  36:20  38: 4  38: 4  42:14  42:14  39: 9  42: 1  44: 3  46: 2
Count:        2     21     20     15     14     10      6      3      2      9      4      2      3      2      4      3      2      3      2
Width:     1994  13236  13219  11012  10913   7920   5239   1761   3082   2233   1173    754   2892   2628   2323   2075   2068    766    884
Strength:  4.40   4.07   4.39   4.63   4.99   4.37   4.21   1.96   5.05   5.05   2.17   1.03   2.81   3.64   1.50   1.91   1.06   1.50   1.38
```

Linguistic Density Plot in Ezekiel 1 - 48

For yc' 311 (8 times)   yc' 312 (20 times)   yc' 313 (2 times)   yc' 314 (6 times)
    yc' 3162 (7 times)

Each Column = 13 Verses.   Separations are: Max = 2071.50, Mean = 635.68, Min = 7.00

Density plot (vertical axis DENSITY with scale markers 25+, 20+, 15+, 10+, 5+, 0+ shown on both sides as +25, +20, +15, +10, +5, +0; horizontal axis REFERENCE).

CLUSTERS:

Start:	1:13	3:22	3:22	9: 7	9: 7	9: 7	10: 7	9: 7	9: 7	10:19	10:19	12:12	12:12	15: 7	16:14	21:24	24:12	27:33	30: 9
End:	16:14	5: 4	3:25	46:10	46: 9	46: 8	33:30	10:19	47:12	47:12	16:14	12:12	24: 6	24: 6	21: 9	19:14	24: 3	42:14	46:10	46:12
Count:	16	4	3	29	26	25	2	5	3	2	10	7	6	6	9	4	3	2	9	2
Width:	6729	626	73	22637	22601	22584	8553	484	212	777	3208	1316	228	123	2879	1401	1994	2548	13015	9152
Strength:	1.41	1.21	1.37	2.41	3.24	3.52	1.40	1.71	1.21	3.68	1.49	1.74	3.02	2.83	3.36	1.23	2.18	3.07	4.12	1.44

GAPS:

Start:	1: 1	9: 7	9: 7	10:19	10:19	12:12	12:12	15: 7	16:14	21:24	24:12	27:33	30: 9
End:	46:10	46:10	46: 9	46: 8	46: 2	24: 6	14:22	24: 6	21: 9	19:14	24: 3	42:14	33:30
Count:	37	29	26	25	22	21	10	8	6	4	3	2	2
Width:	26423	22637	22601	22584	22102	21997	8873	8041	6464	4185	3870	2548	1994
Strength:	2.19	2.41	3.24	3.52	4.20	4.47	1.87	2.35	2.48	2.16	2.99	3.07	2.18

Gaps for yc' 311, yc' 312, yc' 313, yc' 314, yc' 3162, continued.

```
Start:     36:20  39: 9
End:       42:14  42:14
Count:         3      2
Width:      4143   2339
Strength:   3.30   2.74
```

Linguistic Density Plot in Ezekiel 1 - 48

For yc' 311 (8 times)

Each Column = 13 Verses.   Separations are: Max = 6671.50, Mean = 3107.78, Min = 852.00 .

CLUSTERS:

Start:	46: 2
End:	46:12
Count:	2
Width:	222
Strength:	1.03

GAPS:

Start:	1: 1	9: 7	9: 7	15: 7	24: 6
End:	46: 2	46: 2	36:20	36:20	36:20
Count:	8	6	4	3	2
Width:	26265	22479	16234	13343	6879
Strength:	1.22	1.57	1.65	1.93	1.35

Linguistic Density Plot in Ezekiel 1 - 48

For yc' 312 (20 times)

Each Column = 13 Verses.   Separations are: Max = 5456.50, Mean = 1331.90, Min = 12.00 .

REFERENCE

```
25+                                                                           ·  ·  ·
20+
D15+
 E
 N
 S
 I
T10+
 Y
 5+
 0+
```

```
     1 23  4 5 6 7  8 90  1 1  1 1  1 1  1 1  2 2  2 2  2 2  2 2  3 3  3 3  3 3  4 4  4 4  4 4
                          1 2  3 4  5 6  7 8  9 0  1 2  3 4  5 6  7 8  9 0  1 2  3 4  5 6  7 8
                                        REFERENCE
```

CLUSTERS:

Start:	3:23	3:23	10: 7	10: 7	42:14	46: 8	46: 9	46: 9
End:	16:14	5: 4	16:14	12:12	46:10	46:10	46: 9	46:10
Count:	8	3	5	7	3	2		
Width:	5666	615	2936	1044	2262	55	26	14
Strength:	1.30	1.17	1.02	1.41	2.12	1.50	1.04	1.03

GAPS:

Start:	1: 1	1: 1	3:25	12:12	12:12	21:24	21:24	24:12	30: 9
End:	46: 9	46: 8	46: 8	19:14	46: 8	42:14	42:14	42:14	42:14
Count:	18	17	15	10	3	6	4	3	2
Width:	26387	26370	24982	21270	4440	15223	13016	10913	7907
Strength:	1.59	1.99	2.25	3.14	1.01	3.37	4.32	4.71	5.17

Linguistic Density Plot in Ezekiel 1 - 48

For yc' 314 (6 times)

Each Column = 13 Verses.   Separations are: Max = 10137.00, Mean =   3995.71, Min =   133.50 .

CLUSTERS:

Start: 47: 1 47: 8
End: 47:12 47:12
Count: 3   2
Width: 267   125
Strength: 1.72   1.11

GAPS:

Start: 1: 1   1: 1   1: 1 1:13 14:22 14:22
End: 47: 8 47: 1 47: 1 47: 1 47: 1 33:30
Count: 6   5   4   3   2
Width: 26917 26775 26512 20274 11988
Strength: 1.55   2.20   2.96   2.74   2.30

Linguistic Density Plot in Ezekiel 1 - 48

For yc' 3162 (7 times)

Each Column = 13 Verses.   Separations are: Max = 10101.00, Mean = 3496.25, Min = 200.00 .

CLUSTERS:

Start:	44:19	46:10	46:10
End:	47: 3	47: 3	46:12
Count:	4	3	2
Width:	1442	400	70
Strength:	2.00	1.63	1.11

GAPS:

Start:	1: 1	1: 1	10:19	27:33	27:33
End:	46:10	26:18	26:18	46:10	44:19
Count:	6	3	2	3	2
Width:	26423	14369	10101	11412	10370
Strength:	1.98	1.82	2.14	1.09	2.22

Linguistic Density Plot in Ezekiel 1 - 48

For yc' 361 (14 times)   yc' 362 (8 times)   yc' 363 (1 times)   yc' 364 (1 times)
     yc' 3662 (5 times)   yc' 371 (1 times)   yc' 374 (1 times)

Each Column = 13 Verses.   Separations are: Max = 2848.00, Mean = 874.06, Min = 17.50

REFERENCE

CLUSTERS:

Start:	11: 7	11: 7	11: 7	11: 7	12: 4	12: 4	12: 5	12: 7	20: 6	20: 6	20: 9	20:34	46:20	46:20
End:	47: 8	28:18	14:22	12:12	12:12	12: 7	12: 6	28:18	21:10	20:22	21:10	20:41	47: 8	47: 2	46:21
Count:	31	21	9	8	2	6	5	3	2	2	10	5	3	2	4	3	2
Width:	22452	10929	2017	627	168	16	82	41	11	17	5712	1186	431	111	6	465	184	243	112
Strength:	3.19	2.77	2.35	2.72	2.37	1.01	2.12	1.44	1.01	1.68	3.05	1.90	1.38	1.02	1.88	1.32	1.67	1.38	1.02

GAPS:

Start:	1: 1	12:12	12:12	14:22	20:10	21:10	21:10	21:10	28:18	38: 8	42:15
End:	11: 7	20: 9	20: 6	46:20	46:20	34:13	24: 6	34:37: 1	46:20	42: 1	46:20
Count:	2	4	3	17	10	6	4	5	2	2
Width:	4478	4695	4590	3200	16881	15806	10289	9535	7966	2270	3440	5416	2628	2490
Strength:	4.25	1.46	2.41	2.74	1.18	3.62	3.34	3.74	3.76	1.64	1.96	2.06	1.90

Linguistic Density Plot in Ezekiel 1 - 48

For yc' 361 (14 times)

Each Column = 13 Verses.   Separations are: Max = 5144.50, Mean = 1864.67, Min = 26.00 .

CLUSTERS:

Start:	11: 7	11: 7	11: 7	11: 7	12: 4	12: 7	20:14	20:34	21: 8
End:	42:15	21:10	12: 7	11: 9	12: 5	12: 7	21:10	21:10	21:10
Count:	14	11	6	2	4	2	2	5	3	2
Width:	19719	6403	541	16	82	30	17	959	465	44
Strength:	1.90	3.71	2.66	1.05	1.97	1.05	1.05	2.10	1.37	1.04

GAPS:

Start:	1: 1	12: 7	21:10	38: 4	42:15
End:	11: 7	48:35	34:13	48:35	48:35
Count:	2	10	2	5	3	2
Width:	4478	22950	4903	17088	6799	3772
Strength:	1.49	1.80	1.74	3.11	1.29	1.09

Linguistic Density Plot in Ezekiel 1 - 48

For yc' 362 (8 times)

Each Column = 13 Verses.   Separations are: Max = 4957.50, Mean = 3107.78, Min = 636.50 .

REFERENCE

DENSITY

+25
+20
+15
+10
+5
0

REFERENCE

CLUSTERS:

Start:	46:21	
End:	47: 2	
Count:	2	
Width:	103	
Strength:	1.08	

GAPS:

Start:	1: 1	20:38
End:	46:21	37: 1
Count:	8	3
Width:	26696	9915
Strength:	1.34	1.00

Linguistic Density Plot in Ezekiel 1 - 48

For yc' 3662 (5 times)

Each Column = 13 Verses.   Separations are: Max = 16087.00, Mean = 4661.66, Min = 452.50 .

REFERENCE

REFERENCE

DENSITY

CLUSTERS:

Start:	12:12	20: 6	20: 6
End:	20:41	20:41	20: 9
Count:	4	3	2
Width:	5495	905	105
Strength:	1.60	1.68	1.15

GAPS:

Start:	20:41	20:41
End:	48:35	46:20
Count:	3	2
Width:	17369	16087
Strength:	1.61	2.89

Linguistic Density Plot in Ezekiel 1 - 48

For yr' 311 (1 times)   yr' 312 (4 times)

Each Column = 13 Verses. Separations are: Max = 13486.00, Mean = 4661.66, Min = 12.00

CLUSTERS:

Start:	2: 6	2: 6	2: 6	2: 6
End:	11: 8	3: 9	2: 6	2: 6
Count:	5	4	3	2
Width:	3775	289	24	8
Strength:	2.98	2.59	1.86	1.18

GAPS:

Start:	2: 6	2: 6	3: 9	11: 8
End:	48:35	48:35	48:35	48:35
Count:	5	4	3	2
Width:	27253	27237	26972	23486
Strength:	1.72	2.50	3.54	4.77

Linguistic Density Plot in Ezekiel 1 - 48

For yrd 311 (8 times)   yrd 312 (3 times)   yrd 313 (1 times)   yrd 314 (10 times)
     yrd 3162 (1 times)   yrd 361 (2 times)   yrd 362 (1 times)   yrd 363 (1 times)
     yrd 3662 (1 times)   yrd 371 (1 times)

Each Column = 13 Verses. Separations are: Max = 7146.00, Mean = 932.33, Min = 8.50

REFERENCE

(density scatter plot — vertical axis labelled 25+, 20+, D15+, E, N, S, I, T10+, Y, 5+, O+ and +25, +20, +15D, E, N, S, I, +10T, Y, +5, O; horizontal axis labelled in verse/column units with REFERENCE below)

CLUSTERS:

Start:	26:11	26:11	26:11	26:20	26:20	26:20	30:6	30:6	31:12	31:12	31:14	31:16	31:16	32:18	32:18	32:18	32:24
End:	47:8	34:26	28:8	26:20	26:20	34:26	32:30	31:18	31:15	31:18	31:18	31:16	31:17	32:30	32:21	32:19	32:19	32:24
Count:	29	27	7	5	2	19	19	8	3	3	4	2	2	11	4	3	2	7
Width:	12719	4930	1001	216	19	3	2926	1526	844	170	79	55	27	6	291	47	17	5	181
Strength:	10.68	11.30	2.28	2.05	1.47	1.03	6.10	6.19	2.67	2.69	1.02	1.81	1.42	1.46	1.02	3.81	1.82	1.47	1.02	2.69

Start:	32:24	32:29	32:29
End:	32:27	32:24	32:30	32:30
Count:	4	2	3	2
Width:	89	17	32	11
Strength:	1.79	1.01	1.46	1.02

Data for yrd 311, yrd 312, yrd 313, yrd 314, yrd 3162, yrd 361, yrd 362, yrd 363, yrd 3662, yrd 371, continued.

GAPS:

```
Start:      1: 1   1: 1  32:30 32:30 32:30 34:26
End:     26:20 26:11 48:35 48:35 47: 1 47: 1
Count:       4     2     6     5     3     2
Width:   14400 14203 10257 10236  9054  7654
Strength: 7.69 14.71  2.98  3.80  5.73  7.45
```

Linguistic Density Plot in Ezekiel 1 - 48

For yrd 311 (8 times)   yrd 312 (3 times)   yrd 313 (1 times)   yrd 314 (10 times)
     yrd 3162 (1 times)

Each Column = 13 Verses.   Separations are: Max = 7146.00. Mean = 1165.42. Min = 16.00 .

```
                                              REFERENCE
25+

20+

D15+
E
N
S
I
T10+
Y

 5+

 0+
    +--+--+--+--+--+--+--+--+--+--+--+--+--+--+--+--+--+--+--+--+--+--+
    1 23 4 5 6 7  8 90 1 2  3 4 56  7 8  90 1 2  3 4 5 6 7  8 90 1 2  3 4 5 6 7  8 90 1 2  3 4 5 6 7  8
    1 23 4 5 6 7  8 91111   1111    11   1112   2 2 2 2 2  2 2 2 2   3 3 3 3 3  3 3 4 4   4 4 4 4 4  4
                           REFERENCE
```

CLUSTERS:

```
Start:     26:11  26:11  26:11  26:20  26:20  30: 6  30: 6  31:12  31:14  31:16  32:18  32:18  32:24  32:24  32:25  32:29  32:29
End:       47: 8  32:30  27:29  26:20  26:20  32:30  31:17  31:17  31:15  31:17  32:19  32:30  32:27  32:24  32:27  32:30  32:30
Count:     23     21     5      4      2      16     6      5      4      2      10     3      2      7      4      2      3      2
Width:     12719  3530   739    216    1526   816    142    72     9      21     279    5      181    89     17     38     32     11
Strength:  8.35   9.48   1.88   1.77   5.89   2.20   1.85   1.03   1.02   1.02   3.76   1.03   2.81   1.84   1.02   1.00   1.48   1.03
```

GAPS:

```
Start:     1: 1   1: 1   1: 1   1: 1   32:30  32:30  32:30
End:       32:18  31:14  26:20  26:11  48:35  48:35  47: 1
Count:     13     9      4      2      5      4      2
Width:     17454  16951  14403  10257  14203  10236  9054
Strength:  1.24   2.89   5.89   11.66  2.68   3.64   7.05
```

Linguistic Density Plot in Ezekiel 1 - 48

For yrd 311 (8 times)

Each Column = 13 Verses.   Separations are: Max = 9210.00, Mean = 3107.78, Min = 76.00 .

CLUSTERS:

Start:	27:29	27:29	31:17	32:21	32:21	32:27
End:	47: 8	32:30	32:30	32:24	32:30	32:30
Count:	8	7	5	4	2	2
Width:	11980	2770	689	223	63	71
Strength:	2.65	3.80	2.67	2.18	1.09	1.09

GAPS:

Start:	1: 1	1: 1	1: 1	1: 1	32:30	32:30
End:	32:21	31:17	30: 6	27:29	48:35	47: 8
Count:	5	4	3	2	3	2
Width:	17489	17023	16207	14942	10257	9210
Strength:	1.15	1.84	2.71	4.25	1.09	2.19

For yrd 314 (10 times)

Linguistic Density Plot in Ezekiel 1 - 48

Each Column = 13 Verses.   Separations are: Max = 9054.00, Mean = 2542.73, Min = 65.00 .

REFERENCE

DENSITY

REFERENCE

CLUSTERS:

Start:	26:20	26:20	26:20	31:14	31:14	32:18	32:24	32:29
End:	47:1	32:30	26:20	32:30	31:16	32:25	32:25	32:30
Count:	10	9	2	7	5	3	2	2
Width:	12384	3330	16	782	51	279	149	34	32
Strength:	3.37	4.73	1.08	3.60	1.07	2.54	1.58	1.08	1.08

GAPS:

Start:	1: 1	32:30	32:30
End:	26:20	48:35	47: 1
Count:	2	3	2
Width:	14403	10236	9054
Strength:	5.10	1.65	2.80

Linguistic Density Plot in Ezekiel 1 - 48

For yrd 361 (2 times)   yrd 362 (1 times)   yrd 363 (1 times)   yrd 3662 (1 times)
     yrd 371 (1 times)

Each Column = 13 Verses. Separations are: Max = 7602.50. Mean = 3995.71. Min = 223.00.

CLUSTERS:

Start:	26:20	31:16	31:16	31:16
End:	34:26	34:26	32:18	31:18
Count:	6	4	3	2
Width:	4733	2137	446	55
Strength:	3.41	2.01	1.68	1.13

GAPS:

Start:	1: 1	1: 1	34:26
End:	31:16	26:20	48:35
Count:	4	2	2
Width:	16996	14400	8836
Strength:	1.02	3.00	1.39

Linguistic Density Plot in Ezekiel 1 - 48

For yerûšālayim 12 (26 times)

Each Column = 13 Verses.   Separations are: Max = 4852.50, Mean = 1035.93, Min = 32.00 .

```
CLUSTERS:

Start:     4: 1   4: 1   4: 1   4: 1   8: 3   11:15  13:16  14:21  15: 6  16: 2  16: 6  21: 7  21:25
End:      36:38  17:12  12:19   5: 5  12:19   9: 8  12:19  17:12  16: 3  16: 3  16: 3  16: 2  23: 4  21:27  21:27
Count:      26     17     10      4      6      3      7             5      3      2
Width:    18932   6885   3789    491   2022    597   2598    982    251     64     12   3185    387     30
Strength:  5.03   3.73   2.22   1.57   1.53   1.06   1.64   2.04   2.07   1.45   1.02   1.37   1.52   1.21   1.00

GAPS:

Start:    16: 3  16: 3  17:12  21: 7  23: 4  26: 2  26: 2  36:38
End:      48:35  21: 7  21:27  48:35  48:35  33:21  48:35
Count:      12      3      2      8      6      4      2
Width:    21238   4083   2467  16768  15870  13970   4265   7575
Strength:  3.78   1.45   1.43   4.10   5.20   6.53   3.23   6.55
```

Linguistic Density Plot in Ezekiel 1 - 48

For yarkâ 114 (5 times)

Each Column = 13 Verses.   Separations are: Max = 10606.50, Mean = 4661.66, Min = 247.00 .

REFERENCE

CLUSTERS:

Start:	32:23	32:23	38: 6	38: 6
End:	46:19	39: 2	39: 2	38:15
Count:	5	4	3	2
Width:	9149	4191	494	231
Strength:	1.90	1.85	1.77	1.12

GAPS:

Start:	1: 1	1: 1
End:	38: 6	32:23
Count:	3	2
Width:	21212	17515
Strength:	2.38	3.26

Linguistic Density Plot in Ezekiel 1 - 48

For yrs 311 (3 times)   yrs 312 (3 times)

Each Column = 13 Verses. Separations are: Max = 15249.00, Mean = 3995.71, Min = 26.50 .

REFERENCE

CLUSTERS:

Start:	33:24	33:24	33:25	35:10
End:	36:12	33:26	36:12	
Count:	5	3	2	2
Width:	1528	53	16	422
Strength:	2.95	1.77	1.14	1.03

GAPS:

Start:	1: 1	1: 1	7:24	36:12
End:	33:25	33:24	48:35	
Count:	4	3	2	2
Width:	18360	18323	15249	8118
Strength:	1.30	2.31	3.25	1.19

Linguistic Density Plot in Ezekiel 1 - 48

For yiśrā'ēl 12 (186 times)

Each Column = 13 Verses.   Separations are: Max = 1190.00,   Mean = 149.57,   Min = 12.00 .

(Scatter / density plot. Vertical axis labelled DENSITY, marked +25, +20, +15, +10, +5, +0; horizontal axis labelled REFERENCE, marked by chapter : verse reference scale 1–48.)

CLUSTERS:

Start:	2: 3	2: 3	2: 3	3: 1	3: 4	3: 4	4: 3	6: 2	6: 2	8: 4	8: 4	8: 4	8:10	10:19	10:19	12: 6	12: 6	12: 6	12: 6
End:	48:31	14:11	3:17	3: 7	3: 7	4: 4	5: 5	6: 5	8:12	14:11	11:22	8:12	8:12	11:11	11:22	13:16	12:27	12:10	12:19
Count:	186	56	7	5	4	3	3	3	8	39	17	5	9	22	14	6	6	6	6
Width:	27241	5585	319	121	66	47	60	583	179	2978	1560	48	525	1235	753	412	151	73	321
Strength:	2.04	2.84	1.05	1.61	1.49	1.19	1.13	1.19	1.41	3.29	1.45	1.19	1.62	1.15	2.29	2.95	1.63	1.07	1.51

Start:	12:22	12:22	12:22	13: 2	13: 2	14: 1	14: 1	17: 2	17: 2	18: 2	18: 2	18:25	18:25	18:29	20: 1	20:27	20:27
End:	12:27	12:24	13:16	13: 9	13:13	14:11	14:11	22:18	20:13	18: 6	20:13	19: 9	18:30	18:30	20: 5	22:18	21: 8
Count:	4	3	6	5	8	1	7	32	17	3	11	7	3	3	4	11	8
Width:	95	55	288	141	255	47	145	3623	1751	139	707	303	96	29	78	1521	609
Strength:	1.37	1.16	1.39	1.54	2.04	1.19	1.83	1.33	1.12	1.20	1.71	1.65	1.37	1.28	1.05	1.06	1.93

Clusters for yiśrā'ēl 12 , continued.

```
Start:     20:38  33: 7  33: 7  34:13  34:13  35:12  35:12  35:15  36: 8  36: 8  36:17  36:21  36:32  37:11  37:16  37:16
End:       20:40  48:31  40: 4  37:22  36:22  36: 6  36: 1  36: 1  36:12  36:10  36:22  36:22  37:22  37:22  37:22  37:19
Count:         4     88     57     28     19      6     36      4     12      3      9      7      5      3
Width:        63   9962   4514   2993   2048   1188    574    228     76     33     81     36    121     24    619    282    162     80
Strength:   1.50   2.99   4.13   2.81   2.77   2.49   2.64   1.57   1.45   1.26   1.43   1.25   1.27   1.30   1.39   1.71   1.47   1.04

Start:     37:28  37:28  38:14  38:14  38:17  39: 7  39:11  39:11  39:22  43: 2  43: 2  44: 2  44: 9  44: 9  44:22  45: 6  45: 6  45: 6
End:       40: 4  39: 9  39: 9  38:19  38:19  39: 9  40: 4  39:25  39:25  48:31  45:17  44:15  44:12  44:15  45:17  45:17  45: 9  45: 9
Count:        21     12     10      5      3      9      9      6      3     31     22     11      7      4      3      8      4      3
Width:      1329    720    394    134    114    537    306     76   3592    996    354    148     69    592    260     83
Strength:   2.63   1.92   2.17   1.57   1.63   1.59   1.34   1.06   1.19   1.08   1.51   1.17   1.09   1.96   2.03   1.42   1.28

Start:     45:15  47:13  47:18  47:21
End:       45:17  47:22  47:22  47:22
Count:         4      5      4      3
Width:        67    193     94     40
Strength:   1.48   1.37   1.38   1.23

GAPS:

Start:      1: 1   1: 1   1: 1   3: 7   3:17   4: 5   4:13   5: 4   6: 5   7: 2   9: 9  14: 7  14: 7  14: 7  14:11  14:11  14:11  20: 5
End:       36: 1   3: 1   2: 3   4: 3   4: 3   6: 2   6: 3   6: 2   8: 4   8: 4  10:19  20:40  20:38  18:29  18:29  17:23  18: 2  20:27
Count:       115      4      3      3      2      4      2      2     26     24      9     11      4      2      3
Width:     19553    896    841    564    365    740    577    367    877    607    452   4442   4389   3110   3000   2451   2380   1889    561
Strength:   2.51   1.74   2.57   3.31   1.25   1.44   1.13   1.32   1.45   1.66   3.07   1.01   1.41   3.51   4.36   7.81   9.91  11.68   1.24

Start:     20:13  20:27  21: 8  21: 8  21: 8  21:17  21:17  22:18  22:18  25: 6  25:14  25:14  28:25  28:25  28:25  29:21  34:14  39: 9  39:23
End:       20:27  36: 1  34:14  28:24  25: 3  25: 3  22: 6  24:21  25: 3  24: 4  28:24  27:17  34: 2  33:10  33: 7  33: 7  34:30  43: 7  43: 7
Count:      .351     31      2      7     11      6      3      3      2     11      6      5      9      7
Width:      8725   8057   4698   2804   2606   1892   1682   1807    841   3025   2446   2366   1815   2577   2255
Strength:   1.35   5.65   6.54   7.15   6.97   5.30   5.64   1.00   7.58  10.29   6.38   4.64   3.33   5.15   5.98  11.19   1.24   1.94   3.77

Start:     40: 2  40: 4  40: 4  43:10  43:10  45:17  45:17  45:17  45:17
End:       43: 7  43: 7  44: 6  44: 2  47:22  47:21  47:18  47:13
Count:         4      3      2      3      4      2      5      3      2
Width:      2053   1968   1856    548    440   1200   1169   1115   1016
Strength:   6.25   7.95  11.46   1.18   1.94   2.03   2.80   3.88   5.82
```

Linguistic Density Plot in Ezekiel 1 - 48

For   ysb 311 (14 times)   ysb 312 (10 times)   ysb 314 (28 times)   ysb 3162 (2 times)
      ysb 321 (2 times)   ysb 324 (3 times)   ysb 331 (1 times)   ysb 361 (3 times)

Each Column = 13 Verses.   Separations are: Max = 2871.00, Mean = 437.03, Min = 5.00 .

REFERENCE

CLUSTERS:

Start:	2: 6	2: 6	3:15	3:15	11:15	12:19	12:19	23:41	23:41	26:16	26:16	26:16	26:19	28:25	28:25	31: 6
End:	44: 3	3:15	3:15	12:20	12:20	12:20	44: 3	36:35	29:11	29:11	28: 2	27: 3	26:20	29:11	28:26	36:35
Count:	63	4	2	5	3	2	45	32	16	18	9	8	4	3	5	14
Width:	24218	405	10	653	32	5	12093	7496	1559	3021	787	241	40	302	24	3605
Strength:	4.76	1.23	1.43	1.30	1.39	1.00	4.43	3.49	2.87	3.39	2.84	2.83	1.73	1.67	1.72	1.48

Start:	33:24	36:10	36:10	37:25	37:25	37:25	38: 8	38:11
End:	36:35	36:17	36:28	39:26	37:25	38:14	38: 8	38:11
Count:	11	6	3	12	9	6	5	4
Width:	2038	540	157	1214	417	157	93	40
Strength:	1.85	1.76	1.23	2.74	2.68	1.41	1.97	1.73

Data for ysb 311, ysb 312, ysb 314, ysb 3162, ysb 321, ysb 324, ysb 331, ysb 361, continued.

GAPS:

Start:	3:15	8:14	12:20	15: 6	16:46	16:46	16:46	16:46	20: 1	29:11	32:15	38:11	38:12	39: 9	39:26	44: 3
End:	8: 1	11:15	26:17	16:46	26:17	26:16	25: 4	23:41	23:41	31: 6	33:24	48:35	48:35	48:35	48:35	48:35
Count:	3	2	11	4	2	7	6	5	4	3	2	9	7	4	3	3	2
Width:	2023	1594	1151	9064	2421	1037	6632	6620	6600	5941	5138	3266	870	925	6638	6603	6144	5742	3024
Strength:	1.90	2.68	1.65	3.72	1.51	1.39	3.96	4.76	5.77	6.31	7.06	6.57	1.00	1.13	2.73	3.93	6.58	8.06	6.01

Linguistic Density Plot in Ezekiel 1 - 48

For ysb 311 (14 times)   ysb 312 (10 times)   ysb 314 (28 times)   ysb 3162 (2 times)

Each Column = 13 Verses. Separations are: Max = 2871.00, Mean = 508.55, Min = 5.00 .

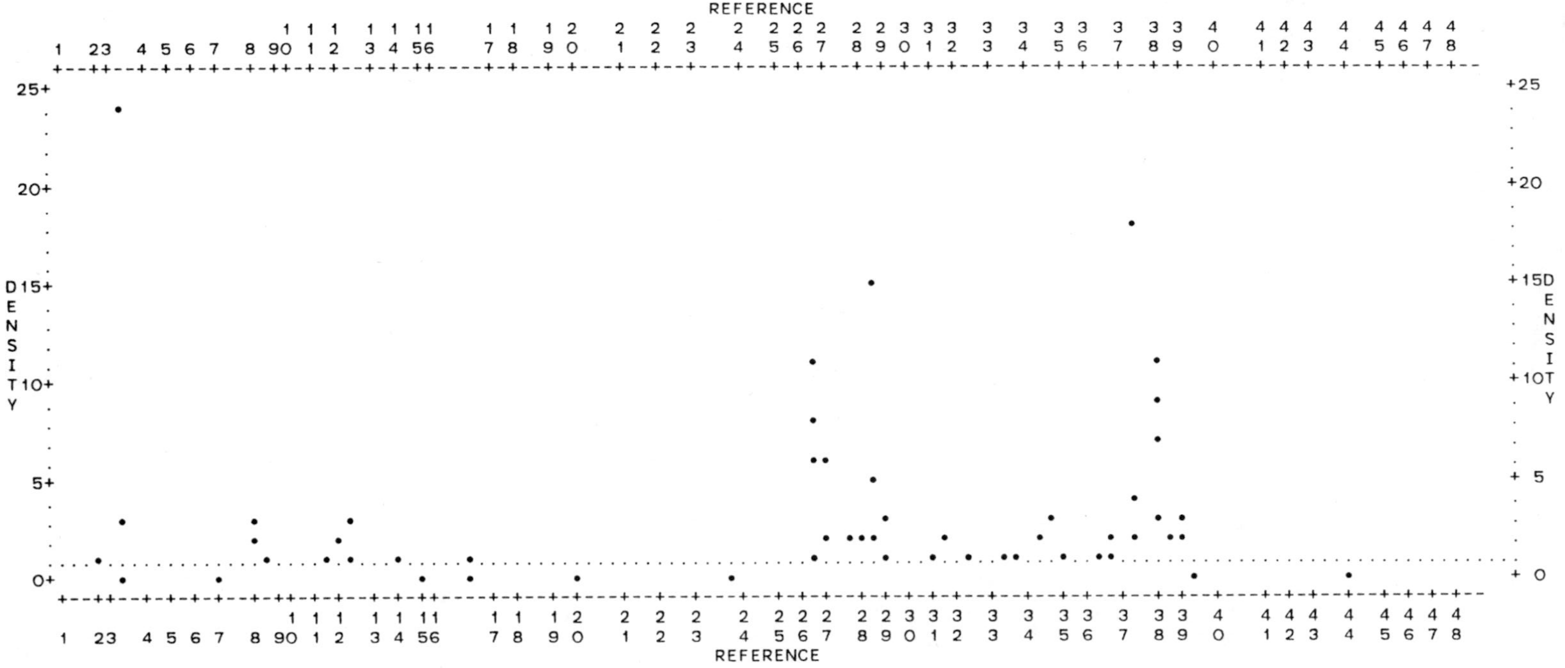

(Density plot — vertical axis labelled DENSITY with gridlines at +25, +20, +15, +10, +5, +0; horizontal axis labelled REFERENCE.)

CLUSTERS:

```
Start:     2: 6   2: 6   3:15   3:15   8: 1  11:15  23:41  23:41  26:16  26:16  26:16  26:16  26:17  26:20  28:25  28:25  31: 6  33:24  34:25
End:      44: 3   3:15   3:15   8: 1  12:19  44: 3  36:35  29:11  28: 2  26:17  29:11  27: 8  29:11  28:26  36:35  35: 9
Count:      54      4      3      2      2     37     25     14     13      6      8      3     11      8      3
Width:    24218    405     10      3      7    648  12093   3021   7496    241   1559    787    302     40    302   3605   2038
Strength:  3.90   1.31   1.43   1.01   1.00   1.03   3.49   2.26   2.54   2.14   2.94   2.22   1.00   1.26   1.78   1.39   1.41   1.02   1.22   1.03
```

```
Start:    37:25  37:25  37:25  37:25  38: 8  38: 8  38:11  38:11
End:      44: 3  39:26  38:14  37:25  38:12  38:14  38:12  38:11
Count:      12     11      8      3      4      5      3      2
Width:    3932   1214    417     17      6    157     93     40      5
Strength:  1.11   2.68   2.52   1.42   1.00   1.93   1.68   1.00   1.39   1.00
```

Data for ysb 311, ysb 312, ysb 314, ysb 3162, continued.

GAPS:

Start:	3:15	3:15	8: 1	8:14	12:19	15: 6	16:46	16:46	16:46	16:46	20: 1	38:11	38:12	39: 9	39:26	44: 3
End:	8: 1	7: 7	26:17	11:15	16:46	16:46	26:16	26:17	23:41	23:41	23:41	48:35	48:35	48:35	48:35	48:35
Count:	3	2	14	2	4	2	4	5	3	2	8	7	4	3	2	
Width:	2023	1594	11184	1151	2426	1037	6600	6632	5138	3266	6638	6603	6144	5742	3024	
Strength:	1.43	2.17	2.87	1.28	1.06	1.05	5.97	4.73	5.88	5.52	2.47	3.04	5.44	6.75	5.03	

Linguistic Density Plot in Ezekiel 1 - 48

For ysb 311 (14 times)

Each Column = 13 Verses.   Separations are: Max = 7551.00, Mean = 1864.67, Min = 8.50 .

```
                                                    REFERENCE
        1   1 1 1 1 1 1 1   1 1 2   2 2 2 2 2   2 2 2 2   2 2 2 2 2 2 2   3 3 3 3 3 3 3 3 3 3   4   4 4 4 4 4 4 4 4
 1 23 4 5 6 7 8 90 1 2 3 456 7 8 9 0 1 2 3 4 5 6 7 8 90 1 2 3 4 5 6 7 8 90 1 2 3 4 5 6 7 8 90 1 2 3 4 5 6 7 8
25+

                                                                                                          +25

20+                                                                                                       +20

D15+
E
N
S
I
T10+
Y

5+                                                                                                         +5

0+                                                                                                          0
        1   1 1 1 1 1 1 1   1 1 2   2 2 2 2 2   2 2 2 2   2 2 2 2 2 2 2   3 3 3 3 3 3 3 3 3 3   4   4 4 4 4 4 4 4 4
 1 23 4 5 6 7 8 90 1 2 3 456 7 8 9 0 1 2 3 4 5 6 7 8 90 1 2 3 4 5 6 7 8 90 1 2 3 4 5 6 7 8 90 1 2 3 4 5 6 7 8
                                                    REFERENCE
```

CLUSTERS:

Start:	23:41	23:41	28: 2	28: 2	28:25	28:25	34:25	34:25	36:28	37:25	37:25	37:25
End:	38: 8	31:17	31:17	28:26	28:26	38: 8	38: 8	34:28	38: 8	38: 8	37:25	37:25
Count:	14	6	5	4	3	2						
Width:	8421	4179	1930	494	24	12	2159	80	1082	260	17	6
Strength:	6.65	1.56	1.78	1.82	1.55	1.06	3.12	1.02	2.50	1.90	1.56	1.06

GAPS:

Start:	1: 1	1: 1	1: 1	1: 1	37:25	38: 8
End:	28:26	28:25	28: 2	23:41	48:35	48:35
Count:	5	4	3	2		
Width:	15583	15571	15101	12852	6939	6696
Strength:	2.62	3.56	4.78	6.29	1.35	2.76

Linguistic Density Plot in Ezekiel 1 - 48

Each Column = 13 Verses.   Separations are: Max = 5536.00, Mean = 2542.73, Min = 779.50 .

REFERENCE

REFERENCE

CLUSTERS:

Start:	26:16	26:16	26:16	
End:	44: 3	35: 9	31: 6	26:20
Count:	7	6	4	2
Width:	10631	5095	2429	110
Strength:	1.15	1.89	1.44	1.04

GAPS:

Start:	1: 1	3:15	35: 9	35: 9
End:	26:16	26:16	48:35	44: 3
Count:	5	4	3	2
Width:	14314	13182	8560	5536
Strength:	1.06	1.54	1.11	1.28

Linguistic Density Plot in Ezekiel 1 - 48

For ysb 314 (28 times)

Each Column = 13 Verses.   Separations are: Max = 3321.50.   Mean = 964.48.   Min = 20.00 .

REFERENCE

DENSITY

CLUSTERS:

Start:	2: 6	2: 6	3:15	7: 7	7: 7	8: 1	8: 1	11:15	12:19	16:46	26:17	26:17	26:17	26:17	26:17	26:17	26:17	36:17	38:11
End:	39: 9	16:46	12:19	3:15	8:14	8:14	8: 1	12:19	12:19	16:46	26:17	33:24	27:35	29: 6	27: 8	26:17	26:17	39: 9	39:11
Count:	28	14	11	8	4	3	2	4	2	2	8	8	5	6	4	6	9	9	5
Width:	21098	6987	4550	2551	402	752	323	648	27	648	3964	7479	701	1403	209	1890	499		
Strength:	3.81	2.18	2.09	1.92	1.17	1.37	1.24	1.44	1.00	1.02	1.27	1.99	1.79	1.77	1.72	1.51	1.90		

Start:	38:11	38:11
End:	38:12	38:11
Count:	3	2
Width:	40	5
Strength:	1.45	1.02

Data for ysb 314, continued.

GAPS:

```
Start:       8: 1 16:46 38:11 38:12 39: 9
End:        26:17 26:17 48:35 48:35 48:35
Count:         10     2     5     4     2
Width:      11184  6632  6638  6603  6144
Strength:    1.05  6.08  1.57  2.38  5.55
```

Linguistic Density Plot in Ezekiel 1 - 48

For ysb 321 (2 times)   ysb 324 (3 times)

Each Column = 13 Verses.   Separations are: Max = 9052.00, Mean = 4661.66, Min = 2737.00 .

CLUSTERS:

Start:	26:17	26:17
End:	38:12	26:19
Count:	4	2
Width:	7021	54
Strength:	1.31	1.16

GAPS:

Start:	1: 1	12:20
End:	26:17	26:17
Count:	3	2
Width:	14334	9052
Strength:	1.00	1.11

Linguistic Density Plot in Ezekiel 1 - 48

For ytr 321 (1 times)   ytr 324 (5 times)   ytr 361 (2 times)   ytr 362 (1 times)

Each Column = 13 Verses.   Separations are: Max = 7736.50, Mean = 2797.00, Min = 71.50 .

REFERENCE

```
            1   1 1  1 1111   11  1 1  2 2 2  2 2  2 2 2  2 2 2  3 3 3  3 3 3  3 3 3  4 4 4  4 4 4  4
   1 23  4 5 6 7  8 90 1 2  3 456  7 8  90  1 2  3 4  5 6 7  8 90 1 2  3 4  5 6 7  8 90 1 2  3 4  5 6 7 8
25+
    ·
20+
    ·
15+ D
    E
    N
    S
    I
10+ T
    Y
    ·
 5+
    ·
 0+
   1 23  4 5 6 7  8 90 1 2  3 456  7 8  90  1 2  3 4  5 6 7  8 90 1 2  3 4  5 6 7  8 90 1 2  3 4  5 6 7 8
```

REFERENCE

CLUSTERS:

Start:	34:18	48:15	48:18
End:	48:21	48:21	48:21
Count:	6	3	2
Width:	8713	143	58
Strength:	1.25	1.61	1.08

GAPS:

Start:	1:1	1:1	1:1	14:22	14:22
End:	48:18	48:15	39:14	39:14	34:18
Count:	9	8	6	3	2
Width:	27636	27551	21964	15473	12490
Strength:	1.55	2.06	1.89	2.92	3.83

Linguistic Density Plot in Ezekiel 1 - 48

For ytr 321 (1 times)   ytr 324 (5 times)

Each Column = 13 Verses.   Separations are: Max = 12490.00, Mean = 3995.71, Min = 71.50

CLUSTERS:

Start:	34:18	48:15	48:18
End:	48:21	48:21	48:21
Count:	5	3	2
Width:	8713	143	58
Strength:	1.48	1.75	1.13

GAPS:

Start:	1: 1	1: 1	1: 1	14:22
End:	48:18	48:15	34:18	34:18
Count:	6	5	3	2
Width:	27636	27551	18981	12490
Strength:	1.71	2.36	2.45	2.45

Linguistic Density Plot in Ezekiel 1 - 48

For ytr 324 (5 times)

Each Column = 13 Verses.   Separations are: Max = 10982.50, Mean = 4661.66, Min = 71.50 .

CLUSTERS:

Start:	34:18	48:15	48:18
End:	48:21	48:21	48:21
Count:	5	3	2
Width:	8713	143	58
Strength:	1.99	1.84	1.16

GAPS:

Start:	1: 1	1: 1	1: 1
End:	48:18	48:15	34:18
Count:	5	4	2
Width:	27636	27551	18981
Strength:	1.80	2.56	3.63